A Record of the Descendants of
Capt. George Denison
of Stonington, Connecticut

WITH NOTICES OF HIS FATHER AND BROTHERS,
AND SOME ACCOUNT OF OTHER DENISONS
WHO SETTLED IN AMERICA
IN THE COLONY TIMES

*John Denison Baldwin
and William Clift*

HERITAGE BOOKS
2013

HERITAGE BOOKS
AN IMPRINT OF HERITAGE BOOKS, INC.

Books, CDs, and more—Worldwide

For our listing of thousands of titles see our website
at
www.HeritageBooks.com

A Facsimile Reprint
Published 2013 by
HERITAGE BOOKS, INC.
Publishing Division
100 Railroad Ave. #104
Westminster, Maryland 21157

Originally published
Worcester:
Printed by Tyler & Seagrave
1881

— Publisher's Notice —
In reprints such as this, it is often not possible to remove blemishes from the original. We feel the contents of this book warrant its reissue despite these blemishes and hope you will agree and read it with pleasure.

International Standard Book Numbers
Paperbound: 978-0-7884-1346-9
Clothbound: 978-0-7884-6922-0

A RECORD

OF THE DESCENDANTS OF

CAPT. GEORGE DENISON,

OF STONINGTON, CONN.

With Notices of His Father and Brothers, and some
account of Other Denisons who settled in
America in the Colony Times.

PREPARED BY

JOHN DENISON BALDWIN

AND

WILLIAM CLIFT.

WORCESTER:
PRINTED BY TYLER & SEAGRAVE.
1881.

ERRATA.

2507 John D., for 2503,	page 125.	2600 for 2400,	page	118
319 for 317,	" 31	2783½ for 2983½,	"	144
317 for 319 Robert,	" 31	4047 for 4147,	"	197
5020 for 5920,	" 281	5446 for 5546,	"	264
1033 for 136,	" 55	Son of 2733½ George for 2983½,		144
1603 for 1633,	" 82	Francis for Frances, 1637,	"	81
2083 for 2101,	" 114	Robert6 for Robert5,	"	257
1810 for 1800,	" 116			

ABBREVIATIONS.

b. means born.
bapt, " baptized.
m. " married.
d. " died.
dau. " daughter.

PREFACE.

This tribute to the memory of our grandmothers, ANNA DENISON CLIFT and SARAH DENISON BALDWIN, daughters of JOHN DENISON and ABIGAIL AVERY DENISON of Stonington, began many years ago, grew into the proposition to publish the volume three years since. Circulars were sent out in 1878, and subscriptions enough were sent in to guard against loss in meeting the expenses of publication, and the printing was commenced in October, 1880. The work of compiling and publishing a genealogy of the descendants of any of the early settlers of New England is necessarily long and tedious. Some of the descendants take no interest in the matter; some who are interested forget to write; others furnish the required information only after repeated requests; and others still, promise and fail to fulfil. The delay in issuing the work has been unavoidable, and has always been in the interest of subscribers. With longer time and more zealous coöperation on the part of some of the descendants, we could have added largely to the list of family records. Our rule, to stop the records with the children of Denison women married with other families, has been departed from in some special cases, bringing the descendants down to the present generation. There are probably enough of descendants bearing the name, and of the Denison women not yet heard from, to make another volume as large as this. The work of collecting and publishing them must be left to other hands.

This genealogical record is not complete; it is seldom or never possible to make such a record complete. It is sent forth with the hope that it will be acceptable to the living members of the family, strengthen the ties of kindred, and stimulate the present and future generations to emulate the piety and the patriotism of the early settlers bearing the name of DENISON.

WORCESTER, MASS., Sept. 1, 1881.
MYSTIC BRIDGE, CONN.

DENISON COAT OF ARMS.

OUTLINE OF THE COAT OF ARMS TAKEN FROM THE TOMB OF MAJOR GENERAL DENISON, OF IPSWICH, MASS.

1. The side-long close helmet, color steel, designates the dignity of a knight. Latin scutifer: he had two to attend him in the wars, who bare his helmet and shield before him, and who held land of him in scutage. Arm, green dress.
2. Chevron, color blue: denotes the founder of his house; engrailed, indicating blows of hail, indenting strokes of war.
3. Bezant, gold color: represents Byzantian coin, medal for crusade service.
4. Ogresses, color black, hemispheres of iron, symbolizing cannon shot, garrison or naval service, doubtless the latter.
5. Ground of shield, gold color.
6. Ribbon, red color.
7. Motto: DOMUS GRATA, hospitable house.
8. Surrounding ornaments, color from taste.

CAPT. GEORGE DENISON,

OF STONINGTON, CONN.;

HIS FATHER, HIS BROTHERS, AND HIS DAUGHTERS.

1 WILLIAM DENISON, b. in England about 1586, came to America in 1631, and settled in Roxbury, Mass., having with him his wife Margaret, his three sons, *Daniel, Edward* and *George*, and John Eliot, who seems to have been a tutor in his family. Mr. Eliot became pastor of the church in Roxbury, and did missionary work among the Indians. Mr. Denison was a deacon of the Roxbury church. He had been liberally educated, and his sons were carefully educated. He died in Roxbury, Jan. 25, 1653; his wife died there, Feb. 23, 1645.

2 DANIEL DENISON, (son of William,) b. in 1612, was married to Patience Dudley, dau. of Gov. Thomas Dudley, lived at Ipswich, Mass., and had two children: *John*, who *m.* a dau. of Deputy Governor, John Symonds; and *Elizabeth*, who *m.* John Rogers, president of Harvard College. He was very prominent in Massachusetts, having been Major General of Militia, Speaker of the House of Representatives, and for 29 years, one of the "Assistants." He died in 1682. It is supposed, but not absolutely certain, that his last male descendant bearing the family name, was an accomplished young clergyman, who died at Ipswich, unmarried, August 25, 1747.

3 EDWARD DENISON, (son of William,) b. in 1614, was married to Elizabeth Welde of Roxbury, and had twelve children. He lived in Roxbury, where he was a man of mark, and died there, April 26, 1668; his wife died there in 1716, aged 91 years. His children:

ELIZABETH, b. in 1642.   MARY, b. in 1653.
JOHN, b. in 1644.   HANNAH, b. in 1655.
EDWARD, b. and d. in 1645. SARAH, b. in 1657.
JOSEPH, b. and d. in 1646. DEBORAH, b. in 1660; d. in 1663.
JEREMIAH, b. in 1647; d. in 1649. WILLIAM, b. in 1664; d. Mar. 22, '18.
MARGARET, b. in '50; m. D. Mason. DEBORAH, b. in 1666; d. in 1667.

Edward Denison's son William m. Dorothy Welde, of Roxbury, and had children; but it is not known to those who have inquired carefully, that any male descendant of this family, bearing the family name, is now living.

4 GEORGE DENISON, (son of William,) b. in 1618,* was married, first, in 1640, to Bridget Thompson, dau. of "John Thompson, *gent.*, of Preston, Northamptonshire, England," whose widow Alice had come to America, and was living in Roxbury. She had in this country, besides Bridget, these three sons: *John Thompson; Anthony Thompson*, recorded in New Haven, Conn., in 1643, as a planter; and *William Thompson*, who died in New Haven in 1683. George and Bridget (Thompson) Denison had two children born in Roxbury:

5 SARAH, b. March 20, 1641; *m.* Thomas Stanton, Jr.
6 HANNAH, b. May 20, 1643; twice married.

The wife, Bridget, died in 1643. George Denison then went to England, served under Cromwell in the army of the Parliament, won distinction, was wounded at Naseby, was nursed at the house of John Borodell, by his daughter Ann, was married to Ann, returned to Roxbury, and finally settled at Stonington, Conn. The children of George and Ann (Borodell) Denison, were as follows:

7 JOHN, b. July 14, 1646; *m.* Phebe Lay.
8 ANN, b. May 20, 1649; *m.* Gershom Palmer.
9 BORODELL, b. in 1651; *m.* Samuel Stanton.
10 GEORGE, b. in 1653; *m.* Mercy Gorham.
11 WILLIAM, b. in 1655; *m.* Sarah Stanton.
12 MARGARET, b. in 1657; *m.* James Brown, Jr.
13 MERCY, b. in 1659; d. March 10, 1671.

George Denison died in Hartford, Oct. 23, 1694, while there on some special business, being 76 years old. His

---

* There is a lack of agreement relative to the birth-date of Capt. George Denison. Some insist that he was born in 1621, because the figures on his gravestone make him 73 years old when he died. Others very strongly doubt the correctness of those figures. We do not accept them as correct, for it seems to us extremely improbable that he was hardly 20 years old when his first child was born, and also, 6 years younger than his second wife. Therefore, we agree with those who say he was born in 1618.

wife, Ann Borodell, died Sept. 26, 1712, aged 97 years. They were both remarkable for magnificent personal appearance, and for force of mind and character. She was always called "Lady Ann." They held a foremost place in Stonington. At the time of their marriage, in 1645, she was 30 years old and he 27. He has been described as " the Miles Standish of the settlement ;" but he was a greater and more brilliant soldier than Miles Standish. He had no equal in any of the colonies, for conducting a war against the Indians, excepting perhaps Capt. John Mason. Miss Calkins, in her history of New London, says of him : " Our early history presents no character of bolder and more active spirit than Capt. George Denison; he reminds us of the border men of Scotland." In emergencies he was always in demand, and he was almost constantly placed in important public positions.

5 SARAH DENISON, (dau. of 4 George,) b. March 20, 1641, was married to Thomas Stanton, Jr., (son of Thomas who was one of the first two settlers in Stonington.) They lived in Stonington. There is no existing public record of either the date of their marriage or of the births of their children, but they were probably married in 1659. The following record of their children is believed to be correct :

  14 MARY, b. in 1660; bapt. Dec. 14, 1674.
  15 THOMAS, b. in 1665; bapt. Dec. 14, 1674; d. in 1683.
  16 SARAH, b. in 1673; bapt. Dec. 14, 1674.
  17 ANN, b. in 1675; bapt. June 30, 1675.
  18 WILLIAM, b. in 1677; bapt. May 6, 1677.
  19 DOROTHY, b. in 1680; bapt. April 24, 1681.
  20 SAMUEL, b. in 1682; bapt. May 21, 1682.

Between Mary and Thomas, and between Thomas and Sarah, there may have been others who died in infancy. Mary *m.* Robert Lay, Jr., of Saybrook, Jan. 22, 1679; Sarah *m.* Nathaniel Chesebro', Jr., Jan. 13, 1692; Ann *m.* Thomas Stanton, her cousin, son of Capt. John ; William *m.* Anna Stanton, his cousin, dau. of Robert, May 7, 1701 ; Dorothy was thrice married; Samuel was twice married. Mr. Thomas Stanton, the father, died in Stonington, April 11, 1718, aged 80 years.

6 HANNAH DENISON, (dau. of 4 George,) b. May 20, 1643, was married to Nathaniel Chesebro', in 1659. He was son of

William and Anna (Stevenson) Chesebro'; and was baptized at Boston, England, Jan. 25, 1630. William Chesebro' was born in 1594. He and Thomas Stanton were the first two settlers in Stonington. Nathaniel and Hannah (Denison) Chesebro' lived in Stonington and had eight children :

 21 ANNA. b. Oct. 12, 1660 ; *m.* Samuel Richardson.
 22 SARAH, b. Jan. 30, 1662.
 23 NATHANIEL, b, April 14, 1666; *m.* Sarah Stanton.
 24 BRIDGET, b. March 25, 1669; twice married.
 25 HANNAH, b. in 1672; bapt. Nov. 14, 1674.
 26 SAMUEL. b. Feb. 14, 1674.
 27 MARGARET, b. in 1676; bapt. April 15, 1617; *m.* Jos. Stanton.
 28 MARY, b. in 1678; bapt. June 30, 1678.

The first six were born previous to the organization of the church in Stonington. Nathaniel Chesebro' was one of the first nine members of the church. He died Nov. 22, 1678 ; and, July 15, 1680, Hannah Denison, his widow, was married to Capt. Joseph Saxton of Stonington, and had :

 29 MARY, b. in 1681; bapt. Sept. 4, 1681; *m.* Benj. Minor.
 30 JERUSHA, b. in 1683; bapt. Dec. 2, 1683.
 31 MERCY, b. in 1686; bapt. May 30, 1686.

Capt. Joseph Saxton was thirteen years younger than his wife. He was born at Boston, May 9, 1656, and was the third son of Thomas Saxton of Boston, and his second wife, Ann (Copp) Atwood. He settled in Stonington, and was largely engaged in the West India trade, by which he became very wealthy. His will, dated July 8, 1715, was admitted to probate in New London, Conn., a few weeks later. By this will, he left one third of all his property to his "loving wife Hannah, to have during her life," and most of the remaining two thirds to his two grandsons, *Saxton Palmer* and *Saxton Bailey*. His widow withheld the will for a time, and there was what is described as "an interesting controversy," before it was admitted to probate. She seems to have had two reasons for being not well pleased with it : first, it gave her only a life interest in one third of the estate, which, as she was then 72 years old, did not appear to be such an interest as she was entitled to ; and, second, she probably thought the great estate was not properly distributed among his grand children.

29 MARY SAXTON, (dau. of 6 Hannah and Capt. Joseph,) was married, first, Nov. 15, 1697, to Benjamin Minor, son of

Capt. Denison's Daughters.

Joseph, and grandson of the first Thomas Minor. They had these children:

32 MARY, b. July 31, 1699.
33 MERCY, b. May 2, 1702.
34 BENJAMIN, b. June 22, 1706.
35 CLEMENT. b. Oct. 1, 1709.
36 SARAH, b. June 10, 1710.

Benjamin Minor died; and she was married, second, to Joseph Page of Stonington, March 5, 1713. She died Oct. 17, 1750. Her children by Joseph Page were baptized in Stonington, as follows:

37 HANNAH, May 30, 1714; m. Simeon Minor, Dec. 29, 1731.
38 ELIZABETH, Sept. 29, 1717; m. John Billings, April 7, 1743.
39 JOSEPH, May 13, 1722; m. Catherine Ranger.
40 PHEBE, July 5, 1724.

30 JERUSHA SAXTON, (dau. of 6 Hannah and Capt. Joseph,) was married Jan. 17, 1699, to Nehemiah Palmer, Jr., son of Nehemiah and Hannah (Stanton) Palmer. He was baptized in Stonington, July 8, 1677; and he and his wife, Jerusha Saxton, had these born there:

41 SAXTON, b. Nov. 29, 1700.
42 THOMAS, b. July 7, 1703.
43 JERUSHA, b. April 30, 1705; m. James Dean.
44 NEHEMIAH, b. Feb. 4, 1707.
45 STEPHEN, b. May 1, 1709; m. Elizabeth Quimby.
46 ABIJAH, b. Sept. 29, 1712.
47 THANKFUL, b. April 24, 1714.
48 DAVID, b. Dec, 22, 1717.
49 MARY, b. 1719.
50 BRIDGET, b. April 8, 1721; m. John Gallup.

Jerusha Saxton had two more husbands, but no more children. Her will was admitted to probate in Windham, Conn.

31 MERCY SAXTON, (dau. of 6 Hannah and Capt. Joseph,) was married to Isaac Bailey of Roxbury, Mass, June 4, 1702. They lived in Stonington until 1707, when they emigrated to Lebanon. Their record after this date has not been secured; but, among their children born in Lebanon, there was a son named Saxton Bailey. They had these two children baptized in Stonington:

51 JOSEPH, July 25, 1703.
52 MARY, March 10, 1706.

27 MARGARET CHESEBRO', (dau. of 6 Hannah and Nathaniel,) was married July 18, 1696, to Joseph Stanton, (son of Capt. John.) She was great grandmother of Hannah Stanton, who was born March 11, 1786, and married to Daniel Baldwin, in 1808. Her children were :

- **53** HANNAH, b. Dec. 15, 1698; *m.* Wm. Morgan.
- **54** MARGARET, b. Oct. 7, 1701; *m.* Jonathan Copp, Dec. 28, 1721.
- **55** ZERVIAH, b. Sept. 24, 1704; *m.* Nehemiah Mason, Jan. 9, 1722.
- **56** SARAH, b. Feb. 22, 1706; *m.* William Halsey, June 19, 1738.
- **57** ANNA, b. Aug. 6, 1708; *m.* John Avery, Feb. 19, 1732.
- **58** DOROTHY, b. and d. in July, 1710.
- **59** JOSEPH, b. May 1, 1712; *m.* Anna Wheeler, Nov. 6, 1735.
- **60** JOHN, b. Sept. 29, 1714; *m.* Prudence Chesebro', Feb. 27, 1737.
- **61** NATHANIEL, b. July 29, 1716; *m.* Mary Colt, dau. of Rev. Joseph Coit, the first minister of Plainfield, Conn., and was grandfather of the above named Hannah Stanton, through his son, Capt. Nathaniel Stanton.

23 NATHANIEL CHESEBRO', Jr., (son of 6 Hannah and Nathaniel,) was married Jan. 13, 1692, to his cousin, Sarah Stanton, dau. of Thomas, Jr., and Sarah (Denison) Stanton. She was born in 1673. Their children :

- **62** SARAH, b. Jan. 3, 1693; d. Jan. 8, 1693.
- **63** SARAH, b. Sept. 25, 1694; d. Nov. 22, 1707.
- **64** HANNAH, bapt. Sept. 5, 1697; d. young.
- **65** NATHANIEL, b. May 11, 1700; d. Aug. 5, 1701.
- **66** THANKFUL, b. April 4, 1703; d. Nov. 6, 1704.
- **67** NATHAN, b. Aug. 2, 1707; *m.* Bridget Noyes.
- **68** KETURAH, b. Sept. 2, 1733; by a second wife.

67 NATHAN CHESEBRO', (son of 23 Nathaniel,) *m.* Bridget Noyes, Nov. 2, 1727. She was dau. of Dr. James Noyes, and grand daughter of Rev. James Noyes; and was born in 1710. Their children :

- **69** NATHAN, bapt. May 4, 1729.
- **70** KETURAH, bapt. Sept. 1732.
- **71** PELEG, bapt. Feb. 13, 1737.
- **72** ROBERT, bapt. April 15, 1739.
- **73** CODDINTON, bapt. March 29, 1741.
- **74** BRIDGET, bapt. Nov. 14, 1742.
- **75** JAMES, bapt. Nov. 4, 1744; d. young.
- **76** ANN, bapt. March 29, 1747.
- **77** JAMES, bapt. Sept. 11, 1749.

26 SAMUEL CHESEBRO', (son of 6 Hannah and Nathaniel,) was married and had 12 children. The records of the First Cong. Church in Stonington say : " July 14, 1695, Mary, wife

Capt. Denison's Daughters.

of Samuel Chesebro', was baptized." On the same day they presented two children for baptism. Their twelve children were baptized in Stonington as follows:

78 SAMUEL, July 14, 1695.
79 WILLIAM, July 14, 1695.
80 JEREMIAH, Oct. 4, 1697.
81 JONATHAN, Oct. 21, 1700.
82 JOSEPH, April 12, 1703.
83 MARY, July 15, 1805; d. young.
84 PRISCILLA, July 15, 1705; m. Jabez Chesebro'.
85 ANN, April 12. 1707; d. young.
86 AMOS, April 24, 1709.
87 MARY, Oct. 22, 1710.
88 ANN, Aug. 24, 1712.
89 SARAH, Oct. 9, 1715.

8 ANN DENISON, (dau. of 4 George,) b. May 20, 1649, was married, Nov. 28, 1667, to Dea. Gershom Palmer; lived in Stonington. He was the sixth child of Walter and Rebecca (Short) Palmer. She d. in 1694; and he m. 2nd, Elizabeth, widow of Maj. Samuel Mason. He d. Sept. 27, 1718. The children:

90 MERCY, b. in 1669; m. John Breed in 1689.
91 GERSHOM, b. in 1672; bapt. Sept. 9, 1677.
92 ICHABOD, b. in 1675; bapt. Sept. 9, 1677.
93 WILLIAM, b. in 1677; bapt. April 25, 1678; m. Grace Minor.
94 GEORGE, b. in 1680; bapt. May 29, 1681.
95 ANN, b. in 1683; bapt. May 20, 1683; d. in 1684.
96 WALTER, b. in 1685; bapt. June 7, 1685; m. Grace Vose.
97 ELIHU, b. in 1688; bapt. May 6, 1688.
98 MARY, b. in 1690; bapt. June 8, 1690.
99 REBECCA, b. in 1694; bapt. July 1, 1694.

90 MERCY PALMER, (dau. of 8 Ann and Dea. Gershom,) b. in 1669, was married April 11, 1689, to John Breed, from Lynn, Mass. He d. in 1751, aged 90; she d. in 1752, aged 83. Their children:

100 MERCY, bapt. March 1, 1691.
101 ANNA, bapt. Nov. 20, 1692; d. in infancy.
102 ANNA, b. Nov. 8, 1693; m. Maj. Israel Hewett.
103 MARY, b. Jan. 8, 1697.
104 JOHN, b. Jan. 26, 1700; m. Mary Prentice.
105 ELIZABETH, b. June 28, 1702.
106 SARAH, b. Feb. 7, 1704; m. James Minor.
107 ZERVIAH, b. Aug. 27, 1706; m. Samuel Hinckley.
108 JOSEPH, b. Oct. 4, 1708; m. Priscilla ———.

109 BETHIAH, b. Dec. 20, 1710.
110 ALLEN, b. Aug. 29, 1714.
111 GERSHOM, b. Nov. 15, 1715; *m.* Dorothy ———.

91 GERSHOM PALMER, Jr., (son of 8 Ann and Dea. Gershom,) b. in 1672, was married, June 28, 1715, to Hannah Spencer, who d. Nov. 22, 1766, aged 77 and over. His children are recorded in Windham, Conn., as follows:

112 JONAH. b. July 18, 1716.
113 PHEBE, b. Nov. 20, 1718.
114 SHUBAEL, b. Jan. 14, 1720.
115 HANNAH, b. May 16, 1726.

92 ICHABOD PALMER, (son of 8 Ann and Dea. Gershom,) was married in 1698, to Hannah Palmer, his cousin, dau. of Nehemiah and Hannah (Stanton) Palmer. Their children:

116 LUCY, b. in 1699; bapt. May 28, 1699.
117 ICHABOD, in 1702; bapt. Jan. 10, 1703.
118 PRUDENCE, b. May 29, 1706; bapt. July 26, 1706.
119 DANIEL, b. in 1703; bapt. Dec. 18, 1709.
120 NATHANIEL, b. Oct. 1, 1709; *m.* Mary Chesebro'.
121 ELIAS, bapt. May 15, 1715.

120 NATHANIEL PALMER, (son of 92 Ichabod,) *m.* Mary Chesebro', June 9, 1731. They lived in Stonington. Their children:

122 ANN, b. March 12, 1732.
123 LUCRETIA, b. Aug. 3, 1734.
124 LUCY, b. Sept. 25, 1737.
125 NATHANIEL, b. Aug. 19, 1740; *m.* Grace Noyes.
126 DAVID, b. Jan. 9, 1742; he was killed at Fort Griswold.
127 MARY, b. July 30, 1744.

125 NATHANIEL PALMER, 2nd, (son of 120 Nathaniel,) *m.* Grace Noyes, Aug. 18, 1765; lived in Stonington. She was dau. of James Noyes, and great grand daughter of Rev. James Noyes. Their children:

128 PAUL, b. May 24, 1766; d. Sept. 17, 1766.
129 NATHANIEL, b. Dec. 15, 1768; *m.* Mercy Brown.
130 GRACE, b. May 25, 1772; *m.* a Durfee and had 4 children, viz., Sarah, Grace N., Nathaniel, and Pauline.
131 LUKE, b. Feb. 14, 1775; *m.* Sally Potter Denison.
132 MARY, b. May 3, 1777; d. Aug. 4, 1777.
133 POLLY, b. Jan. 21, 1780; *m.* Noyes Brown and had 7 children.
134 BETSEY, b. Sept. 8, 1785; *m.* David Smith and had Betsey S.
135 WARREN, b. March 3, 1788.

129 NATHANIEL PALMER, 3rd, (son of 125 Nathaniel, 2d,) *m*. Mercy Brown, March 18, 1798 ; lived in Stonington. Their children :

    136 NATHANIEL B., b. Aug. 8, 1799.
    137 ANN ADELAIDE, b. Nov. 26, 1800; *m.* Chas. T. Stanton.
    138 GRACE NOYES, b. Oct. 18, 1802; *m.* Jos. W. Stanton.
    139 LOUIS LAMBERT, b. Feb. 8, 1804.
    140 ALEXANDER SMITH, b. Jan. 26, 1806.
    141 JULIET, b. Feb. 25, 1808.
    142 MERCY, b. Aug. 8, 1811; d. Aug. 11, 1811.
    143 WILLIAM LORD, b. Nov. 3, 1813
    144 NANCY LORD, b. Nov. 3, 1813, twin to Wm. L.
    145 THEODORE DWIGHT, b. Aug. 29, 1816.

131 LUKE PALMER, (son of 125 Nathaniel, 2nd,) b. Feb. 14, 1775, was married March 11, 1804, to Sally Potter Denison, who was born Sept. 2, 1785 ; lived in Stonington ; d. there Dec. 25, 1822 ; she d. July 9, 1862. Children :

    146 SALLY MARIA, b. Jan. 7, 1805 ; d. Nov. 3, 1874, unmarried.
    147 BETSEY DENISON, b. Nov. 29, 1806; *m.* William Weed, Nov. 6, 1836; d. in Stonington, July 12, 1843; 3 children : Hannah P., Williams, and Luke. Hannah Palmer Weed, the daughter, b. Oct. 6, 1837, at Milwaukee, Wis., *m.* George Sheffield, at Westerly, R. I., Oct. 21, 1857. P. O. Pleasantville, Pa. Their children:
        HENRY, b. April 2, 1859.
        GEORGE, Jr., Nov. 21, 1861.
        WM. WEED, Nov. 21, 1861; d. Sept. 23, 1862.
        JESSIE, b. Nov. 3, 1864.
        FANNY, b. Feb. 12, 1868; d. Feb. 13, 1868.
    148 LUKE, Jr., b. Oct. 19, 1808 ; *m.* Mary E. Holbrook, of Burlington, Iowa, Jan. 8, 1851; two children : Luke, b. Nov. 20, 1851 ; Sarah Maria, b. Oct. 18, 1853 ; *m.* John S. Cameron, Jan. 4, 1876.
    148½ HANNAH WILLIAMS, b. Aug. 4, 1810; *m.* Joshua Noyes, Mar. 8, 1848 ; no child ; P. O. North East, Pa.
    149 GRACE BILLINGS, b. Aug. 28, 1812.
    150 HARRIET NEWELL, b. Aug. 31, 1814; *m.* Theodore Butler, April 24, 1837; d. Jan. 5, 1860; 7 children : Harriet, Grace, Ellen, Sarah Denison, Theodore Hunt, James, Grace, and Frederick. Harriet, *m.* James Peck; has children; P. O. Chicago, Ill.

149 GRACE BILLINGS PALMER, (dau. of 131 Luke,) b. Aug. 28, 1812, *m.* 1st, June 21, 1830, at Stonington, Daniel Carew, b. March, 1808. Their children :

    151 SARAH ELIZABETH, b. Jan. 15, 1833; *m.* James Sheldon.

Capt. Denison's Daughters.

152 ABBIE CHESEBRO', b. Nov. 27, 1834; *m.* Louis H. Kniskern, Oct. 1, 1868; d. at Dubuque, Iowa, July 2, 1870; one child: Grace Gertrude, b. July 1, 1870 ; d. July 1, 1870.
153 DANIEL, Jr., b. Feb. 28, 1837; d. March 20, 1837.

Daniel Carew died at sea, Aug. 19, 1837 ; the widow *m.* 2nd, Nathaniel Wilgus, April 5, 1852. He was born July 24, 1793, and died March 28, 1873. Their child :

154 EDWARD DENISON, b. Nov. 8, 1854, at Buffalo.

151 SARAH ELIZABETH CAREW, (dau. of 149 Grace Billings Palmer and Daniel Carew,) b. Jan. 15, 1833, *m.* James Sheldon, at Buffalo, N. Y., April 4, 1854. Their children :

155 GRACE CAREW, b. March 25, 1855.
156 JAMES, Jr., b. July 20, 1856.
157 SARAH PALMER, b. March 5, 1858.
158 SYLVIA ALEXANDER, b. Oct. 9, 1859.
159 GEORGE, b. Dec. 24, 1860.
160 THEODORE BUTLER, b. Dec. 12, 1862.
161 DANIEL CAREW, b. in 1864; d. in infancy.
162 AGNES DOUGLAS, b. Dec. 1, 1866.
163 HENRY ALEXANDER, b. Sept. 23, 1870.
164 ROBERT CAREW, b. May 10, 1872.

9 BORODELL DENISON, (dau. of 4 George,) b. in 1651, was married to Samuel Stanton, (son of the first Thomas,) June 16, 1680, she being 29 years old and he 23. They lived in Stonington, and had these three children :

165 SAMUEL, b. June 16, 1683; twice married.
166 DANIEL, b. Nov. 4, 1685; *m.* Mary Chesebro'.
167 ANNA, b. July 2, 1688; *m.* Thomas Jackson, of Boston.

12 MARGARET DENISON, (dau. of 4 George,) b. in 1657, was married June 5, 1676, to James Brown, Jr., of Swanzy, Mass. They lived in Swanzy ; had these children recorded there :

168 LYDIA, b. Jan. 23, 1678; d. Feb. 1, 1678.
169 MARY, b. Sept. 11, 1680; d. young.
170 LYDIA, b. July 28, 1684.
171 JAMES, b. Sept. 7, 1685; *m.* Elizabeth Hunt, Dec. 20, 1711.
172 MARGARET, b. July 5, 1687.
173 PELEG, b. Feb. 28, 1689.
174 WILLIAM, b. June 2, 1690.
175 MARY, b. Nov. 25, 1699; *m.* John Thurber, April 8, 1726.
176 ISAAC, b. Dec. 2, 1702.

DESCENDANTS OF

CAPT. JOHN DENISON, OF STONINGTON,

OLDEST SON OF

C A P T. G E O R G E.

CAPT. JOHN DENISON'S DESCENDANTS.

I.

7 JOHN DENISON, (George¹,) b. July 14, 1646, was married Nov. 26, 1667, to Phebe Lay, dau. of Robert and Sarah Lay of Saybrook, Ct. The marriage contract or deed of settlement, arranged between their parents, is recorded in Saybrook. By this deed of settlement, executed before the marriage, the respective parents conveyed to John Denison and Phebe Lay, the farm granted to Capt. George Denison near the mouth of Mystic river in Stonington, and the house and land in Saybrook, which Mr. Lay had formerly bought of John Post. This deed was witnessed by Rev. Simon Bradstreet, and " Ann Denison, Jr." They settled in Stonington, on " the farm near the mouth of Mystic river." He was known as " Capt. John Denison," held a prominent position in Stonington, and in many ways, was a man of mark. He died in 1698, aged 52 years ; his wife died in 1699, aged 49. Their children :

177 JOHN, b. Jan. 1, 1669; lived in Saybrook.
178 GEORGE, b. March 28, 1671; lived in New London.
179 ROBERT, b. Sept. 17, 1673; lived in Mohegan.
180 WILLIAM, b. April 7, 1677; lived in North Stonington.
181 DANIEL, b. March 28, 1680; lived in Stonington.
182 SAMUEL, b. Feb. 23, 1683; d. May 12. 1683.
183 ANN, b. Oct. 3, 1684; twice married; first to Samuel Minor of Stonington; 2nd, to Edward Denison of Westerly, R. I.; no child.
184 PHEBE. bapt. April 6, 1690; *m.* Ebenezer Billings, Jr.
185 SARAH, b. July 20, 1692; *m.* Isaac Williams.

184 PHEBE DENISON, (John², George¹,) b. April 6, 1690, was married, April 2, 1706, to Ebenezer Billings ; lived in Stonington ; he d. July 20, 1760 ; she d. Dec. 30, 1775. Children :

186 ABIGAIL, b. Mar. 1, 1707; *m.* Samuel Prentice.
187 JOHN, b. Dec. 7, 1708; *m.* —— Page.
188 EBENEZER, b. Mar. 20, 1710.

189 SANFORD, b. 1712; d. unmarried.
190 PHEBE, b. Apr. 4, 1714; *m.* Dr. Nathan Palmer.
191 GRACE, b. May 27, 1716; *m.* James Noyes.
192 ANN, b. Jan. 21, 1718; *m.* Samuel Prentice.
193 JABEZ, b. Sept. 29, 1720.
194 CHRISTOPHER, b. Feb., 1723.
195 DANIEL, b. Feb. 10, 1725; d. June 1, 1745.
196 NATHAN, b. April 9, 1727; *m.* Mary Bell.
197 ELIZABETH, b. 173); *m.* —— Spalding.
198 BORODELL, b. April 18, 1732; *m.* Oliver Grant.

185 SARAH DENISON, (John², George¹,) b. July 20, 1692, was married, Nov. 7, 1711, to Isaac Williams ; lived in Stonington. Children :

199 SARAH, b. March 2. 1713; *m.* Joshua Culver.
200 MARTHA, bapt. April 22, 1716.
201 ISAAC, b. March 11, 1717; d. in 1801, aged 84.
202 NATHAN, b. July 22, 1720; *m.* Elizabeth Haley.
203 ASTWOOD, b. April 16, 1723.
204 WARHAM, b. April 2, 1727; *m.* Rebecca Satterly.
205 PHEBE, b. March 26, 1731; *m.* Daniel Brewster.
206 EUNICE, b. Dec. 25, 1732; *m.* Richard Williams.

II.

177 JOHN DENISON, Jr., (John², George¹,) b. Jan. 1, 1669, was married in 1690, to Ann Mason, dau. of Capt. John Mason, who was killed in 1675, in the Narragansett fort fight with the Indians. He lived in Saybrook, Ct.; died in Saybrook in 1699, and had these children recorded there, Jabez excepted :

207 JOHN, b. March 30, 1692; d. in 1732, unmarried.
208 DANIEL, b. Oct. 13, 1693; *m.* Mehitabel Foster.
209 JAMES, b. Feb. 26, 1695; d. in 1717, unmarried.
210 ABIGAIL, b. Aug. 25, 1696; *m.* Dea. Ebenezer Pratt, May 6, 1717; lived and died in Saybrook; no child.
211 JABEZ, b. Aug. 1698; *m.* Dorothy Cogswell.

March 17, 1701, Mrs. Ann (Mason) Denison, his widow, was married to Samuel Cogswell. John Denison Jr., has descendants only through his sons, Daniel and Jabez.

207 JOHN DENISON, (John, Jr.³, John², George¹,) b. March 30, 1692, lived unmarried, in Saybrook, Ct., and died there in 1732, at the age of 40. His will was dated Feb. 17, 1731, and was admitted to probate at Guilford, Ct., Jan. 18, 1733. He

Capt. John Denison's Descendants. 19

had a large estate, chiefly in lands, which he gave mostly to his brothers, Daniel and Jabez; but he gave £100 to establish a school at Essex, and the school is still in existence. The probate of his will is recorded in Vol. 3, at page 53, of the Guilford probate records. Inventory £821—19s—8d.

208 DANIEL DENISON, (John, Jr.[3], John[2], George[1],) b. Oct. 13. 1793, was married, about 1728, to Mehitabel Foster; lived in Saybrook. In 1734 he deeded a real estate right to his brother Jabez. March 15, 1728, land was laid out to him from his father's estate, on account of his marriage, probably. He died in Saybrook at the age of 92. His children:

    212 DANIEL, Jr., b. in 1729; lived in Walpole, N. H.
    213 EBENEZER, b. in 1731; *m.* Lydia Williams.
    214 HEPZIBAH, b. in 1733.
    215 PHEBE, b. in 1735.
    216 ABIGAIL, b. in 1737; *m.* Asa Pratt.
    217 ANN, b. in 1740.

212 DANIEL DENISON, Jr., (Daniel[4], John, Jr.[3], John[2], George[1],) b. in 1729, emigrated to Walpole, N. H., about 1762. He was there in 1786, when he bought Pew No. 22, in the meeting-house. His wife's name is not known; but they had these two children:

    218 JOHN, b. in 1751 probably; *m.* Lucy Wells.
    219 KETURAH, b. after 1762, probably; *m.* Edward Watkins.

218 JOHN DENISON, (Daniel[5], Daniel[4], John, Jr.[3], John[2], George[1],) was married to Lucia (or Lucy) Wells about 1773. He emigrated from Saybrook to Walpole, N. H., with his father, in 1762. He held several town offices there, one of which, held in 1773, was "deer reeve." He probably died in 1796, for, after this date to 1802, the taxes were paid by Widow Lucy Denison. His children:

    220 ELIJAH, b. in 1775; d. in Rochester, N. Y.
    221 LUCY, b. Sept. 25, 1777; *m.* Benj. Marsh.
    222 JOHN, b. Jan. 25, 1780; d. June 7, 1782.
    223 PAUL, b. Feb. 0, 1782; d. Oct. 25, 1784.
    224 JOHN, b. in 1784; *m.* Mary ——.
    225 ZIBA, b. Oct. 25, 1786; *m.* Parnell Graves.

220 ELIJAH DENISON, (John[6], Daniel[5], Daniel[4], John Jr.[3], John[2], George[1],) b. in 1775, emigrated from Walpole, N. H., to Rochester, N. Y., where he died in 1850. He was married and had three sons and one daughter.

221 LUCY DENISON, (John[6], Daniel[5], Daniel[4], John, Jr.,[3] John[2], George[1],) b. Sept. 25, 1777, was married to Benjamin Marsh, of Walpole, N. H. They settled at Coral, McHenry Co., Illinois, and had ten children, five sons and five daughters.

224 JOHN DENISON, 3d, (John[6], Daniel[5], Daniel[4], John, Jr.[3], John[2], George[1],) b. in 1784, was married to Mary ———, about 1806, in Walpole, N. H., and had one son and six daughters. In 1824 he emigrated to Ohio. His oldest child was:

    226 LUCY, b. March 26, 1808.

225 ZIBA DENISON, (John[6], Daniel[5], Daniel[4], John, Jr.[3], John[2], George[1],) b. Oct. 25, 1786, was married Jan. 1, 1811, to Parnell Graves. He lived in Walpole, N. H., until 1817, in which year he paid taxes there on the following property: money at interest $300; a small farm and six cattle; and a house site with an old chimney on it, "about three miles from the town clerk's office, known as the Denison House where he (Ziba,) used to live." In 1817, he went to Herkimer Co., N. Y. He lived in Chenango Co., N. Y., when his youngest child was born, in 1822. He and his wife both died in Warwick Co., Indiana, in 1851. His children:

    227 PAUL, b. Sept. 8, 1811; d. in Indiana.
    228 LEWIS, b. April 5, 1813; twice married; no child; d. March 22, 1864, at Newburg, Indiana.
    229 HIRAM, b. June 15, 1815; m. Huldah Hart.
    230 ALVINA, b. Jan. 10, 1822; m. a Rand in 1848; d. in August, 1849.

227 PAUL DENISON, (Ziba[7], John[6], Daniel[5], Daniel[4], John, Jr.[3], John[2], George[1],) b. Sept. 8, 1811, was married in 1849, to Louisa Oberlin; lived in Missouri and in Illinois; d. in Indiana, July 27, 1870. His children:

    231 FRANCIS MARION.   **231½** WILLIAM ZIBA.

229 HIRAM DENISON, (Ziba[7], John[6], Daniel[5], Daniel[4], John, Jr.[3], John[2], George[1],) b. June 15, 1815, was married, April 14, 1836, to Huldah Hart, who died in Ohio, April 1, 1850. He married 2d, Widow Louisa Macomber, in 1853. He settled in Michigan, with P. O. address in 1877, at Kalamazoo. His children:

    232 WILLIS, b. Jan. 21, 1837.
    233 SELINA, b. March 5, 1838; d. Feb. 22, 1850.
    234 LILLIE IDA, b. April 16, 1856.
    235 CARRIE EUGENIA, b. April 12, 1863.

232 WILLIS DENISON, (Hiram⁸, Ziba⁷, John⁶, Daniel⁵, Daniel⁴, John, Jr.³, John², George¹,) b. Jan. 21, 1837, was married Jan. 1, 1863, to Susan Beach of Kalamazoo, Mich. Settled in Benton, Elkhart Co., Indiana, where his wife died, June 22, 1876. His children:

    236 SILENA, b. April 11, 1864.
    237 SARAH ANN, b. June 26, 1866.
    238 HULDAH JANE, b. Sept. 3, 1867.
    239 ELLA MAY, b. Oct. 17, 1870.
    240 HIRAM JAY, b. Nov. 22, 1875.

219 KETURAH DENISON, (Daniel⁵, Daniel⁴, John, Jr.³, John², George¹,) b. about 1762, was married, Oct. 3, 1786, to Edward Watkins; lived in Walpole, N. H. Children:

    241 MIRIAM, b. March 7, 1791.
    242 IRA, b. April 19, 1793; d. young; fell from a horse.
    243 ALPHEUS, b. May 29, 1797; d. Jan. 3, 1800.
    244 CHARLOTTE, b. July 21, 1799.
    245 ROYAL, b. Dec. 1, 1808.

213 EBENEZER DENISON, (Daniel⁴, John, Jr.³, John², George¹,) b. in 1731, was married to Lydia Williams. He lived in Essex, Ct.; d. there in May, 1821; his wife d. in March, 1810. Their children:

    246 EBENEZER, Jr., b. March 1762; twice married.
    247 WELLS, b. March, 1765; m. Jedidah Tyler.
    248 SABRA, b. in 1767; d. unmarried, aged 82.
    249 LYDIA, b. Oct. 17, 1774; m. J. Clark.

246 EBENEZER DENISON, Jr., (Ebenezer⁵, Daniel⁴, John, Jr.³, John², George¹,) b. March, 1762, was married, first, to Mehitabel Dickerson, who d. childless. In 1795, he was married, second, to 419 Mehitabel Denison, dau. of John and grand dau. of Jabez 1st. She d. Feb. 22, 1849, aged 75; he d. Aug. 1851, aged 89. Their children:

    250 ANN BORODELL, b. Feb. 26, 1797; m. Stephen Gaskill.
    251 MEHITABEL D., bapt. Oct. 26, 1800; m. M. Converse; 7 ch.
    252 LUCRETIA, b. 1803; twice married; 7 ch.
    253 MARY, b. 1805; twice married; 7 ch.
    254 TITUS, b. 1807; twice married; 4 ch.
    255 EUNICE M., b. 1810; m. Wm. Edes.
    256 ERASTUS, b. 1814; died aged 16.

250 ANN BORODELL DENISON, (Ebenezer⁶, Ebenezer⁵, Daniel⁴, John, Jr.³, John², George¹,) b. Feb. 26, 1797, was married in 1820, to Stephen Gaskill. She d. April 17, 1850, aged 53; he d. Sept. 2, 1870, aged 73. Their children:

257 JABEZ, b. April 25, 1821; m. Lydia Wing; he d. July 21, 1876; had three children: Ann Eliza, Philena Jane, W. Adelbert.
258 HELEN JANE, b. Nov. 23, 1823; d. March 27, 1862.
259 OLIVE ELIZA, b. Oct. 23, 1825; m. Daniel S. Douglass, of Clinton, N. Y., March 25, 1856; three children: James Frank, b. March 23, 1859 and d. May 10 1865; Mary Ann, b. Feb. 4, 1862; and Stephen Charles, b. Sept. 1, 1866.

247 WELLS DENISON, (Ebenezer[5], Daniel[4], John, Jr.[3], John[2], George[1],) b. in 1765, was married Feb. 14, 1790, to Jedidah Tyler of Haddam, Ct. He died Sept. 1, 1846, aged 81 years. His children:

260 DANIEL W., b. Nov. 14, 1793; d. Sept. 12, 1864; unmarried.
261 CLARISSA, b. 1795; m. Luther Hull.
262 ABRAHAM, b. July 28, 1804; m. Abby Post.
263 JEDIDAH, b. June 1, 1806; m. David B. Ventris.
264 SELDEN S., b. Sept, 1809; m. Mary Allen.
265 TIMOTHY T., bapt. July 28, 1799; m. Selden S.'s widow.

261 CLARISSA DENISON, (Wells[6], Ebenezer[5], Daniel[4], John, Jr.[3], John[2], George[1],) b. in 1795, was married, May 18, 1819, to Luther Hull, of Killingworth, Ct. She died in July, 1848. Children:

266 LEVI HULL; lives in Centerbrook, Ct.
267 FRANCES J., b. July 19, 1826; m. J. S. Buell.
268 SELDEN T.; lives in Middletown, Ct.; 7 ch.
269 GEORGE L., lives in Portland, Ct.

262 ABRAHAM DENISON, (Wells[6], Ebenezer[5], Daniel[4], John, Jr.[3], John[2], George[1],) b. July 28, 1804, was married to Abby Post, June 16, 1825. He lived in Essex, Ct. Children:

270 EZRA SELDEN, b. March 20, 1826; d. Sept. 10, 1828.
271 CHARLES, b. Nov. 1, 1827; d. Sept. 19, 1828.
272 CLARISSA POST, b. June 29, 1829; unmarried.
273 MARTHA, b. May 9, 1831; m. W. S. Williams.
274 EZRA SELDEN, b. Sept. 10, 1833; unmarried.
275 GEORGE EUGENE, b. March 10, 1836; m. Harriet M. Goodman.
276 CHARLES A., b. June 16, 1838; m. Clara Brewster.
277 ABBY AUGUSTA, b. Aug. 27, 1843; unmarried.

273 MARTHA DENISON, (dau. of 262 Abraham,) b. May 9, 1831, was married, Aug. 27, 1852, to W. S. Williams of Hartford. Children:

279 GELTINE, b. March 7, 1855; d. April 1, 1855.
280 JOSEPHINE, b. April 19, 1857.
281 THATCHER M., b. Jan. 9, 1863; d. Nov. 5, 1865.
282 DENISON P., b. Feb. 23, 1867.

275 GEORGE E. DENISON, (son of 262 Abraham,) b. March 10, 1836, was married Jan. 3, 1859, to Harriet M. Goodman, b. Jan. 26, 1834. He lives in Hartford, Ct. Children:

283 LILLIAN ABBY, b. Nov. 2, 1859.
284 CLARA MARIA, b. Oct. 7, 1861.
285 JULIA BELLE, b. April 22, 1863.
286 HATTIE GOODMAN, b. Dec. 19, 1866.
287 EDGAR FARNSWORTH, b. Feb. 18, 1869; d. July 5, 1870.
288 GRACE WILLIAMS, b. Nov. 8, 1870; d. Jan. 13, 1871.
289 FRANCES EUGENE, b. Dec. 2, 1872.
290 FREDERIC RUSSELL, b. Dec. 8, 1874.

276 CHARLES A. DENISON, (son of 262 Abraham,) b. June 16, 1838, was married July 15, 1873, to Clara Brewster. He lives at Essex, Ct., and has:

291 FRANK DANIEL, b. Jan. 14, 1876.

263 JEDIDAH DENISON, (Wells[6], Ebenezer[5], Daniel[4], John, Jr.[3], John[2], George[1],) b. June 1, 1806, was married, Aug. 29, 1836, to David B. Ventris, of Haddam, Ct. They live in Haddam. Children:

292 ELLEN J., b. June 4, 1837; m. John A. Brainard.
293 NEHEMIAH B., b. March 17, 1839; d. June 22, 1861.
294 FRANCES S., b. June 19, 1842; m. Henry H. Clark.
295 CLARISSA, b. Feb. 2, 1845; d. Sept. 23, 1857.
296 JOHN F., b. Nov. 23, 1847; d. Feb. 17, 1848.
297 ALICE, b. Sept. 29, 1849.

264 SELDEN S. DENISON, (Wells[6], Ebenezer[5], Daniel[4], John, Jr.[3], John[2], George[1],) b. in September, 1809, was married to Mary Allen, of Windham, Ct., May 12, 1830. He died June 24, 1840. Children:

298 OLIVER S. b. Jan. 28, 1837; is in Texas.
299 ELLEN H., b. March 22, 1839; m. Charles S. Munger.

265 TIMOTHY T. DENISON, (Wells[6], Ebenezer[5], Daniel[4], John, Jr.[3], John[2], George[1],) b. in 1799, was married, first, to Eliza Ames, of Chatham, Ct. She died childless, Oct. 29, 1855, aged 55. He married, second, June 8, 1856, Mary, his brother Selden S.'s widow; no child. He d. Aug. 25, 1862; the second wife d. Dec. 8, 1874, aged 65.

299 ELLEN H. DENISON, (dau. of 264 Selden S..) b. March 22, 1839, was married, July 25, 1861, to Charles S. Munger. They live in Essex, Ct. Children :
>**300** HARRIET H., b. Aug. 29, 1862.
>**301** ALLEN SMITH, b. Sept. 28, 1863; d. Sept. 8, 1864.
>**302** FRANK DENISON, b. March 15, 1866.
>**303** EDWIN HOLMES, b. Aug. 13, 1869.
>**304** MARY ELIZA, b. Sept. 22, 1875.

216 ABIGAIL DENISON, (Daniel[4], John, Jr.[3], John[2], George[1],) b. in 1737, was married, Oct. 7, 1759, to Asa Pratt. They lived in Saybrook, Ct. She d. in July, 1830. Their children :
>**305** ASA, b. May, 31, 1761.
>**306** JOHN, b. Aug. 25, 1763.
>**307** ELIAS, b. May 15, 1766.
>**308** JENNETT, b. June 1, 1768.
>**309** LUCINA, b. Nov. 29, 1771; m. John G. Hayden.
>**310** ABIGAIL, b. Dec 8, 1773.
>**311** ANNIE, b. Sept. 25, 1776.
>**312** PIERCY, b. Aug. 7, 1781.

249 LYDIA DENISON, (Ebenezer[5], Daniel[4], John, Jr.[3], John[2], George[1],) b. Oct. 17, 1774, was married, April 13, 1797, to Jonathan Clark, of Haddam, Ct. He d. Feb. 24, 1839, aged 63 ; she d. Oct. 26, 1843, aged 69. Children :
>**313** SABRA DENISON, b. Dec. 13, 1798; m. Samuel Tyler of Haddam; d. Aug. 1, 1848; 7 children.
>**314** LYDIA WILLIAMS, b. Nov. 16, 1800; m. Wm. Wells; 9 ch.
>**315** JONATHAN W., b. Oct. 5, 1813; m. Catherine Smith; 4 ch.

211 JABEZ DENISON, (John, Jr.[3], John[2], George[1],) b. in August, 1698, was married in 1740, to Dorothy Cogswell, and died June 4, 1788. His inventory was £432. He lived in Pettipaug, (Saybrook.) His will was dated in 1783. His children :
>**316** JABEZ, b. Dec., 1740; m. Mary Wheeler.
>**317** JOHN, b. Dec. 2, 1743; m. Mary Post.
>**318** JAMES, b.
>**319** ROBERT, b. in 1745; m. Elizabeth Pelton.
>**320** ABIGAIL, b.
>**321** DOROTHY, b.
>**322** ASHBEL, b. in 1764; m. Susanna ——.

316 JABEZ DENISON, Jr. (Jabez[4], John, Jr.[3], John[2], George[1],) b. in 1740, was married to Mary Wheeler, Jan. 21, 1759 ; lived in Saybrook. Their children :
>**323** MOLLY, b. 1760.

324 Jabez, 3rd, b. Oct. 10, 1765 ; m. Caroline Baldwin.
325 Abigail, b. 1768.
326 Lucy, b. 1770.
327 Eli, b. in 1772; m. Molly Tripp.
328 Dolly, b. Feb. 8, 1775 ; m. R. Buckingham.
329 Rhoda, b. 1778.
330 Robert, b. 1780.

324 Jabez Denison, 3rd, (Jabez[5], Jabez[4], John, Jr.[3], John[2], George[1],) b. Oct. 10, 1765, was married to Caroline Baldwin, Feb. 19, 1795, and lived in Saybrook, and in Bridgewater, N. Y., His wife was born Oct. 10, 1762. Their children :

331 Jabez. 4th, b. July 2, 1797 ; d. Nov. 25, 1820.
332 Wheeler, b. July 15, 1800 ; d. Jan. 29, 1827.
333 Gideon H., b. Aug. 26, 1802 ; m. Christina Dibble.
334 Asa W., b. April 8, 1805 ; m. Eliza R. Clark.
335 Charles B., b. May 11, 1807 ; m. Desire Holbrook.
336 Mary B., b. Sept. 5, 1809 ; m. Charles Coger.

This Jabez Denison, 3rd, emigrated in May, 1814, with his family, to Bridgewater, N. Y., where he died, Feb. 8, 1815. In September, 1836, his widow, with her children, Gideon, Asa, and Mary B., removed to Jackson Co., Michigan ; and in 1847, to Kent Co., Michigan. The widow died Sept. 24, 1854.

327 Eli Denison, (Jabez[5], Jabez[4], John, Jr.[3], John[2], George[1],) b. in 1772, was married to Molly Tripp, Nov. 23d, 1794. He lived in Saybrook ; he died there, Jan. 28, 1854, aged 82 ; his wife died April 15, 1866, aged 94. Their children :

337 Twins, (son and dau.) b. March 14, 1795 ; d. same day.
338 Eli, b. June 7, 1797 ; d. Nov. 20, 1819.
339 Thomas, b. Dec. 19, 1799 ; twice married.
340 Reuben, b. July 5, 1802 ; m. Lucy A. Barker.
341 Charlotte, b. Jan. 11, 1805 ; d. Sept. 21, 1806.
342 Charlotte M., b. April 12, 1807 ; m. Ezra Wright.
343 William, b. Nov. 16, 1809 ; m. Mary C. Bates: no child.
344 Almira A., b. July 21, 1817 ; m. 428 Wm. L. Denison.

339 Thomas Denison, (Eli[6], Jabez[5], Jabez[4], John, Jr.[3], John[2], George[1],) b. Dec. 49, 1797, was married, first, to Charlotte Spencer, Jan. 8, 1823, ; and second, to Mary Ann Southworth, Jan. 14, 1827 ; all of Deep River, Ct. The first wife died, Oct. 26, 1824, aged 20 ; he died July 12, 1875. His children :

345 Eli, b. May 24, 1824 ; m. Adela H. Arnold.

346 FELIX A., b. Aug. 23, 1829; *m.* Hattie E. Keep; no child.
347 EDWARD P., b, June 24, 1833; d. Jan. 11, 1834.
348 EMILY C., b. Aug. 8, 1835; *m.* Jos. A. Smith.
349 THOMAS L., b. July 8, 1838; d. Jan. 4, 1839.
350 HORACE P., b. Sept. 20, 1840; *m.* Adeline C. Hayes.

345 ELI DENISON, 2nd, (son of 339 Thomas, by 1st wife,) b. May 24, 1824, was married to Adela H. Arnold, Oct. 15, 1852; lived at Deep River. His children:

351 LURANA M., b. Jan. 25, 1852; *m.* Irwin S. Watrous.
352 EDWARD C., b. Oct. 7, 1853; *m.* Mary I. Leavenworth.

350 HORACE P. DENISON, (son of 339 Thomas by 2nd wife,) b. Sept. 20, 1840, was married to Adeline C. Hayes, July 3, 1867; lives at Deep River, and has:

353 BERTHA LEE. b. Nov. 9. 1870.
354 LEON HAYES, b. Oct. 17, 1872.

348 EMILY C. DENISON, (dau. of 339 Thomas, by 2nd wife,) b. Aug. 8, 1835, was married to Joseph A. Smith, May 23, 1861. Lives at Deep River. Children:

355 ALLEN JESSUP, b. May 8, 1862.
356 ROBERT EDWIN, b. Feb. 8. 1866.
357 MARY FISK, b. Jan. 8, 1868; d. young.
358 EMMA CHARLOTTE, b. March 28, 1870.
359 LOUIS JOSEPH, b. Aug. 7, 1871.
369 WILBUR FISK, b. July 23, 1873.

340 REUBEN DENISON, (Eli[6], Jabez[5], Jabez,[4] John, Jr.[3], John[2], George[1],) b. July 5, 1802, was married, Nov. 20, 1832, to Lucy A. Barker. She d. July 14, 1846, aged 39; he d. Aug. 22, 1873. Children:

361 SARAH, J., b. Sept. 13, 1833.
362 RICHARD W., b. April 1, 1837.
363 MARY A., b. July 18, 1844; d. Jan. 5, 1872.

342 CHARLOTTE M. DENISON, (Eli[6], Jabez[5], Jabez[4], John, Jr.[3], John[2], George[1],) b. April 12, 1807, was married, Aug. 25, 1830, to Ezra Wright, who d. Jan. 27, 1867. Children:

364 ELIZABETH ELLEN, b. Sept. 9, 1833.
365 FREDERICK WM., b. Aug. 12, 1845; d. May 15, 1867.

333 GIDEON H. DENISON, (Jabez[6], Jabez[5], Jabez[4], John, Jr.[3], John[2], George[1],) b. Aug. 26, 1802, was married April 13, 1825, to Christina Dibble. He was drowned in Lake Michigan, off Grand Haven, by the sinking of the Steamer Ironsides, Sept. 17, 1875. She d. at Spring Lake, Mich., April 22, 1871, aged 66. Their children:

365½ Morris Williams, b. Oct. 31, 1825; lives in Ada, Mich.
366 Thomas Dibble. b. April 1, 1828; m. Eva Van Vulpin.
367 William Wheeler, b. May 27, 1830; d. unmarried in 1867.
368 Charles Millard, b. Feb. 3, 1833; m. Ann M. Beard.
369 Henry Clay, b. in 1837; m. Helen E. Tobias.
370 Mary Louisa, b. Aug. 11, 1841; d. Dec. 25, 1865.
371 Sarah Maria, b. Feb. 10, 1844; m. Henry Millard.

366 Thomas Dibble Denison, (Gideon H.^{7}, Jabez^6, Jabez^5, Jabez^4, John, Jr.^{3}, John^2, George^1,) b. April 1, 1828, was married, April 9, 1853, to Eva Van Vulpin, b. Feb. 1, 1835, in Holland; lives at Spring Lake, Michigan; has two children:

372 Eva La Dell, b. May 5, 1855; m. W. I. Brian, of Chicago, Ill., May 10, 1876.
373 Mary L., b. Feb. 14, 1857; d. Sept. 6, 1857.

368 Charles Millard Denison, (Gideon H.^{7}, Jabez^6, Jabez^5, Jabez^4, John, Jr.^{3}, John^2, George^1,) b. Feb. 3, 1833, was married, Dec. 9, 1857, to Ann M. Beard; lives at Cascade, Mich.; one child:

374 Carrie L., b. March 12, 1863.

369 Henry Clay Denison, (Gideon H.^{7}, Jabez^6, Jabez^5, Jabez^4, John, Jr.^{3}, John^2, George^1,) b. in 1837, was married, Oct. 13, 1858, to Helen E. Tobias, b. Dec. 16, 1838; lives in Ada, Kent Co., Mich. Children:

375 Elmetta J., b. March 17, 1860; d. Feb. 6, 1863.
376 Minnie C., b. Feb. 18, 1862.
377 Nina F., b. Jan. 12, 1865.
378 Marshall H., b. June 5, 1867; d. Sept. 2, 1878.
379 Marshall H., b. June 5, 1867, twin to 378; d. Sept. 9, 1868.
380 Mary L., b. June 20, 1869; d. July 19, 1878.
381 Rhoda E., b. Jan. 7, 1872; d. July 4, 1878.
382 Perry M., b. June 14, 1878.

371 Sarah M. Denison, (Gideon H.^{7}, Jabez^6, Jabez^5, Jabez^4, John, Jr.^{3}, John^2, George^1,) b. Feb. 10, 1844, was married, February, 1867, to Henry Millard, b. Aug. 22, 1838, in Somersetshire, England. They live at Spring Lake, Michigan. One child:

383 Millie M., b. Feb. 1, 1869.

336 Mary B. Denison, (Jabez^6, Jabez^5, Jabez^4, John, Jr.^{3}, John^2, George^1,) b. Sept. 5, 1809, was married, Sept. 4, 1834, to Charles Coger; lives in Cascade, Mich. Children:

384 CAROLINE M., b. June 30, 1837; *m.* Rufus W. Martin; no child.
385 JABEZ D., b. Nov. 14, 1840; *m.* Mary R. Parish, who had two children: Charles R. and Millie Maud. She d. Dec. 17, 1874.
386 HARRIET L., b. May 10, 1843; d. April 12, 1845.
387 HENRY A., b. Jan. 16, 1847; *m.* Julia Reynolds, who had three children: Harley, Lillie, and Willie. She d. March 19, 1877.
388 HARRIET L., b. Sept. 29, 1848; *m.* James G. Ausley.

334 ASA W. DENISON, (Jabez^6, Jabez^5, Jabez^4, John, Jr.^{3}, John^2, George^1,) b. April 8, 1805, was married, Dec. 25, 1828, to Eliza R. Clark. He d. Sept. 9, 1857 ; and she *m.* 2nd, J. P. Johnson. Asa W. Denison lived at Ada, Kent Co., Michigan. His children :

389 HELEN M., b. Nov. 17, 1829; *m.* Lemon Chaple.
390 OLIVE C., b. April 4, 1832; *m.* Highland H. Stewart.
391 WILLIAM C., b. Oct. 24, 1836; *m.* Frances E. Holt.
392 ISADORA, b. Nov. 13, 1841; d. Oct. 2, 1842.
393 MARSHALL, b. July 4, 1843; d. Sept. 3, 1865.
394 ALTHEA E., b. Nov. 24, 1845; *m.* Sanford Fish; no child.

389 HELEN M. DENISON, (dau. of 334 Asa W.,) b. Nov. 7, 1829, *m.* Lemon Chaple, Dec. 25, 1850. Children :

395 AUGUSTA, b. Jan. 28, 1852.
396 ADELINE O., b. Nov. 22, 1854.
397 WILLIAM A., b. July 26, 1856.
398 ELMER E., b. July 28, 1864.
399 ROYAL, b. Oct. 11, 1867.

390 OLIVE C. DENISON, (dau. of 324 Asa W.,) b. April 4, 1832, *m.* H. H. Stewart, Dec. 25, 1854, and d. Jan. 14, 1864. Children :

400 ISADORE M., b. Nov. 17, 1855.
401 HERBERT L., b. Jan. 9, 1858.
402 MARSHALL W., b. Dec. 11, 1863.

391 WILLIAM C. DENISON, (son of 334 Asa W.,) b. Oct. 24, 1836, *m.* Frances E. Holt, Oct. 13, 1858; lives at Grand Rapids, Mich. Children:

403 LAVELLO, b. Feb. 14, 1861.
404 BERTY M., b. March 2, 1875.

335 CHARLES B. DENISON, (Jabez^6, Jabez^5, Jabez^4, John, Jr.^{3}, John^2, George^1,) b. May 11, 1807, was married, Aug. 19, 1830, to Desire Holbrook, b. Dec. 11, 1809 ; lives in Cassville, N. Y. Children :

405 JANE MINERVA, b. Oct. 28, 1833. *m.* Curtis D. Washburn.
406 CHARLES MODUSTUS, b. Jan. 6, 1836; *m.* Merinda Lohnds.
407 JABEZ DARWIN. b. April 3, 1843; *m.* Adeline L. Avery.

405 JANE M. DENISON, (dau. of 335 Charles B.,) m. first, Nov. 4, 1854; and, second, Dec. 25, 1859, to Curtis D. Washburn; lives at Cascade, Mich. Children:

    408 NELLIE, b. July 25, 1855.
    409 DORA A., b. Feb. 20, 1861.
    410 ABBIE, b. Aug. 28, 1870.

406 CHARLES M. DENISON, (son of 335 Charles B.,) b. Jan. 6, 1836, m. May 3, 1853, Merinda Lohnds; lived at Wataga, Ill.; d. May 15, 1862. Children:

    411 CHARLES, and   **411½** LELIA.

407 JABEZ D. DENISON, (son of 335 Charles B.,) b. April 3, 1843, m. Adeline L. Avery, Sept. 8, 1864; lives at Waterville, N. Y. Children:

    412 JAMES AVERY, b. April 9, 1866.
    413 ALICE MAUD, b. Jan. 28, 1868.

317 JOHN DENISON, (Jabez[4], John, Jr.[3], John[2], George[1],) b. Dec. 2, 1744, was married Feb. 25, 1761, to Mary Post. He lived at Saybrook; died there July 29, 1789; his wife died in July, 1809. Their children:

    414 JAMES P., b. Dec. 3, 1861; m. Taphena ———.
    415 JOHN, b. June 20, 1763; killed by a fall, when young.
    416 MASON, b. May 11, 1765; m. Abigail Lane.
    417 MARY, b. Sept 25, 1768.
    418 DAN, b. Oct. 11, 1771; m. Sally Bushnell.
    419 MEHITABEL, b. Jan. 7, 1774; m. 246 Ebenezer Denison, Jr.; had 7 children, and d. Feb. 22, 1849. See his record page 21.
    420 TITUS, bapt. Jan. 30, 1776; m. Margaret Post.
    421 ANNA, bapt. Sept. 26, 1778; d. Oct. 26, 1789.

414 JAMES P. DENISON, (John[5], Jabez[4], John, Jr.[3], John[2], George[1],) b. Dec. 3, 1761, was married to Taphena ———, and had

    422 JOHN, bapt. Oct. 21, 1792.
    423 GEORGE ANSON, bapt. Sept. 21, 1794.
    424 ERASTUS, bapt. March 26, 1786.
    425 NATHANIEL K., bapt. April 5, 1789.
    426 ANSEL, bapt. Aug. 1, 1790.

416 MASON DENISON, (John[5], Jabez[4], John, Jr.[3], John[2], George[1],) b. May 11, 1769, was married April 12, 1804, to Abigail Lane, of Killingworth; lived at Deep River; died there July 27, 1827. Children:

    427 ACHSA, b. March 31, 1805; unmarried.

428 WILLIAM L., b. March 2, 1808; *m.* 344 Almira A. Denison.
429 BETSEY, b. Aug. 11, 1811; *m.* Isaac Schellinger.
430 ELIZA H., b. Nov. 2. 1806; *m.* in Michigan.
431 ANN BORODELL, b. Sept. 19, 1809: *m.* in Michigan.
432 GEORGE MASON. b. June 11, 1813; twice married.
433 JERUSHA H., b. August, 1815; *m.* Joshua Culver, of Westville, Ct.

428 WILLIAM L. DENISON, (Mason[6], John[5], Jabez[4], John, Jr.[3], John[2], George[1],) b. March 2, 1808, was married, March 13, 1841, to 344 Almira A. Denison, (dau. of 327 Eli. He lived at Pittsburg, Pa.; and died there, May 13, 1874. His children :

434 WILLIAM M., b. Feb. 22, 1843; *m.* Mary Caroline Thurlow, Aug. 30, 1876; lives at Pittsburg, Pa.
435 ARTHUR L., b. Nov. 28, 1845.
436 LOUIS A., b. Nov. 17, 1851; *m.* Gertrude Douglas.

429 BETSEY DENISON, (Mason[6], John[5], Jabez[4], John, Jr.[3], John[2], George[1],) b. Aug. 11, 1811, was married, Sept. 12, 1841 to Isaac Schellinger. Lived on Long Island; died May 9, 1875. She had these twin children :

437 ISAAC DENISON, b. May 6, 1844; died July 17, 1
438 JEREMIAH MASON, b. May 6, 1844; lives at Pittsburg, Pa.

432 GEORGE MASON DENISON, M. D., (Mason[6], John[5], Jabez[4], John, Jr.[3], John[2], George[1],) b. June 11, 1813, was married, first, May 20, 1835, to Charlotte Beckwith who died, May 20, 1843 ; and, second, Jan. 12, 1845, to Lucretia Beckwith. Lived at Saybrook. His children :

439 FREDERICK M., b. July 1, 1836.
440 HARRIET PLATT, b. May 12, 1837.
441 AN INFANT SON, b. April 25, 1843; died unnamed.

418 DAN DENISON, (John[5], Jabez[4], John, Jr.[3], John[2], George[1],) b. Oct. 11, 1771, was married to Sally Bushnell, and had these children :

442 MARY ANN, bapt. Nov. 9, 1800.
443 SALLY, bapt. June 30, 1805.
444 ERASTUS, b. 1806; d. June 22, 1811.
445 HANNAH M., bapt. Oct. 9, 1809.
446 LOUISA A., bapt. October, 1816.
447 JABEZ W., bapt. October, 1816.

420 TITUS DENISON, (John[5], Jabez[4], John, Jr.[3], John[2], George[1],) bapt. Jan. 30, 1776, was married, in March, 1812, to Margaret Post, and lived at Deep River. He was b. in Jan-

Capt. John Denison's Descendants.

uary, 1776, and d. March 14, 1859, aged 81; his wife died Aug. 24, 1855, aged 76. Their children:

 448 MARGARET. b. Dec. 22, 1812; m. J. H. Burr.
 449 CYNTHIA, b. April 18, 1815; unmarried.
 450 TITUS K., b. Aug. 18, 1817; twice married, no child.
 451 LINUS S., b. Oct. 3, 1819; m. 1st, Juliet Gladwin; 1 child.
 452 SARAH ANN, b. May 11, 1824; m. Alvin A. Blake; 3 children.

448 MARGARET DENISON, (dau. of 420 Titus,) b. Dec. 23, 1812; m. Jonathan H. Burr, of Haddam, Ct., April 26, 1840. Children:

 453 HARRIET E., b. June 1, 1842; m. Rev. David B. Hubbard, June 9, 1870, and died March 19, 1876, aged 34.
 454 CALISTA, b. Aug. 15, 1844; d. Sept. 24, 1848.
 455 RANDOLPH, b. June 1, 1847; d. Sept. 29, 1847.
 456 MARY E., b. Sept. 17, 1849; d. Aug. 31, 1851.
 457 ALICE R., b. Dec. 29, 1854; m. Rev. David B. Hubbard.

REV. DAVID B. HUBBARD, of Canton Centre, Conn., m. first, Harriet, E. Burr, June 9, 1870, and second, Alice R. Burr. Sept. 17, 1876. They were both daughters of 448 Margaret Denison and J. H. Burr. There were three children by the first marriage, and the second wife has two; as follows:

  EMMA BRAINERD, b. June 29, 1872.
  LENA IRENE, b. Jan. 27, 1874.
  HATTIE E., b. Feb. 26, 1876.
  JOSEPH BURR, b. Nov. 8, 1877.
  HARVEY. b. April 28, 1879.

451 LINUS S. DENISON, (son of 420 Titus,) b. Oct. 3, 1819, was married, first, July 4, 1853, to Julietta Gladwin, who d. Feb. 16, 1857; and, second, Sept. 30, 1867, to Mrs. Susan (Jones) Harding; lives in West Meriden, Ct. 1 child.

 458 LINUS JESSE, b. June 24, 1871.

317 ROBERT DENISON, (Jabez[4], John, Jr.[3], John[2], George[1],) b. in 1745, was m. to Elizabeth Pelton who was born 1749; they were married about 1769 and lived in Saybrook. She died, May 1, 1786, six days after giving birth to a child. He m. 2nd, Jemima Buckingham, Dec. 24, 1786, who died childless, in 1813. He died in January, 1813. His children:

 459 ROBERT, b. Feb. 17, 1771; m. Molly Post.
 460 ELIZABETH, bapt. Aug. 11, 1776.
 461 EZRA, b. 1781; m. Mary Camp.
 462 AN UNNAMED CHILD, b. April 25, 1786; lived two days.

459 ROBERT DENISON, (Robert[5], Jabez[4], John, Jr.[3], John[2], George[1],) b. Feb. 17, 1771, was married, Jan. 8, 1794, to Molly Post; lived in Saybrook; d. there Oct. 21, 1813. His children:

463 DAVID, bapt. Nov. 30, 1794.
464 DEBBY, bapt. April 16, 1797.
465 LIZZIE, bapt. June 9, 1799.
466 ROBERT FORDYCE, bapt. July 12, 1801.
467 ALFRED, bapt. Dec. 11, 1803.
468 AN INFANT, b. and d. in 1805.
469 CLARISSA, b. in 1806, and d. Oct. 6, 1806.

466 ROBERT FORDYCE DENISON, (Robert^6, Robert^5, Jabez^4, John, Jr.^{3}, John^2, George^1,) bapt. July 12, 1801, was married to Fanny Maria Griswold, of Essex or Deep River, Nov. 27, 1823. September 17, 1833, Robert F. Denison fell from a house top, and was killed. May 4, 1840, his widow m. Jonathan Bishop, of Guilford, Ct. She died in Guilford, March 31, 1865, aged 61. His children:

470 MARY ANN G., b. Nov. 5, 1824; m. Geo. C. Bartlett.
471 ROBERT F., b. April 21, 1827; m. Cornelia D. Ford.
472 EDGAR, b. May 31, 1829; d. May 23, 1831.
473 WILLIAM EDGAR, b. in 1831 and d. 1834.

470 MARY ANN G. DENISON, (dau. of 466 Robert F.,) b. Nov. 5, 1824, was married, Sept. 19, 1850, at Guilford, Ct., to Geo. C. Bartlett. They live at Titusville, Pa. Their children:

474 HELEN M., b. March 22, 1852; m. Burton F. Edwards.
475 MARY GRISWOLD, b. Aug. 13, 1856.
476 GEORGE FORDYCE, b. Jan. 31, 1859.
477 CARRIE DENISON, b. May 19, 1863.

471 ROBERT FORDYCE DENISON, JR., (son of 466 Robert F.,) b. April 21, 1827, was married, May 16, 1849, to Cornelia D. Ford. Lives in Brooklyn, N. Y.; does business at No. 31, Pearl Street, N. Y. City. His children:

478 MARY ELIZABETH, b. May 26, 1851.
479 FANNY GRISWOLD, b. July 11, 1854.
480 ROBERT FORD, b. and d. Feb. 22, 1856.
481 ROBERT FORDYCE, b. and d. the same day in 1858.
482 CARRIE FREEMAN, b. in 1860.
483 LOUISA BURGER, b. in 1865.

461 EZRA DENISON, (Robert^5, Jabez^4, John, Jr.^{3}, John^2, George^1,) b. in 1781, was married to Mary Camp, of Durham, Ct., and, in 1818, emigrated to Brunswick Co., Va., where he died in 1823; his wife d. in 1826. He had GUERNSEY L., b. Dec. 19, 1808.

Capt. John Denison's Descendants.

484 GUERNSEY L. DENISON, (son of Ezra,) b. Dec. 19, 1808, was married, in 1831, to Mary Loomis, of Petersburg, Va., and settled at Memphis, Tenn., as a member of the mercantile firm of Orgill Brothers & Co. His children:

- **485** MARIANNA, b. in 1832.
- **486** VIRGINIA A., b. in 1834; m. W. G. Richardson, July 5, 1866.
- **487** WILLIAM E., b. in 1837; killed in Arizona by Indians.
- **488** LELIA J., b. in 1841.
- **490** EMMA, A., b. in 1845.
- **491** GUERNSEY H., b. in 1850.
- **492** LAURA GLYNN, b. in 1843; d. Sept. 13, 1845.
- **493** NORAH GLYNN, b. in 1847; d. Aug. 4, 1848.

322 ASHBEL DENISON, (Jabez[4], John, Jr.[3], John[2], George[1],) b. in 1764, was married, about 1788, to Susanna ———. He lived in East Haddam, Ct., after 1793. He d. in East Haddam, July 11, 1806, aged 42; his wife d. there, March 25, 1825. Their children:

- **494** CHARLES; m. Gertrude de la Montague.
- **495** MARTHA, b. ———
- **496** LYMAN; twice married.
- **497** SYLVESTER P.; m.; had a son Henry.
- **498** ASHBEL J., b. ———

494 CHARLES DENISON, (Ashbel[5], Jabez[4], John, Jr.[3], John[2], George[1],) b. in 1790, was married, in 1812, to Gertrude de la Montague, dau. of a French Huguenot; removed to New York, and died in 1863; Mrs. Gertrude died in 1871. Two children:

- **499** SUSANNA, b. in 1814; m. Samuel B. White.
- **500** CHARLES, JR., b. Sept. 10, 1816; m. Helen M. Cook.

499 SUSANNA DENISON, (Charles[6], Ashbel[5], Jabez[4], John, Jr[3]., John[2], George[1], (b. in 1814, was married, June 10, 1825, to Samuel B. White, of New York. Their children:

- **501** HENRY W., b. July 12, 1836.
- **502** CHARLES D., b. Nov. 25, 1840.
- **503** FRANK S., b. March 3, 1845.
- **504** EDWIN, b. June 25, 1848.
- **506** HELEN, b. May 23, 1856.

500 CHARLES DENISON, Jr.,(Charles[6], Ashbel[5], Jabez[4], John, Jr.[3], John[2], George[1],) b. Sept. 10, 1816, was married, Sept. 19, 1837, to Helen M. Cook, b. March 5, 1819. He lives at Little Silver, N. J., and has an office at 187 Greenwich St., New York City. His children:

507 LYMAN, b. Oct. 25, 1838; twice married.
508 KATE, b. Aug. 23, 1842; m. George Henriques.
509 GERTRUDE, b. Jan. 3, 1844; m. Isaac Ludlow.
510 CHARLES F., b. May 22, 1847; m. Winnifred Austin.
511 WALTER, b. June 9, 1852.
512 EGBERT C., b. Nov. 12, 1858.

507 LYMAN DENISON, (son of 500 Charles, Jr.,) b. Oct. 25, 1838; m. 1st, Mary Amanda Whitemore, April 3, 1862; and 2nd, Mary Sophia Aiken, Nov. 29, 1865. His children:

513 CHARLES, b. Aug. 26, 1866; d. May 1, 1876.
514 MARY A., b. June 19, 1868.
515 HELEN, b. April 11, 1871.

509 GERTRUDE DENISON, (dau. of 500 Charles, Jr.,) b. Jan. 3, 1844, was married, June 15, 1869, to Isaac Ludlam. Children:

516 HELEN DENISON, b. April 3, 1870.
517 PERCY CLIFFORD, b. Dec. 3, 1871.
518 GERTRUDE ETHEL, b. Dec. 17, 1874.

496 LYMAN DENISON,) Ashbel[5], Jabez[4], John, Jr.[3], John[2], George[1],) was twice married, and had these children:

By first wife:	By the second wife, Charlotte:
519 CHARLES.	**522** CHARLES.
520 DAVID.	**523** EMMA WENHAM.
521 SYLVESTER.	**524** FANNY HALSEY.
Three others.	**525** LOUISA.
No further record.	

III.

178 GEORGE DENISON, (John[2], George[1],) b. March 23, 1671, was graduated at Harvard College, studied law, and settled in New London, Conn., where he was town clerk, county clerk, and clerk of probate. He was married, in 1694, to Mrs. Mary (Wetherell) Harris, (dau. of Daniel Wetherell, a very prominent citizen of New London, who was born in Maidstone, County Kent, England, Nov. 29, 1630, and died in New London, April 14, 1719.) George Denison died Jan. 22, 1720. His wife died Aug. 22, 1711. Their children:

526 GRACE, b. March 4, 1695; m. Edward Hallam.
527 PHEBE, b. March 16, 1697; m. Gibson Harris.

Capt. John Denison's Descendants.

528 HANNAH, b. March 28, 1699; m. John Hough.
529 BORODELL, b. May 17, 1701; m. Jonathan Latimer.
530 DANIEL, b. June 27, 1703; m. Rachel Starr.
531 WETHERELL, b. Aug. 24, 1705; m. Lydia Moore.
532 ANN, b. Aug. 15, 1707; twice married.
533 SARAH, b. June 20, 1710; m. Wm. Douglas.

526 GRACE DENISON, (George^3, John^2, George^1,) b. March 4, 1695, was married to Edward Hallam of New London, Dec. 2, 1713, and had :

534 JOHN, b. Sept. 10, 1715; d. in Sept. 1736.
535 GRACE, b. May 25, 1717; d. June, 1717.
536 NICHOLAS, b. April 29, 1718.
537 EDWARD, b. June 8, 1721; d. June, 1726.
538 AMOS, b. March 7, 1725.
539 EDWARD. b. Feb. 21, 1727; d. in 1728.
540 ELIZABETH, b. May, 1732.

527 PHEBE DENISON, (George^3, John^2, George^1,) b. in 1697, was married Jan. 7, 1720, to Gibson Harris; lived in New London and Bozrah; he d. in Bozrah, Conn., in 1761, aged 67. Their children :

541 GEORGE, b. Jan. 18, 1721; m. Ann Lathrop.
542 JOSHUA, b. Feb. 26, 1722.
543 BENJAMIN, b. July 7, 1724; m. Ann Waterman.
544 DANIEL, b. May 25, 1726; m. Prudence Rogers.
545 PHEBE, b. May 21, 1728; m. Jabez Hough.
546 ANN, b. Oct., 1730.
547 MARY, b. Nov. 12, 1732.
548 ELIZABETH, b. 1734.

528 HANNAH DENISON, (George^3, John^2, George^1,) b. March 28, 1699, was married to Capt. John Hough. They were m. Sept. 4, 1718. They settled in Bozrah, Conn. She died there, April 9, 1782. In Oct., 1782, he m. 2nd, Wid. Ann Baldwin. He died Feb 7, 1785. aged 88 years. John and Hannah (D.) Hough had :

549 JOHN, b. Oct. 14, 1719; d. March 6, 1720.
550 DAVID, b. Jan. 27, 1724; twice married.
551 SARAH, b. April 6, 1722; twice married.
552 ABIAH, b. Nov. 18, 1726; m. Simeon Edgerton.
553 HANNAH, b. March 11, 1725; m. Elisha Lathrop.
554 JABEZ, b. Nov. 16, 1728; twice married.
555 JOHN, b. Dec. 17, 1730; m. Abigail Baldwin.
556 GEORGE, b. Feb. 9, 1733; d. unmarried.
557 ESTHER, b. July 29, 1735; m. Zebadiah Wood.

529 BORODELL DENISON, (George³, John², George¹,) b. May 17, 1701, was married, in 1723, to Jonathan Latimer, lived in New London, and had :

    558 JONATHAN, b. 1724; *m.* Lucretia Griswold, Jan. 7, 1747.
    559 ELIZABETH, b. 1726.   **564** HENRY, b. 1737.
    560 LUCY, b. 1728.   **565** DANIEL, b. 1739.
    561 MARY, b. 1729.   **566** JOHN, b. 1741.
    562 LYDIA, b. 1730.   **567** BORODELL, b. 1743.
    563 SAMUEL, b. 1732.

532 ANN DENISON, (George³, John², George¹,) b. August 10, 1707, was married, 1st, to Jabez Hough, Jan. 7, 1725. He d. Jan. 25, 1725. She *m.* Samuel Richards in 1726, and died in 1786. She had :

    568 AN INFANT, b. & d. 1727.   **573** KATHERINE, b. 1736.
    569 LUCY, b. 1728.   **574** DANIEL, b. 1737.
    570 SAMUEL, b. 1732.   **575** JABEZ, b. 1739.
    571 ELIJAH b. 1734.   **576** LOVE, b. 1741.
    572 JERUSHA, b. 1735.   **577** WILLIAM, b. 1743.

533 SARAH DENISON, (George³, John², George¹,) was married to Wm. Douglas, March 4, 1730, and died in 1797. He d. in 1787, aged 80 years. They lived in New London, and had :

    578 WILLIAM, b. Feb. 7, 1732.   **584** LUCY, b. 1743.
    579 SARAH, b. Nov. 1733; d.yg.   **585** SARAH, b. 1745.
    580 MARGARET, b. Oct., 1735.   **586** RICHARD.
    581 JONATHAN, b. July, 1737.   **587** LYDIA.
    582 GEORGE, b. 1739.   **588** ELIZABETH.
    583 ABIAH, b. 1741.   The last three names are in his will only.

530 DANIEL DENISON, (George³, John², George¹,) b. June 27, 1703, was married, Nov. 14, 1726, to Rachel Starr ; lived in New London, Conn.; d. previous to 1760 ; his widow *m.* about 1760, Col. Ebenezer Avery of South Groton, who had twelve children by his first wife, Lucy Latham. She had ten children by her first husband. Of these, Daniel *m.* Col. Ebenezer's daughter Katherine, previous to his mother's second marriage ; and Phebe *m.* his son, Ebenezer Avery, Jr. Mrs. Rachel d. in 1791, aged 86. The children of 530 Daniel and Rachel (Starr) Denison, were as follows :

    589 MARY, b. August 19, 1728; twice married.
    590 DANIEL, b. Dec. 16, 1730; *m.* Katherine Avery.
    591 THOMAS, b. Nov. 4, 1732; *m.* Katherine Starr.

Capt. John Denison's Descendants.

592 RACHEL, b. Sept 20, 1734; *m.* Joseph Copp.
593 SAMUEL, b. Nov. 9, 1736; d. in 1767; no family.
594 HANNAH, b. Jan. 2, 1739; *m.* Henry Jepson.
595 ANNA, b. Sept. 18, 1743; d. Nov. 1767.
596 PHEBE, b. Sept. 18, 1743; *m.* Ebenezer Avery jr.
597 JAMES, b. April 18. 1746; *m.* Esther Brown.
598 ELIZABETH, b. Nov. 19, 1748; *m.* John Barber.

589 MARY DENISON, (Daniel^4, George^3, John^2, George^1,') b. Aug. 17, 1728, was married, first, to William Douglass of New London, in 1749, and had :

599 MARY, b. Jan. 1750.

Wm. Douglass died. In 1752, she *m.* 2nd, James Thompson. They had :

600 JAMES, b. 1753.
601 SARAH, b. 1755.
602 ELIZABETH, b. 1756.
603 PHEBE.
604 ALEXANDER.
605 JOSEPH.
606 MOSES.
607 NATHAN.
608 JOSHUA, b. 1767.
609 REBECCA, b. 1769.
610 ELIAS, b. 1773.

592 RACHEL DENISON, (Daniel^4, George^3, John^2, George^1,) b. Sept. 20, 1734, was married to Joseph Copp, in 1757 ; lived in Groton, and had these :

611 ELIZABETH, b. 1758.
612 JOSEPH, b. 1760.
613 RACHEL, b. 1762.
614 MARGARET, b. 1764; d.1765.
615 ANN, b. 1766; d. 1766.
616 JONATHAN, b. 1767; d. 1774.
617 DANIEL, b. 1770.
618 PEGGY, b. 1773.
619 KATHERINE, b. 1775.
620 JONATHAN, b. 1777.

594 HANNAH DENISON, (Daniel^4, George^3, John^2, George^1,) b. Jan. 2, 1739, was married to Henry Jepson, Jan., 1769. They lived in New London, and had :

621 HANNAH, b. Nov., 1769.
622 ANN, b. 1771.
623 HENRY, b. 1773.
624 DANIEL, b. Jan., 1775.
625 MARGARET, b. Oct. 4, 1776.
626 ESTHER, b. Sept., 1779.
627 JOANNA, b. April, 1783.

596 PHEBE DENISON, (Daniel^4, George^3, John^2, George^1,) b. Sept. 18, 1743, was married, June 11, 1761, to Ebenezer Avery, Jr., of Groton, Conn., son of her mother's second husband. Ebenezer Avery, Jr., was killed in Fort Griswold, Sept. 6, 1781. Their children were as follows :

628 EBENEZER, b. Aug. 8, 1762; *m.* twice; 13 children.
629 LUCY, b. Aug. 4, 1766; *m.* Wm. Morgan.
630 ELIZABETH, b. Oct. 28, 1768; *m.* Dr. John O. Minor.

631 HEZEKIAH, b. July 20. 1772; *m.* Mary Avery.
632 HENRY, b. Sept. 2, 1776; *m.* Lucy M. Fish; had 11 children; d. May 1, 1873, in Salem, Pa.
633 CYRUS, b. July 7, 1779; *m.* Phebe Hewitt.

598 ELIZABETH DENISON, (Daniel[4], George[3], John[2], George[1],) b. Nov. 19, 1748, was married in 1770, to John Barber, son of Rev. Jonathan Barber of Groton. They lived in Groton, and had these children :

634 BETSEY, b. May 12, 1771.
635 SARAH, b. Nov. 6, 1773.
636 THOMAS. b. March 11, 1776.
637 DESIRE W., b. Sept. 20, 1778.
638 NOYES, b. April 28, 1781.
639 JOHN, b. Aug. 25, 1783.
640 NANCY, b. Aug. 29, 1785.
641 REBECCA, b. March 6, 1789.
642 EDWIN, b. May 6, 1793.

590 DANIEL DENISON, Jr. (Daniel[4], George[3], John[2], George[1],) b. Dec. 16, 1730, was married July 1, 1756, to Katherine Avery, dau. of his mother's second husband. He settled in Stephentown, N. Y., about 1773 ; and he and his wife both were buried there. He d. in 1793 ; she d. in 1825, aged 88. Their children were as follows :

643 KATHERINE, b. July 24, 1757; *m.* James Jones.
644 DANIEL, b. Sept. 26, 1758; *m.* Hannah Jones.
645 EBENEZER A., b. Jan. 26, 1760; *m.* Wid. Jones.
646 JONATHAN, b. May 17, 1761; *m.* Sarah Green.
647 GEORGE, b. April 12, 1763; d. in 1786.
648 GRISWOLD, b. Aug. 21, 1765; *m.* Rhoda Tifft.
649 ASENATH, b. Feb. 24, 1767; *m.* Roger Jones.
650 DAVID, b. March 19, 1769; *m.* Wid. Williams.
651 LATHAM, b. March 8, 1771; *m.* Eleanor Tifft.
652 A CHILD UNNAMED, b. and d. Aug. 18. 1773.
653 SAMUEL, b. Aug. 24, 1774; twice married.
654 ELIHU, b. April 14, 1777; *m.* Thankful Stewart.
655 THOMAS, b. May 5, 1779; *m.* Polly Crary.

644 DANIEL DENISON, (Daniel[5], Daniel[4], George[3], John[2], George[1],) b. Sept. 26, 1758, was married to Hannah Jones in 1780 ; lived at Stephentown, N. Y.; d. July 22, 1832; she d. Feb. 14, 1832. Children :

656 DANIEL, b. Feb. 18, 1785; died young.
657 GEORGE, b. Aug. 25, 1786; d. Sept. 12, 1825.
658 HANNAH, b. March 11, 1788; d. young.
659 (REV.) AVERY, b. June 28, 1790; *m.* Mercy L. Benedict.

Capt. John Denison's Descendants.

660 EUNICE, b. Dec. 16, 1791; m. Edward Briggs.
661 CLARISSA, b. Aug. 23, 1793; d. in 1842.
662 ELIAS, b. Oct. 19, 1795; d. in 1848.
663 NANCY, b. March 20, 1797; m. David Lightbody.
664 DANIEL, b. May 12, 1799; d. April 13, 1812.
665 LORENA, b. Feb., 1802.
666 HANNAH, b. Dec. 1, 1803; d. March 7, 1822.
667 RHODA, b. May 22, 1806; m. Jeremy Bement.
668 DELINA, b. Oct. 27, 1809; d. Oct. 13, 1827.

659 REV. AVERY DENISON, (Daniel[6], Daniel[5], Daniel[4], George[3], John[2], George[1],) b. June 28, 1790, in Berne, N. Y., was married in 1814, to Mercy L. Benedict, of Cayuga Co., N. Y. He lived first in Sempronius, N. Y., on an 80 acre farm. In 1831, he went to Avon, Michigan, with a family of nine children. In 1834, he removed to Warren, Macomb Co., Mich., where he lived nineteen years, farming, and preaching in the Baptist Church, with great success. He d. in Bay City, Mich., Oct. 16, 1866, at the home of his son, Elias B; his wife died eighteen days later. His children:

669 DANIEL A., b. July 23, 1815; twice married.
670 WILLIAM A., b. Jan. 29, 1817; m. Clarissa J. Bayley.
671 HENRY A., b. Aug. 12, 1818; m. Agnes E. Phelps.
672 LORENZO N., b. May 2, 1820; m. Almira Alison.
673 JAMES O., b. Jan. 12, 1822; d. March 18, 1842.
674 GEORGE I., b. Oct. 19, 1823; m. Eleanor L. Phelps.
675 DAVID T., b. Oct. 20, 1825; d. July 26, 1853.
676 SOPHRONIA J., b. Sept. 12, 1827; m. Isaiah Davy.
677 THOMAS R., b. April 18, 1830; m. Jennie Flint.
678 CHARLES H., b. Jan 20, 1833; m. Dimis T. Stocking, no ch.
679 ELIAS B., b. Jan. 13, 1837; m. Elizabeth F. Fraser.

669 DANIEL A. DENISON, (son of 659 Rev. Avery,) b. July 22, 1815, was married, first, Jan. 24, 1838, to Elsie Hough, who had one child, and died Oct. 23, 1840; and, second, Jan. 22, 1843, to Fony P. Wilbur; lives at Birmingham, Mich. Children:

680 ELSIE E., b. July 28, 1840; m. Alonzo T. Sharp.
681 AVERY W., b. April 26, 1844; d. April 9, 1873.
682 EUNICE M., b. June 24, 1846; d. April 25, 1871.
683 VICTOR V., b. Sept. 29, 1849.
684 FRANK F., b. Nov. 25, 1856.

680 ELSIE E. DENISON, (dau. of 669 Daniel A.,) b. July 28, 1840, m. Alonzo T. Sharp, Sept. 23, 1858; lives in Livonia, N. Y. Two children:

685 TROY D. C., b. Sept. 2, 1860.
686 BELLE H., b. July 17, 1864.

683 VICTOR V. DENISON, (son of 669 Daniel A.,) b. Sept. 29, 1849, *m.* Sarah Irving, April 1, 1875; lives in Birmingham, Mich. Children:
 687 LION KILE, b. Sept. 1, 1876.
 688 MARK, twin, b. Dec. 20, 1877.
 689 LUKE, twin, b. Dec. 20, 1877.

670 WILLIAM A. DENISON, (son of 659 Rev. Avery,) b. Jan. 29, 1817, was married, Dec. 22, 1842, to Clarissa J. Bayley; lives in Troy, Oakland Co., Mich. Children:
 690 JENNIE B., b. Oct. 18, 1843; *m.* F. M. Wheeler.
 691 HENRY CLAY, b. Aug. 20, 1845.
 692 HERBERT, b. Aug. 23, 1847; d. March 24, 1848.
 693 CLARA, b. May 31, 1851; *m.* G. A. Shannon, Oct. 9, 1879.
 694 EVALYN F., b. Oct. 26, 1855; *m.* Edmund J. Niles; they have Jennie Frank, b. Feb. 26, 1880.
 695 WILL F., b. Oct. 28, 1863.

671 HENRY A. DENISON, (son of 659 Rev. Avery,) b. Aug. 12, 1818, was married, Jan. 19, 1841, to Agnes E. Phelps, lives at Alpine, Kent Co., Mich. Children:
 696 ELIZABETH E., b. Nov. 2, 1841; d. Nov. 3, 1862.
 697 EMELINE R., b. April 30, 1843.
 698 LYDIA J., b. Jan. 23, 1845; *m.* Libeus P. Graves.
 699 HALEY A., b. Nov. 10, 1846; *m.* Alonzo Clement.
 700 CALISTA E., Aug. 12, 1849; *m.* Wm. H. Wright.
 701 CORDELIA S., b. Jan. 18, 1853; *m.* Hiram W. Roy.
 702 JAMES R., b. Sept. 29, 1855.

696 ELIZABETH E. DENISON, (dau. of 671 Henry A.,) *m.* Wm. H. Fox, Jan. 1, 1862; d. Nov. 3, 1862. One child:
 703 WILLIAM R., b. Nov. 3, 1862; d. Dec. 8, 1863.

698 LYDIA J. DENISON, (dau. of 671 Henry A.,) *m.* Libeus P. Graves, Sept. 21, 1862; d. June 15, 1863. One child:
 704 LYDIA J., b. June 13, 1863.

699 HALEY A. DENISON, (dau. of 671 Henry A.,) *m.* Alonzo Clement, Oct. 19, 1869; lives at Grand Rapids, Mich. One child:
 705 EDITH L., b. Dec. 16, 1870.

701 CORDELIA S. DENISON, (dau. of 671 Henry A.,) *m.* Hiram W. Roy, Oct. 11, 1869. One child:
 706 VERNEL A., b. Sept. 16, 1875; d. Sept. 18, 1875.

Capt. John Denison's Descendants. 41

672 LORENZO N. DENISON, (son of 659 Rev. Avery,) b. May 2, 1820, was married, Dec. 25, 1844, to Almira Allison, who d. Aug. 17, 1870. He m. second, Eliza Hamburger, April 17, 1871. Children:

- **707** DAVID A., b. Nov. 25, 1845; d. Jan. 23, 1864.
- **708** SUSAN L., b. March 3, 1848; m. Charles Hinman, Feb. 23, 1867; had one child, and d. Nov. 13, 1872.
- **709** WILLIAM H., b. March 3, 1850; m. Mary Gano.
- **710** SALINDA, b. Sept. 13, 1851; m. Denton A. Smith, Jan. 13, 1873; 1 c
- **711** SARAH A., b. April 26, 1854; m. Robert Siple, March 16, 1873; d Sept. 4, 1874.

709 WILLIAM H. DENISON, (son of 672 Lorenzo N.) b. March 3, 1850; m. Mary Gano, Dec. 25, 1870. Children:

- **712** CARRIE M., b. Sept. 23, 1871.
- **713** ADA L., b. June 7, 1877.

674 GEORGE I. DENISON, (son of 659 Rev. Avery,) b. Oct. 19, 1823, was married June 23, 1850, to Eleanor M. Phelps, b. Dec. 28, 1827. They live at Big Beaver, Mich. Children:

- **714** CELIA LOUISA, b. Oct. 13, 1852.
- **715** ROLL FREMONT, b. May 6, 1855.
- **716** IDA BELL, b. Feb. 15, 1859.
- **717** LILLIAN ETTA, b. July 26, 1861; d. March 25, 1862.
- **718** FRED LINCOLN, b. March 16, 1865.
- **719** RILEY ELIAS, b. Aug. 14, 1867.
- **720** KITTY S., b. Nov. 6, 1871; d. Aug. 20, 1872.

679 ELIAS BENEDICT DENISON, (son of 659 Rev. Avery,) b. Jan. 13, 1837, was married March 17, 1864, to Elizabeth F. Fraser; lives in Bay City, Mich. Children:

- **721** ELEANOR F., b. Nov. 29, 1864.
- **722** JENNIE R., b. July 17, 1866.
- **723** FRANK H., b. July 29, 1869; d. Feb. 23, 1873.
- **724** ERNEST, b. July 13, 1874.
- **725** ALEX. F., b. Dec. 10, 1876.

676 SOPHRONIA J. DENISON, (dau. of 659 Rev. Avery,) b. Sept. 12, 1827, was married, Sept. 12, 1846, to Isaiah Davy, b. in England, May 4, 1822. He d. March 13, 1855, at Warren, Mich. She lives at Detroit, Mich. Children:

- **726** ALONZO MARSHALL, b. July 26, 1847.
- **727** WILLIAM RILEY, b. Oct. 23, 1849.
- **728** ANNA ISORA, b. July 15, 1851; d. March 3, 1855.
- **729** VERNAL ROSECRANZ, b. Aug. 17, 1862.
- **730** LON ELTON, b. July 18, 1869.

677 THOMAS R. DENISON, (son of 659 Rev. Avery,) b. April 18, 1830, was married, Aug. 23, 1857, to Jennie Flint; lives at Bay City, Mich. Children:

    731 FREDDIE, b. July 29, 1858; d. May 14, 1860.
    732 BURT R., b. July 21, 1863.
    733 ELLIS F., b. Oct. 28, 1865.
    734 ROY, b. Dec. 12, 1868.
    735 MARY L., b. Aug. 2, 1872.
    736 WALDO B., b. Dec. 5, 1875; d. Dec. 11, 1876.

660 EUNICE DENISON, (Daniel^6, Daniel^5, Daniel^4, George^3, John^2, George^1,) b. Dec. 16, 1791, was married, Feb. 5, 1818, to Edward Briggs, and d. Feb. 18, 1849. Children:

    737 MELVINA, b. Oct. 14, 1818, m. O. F. Greenman, June 26, 1838, and d. Oct. 2. 1842.
    738 CLARISSA, b. Dec. 23, 1819; m. Wm. Fish.
    739 WILLIAM D., b. March 20, 1822; d. June, 1855; 5 ch.
    740 LOUISA F., b. Aug. 16, 1824; m. Wm. Foster; d. August, 1863.
    741 NANCY, b. Aug. 24, 1828.
    742 FRANK, b. May 28, 1830; d. April, 1850.
    743 SANFORD, b. Nov. 18, 1834; d. in 1835.

663 NANCY DENISON, (Daniel^6, Daniel^5, Daniel^4, George^3, John^2, George^1,) b. March 20, 1797, was married, March 19, 1820, to David Lightbody, lived at Seneca Falls, N. Y., and d. May 2, 1836. Children:

    744 ATILDA, b. July 4, 1821; d. June 15, 1828.
    745 LORENA, b. Feb. 21, 1823.
    746 RHODA, b. Aug. 20, 1825.
    747 GORTON S., b. April 13, 1827; m. Julia A. Martin, Sept. 10, 1853; lives at Pontiac, Mich; seven children.
    748 ALBERT, b. Nov. 27, 1829; killed in the war, May 16, 1863.
    749 ELVIRA, b. in 1832; d. in infancy.
    750 BELLAMY, b. Sept. 7, 1834.
    751 EUNICE, twin, b. April 26, 1836; d. in infancy.
    752 NANCY, twin, b. April 26. 1836; d. in infancy.

667 RHODA DENISON, (Daniel^6, Daniel^5, Daniel^4, George^3, John^2, George^1,) b. May 22, 1806, was married, April 18, 1830, to Jeremy Bement, b. Aug. 8, 1807; lived in Rochester, N. Y., he d. July 28, 1849. Children:

    753 ALONZO SYDNEY, b. March 8, 1831.
    754 ANNA MARIA, b. Nov. 10, 1832.
    755 DENISON, b. Feb. 27, 1834; d. Jan. 2, 1835.
    756 HENRY CLAY, b. Aug. 10, 1835; d. July 5, 1836.
    757 CHARLOTTE AURELIA b. Oct. 19, 1836; d. Aug. 16, 1853.

Capt. John Denison's Descendants.

758 FRANCES FREEMAN, b. Aug. 15, 1838: m. Oscar B. Davis, Nov. 5 1856; 5 children.
759 EDWARD DOUGLASS, b. May 18, 1843; d. July 5, 1843.

645 EBENEZER A. DENISON, (Daniel[5], Daniel[4], George[3], John[2], George[1],) b. Jan. 26, 1760, was married in 1784, to Mrs. Elizabeth (Spencer) Jones. Their children :

760 KATHERINE, b. 1786.
761 EBENEZER A., JR., b. 1788; m. Esther Gallup.
762 HANNAH. b. 1790; m. Isaac Allen.
763 POLLY, b. 1792; m. William Allen.
764 CHILD UNNAMED, b. and d. in 1794.
765 WILLIAM, b. 1795.
766 ALMA, b. 1797.
767 ORPHA, b. 1799; m. Eugene Wood.
768 AVERY, b. 1802.

761 EBENEZER A. DENISON, (Ebenezer A.[6], Daniel[5], Daniel[4], eorge[3], John[2], George[1],) b. in 1788, was married to Esther Gallup ; lived at Rutherford Park, N. J.; and had :

769 AVERY, m. Elizabeth Meigs.
770 ADMETUS, b. April 26, 1824; m. Margaret Farley.
771 EDWIN, lives at Esperance, N. Y.; no child.
772 MARY O., m. J. W. Holmes, Sept. 4, 1847; 1 child, Edwin W., b. March 16, 1856; lives at Mystic River, Conn.
773 ALIDA, m. Albert Reynolds.
774 HANNAH ELIZABETH, m. Wm. Locke of Canada.

769 AVERY DENISON, (son of 751 Ebenezer A., Jr.) m. Elizabeth Meigs, and had :

775 MARIA M., b. 1854.
776 ESTHER.
777 SARAH L.

770 ADMETUS DENISON, (son of 761 Ebenezer A., Jr.,) m. Margaret Farley, June, 1866 ; lives at Vernon Centre, Blue Earth Co. Minnesota. His children :

778 CORNELIA A., b. Oct. 22, 1867.
779 MARY ELIZABETH, b. March 1, 1870.
780 WILLIAM HENRY. b. Jan. 1, 1871.
781 EBENEZER AVERY. b. June 25, 1873; d. April 17, 1876.
782 MINNIE GRACE, b. Dec. 29, 1875.

673 ALIDA DENISON, (dau. of 761 Ebenezer A., Jr.,) m. Albert Reynolds ; lives in Brooklyn, N. Y., and has :

783 NELSON.   **784** AVERY.

774 HANNAH ELIZABETH DENISON, (dau. of 761 Ebenezer A., Jr.,) m. William Lock, of Perth, Canada, Dec. 25, 1846, and has :

785 MINULETA, b. Oct. 4, 1854.
786 JANE ESTHER, b. Nov. 16, 1856.
787 MARY OLIVIA, b. Feb. 7, 1859; d. Dec. 25, 1860.
788 WILLIAM A., b. Sept. 17, 1862.
789 WALTER W., b. Nov. 18, 1866; d. Feb. 4, 1876.
790 JOSEPHINE A., b. Oct. 20, 1864.

646 JONATHAN DENISON, (Daniel^5, Daniel^4, George^3, John^2, George^1,) b. May 17, 1761, was married, in 1786, to Sarah Green; lived in Berlin, N. Y. Children:

791 JAMES, b. Oct. 19, 1789; m. Esther Green.
792 DANIEL, b. Dec. 11, 1791; m. Isabel Niles.
793 BENJAMIN G., b. Oct. 30, 1793; m. Abigail Babcock.
794 POLLY, b. Nov. 14, 1798; m. Holden Sweet.
795 AN INFANT SON, b. and d. Dec. 9, 1801.
796 GORHAM, b. April 19, 1806; twice married.
797 ERI, b. Nov. 10, 1807; d. Oct. 21, 1808.
798 DAVID, twin, b. Dec. 22, 1809; m. Abigail Maxon.
799 JONATHAN, twin, b. Dec. 22, 1809; m. Alzina Allen.

794 POLLY DENISON, (Jonathan^6, Daniel^5, Daniel^4, George^3, John^2, George^1,) b. Nov. 14, 1798, was married Jan 22, 1816, to Holden Sweet. Children:

800 JAMES D.; m.; d. at Berlin, N. Y.
801 BENJAMIN A.; lives in Albany, N. Y.
802 MARY; lives in Albany, N. Y.

791 JAMES DENISON, (Jonathan^6, Daniel^5, Daniel^4, George^3, John^2, George^1,) b. Oct 19, 1789, was married "about 1812," to Esther Green; lived at Berlin, N. Y. His children:

803 SARAH; m. D. O. Mattison; d. at Berlin.
804 JONATHAN G.; m.; two children.
805 MARGARET; m. J. Shaw, of Niles, Mich.
806 MARYETTE; m. E. Dodge of Lawn Ridge, Ill.
807 POLLY; not married; lives with J. Shaw.

792 DANIEL DENISON,(Jonathan^6, Daniel^5, Daniel^4, George^3, John^2, George^1,) b. Dec. 11, 1791, was married to Isabel Niles, Oct. 29, 1815; lived at Berlin, N. Y.; had these:

808 DANIEL ERI, b. July 22, 1816; lived at Berlin, N. Y.
809 ALBERT G.; d. at Berlin, N. Y.
810 RHODA; d. at Berlin, N. Y.
811 MARGARET; m. C. Bly, Marshall, Mich.
812 REBECCA; m. J. T. Davis, East Greenbush, N. Y.
813 SARAH; m. F. Taylor, Berlin, N. Y.
814 GORHAM N.; not married; d. at Berlin, N. Y.

796 GORHAM N. DENISON, (Jonathan^6, Daniel^5, Daniel^4, George^3, John^2, George^1,) b. April 19, 1806, was married to

Eveline Maxon, Oct. 15, 1826, who d. June 19, 1842. He *m.*
2d, Lucy Crandall, who d. Feb. 25, 1852. He d. at Berlin, N.
Y., March 16, 1858. His children:

 815 CHARLOTTE, b. April 21, 1828; d. at Berlin, unmarried, Dec. 24, 1860.
 816 BYRON, b. May 11, 1830; *m.*; d. Feb. 27, 1855, at Berlin.
 817 WILLIAM E., b. Aug. 19, 1834; d. unmarried, April 25, 1853, Berlin.
 818 HERBERT E. b. Sept. 23, 1836; d. unmarried, Dec. 16, 1855, Berlin.
 819 DANIEL G., b. March 27, 1832; d. unmarried. Dec. 27, 1856, Berlin.
 820 FRANCIS A., b. Jan. 16, 1837; d. April 23, 1840, at Berlin.
 821 VICTOR D., b. Feb. 3, 1841; d. Jan. 16, 1856, at Berlin.
 822 OSCAR F., b. Nov. 3, 1843; d. Sept. 13, 1845, at Berlin.

808 DANIEL ERI DENISON, (Daniel^7, Jonathan^6, Daniel^5, Daniel^4, George^3, John^2, George^1,) b. July 25, 1816, was married, January, 1840, to Sarah M. Streeter. They lived and died in Berlin, N. Y. She d. March 9, 1870; he d. Jan. 23, 1877. Four children:

 823 ALFRED G., twin, b. Nov. 1, 1844; d. August, 1845.
 824 ALBERT E., twin, b. Nov. 1, 1844; *m.* Estella Town.
 825 HARVEY S., b. Aug. 6, 1851; *m.* Ida A. Green.
 826 BYRON FRANK, b. March 28, 1856; lives in Troy, N. Y.

824 ALBERT E. DENISON, (son of 808 Daniel Eri,) was married in Aug., 1870, to Estella Town ; lived in Berlin, N. Y.; d. there, Sept 27, 1875. One child:

 827 DANIEL S., b. in May, 1871.

825 HARVEY S. DENISON, (son of 808 Daniel Eri,) was married, Dec. 13, 1871, to Ida A. Green. They lived first in Berlin, but live now in Troy, N. Y., where he became engaged in business in March, 1877. Three children :

 828 BENJAMIN H., b. April 18, 1874.
 829 MILFORD S. b. Dec. 14, 1875.
 830 EDGAR RAY, b. July 28, 1879.

793 BENJAMIN G. DENISON, (Jonathan^6, Daniel^5, Daniel^4, George^3, John^2, George^1,) b. Oct. 30, 1793, was married to Abigail Babcock, Jan. 7, 1816; lived in Greenbush, N. Y.; had these :

 831 TYLER,   **831½** CAROLINE,
 832 SARAH,   **832½** SUSAN.

799 JONATHAN DENISON, (Jonathan^6, Daniel^5, Daniel^4, George^3, John^2, George^1,) b. Dec. 22, 1809, was married to Alzina Allen, April 12, 1832. His children :

833 MARY M., twin, b. Dec. 4. 1833; m. G. D. Jones of Pohegan, Mich.
834 A DAUGHTER, twin, b. Dec. 13, 1833; d. Dec. 13, 1833.
835 EUDORA E., b. Aug. 13, 1839.
836 ALZINA A., b. April 2, 1842.

798 DAVID DENISON, (Jonathan[6], Daniel[5], Daniel[4], George[3], John[2], George[1],) b. Dec. 22, 1809, was married to Abigail Maxon, Oct. 21, 1837. She was born, Aug. 24, 1818; d. Aug. 27, 1849. He m. 2nd, Rebecca A. Sheldon, Oct. 12, 1851. His children:

837 JAIRUS N., b. Dec. 4, 1838; m. Polly C. Holmes, Dec. 24, 1861, and d. Nov. 18, 1870.
838 MARY E., twin, b. April 20, 1843; m. James H. Cranston.
839 MARTHA A., twin, b. April 20, 1843; m. Edwin D. Culver.

838 MARY E. DENISON, (dau. of 798 David,) b. April 20, 1843, m. James H. Cranston, at Berlin, N. Y., Aug. 17, 1864, and d. Sept. 14, 1866. He had one child:

840 MARY E., b. Feb. 8, 1866.

839 MARTHA A. DENISON, (dau. of 798 David.) b. April 20, 1843, m. Edwin D. Culver, June 15, 1864; lives at Peoria, Ill.; has:

841 MARY D., b. March 12, 1866.

648 GRISWOLD DENISON, (Daniel[5], Daniel[4], George[3], John[2], George[1],) b. August 21, 1765, was married in 1793, to Rhoda Tifft. She d. March 22, 1869, aged 91. Three children:

842 GEORGE T., b. March 17, 1795.
843 REBECCA, b. 1797; m. Dr. Emerson Hull; children, Alsen & Julia.
844 ALSON, b. 1798; d. young.

842 GEORGE T. DENISON, (Griswold[6], Daniel[5], Daniel[4], George[3], John[2], George[1],) b. March 17, 1795, was married to Nancy Niles, July 11, 1819,; lived at Berlin, N. Y.; his wife died Oct. 8, 1853; he m. 2nd, Mrs. S. A. Green, and d. Feb. 8, 1874. His children were:

845 PARDEE N., b. Sept. 30, 1820.
846 PORTER G., b. Feb. 19, 1825.
847 HENRY E., b. May 30, 1828.

845 PARDEE N. DENISON, (son of 842 George T.) b. Sept. 30, 1820, m. Aurora F. Streeter of Berlin, N. Y. He died in Berlin, May 31, 1848; she died at Chester, Ill., Oct. 20, 1858. She was born Oct. 6, 1824. Their children:

847 OLIVE ADELAIDE, b. Aug. 12, 1844; m. Daniel J. Hull.
848 NANCY LOUISA, b. Jan 29, 1846; m. James F. Cowee, Troy, N.Y.

846 PORTER G. DENISON, (son of 842 George T.) b. Feb. 19, 1825, m. Mary E. Nichols, Sept. 30, 1852; lives at Clyde, N. Y. Their children:

849 GEORGE H., b. Aug. 30, 1853; d. Oct. 15, 1860.
850 CARRIE A. b. April 6, 1859.
851 CHARLES E., b. March 11, 1861.
852 JAMES P., b. Dec. 5, 1864; d. Sept. 1, 1865.
853 PORTER G., b. Feb. 6, 1870.

847 HENRY E. DENISON, (son of 842 George T.,) b. May 30, 1828, m. Hannah M. Godfrey, of Berlin, N. Y., Dec. 8, 1850. They have had two children:

854 GEORGE P., b. Oct. 28, 1851; d. April 17, 1852.
855 FREDERICK P., b. Oct. 12, 1857.

847 OLIVE ADELAIDE DENISON, (dau. of 845 Pardee N.,) was married, Oct. 18, 1865, to Daniel J. Hull, in Clyde, N. Y.; has:

856 ARTHUR DENISON HULL, b. June 30, 1869.

848 NANCY LOUISA DENISON, (dau. of 845 Pardee N.,) was married, April 22, 1869, to James F. Cowee, in Lansingburg, N. Y.; has:

857 HARVEY DENISON COWEE, b. May 22, 1874.

650 DAVID DENISON, (Daniel[5], Daniel[4], George[3], John[2], George[1],) b. March 19, 1769, was married in 1794 to Mrs. Polly (Jones) Williams. They had:

858 POLLY, b. 1795.
859 ORREL, b. 1797.
860 ANSEL, b, 1799.
861 CAROLINE, b. 1800.
862 FURMAN, b. 1802.

651 LATHAM DENISON, (Daniel[5], Daniel[4], George[3], John[2], George[1],) b. March 8, 1771, was married to Eleanor Tifft. Their children were:

863 HOLLEY, b. 1797; d. young.
864 PEDY, b. 1799; d. young.
865 TERESA, b. 1800.
866 RHODA, b. 1802.
867 GEORGE, b. 1804; d. young.
868 ALONZO, b. 1806.
869 PEDY, b. 1808.
870 HOLLEY, b. 1810.
871 GEORGE, b. 1812.
872 ANGELINE, b. 1814.
873 WELLINGTON, b. 1817.

655 THOMAS DENISON, (Daniel[5], Daniel[4], George[3], John[2], George[1],) b. May 5, 1779, at Stephentown, N. Y., was married Feb. 23, 1801, to Polly Crary. Children:

874 THOMAS C., b. Sept. 24, 1802; m. Charity Schults.
875 MARY, b. April 30, 1804; m. Ezra Orcutt.
876 ISAAC, b. July 21, 1806; m. Mary Dibble.
877 KATHERINE, b. March 27, 1809; m. Nathan Earl.
878 CANDACE, b. July 14, 1811; m. Ichabod Dibble.
879 DANIEL, b. May 21, 1814; m. Eliza Almy.
880 HANNAH, b. Dec. 11, 1815; unmarried; insane.
881 JESSE W., b. April 9, 1818; m. Mary W. Briggs.

874 THOMAS CRARY DENISON, (Thomas^6, Daniel^5, Daniel^4, George^3, John^2, George^1,) b. Sept. 24, 1802, was married to Charity Schults. He lives at Hunt's Landing, Schoharie Co., N. Y. His children:

882 THOMAS N.; lives in Niagara Co., N. Y.
883 JANE; lives in Niagara Co., N. Y.
884 MINOR, b, Jan. 19, 1841; lives at Gallupville, N. Y.
885 CHARITY; m. a Wiley at Gallupville, N. Y.
885 SARAH, b. Nov. 19, 1830; m. Jacob N. Wiedman.
887 JESSE.
888 ALVIRA; m. —— Hostrasser of Pa.
889 EDWARD; of Livingstonville, Pa.

884 MINOR DENISON, (son of 874 Thomas Crary,) b. Jan. 19, 1844, was married Jan. 11, 1866, to Lovisa Welch, b. March 22, 1845. They live at Gallupville, N. Y. Their children:

890 ALTHA J., b. Dec. 4, 1868.
891 IDA MAY, b. Aug. 25, 1876.

886 SARAH DENISON, (dau. of 874 Thomas Crary,) b. Nov. 19, 1830; was married, Oct. 5, 1861, to Jacob N. Weidman, b. Feb. 9, 1827. They live at East Hebron, Pa. Children:

892 LIZETTA, b. April 6, 1863.
893 ULYSSES G., b. Nov. 26, 1865.

875 MARY DENISON, (Thomas^6, Daniel^5, Daniel^4, George^3, John^2, George^1,) b. April 30, 1804, was married, Feb. 22, 1824, to Ezra Orcutt ; lived at Catatonk, Tioga Co., N. Y. Children:

894 WILLIAM, b. March 13, 1825; lives at Candor, N. Y.; m. March 15, 1846, Ruth Sherman, b. Oct. 1, 1823; no child.
895 JOSEPHINE, b. March 21, 1827; m. John Palmatier; 5 children.
896 JAMES E., b. Nov. 20, 1828; m. Elizabeth E. LaGrange; 3 children.
897 AMANDA, b. July 19, 1830; m. Abram LaGrange; 3 children.
898 MARY M., b. Aug. 28, 1833; m. Lucius H. Smith; 4 children.
899 DAVID, b. July 25, 1837; m. Belle G——; one child, Emma Grace, b. July 23, 1817; lives at Candor, N. Y.
900 ISAAC D., b. July 26, 1839; m. Dell Billings; 3 children.
901 HANNAH E., b. March 8, 1842; m. Henry Fox; 7 children.

902 EMMA CORNELIA, twin, b. Nov. 10, 1844; *m*. Alvin T. Robinson; 3 children.

903 AMY PAMELIA, twin, b. Nov. 10, 1844; *m*. M. P. Smith; 1 child.

876 ISAAC DENISON, (Thomas[6], Daniel[5], Daniel[4], George[3], John[2], George[1],) b. July 21, 1806, was married, Dec. 30, 1830, to Mary Dibble, b. Dec. 30, 1810; lived at Hunt's Landing, Schoharie Co., N. Y. Children:

    904 HULDAH, b. Feb. 25, 1832; *m*. Ransom E. Sisson.
    905 DANIEL, b. Aug. 21, 1835; *m*. Lydia Norton.
    906 LEONARD, b. June 15, 1837; d. in 1846.
    907 LEONARD A., b. April 29, 1847; *m*. Olive P. Cook.
    908 WILLIAM A., b. Aug. 4, 1848; *m*. Mary A. Sisson.
    909 EMMA J., b. July 23, 1853.

904 HULDAH DENISON, (dau. of 876 Isaac,) b. Feb. 25, 1832; *m*. Ransom E. Sisson, Oct. 50, 1850. She died Sept. 3, 1864; he d. Aug. 1872, aged 45. Two children:

    910 ALBERT P., b. July, 1851; d. in 1862.
    911 ANGELO, b. March, 1859; lives at Des Moines, Iowa.

905 DANIEL DENISON, (son of 876 Isaac,) b. Aug. 21, 1835, *m*. Lydia Norton, b. April 25, 1834; lives at Westerlo, N. Y. Two children:

    912 MELVIN J., b. Sept. 15, 1859.
    913 WILLIAM, b. June 18, 1858; d. Sept., 1858.

895 JOSEPHINE ORCUTT, (dau. of 875 Mary and Ezra,) was married, Jan. 15, 1851, to John Palmatier, b. Jan. 26, 1828; lives in Candor, N. Y. Children:

    914 JOHN LUTHER, b. July 1, 1854; d. March 30, 1860.
    915 CHAS WESLEY, b. June 9, 1856.
    916 FRANKLIN A., b. March 6, 1858.
    917 WILLARD WINFIELD, b. Jan. 22, 1862; d. March 11, 1862.
    918 DELPHINE, b. April 2, 1868.

896 JAMES E. ORCUTT, (son of 875 Mary and Ezra,) was married, Nov. 8, 1852, to Elizabeth E. LaGrange, b. Aug. 10, 1832. They live at Catatonk, N. Y. Children:

    919 JOHN ALLEN b. Aug. 24, 1859; *m*. Mary E. Campbell, b. in 1855.
    920 ELLEN ORLENA, b. April 8, 1858; *m*. Geo. Taft, Oct. 7, 1875; has one child, Bertha E., b. Oct 14, 1877.
    921 MARY, b. Nov. 11, 1866.

897 AMANDA ORCUTT, (dau. of 875 Mary and Ezra,) was married, Feb. 25, 1850, to Abram LaGrange, b. July 18, 1829; lives at Candor, N. Y. Children:

922 MARY EMMA, b. July 29, 1851; d. Nov. 1, 1861.
923 JOSEPHINE ELIZABETH, b. April 22, 1853; d. Nov. 11, 1861.
924 CHARLES, b. April 18, 1855.

898 MARY M. ORCUTT, (dau. of 875 Mary and Ezra,) was married, Oct. 20, 1852, to Lucius H. Smith, b. Dec. 19, 1827; lives at Candor, N. Y. Children :

925 ADA BELLE, b. June 2, 1856; m. June 16, 1873, John C. Campbell, b. Oct. 6, 1853; has these : Frederick Smith, b. March 1, 1874; May E., b. June 5, 1877.
926 EMMA G., b. Feb. 15, 1858.
927 EVERETT L., b. Feb. 20, 1863.
928 MAMIE, b. Dec. 24, 1875; d. April 14, 1876.

900 ISAAC D. ORCUTT, (son of 875 Mary and Ezra,) was married, Nov 18, 1865, to Dell Billings, b. Aug. 16, 1845. They live at Owego, N. Y. Children :

929 CARRIE, b. Feb. 24, 1867.
930 LOTTIE ELVENIA, b. Oct. 6, 1870.
931 JENNIE, b. Nov. 25, 1875.

901 HANNAH E. ORCUTT, (dau. of 875 Mary and Ezra,) was married, Dec. 28, 1859, to Henry Fox, b. Dec. 18, 1835. They live in Owego, N. Y. Children :

932 WILLARD S., b. March 22, 1862.
933 JOHN E., b. Oct. 22, 1866.
934 LILLIAN, b. Sept. 10, 1867.
935 ADA MARY, b. Dec. 22, 1869; d. Sept. 30, 1870.
936 EDWARD, b. Nov. 15, 1871.
937 KITTIE, b. June 15, 1874.
938 BERTIE, b. Jan. 6, 1877; d. April 16, 1877.

902 EMMA CORNELIA ORCUTT, (dau. of 875 Mary and Ezra,) was married Oct. 21, 1863, to Alvin T. Robinson, b. Dec. 10, 1840. Children :

939 FREDERICK ODELL, b. April 17, 1865.
940 BERT E., b. Jan. 28, 1867.
941 MARTIN T., b. June 12, 1870.

903 AMY PAMELIA ORCUTT, (dau. of 875 Mary and Ezra,) was married, Oct. 21, 1863, to Philemon P. Smith ; lives at Ithaca, N. Y. One child :

942 EDDIE, b. Dec. 24, 1867.

907 LEONARD A. DENISON, (son of 876 Isaac,) b. April 29, 1847, was married, Dec. 23, 1866, to Olive J. Cook, b. July 23, 1843 ; lives at Berne, N. Y. Children :

Capt. John Denison's Descendants. 51

943 WARREN H., b. June 18, 1870.
944 FRED. C., twin, b. May 24, 1874.
945 FLORA B., twin, b. May 24, 1874.

908 WILLIAM A. DENISON, (son of 876 Isaac,) b. Aug. 4, 1838, was married, June 18, 1858, to Mary A. Sisson; lives in Berne, Albany Co., N. Y. Children:

946 FRANK T., b. Aug. 24, 1864.
947 WELLINGTON J., b. Nov. 15, 1872.
948 LAURA E., b. Dec. 14, 1874.
949 HULDAH M., b. Dec. 25, 1875.

877 KATHERINE DENISON, (Thomas[6], Daniel[5], Daniel[4], George[3], John[2], George[1],) b. March 27, 1809, was married to Nathan Earl, in 1828; lived near Grand Rapids, Mich. She d. July 29, 1874. One child:

950 MARIA, b. Jan., 1832; lives near Grand Rapids.

878 CANDACE DENISON, (Thomas[6], Daniel[5], Daniel[4], George[3], John[2], George[1],) b. July 14, 1811, was married March 11, 1832, to Ichabod Dibble. P. O., New Milford, Pa. Children:

951 ALMIRA, b. Dec. 11, 1832; twice married; 6 children.
952 MARIA, b. Aug. 29, 1834; m. Jacob Keyser; 2 children; d. Sept. 19 1865.
953 SYLVESTER, b. Aug. 7, 1836; m. Eliza Dunham; 3 children.
954 JOSEPHINE, twin, b. Aug. 13, 1838; m. Wm. P. Dunham; 3 child'n.
955 EVALINE, twin, b. Aug. 13, 1838; d. April 28, 1839.
956 JESSE D., b. Aug. 29, 1840; m. Hetty Dunham; 7 children.
957 LEWIS D., b. Aug. 23, 1842; d. April 15, 1844.
958 ISAAC V., b. July 1, 1845: m. Mary Conway; 5 children.
959 ICHABOD I., b. Oct. 23, 1847; m. Eva Hill; P. O., Titusville, Pa.
960 DANIEL D., b. May 23, 1850; d. May 1, 1876.
961 WESLEY, b. Sept. 17, 1852; m. Elizabeth Dexter; 1 child.

879 DANIEL DENISON, (Thomas[6], Daniel[5], Daniel[4], George[3], John[2], George[1],) b. May 21, 1814, was married first, December, 1836, to Eliza Almy, who d. May 18, 1848; and second, Dec. 11, 1850, to Mrs. Jane Ann Winchester; lives in Albany, N. Y. Children:

962 CANDACE, b. April 3, 1838; m. Isaac Crary Seabury.
963 JAMES C., b. April 10, 1840; d. March 27, 1841.
964 MARY LOUISA, b. March 11, 1853.
965 HOWARD, b. March 28, 1858.
966 FRANK, b. June 9, 1860.

881 JESSE W. DENISON, (Thomas[6], Daniel[5], Daniel[4], George[3], John[2], George[1],) b. April 9, 1818, was married, first, in 1846, to Mary W. Briggs, dau. of Rev. A. Briggs; and second, Aug. 3, 1859, to Eliza B. Lewis, dau. of Nathan Lewis of Seekonk, Mass. The first wife d. Dec. 27, 1855. He lives at Denison, Iowa. Children:

 967 MARY LOUISA, b. Dec. 5, 1848; *m.* Thos. Hooker, of Hartford, Ct.
 968 JULIA P., b. July 19, 1851; *m.* Rev. A. M. Duboe.
 969 WILLIE S., b. Feb. 1, 1852.
 970 MARIA LOUISA, b. Aug. 17, 1866.
 971 JESSIE L., b. May 13, 1876; d. April 1, 1877.

967 MARY LOUISA DENISON, (dau. of 881 Jesse W.,) was married, June 27, 1872, to Thomas Hooker of Hartford, Conn.; they live at Dallas Centre, Iowa; he is an extensive stock dealer, and works a section farm. Children:

 972 EDWARD D., b. March 28, 1873.
 973 ROBERT, b. in 1874; d. in infancy.
 974 HELEN FOSTER, b. March 28, 1876.

968 JULIA P. DENISON, (dau. of 881 Jesse W.,) was married, June 25, 1874, to Rev. A. M. Duboe, of Livonia, N. Y. Children:

 975 CHARLES HENRY, b. July 15, 1875.
 976 MARY CLARA, b. Jan. 3, 1878.

653 SAMUEL DENISON, (Daniel[5], Daniel[4], George[3], John[2], George[1],) b. Aug. 24, 1774, was married, first, about 1800, to Rhoda Crandall; and second, about 1818, to Nancy Burlingame. His children were as follows:

 977 PAMELA, b. in 1801.
 978 ALVIN, b. in 1803.
 979 KATHERINE, b. in 1805.
 980 SALLY, b. in 1807.
 982 ALSON, b. in 1809; died young.
 983 ALEXANDRA, b. in 1811.
 984 ALSON, b. in 1814.
 985 LUCY, b. in 1815.
 986 AN INFANT, unnamed, b. in 1817.
 987 GEORGE B., b. in 1819.
 988 CHARLES M., b. in 1821.
 989 AN INFANT, unnamed.   Three others.

654 ELIHU DENISON, (Daniel[5], Daniel[4], George[3], John[2], George[1],) b. April 14, 1777, was married, about 1800, to Thankful Stewart, dau. of Alexander and Thankful (Denison) Stewart, of Griswold, Conn. His children:

Capt. John Denison's Descendants.

990 ELIHU,
991 ANNA,
992 THANKFUL,
993 JAMES S.
994 DANIEL,
995 HORACE,
996 KATHERINE,
997 GEORGE,
998 AVERY.

643 KATHERINE DENISON, (Daniel[5], Daniel[4], George[3], John[2], George[1],) b. July 24, 1757, was married to James Jones. He d. in 1803; she d. in 1850. They had:

999 JAMES H., b. March 28, 1779; m. Waity Jerome; lives in Illinois.
1000 KATHERINE,
1001 EUNICE,
1002 JERUSHA,
1003 DANIEL,
1004 WILLIAM,
1005 RACHEL,
1006 AVERY,
1007 ELIAS,
1008 CLARISSA.

649 ASENATH DENISON, (Daniel[5], Daniel[4], George[3], John[2], George[1],) b. Feb. 24, 1767, m. Roger Jones, and had:

1009 ELIPHALET,
1010 ASENATH,
1011 DENISON,
4012 LATHAM,
1013 SALLY,
1014 DRUSILLA,
1015 KATHERINE,
1016 AVERY,
1017 ALANSON,
1018 WILLIAM,
1019 ALVAH,
1020 NANCY.

591 THOMAS DENISON, (Daniel[4], George[3], John[2], George[1],) b. Nov. 4, 1732, was married, Jan. 17, 1759, to Katherine Starr. He died, March, 1813; she died, March, 1817, aged 83 years. They reared their family in New London, Conn., but removed to Hartford, and "about 1790," to Mansfield, Montgomery Co., N. Y. Their children were:

1021 SAMUEL, b. Jan. 5, 1760: m. Hannah Gaylord in 1793; no child. He d. at Mayfield, N. Y., Sept. 28. 1831; she d. May, 1833, aged 72.
1022 ANN, b. Oct. 25, 1761; m. Samuel Easton.
1023 THOMAS, b. March 9, 1764; m. Meribah Cowdry.
1024 ELIZABETH, b. March 7, 1766; m. Asa Seymour.
1025 GRACE, b. June 3, 1769; m. Barout Van Buren.
1026 STARR, b. April 16, 1771; m. Chloe Stone in 1800.
1027 KATHERINE, b. March 20, 1773; died in 1775.
1028 KATHERINE, b. March 22, 1775; m. Ebenezer Warner.
1029 DANIEL, b. Oct. 26, 1779; d. at East Hartford, in 1781.

1022 ANN DENISON, (Thomas[5], Daniel[4], George[3], John[2], George[1],) b, Oct. 25, 1761; m. Samuel Easton, in 1788, at East Hartford. He d. in East Hartford, March, 1800; she d. there, May, 1800. Their children were:

1030 SAMUEL, b. 1790; m. —— Ives, of New Haven, Conn.
1031 STARR, b. 1792; m. —— Burgess of Colchester, Conn.
1032 Thomas, b. 1794.

1023 THOMAS DENISON. (Thomas[5], Daniel[4], George[3], John[2], George[1],) b. March 9, 1764, was married to Meribah Cowdry, of Newport, R. I., in 1791. She was born, Oct., 1764, dau. of Isaac and Eunice Cowdry. He d. in Norwich, Conn., in 1826; she d. there, Aug. 1827. Their children :

1033 THOMAS, b. May 26, 1793; m. Sarah Beebe.
1034 KATHERINE, b. March 1, 1795; m. Joseph Meeker.
1035 CHARLES, b. July 16, 1797; twice married.
1036 EMILY, b. April 17, 1800; twice married.
1037 DANIEL, b. July 20, 1802.
1038 LOUISA A., b. April, 1806; d. Jan., 1807.

1034 KATHERINE DENISON, (Thomas[6], Thomas[5], Daniel[4], George[3], John[2], George[1],) b. March 1, 1795, was married to Joseph Meeker, May, 1814, and d. May 27, 1819. Her children were :

1039 MARY E., b. Aug. 17, 1815.
1040 JOSEPH, twin. b. May 16, 1819; m. Ellen Campbell.
1041 KATHERINE, twin, b. May 16, 1819; m. John P. Lawrence.

1035 CHARLES DENISON, (Thomas[6], Thomas[5], Daniel[4], George[3], John[2], George[1],) b. July 16, 1797, was married, 1st, to Eliza Lester, Jan. 24, 1829 ; she d. Jan. 29, 1836. He married, second, Sarah M. Crocker. The children, all by the first wife :

1042 ELIZABETH M., b. Oct. 27, 1829; d. Oct. 21, 1830.
1043 WILLIAM T., b. Oct. 23, 1831; d. Nov. 11, 1831.
1044 CHARLES F., b. Feb. 15, 1833; m. Mary E. Crumb.
1045 ELIZABETH L., b. Jan. 25, 1835; d. April 30, 1836.

1044 CHARLES F. DENISON, (son of 1035 Charles and Eliza,) b. Feb. 15, 1833, was married to Mary E. Crumb, who d. Feb. 4, 1870, aged 37. Their children:

1046 FREDERICK, b. March 28, 1858; d. May, 1860.
1047 ELIZABETH L., b. March 8, 1860.
1048 HARRIET A., b. April, 1863; d. June, 1867.
1049 AN UNNAMED INFANT, b. and d. in December, 1865.
1050 FREDERICK E., b. 1866; d. Jan. 1867.
1051 DANIEL A.

1033 THOMAS DENISON, (Thomas[6], Thomas[5], Daniel[4], George[3], John[2], George[1],) b. May 26, 1793, was married, Jan.

1, 1820, to Sarah Beebe, of Norwich, Conn. She d. Jan. 1825. He d. Jan. 1, 1857. They had but one child:

1052 JAMES P., b. Nov. 12, 1822.

1052 JAMES P. DENISON, (Thomas[7], Thomas[6], Thomas[5], Daniel[4], George[3], John[2], George[1],) b. Nov. 12, 1822, was married, Nov. 6, 1850, to Ellen Cheney, (dau. of Martin and Nancy,) lives at Norwich, Conn. Children:

1053 MARTIN, b. July 8, 1852; m. Hattie Lillie.
1054 LEWIS C., b. Sept. 27, 1854.
1055 ALACE, b. Sept. 12, 1864; d. Sept. 20, 1865.

136 EMILY DENISON, (Thomas[6], Thomas[5], Daniel[4], George[3], John[2], George[1],) b. April 17, 1800, was married to Hallam Harris, April 3, 1820. He d. in 1836, aged 37. In 1847, she m. 2nd, Wm. Kelley. She d. in Norwich, Conn., Sept. 2, 1851. Her children, all by Hallam Harris, were:

1056 EMILY L., b. Aug., 1821; d. in Aug., 1822.
1057 AN INFANT SON, b. and d. in September, 1822.
1058 KATHERINE D., b. March 24, 1824; m. Wm. S. Hempstead.

1037 DANIEL DENISON, (Thomas[6], Thomas[5], Daniel[4], George[3], John[2], George[1],) b. July 20, 1802, was married to Nancy Williams, of Norwich, Conn., in April, 1828; lived in Cleveland, Ohio; removed to Peoria, Ill., in 1834, where he d. Aug. 15, 1852. His family returned to Cleveland. He had:

1059 NANCY W., b. March 4, 1829; m. Russell Beach.
1060 MERIBAH D., b. June 30, 1830; m. Dr. Andrew J. Gardner, May 5, 1850; they live at Grand Rapids, Mich.; no child.
1061 LOUISA A., b. June 7, 1833; m. Wellington P. Cook.
1062 EDWIN, b. June 21, 1836; m. Julia A. Burwell.
1063 THOMAS, b. June 9, 1839; m. Mary J. Wyville, in 1868.
1064 JEDEDIAH W., b. Nov. 6, 1841; m. Mary Eden Fairchild.
1065 DANIEL, b. Feb. 5, 1844; d. Aug., 1844.
1066 MARIETTA, b. June 16, 1845; m. Geo. Hester.

1059 NANCY W. DENISON, (dau. of 1037 Daniel and Nancy,) b. March 4, 1829, was married to Russell Beach, at Cleveland, Aug. 13, 1848, and had these:

1067 CHARLES R., b. 1849; m. Ida M. Denison, at Saginaw, Mich.; has: Grace Minerva, b. March 21, 1876; Bessie Williams, b. April 19, 1880.
1068 FRANK WILLIS, b. 1850.
1069 ADDIS MAY, b. 1851.
1069½ ANNA WEBSTER, b. 1852.
1070 ELLA LUCILLA, b 1853; m. at Saginaw, Mich., Jan. 1873, Albert J. Linton.

1063 THOMAS DENISON, (son of 1037 Daniel and Nancy,) b. June 9, 1839, was married in 1868, to Margaret J. Wyville; lives in Cleveland, Ohio, and has had:
 1071 JENNIE W., b. April 3, 1869.
 1072 ADDIE C., b. Aug. 19, 1871.
 1073 BELLE, b. Nov. 3, 1873; d. April 4, 1875.

1062 EDWIN DENISON, (son of 1037 Daniel and Nancy,) b. June 21, 1836, was married to Julia A. Burwell, Jan. 20, 1859; lives at Cleveland, Ohio, and has these:
 1074 CHARLES E., b. June 6, 1860.
 1075 MARY A., b. Jan. 11, 1863.
 1076 GEORGE B., b. Sept. 8, 1864.
 1077 JESSE L., b. Nov. 5, 1868.
 1078 DANIEL, b. March 6, 1870.
 1079 JULIA EMELINE, b. June, 1872.
 1080 HATTIE BELLE, b. Dec. 29, 1878.
 1081 GRACE, b. Feb. 18, 1876.

1061 LOUISA ADELAIDE DENISON, (dau. of 1037 Daniel and Nancy,) m. Wellington P. Cook, Nov. 8, 1849. They live in Cleveland, Ohio. Children:
 1082 HENRY E., b. May 7, 1854; m.; has one child.
 1083 ARTHUR W., b. May 7, 1858; d. Jan. 14, 1862.
 1084 ADELAIDE L., b. Feb. 15, 1860.
 1085 MYRTIE DENISON, b. July 7, 1864.

1064 JEDEDIAH WILLIAMS DENISON, (son of 1037 Daniel and Nancy,) m. April 26, 1863, Mary Eden Fairchild, b. April 26, 1844. They live in Cleveland, Ohio. Children:
 1086 NELLIE AGNES, b. Feb. 5, 1864.
 1087 HARRY EDWIN, b. June 21, 1866.
 1088 DANIEL FAIRCHILD, b. March 1, 1872.
 1089 LEROY WILSON, b. Dec. 2, 1874.
 1090 LULU ELLA, b. Aug 24, 1876.

1066 MARIETTA DENISON, (dau. of 1037 Daniel and Nancy,) m. George Hestor, June 18, 1865. They live in Cleveland, Ohio. Children:
 1091 FRANK, b. May 19, 1866.
 1092 FLORA BELLE, b. Sept. 17, 1867.
 1093 EDWIN DENISON, b. April 26, 1869.

1024 ELIZABETH DENISON, (Thomas[5], Daniel[4], George[3], John[2], George[1],) b. March 7, 1766, was married to Asa Seymour, Dec. 17, 1786; of Hartford, Conn. He d. Oct. 28, 1810; she d. Nov. 28, 1846. Their children:

Capt. John Denison's Descendants.

1094 BETSEY, b. Feb. 16, 1788; m. Wm. Wadsworth.
1095 KATHERINE, b. May 30, 1789; m. Joseph Brown.
1096 MARY, b. May 27, 1791; m. Roger Newell.
1097 CHESTER, b. Jan. 10, 1793; m. Florilla Mather.
1098 MABEL, b. May 22, 1795; m. Russell Rollins.
1099 WILLIAM, b. May 26, 1798; d. Oct., 1850.
1100 ANN, b. Dec. 29, 1801; m. David F. Robinson.
1101 ALBERT, twin, b. April 29, 1804; m. Jerusha Ensign.
1102 ALMIRA, twin, b. April 29, 1804; d. Nov. 1866.

1100 ANN SEYMOUR, (dau. of 1024 Elizabeth Denison, and Asa Seymour,) b. Dec. 29, 1801, was married, April 22, 1823, to David F. Robinson, son of David and Catherine (Coe) Robinson, of Granville, Mass. They lived in Hartford, Conn. He d. Jan. 26, 1862; his widow resides in Hartford. Their children:

1103 LUCIUS F., b. Feb. 1, 1824; m. Eliza S. Trumbull.
1104 CHARLES, b. Dec. 22, 1825; d. Nov. 2, 1827.
1105 ANN C., b. Sept. 14, 1827; d. April 1828.
1106 SARAH AMELIA, b. Oct. 26, 1829; m. Hon. J. Hammond Trumbull, Aug. 6, 1855; one child, Ann E., b. March 2, 1857.
1107 HENRY C., b. Aug. 28, 1832; m. Eliza N. Trumbull.
1108 MARY C., b. Aug. 12, 1834; m. Nathaniel Shipman.
1109 ALFRED S., b. April 6, 1836; m. Emily Haynes, Dec. 8, 1869; d. Sept. 26, 1878.

1103 LUCIUS F. ROBINSON, (son of 1082 Ann Seymour and D. F. Robinson,) b. Feb. 1, 1824, was married, Oct. 21, 1850, to Eliza S., dau. of Gov. Joseph and Eliza (Storrs) Trumbull, of Hartford, Conn. He d. March 11, 1861. His children:

1110 ELIZA T., b. Nov. 29, 1857.
1111 ANNIE S., b. Feb. 10, 1855; d. April 11, 1861.
1112 MARY A., b. Sept. 17, 1856.
1113 HARRIET T., Feb. 9, 1859; d. Aug. 19, 1870.

1107 HENRY C. ROBINSON, (son of 1082 Ann Seymour and D. F. Robinson,) b. Aug. 28, 1832, was married, Aug. 28, 1862, to Eliza N., dau. of John F. and Eliza Trumbull of Stonington, Conn.; lives in Hartford. His children:

1114 LUCIUS F., b. June 12, 1863.
1115 LUCY T., b. July 19, 1865.
1116 HENRY S., b. April 16, 1868.
1117 JOHN T., b. April 25, 1871.
1118 MARY S., b. May 17, 1873.

1108 MARY C. ROBINSON, (dau. of 1082 Ann Seymour and D. F. Robinson,) b. Aug. 12, 1834, was married, May 25, 1859,

58 Capt. John Denison's Descendants.

to Nathaniel Shipman, of Hartford, son of Rev. Thos. L. Shipman of Jewett City, Conn. Their children:

1119 FRANK R., b. Feb. 15, 1863.
1120 ARTHUR L., b. Nov. 19, 1864.
1121 MARY, b. July 27, 1868.
1122 THOMAS L., b. in 1870; d. July 31, 1872.
1123 HENRY, b. April, 1877.

1025 GRACE DENISON, (Thomas[5], Daniel[4], George[3], John[2], George[1],) b. June 3, 1769, *m.* Barout Van Buren, in 1792. She d. Aug. 18, 1834; he d. in 1850, aged 86. Children:

1124 HARMON, b. 1793. **1128** PETER, b. 1803.
1125 THOMAS, b. 1795. **1129** KATHERINE, b. 1807.
1126 ANGELICA, b. 1799. **1130** WILLIAM, b. 1812.
1127 SAMUEL, b. in 1801.

1028 KATHERINE DENISON, (Thomas[5], Daniel[4], George[3], John[2], George[1],) b. March 22, 1775, was married to Ebenezer Warner, Nov. 8, 1804. She d. Sept. 23, 1849. She had:

1131 VINE S., b. 1806.
1132 JOHN, b. 1808.
1133 FANNY, b. 1810.

1026 STARR DENISON, (Thomas[5], Daniel[4], George[3], John[2], George[1],) b. April 16, 1771, was married, in 1800, to Chloe Stone. They settled, first, in Mayfield, N. Y. Previous to 1818, they emigrated to Clearfield, Pa. He d. June, 1844; she d. Feb. 1865, aged 84. They had:

1134 ASENATH, b. Aug., 1801; *m.* Simpson Johnson,
1135 VINE, b. Jan., 1803.
1136 DANIEL, b. June, 1804; *m.* Clarissa Swagart.
1137 STARR, b. March, 1806; *m.* Elmira, Wid. of James.
1138 JAMES, b. Dec. 1807; d. in 1810.
1139 THOMAS, b. Aug., 1809; d. in 1840.
1140 ELIZABETH, b. May, 1811; *m.* Wm. Smith.
1141 JAMES, b. Nov., 1812; *m.* Elmira Coleman, in 1836.
1142 KATHERINE, b. Nov., 1814.
1143 CHARLES E., b. 1817; d. in 1838.
1144 EDWARD R., b. April, 1822.
1145 CHLOE, b. Sept., 1824.

1137 STARR DENISON, (Starr[6], Thomas[5], Daniel[4], George[3], John[2], George[1],) b. March, 1806, was married in 1840, to Elmira, widow of his brother James. They emigrated to Wisconsin. Children:

1146 KATHARINE, b. 1840.
1147 JAMES, b. 1843.
1148 MARY J., 1845.
1149 PHEBE B., b. 1848.
1150 STARR, b. 1850.
1151 HENRY, b. 1853.
1152 ANOTHER CHILD, b. 1856.

1136 DANIEL DENISON, (Starr⁶, Thomas⁵, Daniel⁴, George³, John², George¹,) b. June, 1804, was married, in 1830, to Clarissa Swagart, in Pennsylvania. They had:

1152 AMELIA T., b. Feb., 1832.
1153 MARY CHLOE, b. 1833; d. in 1854.
1154 VESTA ANN, b. 1837; d. in 1845.
1155 GEORGE G., b. 1849.

531 WETHERELL DENISON, (George³, John², George¹,) b. Aug. 24, 1705, was married to Lydia More, Nov. 9, 1726. Wetherell Denison lived in New London. I find this record of his children:

1156 GRACE, b. Feb. 8, 1728; m. Park Avery, Dec. 10, 1778; d. Aug. 13, 1809.
1157 GEORGE, b. Jan. 16, 1730.
1158 LYDIA, b. Aug. 6, 1831; m. Daniel Whetmore.
1159 ESTHER, b. March 16, 1735.
1160 LUCY, b. May 5, 1739; m. Rupert Sandiforth, March 24, 1758; had Wetherell, b. June 22, 1759.
1161 SARAH, b. May 31, 1743.

1157 GEORGE DENISON, (Wetherell⁴, George³, John², George¹,) married (wife's name unknown,) and had five children:

1162 A DAUGHTER; m. a Hammond and had two children: Alonzo and Amanda.
1163 A DAUGHTER; m. a Burlingame and had three children: Eliza, Sarah and Chester.
1164 CHARLES.
1165 JAMES.
1166 ESTHER; m. Jonas B. Avery.

1166 ESTHER DENISON, (George⁵, Wetherell⁴, George³, John², George¹,) was married, July 24, 1791, to Jonas B. Avery, son of John Avery. He d. Feb. 2, 1836. Their children:

1167 CLARISSA, b. April 27, 1792; m. Park W. Avery.
1168 NANCY, b. April 1, 1794; m. Ebenezer Avery.
1169 FRANKLIN N., b. Jan 10, 1796; m. Rosanna Brush.
1170 JULIA, b. Jan, 1803; m. Jedediah Brigham.
1171 ALMIRA E., b. Oct. 18, 1806; m. George Leach; P.O. Harford, Pa.

IV.

179 ROBERT DENISON, (John[2], George[1],) b. Sept. 7, 1673, was married, in 1696, to Joanna Stanton, dau. of Robert and Joanna (Gardner) Stanton. He settled in the North Society of New London, (then called Mohegan, now Montville.) In 1710, he bought of Owaneco, chief sachem of the Mohegans, 500 acres of land in Mohegan, on the east side of Gardner's Lake, for which he paid £20. At that time he was "Capt. Robert Denison of Stonington;" but soon afterwards, he settled on the land he had bought of Owaneco. In 1716, he bought of the Mohegans another tract of land. His children:

1172 ANN, b. in 1695; d. young.
1173 ROBERT, b. in 1697; twice married; d. in Nova Scotia.
1174 JOHN, b. March 28, 1698; m. Patience Griswold.
1175 JOANNA, b. in 1699; m. Thomas Morehouse.
1176 MARY, b. in 1700; d. young.
1177 NATHANIEL, b. in 1702; d. in 1722.
1178 ANDREW, b. in 1704; d. in 1727.
1179 SARAH, b. in 1706; d. in 1714.
1180 ANN, b. in 1707; m. James Fitch in 1725.
1181 THOMAS, b. Oct. 20, 1709; m. Elizabeth Bailey.
1182 LUCY, b. in 1711; m. Samuel Rogers.
1183 ELIZABETH, b. in 1712; d. young.
1184 ABIGAIL, b. in 1714; m. Wm. Wattles.
1186 GEORGE, b. in 1715; d. young.

The wife Joanna d. in 1715. In 1717, he m. second, Dorothy, dau. of Thomas Stanton, Jr., and widow of two previous husbands, namely: Thomas Lynde and John Frink. Robert Denison d. in 1737. Two children by the 2nd wife:

1187 GEORGE, b. in 1719; m. Hannah Dodge, in 1742.
1188 DOROTHY, b. in 1721; thrice married.

1080 ANN DENISON, (Robert[3], John[2], George[1],) b. in 1707, was married to James Fitch, (son of Daniel and grandson of Rev. James,) in 1725. He died in Lebanon, in 1789, aged 86. She died in 1792, aged 85. Their children were:

1189 ANN, b. Feb., 1728; m. a Stark.
1190 ELIZABETH, b. June, 1731; m. Jere. Mason.

Capt. John Denison's Descendants.

1184 ABIGAIL DENISON, (Robert[3], John[2], George[1],) b. in 1714, was married, in 1735, to William Wattles, of Lebanon. They had these children :

    1191 ABIGAIL, b. 1738.
    1192 WILLIAM, b. Dec , 1739.
    1193 BESTOR, b. 1743.
    1194 MARY, b. 1744; m. Daniel Hyde.
    1195 SARAH, b. 1746; m. Walter Hyde.
    1196 DENISON, b. 1750; m. 1st.; 2nd, Ann Hyde.
    1197 DANIEL, b. 1756.

1192 LUCY DENISON, (Robert[3], John[2], George[1],) b. in 1711, m. Samuel Rogers, in 1730, and had :

    1198 JAMES, b. in 1740; m. Zelpha Hyde.
    1199 DANIEL, b. in 1745; m. Hannah Latimer.

1175 JOANNA DENISON, (Robert[3], John[2], George[1],) b. in 1699, was married to Thomas Morehouse, Dec. 27, 1721. They lived in Fairfield, Conn., and had :

    1200 JOANNA, b. Nov. 9, 1723.

1173 ROBERT DENISON, (Robert[3], John[2], George[1],) b. in 1697, was a soldier who saw some service. He was a Captain in Gen. Roger Walcott's brigade, at the capture of Louisburg, and won reputation by his gallant behavior in that affair. He was rapidly promoted until he received the rank of Colonel. He was very popular with the British officers with whom he acted. He was married, first, to Deborah Griswold of Lyme, dau. of Matthew and Phebe, Oct. 19, 1721. She d. in 1732 ; and April 4, 1733, he was married, second, to Prudence Sherman, of New Haven, dau. of David and Mercy Sherman, b. Oct. 20, 1706. He lived in Mohegan, now Montville ; but late in life he emigrated, with part of his family, to Horton, Nova Scotia. A deed, dated Sept. 18, 1761, and recorded at New London, mentions him as " Col. Robert Denison, of Horton, Nova Scotia." He d. there in 1766. His children :

    1210 DEBORAH, b. Dec. 9, 1722; m. C. Manwaring.
    1211 ROBERT, b. March 5, 1724; d. May 16, 1724.
    1212 ELIZABETH, b. Feb. 26, 1723; d. in infancy.
    1213 ELIZABETH, b. Sept. 10, 1726; m. Nathan Smith, of Groton.
    1214 DANIEL, b. 1727.
    1215 ANDREW, b. 1728; m. Mary Thompson.
    1216 MARY, b. 1730; d. Dec. 21, 1743.
    1217 ROBERT, b. 1732; d. in 1732.

1218 DAVID SHERMAN, b. Aug., 1734; m. Sarah Fox.
1219 MERCY, b. Oct. 1736; d. Jan. 15, 1743.
1220 ROBERT, b. July 31, 1739; d. Dec. 25, 1743.
1221 GURDON, b. 1744; m. Catherine Fitzpatrick.
1222 SAMUEL, b. 1746; d. unmarried in 1820, aged 74.
1223 SARAH; m. a Capt. Kennedy.
1224 EUNICE; m. John Lothrop.

1210 DEBORAH DENISON, (Robert[4], Robert[3], John[2], George[1],) b. Dec. 9, 1722, was married in 1744, to Christopher Manwaring, son of Richard and Eleanor Manwaring. He d. in 1801; she d. in 1816. Their children:

1225 ROBERT, b. Dec. 16, 1745; m. Elizabeth Rogers in 1772.
1226 DEBORAH, b. Sept. 3, 1747.
1227 HANNAH, b. Oct. 3, 1749.
1228 ELEANOR, b. Sept. 12, 1751.
1229 ANN, b. Sept. 11, 1752.
1230 ELIZABETH, b. Sept. 26, 1754; m. Nathan Hempstead in 1777.
1231 ASA, b. Nov. 28, 1756; d. in 1779.
1232 ROGERS, b. Aug. 27, 1758; m. Ruth Crocker in 1777.
1233 SYBIL, b. June 14, 1760.
1234 SARAH, b. April 1, 1762; m. Andrew Huntington; 2nd wife.
1235 JOHN, b. March 21, 1765; m. Eleanor Raymond in 1790.
1236 LOIS, b. Aug. 16, 1767; m. Andrew Huntington; 1st wife.

1225 ROBERT MANWARING, (Deborah[5], Robert[4], Robert[3], John[2], George[1],) b. Dec. 16, 1745, was married in 1772, to Elizabeth Rogers. Their children:

1237 DEBORAH, b. in 1773; d. unmarried, 1844.
1238 CHRISTOPHER, b. in 1774; m. Sarah Bradley.
1239 FRANCES, b. in 1776; m. Joshua Caulkins.
1240 ELIZABETH, b. in 1778; m. Wm. Raymond.
1241 ELEANOR, b. in 1780; d. young.
1242 LUCRETIA, b. in 1783; m. Henry Nevins.
1243 PHEBE, b. in 1786; d. in 1787.

1238 CHRISTOPHER MANWARING, (son of 1225 Robert,) b. in 1774, was married in 1797, to Sarah Bradley, who d. Oct. 1805. He was married to a second wife in January, 1807. Children:

1244 SARAH, b. in 1798; d. in 1798.
1245 CHRISTOPHER, b. in 1799; m. Catherine Hinsdale.
1246 LUCRETIA, b. in 1803.
1247 Mary W., b. Dec., 1807; m. Edwin Colver.
1248 SIMON W., b. Sept., 1809.
1249 ROBERT A., b. in 1811; m. Ellen Barber.

Capt. John Denison's Descendants.

1239 FRANCES MANWARING, (dau. of 1225 Robert,) b. in 1776, was married in 1792, to Joshua Caulkins, who d. in 1795. In 1806, she was married, second, to Philemon Haven; lived in New London, and in Norwich, Conn.; he d. in 1819; she d. in 1854. Her children:

1250 PARMELIA, b. April, 1793; d. unmarried, in 1860.
1251 FRANCES MANWARING CAULKINS, b. April, 1795; was widely known as an author and genealogist. She wrote important and valuable histories of New London and Norwich. She d. in 1871, unmarried.
1252 ROBERT M. HAVEN, b. in 1808.
1253 PHILEMON HAVEN, b. in 1810; d. in 1816
1254 HENRY P. HAVEN, b. in 1815; d. in 1876.
1255 ELIZABETH, b. in 1819; d. in 1842.

1224 EUNICE DENISON, (Robert[4], Robert[3], John[2], George[1],) m. John Lothrop. Children:

1256 FANNY, b. Oct. 31, 1781; m. Charles Brown.
1257 EUNICE, b. in New Haven, Conn.; m. and d. there; no child.
1258 HENRY; lived in Utica, N. Y., when last heard from.
1259 JULIA; d. young.
1260 JULIA, b. March 8. 1790; m. John Leard.

1256 FANNY LOTHROP, (dau. of 1224 Eunice Denison Lothrop,) b. Oct. 1, 1781, was married about 1799, to Charles Brown. Thirteen children:

1261 CHARLES H., b. Dec. 26, 1800; d. Feb. 15, 1855.
1262 EMMA AMELIA, b. March 30, 1802.
1263 AUGUSTUS, b. Aug. 29, 1803.
1264 EDWARD LOTHROP, b. Sept. 7, 1805.
1265 JULIA, b. Nov. 18, 1807; d. young.
1266 WILLIAM A., b. Jan. 18, 1811.
1267 FRANCES MARIA, b. April 18, 1814.
1268 JOHN LOTHROP, b. Nov. 15, 1815.
1269 SAMUEL DENISON, b. May 12, 1819.
1270 HENRY, b. Jan. 13, 1821.
1271 JULIA, b. Oct. 1, 1822.
1272 ELIZABETH, b. Oct. 1, 1825.
1273 FREDERICK, b. Dec. 28, 1827.

1215 ANDREW DENISON, (Robert[4], Robert[3], John[2], George[1],) b. in 1728, was married, in Feb., 1749, to Mary Thompson. He d. in 1803. His children:

1274 ROBERT, b. Dec. 22, 1749; m. Esther Wade.
1275 CHRISTOPHER, b. Dec. 19, 1751; d. in infancy.
1276 ISAAC, b. Dec. 20, 1753; m. Anna Rogers.
1277 JOHN, b. Sept. 16, 1755; m. Mary Tuman.

1278 MARY, b. June 21, 1757; m. John Moriarty.
1279 ELISHA, b. 1760; returned to the States.
1280 MERCY, b. 1762; d. in Nova Scotia, unmarried.
1281 PHEBE, b. 1765; d. unmarried, in Horton, N. S.
1282 ANNIE, b. 1768.
1283 JAMES, b. 17.2; m. 1336 Lavinia Denison.

1274 ROBERT DENISON, (Andrew[5], Robert[4], Robert[3], John[2], George[1],) b. Dec. 22, 1749, was married to Esther Wade in 1778. He d. previous to 1790, for she was "Wid. Esther," when she d. in 1790. Their children:

1284 ABIGAIL, b. March 16, 1779; m. James Woody.
1285 JOSEPH, b. Nov. 15, 1781; m. Thankful Grant.
1286 CHARLES, b. Sept. 28, 1783; m. Beulah Rose.
1287 ANDREW, b. Jan. 15, 1785; m. Susan Selden.
1288 ROBERT, b. Jan. 11, 1788.

1276 ISAAC DENISON, (Andrew[5], Robert[4], Robert[3], John[2], George[1],) b. Dec. 20, 1753, was married in 1780, to Anna Rogers. Their children:

1289 ANN, b. in 1782; m. Wm. Chappell.
1290 JOHN, b. in 1784; m.; lived in East Lyme, Conn.
1291 ELISHA, b. in 1786; m.; one child that d. in infancy.
1292 POLLY, b. in 1788.

1277 JOHN DENISON, (Andrew[5], Robert[4], Robert[3], John[2], George[1],) b. Sept. 16, 1755, was married in 1810, to Mary Tuman, widow of Amasa Miller, to whom she was married when 15 years old. She was born, June 4, 1782. They lived in Lyme, Conn. He died there in 1842, aged 87. She died in Wisconsin, Dec. 19, 1864, aged 82. Their children:

1293 JAMES, b. Feb. 10, 1813; m. Orinda Bacon, of Lima, N. Y.
1294 PHEBE, b. Sept. 5, 1815; m. Ruel Hoyt, of East Cleveland, Ohio.
1295 WILLIAM, b. Oct. 6, 1816; d. at sea, unmarried.
1296 JOHN H., b. Jan. 10, 1819; m. Marian Johnson.
1297 RICHARD N., twin, b. March 14, 1822; m. Emma Robbins in 1849.
1298 MARTHA N., twin, b. March 14, 1822; m. Henry Robbins, 1843.

1293 JAMES DENISON, (John[6], Andrew[5], Robert[4], Robert[3], John[2], George[1],) b. Feb. 10, 1813, was married, Jan. 8, 1840, to Orinda Bacon, of Lima, N. Y. He d. in Wisconsin, in 1843; she d. May 31, 1847. She was 9 years older than he. They had two children:

1599 WILLIAM B., b. Feb. 29, 1842; d. Sept. 10, 1842.
1300 GEORGE W., b. July 10, 1844; lives at Fox Lake, Wis.

Capt. John Denison's Descendants. 65

1296 JOHN H. DENISON, (John[6], Andrew[5], Robert[4], Robert[3] John[2], George[1],) b. Jan. 10, 1819, was married, Feb. 25, 1852, to Marian Johnson, and live in East Lyme; have one child:

    1301 BENJ. TOLMAN, b. July 17, 1853; *m.* Julia F. Cross, of Rochester, Pa., Oct. 31, 1876; lives at Niantic, Conn.; she was born, April 14, 1858. They have John Francis, b. March 3, 1879.

1297 RICHARD N. DENISON, (John[6], Andrew[5], Robert[4], Robert[3], John[2], George[1],) b. March 14, 1822, was married to Emeline Robbins, Sept. 30, 1849; lives in Lyme; he has:

    1302 MARTHA J., b. July 26, 1850; d. Jan. 25, 1853.
    1303 ALICE M., b. Dec. 2, 1852.
    1304 JOHN, b. April 10, 1855.

1298 MARTHA N. DENISON, (John[6], Andrew[5], Robert[4], Robert[3], John[2], George[1],) b. March 14, 1822, was married to Henry Robbins, in 1843, and had these:

    1305 ALFRED H., b. March 18, 1846; *m.* Vienna Ashley, in 1874.
    1306 RICHARD D., b. March 15, 1849.

1283 JAMES DENISON, (Andrew[5], Robert[4], Robert[3], John[2], George[1],) born in 1772, was a lawyer. He practiced in Nova Scotia, and died there, Aug. 10, 1844, aged 72. He was married to Lavinia Denison, dau. of David Sherman Denison. His wife d. July 17, 1847, aged 69 years. Their children:

    1307 JAMES A., b. Nov. 22 1802; *m.* Louisa Viets.
    1308 ELIZA, b. Dec. 6, 1806; *m.* Asa S. Angus.
    1309 ROBERT W., b. March 24, 1809; *m.* Sarah Starrett; d. Dec. 23,'61.
    1310 JULIA LAVINIA, b. June 24, 1817; *m.* Benj. H. Calkin; no child.

1307 JAMES A. DENISON (James[6], Andrew[5], Robert[4], Robert[3], John[2], George[1],) b. Nov. 22, 1802, studied law with the late Judge Haliburton, (Sam. Slick,) and was admitted to the Nova Scotia bar in 1827. He settled at Digby, and for many years was Judge of Probate for Digby County, N. S. He was married, June 26, 1832, to Louisa Viets, dau. of Rev. Roger M. Viets, Rector of Digby. The Viets family went from Simsbury, Conn., and the father of Roger M., who graduated at Yale College, was the first Rector of Digby. James A. Denison's children:

    1311 EMMA, b. March 16, 1833.
    1311½ JAMES, b. June 14. 1834.

1312 LOUISA, b. Dec. 28, 1835; d. Sept. 17, 1872.
1313 JULIA, b. Feb. 23, 1838; d. May 26, 1873.
1314 GEORGE, b. Sept. 26, 1839; d. Jan. 6, 1869.
1315 FRANK, b. Nov. 8, 1841.
1316 LUCY, b. May 12, 1844.
1317 HERBERT, b. May 16, 1846.
1318 ARCHIBALD, b. Nov. 27, 1848; d. June 9, 1867.
1319 CHARLES, b. June 28, 1851.
1320 ELIZA, twin, b. Oct. 31, 1853.
1321 WALTER, twin, b. Oct. 31, 1853.
1322 WILLIAM, b. Feb. 2, 1858.

1308 ELIZA DENISON, (James⁶, Andrew⁵, Robert⁴, Robert³, John², George¹,) b. Dec. 6, 1806; was married, Oct. 25, 1848, to Asa S. Angus, and died Sept. 13, 1879; no child. He had been married to a first wife, Maria Denison, dau. of 1331 Samuel, Sept. 18, 1834, who died March 14, 1847, and left four children:

1323 SAMUEL D., b. Feb. 15, 1836; d. Aug. 17, 1867.
1324 EDWARD S., b. Dec. 5, 1837.
1325 JOHN STORRS, b. Dec. 9, 1840.
1326 LAVINIA MOORE, b. April 15, 1843; d. Aug. 3, 1849.

1218 DAVID SHERMAN DENISON, (Robert⁴, Robert³, John², George¹,) b. in August, 1734, was married in Montville, about 1752, to Sarah Fox. They emigrated to Nova Scotia; and in 1790, they sold to Jared Comstock, a part of what was her father's estate, being then, the record says, "of Horton, Nova Scotia." He died in Horton in 1796, aged 62; his wife died in 1818. Their children:

1327 ABIGAIL, b. March 9, 1753; *m.* Dr. John Martin.
1328 DAVID, b. Jan. 1, 1755; *m.* Milcah Palmer.
1329 PRUDENCE, b. Jan. 8, 1757; *m.* Asa Davidson.
1330 RACHEL, b. Oct. 22, 1758; *m.* Andrew Davidson.
1331 SAMUEL, b. Oct. 24, 1760; *m.* Mary Gallup.
1332 SARAH, b. Sept. 18, 1763; *m.* Theodocius Palmer.
1333 EUNICE, b. Nov. 22, 1766; *m.* Amasa Harris.
1334 SHERMAN, b. June 17, 1769; *m.* Nancy Crane.
1335 OLIVE, b. Oct. 7, 1771; *m.* Dennis Angus.
1336 LAVINIA, b. Dec. 3, 1774; *m.* 1283 James Denison.

1327 ABIGAIL DENISON, (David Sherman⁵, Robert⁴, Robert³, John², George¹,) b. March 9, 1753, was married to Dr. John Martin, a Chaplain in the British army, of Sussex Vale, N. B. She d. in 1837. They had six children:

Capt. John Denison's Descendants.

1337 RACHEL; unmarried.
1338 MARY; m. Wm. N. Leggett.
1339 ABIGAIL.
1340 MILCAH.
1341 LAVINIA.
1342 JOHN.

Rachel and Mary Martin were teachers in New York city. Rachel was remarkably clever. She taught for many years. In her old age, she went to England, and was presented to the Queen, who gave her a pension of £50 a year for life.

1328 DAVID DENISON, (David Sherman[5], Robert[4], Robert[3], John[2], George[1],) b. Jan. 1, 1755, was married to Milcah Palmer; lived in Nova Scotia. The children:

1343 MARY, b. in 1791; m. Perry Borden, March 10, 1827; no child; died Nov. 26, 1860.
1344 SARAH, b. in 1792; m. Charles Randall.
1345 DAVID S.; unmarried; went to N. Y.
1346 RACHEL; m. Peter Shay.
1347 EUPHEMIA, b. April 3, 1800; m. E. G. Fuller.
1348 LOUIS PALMER, b. July 14, 1803; m. Abigail Coffell.
1349 MARGARET; m. James T. Harris; no child.

1344 SARAH DENISON, (David[6], David Sherman[5], Robert[4], Robert[3], John[2], George[1],) b. in 1792, was married to Charles Randall, and died Oct. 28, 1816, aged 24. Charles Randall died April 25, 1856. One child:

1350 CHARLES DENISON.

1346 RACHEL DENISON, (David[6], David Sherman[5], Robert[4], Robert[3], John[2], George[1],) was married to Peter Shay; both are dead. They had one child, now Mrs. Kendall Holmes, a widow, who lives at Hautzport, N. S.

1347 EUPHEMIA DENISON, (David[6], David Sherman[5]; Robert[4], Robert[3], John[2], George[1],) b. April 3, 1800, was married March 10, 1827, to Eliphalet G. Fuller, b. April 22, 1794. Four children:

1351 MARGARET ANN; d. when 13 years old.
1352 HOWARD, b. Sept. 3, 1834; m. a Wolf.
1353 AMANDA.
1354 ALICE; m. Francis Cook; lived at Canso, N. S.; d. in 1876.

1348 LOUIS PALMER DENISON, (David[6], David Sherman[5], Robert[4], Robert[3], John[2], George[1],) b. July 14, 1803, was married Oct. 25, 1847, to Abigail Coffell, b. April 5, 1823. Their children :

1355 LOUIS P., b. Jan. 30, 1849.
1356 MARY A., b. June 27, 1851.
1357 EMILY E., b. Feb. 25, 1854.
1358 CHARLES M., b. Aug. 19, 1856.
1359 SARAH A., b. Oct. 9, 1858.
1360 EMMA N., b. July 8, 1862.
1361 FRANCES E., b. Jan. 6, 1865.

1329 PRUDENCE DENISON, (David Sherman[5], Robert[4], Robert[3], John[2], George[1],) b. Jan. 8, 1775, was married, April 30, 1782, to Asa Davidson. Three children :

1362 RACHEL, b. Mar. 12, 1784; twice married; 1st, to John R. Angus, by whom she had Asa S. and Mary Kine; 2nd to a Mr. Chelsy; left several children.
1363 DAVID.
1364 SAMUEL.

1331 SAMUEL DENISON, (David Sherman[5], Robert[4], Robert[3], John[2], George[1],) b. Oct. 20, 1760, d. 1833, was married in 1790, to Mary Gallup; lived at Kentville, N. S. Children :

1370 REBECCA, b. in 1792; m. John Mitchell, 1833; d. May 8, 1876.
1371 WM. ANTIL, b. in 1794; m. Mary J. Angus.
1372 SAMUEL, b. in 1797; m. Susan Pines.
1373 MARY, b. in 1799; unmarried.
1374 ABIGAIL. b. in 1801; twice married; no child.
1375 MARIA, b. April 21, 1803; m. Asa S. Angus.
1376 ELIZA, b. in 1808; unmarried; d. in 1875.

1371 WILLIAM ANTIL DENISON, (Samuel[6], David Sherman[5], Robert[4], Robert[3], John[2], George[1],) b. in 1794, was married, Nov. 21, 1832, to Mary J. Angus; d. July 7, 1850; lived in Kentville, N. S. His children :

1377 ADELAIDE, b. Dec., 1833.
1378 WM. HENRY, b. April, 1836.
1379 GEO. ALBERT, b. Nov. 17, 1838; m. Margaret Alice Forsyth.
1380 JOHN HARRIS, b. Jan. 7, 1841; m. Phebe Bryson.
1381 WILHELMINA, b. Jan 7, 1843; d. May 13, 1849.
1382 LUCILLA C., b. Dec., 1845; d. April 14, 1849.
1383 ASA SAM'L ANGUS, b. 1847; d. July 4, 1870.
1384 MARY JANE, b. 1849; d. Sept. 29, 1861.

1378 GEORGE ALBERT DENISON, (son of 1371 Wm. Antil,) b. Nov. 17, 1838, was married to Margaret Alice Forsyth, Sept. 22, 1864; lives at Kentville, N. S. Children :

1385 LESLIE EUGENE, b. March 30, 1866.
1386 WILLIE BRENTON, b. April 23, 1868; d. Feb. 27, 1869.
1387 ALBERT FREEMAN, b. April 26, 1871.
1388 GEO. ARCHIBALD, b. March 18, 1873.
1389 JAMES AUBREY, b. Oct. 15, 1876.

1380 JOHN HARRIS DENISON, (son of 1371 Wm. Antil,) b. Jan. 7, 1841, was married to Phebe Bryson, June 14, 1865; lives at Kentville, N. S. Children :

1390 HARRY LIVINGSTON, b. June 1, 1866.
1391 FRANK EVELYN, b. Sept. 22, 1871.
1392 JOHN WILLIAM. b. Aug. 1, 1873.
1393 HENRIE SHAW, b. Sept. 21, 1876; d. Nov. 28, 1879.

1372 SAMUEL DENISON, (Samuel^6, David Sherman^5, Robert^4, Robert^3, John^2, George^1,) b. in 1797, was married, Jan. 29, 1835, to Susan Pines ; lived in Kentville, N. S. Children :

1394 SAMUEL ANTIL, b. Nov. 17, 1835; m. Emma Denison.
1395 EDWIN, b. April 29, 1838; m. Amelia Davis.
1396 JOSEPH, b. April 19, 1841; m. Susan Woodbury.
1397 NANCY, b. June 14, 1846; m. Horatio T. James.
1398 HERBERT, b. Nov. 5, 1852; unmarried in 1877.

1394 SAMUEL ANTIL DENISON, (son of 1372 Samuel, Jr.,) b. Nov. 17, 1835, was married, Dec. 29, 1863, to 1311 Emma Denison, dau. of 1307 James A. He lives in Bridgetown, N. S. Their children :

1399 MAUD C., b. Jan. 15, 1865.
1400 FREDERICK A., b. April 5, 1868.
1401 LOUISA G., b. March 1, 1870; d. April 2, 1871.
1402 WILLIAM N., b. June 23, 1872; d. Dec. 3, 1872.

Mrs. Emma Denison died, Dec. 13, 1873 ; and he married second, Adelia DeWitt, June 13, 1877.

1395 EDWIN DENISON, (son of 1372 Samuel, Jr.,) b. April 29, 1838, was married, Dec. 2, 1862, to Amelia Davis ; lives at Kentville, N. S. Children :

1406 FANNIE DAVIS, b. Oct. 18, 1863.
1407 BLANCHE ANNIE, b. April 8, 1865.
1408 JOSEPH GEORGE, b. Oct. 21, 1866.
1409 STEWART MELBOURNE, Feb. 8, 1868.
1410 ARTHUR PUTTERILL, b. Feb. 1, 1869.
1411 ELIZABETH MARY, b. Dec. 11, 1870.
1412 CHARLES EDWARD, b. July 20, 1872.

1396 JOSEPH DENISON, (son of 1372 Samuel, Jr.,) b. April 19, 1841, was married, Nov. 21, 1867, to Susan Woodbury; lives at Bridgetown, N. S. Children:

    1413 ARCHIE SAYRE, b. Dec. 19, 1869.
    1414 JOSEPH WARREN, b. Nov. 17, 1871; d. Aug. 4, 1872.
    1415 IDA MARIA, b. Nov. 17, 1874.
    1416 NELLIE J., b. Feb. 1, 1877.

1397 NANCY DENISON, (dau. of 1372 Samuel, Jr.,) b. June 11, 1846, was married, May 24, 1871, to Horatio T. James; lives in Lawrencetown, N. S. Children:

    1417 HERBERT HORATIO, b. March 25, 1872.
    1418 BERYL GREATOREX, b. Jan. 1, 1875.
    1419 WILLIS GEORGE, b. March 18, 1877.

1333 EUNICE DENISON, (David Sherman[5], Robert[4], Robert[3], John[2], George[1],) b. Nov. 22, 1766, was married to Amasa Harris; had one child:

    1420 JOHN, b. in 1797, and d. in 1853; he *m.* Sophia Hamilton, (sister of Dr. C. C. Hamilton,) and had a daughter, Eunice Sophia, who *m.* Senator H. A. N. Kaulback. She lives at Lunenburg, N. S.

1334 SHERMAN DENISON, (David Sherman[5], Robert[4], Robert[3], John[2], George[1],) b. June 17, 1769, was married, March 12, 1792, to Nancy Crane. He was a man of mark in Nova Scotia, where he served in the House of Assembly, and as a Colonel in the militia. Tradition says, he was "the finest looking man in the Province." He died at the age of 82. His Children:

    1421 SHERMAN DAVID, b. June 26, 1797; *m.* Nancy Hamilton.
    1422 WILLIAM CRANE, b. Oct. 8, 1801; d. unmarried in Mississippi.
    1423 JOSEPH ALLISON, b. August 15, 1807; d. in Mississippi.
    1424 NANCY, b. Jan. 20, 1793; *m.* John M. Latchley.
    1425 LAVINIA, b. March 3, 1795; d. unmarried, March 13, 1876.
    1426 REBECCA, b. Aug. 10, 1799; *m.* Edward Bayers.
    1427 SOPHIA, b. Feb. 10, 1804; *m.* Robert DeWolf.
    1428 MARY, b. Nov. 30, 1809; d. unmarried, May 7, 1870.

1421 SHERMAN DAVID DENISON, (Sherman[6], David Sherman[5], Robert[4], Robert[3], John[2], George[1],) b. June 26, 1797, was married, July 6, 1836, to Nancy Hamilton; lived in Lower Horton, N. S.; died there Jan. 21, 1864. Two children:

    1429 ANNIE, b. in 1837.
    1430 MINNIE, b. in 1841; d. Jan. 4, 1876, aged 34.

Capt. John Denison's Descendants. 71

1426 REBECCA DENISON, (Sherman[6], David Sherman[5], Robert[4], Robert[3], John[2], George[1],) b. Aug. 10, 1799, was married July 13. 1819, to Edward Bayers: lived at Halifax, N. S.; died in 1833, aged 34; Mr. Bayers d. May 10, 1858, aged 60. Her children:

    1431 ELIZABETH MARY, b. in 1820; m. Rev. Henry H. Hamilton, July 8, 1846, and had these: Geo. Augustus, Georgiana A. L., and Henry Harris.
    1432 WILLIAM, b. in 1821; d. when 7 years old.
    1433 JOSEPH A., b. in 1823; d. when 4 years old.
    1434 SHERMAN D., b. in 1825.
    1435 EDWARD, b. in 1827.
    1436 Rebecca, b. in 1829.
    1437 LAVINIA, b. in 1831; m. Stitt McLelland.
    1438 C. LOUISA, b. in 1833.

1427 SOPHIA DENISON, (Sherman[6], David Sherman[5], Robert[4], Robert[3], John[2], George[1],) b. Feb. 10, 1804, was married Sept. 27, 1827, to Robert DeWolf; lived in Halifax, N. S. One child:

    1439 MARY; m. a Reid.

1221 DR. GURDON DENISON, (Robert[4], Robert[3], John[2], George[1],) b. in 1744, was married in 1778, to Catherine Fitzpatrick, of Halifax, N. S. He practiced medicine successfully, was a member of the Assembly of Nova Scotia, and in many ways was a very popular man. He d. in 1807. His children:

    1440 GURDON, b Nov. 13, 1779; m. Mary Wakefield.
    1441 CATHERINE, b. Oct. 1, 1781; d. unmarried.
    1442 NANCY, b. Oct. 5, 1785; m. William Fuller; 2 daughters.
    1443 SAMUEL, b. Dec. 5, 1787; d. unmarried.
    1444 PRUDENCE, b. April 9, 1789; d. unmarried, March 4, 1852.
    1445 WILLIAM, b. June 12 1791; d. unmarried, Sept. 9, 1859.
    1446 ELIZABETH. b. Jan. 16, 1793; m. Oliver Fuller.
    1447 SOPHIA, b. Dec. 6, 1794; d. unmarried.
    1448 MARIE, b. June 19, 1796; m. Mark Wright.
    1449 AMELIA, b. Aug. 7, 1798; d. unmarried.

1440 GURDON DENISON, Jr., (Dr. Gurdon[5], Robert[4], Robert[3], John[2], George[1],) was a merchant on Washington street, Boston. He married Mary Wakefield, of Boston, and had:

    1450 EDWARD, and two daughters.

1442 NANCY DENISON, (Dr. Gurdon[5], Robert[4], Robert[3], John[2], George[1],) m. William Fuller, and had:

1451 THOMAS; left home when young.
1452 CATHERINE; *m.* Andrew Borden; P. O. Grand Pre, N. S.
1453 ANN; *m.* David Borden.

1446 ELIZABETH DENISON, (Dr. Gurdon[5], Robert[4], Robert[3], John[2], George[1],) *m.* Dec. 18, 1817, Oliver Fuller, b. in 1791, and d. July 26, 1866; lived at Avon Port, Kings Co., N. S. Children :

1454 GURDON ELIHU, b. Dec. 17, 1818: lives in Chelsea, Mass.
1455 OLIVER, b. Jan. 21, 1820; *m.* Mary Elizabeth Rathburn.
1456 MARGARET ANN, b. Nov. 16, 1821; *m.* Geo. H. Gillmar.
1457 AMELIA, b. Oct. 6, 1823; *m.* Lemuel L. Gilmar.

1448 MARIE DENISON, (Dr. Gurdon[5], Robert[4], Robert[3], John[2], George[1],) *m.* Dec. 24, 1817, Mark Henry Hector Wright, son of an English officer. She d. in 1876. Her children:

1458 CATHERINE, b. Nov. 1, 1818; *m.* David A. Dickson, Pictou.
1459 SOPHIA, b. April 23, 1820; *m.* Samuel G. Black.
1460 ELEANOR, b. Sept. 30, 1821; d. young.
1461 JOHN P. C., b. Oct. 9, 1823; d. young.
1462 EMILY ELIZABETH, b. March 1, 1827; d. young.

1459 SOPHIA WRIGHT, (Marie[6], Dr. Gurdon[5], Robert[4], Robert[3], John[2], George[1],) b. April 23, 1820, was married, Jan. 12, 1846, to Samuel Gay Black. They live at Brookville, Windsor, Nova Scotia. Children :

1463 WILLIAM ANDERSON, b. Oct. 9, 1847.
1464 MARY MARIA, b. Oct. 17, 1849.
1465 KATE DICKSON, b. June 4, 1851.
1466 ELIZABETH WILMOT, b. Oct. 1, 1853.
1467 LAURA SOPHIA, b. Feb. 7, 1856.
1468 ELLEN AMELIA, b. Feb. 10. 1858.

1174 JOHN DENISON, (Robert[3], John[2], George[1],) b. March 28, 1698, was married to Patience Griswold, dau. of Matthew Griswold, in 1724. They lived and died in Lyme, Conn. He d. Nov. 28, 1776 ; she d. Nov. 8, 1776, aged 78. Their children :

1470 DOROTHY, b. 1726.
1471 JOHN, b. July 31, 1731; d. Dec. 14, 1736.
1472 SAMUEL, b. Aug., 1733; d. Dec. 6, 1739.
1473 PATIENCE, b. 1735; *m.* John Walworth.
1474 JOHN, b. Feb. 6, 1737; twice married.
1475 PHEBE, b. April 21, 1739; d. Dec. 28, 1741.
1476 SAMUEL, b. June 8, 1741; d. July 15, 1741.
1477 SAMUEL, b. March 11, 1742; twice married.
1478 PHEBE, b. Nov., 1746; *m.* Josiah G. Ely.

Capt. John Denison's Descendants. 73

1474 JOHN DENISON, (John[4], Robert[3], John[2], George[1],) b. Feb. 6, 1737, was married, first, to Mary Sears, Aug. 9, 1764. He settled first in Lyme; next lived in Stonington; then went to Middletown, Conn., where his wife, Mary, died, April 6, 1782. He m. second, a Widow Collins, and settled in Northampton, Montgomery Co., N. Y., where he was Town Clerk, etc. He was a wealthy man and a farmer. He d. in 1804. Most of his property was lost in the revolutionary war. His children, (all by the first wife,) were:

- **1479** JOHN SEARS, b. July 28, 1865; died at sea.
- **1480** SAMUEL b. July 6, 1767; m. Phebe Topping.
- **1481** ROBERT, b. April 13, 1771; d. at sea, unmarried.
- **1482** ELIZABETH, b. April 16, 1769; m. Benj. Colt, of Lyme, Conn.
- **1483** NANCY, b. April 12, 1773; m. Wm. Colt, in 1796.
- **1484** PHEBE, b. Nov. 26, 1775; m. Benj. Grinnell, in 1793.
- **1485** GEORGE W., b. Aug. 4, 1778; m. and d. at Milton, N. Y.
- **1486** OLIVER, b. March 12, 1782; d. in 1782.

1480 SAMUEL DENISON, (John[5], John[4], Robert[3], John[2], George[1],) b. July 6, 1767, was married to Phebe Topping. He was a cloth dresser; but he settled at Sag Harbor, Long Island, and became a shipmaster. He died in 1820; his wife died in 1840. Their children:

- **1487** PHEBE T.; m. William A. Folger, of Nantucket, a New York merchant; d. in 1835; had a son who was a shipmaster, in California, in 1858.
- **1489** MARY A., b. 1798; m. John Stone, a New York merchant; they had two children; John and Thomas.
- **1490** FANNY E.; m. Jeremiah Rogers; d. in 1832.
- **1491** CAROLINE; m. Nathan Rogers.
- **1492** WILLIAM S., b. 1808; twice married.
- **1493** SAMUEL, b. 1813; m. Jane Sayre, of Sag Harbor; emigrated to Texas; d. in California, in 1857: two children: Thomas and Caroline.

1492 WILLIAM S. DENISON, (Samuel[6], John[5], John[4], Robert[3], John[2], George[1],) b. in 1808, m. 1st, Jane M. Woodruff, who d. in 1844. He m. 2nd, Dec. 1844, Susan M. Halsey. He lived at Sag Harbor; was captain of a whale ship; received from the French government a first class medal, for rescuing six French sailors from shipwreck on the coast of California. Two children:

- **1494** WILLIAM E.   **1495** FANNIE E.

1491 CAROLINE DENISON, (Samuel[6], John[5], John[4], Robert[3], John[2], George[1],) was married to Nathan Rogers, a miniature portrait painter. Their children:

1496 DENISON; studied theology at Princeton; d. in 1852.
1497 GEORGE T.; *m.* Fanny Minor; lived in N. Y. city.
1498 EDMUND; *m.* Maria Topping; lived in Wisconsin.
1499 JAMES H.; grad. of Williams; d. unmarried.
1500 HELEN; *m.* Henry C. Manning, banker, at Madison, Wis.

1483 NANCY DENISON, (John[5], John[4], Robert[3], John[2], George[1],) b. April 12, 1773, was married to Dea. Wm. Colt, Oct. 23, 1796, and had these:

1501 WILLIAM E., b. June 24, 1797.
1502 ABIGAIL M., b. July 6, 1800; d. Jan. 9, 1828, unmarried.
1503 ANNA, b. July 5, 1802; d. in infancy.

1482 ELIZABETH DENISON, (John[5], John[4], Robert[3], John[2], George[1],) b. April 16, 1769, was married to Benj. Colt, in 1788; lived in Lyme, Conn. Children:

1504 NANCY MARIA, b. Oct. 28, 1790; *m.* Judah Ransom; 3 ch.
1505 BENJ. GARDNER, b. Jan. 10, 1793; d. in 1813.
1506 JOHN DENISON, b. May 10, 1795; d. in April, 1796.
1507 MARY SEARS, b. Feb. 19, 1797; d. unmarried.
1508 JOHN DENISON, b. Aug. 10, 1799; *m.* Frances Miller.
1509 JOSEPH HARRIS, b. Aug. 10, 1801; *m.* Adeline Ripley; 6 ch.
1510 GEORGE ROBERT, b. Oct. 20, 1804; *m.* Catherine Calkins.

1484 PHEBE DENISON, (John[5], John[4], Robert[3], John[2], George[1],) b. Nov. 26, 1775, was married to Benj. Grinnell, June 20, 1793. They settled at Greenfield, N. Y., and had:

1511 BENJAMIN C., b. July 28, 1794; *m.* Elizabeth Moon; 6 ch.
1512 PHEBE, b. Nov. 15, 1796; d. July 15, 1798.
1513 ALVAH D., b. May 6, 1799; *m.* Eliza Keeler; 8 ch.
1514 PHEBE, b. Aug. 30, 1801; d. July 7, 1803.
1515 JOHN SEARS, b. Dec. 8, 1804; *m.* A. Morehouse; 8 ch.

1477 SAMUEL DENISON, (John[4], Robert[3], John[2], George[1],) b. Jan. 8, 1741, was married in 1760, to Mary Champlin of Lyme, Conn. She d. in 1800, at Bridgewater, Vt. He married, second, Wid. Cleveland. He d. in 1836, aged 94. His children:

1516 PATIENCE, b. 1762; *m.* Dea. J. Perkins, Bridgewater, Vt.
1517 ELIZABETH, b. 1764; *m.* Henry Boyce.
1518 SARAH, b. 1776; *m.* Francis Perkins.
1519 MARY, b. 1768; *m.* Sylvanus Griswold.
1520 WILLIAM H., b. Nov. 26, 1776; *m.* Iola Higley.

Capt. John Denison's Descendants.

1521 CHARLOTTE, b. Jan 5, 1779; m. John Purdy.
1522 HENRY C., b. March 8, 1781; m. Lucy Perrin.
1523 FRANCES, b. Oct. 23, 1785; m. Rev. Paul Dean.
1524 JOHN, (Rev.) b. May 3, 1788; m. Lucretia Kellog.

1520 WILLIAM H. DENISON, (Samuel[5], John[4], Robert[3], John[2], George[1].) b. Nov. 26, 1776, was married, March 25, 1800, to Iola Higley, and settled in Rutland, Vt., where he was a man of some mark. He carried on the business of tanning, currying, and shoe-making. His wife Iola died; and he m. second, Wid. Mercy B. Gridley, Feb. 25, 1825. He d. at Castleton, Vt., May 7, 1856; his second wife d. Dec. 31, 1854. His children:

1525 PHILA, twin, b. Jan. 27, 1801; d. March 13, 1801.
1526 ELIZA, twin, b. Jan. 27, 1801; m. Henry Lost.
1557 FANNY, b. May 16, 1805; m. John T. Duncan.
1528 IOLA, b. March 25, 1807; twice married.
1529 WM. COWPER, b. Dec. 31, 1809; m. Wealthy Cushman.
1530 FRANCIS L. C., b. May 15, 1813; thrice married.
1531 EDWARD H., b. Sept. 29, 1817; m. Sarah Robinson.
1532 MARY, b. March 20, 1821; m. Horace Lyman.
1533 MERCY WEBSTER, b. Jan. 26, 1826; d. Dec. 22, 1838.

1529 REV. WM. COWPER DENISON, (William H.[6], Samuel[5], John[4], Robert[3], John[2], George[1].) b. Dec. 31, 1809, was married, first, Oct. 16, 1832, to Wealthy Cushman, who d. in 1844; and, second, April 30, 1846, to Gertrude Russell. He lived first, in Castleton, Vt. In 1843, he emigrated to Dexter, Mich. In 1875, he and his second wife returned to Castleton, where she d. He was living there in 1880. Children:

1534 WILLIAM C., Jr., b. Jan. 8, 1836; d. April 13, 1842.
1535 FRANCES, b. June 17, 1839; m. J. W. Taylor; lives at Kalamazoo, Mich.; 4 children; she died in 1864; one child, Eliza W., living.
1536 A CHILD, b. and d. in 1844, at Dexter, Mich.

1530 FRANCIS L. C. DENISON, (William H.[6], Samuel[5], John[4], Robert[3], John[2], George[1],) b. May 15, 1813, was married three times; first, Nov., 1839, to Elizabeth Everett, who bore a child that did not survive its birth, and d. in 1840, at Dundee, Mich.; second, March, 1842, to Betsey Chandler, who d. Sept., 1843; third, in 1845, to Caroline W. Taylor. He lives in Kalamazoo, Mich. Children:

1537 WILLIAM, b. February, 1846; d. in 1847.

1538 HERBERT G., b. May 28, 1848; m. Sarah Hurd, in 1872; is a graduate of Olivet College; lives at Ripon; is Superintendent of Preparatory Dept. of Ripon College.
1539 FRANCIS W., b. Oct. 1, 1855; a graduate of Olivet College; was Prof. of Greek in Adrian College; lives now at Marshall, Wis.
1540 CHARLES, b. Feb., 1856; d. in 1857.

1531 EDWARD H. DENISON, (Wm. H.[6], Samuel[5], John[4], Robert[3], John[2], George[1],) b. Sept. 29, 1817, was married, Oct. 19, 1840, to Sarah Robinson, at Castleton, Vt.; d. at Middlebury, Vt. His children:

1541 ANN ELIZA, b. Dec. 28, 1841; m. Rev. John K. Williams.
1542 WILLIAM TYLER, b. June 9, 1844; m. Emilie H. Drake.
1543 FRANCIS C., b. June 20, 1850; m. Anna E. Rice.
1544 EDWARD R., b. April 14, 1853.
1545 SAMUEL, b. April 14, 1856.

1541 ANN ELIZA DENISON, (dau. of 1531 Edward H.) was married, Sept. 25, 1866, to Rev. John K. Williams. P. O., West Rutland, Vt. Children:

1546 CHARLES ADAMS, b. May 28, 1867.
1547 EDWARD DENISON, b. Sept. 15, 1868.
1548 ALICE ELIZABETH, b. Dec. 27, 1870.
1549 SARAH MCKEEN, b. Nov. 25, 1873.
1550 JOHN KIRK, b. Nov. 23, 1875.
1551 WILLIAM RENSALAER, b. May 3, 1878.

1542 WILLIAM T. DENISON, (son of 1531 Edward H.,) was married to Emilie H. Drake, March 25, 1874. He lives in Pittsford, Vt.; is a merchant, tax collector, constable, and leads a busy and useful life. He has:

1552 GRACE ELIZABETH, b. Jan. 20, 1879.

1543 FRANCIS C. DENISON, (son of 1531 Edward H.,) was married to Anna E. Rice, of Castleton, Vt., Jan. 21, 1874. He is Postmaster at Pittsford, Vt., and, also, of the firm of Denison Brothers, in Pittsford. Children:

1553 SARAH C., b. Aug. 31, 1874.
1554 JESSIE C., b. Dec. 9, 1875.
1555 ANNA T., b. Jan. 7, 1879.

1526 ELIZA DENISON, (Wm. H.[6], Samuel[5], John[4], Robert[3], John[2], George[1],) b. Jan. 27, 1801, was married, Sept. 19, 1822, to Henry Post; lived first in Rutland, Vt; lives now at Victor, Michigan. Children:

Capt. John Denison's Descendants.

1556 Henry D., b. March 26, 1824, at Rutland.
1557 Hoyt G., b. Nov. 26, 1827, at Rutland.
1558 Helen M., b. Feb. 15, 1830, at Rutland.
1559 Charles T., b. March 2, 1834, at London, Mich.
1560 Edward D., b. Sept. 8, 1836, at London, Mich.
1561 Mary Elizabeth, b. Jan. 20, 1841, at London, Mich.

1527 Fanny Denison, (Wm. H.[6], Samuel[5], John[4], Robert[3], John[2], George[1],) b. May 16, 1805, was married, July 25, 1822, to John T. Duncan; lived at Clintonville, N. Y. He died in 1872. Children:

1562 Robert W. b. Feb. 25, 1824; lives at Godhaven, Mich.
1563 John T., b. April 1, 1829; a lawyer at Vineland, N. J.
1564 James D., b. July 14, 1831.
1565 Francis E., b. Sept. 29, 1834.
1566 Charles, b. Oct. 14, 1836; d. in 1839.
1567 Margaret, b. June 12, 1838.
1568 Charles, b. July 12, 1841.
1569 Eliza B., b. May 28, 1846.

1528 Iola Denison, (Wm. H.[6], Samuel[5], John[4], Robert[3], John[2], George[1],) b. March 25, 1807, was married, first, in 1828, to Hoyt Guernsey, of Poultney, Vt, who d. Jan., 1835; and second, in 1848, to Dr. Perkins of Castleton, Vt., who d. in 1872. Children:

1570 William C., b. in 1830; lives at Castleton, Vt.
1571 Herbert D., b. in 1832; d. in 1847.
1572 Lucy Ann, b. in 1834; m. a Mr. Geer of Ogdensburg, N. Y.

1532 Mary Denison, (Wm. H.[6], Samuel[5], John[4], Robert[3], John[2], George[1],) b. March 20, 1821, was married, in 1848, to Rev. Horace Lyman, and d. in 1873. They lived in Portland, Oregon. He is a Professor in Pacific University. Children:

1573 Sarah, b. in 1850.
1574 William D., b. in 1852.
1575 Mary, b. in 1855.
1576 Horace, b. in 1860.

1522 Henry Champlin Denison, (Samuel[5], John[4], Robert[3], John[2], George[1],) b. March 8, 1781, was married to Lucy Perrin, Oct. 14, 1804. He studied law and settled at Woodstock, Vt.; was a judge. His children, by the wife Lucy were:

1576½ Mary C., b. Aug. 14, 1805; m. O. A. Dana, Oct., 1847.
1577 Henry C., b. Jan. 19, 1807; was a physician; d. in June, 1832, at St. Jago de Cuba.
1578 Lucy P., b. June 9, 1808; m. Nahum Haskell.

1579 FRANCES D , b. Jan. 28. 1810; *m.* H. H. Smith.
1580 JOHN, b. March 20, 1812; d. April 2, 1812.

The wife Lucy died; and Nov. 24, 1822, he *m.* 2nd, Mary Eddy, who d. March 8, 1825. Sept. 18, 1826, he *m.* 3rd, Amy Smith, by whom he had:

1581 CHARLES EDWARD, b. May 30, 1827; twice married.
1582 JOHN, b. Jan. 21, 1829; d. Oct. 2, 1833.
1583 EDWARD C., b. Aug. 20, 1831; was an architect.
1584 HENRY C., b. April 20, 1835.
1585 ELIZABETH W., b. Oct. 26, 1836.
1586 FRANCES SMITH, b. July 15, 1839.

Judge Henry C. Denison died, May 16, 1853; his wife Amy died March 8, 1848.

1576½ MARY C. DENISON, (dau. of 1522 Judge Henry C.,) *m.* O. A. Dana, Oct., 1847, and had:

1587 DENISON.
1588 MARY FRANCES; *m.* Geo. H. Slade; 6 ch.

1578 LUCY P. DENISON, (dau. of 1522 Judge Henry C.,) *m.* Nahum Haskell, and had:

1589 SARAH D.; *m.* Henry S. Chase; 4 ch.
1590 HENRY C. D.; *m.*
1591 JAMES N.
1592 LUCY PERRIN, b. at Woodstock, Vt.

1581 CHARLES EDWARD DENISON, (son of 1522 Judge Henry C.) *m.* 1st, Harriet H. Stevens, Nov. 20, 1849, who d. Sept. 21, 1852. He *m.* 2nd, her sister, Mary J. Stevens, March 29, 1854, and went from Newbury, Vt., to Peoria, Ill. His children:

1593 HARRIET STEVENS, b. Sept., 1850, at Newbury, Vt.
1594 CHARLES, b. April 17, 1856, at Peoria, Ill.

1579 FRANCES D. DENISON, (dau. of 1522 Judge Henry C.,) *m.* H. H. Smith; they emigrated to Michigan; had one child:

1595 FRANCES DENISON.

1524 REV. JOHN DENISON, (Samuel[5], John[4], Robert[3], John[2], George[1],) b. May 3, 1798, was married in 1810, to Lucretia Kelley, and d. in 1812, at Jericho, Vt., where he was pastor of the Congregational church. He had one child:

1596 JOHN NEWTON, b. June 22, 1811; *m.* Mary F. Dean.

1596 JOHN N. DENISON, (son of 1524 Rev. John,) *m.* Jan. 1839, Mary F. Dean, dau. of Rev. Paul Dean, and had:

Capt. John Denison's Descendants.

1597 FRANCES L., b. Nov. 1839; d. Sept., 1840.
1598 JOHN HENRY, Rev., b. March, 1841; grad. at Williams Col.; m. a dau. of Pres. Mark Hopkins.
1599 AURELIA, b. in 1842; d. in 1843.
1600 CLARA AUGUSTA, b. July 27, 1845.
1601 CHARLES DEANE, b. Dec. 30, 1849.

1521 CHARLOTTE DENISON, (Samuel[5], John[4], Robert[3], John[2], George[1],) b. Jan. 5, 1779, was married, Nov. 3, 1803, to John Purdy, and settled at Rutland, Vt. They had two children:

1602 LUCIUS M., b. May 28, 1805; m. Laura E. Ward; 3 ch.; he was an Episcopal clergyman; he d. at St. Mary's, Ga., in May, 1853.
1603 EDWARD C., b. Dec. 9, 1806; m. Louisa Gage; was editor of the Rutland Herald, Lowell Journal, and other papers; no child.

1523 FRANCES DENISON, (Samuel[5], John[4], Robert[3], John[2], George[1],) b. Oct. 23, 1785, was married to Rev. Paul Dean, June 30, 1805. He was son of Seth Dean, grandson of Paul Dean, gr. grandson of Seth Dean of Taunton, and gr. gr. grandson of Ezra of Taunton. They lived in Vermont, in New York, and in Boston where he was pastor of the Bulfinch St. Church. Their children:

1604 PAUL D., b. May 9, 1808; d. July, 1810.
1605 MARY F., b. Aug. 11, 1811; m. John N. Denison, Jan., 1839.
1606 CHARLOTTE A., b. Dec. 9, 1813; d. in infancy.
1607 AMELIA A., b. Dec. 25, 1815; m. John G. Read; d. in 1848.
1608 PAUL D., b. Oct. 9, 1819; d. Dec. 29, 1823.
1609 CHARLOTTE L., b. Nov. 13, 1821; m. John W. Brooks; 3 ch.
1510 MARCIA P., b. Aug. 12, 1825; m. E. B. Johnson; 2 ch.
1611 JULIET S., b. April 21, 1827; d. Oct. 9, 1830.

1473 PATIENCE DENISON, (John[4], Robert[3], John[2], George[1],) b. in 1735, was married to John Walworth, being his second wife. His first wife was Mary Minor of Stonington, Conn., by whom he had a son, John W., b. March 19, 1755, and m. to Mercy Rogers. This son of the first wife lived at Hoosic, N. Y. John and Patience removed to Hoosic. They were there Aug. 16, 1777, when the battle of Bennington was fought, and he was captured by the Indians, who took him to the British camp. Mr. Walworth and his wife Patience both died at Hoosic. They had four children:

1612 GRISWOLD; m. Lydia Eldridge.
1613 MARY; m. Samuel Whitman; lived in Burlington, N. Y.
1614 ELIZABETH, m. George Tibbitts: lived in Monkton, Vt.
1615 ABIGAIL.

1478 PHEBE DENISON, (John⁴, Robert³, John², George¹,) b. Nov., 1746, was married Aug. 1, 1765, to Josiah Griswold Ely. He d. in 1826. Their children:

1616 JOSIAH G., b. Aug. 26, 1766; *m.* Elizabeth Sill.
1617 ENOCH, b. Feb. 10, 1769; *m.* Keziah Durkee.
1618 PHEBE, b. Jan. 5, 1771; *m.* Abner Lord.
1619 DAVID, b. Jan. 13, 1774.
1620 RICHARD, b. Jan. 6, 1777; *m.* Mary Peck.

1181 THOMAS DENISON, (Robert³, John², George¹,) b. in 1709, was married to Elizabeth Bailey. He was a clergyman; first a Congregationalist, next a Separatist, then a Baptist, and finally a Congregationalist again, preaching at various places in New London and Windham Counties, Conn. He died in Pomfret, Conn., Oct. 24, 1787. In a letter which he addressed to President Stiles of Yale College, he said: " My first American ancestor, William Denison, came from Hartford, England." His children were:

1621 JABEZ; *m.* Rachel Chandler.
1622 NATHANIEL; his estate was settled at Plainfield, Conn., in 1805.
1623 ELEAZER.
1624 DAVID, b. Dec. 30, 1756.
1625 ABIGAIL.
1626 SARAH.
1627 PRUDENCE.
1628 EBENEZER.

The names of his children, (except Ebenezer,) are found in his will, which was dated at Pomfret, Jan. 29, 1785. After the introductory words, his will reads as follows: " First, I give my loving wife Elizabeth, for the term of her life, the use and improvement of my house and land, and the use and improvement of all my household goods, stock, &c. To my son, Jabez, six shillings; to my son Nathaniel, my land in Voluntown; to my son, Eleazer, six shillings; to my son David, my house and land after the decease of my wife; to my daughter, Abigail, one pound five shillings; to my daughter, Sarah, one pound five shillings; to my daughter, Prudence, one cow, one feather bed and coverings, and fifteen pounds."

The inventory of his estate was £180. His estate was considerably larger twenty-five or 30 years earlier; for in 1763, he sold his land in Norwich for £201, 6s, and at that time had

Capt. John Denison's Descendants. 81

other property. The Norwich land he had owned from 1747 to 1763.

1624 DAVID DENISON, (Thomas[4], Robert[3], John[2], George[1],) b. Dec. 30, 1756, was married, first, Dec. 9, 1779, to Sarah Spaulding, b. March 18, 1757; and, second, Dec. 3, 1789, to Anne Paine, b. March 20, 1764. The first wife d. Aug. 20, 1787; the second wife d. Sept. 3, 1849; he d. May 23, 1838. He lived in Pomfret, Conn., and in Guildhall, Vt. His children:

1629 GEORGE. b. Aug. 18, 1780; m. Martha Kyle.
1630 ELIZABETH, b. Jan. 19, 1782: m. a Beach; d. in Canaan, N. H.
1631 PRUDENCE, b. Nov. 26, 1783; d. July 20, 1812.
1632 FRANCES, b. March 31, 1795; m. S. W. Cone.
1633 ANNA, b. June 7, 1798; m. Anderson Dana.
1634 DAVID E., b. May 28, 1806; m. Esther K. Goodrich.
1635 JOHN P., b. Sept. 8, 1808; m. Mercy S. Cooper.

1629 GEORGE DENISON, (David[5], Thomas[4], Robert[3], John[2], George[1],) b. Aug. 18, 1780, was married, in 1808, to Martha Kyle; lived in Philadelphia. His children:

1636 FREDERICK. b. in 1809; d. in 1810.
1637 FRANCIS ANNA, b. in 1813; m. John Rumsey of Md.; no child.
1638 OPHELIA, b. in 1816; d. in 1818.
1639 GEORGE, b. in 1815; d. in 1824.
1640 DAVID, b. in 1818; d. in 1867.
1641 MARTHA K., b. in 1819; m. Geo. H. Stuart.
1642 FREDERICK, b. in 1823; d. in 1825.

1641 MARTHA K. DENISON, (George[6], David[5], Thomas[4], Robert[3], John[2], George[1],) b. in 1819, was married, May 11, 1837, to George H. Stuart, of Philadelphia. Their children:

1643 FRANCES R., b. May 17, 1838; d. May 13, 1843.
1644 WM. DAVID, b. Aug. 10, 1840; m. Mary E. Johnson; and died, Apri 7, 1863.
1645 GEORGE HAY, Jr., b. May 16, 1842; d. April 28, 1843.
1646 ELLEN, b. April 8, 1845: m. Christopher S. Paterson.
1647 MARY. b. Dec. 20, 1846: m. Herbert B. Tyson.
1648 GEORGE HAY, Jr., b. Feb. 11. 1849; m. Hannah B. S., dau. of E. S. Tobey, Boston,
1649 FRANK, b. 1851.
1650 CHARLES DUFF, b. Oct. 31, 1853; d. Jan. 10, 1855.
1651 MARTHA.

1646 ELLEN STUART, (dau. of 1641 Martha K. and George H.,) was married, Oct. 16, 1867, to Christopher S. Paterson, of Philadelphia. Children:

1652 GEORGE STUART, b. Oct. 10, 1868.
1653 JOSEPH HENRY, b. June 1, 1870.
1654 CHRISTOPHER STUART, b. Dec. 10, 1871.
1625 ELEANOR CUYLER, b. Oct. 29, 1873.
1656 FRANCIS DENISON, b. June 21, 1875.
1657 ALICE KYLE, b. Nov. 29, 1877; d. May 1, 1878.

1647 MARY STUART, (dau. of 1641 Martha K. and George H.,) was married Nov. 18, 1868, to Herbert B. Tyson of Philadelphia. Children:

1658 CAROLINE, b. Sept. 19, 1869.
1659 MARY STUART, b. Feb. 24, 1871.
1660 STUART LAWRENCE, b. Nov. 12, 1873.
1261 ESTHER FIELDING, b. Oct. 22, 1876.
1662 EDITH B., b. Oct. 1, 1875.
1563 MARTHA STUART, b. Aug. 26, 1878.

1648 GEORGE HAY STUART, JR., (son of 1641 Martha K. and Geo. H.,) b. Feb. 11, 1849, was married Dec. 21, 1871, to Hannah B. S. Tobey, dau. of Edward S. Tobey of Boston, Mass. He lives in Philadelphia. Children:

1664 GEORGE HAY, b. Oct. 12, 1872.
1665 EDWARD TOBEY, b. Oct. 19, 1876.
1666 ELIZABETH SPRAGUE, b. Aug. 19, 1878.

1603 ANNA DENISON, (David[5], Thomas[4], Robert[3], John[2], George[1],) b. at Brooklyn, Ct., June 7, 1798, was married, Jan. 2, 1818, to Anderson Dana, b. June 15, 1790, at Enfield, Conn. They were married at Guildhall, Vt., and lived at Hinsdale, N. H., at Gaines, N. Y., and at Farmington, Ohio. He died at Farmington in April, 1876. She died at Gaines, N. Y., Sept. 7, 1828. Their children:

1669 CHARLES A., b. Aug. 8, 1819, at Hinsdale, N. H.
1670 JUNIUS, b. April 23, 1821, at Hinsdale, N. H.; *m.* Martha Potter, July 8, 1844; two children, William and Alice; is devoted to music.
1671 ANN MARIA, b. Nov. 17, 1825, at Gaines, N. Y.
1672 DAVID DENISON, b. Sept. 7, 1828, at Gaines, N. Y.

1669 CHARLES A. DANA, (Anna[6], David[5], Thomas[4], Robert[3], John[2], George[1].) b. Aug. 8, 1819, was married, March 2, 1846, to Eunice McDaniel; lives in New York City; is editor of the N. Y. Sun. Children:

1673 ZOE, b. March 4, 1847.
1674 RUTH, b. April 13, 1850.
1675 PAUL, b. Aug. 20, 1852.
1676 EUNICE, b. Aug. 27, 1854.

Capt. John Denison's Descendants. 83

1635 JOHN P. DENISON, (David[5], Thomas[4], Robert[3], John[2], George[1],) b. Sept. 8, 1808, was married, May 9, 1841, to Mary S. Cooper ; lives at Wyandotte, Kansas. Children :

    1677 CHARLES P., b. Feb. 3, 1842.
    1678 FRANCES M., b. March 19, 1844; d. June 29, 1866.
    1579 HENRY W., b. May 11, 1846; m. Nellie W. Cross, Feb. 6, 1873, and went to Yokohama, Japan.
    1680 NELLIE S., b. May 11, 1850.
    1681 JOHN C., b. Nov- 30, 1852.

1634 DAVID E. DENISON, (David[5], Thomas[4], Robert[3], John[2], George[1],) b. March 28, 1806, was married in December, 1827, to Esther K. Goodrich. They lived at Hadley, Mass.; she d. Sept. 17, 1837 ; he d. Dec. 31, 1848 ; but he *m*. 2nd, Parmelia Nelson, of Guildhall, Vt. The first wife had two children, and the 2nd, three, as follows :

    1682 ALMIRA GOODRICH.
    1683 ESTHER ANN ; *m*. and left a daughter and a son. The daughter is now Bessie Goodale Moseman, Waterbury, Conn.
    1684 SARAH HOVEY; *m*. a Meacham; P. O. Guildhall, Vt.
    1685 ELIZABETH.
    1686 HARRIET.

1632 FRANCES DENISON, (David[5], Rev. Thomas[4], Robert[3], John[2], George[1],) *m*. Sylvester Wells Cone, Jan. 26, 1815. He d. Feb. 8, 1838 ; she d. Oct. 28, 1844. Their children :

    1687 A DAUGHTER, b. and d. Nov. 12, 1815.
    1688 ELIZABETH JANE, b. Jan. 9, 1817; *m*. Joseph B. Smith.
    1689 SARAH ANN, b. April 22, 1819; d. July 17, 1819.
    1690 GEORGE D., b. Nov. 22, 1820; d. Nov. 8, 1844.
    1691 CAROLINE ANN, b. Feb. 6, 1823 ; d. Nov. 2, 1844.
    1692 SUSAN C., b. Sept. 15, 1825 ; *m*. Michael Carleton.
    1693 DAVID D., b. April 15, 1828; *m*. Ellen Gronard, April 5, 1863; P. O., Washington, D. C.
    1694 SYLVESTER WELLS, b. Dec. 10, 1830; *m*. Anna W. Cone in 1874.
    1695 FRANCIS MARION, b. June 1, 1833;
    1696 JOHN PAINE, b. Feb. 8, 1836; *m*. Amanda Sappin.

1692 SUSAN C. CONE, (dau. of 1632 Frances and Sylvester,) *m*. Jan. 26, 1845, Michael Carlton, of Haverhill, N. H. Children :

    1697 CHARLES KIMBALL, b. Aug. 8, 1846.
    1697½ ANNA CAROLINE, b. April 25, 1850.
    1698 HATTIE E., b. March 12, 1855; d. May 19, 1860.
    1698½ GEORGE DENISON, b. April 27, 1857; d. Oct. 11, 1861.

1699 ELIZABETH DENISON, b. March 26, 1863.
1699½ ARTHUR MERRILL, b. Jan. 26, 1868; d. March 3, 1868.
Two others died in infancy.

1187 GEORGE DENISON, (Robert[3], John[2], George[1],) b. in 1719, was married, in 1742, to Hannah Dodge, and had :

1700 GEORGE, b. in 1744.

The following is from a will found in the probate records of New London, Conn., and dated in 1777 : " I bequeath to my wife Margaret, the use and improvement of my real estate, if she remains my widow ; but, if she gets married, the property to be divided among my children, except Ann Johnson : I give her £5 ; she had hers in getting married. Margaret, my wife, Executrix, and son George, Executor. Signed, GEORGE DENISON ; before Justice Hillhouse." This indicates that he had a second wife and more children.

1188 DOROTHY DENISON, (Robert[3], John[2], George[1],) b. in 1721, was married three times : 1st, to Ebenezer Rogers, about 1741 ; 2nd to David Copp ; 3rd, to Jonathan Avery, (son of the 2nd James,) Oct. 18, 1752. Her children by Jonathan Avery, 3rd husband, were as follows :

1700½ ANN, (Avery,) b. July 10, 1753.
1701 LUCY, (Avery,) b. July 16, 1755.
1701½ DAVID, (Avery,) b. Dec. 27, 1759.

V.

180 WILLIAM DENISON, (John[2], George[1],) b. April 7, 1677, was married in 1698, to Mary, dau. of the first John Avery, of Groton, Conn.; lived in North Stonington, Conn., and d. there, Jan. 30, 1730. His widow, being 52 years old, was married, Jan. 12, 1732, to Daniel Palmer, who was 59 years old, outlived him, and d. in 1762, aged 82 years. Daniel Palmer was son of Nehemiah and Hannah (Stanton) Palmer. He had had nine children by a first wife. William Denison's children :

1702 MARY, b. in 1699; bapt. Sept. 3, 1699; d. in 1699.
1702½ MARY, twin, b. in 1701; bapt. June 6, 1701.
1703 PHEBE, twin, b. in 1701; bapt. June 6, 1701.
1704 ANN, b. in 1703; m. John Denison, son of Edward, in 1720, and was drowned in a well in 1721.

Capt. John Denison's Descendants. 85

1705 WILLIAM, b. in 1705; twice married.
1706 ABIGAIL, b. in 1708; m. Roger Billings.
1707 LUCY, b. in 1710; m. John Swan, 2d.
1708 AVERY, b. in 1712; m. Thankful Williams.
1709 THANKFUL, b. in 1714; m. Joseph Billings.
1710 DESIRE, b. in 1716; m. John Stanton.
1711 CHRISTOPHER, b. in 1719; m. Abigail Tyler.
1712 JOHN, b. Feb. 23, 1722; m. Martha Wheeler.

1702 MARY DENISON, (William^3, John^2, George^1,) was married to Edward Herrick of Preston, Conn., in 1725, and died in 1735. Her children:

1713 MARY, b. in 1726.
1714 EBENEZER, b. in 1731.
1715 RUFUS, b. in 1734.

1703 PHEBE DENISON, (William^3, John^2, George^1,) was married, first, to Benj. Gile, of Preston, Conn., July 6, 1719. He d. in 1725, and she m. second, Stephen Herrick, who was appointed guardian of her children in 1738. No record of children by the second husband has been found. By the first she had:

1716 WILLIAM, b. March 1, 1723.
1717 PHEBE, b. Jan. 22, 1725.

1707 LUCY DENISON, (William^3, John^2, George^1,) b. in 1710, was married, March 5, 1726, to John Swan, Jr., who was born in Haverhill, Mass., Dec. 26, 1700. He was son of John Swan, of Haverhill, who removed from that place to North Stonington, about 1708, and whose wife, Susannah, died in Stonington, Dec. 20, 1772, in the hundredth year of her age. The following were children of John, Jr., and Lucy (Denison) Swan:

1718 ANNA, b. March 10, 1727.
1719 LUCY, b. Nov. 3, 1729.
1720 JOHN, Jr., b. Sept. 24, 1731; m. Mary Prentice.
1721 JOSEPH, b. March 12, 1734.
1722 JOSHUA, b. Nov. 15, 1736.
1723 PEREZ, b. Oct. 3, 1739.
1724 THOMAS, b. March 18, 1742.
1725 EUNICE, b. Sept. 15, 1744.
1726 EDWARD, b. Nov. 12, 1746.
1727 GEORGE, b. Aug. 26, 1750; m. Abigail Randall.

1706 ABIGAIL DENISON, (William^3, John^2, George^1,) born in 1708, was married to Roger Billings, July 20, 1729. Her children:

1728 ABIGAIL, b. Feb. 7, 1730; *m.* Benj. Coit, 1753.
1729 JOHN, b. Dec. 15, 1732; *m.* Eunice Gallup, 1757.
1730 WILLIAM, b. May 8, 1734.
1731 PELEG, b. June 26, 1738.
1732 DOROTHY, b. April 18, 1740.
1733 BENJAMIN, b. Oct. 10, 1743.
1734 HENRY, b. April 9, 1746.
1735 SABRA, b. Jan. 4, 1751; *m.* Elias Brown.
1736 MARY, b. May 24, 1755; *m.* Darius Denison, 1771.

1710 DESIRE DENISON, (William³, John², George¹,) b. in 1716, was married, April 8, 1735, to John Stanton, 3d, of Preston, Conn., oldest son of John Stanton, 2nd, son of Capt. John Stanton of Stonington. He d. in August, 1774. His will names all his children, and shows that Lucy, Esther, and Abigail were then unmarried. The children were as follows:

1737 MARY, b. Jan. 1, 1736; *m.* Amos Crary, in 1756; H. Babcock, 1764.
1738 SARAH, b. Feb., 1738; *m.* Eleazer Prentice, 1758.
1739 AMY, b. June, 1740; *m.* Benj. Crary, 1762.
1740 DESIRE, b. Oct., 1742; *m.* Elisha Geer, 1770.
1741 LUCY, b. Aug., 1745.
1742 PRUDENCE, b. Feb., 1748; *m.* Daniel Meach, 1769.
1743 JOHN, b. Nov. 13, 1750; *m.* Huldah Freeman, 1775.
1744 JOSEPH, b. Aug. 13, 1754.
1745 ESTHER, b. Nov., 1756.
1746 ABIGAIL, b. Nov., 1759.

1709 THANKFUL DENISON, (William³, John², George¹,) b. in 1714, was married to Joseph Billings, Nov. 10, 1737. Her children:

1747 COMFORT, b. Sept. 24, 1740.
1748 SARAH, b. Jan. 15, 1746.
1749 NATHAN, b. June 9, 1748.

1705 WILLIAM DENISON, (William³, John², George¹,) b. in 1705, lived in North Stonington. He was married, first, Jan. 30, 1732, to Hannah Burrows, who d. Jan. 5, 1737; 2nd, Jan. 30, 1738, to Hannah Tyler, who d. in 1797, aged 86. He died, Jan. 29, 1760. The inventory of his estate was £2268, 17s, 8d. His children:

1750 WILLIAM, bapt. Feb. 17, 1733; d. Oct. 21, 1736.
1751 JOSEPH, b. Oct. 24, 1736; *m.* Mary Babcock.
1752 HANNAH, b. Dec. 25, 1736; *m.* Dr. Charles Phelps.
1753 NATHAN, b. Feb. 24, 1739; d. May 28, 1742.
1754 DANIEL, b. July 20, 1740; *m.* Martha Geer.
1755 AMY, b. March 27, 1742; *m.* Thomas Swan.

Capt. John Denison's Descendants.

1756 ANN, b. Sept. 12, 1744; *m.* George Palmer.
1757 ESTHER, b. April 23, 1746; *m.* John James.
1758 SARAH, b. Feb. 7, 1748; *m.* John W. Geer.
1759 JOHN, b. Nov. 5, 1749; *m.* Abigail Minor.
1760 ELIJAH, b. Nov. 6, 1751; *m.* Mary Geer; no child.

1752 HANNAH DENISON, (William[4], William[3], John[2], George[1],) b. Dec. 25, 1736, was married, Nov. 10, 1757, to Dr. Charles Phelps; died Sept. 10, 1775; lived in Stonington, Conn. Her children:

1761 WILLIAM, b. Sept. 26, 1758; d. Nov. 5, 1786.
1762 HANNAH, b. Dec. 15, 1760; *m.* Andrew Huntington, 1777.
1763 CHARLES, b. Feb. 23, 1763; d. Dec. 2, 1791.
1764 HEPZIBAH, b. May 13, 1765; *m.* Ephraim Williams.
1765 MARTHA, b. May 8, 1767.
1766 JOSEPH D., b. May 15, 1769; *m.* Hannah Babcock.
1767 STILES, b. June 20, 1771.
1768 ANNE, b. Aug. 8, 1772.
1769 JOHN, b. July 8, 1774; d. Oct. 16, 1775.
1770 JONATHAN, b. Oct. 30, 1779.
1771 POLLY, b. June 10, 1785.

1764 HEPZIBAH PHELPS, (dau. of Hannah (Denison) and Dr. Charles Phelps,) b. May 13, 1765, was married, Dec. 23, 1787, to Ephraim Williams of Stonington, Conn. He was son of William, who was son of John, who was son of John, who was son of Isaac, who was son of Robert Williams. He d. in Stonington, July 6, 1804, aged 48; she d. April 16, 1837, aged nearly 72. Children:

1772 EHPRAIM, b. July 3, 1791; *m.* Hannah E. Denison.
1773 SARAH P., b. July 15, 1802; d. July 24, 1824.
1774 CHARLES P., b. July 11, 1804.

1772 EPHRAIM WILLIAMS, JR., (son of Ephraim and Hepzibah,) b. July 3, 1791, was married, April 13, 1815, to Hannah Eliza Denison, dau. of Amos, who was son of Dea. Joseph and gr. grandson of George Denison of Westerly. They lived in Stonington. He d. March 23, 1861, aged not quite 70; she d. June 20, 1877, aged 78. Their children:

1775 HEPZIBAH P., b. Feb. 9, 1816; *m.* Dr. Wm. Hyde, Jr.
1776 HANNAH ELIZABETH, b. Nov. 16, 1817; *m.* Courtland P. Dixon.
1777 MARTHA D., b. March 15, 1820; d. Nov. 29, 1820.
1778 EPHRAIM, b. Jan. 25, 1822; d. Oct. 27, 1822.
1779 SARAH P., b. May 1, 1825; *m.* Wm. L. Palmer.
1780 EPHRAIM, b. Dec. 1, 1826; *m.* Pauline Denniston.
1781 EDWARD, b. April 21, 1830; d. Sept. 11, 1830.

1782 CHARLES P., b. Sept. 18, 1828; d. May 16, 1832.
1783 EMELINE P., b. May 18, 1832; m. Jabez Holmes.
1784 AMOS D., b. June 30, 1834; m. Elizabeth Fitch.
1785 JOSEPH P., b. Aug. 8, 1836; m. Elizabeth Town.
1786 MARTHA JANE, b. July 27, 1838; m. John H. Hunter.
1787 CHARLES P., b. Aug. 19, 1840; m. Fanny Mallory.

1775 HEPZIBAH P. WILLIAMS, (dau. of Ephraim, Jr., and Hannah E. (Denison) Williams,) b. Feb. 9, 1816, was married, March 2, 1836, to Dr. William Hyde, Jr. They lived in Stonington, Conn.; she d. May 2, 1841; and Sept. 11, 1843, Dr. Hyde was married, second, to Ellen Williams, who had no child. Mrs. Hepzibah E. P. W. Hyde, the first wife, had these children:

1788 WM. WILLIAMS, b. Nov. 17, 1836; d. July 20, 1856.
1789 CHARLES W., b. April 1, 1838; d. Jan. 14, 1839.
1790 EDWARD, b. Oct. 12, 1839; d. Dec. 22, 1839.
1791 A SON, b. April 29, 1841; d. May 6, 1841.

Dr. William Hyde, Jr., b. Oct. 57, 1808, was son of Dr. William Hyde, of Stonington, and followed the profession of his father, in the same community. Notwithstanding a lifelong struggle with pulmonary disease, he gained a large practice, was highly esteemed in the profession, and greatly beloved by his patients. He died, Sept. 25, 1873.

1776 HANNAH ELIZABETH WILLIAMS, (dau. of Ephraim, Jr. and Hannah E. (Denison) Williams,) b. Nov. 16, 1817, was married, Sept. 9, 1841, to Courtland P. Dixon; lives in Brooklyn, N. Y. Children:

1792 NATHAN, F., b. Aug. 24, 1842; d. July 23, 1843.
1793 COURTLAND P., b. May 10, 1845; d. July 31, 1847.
1794 WILLIAM P., b. March 19, 1847; m. Evelina F. Babcock.
1795 HANNAH E., b. Feb. 16, 1849; m. Henry Barnes.
1796 PRISCILLA P., b. Feb. 25, 1851; m. Thomas Sloane.
1797 COURTLAND P., b. July 8, 1853.
1798 EPHRAIM W., b. Feb. 18, 1855; d. Jan. 7, 1857.
1799 GEORGE A., b. May 6, 1857.
1800 EPHRAIM W., b. April 14, 1859.
1801 PAULINE W., b. Jan. 4, 1862.

1779 SARAH POTTER WILLIAMS, (dau. of Ephraim, Jr. and Hannah E. (Denison) Williams,) b. May 1, 1825, was married, Oct. 21, 1846, to Wm. L. Palmer. She d. May 18, 1877. Her children:

1802 WILLIAM L., b. Sept. 16, 1847.
1803 THEODORE D., b. April 5, 1849; m. Elizabeth L. Denison.
1804 SARAH W., b. Nov. 2, 1858.

1780 EPHRAIM WILLIAMS, 3d, (son of Ephraim, Jr., and Hannah E. (Denison) Williams,) b. Dec. 1, 1826, was married Oct. 19, 1849, to Pauline Denniston, who d. Nov. 26, 1870. He m. second, July 3, 1873, May Denison Babcock, dau. of Giles and Ann (Denison) Babcock. One child by the first wife, and two by the second:

1805 EPHRAIM, b. Dec. 30, 1850; d. March 14, 1853.
1806 MAUD CLEVELAND, b. April 22, 1874.
1807 EPHRAIM, b. June 13, 1875.

1783 EMELINE PENDLETON WILLIAMS, (dau. of Ephraim, Jr. and Hannah E. (Denison) Williams,) b. May 18, 1832, was married, Oct. 23, 1855, by Rev. Wm. Clift, to Jabish Holmes. Their children:

1808 SARAH WILLIAMS, b. July 3, 1856, at Stonington, Conn.
1809 JABISH, b. Aug. 14, 1857, at Detroit, Mich.
1810 ELIZABETH DENISON, b. May 6, 1861, at Detroit, Mich.

Mr. Jabish Holmes, b. in Stonington, Oct. 26, 1812, was son of Jabish Holmes and his wife Lydia Clift. His father, Jabish Holmes, Senr., son of John Holmes of Stonington and Hannah Halsey, of Long Island, was born May 20, 1753, and died in Stonington, Aug. 23, 1831, aged 78. His mother, Lydia Clift, dau. of Amos and Esther W. Clift, was born, Dec. 29, 1792, and died June 20, 1879, in Stonington. Mr. Holmes, after spending most of his years in mercantile pursuits, in New York City, and in Detroit, Mich., is spending the evening of his days in his native village.

1784 AMOS DENISON WILLIAMS, (son of Ephraim, Jr., and Hannah E. (Denison) Williams,) b. June 30, 1834, was married, Dec. 24, 1860, to Elizabeth Fitch. Children:

1811 AMOS D., b. Nov. 21, 1870.
1812 EPHRAIM, b. April 12, 1872.

1785 JOSEPH PHELPS WILLIAMS, (son of Ephraim, Jr. and Hannah E. (Denison) Williams,) b. Aug. 8, 1836, was married, Oct. 24, 1866, to Elizabeth Town. Children:

1813 JOSEPH, b. Nov. 2, 1867.
1814 ELIZABETH T., b. Nov. 7, 1871.
1815 A SON, b. Oct. 14, 1878.

1786 MARTHA JANE WILLIAMS, (dau. of Ephraim, Jr., and Hannah E. (Denison) Williams,) b. July 27, 1838, was married, Sept. 9, 1868, to John H. Hunter. Children :

1816 ESTHER S., b. Jan. 15, 1871.
1817 EMELINE W., b. March 6, 1873.
1818 Two children died young.

1787 CHARLES P. WILLIAMS, (son of Ephraim, Jr., and Hannah E. (Denison) Williams,) b. Aug. 19, 1840, was married Oct. 28, 1868, to Fanny Mallory. Children :

1819 FANNY M., b. July 13, 1869.
1820 CHARLES M., b. Oct. 16, 1872.
1821 KATE M., b. March 19, 1874.

1555 AMY DENISON, (William[4], William[3], John[2], George[1],) b. March 27, 1742, was married, Feb. 2, 1764, to Thomas Swan. Lived at North Stonington, Conn. Her children :

1822 REBECCA, b. March 27, 1765 ; d. young.
1823 THOMAS, b. Oct. 17, 1766 ; m. Fanny Palmer.
1824 CYRUS, b. Oct. 1, 1768.
1825 DANIEL, b. Sept. 7, 1770.
1826 SALLY, b. Oct. 5, 1772.
1827 AMY, b. Oct. 25, 1774.
1828 REBECCA, b. 1776.
1829 SAMUEL, b. 1779.
1830 HENRY, b. 1781.
1831 ABIGAIL, b. 1784.
1832 JOHN, b. Jan. 30, 1788.

1557 ESTHER DENISON, (William[4], William[3], John[2], George[1],) b. April 23, 1746, was married to John James, in 1763 ; lived in Preston, Conn. Her children :

1833 SUSANNA, b. Oct. 1764.
1834 ANNA, b. July, 1766.
1835 WILLIAM, b. May, 1769.
1836 JOHN, b. June, 1771.
1837 HANNAH, b. Dec., 1773.
1838 ESTHER, b. 1775 ; d. in 1776.
1839 NABBY, b. March, 1777.
1840 POLLY, b. July, 1779.
1841 THOMAS, b. March, 1781.
1842 ESTHER, b. June, 1783.
1843 SAMUEL, b. April, 1785.

1823 THOMAS SWAN, JR., (Amy Denison[5], William[4], William[3], John[2], George[1],) was married, April 22, 1798, to Fanny

Palmer; lived in Stonington, Conn.; d. March 19, 1819; only one child :

1844 SARAH ANN, b. Feb. 23, 1799; m. Gurdon Trumbull.

1844 SARAH ANN SWAN, (dau. of 1823 Thomas, Jr.) b. Feb. 23, 1799, and married, May 1, 1817, to Gurdon Trumbull, of Stonington. Children:

1845 GURDON SWAN, b. May 28, 1818; d. Oct. 2, 1819.
1846 FRANCES SWAN, b. Feb. 6, 1820; d. Feb. 1, 1821.
1847 JAMES HAMMOND, b. Dec. 20, 1821; m. Sarah A. Robinson, of Hartford, Conn., Aug. 6, 1855; lives in Hartford; is Secretary and Librarian of the Connecticut Historical Society.
1848 WILLIAM PALMER, b. May 3, 1825; d. Sept. 8, 1826.
1849 MARY, b. Aug. 5, 1827; m. William C. Prime, of New York City, author of various books, and writer for the New York Journal of Commerce. She d. April 3, 1872.
1850 HENRY CLAY, b. June 8, 1830; m. Alice C. Gallaudet; is a clergyman, author, and editor.
1851 CHARLES EDWARD, b. Oct. 31, 1832; d. March 17, 1856.
1852 THOMAS SWAN, b Feb. 15, 1835; d. March 30, 1865.
1853 ANNA, b. May 18, 1838; m. Edward Slosson.
1854 GURDON, b. May 5, 1841; m. Anna F. Niles.

1756 ANN DENISON, (William[4], William[3], John[2], George[1],) b. Sept. 12, 1744, was married to Capt. George Palmer, in 1773; lived in Preston, Conn., and had these :

1855 DENISON, b. Nov. 25, 1774; m. Lavinia Harvey, April 19, 1809; lived at Preston City, Conn.; had five children, as follows:
   NATHAN, b. Feb. 25, 1810.
   MARIA FOWLER, b. Dec. 8, 1811.
   RUTH ANN, b. Jan. 30, 1816.
   EUNICE GEER, b. March 23, 1818.
   CYNTHIA BILLINGS, b. Oct. 27, 1820.
1856 HENRY, b. Nov. 9, 1776; d. unmarried.
1857 WILLIAM, b. 1778; m.
1858 POLLY, b. 1780; d. unmarried.
1859 NANCY, b. 1782; d. unmarried.

1758 SARAH DENISON, (William[4], William[3], John[2], George[1],) b. Feb. 7, 1748, was married to John W. Geer, Sept. 6, 1778; lived in Griswold, Conn., and had these :

1860 JOHN, b. June 11, 1779.
1861 NATHAN, b. April 30, 1781; m. Ann Denison.
1862 ELIJAH D., b. April 17, 1783; m. Dorothy ———.
1863 SALLY, b. Jan. 25, 1785; d. March 14, 1857.
1864 MOSES T., b. Jan. 11, 1787; m. Hannah Denison.
1865 MARY, b. March 28, 1792; d. Oct. 13, 1842.
1866 SAMUEL, b. Nov. 30, 1788.

1751 JOSEPH DENISON, (William⁴, William³, John², George¹,) b. Oct. 24, 1735, was married to Mary Babcock, Oct. 10, 1765; lived in Stonington. He died, Nov. 15, 1785, aged 50; his wife died Dec. 15, 1798, aged 52. Their children:

 1867 MARY, b. April 16, 1767; *m.* Nathan Smith.
 1868 HANNAH, b. Oct. 6, 1768; *m.* Stephen Brown.
 1869 DORCAS, b. Aug. 9, 1770; *m.* Benj. Eells.
 1870 AMY, b. Nov. 4, 1771; *m.* Paul Rhodes.
 1871 ABIGAIL, b. Feb. 18, 1776; *m.* Oliver Cobb.
 1872 JOSEPH, b. Feb. 12, 1778; *m.* Prudence Denison.
 1873 BETSEY, b. June 19, 1780; *m.* Peter Crary, of New York, and had these: Lucretia, Eveline, Edward.
 1874 SAMUEL F., b. Sept. 19, 1782; *m.* Mary Cleveland.
 1875 CHARLES P., b. Feb. 16, 1785; *m.* Rebecca Shearwood; no child.
 1876 SARAH, b. Dec. 14, 1773; *m.* Thomas Butler.

1872 JOSEPH DENISON, JR., (Joseph⁵, William⁴, William², John², George¹,) b. Feb. 12, 1778, was married to Prudence Denison, his cousin, Feb. 12, 1797, lived in Chenango Co., N. Y. His children:

 1877 MARY, b. in 1797; d. young.
 1878 SARAH, b. in 1800; d. unmarried.
 1879 ELIZA, b. in 1802; d. unmarried
 1880 PRUDENCE, b. i : 1804; d. unmarried.
 1881 JOSEPH, b. in 1806; d. unmarried.

1867 MARY DENISON, (Joseph⁵, William⁴, William³, John², George¹,) b. April 16, 1767, was married, June 8, 1788, to Nathan Smith. Her children:

 1882 EVELINA, b. in 1790; d. unmarried.
 1883 MARY D., b. in 1792; *m.* Elisha Faxon, Jr.
 1884 NATHAN S., b. in 1794.
 1885 OLIVER, b. in 1797.

1869 DORCAS DENISON, (Joseph⁵, William⁴, William³, John², George¹,) b. Aug. 9, 1770, was married, Dec. 20, 1789, to Benj. Eells, (son of Rev. Nathaniel); lived in Stonington; he died, March 6, 1799; she died Jan. 28, 1856. Their children:

 1886 MARIA, b. Sept. 22, 1790; *m.* B. F. Babcock.
 1887 LYDIA, b. Nov. 13, 1791; d. July 25, 1794.
 1888 CHARLOTTE D., b. July 12, 1793; *m.* Nathan Smith.
 1889 BENJAMIN S., b. June 12, 1795; d. Sept. 5, 1796.
 1890 ELIZABETH, b. Dec. 30, 1798; *m.* Rev. Oliver Brown.

Capt. John Denison's Descendants.

1870 AMY DENISON, (Joseph[5], William[4], William[3], John[2], George[1],) b. Nov. 4, 1771, was married, in 1793, to Paul Rhodes ; lived in Westerly, R. I. Her children :

1891 CHARLES D., b. 1794; *m.* Harriet D. Butler.
1892 ABBY.
1893 EMMA.
1894 MARY ANN.
1895 RALPH E.
1896 FRANCIS B.
1897 HORACE S.

1876 SARAH DENISON, (Joseph[5], William[4], William[3], John[2], George[1],) b. Dec. 14, 1773, was married, about 1792, to Thomas Butler, son of Benj. and Diadama Hyde Butler, of Norwich, Ct. They lived in Stonington, Ct., in Oxford, N. Y., and in Plainfield, Ct., where he died, Aug. 7, 1822. She d. Nov. 13, 1839. Her children :

1898 FRANCES HYDE, b. Jan. 9, 1793; d. June 15, 1801.
1899 HARRIET DENISON, b. Feb. 12, 1795; *m.* Charles D. Rhodes.
1900 CAROLINE HYDE, b. July 23, 1804; *m.* Edward Butler.

1899 HARRIET DENISON BUTLER, (dau. of 1876 Sarah Denison and Thomas Butler,) b. Feb. 12, 1795, *m.* Charles Denison Rhodes, of Boston, son of Paul and 1870 Amy Denison Rhodes, May 23, 1816. He d. Sept. 1867 ; she d. Aug. 23, 1832. Children :

1901 HARRIET ADELE, b. March 15, 1818.
1902 HELOISE FLORENTHE, b. Aug. 17, 1819.
1903 CHARLES BUTLER, b. in 1822; d. in infancy.
1904 LUCIA BUTLER, b. Aug. 24, 1824; d. Nov. 1876.
1905 ABBY GOODWIN, b. Aug. 14, 1829; *m.* Horatio N. Slater, of Webster, Mass., Sept. 29, 1869.

1901 HARRIET ADELE RHODES, (dau. of Harriet Denison Butler and Charles Denison Rhodes), *m.* Charles G. Carleton, of New York, May 25, 1835. He d. Sept. 29, 1854. Their children :

1906 EMILY, b. March 31, 1836; d. Oct. 30, 1839.
1907 HARRIET RHODES, b. in 1837; d. young.
1908 FLORENCE, b. Feb. 25, 1838.
1909 MEDORA, b. Jan. 18, 1841; d. Nov. 1876.
1910 CHARLES GUY, b. Oct. 11, 1843; *m.* Fanny High, of Chicago, in 1875; one child, RICHARD, b. in 1876.

1900 CAROLINE HYDE BUTLER, (dau. of 1876 Sarah Denison and Thomas Butler), b. July 23, 1804 ; *m.* at Plainfield, Ct., Sept. 22, 1822, Edward Butler, of Boston, son of Simeon and Mary Hunt Butler, of Northampton. He d. July 12, 1849, aged 52. Their children :

1911 SARAH CAROLINE, b. May 25, 1824.
1912 THOMAS E., b. March 19, 1827.
1913 EDWARD, b. March 12, 1829.
1914 THEODORE HUNT, b. May 10, 1831.
1915 HUNT MILLS, b. May 20, 1834.
1916 HARRIET DENISON, b. Aug. 20, 1837; *m.* Thomas Buchanan Read, the well known poet and artist, of Chester Co., Pa., July 8, 1856; he d. May 11, 1872.
1917 ROBERT MORRIS b. Oct. 9, 1838.
1918 MARY HUNT, b. March 7, 1841.
1919 CAROLINE HYDE, b, Aug. 23, 1844.
1920 FRANKLIN DELANO, b. April 13, 1846; d. Dec. 26, 1875.

In 1852, Mrs. Caroline Hyde Butler *m.*, second, Hugh Laing of New York, who was long president of the Clinton Fire Insurance Co. He d. in 1869, aged 86 years.

1911 SARAH CAROLINE BUTLER,(dau. of 1900 Caroline Hyde and Edward Butler,) b. May 25, 1824, was married at New York to James Emott Caldwell of Philadelphia, Pa., Sept. 1, 1842. Children :

1921 JAMES ALBERT, b. Nov. 9, 1844; *m.* Annie Lafoucade, of Philadelphia, Pa., Jan. 14, 1869. Children: James, d. in infancy; James Albert, b Dec. 7, 1872.
1922 LAURA EMOTT, b. Nov. 7, 1846.
1923 CAROLINE ELIZABETH, b. July 18, 1849; *m.* Feb. 24, 1878, Dr. William Barton Brewster, U. S. N., son of Judge Carroll Brewster.
1924 RICHARD NELSON, b. Feb. 24, 1854.
1925 CLARENCE EDMUND, b. Oct. 18, 1857.
1926 BELINDA EMOTT, b. May 23, 1862.

1913 EDWARD BUTLER, (son of 1900 Caroline Hyde and Edward Butler,) b. March 12, 1829, married Justine Curtis, dau. of Samuel and Sarah Curtis, of Brooklyn, L. I., Sept. 22, 1849. He d. July, 1870 ; she d. June, 1866, aged 35. Children :

1927 FRANCES LATHROP, b. June 14, 1850; *m.* Samuel E. Johnson of Brooklyn, L. I. Children: Caroline Hyde Butler, b. Oct. 17, 1878; Samuel, b. Dec. 29, 1879.
1928 EDWARD, b. Jan. 14, 1854; d. Oct. 9, 1880.
1929 CAROLINE HYDE, b. Nov. 10, 1856.
1930 HUGH LAING, b. Feb. 26, 1861.
1931 JUSTINE, b. March, 1866; d. in infancy.

Capt. John Denison's Descendants. 95

1914 THEODORE HUNT BUTLER, (son of 1900 Caroline Hyde and Edward Butler,) b. May 10, 1831, *m*. Bertha Fairfield Cooke, dau. of Daniel and Mary Cushman Cooke, of Norristown, Pa., April 29, 1857. Children :
- **1932** ROBERT CUSHMAN, b. March 9, 1858.
- **1933** RALPH HYDE, b. May 14, 1860.
- **1934** FREDERIC COOKE, b. Oct 15, 1861.
- **1935** AMY DENISON, b. Aug. 24, 1864.
- **1936** GERTRUDE, b. Aug. 16, 1869; d. infancy.
- **1937** BERTHA, b. Dec. 14, 1872; d. in infancy.

1915 HUNT MILLS BUTLER, (son of 1900 Caroline Hyde and Edward Butler,) b. May 20, 1824, *m*. first, Rebecca Jackson, dau. of Gen. W. Jackson, U. S. A., Oct. 15, 1862. Children :
- **1938** EDWARD PITCAIRN, b. March 30, 1865; d. in infancy.
- **1939** ANNIE J., b. March 18, 1866; d. in infancy.
- **1940** CHARLES B., b. Aug. 26, 1867.
- **1941** HUNT MILLS, b. Jan. 5, 1869; d. in infancy.
- **1942** WALTER R., b. Oct. 18, 1870.
- **1943** REBECCA J., b. Nov. 5, 1871.

The first wife d. March 15, 1872, aged 31 years ; and in Nov., 1873, he *m*. second, Miss Kate Laufman, of Pittsburg, Pa. Their children :
- **1944** HARRINGTON LAUFMAN, b. Aug. 6. 1874.
- **1945** THEODORE HUNT, b. March 11, 1880.

1918 MARY HUNT BUTLER, (dau. of 1900 Caroline Hyde and Edward Butler,) b. March 7, 1841. *m*. James J. Reeves, of Bridgeton, N. J., June 7, 1866. Children :
- **1946** HUGH LAING, b. May 7, 1867.
- **1947** SARAH CALDWELL, b. Oct. 7, 1868.
- **1948** HARRIET DENISON, b. March 1, 1872.
- **1949** BERTHA BUTLER, b. Oct. 28, 1875.

1919 CAROLINE HYDE BUTLER, (dau. of 1900 Caroline Hyde and Edward Butler,) b. Aug. 23, 1844, *m*. Whitehead Cornell Duyckinck, of Brooklyn, L. I., April 29, 1869. Children :
- **1950** RICHARD BANCHER, b. April 21, 1870.
- **1951** THOMAS BUTLER, b. Sept. 29, 1875.
- **1952** HARRIET DENISON, b. Oct. 7, 1879.

1922 LAURA EMOTT CALDWELL, (dau. of 1911 Sarah Caroline and James Emott Caldwell,) *m*. Justus L. Bulkley, of New York, Feb. 14, 1871. . Children :

1953 JOSEPHINE, b. Aug. 12, 1872.
1954 JOSEPH, b. Dec. 4, 1876.
1955 HELEN CALDWELL, b. July 31, 1879.

1871 ABIGAIL DENISON, (Joseph^5, William^4, William^3, John^2, George^1,) b. Feb. 18, 1776, was married to Oliver Cobb, Nov. 1, 1795, and had these:

1956 JULIAN, b. Aug. 6, 1796; d. Aug. 6, 1797.
1957 MARIA, b. Jan. 24, 1798.
1958 OLIVER E., b. Aug. 5, 1799; d. Sept. 24, 1801.
1959 OLIVER E., (again,) b. March 6, 1802.
1960 SAMUEL D., twin, b. Oct. 4, 1804; d. Sept. 3, 1805.
1961 CHARLES D., twin, b. Oct. 4, 1804.
1962 SANFORD, b. Dec. 12, 1806.
1963 ABBY D., b. Sept. 27, 1809.

1874 SAMUEL F. DENISON, (Joseph^5, William^4, William^3, John^2, George^1,) b. Sept. 19, 1782, was married, Nov. 6, 1804, to Mary Cleveland of Plainfield, Conn. He died Jan. 28, 1855; she d. Oct. 11, 1866. They lived in Stonington, and had:

1964 MARY E., b. Aug. 18, 1805; d. Sept. 6, 1806.
1965 CAROLINE G., b. Feb. 21, 1807; d. Aug. 18, 1808.
1966 WILLIAM C., b. Dec. 11, 1808; d. unmarried.
1967 REV. SAMUEL D., b. Oct. 7, 1810; m. Sarah F. Bleeker.
1968 MARY C., b. July 13, 1812; m. Wm. H. Plummer.
1969 ANN E., 1814; m. Giles Babcock.
1970 JANE ISABEL, b. March 31, 1816; m. John A. Burnham.
1971 HARRIET MARIA, b. Aug. 20, 1818; m. Joseph Bennett.
1972 HENRY C., b. Sept. 10, 1820.
1973 EVELINA C., twin, b. Sept. 14, 1822; m. Stephen D. Thatcher.
1974 EDWARD, twin, b. Sept. 14, 1822; m. Elizabeth L. Lathrop.
1975 PULASKI, b. Feb. 4, 1825; d. Feb. 15, 1827.
1976 FRANKLIN B., b. July 16, 1832; d. Feb. 22, 1833.

1967 REV. SAMUEL DEXTER DENISON, (Samuel F.^{6}, Joseph^5, William^4, William^3, John^2, George^1,) b. Oct. 7, 1810, was married, June 7, 1832, to Sarah F. Bleeker, (dau. of James W. Bleeker, of New York City,) He died at White Plains, N. Y., Sept. 3, 1880. He was a minister of the Protestant Episcopal Church, and was chosen Home Secretary of its Domestic and Foreign Missionary Society, at the age of 32, which position he held constantly until his death in his seventieth year. His children:

1977 MARY C., b. Aug. 19, 1833.
1978 SAMUEL, b. July 4, 1837; d. April 3, 1844.

Capt. John Denison's Descendants.

1979 SARAH B., b. Aug. 14, 1840.
1980 CAROLINE L., b. March 8, 1843.
1981 EDMUND F., b. July 4, 1845.
1982 ANNA, b. Nov. 2, 1847.
1983 AMIE, b. Aug. 1, 1850.
1984 HENRY, b. Oct. 18, 1853.

1969 ANNA E. DENISON, (Samuel F.[6], Joseph[5], William[4], William[3], John[2], George[1],) b. in 1814, was married, Oct., 1832, to Giles Babcock, who d. in Stonington, Conn., March 4, 1862. They had these children :

1985 GILES, b. March 4, 1834; d. Aug. 26, 1834.
1986 SAMUEL, b. March 16, 1835; d. July 5, 1836.
1987 ANNA, b. Nov. 15, 1837; *m.* Samuel Wood of Albany; 2 ch.
1988 GILES, b. Sept. 3, 1840; *m.* Sarah Smith; one child, a son.
1989 JOHN B., b. Feb. 7, 1843; *m.* Blandina Stanton, dau. of Samuel and Lydia.
1990 MARY D., b. June 5, 1846; *m.* Ephraim Williams; 2 child.
1991 LUCY BELL, b. May 29, 1849.
1992 NATHANIEL P., b. Dec. 28, 1851.
1993 STEPHEN T., b. Sept. 2, 1859.

1971 HARRIET M. DENISON, (Samuel F.[6], Joseph[5], William[4], William[3], John[2], George[1],) b. Aug. 20, 1818, *m.* Joseph Bennett, Sept. 12, 1838, and had :

1994 CATHERINE, b. in 1839; *m.* Cortland Palmer, Jr. of N. Y.; 5 ch.

1970 JANE ISABEL DENISON, (Samuel F.[6], Joseph[5], William[4], William[3], John[2], George[1],) b. March 31, 1816, was married, Sept. 9, 1839, to John A. Burnham ; lives in Boston ; has had :

1995 JOHN A., b. Aug. 1, 1840; *m.* Mary W. Clark of Philadelphia, Oct. 18, 1866.
1996 WILLIAM A., b. Sept. 3, 1844; d. Aug. 5, 1846.
1997 MARIA D., b. May 15, 1849.
1998 WILLIAM A., b. Feb. 17, 1852.
1999 HENRY D., b. Nov. 24, 1857.
2000 JANE D., b. Dec. 2, 1846; *m.* 1st, J. H. Clark, Dec. 25, 1865; 2d, Geo. Sharswood, Jr., Sept. 15, 1874.

1968 MARY C. DENISON, (Samuel F.[6], Joseph[5], William[4], William[3], John[2], George[1],) b. July 13, 1812, was married, Jan. 6, 1835, to William H. Plummer. They have had :

2001 ANNIE D., b. Jan. 31, 1837, at Manchester, Eng.
2002 WILLIAM H., b. Jan. 9, 1840, in New York.
2003 CAROLINE.

1974 EDWARD DENISON, (Samuel F.[6], Joseph[5], William[4], William[3], John[2], George[1],) b. Sept. 14, 1822, was married, Oct. 3, 1844, to Elizabeth L. Lathrop, and had :

2004 Evelina T., b. Dec. 7, 1845.
2005 Elizabeth L., b. Nov. 26, 1847; *m.* Theo. Palmer. June 25, 1872.

1973 Evelina C. Denison, (Samuel F.[6], Joseph[5], William[4], William[3], John[2], George[1],) b. Sept. 14, 1822, was married, June 9, 1841, to Stephen D. Thatcher. They have had :

2006 Evelina, b. April 27, 1842; d. Sept. 3, 1844.

1754 Daniel Denison, (William[4], William[3], John[2], George[1]) b. July 20, 1740, was married to Martha Geer, May 28, 1771; lived first in North Stonington. About the year 1800, he emigrated to Pharsalia, Chenango County, N. Y., and settled on lot 70 in that town. His children :

2007 Hannah, b. Sept. 29, 1772; *m.* Wm. Popple.
2008 Prudence, b. Dec. 15, 1775; *m.* Joseph Denison, Jr.
2009 William, b. March 20, 1777; *m.* Betsey Ledyard.
2010 Martha, b. June 2, 1779; *m.* a Spaulding.
2011 Mary, b. April 3, 1782; d. unmarried.
2012 Amy, b. Oct. 23, 1784; d. unmarried.
2013 Daniel, b. March 20, 1787; *m.* Betsey Hunt.

2013 Daniel Denison, Jr. (Daniel[5], William[4], William[3], John[2], George[1],) b. March 20, 1787, was married to Betsey Hunt of Oxford, Chenango Co., N. Y.; lived in Oxford ; d. there June 28, 1865 ; his wife d. there. Their children :

2014 Emma Amelia, b. Jan. 17, 1815; *m.* Van Rensaeller Richmond.
2015 Betsey Ann, b. March 21, 1816; d. Oct. 7, 1831.
2016 Jane Maria, b. Aug. 20, 1817; *m.* Charles McNeil.
2017 William Henry, b. March 11, 1819; *m.*; two children:
2018 Charlotte Rebecca, b. Dec. 9, 1820; *m.* Nelson P. Purdy.
2019 Cornelia S., b. Dec. 20, 1825; d. Aug. 15, 1826.

2016 Jane Maria Denison, (dau. of 2013 Daniel, Jr.,) *m.* Charles McNeil, Sept. 22, 1838. Children :

2020 Frank P., b. May 22, 1841; *m.* Lois Sorate.
2021 William D., b. May 11, 1844; d. Aug. 25, 1864.
2022 Abbie Jane, b. June 8, 1850.

2018 Charlotte Rebecca Denison, (dau. of 2013 Daniel, Jr.,) *m.* Nelson P. Purdy, Nov. 14, 1843. Children :

2023 Henry Denison, b. Aug. 25, 1845; *m.* Mary Withington.
2024 John Nelson, b. April 2, 1851; d. Nov. 1, 1851.
2025 Helen Emma, b. Nov. 5, 1853; d. July 14, 1859.

2017 William Henry Denison, (son of 2013 Daniel, Jr.,) *m.* (wife not known.) Children :

2026 Lorin G.
2027 Lydia ; adopted by her aunt Purdy; *m.* Geo. H. Poole.

2023 Henry Denison Purdy, (son of 2018 Charlotte Rebecca and Nelson P.,) was married, Dec. 22, 1869, to Mary Withington. Children :

    2028 Lee Nelson. b. March 20, 1872.
    2029 Van Rensalaer, b. Jan. 5, 1874.
    2030 Helen Maria, b. Jan. 30, 1877.

1759 John Denison, (William[4], William[3], John[2], George[1],) b. Nov. 5, 1749, was married, Sept. 6, 1772, to Abigail Minor, dau. of Nathaniel and Ann (Denison) Minor. They lived and died in Stonington, " on Rev. Mr. Rossiter's farm," which John Denison bought. He died July 12, 1801 ; his wife d. May 25, 1795. Their children :

    2031 Moses T., b. Sept. 27, 1776; d. Aug. 26, 1779.
    2032 Nathaniel, b. Nov. 29, 1777; d. March 30, 1778.
    2033 Nancy, b. Nov. 18, 1780; m. Jesse Dean.
    2034 Lois, b. March 11, 1783; m. Elisha Williams.
    2035 Edward, b. July 12, 1785; d. June 4, 1789.
    2036 Ethan A., b. July 4, 1787; m. Eliza Williams.
    2037 Hannah P., b. Dec. 17, 1789; m. Moses T. Geer.
    2038 Fanny B., b. Dec. 6, 1791; m. David Smith.
    2039 Abby, b. in 1795; d. young.

2036 Ethan A. Denison, (John[5], William[4], William[3], John[2], George[1],) b. July 4, 1784, was married, March 14, 1809, to Eliza Williams. They lived in Stonington, " on Rev. Mr. Rossiter's farm," inherited from his father ; he d. Oct. 2, 1814. Children :

    2040 Nancy, b. Jan. 24, 1810; m. Nathan S. Noyes.
    2041 Lois W., b. Oct. 4, 1811; m. Joseph Griswold.
    2042 Abby Eliza, b. March 14, 1813; d. July 25, 1821.

2040 Nancy Denison, (Ethan A.[6], John[5], William[4], William[3], John[2], George[1],) b. Jan. 24, 1810, was married, Nov. 23, 1828, to Nathan S. Noyes ; lives in Mystic ; her children are :

    2043 An Unnamed Infant Son, b. and d. Sept., 1829.
    2044 An Unnamed Infant Son, b. and d. Feb. 7, 1831.
    2045 Nathan D., b. Jan. 20, 1832; m. Adelia M. Randall.
    2046 William H., b. March 19, 1834; d. Sept. 5, 1837.
    2047 Elisha E., b. Feb. 7, 1836; d. Sept. 2, 1837.
    2048 An Infant Daughter, b. and d. June, 1838.
    2049 Harriet Eliza, b. Oct. 11, 1839 .
    2050 Ann Louisa, b. March 19, 1842; m. B. F. Williams.
    2051 Fanny Smith, b. May 11, 1844; m. David L. Gallup.
    2052 Henry Clay, b. March 19, 1848; m. Sarah M. Heath.

2041 LOIS W. DENISON, (Ethan A.⁶, John⁵, William⁴, William³, John², George¹,) b. Oct. 4, 1811, was married, Nov. 23, 1828, to Joseph Griswold. He lives in Griswoldville, Mass.; she died in March, 1879. Their children:

    2053 ETHAN D., b. March 11, 1831; m. Sarah D. Wilson.
    2054 JOSEPH W., b. Dec. 26, 1832; died young.
    2055 CHESTER A., b. June 18, 1834; died young.
    2056 MARIA LOUISE, b. Dec. 2, 1836; m. Dr. A. C. Deane.
    2057 EMMA L., b. June 11, 1837; died young.
    2058 WHITING, b. April 17, 1839; died young.
    2059 JOSEPH, b. July 9, 1840; m. Fanny E. Cottrell.
    2060 WAYNE, b. July 2, 1841; died young.
    2061 LORENZO, b. Jan. 5, 1847; m. Lizzie Shaw.
    2062 CHESTER A., b. Feb. 15, 1844; died young.
    2063 WAYNE, b. Oct. 4, 1845.
    2064 MYRA, b. Nov. 20, 1848; m. Wm. W. Ballard.
    2065 HORACE, b. June 19, 1851; d. Nov. 9, 1851.

2034 LOIS DENISON, (John⁵, William⁴, William³, John², George¹,) b. March 11, 1783, was married, March 22, 1807, to Elisha Williams, and died in 1808. She had:

    2066 HANNAH, b. Aug. 22, 1808; d. May 8, 1827.

Elisha Williams married, 2nd, Mrs. Rebecca Mumford, May 5, 1815.

2033 NANCY DENISON, (John⁵, William⁴, William³, John², George¹,) b. Nov. 15, 1780, was married, to Jesse Deane of Stonington, and died Aug. 21, 1807. Her children were:

    2067 NANCY, b. Jan. 2, 1803; m. Ezra Chesebro, Dec. 28, 1828.
    2068 JESSE, b. Oct. 22, 1804.
    2069 FANNY, b. Nov. 23, 1806; m. Elias Gallup, Sept. 28, 1828.

2037 HANNAH P. DENISON, (John⁵, William⁴, William³, John², George¹,) b. Dec. 17, 1789, was married, Feb. 1, 1816, to Moses T. Geer, and d. Feb. 26, 1864. Her children:

    2070 HARRIET A., b. Oct. 28, 1817; m. Ethan Pierce.
    2071 MOSES E., b. Dec. 24, 1819; d. unmarried, Sept. 19, 1843.
    2072 ETHAN D., b. April 13, 1823; d. Aug. 31, 1843.
    2073 NATHANIEL M., b. and d. Aug. 1825.
    2074 HANNAH L., b. July 26, 1826; m. Mark P. Masten.
    2075 JOHN W., b. Dec. 16, 1828.
    2076 FANNY A., b. June 11, 1831; d. Aug. 23, 1831.
    2077 SARAH C., b. Oct. 22, 1832; d. Feb. 14, 1851.

2038 FANNY DENISON, (John⁵, William⁴, William³, John², George¹,) b. Dec. 6, 1791, was married, Feb. 27, 1815, to David

Capt. John Denison's Descendants. 101

Smith. They emigrated to Coleraine, Mass., where she died, Aug. 17, 1847. No child.

1708 AVERY DENISON, (William[3], John[2], George[1],) b. in 1712, was married to Thankful Williams, Jan. 31, 1734. They lived in North Stonington; he d. April 3, 1775; she d. May 3, 1767. Their children:

2078 ELISHA, b. Nov. 3, 1734; *m.* Keturah Minor.
2079 NATHAN, b. Aug. 12, 1736; d. Oct. 3, 1737.
2080 WILLIAM, b. March 22, 1738; *m.* Susanna Swan.
2081 DESIRE, b. June 5, 1739; *m.* Thos. Minor.
2082 MOLLY, b. Nov. 8, 1741; *m.* Jesse Denison.
2083 PRUDENCE, b. Oct. 3, 1743; *m.* Joseph Noyes.
2084 MERCY, b. Nov. 7, 1745; *m.* Edward Eells.
2085 THANKFUL, b. July 17, 1747; *m.* Alexander Stewart.
2086 ZERVIAH, b. July 13, 1751; d. unmarried.
2087 REBECCA, b. March 24, 1754; d. unmarried.
2088 AVERY, b. April 10, 1756; *m.* Prudence Brown, Aug. 17, 1778; no child; he d. Aug. 23, 1800; she d. in 1847, aged 91 years.

1708 AVERY DENISON'S WILL.

I, AVERY DENISON, of [Stonington] in the County of New London, and Colony of Connecticut, being sick and weak in body, but by the blessing of God am sound in my understanding, mind and memory; calling to mind the mortality of my body, and that it is appointed for all men once to die, and considering my present weakness as a symptom of the close of my days, I do make and ordain this my last will and testament.

First, I recommend my soul to God who gave it me, and my body to the dust to be buried in a decent Christian manner, at the direction of my Executor hereafter named; and as to the worldly interest it hath pleased God to bless me with, I give and dispose of it in manner and form as follows:

It is my will that all my just debts and funeral charges should first of all be paid by my executor out of the legacy given him in the will.

I give to my beloved son, Elisha Denison, all the lands that I own, called the Sterry farm: viz., all the lands that I purchased, which formerly belonged to Cyperan Sterry, with all the appurtenances, except about three acres and one half which lies locked in with John James' land; he the said Elisha paying such legacies as are hereafter mentioned for him to pay.

I give to my beloved son, Wm. Denison, who lately moved to the westward of ——— ———— *river, all my homestead farm that I now live on, with all the buildings and appurtenances, to be and remain to him and his heirs and assigns forever, upon conditions, that he, the said William, discharge one certain note of hand he hath against me of about seventy pounds lawful money, and comply with such other directions and provisions as are mentioned in this will relating to him.

I give to my beloved son, Avery Denison, my sorrel horse and the saddle he now uses and bridle; my gold sleeve buttons and one-third part of my wearing apparel, with half a score of sheep, (to be provided and delivered by my executor,) at the age of twenty-one years; I also give to my said son Avery forty pounds lawful money to be paid him by my executor at the age of twenty-two years; also forty pounds lawful money to be paid him by my son Elisha, ten pounds at the age of twenty-one years and thirty pounds at the age of twenty-two years.

I give to my daughter Desire ten shillings lawful money, to be paid her by my executor, which together with what she has had, is the full of her share of my estate.

I give to my daughter, Prudence Noyce, ten shillings, which, with what she has had, is her share of my estate.

I give to my daughter, Mercy Ellis, [Eells,] six silver tea spoons, and five pounds lawful money, to be paid by my said son Elisha, within two years after my decease, which with what she hath already had, is the full of her share of my estate.

I give to my daughter, Thankful Stewart, one gold necklace of the value of forty-eight shillings, and one gold ring of the value of fifteen shillings, to be procured and delivered to her by my executor within two years after my decease, which will complete her portion of my estate.

I give to my two daughters, Zerviah and Rebecca, each one-third part of my household stuff, after the things that are individually given away are taken out; I also give to my two daughters, Zerviah and Rebecca, my side saddle and pillion, my yearling colt and last spring's colt; and to each of them half a score of sheep, to be procured and delivered to them by my executor within three years after my decease; and to each of them four silver table spoons and one gold ring which are now in the house. I also give to my two daughters, Zerviah and Rebecca, together with my granddaughter Mary Denison, the privilege of living in the west part of my house, with firewood during the time they each of them remain unmarried. I also give to my said daugh-

*Name not legible.

ter Zerviah, one brown silk gown that was her mother's. I also give to my said grandaughter, Mary, and her little sister Betsey, who is in the West Indies, one third part of my household stuff, after the things that are individually given away are taken out; three quarters of said third to said Mary, and one quarter to said Betsey; and in case s'd Betsey should never call for her said part, then the same is to belong to said Mary forever. And farther, my will is that my said son William, for two years after my decease, shall furnish to my s'd two daughters, Zerviah and Rebecca, one good riding beast for going to meeting, and other necessary business, and keep the colts given them in this will, if they live; And also provide them with thirty weight of flax and twenty weight of wool, each of said two years, together with the privilege of their summer and winter apples during the time they may live in my said house; and also my s'd son Wm. is to deliver and give or pay to s'd Zerviah, Rebecca, and Mary, ten bushels of corn and three bushels of wheat, every year, during the space of three years after my decease.

And I do farther give to my said son Elisha my great Bible and my spectacles, and one-third part of my wearing apparel.

And I do farther give my s'd son William one-third part of my wearing apparel, and three acres and half of land reserved of my Sterry farm, and all my stock and farming tools, and all other of my estate both real and personal, of every kind, except what is heretofore or hereafter otherwise particularly given away in this will.

I farther give to my s'd son Wm. the age and improvement of my Indian boy Peter, during the time for which he is bound, and that s'd Wm. fulfil the indenture of s'd boy, and that my said son Wm. be guardian to my son Avery through his minority. I give to my said son Avery Denison one case of bottles now in the house; and I give to my grandson, Avery Denison Noyes, my silver shoe and knee buckles; and I do make and ordain my said son Wm. Denison, Executor of this my last will and testament, wholly revoking any will heretofore by me made, and declareing this only to be my last.

In witness whereof I have hereunto set my hand and seal, this third day of January, Anno Domini, 1775. Signed, sealed, published, pronounced, and declared, in presence of

JOSEPH SMITH,
DANIEL SMITH,   AVERY DENISON. [Seal.]
LEMUEL SMITH.

2078 ELISHA DENISON, (Avery[4], William[3], John[2], George[1],) b. Nov. 3, 1734, was married, Feb. 23, 1758, to Keturah Minor, lived in Stonington, Conn., and Ludlow, Vt.; he died May 6, 1809; his wife died March 24, 1813; they had these children, all born in Stonington:

 2089 SIMEON, b. Oct. 22, 1758; d. Dec. 9, 1776, in the revolu. army.
 2090 GRACE, b. Nov. 11, 1760; d. July 16, 1780.
 2091 DESIRE, b. Dec. 7, 1762; *m.* David Blossom.
 2092 EUNICE, b. Jan. 16, 1764; *m.* Arima Smith.
 2093 NATHAN, b. Feb. 3, 1766; twice married.
 2094 THANKFUL, b. Aug. 2, 1767; d. May 8, 1785.
 2095 ELISHA, b. Aug. 28, 1769; *m.* Ruth Robinson.
 2096 HANNAH, b. Sept. 18, 1771; d. Oct. 24, 1775.
 2097 ZERVIAH, b. Oct. 23, 1773; d. July 4, 1780.
 2098 AVERY, b. Dec. 15, 1775; *m.* Eunice Williams.
 2099 ISAAC, b. April 23, 1778; *m.* Electa Newell.
 2100 LOIS, b. Aug. 14, 1780; *m.* J. Spaulding; no child.
 2101 PRUDENCE, b. Oct. 26, 1782; *m.* George Fyler.

2091 DESIRE DENISON, (Elisha[5], Avery[4], William[3], John[2], George[1],) b. Dec. 7, 1762, was married to David Blossom, (being his second wife,) and had these three children:

 2102 MINOR.
 2103 LEVI.
 2104 ALMA M., b. Aug. 30, 1803; *m.* Anthony Rhodes, Dec. 22, 1824; *m.* 2nd, A. B. Cooper; d. Dec. 2, 1871.

2092 EUNICE DENISON, (Elisha[5], Avery[4], William[3], John[2], George[1],) b. Jan. 16, 1764, was married, Feb. 15, 1797, to Arima Smith, who was born Aug. 9, 1766. Their children:

 2105 ELISHA D., b. May 29, 1798.
 2106 ENOCH, b. March 22, 1800.
 2107 SOCRATES, b. Oct. 21, 1801.
 2108 NATHAN J., b. March 8, 1804.
 2109 LOUISA A., b. Sept. 9, 1805.
 2110 SENECA, b. Feb. 19, 1807.

2093 NATHAN DENISON, (Elisha[5], Avery[4], William[3], John[2], George[1],) b. Feb. 3, 1766, was married, first to Nabby Lines, and second to Betsey Frasier, widow of William Stevens; lived at Massena, N. Y.; died in Massena, March, 1827; had one child by the second wife:

 2111 ELISHA M., born March 28, 1807.

2111 ELISHA M. DENISON, (Nathan[6], Elisha[5], Avery[4], William[3], John[2], George[1],) was married to Betsey Ann Ramsey,

Capt. John Denison's Descendants.

Oct. 17, 1827; lived at Massena, N. Y.; had these twelve children :

2112 BETSEY ANN, b. July 21, 1828; *m.* William Stevens.
2113 ISAAC MINOR, b. May 8, 1830; *m.* Augusta Higby.
2114 FRANCIS AVERY, b. April 13, 1832; *m.* Lucretia E. Polley.
2115 JASON, b. May 26, 1834; d. Dec. 28, 1834.
2116 JASON H., b. Feb. 5, 1836; *m.* Amelia A. Hopson.
2117 MARTHA A., b. April 27, 1838; *m.* Alvin Hackett.
2118 NATHAN H., b. April 21, 1840; twice married.
2119 LOUISA A., b. April 27, 1842; *m.* Geo. H. Strader.
2120 ELISHA GILBERT, b. May 18, 1844; *m.* Emma Perkins.
2121 SIMEON, b. Oct. 11, 1846; d. Jan. 6, 1847.
2122 SAMANTHA L., b. Jan. 6, 1848; *m.* James Kinsley.
2123 RILAN H., b. May 15, 1850; *m.* Emma A. Howard.

2112 BETSEY ANN DENISON, (Elisha M.[7], Nathan[6], Elisha[5], Avery[4], William[3], John[2], George[1],) was married, April 6, 1847, to William Stevens, ; lives in Augusta, Wis.; their children :

2124 WILLIAM DON, b. April 28, 1848; d. Aug. 12, 1852.
2125 FRASIER DENISON, b. Oct. 21, 1850.
2126 SUSAN, b. Aug. 25, 1855; d. Oct. 3, 1855.
2127 WILLIAM DON, b. Jan. 5, 1858.
2128 FRANK M., b. July 26, 1861; d. Sept. 14, 1863.
2129 FRANK M., b. Jan. 3, 1864.
2130 ELECTA LOUISA, b. Nov. 30, 1865.

2114 FRANCIS A. DENISON, (Elisha M.[7], Nathan[6], Elisha[5], Avery[4], William[3]; John[2], George[1],) was married, Jan. 1, 1854, to Lucretia E. Polley ; lives in Augusta, Wis. His children :

2130½ GEORGE M., b. Dec. 6, 1854; d. June 6, 1857.
2131 GUY S., b. Jan. 19, 1857; d. Sept. 20, 1862.
2132 IDA M., b. Sept. 14, 1859; d. Oct. 9, 1862.
2133 INEZ M., b. Aug. 2, 1862.
2134 IMOGENE L., b. Nov. 11, 1864.
2135 FRANCES A., b. April 13, 1868.
2136 ELISHA AMOS, b. Feb 20, 1870.
2137 GEORGE H., b. Dec, 6, 1871.
2138 ZENE M., b. Aug. 16, 1873.
2139 GUY AVERY, b. March 1, 1876.
2140 CORA LUCRETIA, b. July 14, 1878.

2116 JASON H. DENISON, (Elisha M.[7], Nathan[6], Elisha[5], Avery[4], William[3], John[2], George[1].) was married, Jan. 1, 1861, to Amelia A. Hopson ; lives in Augusta, Wis. Their children :

2141 BURT M., b. Oct. 29, 1861.
2142 ELLA ELIZA, b. Aug. 19, 1863.
2143 DELLA ANN, b. March 26, 1866.

2144 Lydia A., b. Oct. 31, 1868.
2145 Martin E., b. June 9, 1871.
2146 Mary Louisa, b. Nov. 29, 1873.
2147 Rena, b. Feb. 29, 1876.

2113 Isaac Minor Denison, (Elisha M.[7], Nathan[6], Elisha[5], Avery[4], William[3], John[2], George[1],) was married, July 2, 1852, to Augusta Higby, who died Sept 14, 1872; and, second, July 3, 1876, to Addie H. Gowan; lives at Red Wing, Minnesota. His children:

2148 Allen, b. July 15, 1853.
2149 Addie, b. Dec. 15. 1857.

2119 Louisa Ann Denison, (Elisha M.[7], Nathan[6], Elisha[5], Avery[4], William[3]; John[2], George[1],) was married, Feb. 6, 1867, to George H. Strader. Children:

2150 Fred Elisha, b. April 24, 1868.
2151 Lee Denison, b. Nov. 3, 1869.
2152 Georgia Louisa, b. June 26. 1874.
2153 Mabel Grace, b. March 16, 1878.

2120 Elisha Gilbert Denison, (Elisha M.[7], Nathan[6], Elisha[5], Avery[4], William[3], John[2], George[1],) was married, Feb. 11, 1874, to Emma Perkins. They have:

2154 Elisha Adelbert, b. March 26, 1878.

2117 Martha A. Denison, (Elisha M.[7], Nathan[6], Elisha[5], Avery[4], William[3], John[2], George[1],) was married, July 1, 1860, to Alvin Hackett. Their children:

2155 Elisha I., b. June 16, 1865.
2156 Luman A., July 12, 1878.

2118 Nathan H. Denison, (Elisha M.[7], Nathan[6], Elisha[5], Avery[4], William[3], John[2], George[1], b. April 21, 1840, was married, Feb. 21, 1865, to Rowena M. Hopson. Their children:

2157 Nellie, b. May 12, 1867.
2158 Nathan F., b. June 17, 1876.

Mrs. Rowena Denison died July 19, 1876; and, Nov. 7, 1877, Nathan H. Denison was married to Lottie Forsyth.

2122 Samantha L. Denison, (Elisha M.[7], Nathan[6], Elisha[5], Avery[4], William[3], John[2], George[1],) was married, Oct. 30, 1871, to James Kinsley. Their children:

2159 William Clinton, b. Aug. 8, 1872.
2160 Another Child, b. Dec. 15, 1878.

2123 Rilan H. Denison, (Elisha M.[7], Nathan[6], Elisha[5], Avery[4], William[3], John[2], George[1],) b. May 15, 1850, was married, Feb. 3, 1872, to Emma A. Howard. Children:

    2161 Byron R., b. Oct. 30, 1872.
    2162 Delia L., b. Oct. 25, 1875.

2095 Elisha Denison, (Elisha[5], Avery[4], William[3], John[2], George[1],) b. Aug. 28, 1769, was married, Feb. 11, 1798, to Ruth Robinson of Massena, N. Y., who was born, May 13, 1769. They lived in Massena; he died there, August, 1857. Their children:

    2163 Cyrus R., b. Jan. 7, 1799; d. Oct. 10, 1803.
    2164 Louisa A., b. May 17, 1809; d. July 21, 1804.
    2165 Cassius A., b. June 21, 1802; d. Oct. 7, 1803.
    2166 Louisa A., b. Aug. 31, 1806; m. Luke Boynton.
    2167 Mary Ann, b. July 10, 1808; m. Dr. E. Whitney.

2166 Louisa A. Denison, (Elisha[6], Elisha[5], Avery[4], William[3], John[2], George[1],) was married, March 17, 1825, to Luke Boynton. He was born, Oct. 10, 1798, and died March 15, 1862; she died, Aug. 7, 1877. Their children:

    2168 Lydia Louisa, b. March 19, 1826; m. J. D. Bridges.
    2169 Mary Ann, b. Sept. 1, 1829; m. A. Wheeler.
    2170 Cyrus A., b. June 9, 1831; m. Amarilla Barnhart.
    2171 Elisha, b. Aug. 20, 1837; d. Sept. 29, 1837.

2167 Mary Ann Denison, (Elisha[6], Elisha[5], Avery[4], William[3], John[2], George[1],) was married, Dec. 21, 1834, to Dr. Ephraim Whitney, of Massena. Their children:

    2172 Ephraim, b. Oct. 31, 1835; a widower with one child.
    2173 Josephine A., b. March 14, 1838; is insane.
    2174 Mary Louisa. b. Oct. 14, 1839; m. Jerome Nightingale.
    2175 Jane Elizabeth, b. Oct. 13, 1844; m. Thomas Kenney.

2098 Avery Denison, (Elisha[5], Avery[4], William[3], John[2], George[1],) b. Dec. 15, 1775, m. in September, 1800, Eunice Williams, who was born Jan. 3, 1777; settled in Shipton, Canada East; died their June 18, 1826; she died, Sept. 19, 1856. Their children:

    2176 Simeon Minor, b. April 2, 1801; m. Mary Moore.
    2177 John Williams, b. May 1, 1807; m. Mary Jane Munroe.
    2178 Malvina C., b. March 28, 1810; m. Sereno W. Graves.
    2179 Eunice Maria, b. Sept. 6, 1813; d. in 1846, unmarried.

2176 Simeon Minor Denison, (Avery[6], Elisha[5], Avery[4], William[3], John[2], George[1],) b. April 2, 1801, was married,

May 18, 1834, to Mary Moore; lived in Shipton, Canada East. His children :

2180 WILLIAM AVERY, b. Oct. 19, 1835; *m.* Eleanor Leet.
2181 ISAAC WILLIAMS, b. June 11, 1837; unmarried in 1878.
2182 JOSEPH ROOT, b. May 27, 1839; *m.* Amelia Rossetta Hunton.

2180 WILLIAM AVERY DENISON, (son of 2176 Simeon Minor,) was married, Jan. 5, 1859, to Eleanor Leet, of Shipton, C. E.; lives in Shipton. His children :

2183 CORA LOUISA, b. July 3, 1860.
2184 ADNEY NORMAN, b. June 13. 1862.
2185 LILLIA MAY, b. Dec. 11, 1864.
2186 SIMEON MINOR, b. Sept. 11, 1866.
2187 MARY INEZ, b. June 8, 1869.
2188 ARTHUR ELWYN, b. Sept. 9, 1877.

2182 JOSEPH ROOT DENISON, (son of 2176 Simeon Minor,) was married, Feb. 5, 1866, to Amelia Rosetta Hunton, who died, March 26, 1870. He lives at Denison's Mills, near Shipton, C. E. His children :

2189 WILLIAM SIMEON, b. June 4, 1866.
2190 CORILLA EMMA AMELIA, b. March 22, 1870; d. June 16, 1870.

2177 JOHN WILLIAMS DENISON, (Avery[6], Elisha[5], Avery[4], William[3], John[2], George[1],) was married, July 8, 1844, to Mary Jane Munroe; lived in Shipton, C. E.; d. Dec. 3, 1872; had these five daughters :

2191 HELEN MARIA, b. June 13, 1845; unmarried in 1878.
2192 MALVINA CAROLINE, b. March 29, 1847; *m.* John Smith.
2193 MARY ANNE, b. June 3, 1849; unmarried in 1878.
2194 EUNICE LOUISA, b. April 12, 1852; d. Jan. 22, 1858.
2195 ELIZABETH AUGUSTA, b. Oct. 31, 1856; unmarried in 1878.

2192 MALVINA CAROLINE DENISON, (dau. of 2177 John Williams,) b. March 28, 1847, was married, Nov. 2, 1869, to John Smith. Their children :

2196 EUNICE MINA, b. Dec. 3, 1870.
2197 ANNIE ELLENA, b. June 30, 1872.
2198 JOHN DENISON, b. Nov. 7, 1875.

2178 MALVINA C. DENISON, (Avery[6], Elisha[5], Avery[4], William[3], John[2], George[1],) b. March 28, 1810, was married, March 20, 1843, to Sereno W. Graves, and died Dec. 26, 1845. Her child :

2198½ AVERY DENISON, b. Nov. 28, 1844; d. Nov. 22, 1864.

2099 Isaac Denison, (Elisha[5], Avery[4], William[3], John[2], George[1],) b. in Stonington, Conn., was married, Oct. 21, 1793, in Tinemouth, Vt., to Electa Newell who was born in Farmington, Conn., Sept. 10, 1780. He died in Norway, Me., Jan. 9, 1837. Their children :

 2199 Nancy Curtis, b. Sept. 25, 1799; m. Titus O. Brown.
 2200 Almira, b. Jan. 14, 1802; m. Silas Gilkey.
 2201 Lucius, b. July 27, 1803; twice married.
 2202 Maria, b. Oct. 13, 1806; d. May 31, 1813.
 2203 Rev. Nathan, b. April 2, 1809; m. Sila Stoddard.
 2204 Rebecca N., b. May 5, 1811; m. Alonzo Bemis.
 2205 Minerva C., b. June 13, 1813; m. Edwin Fisher.
 2206 Adna C., b. Nov. 15, 1815; m. Hannah True.
 2207 Oscar Alanson, b. Dec. 13, 1817; thrice married.
 2208 Isaac Avery, b. June 18, 1820; m. Lauristine S. Bemis.
 2209 Rosalie S., b. Aug. 12, 1823; m. Harley M. Hall, Feb. 26, 1846; lives in Burke, Vt.; no child.

2199 Nancy Curtis Denison, (Isaac[6], Elisha[5], Avery[4], William[3], John[2], George[1],) was married, Nov. 13, 1827, to Titus O. Brown; he died April 2, 1878; she died in Norway, Me., Sept. 6, 1861. Their children :

 2210 Persis Sophia, b. Oct. 11, 1829; m. Sewall W. Danforth.
 2211 Nancy A., b. Jan. 5, 1831; d. March 18, 1831.
 2212 Rosalie D., b. Nov. 19, 1832; m. —— Kimball.
 2213 Eliza Jane, b. Aug. 31, 1834; d. July 20, 1837.
 2214 Charles Denison, b. Feb. 16, 1836.
 2215 Electa A., b. April 4, 1839.
 2216 Annie M., b. July 12, 1844; m. Charles B. Noble.
 2217 Ellen F., b. March 22, 1846.

2200 Almira Denison, (Isaac[6], Elisha[5], Avery[4], William[3], John[2], George[1],) was married April 14, 1822, to Silas Gilkey, who was born March 24, 1792. He died in Burke, Vt., April 7, 1847; she died in Milo, Michigan. Their children:

 2218 Saderna E., b. April 21, 1823; m. David Marcut.
 2219 Isaac Denison, b. Feb. 24, 1825.
 2220 Sullivan Newell, b. April 18, 1826.
 2221 Rosalie E. b. April 20, 1830.
 2222 Marietta S., b. Feb. 26, 1833; m. Dr. Hawley.
 2223 Lois Maria, b. Oct. 11, 1835.
 2224 Rebecca M., b. Aug. 24, 1841.
 2225 Malvina A., b. Oct. 1, 1846.

2201 Lucius Denison, (Isaac[6], Elisha[5], Avery[4], William[3], John[2], George[1],) b. July 27, 1803, was married, first, Nov. 24, 1827, to Catherine Bemis, who was born October, 1805, and died Dec. 5, 1841; and second, Nov. 21, 1842, to Adaline C. Hobart. He lives in Norway, Me., and has had these twelve children:

 2226 CAROLINE N., b. Sept. 5, 1828.
 2227 ELIAS BEMIS, b. Feb. 6, 1831.
 2228 WILLIAM B., b. April 20, 1833.
 2229 KATE S., b. Oct. 7, 1843; d. March 12, 1875.
 2230 ELLEN J., b. Feb. 7, 1845.
 2231 ARTHUR E., b. Dec. 5, 1847.
 2232 ALICE, b. Nov. 8, 1849.
 2233 ADALINE M., b. June 27, 1853.
 2234 EMMA M., b. Nov. 21, 1856.
 2235 LUCIUS H., b. July 7, 1858.
 2236 HERBERT R., b. June 5, 1863.
 2237 NATHAN N., b. May 1, 1865.

2226 CAROLINE N. DENISON, (dau. of 2201 Lucius,) *m.* G. W. Higgins, Jan. 1, 1853, and has:

 2238 WILLIAM D., b. June 15, 1854.
 2239 HELEN A., b. Aug. 8, 1856.
 2240 GEORGE, b. Jan. 12, 1858; d. Nov. 1, 1858.
 2241 LUCY A., b. Aug. 9, 1860.
 2242 EDWARD, b. April 4, 1864.

2227 ELIAS B. DENISON, (son of 2201 Lucius,) was married, May 3, 1871, to Mary S. Thaxter. Their children:

 2243 EDWARD E., b. March 9, 1872.
 2244 WINIFRED T., b. June 30, 1873.
 2245 ROBERT L., b. May 28. 1875.

2228 WILLIAM B. DENISON, (son of 2201 Lucius,) was married, Feb. 23, 1862, to Elvira P. Kendall. Their children:

 2246 WILLIAM KENDALL, b. May 17, 1869.
 2247 GRACE M., b. Dec. 12, 1872.

2229 KATE S. DENISON, (dau. of 2201 Lucius,) was married, Oct 10, 1866, to C. S. Tucker, and died March 14, 1875. Her children:

 2248 KATE, b. Dec. 7, 1869; d. July 2, 1876.
 2249 CARRIE, b. Sept. 1, 1871.
 2250 AGNES, b. March 8, 1875.

2230 ELLEN J. DENISON, (dau. of 2201 Lucius,) was married, May 18, 1865, to Amos L. Millet, and has:

 2251 HELEN, b. Dec. 11, 1871.

2232 ALICE DENISON, (dau. of 2201 Lucius,) was married Jan. 2, 1870, to H. Cole, and has:

2252 EDWARD, b. Aug. 19, 1871.
2253 HERBERT D., b. Aug. 20, 1873.
2254 ANNA, b. July 12, 1875.

2203 REV. NATHAN DENISON, (Isaac[6], Elisha[5], Avery[4], William[3], John[2], George[1],) b. April 2, 1809, was married April 12, 1830, to Sila Stoddard, who was born Jan. 5, 1807; was a Baptist preacher. He died at Mendota, Ill., Nov. 30, 1854. His children:

2255 ADALINE N., b. Aug. 17, 1831; m. Whipple Warner.
2256 OSCAR ISAAC, b. July 6, 1833; m. Maggie G. Blair.
2257 ELIZA ANN, b. June 17, 1835; m. Clark Lamb.
2258 JEPTHA SPAULDING, b. June 4, 1837; d. May 17, 1838.
2259 JEPTHAH CURTIS, b. March 3, 1839; m. Sarah A. Evans.
2260 NATHAN LINCOLN, b. June 11, 1841; unmarried.
2261 HENRY HOVEY, b. May 22, 1844; m. Jennie M. Burdick.
2262 GEORGE STODDARD NORCROSS, b. May 1, 1846; m. Hattie Carpenter.
2263 MARY MARIE, b. Sept. 21, 1849; m. Frank E. Towsley.
2264 FRANK HERBERT, b. Aug. 17, 1852; m. Ella Maud Saunders.

2255 ADALINE N. DENISON, (dau. of 2203 Rev. Nathan,) was married, March 25, 1864, to Whipple Warner, of Hardwick, Vt., and died April 3, 1871. Her children:

2265 HATTIE MAY, b. Jan. 16, 1866.
2266 NATHAN, b. Aug. 9, 1867.
2267 FRANKIE D., b. June 9, 1869.

2256 OSCAR ISAAC DENISON, (son of 2203 Rev. Nathan,) was married, Sept. 7, 1856, to Maggie G. Blair, of Hardwick, Vt.; lives at Oakland, Cal. His children:

2268 ADNA A., b. June 7, 1861.
2269 ALBERT NATHAN, b. March 25, 1864.
2270 WILLIAM BLAIR, b. July 25, 1865.
2271 LELAND WALTER, b. June 20, 1869.
2272 LINCOLN LAIRD, b. January 4, 1871.
2273 GEORGE HAIGH, b. July 2, 1875.

2257 ELIZA ANN DENISON, (dau. of 2203 Rev. Nathan,) was married, Sept. 2, 1856, to Clark Lamb, of Hardwick, Vt.; they live at Red Oak, Iowa. Their children:

2274 ADA EDNA, b. May 22, 1858.
2275 WILLIS HILL, b. Aug. 14, 1860; d. Jan. 4, 1861.
2276 HENRY DENISON, b. July 17, 1864.
2277 LIDA MAY, b. Jan. 1, 1866.
2278 ALICE ANGIER, b. Sept. 28, 1867.

2259 JEPTHAH CURTIS DENISON, (son of 2203 Rev. Nathan,) was married, Oct. 18, 1865, to Sarah A. Evans, who was born in Binghampton, N. Y., March 23, 1838; lives in Chicago. They have:

 2272 GEORGE W., b. July 10, 1867.
 2280 LEO EVANS, b. March 3, 1873; d. June 8, 1875.
 2281 MABEL ELIZABETH, b. Jan. 1, 1877.

2261 HENRY HOVEY DENISON, (son of 2203 Rev. Nathan,) was married Nov. 26, 1869, to Jennie M. Burdick. Their children:

 2282 LIZZIE MAY, b. May 30, 1871.
 2283 ELLA, b. Aug. 30, 1872; d. Sept. 7, 1874.
 2284 HARRY H., b. Feb. 19, 1876.

2263 MARY MARIA DENISON, (dau. of 2203 Rev. Nathan,) was married, Jan. 1, 1871, to Frank Erwin Tousley. Their children:

 2285 ERWIN GRAHAM, b. Feb. 23, 1873.
 2286 EDWIN DENISON, b. Jan. 1, 1875; d. Feb. 12, 1876.

2264 FRANKLIN HERBERT DENISON, (son of 2203 Rev. Nathan,) was married, Jan. 2, 1875, to Ella Maud Saunders. Their children:

 2287 EDNA A., b. Oct. 22, 1875.
 2288 HERBERT I., b. Feb. 18, 1878.

2262 GEORGE STODDARD NORCROSS DENISON, (son of 2203 Rev. Nathan,) was married, in Mendota, Illinois, Sept. 30, 1873, to Hattie G. Carpenter, who was born August, 1852. Their children:

 2289 MARY GERTRUDE, b. Jan. 3, 1876.
 2290 MARGUERITE EDITH, b. May 30, 1877.

2205 MINERVA C. DENISON, (Isaac[6], Elisha[5], Avery[4], William[3], John[2], George[1],) b. June 13, 1813, was married, Feb. 18, 1834, to Edwin Fisher, who was born March 4, 1809. They live in Parkersburg, Iowa. Their children:

 2291 AMANDA MALVINA, b. Nov. 27, 1834; m. Abner Howland.
 2292 CURTIS, b. Feb. 25, 1836; d. Aug. 20, 1856.
 2293 ELECTA DENISON, b. June 6, 1837; d. Aug. 12, 1854.
 2294 ROSETTA TYLER, b. May 25, 1839.
 2295 LUCIA MATILDA, b. Aug. 8, 1841.
 2296 LUCIUS DENISON, b. Jan. 29, 1843.
 2297 ADALINE C., b. May 4, 1846; m. Dr. C. S. Cahoon.
 2298 EMILY EVANS, b. Feb. 13, 1855.

Capt. John Denison's Descendants.

2206 ADNA C. DENISON, (Isaac[6], Elisha[5], Avery[4], William[3], John[2], George[1],) b. Nov. 15, 1815, was married Sept. 13, 1838, to Hannah True, who was born May 22, 1818 ; lives at Mechanics Falls, Me.; is a paper maker ; has only two children :

    2299 ADNA TRUE, b. Sept. 1, 1839.
    2300 FRANCES MARY, b. Jan. 15, 1847; m. Calvin Cram.

2204 REBECCA N. DENISON, (Isaac[6], Elisha[5], Avery[4], William[3], John[2], George[1],) b. May 5, 1811, was married, Aug. 12, 1832, to Alonzo Bemis, who was born in Lyndon, Vt., Feb. 26, 1809. They live in Brighton, Vt. Their children :

    2301 ADNA DENISON, b. May 21, 1834; m. Ellen Young.
    2302 ANNIE S., b. Aug. 31, 1836; m. J. L. Tuttle of Winsted, Ct.
    2303 ISAAC DENISON, b. Sept. 13. 1841; m. Kate Cushing.
    2304 LAURA A., b. June 3, 1845; m. Freedom Cobleigh.
    2305 ELIAS A., b. Feb. 25, 1848; m. Diana and Mary Cobleigh.

2207 OSCAR ALANSON DENISON, (Isaac[6], Elisha[5], Avery[4], William[3], John[2], George[1],) b. Dec. 13, 1817, was married, first, Sept. 26, 1837, to Mary K. Evans, who was born Jan. 15, 1815, and died June 30, 1839 ; second, Dec. 17, 1844, to Adaline Stoddard, who died May 15, 1850 ; third, Sept. 1, 1850, to Lydia Putney, who was born Feb. 4, 1817. He lives in Burke, Vt.; has two children :

    2306 AVERY ELISHA, b. Sept. 1, 1838.
    2307 ADELBERT STODDARD, b. March 3, 1846.

2306 AVERY ELISHA DENISON, (son of 2207 Oscar Alanson,) was married, first, May, 1864, to Diantha Godding, who was born March 18, 1838, and died Oct. 15, 1869 ; second, Jan. 1, 1871, to Cynthia Wells. Two children :

    2308 MARY H., b. May 17, 1869.
    2309 HATTIE L., b. Sept. 18, 1872.

2307 ADELBERT S. DENISON, (son of 2207 Oscar Alanson,) was married Dec, 1869, to Estelle Mattocks, who was born Nov., 1851. They have :

    2310 EVA M., b. April 23, 1872.

2208 ISAAC AVERY DENISON, (Isaac[6], Elisha[5], Avery[4], William[3], John[2], George[1],) b. June 18, 1820, was married, April 23, 1844, to Laurestine S. Bemis ; lives at Mechanics Falls, Me.; they have :

    2311 HULDA ELECTA, b. Jan. 22, 1845.

2312 ROSALIE H., b. May 24, 1846; d. Sept. 8, 1852.
2313 JULIA LAURESTINE, b. Dec. 23, 1849; d. Jan. 12, 1868.
2314 CLARA REBECCA, b. July 14, 1854.
2315 KATIE LOUISE, b. March 23, 1859.

2311 HULDA ELECTA DENISON, (dau. of 2208 Isaac Avery,) was married to Rev. Webster Woodbury. They have:

2316 HAROLD DENISON, b. Sept. 9, 1869.
2317 CLARENCE HALE, b. Feb. 13, 1873.

2083 PRUDENCE DENISON, (Elisha[5], Avery[4], William[3], John[2], George[1],) b. Oct. 28, 1782, was married, June 13, 1808, to George Fyler, who was born in Torrington, Conn., Feb. 10, 1782. They lived in Burke, Vt. He died May 17, 1869; she died April 13, 1858. Their children:

2318 GEORGE DENISON, b. Feb. 5, 1810.
2319 ELHANAN W., b. July 17, 1811.
2320 ADALINE ROXANNA, b. Nov. 26, 1812.
9321 LOIS MARIA, b. Oct. 6, 1814.
9322 MARY CATHERINE, b. June 28, 1816.
2323 OCTAVIA D., b. Feb. 10, 1818.
2324 AURORA ROSALIE, b June 18, 1821; d. April 4, 1823.
2325 ALFRED REUBEN, b. March 23, 1823; d. April 2, 1855.
2326 STEPHEN M., b. Sept. 17, 1827; d. May 29, 1840.
2327 AZRO ASHLEY, b. Feb. 19, 1829; d. Feb. 19, 1829.

2080 WILLIAM DENISON, (Avery[4], William[3], John[2], George[1],) b. March 22, 1738, was married, Feb. 25, 1762, to Susanna Swan. They lived in North Stonington, Conn., until about the year 1788, when they emigrated to Strafford, Vt., where he seems to have been a man of mark. He died there, June 3, 1799; his wife died in 1809. Their children:

2328 LYMAN, b. Dec. 24. 1762; d. on the Jersey Prison Ship.
2329 MARY, b. May 19, 1764; m. Philip Caverly.
2330 ABIGAIL, b. Nov. 4, 1766; m. Rev. Abisha Colton.
2331 THANKFUL, b. May 28, 1769; m. Daniel Colton; no child.
2332 MERCY, b. Oct. 12, 1771; d. in 1773.
2333 REBECCA, b. Jan. 27, 1774; twice married.
2334 BETSEY, b. May, 1776; m. Thomas Hurlburt, Aug. 7, 1794.
2335 ASA S., b. Nov. 1778; m. Betsey Smith.
2336 LUCY, b. April 12, 1781; m. Edmund McIntyre.
2337 WILLIAM A., b. 1783; m. Sally Brown, Oct. 30, 1811; lived at Conneaut, Ohio, and died there.
2338 ASAHEL C., b. 1786; m. Bathsheba Blake.

2329 MARY DENISON, (William[5], Avery[4], William[3], John[2], George[1],) b. May 19, 1764, was married in August, 1781, to

Capt. John Denison's Descendants. 115

Philip Caverly of New London, Conn. They lived in Waterford, Conn., and died there. Their children:

2339 MARY, b. Sept. 1782; d. in infancy.
2340 PHILIP, b. Dec., 1783; d. Feb. 11, 1818.
2341 MARY, b. Jan., 1789; d. May 6, 1858.
2342 WILLIAM D., b. June, 1791; d. Nov. 19, 1818.
2343 ALFRED, b. Dec. 1793; d. in 1876.
2344 LYMAN, b. July 15, 1796; d. Dec. 1, 1864.
2345 JOHN, b. June 24, 1799; d. March 4, 1845.
2346 HIRAM, b. July, 1801; d. July 29, 1851.
2347 JOSEPH D., b. Oct., 1803; d. O:t. 5, 1871.

2330 ABIGAIL DENISON, (William[5], Avery[4], William[3], John[2], George[1],) b. Nov. 4, 1766, was married to Rev. Abisha Colton, pastor of a Congregational Church in Sandgate, Vt. Their children:

2348 ALONZO.
2349 CALVIN.
2350 RUFUS.

2333 REBECCA DENISON, (William[5], Avery[4], William[3], John[2], George[1],) b. Jan 27, 1774, was married, first, to Elijah Hurlburt; and second, in May, 1804, to Isaac Fellows, of Hanover, N. H. She died in Hanover, Dec. 14, 1818. Her children:

2351 ASA DENISON, b. Dec., 1797.
2352 JERUSHA, b. Dec., 1799.
2353 WILLIAM D., b. March, 1802.
2354 LYMAN, b. May 10, 1805; d. July 5, 1878.
2355 REBECCA, b. Nov. 14, 1806; d. May 17, 1843.
2355½ ELIJAH, b. April 1, 1809; d. March 6, 1826.
2356 FANNY, b. March 15, 1812; m.
2357 MARY C., b. May 12, 1814; d. July 30, 1815.
2358 ALVAN, b. June 28, 1817.

2335 ASA S. DENISON, (William[5], Avery[4], William[3], John[2], George[1],) b. in 1778, was married in 1800, to Betsey Smith; lived in Strafford, Vt.; and also in Willsboro', Essex Co., N. Y., where he died Dec. 12, 1842. Children:

2359 SOPHIA, b. 1802; twice married; d. Aug., 1868.
2360 DUDLEY C., b. Jan. 5, 1805; m. Laura H. Thompson; d. June 14, 1868.
2361 STRATTON, b. Dec. 1806; m. Wealthy Robinson, April 3, 1835.
2362 ELIZA, b. Dec. 6, 1808; m. Aaron Hoyt.
2363 THIRZA, b. 1811; m. James Lougee.
2364 AMANDA, b. 1813; m. Robert Rogers, Feb., 1830; d. May 11, '51.

2360 DUDLEY C. DENISON, (Asa S.[6], William[5], Avery[4], William[3], John[2], George[1],) b. Jan. 5, 1805, was married, Oct. 12, 1834, to Laura H. Thompson; he d. June 14, 1868. Children:

 2365 HARRIET B., b. Dec. 28, 1839.
 2366 NATHAN W., b. Oct. 7, 1841. On his twenty-first birth day, Oct. 7, 1862, he enlisted in the 92nd Regt. of N. Y. Volunteers; and *m.* Irene B. Yerrington, of Potsdam, N. Y., Oct. 20, 1862. He served in the war, with this regiment, three years, and was honorably discharged at Fredericksburg, Va., Oct. 20, 1865. He lives at Strafford, Vt.; no child.

2363 THIRZA DENISON, (Asa S.[6], William[5], Avery[4], William[3], John[2], George[1],) b. Jan. 1811, was married to James Lougee, of Lawrence, Mass. Children:

 2367 ANNETTE, b. Feb. 29, 1837; d. Dec. 7, 1854.
 2368 JAMES HENRY, b. Jan. 4, 1839; an untraced wanderer.
 2369 ADELAIDE, b. Aug. 16, 1843; *m.* Geo. I. Sargent.

2336 LUCY DENISON, (William[5], Avery[4], William[3], John[2], George[1],) was married in 1810, to Edmund McIntyre. He died, June 2, 1846, aged 68 years and 6 mos. She died Jan. 26, 1862. They lived in Strafford, Vt. Their children:

 2370 LUCIA, b. July 9, 1801; d. Dec. 12, 1835.
 2371 WILLIAM D., b. Dec. 3, 1802; *m.* Mary Carpenter.
 2372 WEALTHY M., b. Sept. 25, 1804; d. July 23, 1853.
 2373 POLLY C., b. Sept. 5, 1806; d. March 5, 1838.
 2374 SALLY, b. June 25, 1808; d. July 20, 1865.
 2375 HIRAM C., b. May 1, 1810; d. Nov. 11, 1876.
 2376 MATILDA, b. Nov. 16, 1813.
 2377 EDMUND G., b. April 12, 1815.
 2378 LUCY, b. Sept. 9, 1820; d. Oct. 14, 1841.

2334 BETSEY DENISON, (William[5], Avery[4], William[3], John[2], George[1],) b. in 1776, was married, August 7, 1794, to Thomas Hurlburt, b. in 1775, and d. in 1837; she d. Jan. 28, 1828. Their children:

 2379 THANKFUL, b. Aug. 13, 1795; d. May 2, 1799.
 2380 POLLY, b. Dec. 15, 1796; *m.* Sheldon Tenney.
 2381 SUKEY, b. April 11, 1798; *m.* Moody Howes.
 2382 THOMAS S., b. Feb. 7, 1800; *m.* Elizabeth Brown.
 2383 BETSEY, b. Nov. 19, 1801; d. Sept. 16, 1804.
 2384 LUCY, b. March 15, 1803; *m.* Wm. Flagg Moore.
 2385 ASAHEL, b. Aug. 11, 1804; *m.* Samantha Carpenter.
 2386 CORDELIA, b. May 8, 1806; *m.* Isaac P. Jenks.
 2387 OZRO, b. Jan. 8, 1808; d. April 28, 1870.
 2388 WILLIAM D., b. Oct. 21, 1809; d. April 16, 1877.

Capt. John Denison's Descendants. 117

2389 BETSEY ANN, b. Feb. 13, 1811; m. Willard Moore.
2390 DON PEDRO, b. March 22, 1813; d. in 1833.
2391 AMANDA, b. April 26, 1817; d. in 1833.

2382 THOMAS STEWART HURLBURT, (son of 2334 Betsey Denison and Thomas Hurlburt,) b. Feb. 7, 1800, m. Elizabeth Brown, dau. of Hiram and Mercy (Walcott) Brown, of Surrey, N. H., March 21, 1822. Seven children :

2392 ISABELLA AMANDA, b. Oct. 20, 1823; twice married.
2393 GEORGE DENISON, b. May 10, 1825; d. March 2, 1857.
2394 THOMAS NEWTON, b. March 21, 1828; m. Hannah Maria Maynard; d. Dec. 13, 1860.
2394½ DELIA, b. March 18, 1827; d. May 14, 1827.
2395 WILLIAM MOORE, b. Sept. 20, 1830; m. Helen M. Fifield.
2396 DELIA ELIZABETH, b. Jan. 14, 1833; m. Daniel Seagrave.
2397 BETSEY DENISON, b. Oct. 5, 1835; m. Edward Denney.

2338 ASAHEL C. DENISON, (William[5], Avery[4], William[3], John[2], George[1],) b. in 1786, was married, Jan. 22, 1811, to Bathsheba Blake ; lived in Vermont ; died in 1836 ; his wife d. Sept. 5, 1845, aged 55. Their children :

2398 ALPHA MARIA, b. in Nov., 1811; d. in 1815.
2399 ALMOND, b. in 1813; deaf and dumb; m. a deaf mute.
2400 ELIJAH B., b. June 6, 1816; m. Lydia W. Ramsdell ; 10 ch.
2401 SAMUEL A., b. Sept. 14, 1818; m. Phebe Hood.
2402 ALPHA MARIA, b. 1820; deaf and dumb; d. March 5, 1842.
2403 GRATIA, b. 1823; deaf and dumb.
2404 LYMAN, b. July 30, 1826; m. Harriet Lewis.
2405 HARRIET, b. Nov. 21. 1830; m. John Bolton.

2399 ALMOND DENISON, (Asahel C.[6], William[5], Avery[4], William[4], John[2], George[1],) b. in 1813, was a deaf mute ; he married Mercy Deniston, also a deaf mute ; their children were not deaf mutes. He lived in California, and died there in 1851. His children :

2406 JOHN CLARK.
2407 FRANCELIA.
2408 ALMOND C.

2404 LYMAN DENISON, (Asahel C.[6], William[5], Avery[4], William[3], John[2], George[1],) b. July 30, 1826, was married to Harriet L. Lewis, of Washington, N. H., April 15, 1855. Their children :

2409 CARRIE, b. Oct. 10, 1856; m. Frank Underhill in 1876.
2410 WALTER, b. March 29, 1858.
2411 EDWIN, b. March 5, 1864.

2600 ELIJAH B. DENISON, (Asahel C.[6], William[5], William[3], John[2], George[1],) b. June 6, 1816, was married to Lydia W. Ramsdell, Dec. 2, 1838. Lives in Vermont. Children:

    2412 HENRY M. b. Dec. 27, 1839; d. April 5, 1844.
    2413 CHARLES H., b. July 21, 1844; d. Feb. 16, 1846.
    2414 EMILIE H., b. March 3, 1848; m. Curtis O. Slack.
    2415 LYMAN, b. Dec. 30, 1850; m. Hattie Yaratau.
    2416 JOHN R., b. May 31, 1852; m. Myra Downing.
    2417 ASAHEL, b. Dec. 9, 1853; d. Feb. 16, 1856.
    2418 ELLA, b. July 8, 1861; d. Jan. 9, 1862.
    2419 ADAH, b. Sept. 21, 1863.
    2420 MYRA, b. Feb. 22, 1867.
    2421 ARTHUR, b. Sept. 18, 1870.

2401 SAMUEL A. DENISON, (Asahel C.[6], William[5], Avery[4], William[3], John[2], George[1],) b. Sept. 14, 1818, was married, Jan. 1, 1842, to Phebe Hood. Lives in Vermont. One child.

    2422 ALBERT H., b. Aug. 5, 1847; m. Delia Bickford.

2405 HARRIET DENISON, (Asahel C.[6], William[5], Avery[4], William[3], John[2], George[1],) b. Nov. 21, 1830, was married, Feb. 8, 1854, to John Bolton, of Danville, Vt. Children:

    2423 CARRIE H., b. Feb. 24, 1855; m. Francis H. Goodale, of Cabot, Vt., March 5, 1877.
    2424 ABBIE W., b. Dec. 21, 1857.
    2425 JOHN W., b. Jan. 16, 1860.
    2426 AARON W., b. Nov. 12, 1869.
    2427 MABEL H., b. May 12, 1874; d. Feb. 7, 1877.

2081 DESIRE DENISON, (Avery[4], William[3], John[2], George[1],) b. June 5, 1739, was married, Feb. 10, 1757, to Thomas Minor, of Stonington, Conn. Children:

    2441 WILLIAM, b. Feb. 24, 1759.
    2442 THANKFUL, b. May 1, 1761.
    2443 ISAAC, b. June 17, 1764.
    2444 THOMAS, b. March 20, 1767; d. March 31, 1767.
    2445 DESIRE, b. Aug. 10, 1768.
    2446 THOMAS, b. Sept. 12, 1771.

2082 MOLLY or MARY DENISON, (Avery[4], William[3], John[2], George[1]) b. Nov. 8, 1741, was married to Jesse Denison, Jan. 24, 1759. They lived in the island of St. Eustatia, where he died after having two children, named Mary and Betsey. She m., 2nd, a Dr. Boscawen, and died in Jamaica. See record of Jesse Denison, son of John, and great grandson of George Denison of Westerly, R. I.

Capt. John Denison's Descendants.

2083 PRUDENCE DENISON, (Avery[4], William[3], John[2], George[1],) b. Oct. 8, 1743, was married, Jan. 27, 1763, to Joseph Noyes; lived in Stonington, Conn., and had these:

2447 PRUDENCE, b. March 5, 1764.
2448 SARAH, b. Feb. 18, 1766.
2449 JOSEPH, b. Sept. 30, 1768.
2450 AVERY, b. Feb. 13, 1771; m. Polly Slack, Feb. 13, 1799.
2451 THANKFUL, b. Oct. 29, 1773.
2452 ZERVIAH, b. Oct. 5, 1775.
2453 JOHN, b. Aug. 6, 1777.
2454 ANN, b. Jan. 13, 1780.
2455 REBECCA, b. March 6, 1782.
2456 POLLY, b. March 6, 1785.
2457 DENISON, b. March 3, 1788.

2084 MERCY DENISON, (Avery[4], William[3], John[2], George[1],) b. Nov. 7, 1745, was married to Edward Eels, May 10, 1764, and died Dec. 3, 1790; lived in Preston, Conn., and had these:

2458 LUCRETIA, b. in 1765.
2459 SAMUEL, b. in 1766.
2460 CUSHING, b. 1770.
2461 EDWARD, b. in 1772.
2462 REBECCA, b. in 1774.
2463 NATHANIEL, b. in 1776.
2464 NATHAN, b. in 1778.
2465 JOHN, b. in 1780.
2466 SARAH, b. in 1781.

2085 THANKFUL DENISON, (Avery[4], William[3], John[2], George[1],) b. July 17, 1747, was married, April 5, 1770, to Alexander Stewart of Griswold, Conn. They had these children:

2467 BETSEY, b. Sept. 28, 1771.
2468 SUSAN, b. Aug. 10, 1773; m. Capt. David Baldwin.
2469 PATTY, b. July 15, 1775.
2470 THOMAS, b. Sept. 18, 1779; d. young.
2471 THANKFUL, b. April 24, 1777; m. 654 Elihu Denison.
2472 POLLY, b. April 18, 1782.
2473 ALEXANDER, b. June 6, 1784.
2474 THOMAS, b. April 4, 1786.
2475 ELIZABETH, b. Aug. 5, 1789.

2088 AVERY DENISON, (Avery[4], William[3], John[2], George[1],) b. April 10, 1756, m. Prudence Brown, Aug. 13, 1778, but had no child. He died, Aug. 28, 1800, in North Stonington. She d. there in 1847, aged 91 years.

1712 JOHN DENISON, (William[3], John[2], George[1],) b. Feb. 23, 1722, was married to Martha Wheeler, Jan. 13, 1647. They had:

2476 ZERVIAH, b. Oct. 7, 1749; d. April 5, 1751.

They lived in North Stonington. Tradition says they had no other child. An old record of Miss Eunice A. Denison says, they had no other child, and that they " left no child."

1711 CHRISTOPHER DENISON, (William[3], John[2], George[1],) b. in 1719, m. Abigail Tyler and had :

 2477 MARY, b. Oct. 13, 1746.
 2479 ANNA, b. June 1, 1748.
 2480 NATHAN, b. Nov. 3, 1749.
 2481 AMOS, b. Dec. 20, 1751. No further record.

VI.

181 DANIEL DENISON, (John[2], George[1],) b. March 28, 1780, was a Deacon of the first Congregational Church in Stonington, Conn. He was married, first, Jan. 1, 1703, to Mary Stanton, dau. of Robert and Joanna (Gardiner) Stanton, and the mother of his eleven children. She d. Sept. 2, 1724, in the 38th year of her life. She was born Feb. 3, 1687, and married when not quite sixteen years old. He m., second, Jane Cogswell, of Long Island, Oct. 27, 1726, ; and third, Nov. 17, 1737, Mrs. Abigail (Fish) Eldridge, who outlived him about 37 years, and d. June 17, 1784, aged 94. He d. Oct. 13, 1747, aged over 67. His childen, all by Mary Stanton, the young first wife, were as follows :

 2501 MARY, b. Aug. 29, 1705 ; m. Nathan Smith.
 2502 DANIEL, b. Nov. 11, 1707 ; d. March 29, 1718,
 2503 BEEBE, b. Jan. 27, 1709 ; m. Sarah Avery.
 2504 RACHEL, b. July 16, 1710.
 2505 ESTHER, b. March 22, 1712 ; m. Isaac Smith.
 2506 LUCY, b. Oct. 13, 1714 ; m. Jonas Prentice.
 2507 JOHN, b. May 21, 1716 ; m. Abigail Avery.
 2508 PRUDENCE, b. Jan. 27, 1718 ; m. William Denison, oldest son of Wm. and Mercy (Gallup) Denison ; 6 children ; see his record.
 2509 DANIEL, b. March 22, 1720 ; m. Esther Wheeler.
 2510 PHEBE, b. April 24, 1723 ; m. Wm. Avery ; no child.
 2511 SARAH, b. Aug. 25, 1724.

2501 MARY DENISON, (Daniel[3], John[2], George[1],) b. Aug. 29, 1705, was married, Dec. 5, 1723, to Nathan Smith, of Groton, Conn.; lived in Groton, and had seven children :

Capt. John Denison's Descendants.

2512 NATHAN, b. Sept. 18, 1724; *m.* Elizabeth Denison, dau. of 1173 Col. Robert, son of Robert of Mohegan.
2513 MARY, b. Oct. 1, 1726.
2514 DOROTHY, b. April 18, 1729; *m.* Samuel Edgecomb.
2515 JANE, b. Jan. 13, 1731; *m.* George Denison, son of George and Lucy (Gallup) Denison. See his record.
2516 ELIZA, b. May 2, 1736.
2517 OLIVER, b. April 27, 1739; *m.* Mary Denison, dau. of John, son of of Edward, and grandson of 10 George; see her record.
2518 GILBERT, (Dea.) b. April 2, 1742; *m.* Eunice Denison, dau. of Amos, son of Joseph, and grandson of 10 George. She d. Jan. 30, 1793. and he *m.* Widow Phebe (Denison) Chesebro', dau. of Daniel Denison, Jr., son of Dea. Daniel. Dea. Gilbert Smith died, and Mrs. Phebe, his widow, *m.* Rev. Silas Burrows. For Dea. Gilbert Smith's children, see the record of Eunice, his first wife.

2505 ESTHER DENISON, (Daniel^3, John^2, George^1,) b. March 22, 1712, was married, Nov. 4, 1729, to Isaac Smith of Groton. Their children:

2519 DENISON, b. Dec. 1, 1730; d. Oct. 2, 1753.
2520 AMOS, b. Dec. 13, 1732.
2521 ESTHER, twin, b. Aug. 9, 1734; d. Aug. 18, 1734.
2522 HANNAH, twin, b. Aug. 9, 1734; d. Jan. 15, 1736.
2523 SIMEON, b. June 9, 1738; *m.* Eunice Wallsworth.
2524 ABIGAIL, b. Feb. 15, 1740; d. Nov. 4, 1760.
2525 MARY, b. Nov. 15, 1743; *m.* Elder Silas Burrows.
2526 LUCY, b. Nov. 11, 1746; *m.* Elisha Packer.
2527 WILLIAM, b. Oct. 26, 1749; *m.* Sarah Smith.
2528 SILAS, twin, b. Oct. 18, 1752; d. Oct. 18, 1752.
2529 PHEBE, twin, b. Oct. 18, 1752; d. Oct. 28, 1760.

2506 LUCY DENISON, (Daniel^3, John^2, George^1,) b. Oct. 13, 1714, was married to Jonas Prentice, Nov. 29, 1733. He d. June 7, 1766, aged 56. They had:

2530 MARY, b. Sept. 6, 1734; *m.* Capt. John Swan.
2531 SAMUEL, b. Oct. 4, 1736; *m.* Phebe Billings.
2532 ESTHER, b. Sept. 1, 1738; *m.*
2533 DANIEL, b. Jan. 31, 1740.
2534 THOMAS, b. April 7, 1743.
2535 NATHAN, b. May 4, 1745.
2536 LUCY, b. March 22, 1747; *m.* Capt. Thos. Wheeler, grandfather of Hon. Thos. W. Williams of New London, and Gen. Wm. Williams of Norwich, Conn.

2503 BEEBE DENISON, (Daniel^3, John^2, George^1,) b. Jan. 27, 1709, was married, Jan. 10, 1734, to Sarah Avery, dau. of Benj. and Sarah (Denison) Avery. He d. March 24, 1745;

and Oct. 18, 1752, she *m.* Benadam Denison (Wm.[3], Wm.[2], George[1].) Beebe Denison's children :

2537 MARY, b. Jan. 24, 1735; *m.* Wm. Hillard.
2538 DANIEL, b. Feb. 9, 1737; d. young.
2539 SARAH, b. Sept. 11, 1739; *m.* William Latham.
2540 DANIEL, b. Nov. 9, 1742; *m.* Dorothy Denison.

2540 DANIEL DENISON, (Beebe[4], Daniel[3], John[2], George[1],) b. Sept. 19, 1742, was married, in 1770, to Dorothy Denison dau. of Geo. and Jane (Smith) Denison. He d. Jan. 17, 1808; She d. Feb. 22, 1803. Their children :

2541 OLIVER; d. unmarried in the war of 1812.
2542 SAMUEL; *m.* Aliph Woodward; lived in Stonington.
2543 BETSEY; *m.* Arnold C. Chesebro'; went to Knox, N. Y.
2544 FANNY,; *m.* Robert Holmes; went to Knox, N. Y.
2545 DOROTHY; *m.* Peleg Williams of Stonington.
2546 DANIEL; d. unmarried.
2547 JANE; *m.* a Porter; went to Knox, N. Y.
2548 NANCY; *m.* Daniel Gallup; went to Knox, N. Y.

2542 SAMUEL DENISON, (Daniel[5], Beebe[4], Daniel[3], John[2], George[1],) was married to Aliph Woodward, and died Sept. 20, 1843. His children :

2545½ ALIPH, b. Aug., 1798; d. April, 1845.
2546½ SAMUEL W., b. June 5, 1800; *m.* Mary Grinnell.
2547½ WILLIAM W., b. 1802; *m.* Sally M. Howell.
2548½ JOHN I., b. 1804; *m.* Laura O. Gillson.
2549 SILAS, b. 1802; *m.* Diana Burrows.
2550 STEPHEN A., b. 1816; *m.* Ann E. Denison.
2551 DUDLEY, b. 1818; d. in California, unmarried.
2552 DANIEL, b. 1820; d. young.

2546½ SAMUEL WASHINGTON DENISON, (Samuel[6], Daniel[5], Beebe[4], Daniel[3], John[2], George[1],) b. June 5, 1800, was married to Mary Grinnell, Oct. 31, 1824; lived at Head of Mystic, Conn.; d. Dec. 9, 1869. He had :

2553 MARY, b. June 19, 1825; *m.* Wm. Collins.
2554 ABBY J., b. May 3, 1827; *m.* David S. Bryant,
2555 CYNTHIA, b. Jan., 1841; *m.* Charles Darling; no child.
2556 STEPHEN, b. Dec. 20, 1837.
2557 ELLEN, b. Nov. 11, 1831; *m.* Thomas Sheffield; no child.
2558 SAMUEL, b. April 1, 1845.
2559 HARRIET, b. Nov. 27, 1829; *m.* John McDonald; no child.

2553 MARY DENISON, (dau. of 2546½ Samuel W.,) b. June 19, 1825, *m.* Wm. Collins, May 19, 1845; they lived at the

Head of Mystic, Conn.; he d. Sept. 3, 1870, aged 49. Children :

 2560 MARY E., b. April 14, 1846; d. May 21, 1861.
 2561 WILLIAM E., b. Dec. 28, 1847; d. April 18, 1848.
 2562 HARRIET E. b. June 29, 1851; d. April 12, 1852.
 2563 WILLIAM E., b. Jan. 28, 1856.
 2564 CHARLES D., b. March 5, 1858.
 2565 CASSIUS H., b. March 11, 1860.
 2566 JOHN M., b. April 16, 1863.
 2567 FLORENCE E., b. June 16, 1865.

2554 ABBY J. DENISON, (dau. of 2546½ Samuel W.,) b. May 3, 1827, was married, Aug. 6, 1845, to David S. Bryant, of Westerly, R. I., who died Sept. 27, 1867, aged 44. They had :

 2568 JOHN E., b. March 11, 1847; d. Oct. 15, 1848.
 2569 DAVID H., b. July 11, 1849; d. April 3, 1860.
 2570 JOHN W., b. Sept. 16, 1851; d. Feb., 1853.
 2571 EDWIN H., b. July 11, 1856.
 2572 D. HENRY, b. Nov. 13, 1862.

2547½ WILLIAM W. DENISON, (Samuel⁶, Daniel⁵, Beebe⁴, Daniel³, John², George¹,) was married to Sally M. Howell, had three children, and died. His children :

 2573 SALLY M., b. 1828; m. Rufus B. Lawton.
 2574 WILLIAM H., b. 1830; m. Eliza Williams; lives at Saginaw, Mich.
 2575 EDWIN N., b. Nov. 23, 1832; M. Harriet N. Kenyon, Nov. 23, 1856; lives in Westerly; no child.

2573 SALLY M. DENISON, (dau. of 2547½ Wm. W.,) b. in 1828, m. Rufus B. Lawton, in Thompson, Conn., Oct. 26, 1845, lives in Providence, R. I.; has had :

 2576 MARY S., b. Oct. 22, 1847; d. March 9, 1876.
 2577 JULIA E., b. Sept. 27, 1851.
 2578 GEORGE H., b. March 31, 1856.

2548½ JOHN I. DENISON, (Samuel⁶, Daniel⁵, Beebe⁴, Daniel³, John², George¹,) b. in 1804, was married, Feb. 13, 1828, to Laura O. Gillson; lived and died in Norwich, Conn. His children :

 2579 GEORGE W., b. July 8, 1828; m. Fanny M. Brown.
 2580 WILLIAM H., b. Oct., 1829; m. Eliza Reed.
 2581 SILAS, b. Dec. 1830; d. at sea.
 2582 ANDREW, b. 1833; m. Harriet Wise.
 2583 MARY A., b. 1835; m. Walter Ingalls of Pa.
 2584 NATHAN, b. 1837.
 2585 ELIZA J., b. March 22, 1840; m. Gershom Child, and had : Minnie
  D., b. Oct. 11, 1861; and Fannie I., b. March 4, 1865.
 2586 JOHN I., Jr., b. Aug. 4, 1841.

2579 GEORGE W. DENISON, (son of 2548½ John I.,) b. July 8, 1828, was married, first, May 5, 1850, to Fanny M. Brown; and second, June 5, 1864, to Mrs. Hannah Strong. The first wife d. Feb. 25, 1821. He lives in Norwich, Conn. Children:

    2587 ALIDA E., b. June 3, 1854.
    2588 JENNIE VIOLA, b. April 24, 1856.
    2589 FANNY ESTELLE, b. July 21, 1858.
    2590 SILAS EDSON, b. March 12, 1870.
    2591 GEORGE W., b. June 21, 1875.

2586 JOHN I. DENISON, Jr., (son of 2548½ John I.,) b. Aug. 4, 1841, was married, in 1867, to Mary Covell, and had:

    2592 CLARA MAY, b. Jan. 21, 1870.

2550 STEPHEN A. DENISON, (Samuel[6], Daniel[5], Beebe[4], Daniel[3], John[2], George[1],) b. in 1816, was married to Ann E. Denison, Nov. 5, 1839. They live at Mystic River, and have had:

    2593 GEORGE A., b. March 4, 1843; d. Sept. 22, 1843.
    2594 MARIA E., b. March 3, 1846; m. Charles B. Wilcox, Oct. 30, 1866.
    2595 DIANA, b. Oct. 8, 1847.
    2596 ADELAIDE, b. July 6, 1849; m. W. W. Pendleton, Nov. 24, 1868.
    2597 ELLEN, b. May 18, 1852; m. Geo. A. Kinney, Aug. 12, 1873.
    2598 EUDORA, b. March 2, 1855.
    2599 MARY B., b. May 16, 1857.
    2600 ESTELLE, b. Jan. 20, 1860.

2545 DOROTHY DENISON, (Daniel[5], Beebe[4], Daniel[3], John[2], George[1],) was married, in 1800, to Peleg Williams. Their children:

    2601 MARY ANN; m. John Harris of Preston.
    2602 ELIAKIM; m. Mary Wightman.
    2603 ERASTUS; m. 1st, Mercy Wightman; 2nd, Sarah Weeden.
    2604 DUDLEY; m. Lydia Harris of Preston.
    2605 CHARLES; m. Aurelia Gore.
    2606 JANE; m. Barton Sanders.
    2607 BETSEY; m. Capt. Thomas Eldridge.
    2608 NANCY; m. Albert Sanders.
    2609 CLARK; unmarried.
    2610 FANNY; unmarried.

2544 FANNY DENISON, (Daniel[5], Beebe[4], Daniel[3], John[2], George[1],) was married to Robert Holmes, Oct. 27, 1808; removed from Stonington to Knox, N. Y. They had:

    2611 DENISON, b. Sept. 16, 1809.

2537 MARY DENISON, (Beebe⁴, Daniel³, John², George¹,) b. Jan. 24, 1735, was married to William Hillard, Feb. 20, 1755. Their children :

    2612 JOHN, b. Oct. 4, 1756.
    2613 WILLIAM, b. Jan. 10, 1759.
    2614 AZARIAH, b. Jan. 25, 1761.
    2615 MARY, b. April 13, 1763.
    2616 PHEBE, b. Oct. 24, 1765.
    2617 PRISCILLA, b. March 11, 1769.
    2618 GURDON, b. Feb. 10, 1771.

2506 JOHN DENISON, (Daniel³, John², George¹,) b. Oct. 21, 1716, was married, about 1738, to Abigail Avery, dau. of the 2nd John Avery of Groton, Conn. They lived in Stonington and had these ten children :

    2619 ABIGAIL, b. in 1740; m. Zebulon Elliot.
    2620 DESIRE, b. 1742; d. unmarried, aged 82, Dec. 2, 1824.
    2621 AVERY, b. 1744; d. young.
    2622 ANNA, b. 1746; twice married.
    2622½ LUCY, b. 1748; d. unmarried, aged 64, May 1, 1812.
    2623 MARY, b. 1750; m. Stephen Avery; no child; d. Feb. 27, 1816.
    2624 SARAH, b. May 2, 1752; m. John Baldwin.
    2625 NATHAN, b. 1754; m. Betsey Conklin.
    2626 JULIA, b. 1758; m. Pierre LaRoche.
    2627 ANDREW, b. Dec. 3, 1761; m. Sally Williams.

2622 ANNA DENISON, (John⁴, Daniel³, John², George¹,) b. in 1746, was married, April 23, 1766, to Nehemiah Avery, son of John and Lydia (Smith) Avery, b. in 1744. They lived in Norwich, Conn.; he d. Sept. 26, 1789. She m. second, Sept. 2, 1798, Amos Clift, and lived in Preston, Conn. She had these four children by the first husband :

    2628 DAVID, b. May 4, 1768; m. Abigail Goddard.
    2629 BEEBE, b. June 8, 1771; m. Rebecca Saterlee.
    2630 WILLIAM, b. 1775; d. June 15, 1790, at Mystic.
    2631 NANCY, b. Sept. 12, 1785; m. Wm. Clift, June 15, 1813.

2628 DAVID AVERY, (Anna⁵, John⁴, Daniel³, John², George¹,) b. May 4, 1768, m. Abigail Goddard, Dec. 8, 1792. She was born, Feb. 26, 1769. They lived in Old Lyme, Conn. He d. Sept. 20, 1815; she d. April 14, 1856. The children :

    2632 MARY ANN, b. May 20, 1795.
    2633 WILLIAM, b. Sept. 11, 1800.
    2634 ABBY G., b. May, 1802.

2634 ABBY G. AVERY, (David[6], Anna[5], John[4], Daniel[3], John[2], George[1],) b. May, 1802, was married to J. H. Conklin, Nov. 20, 1836. They live in Old Lyme, Conn. The children:

    2635 HARRIET A., b. Oct. 15, 1837.
    2635½ JOHN A., b. Aug. 17, 1839.
    2636 JANE M., b. Nov. 2, 1840.
    2637 ANN A., b. April 4, 1842.

2629 BEEBE AVERY, (Anna[5], John[4], Daniel[3], John[2], George[1],) b. June 8, 1771, was married, to Rebecca Saterlee; lived in Rutland, Vt. Their children:

    2638 NANCY.
    2639 WILLIAM, b. 1804.
    2640 ELIZA, b. 1806.
    2641 CHARLES, b. 1808.
    2642 ELISHA SATERLEE, b. 1810; m.; lives in Detroit, Mich; no ch.

2631 NANCY AVERY, (Anna[5], John[4], Daniel[3], John[2], George[1],) b. Sept. 12, 1785, was married, June 5, 1813, to William Clift, (son of Amos,) who was born, Aug. 28, 1763, and d. Jan. 30, 1831. She d. Nov. 27, 1871. Two children:

    2643 WILLIAM, b. Sept. 12, 1817.
    2644 SAMUEL, b. June 4, 1820; m. Mary Jane Prentice about 1853; lives in Jersey City, N. J.; no child.

2643 WILLIAM CLIFT, (Nancy Avery[6], Anna[5], John[4], Daniel[3], John[2], George[1],) b. Sept. 12, 1817, was graduated from Amherst College, Mass., in 1839, and from Union Theological Seminary, N. Y. City, in 1843; was Pastor of the Congregational Church, Stonington Boro', from 1844 to 1864, and Pastor of Mystic Bridge Congregational Church, from 1869 to 1878. He was married, Jan. 1, 1845, to Harriet Adaline Peters, dau. of Rev. Absalom Peters, D. D., and Harriet H. Peters, of New York City. They live at Mystic Bridge, Conn. Their children:

    2645 HARRIET A., b. Dec. 8, 1845; d. Dec. 8, 1845.
    2646 WILLIAM, b. Jan. 23, 1847.
    2647 GEORGE DENISON, b. Jan. 15, 1851.

2646 WILLIAM CLIFT, Jr. (son of 2643 Rev. Wm. Clift,) b. Jan. 23, 1847, was married, Sept. 29, 1873, to Angeline A. Hershey; resides in Kirwin, Kansas. Children:

    2648 WILLIAM A., b. July 17, 1874.
    2649 HARRIET A., b. March 16, 1878.

2647 GEORGE DENISON CLIFT, (son of 2643 Rev. William Clift,) b. Jan. 15, 1851, was married, Oct. 29, 1879, to Mary Esther Miner; he is a practising physician in New York City.

2624 SARAH DENISON, (John[4], Daniel[3], John[2], George[1],) b. May 2, 1752, was married, Jan. 23, 1772, to Major John Baldwin of North Stonington. She died June 19, 1813; he died Aug. 3, 1814. She was ten days older than he. Their children:

    2650 JOHN, b. Oct. 28, 1772; m. Abigail Boardman; 8 children.
    2651 EUNICE, b. March 16, 1775; m. Stephen Tucker.
    2652 DENISON, b. March 28, 1778; d. unmarried.
    2653 ANDREW, b. Dec. 15, 1780; m. Mary Boardman; 10 children.
    2654 DANIEL, b. May 21, 1783; thrice married.
    2655 MARY, b. Feb. 1, 1786; m. Stephen Frink; 4 children.
    2656 GEO. WASHINGTON, b. July 21, 1788; m. Mary C. Kinney; 12 ch.
    2657 SARAH, b. 1790; m. Thos. Holmes; one child.
    2658 NANCY, b. Oct. 23, 1793; d. Dec. 8, 1834, unmarried.

2654 DANIEL BALDWIN, (Sarah[5], John[4], Daniel[3], John[2], George[1],) b. May 21, 1783, was gr. gr. great grandson of John and Rebecca (Palmer) Baldwin of Stonington, Conn. He was married, 1st, April 22, 1804, to Eunice Frink, who died childless, May 1, 1805; 2nd, Jan. 22, 1806, to Lucy Boardman, who died childless, Aug, 27, 1806; 3d, to Hannah Stanton, April 21, 1808, by whom he had these nine children:

    2659 JOHN DENISON, b. Sept. 28, 1809; m. Lemira Hathaway.
    2660 DANIEL AVERY, b. July ?, 1811; m. twice; 10 children.
    2661 SALLY ADELINE, b. July 17, 1813; d in 1814.
    2662 NANCY ADELINE, b. April 27, 1815; m. Frederic Frink; no ch.
    2663 ANDREW, b. and d. in April, 1817.
    2664 MARY ANN, b. May 8, 1818; m. C. D. Smith; 2 children.
    2665 ROBERT STANTON, b. Aug. 21, 1822; drowned June 3, 1838.
    2666 HANNAH, b. Oct. 9, 1820; d. in 1821.
    2667 AMY AVERY, b. Sept. 9, 1825; m. James Boardman; no child.

Daniel Baldwin died, Oct. 28, 1855. His wife, Hannah Stanton, died March 19, 1877, aged 91 years and 8 days. She was born, March 11, 1786, and was a lineal descendant of the first Thomas Stanton of Stonington, Conn., being a dau. of Capt. Nathaniel Stanton of Groton, Conn, who was a son of Nathaniel of Preston, who was son of Joseph of Stonington, who was son of Capt. John of Stonington, who was son of the first Thomas. She was also, through her mother, Amy Avery, a descendent of both the first James Avery and the first James Morgan of Groton; and her grandmother Stanton was a daughter of Rev. Joseph Coit, first minister of Plainfield, Conn., whose wife was Experience Wheeler of Stonington. Her gr. grandmother Stanton was Margaret Chesebro', dau. of Capt. George Denison's dau. Hannah.

2659 JOHN DENISON BALDWIN, (Daniel[6], Sarah[5], John[4], Daniel[3], John[2], George[1],) b. Sept. 28, 1809, was married April 3, 1832, to Lemira Hathaway, dau. of Capt. Ebenezer Hathaway of Dighton, Mass. He studied at New Haven, received the degree of A. M. from Yale College, and graduated from the New Haven Theological Seminary in 1834. After passing some years with Congregational Churches in Woodstock, North Branford, and Killingly, Conn., he became a journalist; first, as owner and editor of "The Republican," at Hartford, Conn.; next, as editor and in part owner of the Daily and Weekly Commonwealth, at Boston, Mass.; and, finally, in 1859, as owner (with his sons,) and editor, of the Daily and Weekly Spy, at Worcester, Mass. He represented the Worcester District in Congress, six years, from 1863 to 1869. He has written two books, "Pre-Historic Nations" and "Ancient America," which have been successfully published by Harper & Brothers. He was b. in N. Stonington, Conn. Four Children:

2668 ELLEN FRANCES, b. Jan 19, 1833; d. March 10, 1854.
2669 JOHN STANTON, b. Jan. 6, 1834; m. Emily Brown.
2670 CHARLES CLINTON, b. May 4, 1835; m. Ella L. T. Peckham.
2671 MARY JANE, b. May 6, 1836; d. Dec. 29, 1850.

2669 JOHN STANTON BALDWIN, (son of 2659 John Denison,) b. Jan. 6, 1834, in New Haven, Conn., was married, Oct. 19, 1863, to Emily Brown, dau. of Albert and Mary (Eaton) Brown, of Worcester, Mass. She was born in Worcester. They live in Worcester, and have these children:

2672 MARY ELEANOR, b. Nov. 25, 1864.
2673 ROBERT STANTON, b. Dec. 17, 1865.
2674 ALICE HATHAWAY, b. Nov. 26, 1867.
2675 JOHN DENISON. b. May 26, 1871.
2676 EMILY BROWN, b. March 27, 1823; d. May 24, 1874.
2677 ROSAMOND, b. Sept. 24, 1874: d. Sept. 2, 1876.
2678 HENRY BROWN, b. Aug. 9, 1877.

Capt. John Denison's Descendants.

2670 CHARLES CLINTON BALDWIN, (son of 2659 John Denison,) b. in Woodstock, Conn., May 4, 1835, was married, Oct. 1, 1868, to Ella L. T. Peckham, dau. of Dr. Fenner H. Peckham, of Providence, R. I. They live in Worcester, and have these children:

    2679 KATHERINE TORREY, b. July 17, 1869.
    2680 EDITH ELLA, b. Nov. 19, 1870.
    2681 GRACE PECKHAM, b. May 16, 1874.

2660 DANIEL AVERY BALDWIN, (Daniel[6], Sarah[5], John[4], Daniel[3], John[2], George[1],) b. July 2, 1811, was married, first, May 23, 1835, to Betsey Rogers, of Lyme, Conn., who d. April 17, 1851, aged 37; and, second, May 22, 1853, to Amanda Colgrove, of Voluntown, Conn. He was well educated in the common schools, and by his own private reading and study. He lives in New London, Conn., and is a shipmaster, but has given part of his life to the business of farming. His children by the two wives were born and named as follows:

    2682 DANIEL MATHER, b. Nov. 19, 1836; d. June 10, 1862.
    2683 HANNAH STANTON, b. April 18, 1839; d. July 13, 1840.
    2684 ROBERT STANTON, b. and d. April 20, 1841.
    2685 GEORGE PRENTICE, b. July 4, 1843.
    2686 HARRIET EMMA, b. Oct. 7, 1848; d. May 5, 1851.
    2687 WILLIAM JAMES, b. Jan. 17, 1851.
    2688 FREDERIC R., b. Feb. 14, 1855; d. Sept. 24, 1855.
    2689 FRANCIS, b. Oct. 11, 1858; d. July 20, 1860.
    2690 CHARLES CLINTON, b. March 1, 1860.
    2691 ELLEN FRANCES, b. Dec. 2, 1863.

2664 MARY ANN BALDWIN, (Daniel[6], Sarah[5], John[4], Daniel[3], John[2], George[1],) b. May 8, 1818, was married, Nov. 1, 1837, to Charles Dwight Smith, of Woodstock, Conn. She lives with him in Worcester, Mass.; has had two children:

    2692 EBENEZER, b. Nov. 7, 1839; twice married; no child.
    2693 HANNAH AMELIA, b. Sept. 16, 1845; *m.* Samuel Woodward of Sturbridge, who now does business in Quincy Market, Boston. One child:
        2694 CHARLES SMITH WOODWARD, b. Sept. 16, 1868.

2627 ANDREW DENISON, (John[4], Daniel[3], John[2], George[1],) b. Dec. 3, 1761, was married, in 1782, to Sally Williams. He lived in Stonington, and after 1809, in Vermont. He died in Bennington, Vt., March 25, 1813. His wife died in North

Stonington, Jan. 12, 1853, aged 92 years. He was a hatter. His children :

2694½ CHARLES H., b. March 1, 1784; d. young.
2695 BENJAMIN F., b. June 1, 1785; *m.* Nancy Stark, Jan. 11, 1858.
2696 STEPHEN W., b. Feb. 16, 1787; d. young.
2697 SALLY, b. June 10, 1789; *m.* John Brown.
2698 ABIGAIL, b. May 12, 1791; d. young.
2699 JOHN, b. June 4, 1793; *m.* Mary Chesebro'.
2700 DESIRE, b. March, 1795; d. young.
2701 SOPHIA, b. March 6, 1797; d. young.
2702 LUCY ANN, b. Feb. 18, 1799; *m.* Matthew Brown.

2695 BENJAMIN F. DENISON, (Andrew[5], John[4], Daniel[3], John[2], George[1],) b. June 1, 1785, was married to Nancy Stark; lived at Bennington, Vt., and elsewhere, and had these :

2703 CHARLES.   **2704** NANCY.   **2705** RHODA.

2699 JOHN DENISON, (Andrew[5], John[4], Daniel[3], John[2], George[1],) b. June 4, 1793, was married, May 3, 1818, to Mary Chesebro'. He d. Oct., 1854; she d. Aug. 21, 1841. They had :

2706 GILBERT W., b. June 7, 1820; *m.* Sarah A. Swan; no child.
2707 CHARLES, b. Jan. 21, 1828; *m.* Sarah M. Chesebro'.
2708 ANDREW, b. Feb. 9, 1833; *m.* Viania Pitcher.
2709 ELI, b. May 9, 1830; d. in Libbey Prison in 1863.
2710 JULIA ANN, b. Oct. 21, 1822; not married.
2711 MARY JANE, b. Oct. 5, 1825; *m.* Peter Clickman.

2707 CHARLES DENISON, (John[6], Andrew[5], John[4], Daniel[3], John[2], George[1],) *m.* Dec. 22, 1859, Sarah M. Chesebro', of Guilderland, N. Y. She has a Delft platter brought over by Ann Borodell. They have :

2712 LYDIA A., b. Feb. 17, 1861.
2713 EDWARD M., b. Dec. 15, 1862.
2714 WILLIAM, b. March 11, 1867.

2711 MARY J. DENISON, (John[6], Andrew[5], John[4], Daniel[3], John[2], George[1],) b. Oct. 5, 1825, was *m.* to Peter Clickman, Feb. 21, 1854. Their children :

2715 EMMA J., b. 1857.
2716 GEORGE DENISON, b. 1859.
2717 ANNIE BORODELL, b. 1860.
2718 WILLIAM, b. 1862.

2708 ANDREW DENISON, (John[6], Andrew[5], John[4], Daniel[3], John[2], George[1],) *m.* Viania Pitcher, Feb. 5, 1863, and has :

2719 MARY ELIZABETH, b. in 1865.

*John Denison Baldwin,
Worcester, Mass.*

Capt. John Denison's Descendants.

2697 SALLY DENISON, (Andrew[5], John[4], Daniel[3], John[2], George[1],) b. June 10, 1789, was married to John Brown, Aug. 13, 1807; lived in North Stonington, Conn. He d. June 2, 1866, aged 91; she d. at Stonington, Ill., Jan. 12, 1877. Their children :

> **2720** JOHN DENISON, b. March 23, 1809; m. Mary Ann Wheeler; 3 children; lives at Stonington, Ill.
> **2721** SALLY ANN, b. Oct. 9, 1814; m. Benj. B. Hewett; 3 children.
> **2722** BENJAMIN F., b. Aug., 1816; m.; went to Texas; had children.
> **2723** STEPHEN E., b. Aug. 8, 1834; d. July 3, 1865; no child.

2702 LUCY ANN DENISON, (Andrew[5], John[4], Daniel[3], John[2], George[1],) b. Feb. 1799, was married to Matthew Brown, July 4, 1816. She d. July 20, 1848. Lived in North Stonington, Conn., and had these :

> **2724** DANIEL, b. May 22, 1817; m. Jerusha Brown, April 8, 1842; 2 ch.
> **2725** ANDREW D., b. Sept. 24, 1818; m. Adeline Partlow, Sept. 20, 1854; 2 children; lives in Minnesota.
> **2726** LUCY E., b. May 16, 1823; m. Reuben W. York, Oct. 8, 1840; 3 c.
> **2727** HOSMER A., b. Sept. 7, 1830; m. Mary Frink, Jan. 1, 1869; lives in Minnesota.

2626 JULIA DENISON, (John[4], Daniel[3], John[2], George[1],) b. in 1758, was m. to Pierre LaRoche, a Frenchman, about 1793. They lived in New London and in New York City. He d. and after his death, his children inherited property in France, after which the widow lived at Preston City, Conn. The children were :

> **2728** PIERRE, b. 1798; lived in New York City.
> **2729** MARY ANN, b. in 1795; m. Luke Wheeler.

2509 DANIEL DENISON, JR., (Daniel[3], John[2], George[1],) b. March 22, 1721, was married, May 27, 1742, to Esther Wheeler, who was b. Feb. 15, 1722, and d. March 31, 1814. He d. in Stonington. May 9, 1776. He had thirteen children, as follows :

> **2731** ESTHER, b. Oct, 11, 1743; m. William Gardiner.
> **2732** DANIEL, b. Dec. 9, 1745; m. Elizabeth Andross.
> **2733** PHEBE, b. Dec. 5, 1747; thrice married.
> **2734** ROBERT, b. Dec. 12, 1749; m. Anna Chesebro'.
> **2735** ISAAC, b. Dec. 20, 1751; m. Eunice Williams.
> **2736** HENRY, b. Nov. 26, 1753; m. Mary Gallup.
> **2737** HANNAH, b. Feb. 13, 1755; d. young.
> **2738** MARY, b. Nov. 6, 1757; twice married.
> **2739** HANNAH, b. Oct. 16, 1759; m. John Gallup.

2740 BEEBE, b. Feb. 22, 1761; twice married.
2741 FREDERICK, b. Sept. 21, 1762; *m.* Hannah Fish.
2742 EUNICE, b. May 18, 1764; *m.* Reuben Hatch.
2743 ANN B., [or Nancy,] b. Oct. 2, 1769; *m.* John Wheeler.

2731 ESTHER DENISON, (Daniel[4], Daniel[3], John[2], George[1],) b. Oct. 11, 1743, was married, April 16, 1761, to William Gardiner, of Gardiner's Island. Their children:

2744 WILLIAM, b. in 1762.
2745 JOHN, b. in 1765.
2746 SARAH, b. in 1767.
2747 ESTHER, b. in 1769.
2748 JOSEPH, b. in 1771.
2749 HANNAH, b. in 1773.
2750 DANIEL D., b. in 1774; *m.* Eunice Otis; 6 children.
2751 HENRY G., b in 1775: *m.* Ruth Percival; 6 children.
2752 ANGELINE, b. in 1778.
2753 ISAAC, b. in 1782.

2733 PHEBE DENISON, (Daniel[4], Daniel[3], John[2], George[1],) b. Dec. 5, 1747, was married, first, to Elihu Chesebro', May 19, 1768; lived at Stonington; had these:

2754 ELIHU, b. March 26, 1769; *m.* Lydia Chesebro'.
2755 DANIEL, b. Jan. 12, 1771; *m.* Fanny Williams.
2756 PHEBE, b. March 11, 1773; *m.* Zebulon Chesebro'.
2757 HENRY; d. young.
2758 ESTHER; d. young.
2759 NANCY, b. Oct. 5, 1780; *m.* Mr. Curran of L. I.

Elihu Cheseboro' died. She had two other husbands, but no other child. She *m.* 2nd, Dea. Gilbert Smith, of Groton; and 3rd, Rev. Silas Burrows.

2738 MARY DENISON, (Daniel[4], Daniel[3], John[2], George[1],) b. Nov. 6, 1757, was married, Jan. 1778, to Jeremiah Holmes; lived in Stonington. Their children:

2759 MARY, b. Oct. 8, 1778; *m.* Thomas Crary.
2760 PHILURA, b. Sept. 14, 1780; *m.* Capt. Theophilus Baldwin.
2761 JEREMIAH, b. Sept. 6, 1782; *m.* Ann B. Denison.
2762 ESTHER, b. March 27, 1785; twice married.
2763 DANIEL D., b. Sept. 17, 1787; *m.* Melinda Lee.
2764 FREDERIC, b. Feb. 19, 1789; *m.* a Pettis.

Mr. Jeremiah Holmes d. March 8, 1790. She *m.* 2nd, Jedediah Lee, about 1797, and they emigrated to Stanstead, Canada, where he d. Oct., 1824. She d. there, April 29, 1828. They had two children:

Capt. John Denison's Descendants.

2765 ERASTUS. b. 1798; d. in Stanstead, March 21, 1866.
2766 LUCY, b. Jan. 1, 1801; m. Benj. Pomroy.

2763 DANIEL DENISON HOLMES, (son of 2738 Mary Denison and Jeremiah Holmes,) b. Sept. 17, 1787, m. Malinda Lee, who was born at Pitsford. Vt., March 23, 1791. He d. Jan'y 7, 1857. She d. Feb. 26, 1871. Children :

2767 HORACE DENISON, b. in 1811; d. March 12, 1820.
2768 WM. HENRY, b. April 25, 1814.
2769 LEWIS FRANKLIN, b. in 1815; d. Aug. 9, 1820.
2770 ALONZO HIRAM, b. Aug. 19, 1817; d. Oct. 29, 1845.
2771 HORACE DENISON. b. Feb. 8, 1821; m. Mary Ann Bagley, Sept. 16, 1865; no child.

2768 WM. HENRY HOLMES, (son of Daniel D.,) b. April 25, 1814, m. Julia Granby Moulton, Aug. 24, 1842. He d. Oct. 16, 1877; she d. July 2, 1877. Children :

2772 JULIA GERTRUDE, b. Jan. 18, 1844; m. Francis B. Denio.
2773 ALONZO LEE. b. June 17, 1846; m. Mary Wilder Pierce, July 7, 1873, and has : Charles William, b. April 23, 1874.

2766 LUCY LEE, (dau. of 2738 Mary Denison and Jedediah Lee,) b. Jan. 1, 1801, m. Benjamin Pomroy, of Stanstead, in 1824. Children :

2774 SELAH JEDEDIAH, b. Jan. 1, 1825.
2775 MARY LEE, b. Aug. 16, 1827.
2776 ERASTUS LEE, b. June 3, 1837; d. May 6, 1841.

2774 SELAH JEDEDIAH POMROY, (son of Lucy Lee and Benj. Pomroy,) b. Jan. 1, 1825, m. Victoria S. Adams, June 30, 1857. Their children :

2777 LIZZIE V., b. May 15, 1858.
2778 MARY AGNES, b. Nov. 2, 1860.
2779 BENJAMIN A., b. July 5, 1861.
2780 ALBERT LEE, b. July 17, 1863.
2781 AARON ALEXANDER, b. July 13, 1865.
2782 LUCY LEE, b. Nov. 7, 1870.
2783 ELSIE B., b. Sept. 13, 1872.

2775 MARY LEE POMROY, (dau. of Lucy Lee and Benjamin Pomroy,) b. Aug. 16, 1827, m. Albert Phelps Ball, Feb. 12, 1850. Children :

2784 WILLIAM LEE, b. Feb. 7, 1851.
2785 BENJ. POMROY, b. May 8, 1854; d. May 9, 1860.
2786 ALBERT LISPENARD CALEB, b. Nov. 14, 1855; d. May 9, 1860.
2787 LUCY LEE, b. Nov. 14, 1857; d. May 10, 1860.
2788 BENJ. POMROY, b. March 7, 1860.
2789 CHARLES, b. Jan. 27, 1862; d. June, 1862.

2790 ERASTUS PHELPS, b. Aug. 2, 1863.
2791 ALBERT EASTON, b. Sept. 7, 1864; d. June, 23, 1865.
2792 MARY ELIZA, b. June 7, 1866; d. Sept. 10, 1866.
2793 JAMES TURNER, b. July 16, 1868.
2794 HENRY TENNEY, b. July 18, 1871.

2762 ESTHER HOLMES, (dau. of 2738 Mary Denison and Jeremiah Holmes,) b. March 27, 1785, was married, first, to Joel Marsh, March 2, 1803, who d. Dec. 1, 1812; and, second, to Joshua Blodgett, June 20, 1819. She d. June 6, 1870; Mr. Blodgett d. Feb. 7, 1876. There were nine children by the two husbands, as follows:

2795 HANNAH M, b. Jan. 11, 1806; m. Wm. Fling.
2796 ALBERT, b. Sept. 9, 1807; m. Elizabeth Tyler.
2797 ALONZO, b. Sept. 7, 1809.
2798 JOEL, b. Jan. 11, 1812; m. Mary H. Coats.
2799 MARY ESTHER, (Blodgett,) b. Sept. 3, 1822.
2799½ LEWIS FRANKLIN, b. April 1, 1820; twice married.
2800 HARRIET MELISSA, b. Nov. 19, 1824; m. Chauncey Wilson.
2801 JEREMIAH WM., b. Jan. 14, 1827; m. Susie W. Watson.
2802 ERASTUS LEE, b. Jan. 24, 1829; m. Maria E. Selleck.

2799 MARY ESTHER BLODGETT, (daughter of 2762 Esther Holmes and Joshua Blodgett, and grand-dau. of 2738 Mary Denison,) b. Sept. 3, 1822, was married June 4, 1843, to James Dean Fish, son of Asa and Prudence (Brown Dean) Fish, of Mystic Bridge, Conn. Their children:

2803 ASA, b. Aug. 18, 1844; m. Joanna, dau. of Noyes P. Brown, Stonington.
2804 JOHN DEAN, b. June 19, 1846; m. Julia B. Force, Brooklyn, N.Y.
2805 HANNAH, b. Jan. 29, 1849.
2806 CHARLES. b. Dec. 30, 1850.
2807 ANNIE, b. Sept. 9, 1854.
2808 IRVING, b. Jan. 4, 1861.
2809 DEAN, b. April 30, 1864.

Mrs. Mary E. B. Fish, d. July 17, 1868, at Brooklyn, N. Y. Mr. Fish was married, second, March 18, 1872, to Isabella Rogers, dau. of Dr. Samuel Rogers of Quincy, Ill. She was born March 4, 1837, and d. Dec. 29, 1879, in New York City. One child:

2810 PAUL ROGERS, b. Nov. 29, 1872.

2739 HANNAH DENISON, (Daniel[4], Daniel[3], John[2], George[1],) b. Oct. 16, 1759, was married to Col. John Gallup, Jan. 3, 1782. They settled in Knox, N. Y. He d. Dec. 8, 1825. She d. Sept. 1, 1830. Their children:

Capt. John Denison's Descendants. 135

2811 JOHN, b. Aug. 7, 1782; m. Ann B. Denison; no child.
2812 HANNAH, b. May 24, 1786; m. Nathan Crary.
2813 DANIEL, b. Sept. 12, 1789; twice married.
2814 JOSEPH, b. Dec. 9, 1791; m. Lucy A. Fowler.
2815 LUCRETIA, b. Aug. 22, 1784; m. Henry Gardiner.
2816 MARY, b. Jan. 23, 1794; not married.
2817 BEEBE, b. April 22, 1796; d. Aug. 25, 1843.
2818 GURDON, b. June 12, 1798; m. Eve Haverly; 9 children.
2819 ESTHER, b. July 19, 1800; m. Ebenezer Denison.
2820 JOHN G., b. Sept. 15, 1805; not married.

2743 ANN BORODELL DENISON, (called Nancy,) (Daniel[4], Daniel[3], John[2], George[1].) b. Oct. 2, 1769, was married to John Wheeler, July 8, 1790. Their children:

2821 JOHN D., b. June 10, 1791.
2822 DANIEL, b. July 14, 1793.
2823 ERASTUS, b. Oct. 16, 1795.
2824 NANCY, b. March 27, 1798.
2825 PRUDENCE, b. June 18, 1800.
2826 MARY ESTHER, b. Nov. 30, 1802.
2827 ELIAS H., b. April 13, 1807.
2828 EMILY A., b. Feb. 26, 1814.
2829 EUNICE H., b. Aug. 8, 1816.

2742 EUNICE DENISON, (Daniel[4], Daniel[3], John[2] George[1],) b. March 18, 1764, was married to Reuben Hatch, May 9, 1784. Their children:

2830 DANIEL D., b. Sept. 17, 1784; m. Fanny Newcomb.
2831 JOHN, b. July 10, 1786; m. Sarah Edwards.
2832 HORACE, b. May 23, 1788; m. Mary Y. Smith.
2833 ELIZABETH, b. Nov. 1, 1790; m. Darius Jones.
2834 FANNY, b. April 19, 1792; m. Joseph Cutting.
2835 AURORA, b. April 22, 1794; m. Luther Dyer.
2836 HARRIET HINCKLEY, b. April 2, 1796; m. Rev. Absalom Peters.
2837 ADALINE, b. April 3, 1798; m. Hon. Milo L. Bennett.
2838 LUCY C., b. Aug. 4, 1800; m. Rev. Rufus W. Bailey.
2839 ALBERT G., b. Dec. 26, 1802; m. Harriet Lemex.
2840 ELLEN A. B., b. Dec. 6, 1804; d. in 1807.
2841 ANN BORODEL, b. in 1807; d. in 1813.
2842 JOSEPH D., b. Jan. 21, 1811; m. Francis Forbes.

2830 DANIEL D. HATCH, (Eunice[5], Daniel[4], Daniel[3], John[2], George[1],) b. Sept. 17, 1784, was married, Nov. 22, 1810, to Fanny Newcomb, dau. of Hon. Daniel Newcomb, of Keene, N. H. He was born in Stonington, Conn., and died in Rochester, N. Y., Dec. 17, 1837. He had seven children; the first two were born at Keene, N. H., the other five in Rochester, N. Y., as follows:

2843 Fanny Newcomb, b. Nov. 19, 1811; *m.* Levi Burnell.
2844 Henry Denison, b. Dec. 7, 1815; *m.* twice.
2845 Frederick William, b. Nov. 6, 1817; *m.* Elizabeth W. Capps.
2846 Harriet Stearns, b. Dec. 2, 1822; d. young.
2847 Maria Allyn, b. Dec. 12, 1824; *m.* Riley Bristol.
2848 Ellen Ann, b. Dec. 29, 1826; *m.* W. H. Taylor.
2849 Emily Stearns, b. Sept. 10, 1831; *m.* Rev. J. E. Roy.

Mrs. Fanny (Newcomb) Hatch, after D. D. H.'s death, in 1837, *m.* 2nd, Dea. Richard Bristol, and died at Farmington, Ill., May 31, 1853. She was born, Oct. 31, 1791.

2843 Fanny Newcomb Hatch, (dau. of 2830 Daniel D.,) b. Nov. 19, 1811, was married to Levi Burnell, April 15, 1830. He was born in Chesterfield, Mass., May 27, 1803. Their children :

2850 Harriet Peters, b. Jan. 23, 1831, at Rochester, N. Y.
2851 Albert, b. June 6, 1832, at Rochester, N. Y.; d. Jan. 14, 1833.
2852 Joseph Hatch, b. Jan. 26, 1834, at Elyria, Ohio.
2853 Martha Gilbert, b. March 5, 1836, at Oberlin, Ohio.
2854 Fanny Newcomb, b. March 18, 1838, at Oberlin, Ohio; unmarried; an Oberlin graduate.
2855 Mary Elmira, b. Nov. 13, 1840, at Oberlin, Ohio.
2856 Samuel Levi, b. Jan. 1, 1843, at Oberlin, Ohio.
2857 Daniel Gilbert, b. Jan. 21, 1844, at Oberlin, Ohio; d. July 30, 1844.

2852 Joseph Hatch Burnell, (Capt.) practical master of the art of book-keeping, lives in Milwaukie, Wis., unmarried.

2853 Martha Gilbert Burnell, *m.* Samuel N. Millard, Oct. 13, 1857 ; 2 ch. He was cashier of the Milwaukie Farmer's Bank ; is now a lay evangelist.

2855 Mary Elmira Burnell, *m.*, Feb. 9, 1867, Jefferson Robinson, M. D., of Manhattan, Kansas. They have had 5 children ; only 2 are living : Charles Nash, b. Feb. 20, 1869 ; and Stanley Russell, b. Feb. 18, 1874.

2856 Samuel Levi Burnell, *m.* Anne Amelia Bigelow, Jan. 1, 1872. They have one child : Guy Chase, b. Oct. 6, 1874. S. L. Burnell is a hardware merchant in Milwaukie, Wis.

2844 Henry Denison Hatch (son of 2830 Daniel D.,) b. Dec. 7, 1815, was *m.* 1st, to Jane Parks, who died childless,

Oct. 30, 1864 ; 2nd, to Adeline Eliza Collins, Nov. 24, 1867. They live at Lockport, Ill., and have but one child :

 2858 EMILY ELLEN, b. Dec. 27, 1869.

2845 FREDERICK WILLIAM HATCH, (son of 2830 Daniel D.,) b. Nov. 6, 1817, was married to Elizabeth Wilson Capps, Sept. 23, 1843, at Farmington, Ill. She was born in Highland Co., Ohio, Feb. 10, 1827. Their children :

 2859 EMILY AUGUSTA, b. Dec. 21, 1846, at Farmington, Ill.; d. Sept. 23, 1847.
 2860 FREDERICK, b. May 28, 1849, at Farmington, Ill.
 2861 OSCAR, b. April 3, 1855, at Farmington, Ill.; is a printer.
 2862 MARTHA ANN, b. May 3, 1863, at Farmington, Ill.

2860 FREDERICK HATCH, (son of Frederick Wm.,) of Farmington, Ill., omnibus proprietor, was married, Nov. 18, 1876, to Mattie Jane Lull of Boscobel, Wis., a school teacher.

2847 MARIA ALLYN HATCH, (dau. of 2830 Daniel D.,) b. Dec. 12, 1824, was married to Riley Bristol, Nov. 2, 1843, at Farmington, Ill. He was born in Harwinton, Conn., May 18, 1822. They live at Farmington, Ill., and have had these four children, all born there :

 2863 ELLEN ANN, b. May 6, 1846.
 2864 CHARLES NEWCOMB, b. Oct. 15, 1850.
 2865 EMILY HATCH, b. Jan. 2, 1854.
 2866 HENRY RICHARD, b. Aug. 22, 1855.

2863 ELLEN ANN BRISTOL, m. April 6, 1865, Wm. S. Woodford, a merchandize broker, of Kansas City, Mo. They have two children, namely : Harry Bristol, b. Aug. 17, 1866 ; and Maud Emma, b. April 8, 1870.

2864 CHARLES NEWCOMB BRISTOL, of Farmington, Ill., m. Alice Ida Reid. He is express messenger on the T. P. & W. R. R.

2866 HENRY RICHARD BRISTOL, merchant and druggist, with his father, in Farmington, Ill., m. Ella Frances Gonard, Aug. 27, 1876.

2848 ELLEN ANN HATCH, (dau. of 2830 Daniel D.,) b. Dec. 29, 1826, was married to Walter Howell Taylor, of New York City, Oct. 30, 1846, at Lockport, N. Y. They live in Jersey City. Their children :

2867 LAMROEAUX HATCH, b. Dec. 4, 1852; d. young.
2868 FANNY HATCH, b. Feb. 22, 1854; m. Albert L. Stetson, of Farmington, Ill.
2869 FRANK BLISS, b. Dec. 31, 1855; d. April 3, 1860.
2870 FRED. LAMOREAUX, b. April 10, 1861.
2871 NELLIE ELIZABETH, b. March 20, 1864.

2849 EMILY STEARNS HATCH, (dau. of 2830 Daniel D.,) b. Sept. 10, 1831, was married to Rev. Joseph Edwin Roy. He was born at Martinsburg, Ohio, Feb. 7, 1827. They were married at Farmington, Ill., June 21, 1853. Their children:

2872 JOHN BLANCHARD, b. May 3, 1854, at Brimfield, Ill.
2873 FANNY ALMIRA, b. May 23, 1856, at Chicago, Ill.
2874 JOHN, b. July 6, 1858, at Chicago, Ill.
2875 EMILY HATCH, b. Aug. 16, 1860, at Chicago, Ill.
2876 CATHERINE MARIA, b. June 25, 1863, at Chicago, Ill.
2877 JOSEPH HENRY, b. Oct. 18, 1866, at Chicago, Ill.
2878 FREDERIC EDWIN, b. March 6, 1873, at Oak Park, Ill.

2850 HARRIET PETERS BURNELL, m. Henry S. Northrop, an Oberlin graduate, June 6, 1856, who d. Feb. 22, 1857. No child. She is a teacher of pencil drawing and oil painting, in Olivet College, Michigan.

2831 JOHN HATCH, (son of 2742 Eunice and Reuben,) b. July 10, 1786, was married, March 6, 1811, to Sarah Edwards, dau. of Thomas and Matilda C. He d. at Keene, N. H., April 25, 1837; his wife d. there Oct. 6, 1851. Their children:

2879 JOHN CHANDLER, b. June 17, 1811. He m. Charlotte Adams, of Providence, R. I., Oct. 4, 1836; she d. Dec. 9, 1838. He. m. second, April 2, 1840, Sarah Everett, of Dubuque, Iowa, who d. April 15, 1846, at Keene; he d. there, Nov. 29, 1850. He had two children: 1, Sarah Edwards, b. Jan. 5, 1841; m. Henry R. Austin, of Malone, N. Y.; 2, Frank Everett, b. July 17, 1844, who served 3 years in the 15th Reg't of Mass. Volunteers, and one year in the first New Jersey Cavalry, in the war of Rebellion; lives in N. Y. City.
2880 THOMAS E., b. April 1, 1820; d. March 22, 1821.
2881 THOMAS E., b. Aug. 11, 1822; m. Harriet M. Handerson, June 12, 1852, dau. of Hon. Phineas and Hannah; lives in Keene, N. H. Two children: Mabel, b. Aug. 26, 1856; Robert Denison, b. Sept. 2, 1859.
2882 REUBEN, b. July 3, 1825; m. Phebe A. Sparhawk, May 6, 1852; lives in Chicago.
2883 A SON, b. and d. in 1828.

2832 DR. HORACE HATCH, (son of 2742 Eunice and Reuben,) b. May, 1788, was married, Jan. 21, 1821, to Mary Y.

Capt. John Denison's Descendants.

Smith, at Norwich, Vt. He was a highly esteemed practising physician, in Vermont. He d. Oct. 18, 1873, in N. Y. City, his wife d. Aug. 6, 1849, at Burlington, Vt. His children:

2884 HORACE, b. Feb. 5, 1822; homeopathic physician; lives in Washington, D. C.; is married, but has no child.
2885 WILLIAM BAILEY, b. Dec. 24, 1823; of the firm of Fairbanks & Co., N. Y.
2886 MARY YATES, b. Sept. 5, 1825.
2887 TWIN SONS, b. and d. March 6, 1823.
2889 ALFREDERIC SMITH, b. July 24, 1829.
2890 EDWARD PAYSON, b. July 11, 1832.

2886 MARY YATES HATCH, (dau. of 2832 Dr. Horace,) m. Lucius E. Chittenden, Sept. 15, 1852; lives in New York City. Children:

2891 HORACE HATCH, b. Jan. 24, 1855.
2892 MARY HATCH, b. Oct. 19, 1860.
2893 BESSIE BORODELL, b. Oct. 5, 1864.

2833 ELIZABETH HATCH, (dau. of 2742 Eunice and Reuben,) b. April, 1790, was married March 4, 1807, to Darius Jones, at Weathersfield, Vt. She d. Oct. 13, 1876, in New York City. Children:

2894 ELLEN A. B, b. Jan. 10, 1808; d. Feb. 28, 1837; m. Walter J. Shepherd; no child.
2895 MARY, b. Jan. 8, 1810; m. Geo. B. Green.
2896 HARRIET H., b. Oct. 21, 1813; twice married.
2897 REUBEN HATCH. Sept. 4, 1816; m. Georgiana Crane.
2898 ALBERT D., b. Sept. 23, 1828; lives in New York City unmarried.
2900 ANNA GREEN.

2897 REUBEN HATCH JONES, (son of 2833 Elizabeth and Darius,) m. Georgiana Crane, Nov. 29, 1843; lives in New York City. Two children:

2901 GEORGE A., b. Sept. 21, 1844; m. Elizabeth A. Conover, Nov. 24, 1869, and has these: Mary C., b. July 31, 1870; Edward M., b. May 22, 1873; William P., b. June 8, 1876.
2902 ELIZABETH A., b. Oct. 7, 1846.

2834 FANNY HATCH, (dau. of 2742 Eunice and Reuben,) b. April 19, 1792, was married, Feb. 1, 1809, at Norwich, Vt., to Joseph Cutting. He d. at Lockport, Ill., aged 69; she d. June, 1853, in N. Y. City, aged 61. Their children:

2903 ALBERT H., b. Dec., 1809; d. in infancy.
2904 JOHN H., b. July, 1811; m. Abigail Emerson.
2905 ANN M., b. Oct. 19, 1813; m. William Gooding.

2906 Reuben H., b. Dec., 1815; no family; fate unknown.
2907 Eunice D., b. Feb., 1816; m. Jasper A. Gooding; 8 children.
2908 Mary A., b. Dec., 1819; m. Isaac Hardy, Chicago.
2909 Catherine M., b. in 1823; d. young.
2910 Catherine F. G., b. Feb. 14, 1829; m ; P. O., Hyde Park, Ill.
2911 Jospeph H., b. Nov. 14, 1831; went to Colorado.
2912 George, b. in 1833; d. in infancy.
2913 Harriet L. B., b. in 1835; m. a Baldwin, Chicago.

2835 Aurora Hatch, (dau. of 2742 Eunice and Reuben,) b. April 22, 1794, was married, Jan. 6, 1813, to Luther Dyer. She d. Nov. 7, 1873. Two children:

> **2914** Almeda, b. April 5, 1816, and d. Oct. 6, 1868; m. first, a Phelps, and had Hattie; m. second, John Ranney, and had: Frank, b. April 23, 1840; Henrietta, b. Dec. 25, 1841; Jessie, b. Nov. 12, 1851.
> **2915** Cornelia, b. July 2, 1821; m. a Diedrich, and had: William, b. Feb. 8, 1841; and Louisa, b. Jan. 29, 1843, d. Nov. 21, 1846.

2836 Harriet Hinckley Hatch, (dau. of 2742 Eunice and Reuben,) b. April 2, 1796, was married, Oct. 25, 1819, to Rev. Absalom Peters, D. D. He was born at Wentworth, N. H., Sept. 19, 1793; was a graduate of Dartmouth College and of Princeton Theological Seminary; was pastor of the Congregational Churches in Bennington, Vt., and in Williamstown, Mass.; was Professor in Union Theological Seminary, N. Y.; and for many years was Secretary of the American Home Missionary Society. He d. May 18, 1869. The children:

> **2916** George Absalom, b. May 12, 1821; is a physician.
> **2917** Harriet Adaline, b. June 13, 1823; m. Rev. Wm. Clift.
> **2918** Horace Hatch, b. Nov. 4, 1825; d. Sept. 15, 1827.
> **2919** Edward Payson, b. Oct. 9, 1828.
> **2920** Frances Margaretta, b. March 6, 1831; d. May 4, 1832.
> **2921** Mary Elizabeth, b. May 13, 1835; m. Albert S. Ward.
> **2922** James Hugh, b. Nov. 13, 1837; m. Mary Booth.

2916 Dr. George A. Peters, (son of 2836 Harriet and Rev. Absalom,) was married, April 10, 1849, to Julia Coggill; lives in New York City. She d. Sept. 17, 1873. Two children:

> **2923** Frederick Denison, b. Nov. 25, 1852; d. May 3, 1859.
> **2924** Bertha Borodell, b. Feb. 13, 1855. She m. Horace H. Chittenden, Oct. 11, 1877. He was b. Feb. 13, 1855. They live in New York City, and have: George Peters, b. July, 1879.

2917 Harriet Adaline Peters, (dau. of 2836 Harriet and Rev. Absalom,) b. June 13, 1823, was married, Jan. 1, 1845,

Capt. John Denison's Descendants. 141

to Rev. William Clift. They live at Mystic Bridge, Conn. Three children : see Nos. 2645, 2646, 2647.

2921 MARY ELIZABETH PETERS, (dau. of 2836 Harriet and Rev. Absalom,) was married, June 1, 1854, to Albert S. Ward. Three children :

    2928 HARRIET PETERS, b. Aug. 7, 1856.
    2929 MARY ELIZABETH, b. Sept. 7, 1858.
    2930 FREDERICK, b. July 17, 1861.

2922 JAMES HUGH PETERS, (son of 2836 Harriet and Rev. Absalom,) was married, Feb. 1, 1866, to Mary Booth ; lives at Englewood, N. J. Children :

    2931 THEODORE LEWIS, b. June 25, 1869.
    2932 GEORGE A., b. Oct. 14, 1871; d. Oct. 17, 1871.
    2933 LOUISA EDGAR, b. Nov. 25, 1872.
    2933½ HUGH, b. May 6, 1880.

2837 ADELINE HATCH, (dau. of 2742 Eunice and Reuben,) b. April 3, 1798, was married, March 10, 1822, to Hon. Milo L. Bennett, of Burlington, Vt. He was born in Sharon, Conn., May 28, 1789, graduated at Yale College in 1811, studied law at Litchfield, and went to Manchester, Vt. In 1817, he *m.* Susan R. Howe, who had two daughters, and d. in 1820. He was Judge of Probate and State Attorney for the County of Burlington, Vt. In 1850, he was elected Judge of the Supreme Court of Vermont, which office he held until 1860. He received from Dartmouth the degree of LL.D. He was made head of the commission to revise the general laws of Vermont ; and afterwards edited an American edition of Shelford on Railways. Judge Bennett d. in Taunton, Mass, July 7, 1868 ; his wife Adeline d. at Burlington, Vt., Aug. 9, 1867. Their children :

    2934 MARY HOWE, b. Feb. 16, 1823.
    2935 EDMUND HATCH, b. April 6, 1824.
    2936 HENRY M., b. March 2, 1831.

2935 EDMUND HATCH BENNETT, (son of 2837 Adeline and Judge Milo,) was graduated at Vermont University in 1843, admitted to the bar in 1847, and settled in Taunton, Mass., in 1848. In 1858, he was made Judge of Probate and Insolvency, which office he still holds. He edited all Judge Story's legal works ; is lecturer in the Dane Law School, at Cambridge, and Prof. and Dean in the Boston University Law School, and has received from the Vermont University the degree of LL D. In the years 1864, 1865, 1866, 1867, he was Mayor of the City of Taunton. He was married, June 29, 1853, to Sally Crocker, dau. of Hon. Samuel Crocker of Taunton. Their children:

    2937 CAROLINE CROCKER, b. Oct. 9, 1854; d. July 25, 1855.
    2938 EDMUND NEVILLE, b. May 23, 1856.
    2939 SAMUEL CROCKER, b. April 19, 1858.
    2940 MARY ANDREWS, b. Jan. 18, 1861.

2838 LUCY C. HATCH, (dau. of 2742 Eunice and Reuben,) b. August, 1800, was married in 1820, to Rev. Rufus W. Bailey, D. D. He was b. April 18, 1793, in North Yarmouth, Me., graduated at Dartmouth College, was a tutor there for several years, was a pastor in Norwich, Vt., and in Pittsfield, Mass., and was a teacher in North Carolina and in Texas. He d. at Huntsville, Texas, April 25, 1863. His wife d. in 1832, at Columbia, S. C. Their children:

    2941 MARY ELIZABETH, b. June 5, 1822.
    2942 HARRIET PETERS, b. April 18, 1824.
    2943 SUSAN SKINNER, b. in 1826; d. in 1828.
    2944 FRANCIS BROWN, b. Aug. 8, 1829.

2839 ALBERT G. HATCH, (son of 2742 Eunice and Reuben,) b. Dec. 26, 1802, was married, Sept. 7, 1829, to Harriet Lemmex, who d. Feb. 21, 1854. He is postmaster at Windsor, Vt.. Children:

    2945 HENRY L., b. Sept. 29, 1830; m. H. K. Durrie; lives in Chicago.
    2946 JANE E., b. June 24, 1836; m. N. P. Lovering, of Boston.
    2947 MARY E., b. Jan. 10, 1845; m James R. Gardner.

2941 MARY E. BAILEY, (dau. of 2838 Lucy C. and Rev. Rufus W.,) was married, in 1846, to John F. Rives, of Edwards Station, Hinds Co., Miss. She d. in 1857. Children:

    2948 BETTIE EARLY.
    2949 MARY GREEN.
    2950 JOHN FLETCHER.

2942 HARRIET P. BAILEY, (dau. of 2838 Lucy C. and Rev. Rufus W.,) was married, July 8, 1846, to Prof. John L. Campbell, of Lexington, Va. Children:

    2951 WM. BAILEY, b. May 5, 1847; d. Sept. 17, 1848.
    2952 MARY, b. April 26, 1849; d. Nov. 24, 1850.

2953 Lucy Bailey, b. Dec. 4, 1850; m. Rev. Wm. A. Dabney, of Atlanta, Ga., Aug. 11, 1873; Children: Matilda Williams, b. Sept., 1874; Wm. Lyle, b. May, 1876.
2954 Susan Esther, b. July 20, 1852; d. Aug. 6, 1853.
2955 John Lyle, b. March 28, 1854; a lawyer.
2956 Edmund D., b. Jan. 1, 1857.
2957 Robert F., b. Dec. 12, 1858.
2958 Harriet Hatch, b. July 1, 1860.
2959 Harry Donald, b. July 29, 1862.
2960 Virginia Waddell, June 13, 1865.

2944 Francis Brown Bailey, (son of 2833 Lucy C. and Rev. Rufus W.,) was married, March 8, 1860, to Ellen Hartley, of Alexandria, Va., b. Aug. 26, 1827. She d. Oct. 4, 1867, and, July 20, 1871, he m. Virginia Ellen Butt, b. Jan. 17, 1845. He lives at Palestine, Texas. Children:

2961 Mary F., b. May 8, 1863.
2962 Rufus W., b. April 8, 1865.
2963 Joseph F., b. Sept. 5, 1872.
2964 Marvin C., b. Feb. 10, 1874.
2965 H. Elizabeth, b. Feb. 3, 1877.
2966 John Campbell, b. Feb. 14, 1880.

2842 Joseph D. Hatch, (son of 2742 Eunice and Reuben,) b. Jan. 21, 1811, was married, April 5, 1832, to Frances S. Forbes; residence, Burlington, Vt. Children:

2967 Elizabeth, b. April 8, 1833; m. Isaac Green; d. June 17, 1860.
2968 Martha, b. May 26, 1839; m. Daniel Lindsey.
2969 William D., b. May 11, 1846; d. July 6, 1846.
2970 Josie, b. Nov. 13, 1847; m. Rodney S. Wires.

2889 Alfrederic S. Hatch, (son of 2832 Dr. Horace,) b. July 24, 1829, was married, May 4, 1854, to Theodosia Ruggles, b. Feb. 27, 1829. He lives in New York City, and belongs to the firm of Fiske & Hatch, bankers. Children:

2971 John, b. April 7, 1855.
2972 Mary Yates, b. Dec. 15, 1856.
2973 Wm. Denison, b. July 13, 1858.
2974 Emily Theodosia, b. Oct. 17, 1860.
2975 Frederick Horace, b. May 2, 1862.
2976 Linsay Fiske, b. Feb. 9, 1864.
2977 Jane Storrs, b. June 24, 1865.
2978 Horace, b. Feb. 22, 1867.
2979 Edward Payson, b. July 17, 1868.
2980 Jessamine, b. March 18, 1870.
2981 Emily Nichols, b. Aug. 2, 1871.

2732 DANIEL DENISON, 3rd, (Daniel[4], Daniel[3], John[2], George[1],) b. Dec. 9, 1745, was married to Elizabeth Andross about 1767. He lived in Vermont, went to Knox, N. Y., lived in Canada, and died, Oct. 15, 1802, "in Bennington or Pawlet, Vt." His widow lived in the family of her son Asa, in Richmond, N. Y., and died there, June 11, 1826, aged 78 years. Children:

    2982 DANIEL, 4th., b. in 1768, had a family.
    2983 ASA, b. May 16, 1770; m. Sylvia Horsford.
    2984 ESTHER, b. in 1776; m. Minor Waldron, at Knox, N. Y.
    2985 ELIZABETH, b. about 1782.
    2986 W. WHEELER, b. Aug. 19, 1788; d. unmarried, aged 80.
    2987 LAWTON, b. Dec. 19, 1791; drowned in the Ohio River.

2982 DANIEL DENISON, 4th, (Daniel[5], Daniel[4], Daniel[3], John[2], George[1],) b. in 1768, was married and had a family. We have not been able to secure a complete record of his family. The following appears to be correct, as far as it goes. He had two sons:

    2983½ GEORGE, b. about 1791.
    2984½ STANTON, d. in Herkimer Co., N. Y., childless.

2983½ GEORGE DENISON, (son of 2982 Daniel,) m. a wife who was living at the age of 86 years, in August, 1880; and consequently, was born in 1794. All we know of their children is, that they had a son Daniel who says he was their only son.

2985½ DANIEL DENISON, (son of 2783½ George,) lives in Richmond, Ill. He has a family, and is a large farmer, and raises much stock. His report is, that he keeps from 70 to 80 cows, and usually has on hand from 30 to 50 horses. He has two sons:

    2986½ CLARENCE.
    2987½ LINCOLN.

2983 ASA DENISON, (Daniel[5], Daniel[4], Daniel[3], John[2], George[1],) b. May 16, 1770, was married, Oct. 27, 1795, to Sylvia Horsford. She was born Feb. 26, 1780. He settled in Richmond, N. Y., in 1795. It was then a wilderness. He had but little money; but he worked and prospered. The land he bought and cleared, is now the seat of a thriving place known as " Denison's Corners." This being the chief stopping place on the old stage road between Canandaigua and Geneseo, he built a large tavern, which became the centre of a large village. He was the landlord of this " half-way house," for about forty years. Asa Denison died, Jan. 15, 1855. His children :

 2988 ANN, b. Oct. 5, 1796; *m.* Adolphus F. Morrison.
 2989 ZEBADIAH, b. Sept. 21, 1798; *m.* Harriette Mead.
 2990 AHIRA, b. May 13, 1800; d. June 3, 1813.
 2991 CYNTHIA, b. March 1, 1802; *m.* Franklin Green.
 2992 CHLOE b. April 24, 1804; *m.* John Morrison.
 2993 SMEDLEY, b. Feb. 19, 1806; *m.* Polly Woodruff.
 2994 ASA, Jr., b. March 31, 1808; *m.* Asenath Frost.
 2995 JULIA ANN, b. Oct. 1, 1810; *m.* John Wright; no child. They lived in Detroit, Mich.; she d. June 5, 1849.

Asa Denison's wife, Sylvia, d. Feb. 26, 1812 ; he married, 2nd, Phebe Crooks, who had four children, and died, March 3, 1819. Her children :

 2996 SYLVIA, b. June 21, 1813; *m.* Benajah Tubbs.
 2997 MARYETTE, b. in 1814; *m.* Daniel Stanley.
 2998 SANFORD, b. in 1816; d. Aug. 3, 1829.
 2999 JEROME B., b. Jan. 11, 1819; *m.* Almira Stanly, July 4, 1841; he d. May 30, 1870; no child.

Asa Denison married, 3d, Laurena Morrison, Dec. 18, 1841 ; no other child.

2988 ANN DENISON, (Asa[6], Daniel[5], Daniel[4], Daniel[3], John[2], George[1],) b. Oct. 5, 1796, was married to Adolphus F. Morrison, Jan. 26, 1829. Residence, Erie, Pa.; has had but one child :

 3000 LEVERITT; *m.* Missouri Bliss.

2989 ZEBADIAH DENISON, (Asa[6], Daniel[5], Daniel[4], Daniel[3], John[2], George[1],) b. Sept. 21, 1798, was married to Harriette Mead, Feb. 4, 1821, and d. in 1870. Residence, Ashtabula, Ohio. Two children :

 3001 THALIE ANN; *m.* Dr. Fox.
 3002 HARRIETTE; *m.*

2991 CYNTHIA DENISON, (Asa[6], Daniel[5], Daniel[4], Daniel[3], John[2], George[1],) b. March 1, 1802, was married to Franklin Green, June 22, 1828. Residence, Badger, Wis. Two children :

 3003 JEROME B., b. June 12, 1831 ; *m.* Louisa Hardy.
 3004 CARLETON L., b. July 27, 1837; *m.*

2992 CHLOE DENISON, (Asa⁶, Daniel⁵, Daniel⁴, Daniel³, John², George¹,) b. April 24, 1804, was married to John Morrison, Sept. 29, 1825; lived at Meadville, Pa.; d. Dec. 14, 1872. Six children :

    3005 ANN E., b. June 27, 1827; m. Sam'l R. Chesebro', of Rochester, N. Y.
    3006 CARLTON J, b. Dec. 20, 1828; m. in San Francisco, Cal.
    3007 AMELIA. b. Feb. 2, 1831; m. Charles Candee, of St. Louis. Mo.
    3008 MARY JANE, b. Dec. 12, 1832, not married, lives in Rochester. N. Y.
    3009 LIZZIE S., b. April 23, 1837; m. —— Parsons of Rock Island, Ill.
    3010 JULIA E., b. March 18, 1840; m. Edwin Burt, of Meadville, Pa.

2994 ASA DENISON, JR., (Asa⁶, Daniel⁵, Daniel⁴, Daniel³, John², George¹,) b. March 31, 1803, was married to Asenath Frost, Oct. 14, 1835. Residence, Richmond, N. Y. Two children :

    3011 CHLOE ANN, b. March 9, 1837; not married.
    3012 HENRY S., b. Sept. 18, 1840; m. Lydia A. Cornell.

3012 HENRY S. DENISON, (Asa, Jr.⁷, Asa⁶, Daniel⁵, Daniel⁴, Daniel³, John², George¹,) b. Sept. 18, 1840, was married to Lydia A. Cornell, March 5, 1873; lives in Maywood, Kansas. His children :

    3013 GEORGE M., b. Dec. 19, 1873.
    3014 AUGUSTA M., twin, b. Aug. 27, 1877.
    3015 ANNIE C., twin, b. Aug. 27, 1877.

2993 SMEDLEY DENISON, (Asa⁶, Daniel⁵, Daniel⁴, Daniel³, John², George¹,) b. Feb. 19, 1806, was married to Polly Woodruff, Aug. 27, 1829. He lived at Erie, Pa., and died Oct. 29, 1872. They had :

    3016 CAROLINE. b. 1830; m. —— Magee.
    3017 MARY, b. 1832; m. John Slausen.
    3018 SARAH, b. 1835; m. —— Sayer.
    3019 FRANCES, b. 1838.
    3020 SAMUEL, b. 1840; went to Texas.
    3021 ASA, b. 1844.
    3022 ELLEN, b. 1847.
    3023 DANIEL, b. 1850; m.; went to Texas.

2996 SYLVIA DENISON, (Asa⁶, Daniel⁵, Daniel⁴, Daniel³, John², George¹,) b. in 1813, was married to Benajah Stubbs, Oct. 3, 1835. Residence, New York City. Three children :

    3024 FANNIE, b. Dec. 25, 1837; m. Joseph Page of Oakland, Cal.

3025 MARY, b. Feb. 8, 1840; m. John Browning of New York City.
3026 WILLIE, b. April 27, 1844; m. Sarah Frances Wood of N. Y. City.

2997 MARYETTE DENISON, (Asa[6], Daniel[5], Daniel[4], Daniel[3], John[2], George[1],) b. in 1814, was married to Daniel Stanley, in 1841. Residence, Lima, N. Y. But one child:

3027 CHARLES D., b. June 21, 1852; not married.

2734 ROBERT DENISON, (Daniel[4], Daniel[3], John[2], George[1],) b. Dec. 12, 1749, was married, March 17, 1774, to Anna Chesebro', of Stonington. About 1793, he emigrated from Stonington to Knox, N. Y. His children:

3028 ANNA b. 1775; m. Daniel Chesebro'.
3029 ROBERT, b. 1777; d. young.
3030 CLARISSA, b. 1779; m. Nicholas VanDerbogert; no child.
3031 NATHAN, b. March 2, 178.; m. Elizabeth Thompson.
3032 PHEBE, b. Dec. 30, 1782; m. Amos Chesebro'.
3033 RENSALAER, b. March 2, 1784; m. Mary Wood.
3034 MARTHA, b. Aug. 26, 1787; m. Dr. John Wood.
3035 ESTHER, b. Nov. 15, 1790; m. Alexander Thompson.
3036 POLLY, b. 1792; m. William VanDerbogert.

3032 PHEBE DENISON, (Robert[5], Daniel[4], Daniel[3], John[2], George[1],) b. Dec. 30, 1782, was married to Amos Chesebro', July 20, 1801. They lived in Stonington, Conn. She died Oct. 9, 1846; her husband died Aug. 3, 1846, aged 73. Their children:

3037 GRACE, b. July 13, 1803; unmarried.
3038 EDMUND, b. Aug. 26, 1805; m. Nancy D. Clift; no ch.; d. 1879.
3039 HENRY D., b. Dec. 5, 1807; m.
3040 RICHARD C., b. May 4, 1810; m. at Red Creek, N. Y.
3041 AN INFANT SON, b. 1812; d. unnamed.
3042 SAMUEL, b. Oct. 8, 1814; died unmarried.
3043 AMOS, b. Dec. 22, 1816; m.
3044 GIDEON, b. Aug. 17, 1823; m.

3034 MARTHA DENISON, (Robert[5], Daniel[4], Daniel[3], John[2], George[1],) b. Aug. 26, 1787, was married to Dr. John Wood, Nov. 25, 1807, and had eleven children. They lived in Duanesburg, N. Y. Their children:

3045 BENJAMIN F.
3046 JOHN D.
3047 J. R. T.
3048 ANGELICA L.; m. Henry Sherburn.
3049 ANGELINE L.; m. Wm. E. Knight.
3050 IDA L.; m. B. W. Jarvis.

3035 ESTHER DENISON, (Robert[5], Daniel[4], Daniel[3], John[2], George[1],) was married to Alexander Thompson, Oct. 31, 1815, and died Feb. 22, 1855; he died Dec. 24, 1869. Residence, Napanee, Ont., Can. Their children:

    3051 ALEXANDER, b. Sept. 13, 1816; m. Nancy McKim; 3 children.
    3052 RENSSALAER, b. June 22, 1818; m. Nancy McBride.
    3053 ROBERT D., b. Aug. 31, 1820; m. Alice E. Bowen.
    3054 NATHAN, b. May 23, 1822; d. May 25, 1822.
    3055 ANNA MARIA, b. Jan. 7, 1824; m. Wm. Rose.
    3056 EMILY C., b. May 9, 1826; not married.
    3057 EUNICE E., b. June 18, 1828; not married.
    3058 CLARISSA, b. Jan. 6, 1832; d. Jan. 12, 1844.

3036 POLLY DENISON, (Robert[5], Daniel[4], Daniel[3], John[2], George[1],) was married to Wm. VanDerbogart, in June, 1817; lived in Canada. Their children:

    3059 SUSANNA, b. Jan. 10, 1819; m. Peter Fretz.
    3060 ANN, b. June 19, 1830; m. E. B. Miles.
    3061 FRANCIS, b. Feb. 2, 1836; m.; large family.
    3062 NATHAN, b. 1825; d. in 1832.

3059 SUSANNA VANDERBOGART, (dau. of 3036 Polly and William,) was married Oct. 14, 1840, to Peter Fretz; lives in Napanee, Canada. Children:

    3063 MARY ALMEDA, b. Sept. 26, 1841; not married.
    3064 WILLIAM EDWIN, b. Feb. 9, 1843; m. Mary J. Scott, March 28, 1865, and died in Virginia City, Nevada, in 1868.
    3065 ESTHER ANN, b. Aug. 2, 1847; d. May 24, 1875.
    3066 FRANCIS AMASA, b. July 26, 1851; m. Martha Wattam.

3060 ANN VANDERBOGART, (dau. of 3036 Polly and Wm,) was married, Nov. 16, 1851, to E. B. Miles; lives in Napanee, Canada. Children:

    3067 POLLY ANN, b. March 6, 1852; m. Marshal Seymour.
    3068 DELIA JANE, b. June 6, 1857.
    3069 WILLIAM TAYLOR, b. May 25, 1860.
    3070 JONATHAN HOMER, b. Nov. 29, 1862.
    3071 REUBEN WRIGHT, b. May 17, 1866.

3031 NATHAN DENISON, (Robert[5], Daniel[4], Daniel[3], John[2], George[1],) b. March 2, 1781, was married to Elizabeth Thompson, Dec. 15, 1803, and settled in Napance, Ontario, Canada. He d. there, Nov. 16, 1849; she d. Nov. 19, 1873. They had:

    3072 AMOS, b. May 8, 1805; m. Mary Rose.
    3073 ALEXANDER, b. April 25, 1807; m. Nancy Davis.
    3074 MARY ANN, b. Dec. 18, 1809; m. Samuel D. Shorts.

3075 PHEBE, b. April 1, 1812; m. Wm. Caton.
3076 ELIZA, b. Feb. 15, 1815; m. Daniel Ungar; d. July 3, 1858.
3077 ANGELINE, b. Nov. 20, 1817; m. John McKim; d. Dec. 8, 1854; had a dau. Martha A., who m. Edmund Swifzer, June 26, 1873.
3078 ROBERT, b. Oct. 20, 1821; m. Mary Grange; no child.
3079 DANIEL, b. Sept. 5, 1824; m. Hannah Shorts Hughes.
3080 JOHN W., b. Nov. 4, 1827; m. Phebe Jane Casey.

3072 AMOS DENISON, (Nathan[6], Robert[5], Daniel[4], Daniel[3], John[2], George[1],) b. May 8, 1805, was married to Mary Rose, March 13, 1827; lives at Napanee, Canada. Has had:

3081 NATHAN, b. April 6, 1828; m. Cynthia M. Dafoe.
3082 WILLIAM, b. Feb. 14, 1830; d. Aug. 20, 1831.
3083 NANCY J., b. May 2, 1832; m. Benj. C. Martin.
3084 JAMES R., b. Aug. 18, 1834; m. Mary E. Windover.
3085 ELIZABETH, b. June 5, 1838; m. Augustus Hughes.
3086 DANIEL E., b. April 14, 1839; m. Mary Ellen Hughes.
3087 GEORGE, b. Oct. 5, 1841; m. Mary Ellen Kirkley.
3088 SARAH A. b. Feb. 27, 1844; m. Wm. J. Hughes.
3089 JOHN A., b. Aug. 28, 1846; m. Elizabeth Richmond.
3090 ROBERT, b. April 19, 1849; m. Mary A. Parrison.

3081 NATHAN DENISON, (Amos[7], Nathan[6], Robert[5], Daniel[4], Daniel[3], John[2], George[1],) b. April 6, 1828, m. Cynthia M. Dafoe, July 30, 1849. He lives at Forest Mills, Ontario County, Canada. Children:

3091 PHEBE JANE, b. April 3, 1850; m. Alonzo Milden, Sept. 19, 1868; 1 child: Myrtie Blanche, b. July 27, 1877.
3092 ELIZABETH A., b. March 11, 1859; m. Nelson Richmond, Nov. 2, 1875; 1 child: Matie B., b. Oct. 1, 1876.

3083 NANCY J. DENISON, (Amos[7], Nathan[6], Robert[5], Daniel[4], Daniel[3], John[2], George[1],) b. May 2, 1832, was married to Benj. C. Martin, Oct. 22, 1860. They have:

3093 GEORGE ALBERT, b. Oct. 29, 1861.
3094 CEPHAS E., b. May 19, 1866.

3084 JAMES R. DENISON, (Amos[7], Nathan[6], Robert[5], Daniel[4], Daniel[3], John[2], George[1],) b. Aug. 18, 1834, m. Mary E. Windover, April 5, 1865; lives at Forest Mills, Ont., Canada, and has these:

3095 EVA JANE, b. July 14, 1866.
3096 MARY ANN, b. Jan. 21, 1868.
3097 ANSON, b. June 24, 1871.
3098 AMOS, b. May 11, 1874.

150   *Capt. John Denison's Descendants.*

3085 ELIZABETH DENISON, (Amos[7], Nathan[6], Robert[5], Daniel[4], Daniel[3], John[2], George[1],) b. June 5, 1838, *m*. Augustus Hughes, of Roblin, Ont., Canada, and has :
    3099 THOMAS G., b. Feb. 19, 1864.
    3100 AMOS D., b. May 14, 1871.
    3101 PHEBE E., b. Sept. 17, 1873.
    3102 JOHN A., b. Dec. 17, 1875.

3086 DANIEL E. DENISON, (Amos[7], Nathan[6], Robert[5], Daniel[4], Daniel[3], John[2], George[1],) b. April 14, 1839, *m*. Mary Ellen Hughes, Aug. 10, 1862 ; lives in Leinster, Ont., Canada, and has :
    3103 ALBERT E., b. May 27, 1865; d. March 11, 1866.
    3104 AURELIA J., b. Oct. 19, 1866.

3087 GEORGE DENISON, (Amos[7], Nathan[6], Robert[5], Daniel[4], Daniel[3], John[2], George[1],) b. Oct. 5, 1841, *m*. Mary Ellen Kirkley, Feb. 21, 1874, and has :
    3105 NANCY MARIA, b. Feb. 3, 1875.

3088 SARAH A. DENISON, (Amos[7], Nathan[6], Robert[5], Daniel[4], Daniel[3], John[2], George[1],) b. Feb. 27, 1844, *m*. William J. Hughes, of Roblin, Ont., and had :
    3106 MARY ETTA, b. Nov. 4, 1864.
    3107 IDA J., b. June 6, 1869.
    3108 ELLA A., b. Oct. 1, 1872.
    3109 BERTHA, b. Feb. 6, 1874.

3089 JOHN A. DENISON, (Amos[7], Nathan[6], Robert[5], Daniel[4], Daniel[3], John[2], George[1],) b. Aug. 28, 1846, *m*. Elizabeth Richmond, Jan. 10, 1867 ; lives at Napanee, Ont., Canada, and has these :
    3110 SARAH ALICE, b. Jan. 3, 1868.
    3111 MARY ELIZABETH, b. July 9, 1870 ; d. Feb. 17, 1873.
    3112 EFFA ANNIE, twin, b. Feb. 3, 1875.
    3113 EMMA MAY, twin, b. Feb. 3, 1875.

3090 ROBERT DENISON, (Amos[7], Nathan[6], Robert[5], Daniel[4], Daniel[3], John[2], George[1],) b. April 19, 1849, *m*. Mary A. Parrison, Oct. 27, 1869 ; lives at Napanee, Ont., Canada, and has these .
    3114 HANNAH M., b. Oct. 9, 1870.
    3115 THEODORE, b. Aug. 25, 1874.

3073 ALEXANDER DENISON, (Nathan[6], Robert[5], Daniel[4], Daniel[3], John[2], George[1],) b. April 25, 1807, was married to

Capt. John Denison's Descendants.

Nancy Davis, March 22, 1860, and died May 25, 1862. One child :

    3116 ANGELINE, b. May 20, 1860.

3074 MARY ANN DENISON, (Nathan[6], Robert[5], Daniel[4], Daniel[3], John[2], George[1],) b. Dec. 18, 1809, was married to Samuel D. Shorts, April 10, 1832, and died March 9, 1874. Her children :

    3117 ELIZABETH, b. April 9, 1833; *m.* R. Abbott.
    3118 JANE, b. Feb. 8, 1835.
    3119 ALEXANDER, (Rev.) b. Dec. 8, 1837; lives at Inkermann, Ont.
    3120 ANDREW, b. Jan. 16, 1840.
    3121 HANNAH, b. Jan. 27, 1846; *m.* J. L. Arnold, of Michigan.
    2122 ROBERT, (Rev.) b. July 18, 1850; lives at Bellville, Ont.

3079 DANIEL DENISON, (Nathan[6], Robert[5], Daniel[4], Daniel[3], John[2], George[1],) b. Sept. 5, 1824, was married to Hannah Shorts Hughes, March 23, 1847 ; lives at Coral, Mich. His children :

    3123 WILLIAM SHORTS, b. Feb. 15, 1848.
    3124 HENRY PERRY, b. May 5, 1853.
    3125 ANGELINE MCKIM, b. Jan. 11, 1855.
    3126 EMMA JANE, b. Aug. 29, 1864.

3075 PHEBE DENISON, (Nathan[6], Robert[5], Daniel[4], Daniel[3], John[2], George[1],) b. April 1, 1812, was married to William Caton, March 3, 1836 ; lives at Napanee, Ont. Her children :

    3127 ARCHIBALD, b. Jan. 15, 1837; d. March 26, 1855.
    3128 NATHAN A., b. Jan. 21, 1839; *m.* Jane Perry.
    3129 MILES, b. Aug. 12, 1841; d. June 1, 1854.
    3130 MARY, b. Jan. 28, 1844; d. Aug. 25, 1844.
    3131 MARIA, b. Sept. 17, 1846.
    3132 LYDIA A., b. Jan. 24, 1849.
    3133 HESTER A., b. May 17, 1851.
    3134 MARY E., b. Oct. 31, 1853.

3128 NATHAN A. CATON, (son of 3075 Phebe and William,) b. Jan. 21, 1839, was married Sept. 4, 1865, to Jane Perry ; lives at Napanee, Canada. Children :

    3135 FRANK A., b. Aug. 9, 1866.
    3136 SOLA HELENA, b. July 2, 1868.
    3137 LAURA BLANCHE, b. July 5, 1870.
    3138 FLORENCE E., b. Feb. 5, 1872.
    3139 EDITH L., b. Aug. 8, 1874.
    3140 MABEL J., b. Nov. 14, 1876.

3080 JOHN WESLEY DENISON, (Nathan[6], Robert[5], Daniel[4], Daniel[3], John[2], George[1],) b. Nov. 4, 1827, was married to Phebe Jane Casey, Dec. 2, 1856; lives at Napanee, Ont. His children:

 3141 SAMUEL C., b. Sept. 13, 1857.
 3142 RHODA E., b. March 26, 1860.
 3143 ROBERT S., b. Sept. 11, 1863.
 3144 JOHN BURNELL, b. July 29, 1865.
 3145 ADOLPHA A., b. July 3, 1869.
 3146 HANNAH LAURA, b. May 14, 1872.

3076 ELIZA DENISON, (Nathan[6], Robert[5], Daniel[4], Daniel[3], John[2], George[1],) m. Daniel Ungar, Nov. 11, 1834; lives at Napanee, Canada. They have had:

 3147 NATHAN D., b. Sept. 16, 1835; m. Rhoda H. Vanblaricom.
 3148 ELI, b. Dec. 13, 1837; d. July 12, 1848.
 3149 RACHEL, b. March 10, 1840.
 3150 ANGELINE, b. May 31, 1842; m. Geo. S. Johnson, July 28, 1875.
 3151 NELSON, b. Oct. 23, 1844; m. Melissa J. Hamley, Nov. 9, 1869.
 3152 JOHN W., b. Sept. 13, 1846; m. Sarah M. R. McQuin, Nov. 3, '75.
 3153 MARY, b. Oct. 19, 1848.
 3154 DANIEL, b. March 19, 1851; m. Amoretta Williams, June 23, '75.

3033 RENSALAER DENISON, (Robert[5], Daniel[4], Daniel[3], John[2], George[1],) b. March 2, 1784, was married to Mary Wood, and lived in Canada. He died Sept. 28, 1871. His children:

 3155 DATUS, b. May 10, 1821; m. Phebe Bicknell, June 12, 1860.
 3156 SARAH A., b. Feb. 14, 1823; m. Wm. Grange, Dec. 10, 1847.
 3157 MARY E., b. Feb. 8, 1826; m. Elias Hoffman, April 14, 1848.
 3158 ROBERT S., b. Dec. 8, 1828; m. April 16, 1851.
 3159 AMELIA, b. Oct. 14, 1832; m. James Sweet, March 8, 1856.
 3160 CLARISSA, b. Sept. 5, 1834; m. Hiram Osborn, July, 1872.
 3161 MARTHA, b. Nov. 9, 1837; m. Sylvester H. Azeltine.
 3162 ELIZABETH, b. April 6, 1839; m. Geo. Lott, March 15, 1859.

3158 ROBERT S. DENISON, (Rensalaer[6], Robert[5], Daniel[4], Daniel[3], John[2], George[1],) b. Dec. 8, 1828, was married April 16, 1851; residence, Selby, Ont., Can. Children:

 3163 ANNA E., b. April 9, 1852.
 3164 EMMA, b. April 20, 1855.
 2165 BENJAMIN F., b. Jan. 8, 1860.
 3166 JAMES R., b. Jan. 4, 1863.
 3167 DATUS R., b. April 18, 1866.
 3168 ALEXANDER, b. March 7, 1870.

3155 DATUS DENISON, (Rensalaer[6], Robert[5], Daniel[4], Daniel[3], John[2], George[1],) b. May 10, 1822, was married, June 12,

1860, to Phebe Bicknell, b. April 13, 1837 ; lives at Napanee, Canada. Children :

    3169 ANNETTA MARIA, b. April 13, 1861.
    3170 EMMA JANE, b. Sept. 29, 1863.
    3171 ROBERT WILSON, b. May 18, 1865.

3157 MARY E. DENISON, (Rensalaer[6], Robert[5], Daniel[4], Daniel[3], John[2], George[1],) b. Feb. 8, 1826, was married April 25, 1848, to Elias Hoffman, of Moscow, Ont. Children :

    3172 MIROW TILLISON, b. April 9, 1849.
    3173 DATUS ENSIGN, b. June 25, 1851 ; *m.* ; lives in Ontario.
    3174 ALMIRA C., b. July 18, 1853 ; *m.* Samuel Azeltine.
    3175 WILLIAM, b. May 18, 1856.
    3176 AMOS E., b. Sept. 11, 1858.
    3177 GEORGE ELIAS, b. Oct. 29, 1860.
    3178 AMELIA, b. Dec. 27, 1862.
    3179 ISAAC, b. March 8, 1865 ; d. Feb. 7, 1867.
    3180 BERTHA MAY, b. Oct. 8, 1871 ; d. Jan. 2, 1873.

3159 AMELIA DENISON, (Rensalaer[6], Robert[5], Daniel[4], Daniel[3], John[2], George[1],) b. Oct. 14, 1832, was married March 8, 1856, to James Sweet ; live at Selby, Ont., Can. Children :

    3181 ESTHER, b. April 21, 1857.
    3182 MARY J., b. May 29, 1860 ; d. Sept. 3, 1861.
    3183 ALMIRA, b. Jan. 17, 1862.
    3184 ELMA, b. Dec. 23, 1863.
    3185 HENRY R., b. July 8, 1866.
    3186 LOUISA, b. June 19, 1869.

3160 CLARISSA DENISON, (Rensalaer[6], Robert[5], Daniel[4], Daniel[3], John[2], George[1],) b. Sept. 5, 1834, was married, first, Sept. 11, 1856, to John D. Gallup, who d. Feb. 6, 1864 ; second, to Hiram Osborn, in 1872 ; lives at Arden, Ont. Children :

    3187 MARY ELIZABETH, b. Dec. 7, 1857.
    3188 ANN MARIA, b. Nov. 28, 1859 ; d. Nov. 15, 1864.
    3189 JOHN GARDNER, b. May 6, 1862.
    3190 AMELIA ADELAIDE, b. Aug. 24, 1864.
    3191 WILLIAM THOMAS, b. March 28, 1868.
    3192 EMMA LOVINA, b. Sept. 18, 1872.
    3193 ABBY O. ZUETTA, b. Sept. 20, 1875.

3161 MARTHA DENISON, (Rensalaer[6], Robert[5], Daniel[4], Daniel[3], John[2], George[1],) b. Nov. 9, 1837, was married, July 17, 1862, to Sylvester H. Azeltine ; lives in Moscow, Canada. Children :

    3194 ROBERT E., b. April 25, 1863.
    3195 CORNELIA ETNA, b. July 17, 1867.

Capt. John Denison's Descendants.

3162 ELIZABETH DENISON, (Rensalaer[6], Robert[5], Daniel[4], Daniel[3], John[2], George[1],) b. April 6, 1839, was married, March 17, 1859, to George Lott; lives in Napanee, Ont. Children:

- **3196** FRANKLIN, b. Jan. 26, 1860; d. March 6, 1860.
- **3197** ALBERT, b. March 30, 1861.
- **3198** WILLIAM, b. June 14, 1864.
- **3199** JOSEPH, b. Jan. 6, 1870; d. May 17. 1863.

2735 ISAAC DENISON, (Daniel[4], Daniel[3], John[2], George[1],) b. Dec. 20, 1751, was married, Nov. 10, 1773, to Eunice Williams; lived at Stonington, Conn.; d. there Feb. 14, 1817. He had these twelve children:

- **3200** EBENEZER, b. July 10, 1774; twice married.
- **3201** ESTHER, b. April 26, 1776; twice married.
- **3202** SARAH, b. April 9, 1778; m. Elam Burrows.
- **3203** THANKFUL, b. May 20, 1780; m. Amos Clift.
- **3204** EUNICE, b. May 20, 1782; m. Nathaniel Clift.
- **3205** ANN B., b. Sept. 22, 1784; twice married.
- **3206** MERCY, b. Feb. 9, 1787; m. Zebediah Gates.
- **3207** ISAAC, b. Feb. 1, 1790; m. Lavina Fish.
- **3208** DANIEL, b. April 26, 1791; drowned, Feb. 2, 1800.
- **3209** FREDERIC, b. Dec. 27, 1795; d. Nov. 1, 1814.
- **3210** ELISHA W., b. April 3, 1798; m. Fanny C. Hicks.
- **3211** HEZEKIAH, b. July 19, 1803; d. Jan. 30. 1804.

3200 EBENEZER DENISON, (Isaac[5], Daniel[4], Daniel[3], John[2], George[1],) b. July 10, 1774, was married, first, Feb. 10, 1798, to Jane (Branch) Williams, and had:

- **3212** DANIEL, b. May 15, 1800; d. June 15, 1802.
- **3213** EBENEZER, b. May 30, 1802; twice married.
- **3214** SALAH B., b. July 22, 1805; d. Nov. 29, 1809.

The first wife, Jane, died March 19, 1806; and Sept. 12, 1816, he m. 2nd, Phebe M. Smith, but had no more children. He died Dec. 20, 1856; she died April 4, 1840. This Ebenezer Denison lived in Stonington, and was a deacon.

3213 EBENEZER DENISON, JR., (Ebenezer[6], Isaac[5], Daniel[4], Daniel[3], John[2], George[1],) b. May 20, 1802, was married to Mary Niles Hazard, Nov. 5, 1831, and had:

- **3215** JOSHUA H., b. Aug. 12, 1833; d. unmarried, aged 32.
- **3216** JANE E., b. Aug. 19, 1835; d. unmarried, aged 27.
- **3217** MARY PHEBE, b. Aug. 14, 1838; d. Oct. 28, 1838.
- **3218** PHEBE MOORE, b. Dec. 19, 1840; d. April 10, 1842.
- **3219** MARY LUNDIE, b. Feb. 28, 1843; m. J. A. Chappell; lives in Illinois; has Urania, b. Aug. 1872, and Denison, b. May, 1874; George S., b. Aug. 6, 1876; Aleck F. b. March 12, 1878.

3220 Albert Hale, b. Feb. 24, 1845; d. Dec. 27, 1845.
3221 Elias Cornelius, b. Dec. 2, 1846; d. May 2, 1847.

The first wife, Mary N., died, Dec. 23, 1846, and April 9, 1849, he was married, 2nd, to Lydia S. Noyes. This Ebenezer Denison, Jr., was also a deacon. He lived in Stonington, at Mystic, and died there, Dec. 26, 1869. His children by the second wife were as follows:

3222 Albert, b. Aug. 19, 1850.
3223 Harriet B., b. Dec. 24, 1853; m. Edmund B. Hart, in 1878; lives at Meriden, Conn.; has Edmund Denison, b. Oct. 26, 1879.
3224 Franklin H., b. July 24, 1852; d. March 13, 1853.
3225 Anna C., b. March 25, 1856.
3226 Eliza M., b. May 17, 1858.

3210 Elisha W. Denison, (Isaac^5, Daniel^4, Daniel^3, John^2, George^1,) b. April 3, 1798, was married to Fanny Hicks, June 5, 1820. They lived at Mystic River, Conn.; he died Oct. 7, 1849; she d. Oct. 18, 1846, aged 51. Their children:

3227 Elisha A., b. April 8, 1821; lives in New London.
3228 Frances I., b. Aug. 25, 1823; m. Robert Greene.
3229 Phebe E., b. Sept. 22, 1825; m. John Prentice.
3230 Hiram C., b. Nov. 27, 1829; m. Eliza A. Minor.
3231 Abby C., b. Aug. 29, 1827; m. Wm. B. Noyes.
3232 Eunice C., b. June 8, 1833; m. Henry Palmer Hewitt.
3233 Sarah M., b. Dec. 8, 1835; m. Caleb Burdick.
3234 Ann E., b. April 11, 1841; d. June 25, 1841.

3227 Elisha A. Denison, (Elisha W.^{6}, Isaac^5, Daniel^4, Daniel^3, John^2, George^1,) m. Susan A. Dickinson, Feb. 2, 1845, lives in New London, Conn.; one child:

3235 Fanny, b. Oct. 6, 1846.

3230 Hiram C. Denison, (Elisha W.^{6}, Isaac^5, Daniel^4, Daniel^3, John^2, George^1,) m. Eliza A. Minor, Feb. 13, 1862; lives at Mystic River, Conn.; two children:

3236 Ira Warren, b. July 16, 1865.
3237 Charles Hiram, b. Dec. 2, 1869.

3233 Sarah M. Denison, (Elisha W.^{6}, Isaac^5, Daniel^4, Daniel^3, John^2, George^1,) b. Dec. 8, 1855, m. Caleb Burdick; lived at Mystic River; married Oct. 24, 1852; d. Dec. 5, 1870. Her children:

3238 Frank. b. June 13, 1854.
3239 Eugene, b. Oct. 20, 1856.
3240 Walter, b. Sept. 18, 1858.
3241 Thomas, b. Jan. 14, 1867.

3228 FRANCES I. DENISON, (Elisha W.[6], Isaac[5], Daniel[4], Daniel[3], John[2], George[1],) b. Aug. 24, 1823, was married to Robert Greene of New London, Aug. 6, 1843, and d. Nov. 22, 1848. He married a second wife and went to California. Her children :

    3242 FRANCES, b. Feb. 6. 1845 ; d. Sept. 1, 1846.
    3243 FRANCIS J., b. Nov. 5, 1848; m.: lives in N. Y. City.

3229 PHEBE E. DENISON, (Elisha W.[6], Isaac[5], Daniel[4], Daniel[3], John[2], George[1],) b. Sept. 22, 1825, m. John Prentice, Feb. 14, 1847, and died, Oct. 15, 1858, lived at Mystic River, and had :

    3244 CHARLES M., b. July 19, 1848.
    3245 WILLIAM H., b. Sept. 17, 1850.
    3246 MARY A., b. Jan. 26, 1853.

John Prentice m. 2nd, Lucy Fitch, in 1859, and had three more children : Eleanor A., b. March 9, 1866 ; Henry A., b. Nov. 8, 1862 ; Anna, b. Feb. 6, 1868.

3231 ABBY C. DENISON, (Elisha W.[6], Isaac[5], Daniel[4], Daniel[3], John[2], George[1],) b. Aug. 29, 1827, m. Wm. D. Noyes, Aug. 23, 1845 ; lives at Mystic River ; and has these :

    3247 SADA M., b. June 29, 1849; d. Feb. 16, 1850.
    3248 IDA, b. Feb. 22, 1852; d. March 9, 1852.
    3249 SADA M., b. May 27, 1853 ; m. B. F. S. Davis, April 13, 1870.
    3250 NETTIE A., b. Jan. 18, 1857.
    3251 WILLIE R., b. Aug. 1, 1858 ; d. Sept. 7, 1860.
    3252 LEWIS B., b. Nov. 22, 1860.
    3253 FANNY S., b. June 3, 1863; d. July 21, 1873.

3232 EUNICE C. DENISON, (Elisha W.[6], Isaac[5], Daniel[4], Daniel[3], John[2], George[1],) b. June 8, 1833, m. Henry Palmer Hewett, of Chesterfield, Conn., Aug. 26, 1849 ; lives in Groton, Conn. Their children :

    3254 HIRAM P., b. June 14, 1852; d. Aug. 29, 1852.
    3255 ALBERT F., b. Sept. 5, 1858.
    3256 IDA ALBINO, b. Feb. 24, 1862.
    3257 INEZ IRENE, b. March 16, 1865; d. Aug. 25, 1867.
    3258 FANNY ESTELLA, b. July 16, 1867.
    3259 LENA CLIFT, b. July 29, 1870.
    3260 OSCAR JEFFERSON, b. May 1, 1875 ; d. May 8, 1875.

3207 ISAAC DENISON, (Isaac[5], Daniel[4], Daniel[3], John[2], George[1],) b. Feb. 1, 1790, was married, Feb. 18, 1817, to Levina Fish, and died Aug. 28, 1855. His children :

ISAAC DENISON.
[No. 3207.]

Born Feb. 1st, 1790.
Died August 28th, 1855.

Copied from a Daguerreotype taken March 24th, 1852.

LEVINA DENISON.
WIFE OF ISAAC DENISON.

Born October 1st, 1794.

Taken from life May 20th, 1881.

3271 Isaac W., b. Nov. 20, 1817; twice married.
3272 Rev. Frederick, b. Sept. 28, 1819; *m.* Amy R. Manton.
3273 Charles C., b. Sept. 20, 1821; died July 5, 1847.
3274 Bridget G., b. March 13, 1824; *m.* Cyrus W. Noyes.
3275 John L., b. Sept. 19, 1826; twice married.
3276 Daniel W., b. Sept. 5, 1828; *m.* Eleanor C. Harris.
3277 Emily F., b. March 13, 1831; *m.* George W. Noyes.
3278 Eliza F., b. Aug. 12, 1833; *m.* Dudley W. Stewart.
3279 Frances L., b. May 8, 1837; *m.* Benj. Burrows, Jr., March 26, 1867. He was a widower with two children. No child of hers is reported.

3271 Isaac W. Denison, (Isaac⁶, Isaac⁵, Daniel⁴, Daniel³, John², George¹,) b. Nov. 20, 1817, was married, May 10, 1843, to Eunice E. Burrows, who bore nine children, and died Feb. 16, 1861, aged nearly 38. He was married, second, July 15, 1862, to Julia M. Wilbur. His children, all by the first wife, are as follows:

3280 Ann B., b. Feb. 9, 1844; *m.* John H. Cranston.
3281 Hannah B., b. Aug. 19, 1845; *m.* Jefferson B. Meservey.
3282 Sarah A., b. Aug. 16, 1847.
3283 Lavinia F., b. Aug. 29, 1850.
3284 Charles, b. Sept. 18, 1852; d. June 12, 1853.
3285 Edward P., b. May 19, 1854; *m.* Ella L. Garfield.
3286 Frederic, b. April 15, 1856.
3287 Emily, twin, b. Jan. 3, 1859.
3288 Eliza, twin, b. Jan. 3, 1859.

3281 Hannah B. Denison, (dau. of 3721 Isaac W.,) b. Aug. 19, 1845, *m.* Jefferson B. Meservey, July 27, 1869. He is a farmer in East Bridgewater, Mass. She is a second wife. They have:

3289 Charles Denison, b. Sept. 29, 1873.
3290 Edward Bethel, b. Dec. 2, 1876.
3291 Louisa Burrows, b. Dec. 1, 1879.

3272 Rev. Frederick Denison, (Isaac⁶, Isaac⁵, Daniel⁴, Daniel³, John², George¹,) b. Sept. 28, 1819, is a Baptist clergyman. He has been pastor of Baptist churches in Westerly, R. I., Norwich, Conn., New Haven, Conn., and Woonsocket, R. I.; and he has some reputation as a writer and an antiquarian. He was married, Jan. 12, 1848, to Amy R. Manton, of Providence, R. I. Two children:

3292 Frederica, b. July 30, 1853.
3293 Amy, b. July 20, 1857; d. March 23, 1858.

3274 BRIDGET G. DENISON, (Isaac⁶, Isaac⁵, Daniel⁴, Daniel³, John², George¹,) b. March 13, 1824, was married, May 11, 1843, to Cyrus W. Noyes, son of Avery and Mary Noyes. She d. March 22, 1876. Their children :
- **3294** GEORGE D., b. and d. in April. 1844.
- **3295** JANE M., b. April 3, 1847; m. James Ryley.
- **3296** CHARLES D., b. Oct. 31, 1850.
- **3297** FANNY E., b. Nov. 15, 1856; d. July 1, 1862.
- **3298** IRA C., b. June 5, 1859.
- **3299** ANNIE, b. May 23, 1863.
- **3300** EVERETT, b. March 10, 1865.

3275 JOHN L. DENISON, (Isaac⁶, Isaac⁵, Daniel⁴, Daniel³, John², George¹,) b. Sept. 19, 1826, m. first, Mary E. Burrows, May 10, 1853, who d. June 16, 1860 ; 2nd, Frances M. Breed, March 5, 1861; lived in Norwich, Conn. Children :
- **3301** EDWIN C., b. May 19, 1855; d. Oct. 21, 1861.
- **3302** JOHN B., b. June 29, 1857; d. June 21, 1864.
- **3303** MARVIN B., b. June 11, 1860.
- **3304** LEARNED B., b. Aug. 16, 1864.
- **3305** FRANCES R., b. July 16, 1868.

3276 DANIEL W. DENISON, (Isaac⁶, Isaac⁵, Daniel⁴, Daniel³, John² George¹,) b. Sept. 5, 1828, was married, Jan. 16, 1856, to Eleanor C. Harris ; lived at Mystic River, Conn.; d. Jan. 7, 1877. Their children :
- **3306** ADDIE, b. and d. in December, 1856.
- **3307** JAMES T. H., b. Oct. 18, 1860.

3277 EMILY F. DENISON, (Isaac⁶, Isaac⁵, Daniel⁴, Daniel³, John², George¹.) b. March 13, 1831, m. Geo. W. Noyes, Jan. 16, 1856. He d. Feb. 26, 1866. For many years he was Cashier of Mystic River Bank. They had a child that died unnamed, and also :
- **3308** GEORGE FREDERIC, b. July 20, 1858.

Mr. Noyes had been previously married. His first wife's name was Hannah De——, by whom he had seven children : two Georges, two Josephs, two Pelegs, and one other.

3278 ELIZA F. DENISON, (Isaac⁶, Isaac⁵, Daniel⁴, Daniel³, John², George¹,) m. Dudley W. Stewart, May 6, 1856. They live at Milltown, in North Stonington, Conn. Three children :
- **3309** CHARLES E., b. Dec. 20, 1859.
- **3310** HENRY T., b. Sept. 16, 1863; d. Dec. 10, 1864.
- **3311** FRANCES D., b. Oct. 18, 1866.

Capt. John Denison's Descendants.

3201 ESTHER DENISON, (Isaac[5], Daniel[4], Daniel[3], John[2], George[1],) b. July 26, 1776, was married to Charles Cottrell, Oct. 18, 1795. They had one child. He died; and, Dec. 11, 1803, she was married to Isaac Minor. Her children were:

- **3312** JOSEPH COTTRELL, b. in 1797.
- **3313** ISAAC D. MINOR, b. Nov. 26, 1804; m. Phebe Burrows.
- **3314** HANNAH " b. Oct. 5, 1806; m. David Thompson of Coleraine, Ms.
- **3315** LYDIA " b. Feb. 7, 1809; d. April 5, 1812.
- **3316** EUNICE " b. March 12, 1811; d. Sept. 21, 1874.
- **3317** LYDIA " b. April 7, 1813; m. Chas. Johnson; d.Oct. 21,'60·
- **3318** FREDERICK D., b. Sept. 18, 1815; d. Jan. 28, 1841; unmarried.
- **3319** MANASSEH " b. Aug. 5, 1818; m. Fanny Hooper.
- **3320** ESTHER " b. Feb. 22, 1821; m. Gurdon Gates.

3202 SARAH DENISON (Isaac[5], Daniel[4], Daniel[3], John[2], George[1],) b. April 9, 1778, was married, Oct., 1797, to Elam Burrows, and had these:

- **3321** JOHN, b. Oct. 28, 1798.
- **3322** EUNICE, b. March 29, 1801.
- **3323** ISAAC D., b. Oct. 7, 1804; d. Jan. 10, 1861; not married.
- **3324** HANNAH, b. June 15, 1806; d. May 21, 1832; not married.
- **3325** PHEBE, b. Feb. 19, 1809; m. J. D. Miner.
- **3326** SARAH, b. May 22, 1811; m. Nathan Noyes.

3206 MERCY DENISON, (Isaac[5], Daniel[4], Daniel[6], John[2], George[1],) b. Feb. 9, 1787, m. Zebediah Gates, June 7, 1820, (2nd wife,) and had:

- **3327** ELISHA, b. April 23, 1821; d. an infant.
- **3328** ISAAC, b. Dec. 27, 1822; m. Prudence D. Gallup, Sept. 24, 1851.
- **3329** GEORGE W., b. April 13, 1825; m. Julia Fish, Nov. 21, 1853.
- **3330** EUNICE, b. April 23, 1827; m. Amos Chesebro', Sept. 24, 1851.
- **3331** CHARLES H., b. July 13, 1829; m. Jane Latham, Aug. 21, 1851.

3205 ANN B. DENISON, (Isaac[5], Daniel[4], Daniel[3], John[2], George[1],) b. Sept. 22, 1784, was married, first, Dec. 12, 1803, to John G. Gallup. No child. He died; and Sept. 8, 1809, she was married, second, to Jeremiah Holmes. They had:

- **3332** JEREMIAH, b. Sept. 10, 1811; d. Sept. 19, 1811.
- **3333** ISAAC D., b. Nov. 12, 1812; m. Ellen Kemp of Groton, Aug. 8,'37.
- **3334** MARY A., b. Nov. 14, 1814; m. Randall Brown.
- **3335** ESTHER C., b. March 23, 1816; m. Benj. Latham.
- **3336** JEREMIAH H., b. Aug. 8, 1819; d. March 16, 1823.
- **3337** BENJAMIN F., b. July 8, 1822; m. Lucy M. Lewis, Sept. 20, '48.
- **3338** JOSEPH W., b. April 1, 1824; m. Mary O. Denison of Stillwater, N. Y., Sept. 4, 1847.
- **3339** HIRAM C., b. Jan. 22, 1826; m. Hannah F. Denison.
- **3340** ERASTUS L., b. April 7, 1830; d. April 30, 1832.

3203 THANKFUL DENISON, (Isaac[5], Daniel[4], Daniel[3], John[2], George[1],) b. May 20, 1780, was married, Aug. 4, 1798, to Amos Clift. They had these:

    3341 ESTHER, b. Nov. 15, 1800.
    3342 MARGERY, b. July 4, 1802; d. young.
    3343 AMOS, b. Aug. 7, 1805; m. Charity Morgan.
    3344 JOHN G., b. May 2, 1807; m. Lydia P. Gillson.
    3345 WATERMAN, b. Sept. 17, 1809; m. Esther Hazard.
    3346 HORATIO, b. March 24, 1811; d. May 24, 1811.
    3347 FREDERICK D., b. Oct. 10, 1814; m. Prudence A Welsh.
    3348 NANCY D., b. March 23, 1817; m. Edmund Chesebro, Sept. 30, 1840: lived in Stonington; she d. Sept. 12, 1880; no child.

3343 AMOS CLIFT, JR., (son of 3203 Thankful Denison and Amos Clift,) b. Aug. 7, 1805, was married, Jan. 29, 1829, to Charity Morgan; lived at Mystic River, and was known as "Hon. Amos Clift." He d. Aug. 18, 1878. The children:

    3349 AMOS, 3d, b. May 15, 1830.
    3350 LEMUEL, b. Nov. 27, 1832; d. Dec. 31, 1832.
    3351 LEMUEL, b. Nov. 30, 1833.
    3352 LYDIA HOLMES, b. Feb. 4, 1836.
    3353 EDWIN, b. June 2, 1838; d. July 17, 1839.
    3354 HORACE, b. May 28, 1840.
    3355 EDMUND CHESEBRO', b. May 19, 1842.
    3356 SARAH S., b. June 1, 1845; m. Wm. S. Williams, May, 1853; lived in Stonington; had Lydia Clift, b. April 1. 1854.

3344 JOHN G. CLIFT, (son of 3203 Thankful Denison and Amos Clift,) b. May 2, 1807, was married, Sept. 30, 1828, to Lydia P. Gillson. Lived at Mystic River. He d. Feb. 18, 1875; she d. Feb. 12, 1877. The children:

    3357 FRANCIS M., b. May 5, 1830; d. June 13, 1831.
    3358 MARY E., b. June 2, 1833; m. Geo. B. Clark; went to Remington, Ind.
    3359 JOSEPH WILLS, b. Nov. 6, 1834; d. Aug. 27, 1835.
    3360 FRANCES JANE, b, May 5, 1838; d. Sept. 12, 1839.

3345 WATERMAN CLIFT, (son of 3203 Thankful Denison and Amos Clift,) b. Sept. 17, 1809, was married, Aug. 31, 1835, to Esther H. Hazard. The children:

    3361 ROBERT H., b. April 13, 1838.
    3362 CHARLES WATERMAN, b. April 22, 1841.
    3363 JOHN G., d. March 25, 1846.
    3364 DANIEL W., b. June 25, 1852; d. Nov. 23, 1871.
    3365 THANKFUL A., b. May 9, 1854; m. Benj. Holmes, Oct. 30, 1880; lives at Mystic River, Conn.
    3366 STANTON H., b. June 10, 1857.

Capt. John Denison's Descendants.

3349 AMOS CLIFT, 3d, (son of 3343 Amos, Jr.,) b. May 15, 1830, was married Feb. 7, 1831, to Hannah Morse lives at Mystic River. The children:

    3367 WILLIAM M., b. Jan. 7, 1864.
    3368 ADAH B., b. Sept. 30, 1866; d. May 31, 1874.
    3369 KATE N., b. May 29, 1868.
    3370 ANNA L., b. Dec. 10, 1870.
    3371 LEONARD A., b. Sept. 14, 1873.

3361 ROBERT H. CLIFT, (son of 3345 Waterman,) b. April 13, 1838, was married, Feb. 14, 1864, to Eusebia Watson; lived in Jersey City, N. J. In the late war, he served three years in the 22d Illinois Regiment, and received a medal with the roll of his twelve battles. He d. Sept. 1, 1869. One child:

    3372 JESSE WATERMAN, b. Dec. 4, 1865.

3362 CHARLES WATERMAN CLIFT, (son of 3345 Waterman,) b. April 22, 1841, was married, Nov. 3, 1862, to Jane Forsyth, b. Jan. 7, 1840. He lives at Mystic Bridge, Conn. She died Oct. 31, 1880. Their children:

    3373 ESTHER H., b. Nov. 30, 1866.
    3374 ELLEN E., b. May 15, 1872.
    3375 WILLIAM F., b. Feb. 17, 1874; d. June, 1874.

3363 JOHN G. CLIFT, (son of 3345 Waterman,) b. March 25, 1846, was married, July 27, 1871, to Mary E. Packer; lives at Mystic River. Children:

    3376 EDITH A., b. Dec. 4, 1876; d. March 27, 1880.
    3377 ROBERT MORTON, b. Nov. 9, 1878; d. Nov. 16, 1879.
    3378 JANE F., b. Dec. 1, 1880.

3347 FREDERIC DENISON CLIFT, (son of 3303 Thankful Denison and Amos Clift,) b. Oct. 10, 1814, was married July 11, 1837, to Prudence Ann Welch; lived at Mystic River; d. Dec. 25, 1863. Children:

    3379 PRUDENCE ANN, b. Sept. 29, 1838; m. Thomas C. Forsyth, Aug. 13. 1863; has had no child.
    3380 FREDERICK D., b. Dec. 16, 1840; d. June 24, 1841.
    3381 SAMUEL W., b. May 21, 1842; d. May 26, 1843.
    3382 ELIZA JANE, b. Feb. 6, 1844.
    3383 WILLIAM S., b. July 29, 1848; d. in 1848.
    3384 ADRIAN F., b. April 29, 1853.
    3385 HELEN, b. March 16, 1859.

3204 EUNICE DENISON, (Isaac[5], Daniel[4], Daniel[3], John[2], George[1],) b. May 11, 1782, was married, Aug. 5, 1801, to Nathaniel Clift; lived at Mystic, Conn. Their children:

Capt. John Denison's Descendants.

3386 HIRAM, b. April 3, 1803; m. Mary Esther Crary, June 1, 1852; lived at Knox, N. Y.; d. Nov. 15, 1874; no child.
3387 WILLIAM, b. April 20, 1805; m. Bridget Fish.
3388 NATHANIEL, b. May 20, 1807; d. an infant.
3389 MARY COIT, b. Nov. 26, 1808; m. John Holdredge.
3390 NATHANIEL, b. May 20, 1811; m. Martha A. B. Denison.
3391 HARRIET W., b. Feb. 10, 1816; m. Benj. F. Hoxie.
3392 IRA HART, b. April 27, 1818; m. Frances A. Leeds, April 22, 1846, at Mystic Bridge; d, April 23, 1856; no child.
3393 EUNICE, b. July 19, 1819; m. Charles H. Mallory.
3394 HORACE H., b. Feb. 8, 1821; m. Frances E. Burrows.
3395 ISAAC D., b. Oct. 14, 1822; m. Elizabeth I. Tift.

3387 WILLIAM CLIFT, (son of 3204 Eunice and Nathaniel,) b. April 4, 1805, was married to Bridget Fish, June 18, 1833, and lives at Mystic River; two children:

3396 MARY H., b. April 10, 1836; m. Edward Y. Foot of New Haven.
3397 HANNAH F., b. May 8, 1838.

Mrs. Bridget, b. Aug. 21, 1811, d. Sept. 17, 1845; and Wm. Clift m. second, Sept. 16, 1846, Eliza A. Burrows; no other child. She was b. Aug. 14, 1811, and d.

3389 MARY COIT CLIFT, (dau. of 3204 Eunice and Nathaniel,) b. Nov. 26, 1808, was married, Jan. 14, 1829, to Capt. John Holdredge, at Mystic Bridge, Conn. He d. Oct. 25, 1872, aged 75; she d. Dec. 26, 1878, aged 70. No child.

3390 NATHANIEL CLIFT, JR., (son of 3204 Eunice and Nathaniel,) b. May 22, 1811, m. Martha A. B. Denison, dau. of Oliver, May 11, 1837. He d. of yellow fever, Aug. 2, 1841, at St. Marks, Fla. Two children:

3398 HIRAM, b. March 8, 1838.
3399 NATHANIEL, b. Jan. 29, 1841; lives in San Francisco, California; m. Esther Caswell, April, 1880.

3391 HARRIET W. CLIFT, (dau. of 3204 Eunice and Nathaniel,) b. Feb. 10, 1816, was married, Nov. 19, 1843, to Benj. F. Hoxie. They live at Mystic Bridge, Conn. The children:

3400 JOHN HOLDREDGE, b. Sept. 6, 1844; m. Mary Van Ryker, Nov. 22, 1867.
3401 IRA CLIFT, b. April 14, 1846; m. Belle Ward, Oct. 1877.
3402 MARY HOLDREDGE, b. Dec. 27, 1847; m. Joseph Lambert.
3403 HARRIET ELIZABETH, b. Nov. 5, 1849; m. Erastus Barnes, March 4, 18 3; d. July 24, 1874.
3404 FRANK, b. March 21, 1852; d. Dec. 8, 1871.
3404½ CHARLES, b. Nov. 17, 1853.

3405 FANNIE H., b. July 13, 1856; *m.* Morton P. Hunt, Oct. 7, 1878.
3406 NELLIE DENISON, b. Aug. 15, 1858; *m.* Frank E. Belden, Nov. 13, 1880.

3393 EUNICE CLIFT, (dau of 3204 Eunice and Nathaniel,) b. July 19, 1819, was married, July 25, 1841, to Charles Henry Mallory. They live in Brooklyn, N. Y. Children:

3407 CHARLES, b. Jan. 18, 1845; *m.* Maria S. Dimon, Oct. 23, 1872.
3408 FANNY E., b. Jan. 18, 1847; *m.* Chas. P. Williams, Oct. 28, 1868.
3409 HENRY R., b. Sept. 21, 1848; *m.* Cora N. Pynchon, Dec. 2, 1873.
3410 KATE, b. March 14, 1852.
3411 ROBERT, b. Sept. 23, 1856.

The children were all born at Mystic Bridge, Conn., and this is still the summer residence of the family.

3394 HORACE HATCH CLIFT, (son of 3204 Eunice and Nathaniel,) b. Feb. 8, 1821, was married, Oct. 25, 1848, to Frances E. Burrows, dau. of John and Roxanna Burrows. She was b. May 23, 1825. They live at Mystic River, Conn. Children:

3412 JOHN BURROWS, b. Oct. 10, 1849.
3413 WM. HORACE, b. March 6, 1852.
3414 HENRY M., b. Jan. 4, 1854.
2415 FANNY, b. March 6, 1856.
3416 MARY E., twin, b. June 24, 1858.
3417 WALTER, twin, b. June 24, 1858.

3395 ISAAC DENISON CLIFT, (son of 3204 Eunice and Nathaniel,) b. Oct. 14, 1822, was married, Oct. 5, 1853, to Elizabeth I. Tift. They live at Mystic River, Conn. Children:

3418 RUBIE, b. Nov. 13, 1855.
3419 IRA, b. April 7, 1858.

2736 HENRY DENISON, (Daniel[4], Daniel[3], John[2], George[1],) b. Nov. 26, 1753, was married to Mary Gallup, in 1778, in Stonington. He went to Knox, but did not remain there. He d. in Stonington, in 1836; his wife d. Jan., 1843. They had:

3420 SARAH, b. Dec. 9, 1780; d. in 1817, unmarried.
3421 HENRY, b. May 15, 1783; *m.* Deborah Pierce.
3422 MARY, b. in 1785; d. young.
3423 DANIEL, b. March 31, 1787; was a physician.
3424 MARY, b. May 17, 1789; *m.* Amos Crary.
3425 GIDEON, b. Feb. 4, 1793; d. Feb., 1826, unmarried.
3426 LOIS, b. Jan. 21, 1796; *m.* John L. Freeman.
3427 ESTHER, b. May 22, 1800; *m.* Anson H. Taylor; 2 ch.

3421 HENRY DENISON, Jr., (Henry[5], Daniel[4], Daniel[3], John[2], George[1],) b. May 15, 1783, was married to Deborah Pierce,

Feb. 12, 1809. He died in Nichols, Tioga Co., N. Y., Oct. 14, 1846. His children:

 3428 JAMES P., b. March 7, 1813; d. Dec. 6, 1855, unmarried.
 3429 SARAH b. July 7, 1818; d. March 29, 1847, unmarried.
 3430 HARMON H., b. Nov. 20, 1820; m. Mary J. Yocum.
 3431 LUCIUS, b. April 2, 1824; d. Aug, 1836.
 3432 MARIA D., b. June 2, 1826; m. Dr. Samuel D. Evans.
 3433 WILLARD G., b. Oct. 9, 1828; m. twice; 3 ch.

3432 MARIA D. DENISON, (Henry, Jr.^{6}, Henry^5, Daniel^5, Daniel^3, John^2, George^1,) b. June 2, 1826, was married to Dr. Samuel D. Evans, of Ocean Grove, N. J., June 11, 1848, and had:

 3434 JAMES H., b. April 8, 1849; d. Nov. 15, 1855.
 3435 SARAH P., b. April 25, 1855; m. Dr. J. A. W. Hetrick, March 23, 1875.

3433 WILLARD G. DENISON, (Henry, Jr.^{6}, Henry^5, (Daniel^4, Daniel^3, John^2, George^1,) b. Oct. 9, 1828, lives in Smithboro', N. Y., was married, first, to Palmyra Eaton, March 30, 1851, who d. May 16, 1871. Her children:

 3436 GEORGE, b. June 2, 1852; d. Dec. 4, 1852.
 3437 HARRIS A., b. March 29, 1856.

He married, 2nd, Laura Pressure, Sept. 24, 1871, and had:

 3439 PERRY, b. Feb. 17, 1873.

3423 DR. DANIEL DENISON, (Henry^5, Daniel^4, Daniel^3, John^2, George^1,) b. March 31, 1787, lives in Pompey, N. Y. He is a physician and farmer; is married, and has these:

 3440 HENRY. **3441** WILLIAM. **3442** DUANE.

3430 HARMON H. DENISON, (Henry, Jr.^{6}, Henry^5, Daniel^4, Daniel^3, John^2, George^1,) b. Nov. 20, 1820, was married, Aug. 26, 1855, to Mary Jane Yocum; lives at Mainville, Pa. Their children:

 3443 DEBORAH ANN, b. Dec. 14, 1858; d. March 17, 1863.
 3444 JACOB HENRY, b. Sept. 27, 1861.
 3445 DELILAH ELIZA, b. June 2, 1864.
 3446 ELMER ELLSWORTH, b. May 18, 1867.
 3447 CHARLES WILLIAM, b. Dec. 9, 1870.
 3448 MARY ELIZABETH, b. Oct. 17, 1874.

3424 MARY DENISON, (Henry^5, Daniel^4, Daniel^3, John^2, George^1,) b. May 17, 1789, was married to Amos Crary, April 14, 1811. They lived in Knox, N. Y. She died there, July 28, 1840. He died there, Dec. 11, 1869, aged 81. Children:

3449 DENISON, b. June 30, 1812; m. Henriette M. Williams, June 16, 1856.
3450 THOMAS, b. April 26, 1817; d. April 30, 1818.
3451 HORACE, b. Sept. 14, 1819; m. Harriet Barclay, Oct. 2, 1855.
3452 SALLY ANN, b. Oct. 8, 1821; not married.
3453 SUSAN M., b. May 18, 1814; m. A. W. Allen, Sept. 1, 1842, of Plymouth, Iowa.
3454 DOROTHY ESTHER, b. Sept. 23, 1831; m. A. S. Faville, Oct. 2, 1855; Mitchell, Iowa.

3426 LOIS DENISON, (Henry[5], Daniel[4], Daniel[3], John[2], George[1],) b. Jan. 21, 1796, was married to John Salter Freeman, in 1830. He was murdered and robbed, near Albany, N. Y., in Jan., 1831, about two months previous to the birth of their only child. She died in Milwaukee, Wis., April 25, 1859. Their child was:

3455 MARY ELLEN, b. March 13, 1831; m. Sherburne Sanborn Merrill, of Milwaukee.

3455 MARY ELLEN FREEMAN, (dau. of 3426 Lois Denison and John S. Freeman,) m. Sherburne Sanborn Merrill, of Milwaukee, May 6, 1858. He is a prominent and wealthy business man. They have had:

3456 SHERBURNE, b. July 17, 1859; d. Feb. 8, 1861.
3457 MARION, b. Dec. 19, 1861.
3458 FREDERIC, b. Aug. 1, 1864.
3459 RICHARD, b. Dec. 27, 1866.

3427 ESTHER DENISON, (Henry[5], Daniel[4], Daniel[3], John[2], George[1],) b. May 22, 1800, was married to Anson Hawley Taylor. Their children:

3460 MARY, m. Kellogg Sexton, a Milwaukee merchant, Sept. 19, 1854. He was born March 29, 1805. Their four children:
    3461 MARY A., b. July 1, 1857; d. April 29, 1858.
    3462 ELEANOR, b. Jan., 1859; d. in infancy.
    3463 ARTHUR T., b. Aug. 22, 1860.
    3464 PAUL DENISON, b. May 11, 1866.
3465 ANSON HAWLEY, JR., m. Emma Gooding, his cousin, g.-daughter of Eunice Denison Hatch; lives in Havana, Cuba; has had:
    3466 WILLIAM, who died young.

2740 BEEBE DENISON, (Daniel[4], Daniel[3], John[2], George[1],) b. Feb. 22, 1761, was married, Nov. 21, 1784, to Hannah Chesebro', in Stonington. They had these:

3467 HANNAH, b. in 1785; m. Moses Root.
3468 KETURAH, b. Sept. 20, 1787; m. Dr. Enos Lewis.

3469 NANCY, b. in 1790; m. Solomon White.
3470 BEEBE, Jr. b. July 28, 1794; m. Harriet Thompson.
3471 JEREMIAH, b. in 1796; d. young.
3472 WILLIAM, b. in 1797; d. young.
3473 JOHN, b. April 6, 1799; m. Jane Fairchild.

Mrs. Hannah (C.) D., died. He m. 2nd, Phebe Hinckley, March 10, 1805. She was born, Feb. 10, 1777. She d. Feb. 25, 1852; he d. Nov. 6, 1839. They had two children:

3474 WM. HORACE, b. Jan. 4, 1809; m. Caroline Turner.
3475 GILBERT PERRY, b. July 24, 1813; m. Betsey E. Andrews.

3470 BEEBE DENISON, JR., (Beebe[5], Daniel[4], Daniel[3], John[2], George[1],) b. July 28, 1794, was married to Harriet Thompson, March 12, 1820. He died March 13, 1866; she died Aug. 9, 1856. They lived in Michigan, and had these children:

3476 HARRIET H., b. March 17, 1821; m. Amos Andrews, Oct. 6, 1853; no child.
3477 LAURA E., July 27, 1823; m. Jer. White, May 9, 1845; one child.
3478 HIRAM T., b. Oct. 17, 1825; m. Azuba E. Pulman.
3479 BEEBE D., b. March 23, 1828; m. Maria L. Pulman, Oct. 23, 1840; d. June 14, 1865; no child.
3480 WYLLYS N., b. May 4. 1831; d. Sept. 11, 1844.
3481 WILLIAM H., b. Dec. 12, 1833; Lany Ann Snyder.

3477 LAURA E. DENISON, (Beebe, Jr.[6], Beebe[5], Daniel[4], Daniel[3], John[2], George[1],) b. July 27, 1823, was married to Jeremiah White, May 9, 1845, and d. March 9, 1863. They had one child:

3482 PERLEYETT, b. July 11, 1848.

3478 HIRAM T. DENISON, (Beebe, Jr.[6], Beebe[5], Daniel[4], Daniel[3], John[2], George[1],) b. Oct. 17, 1825, was married, June 13, 1854, to Azuba E. Pulman, who was born April 11, 1830. He lives in Bronson, Branch Co., Michigan. They have had these children:

3483 MARY M., b. Dec. 5, 1855; m. Charles F. Preston.
3484 ELLA E., b. June 22, 1861.
3485 WILLIS S., b. Nov. 10, 1862.

3481 WILLIAM H. DENISON, (Beebe, Jr.[6], Beebe[5], Daniel[4], Daniel[3], John[2], George[1],) b. Dec. 12, 1833, was married to Lany Ann Snyder, April 29, 1858, and died Oct. 4, 1870. He lived in Michigan, and had these two children:

3486 HARRIET L., b. Feb. 27, 1861.
3487 ADELLA M., b. June 21, 1863.

Capt. John Denison's Descendants.

3474 WILLIAM HORACE DENISON, (Beebe[5], Daniel[4], Daniel[3], John[2], George[1],) b. Jan. 4, 1809, was married May 4, 1829, to Caroline Turner, who was b. Feb. 29, 1810. He lived in Michigan, and died, Oct. 28, 1859. His children were:

    3488 ERASTUS B., Nov. 1, 1830; *m.* Nellie Wallace.
    3489 ANDREW J., b. Jan. 31, 1833; *m.* Charlotte L. Jones.
    3490 MARY ESTHER, b. Sept. 2, 1835; d Oct. 29, 1835.
    3491 DANIEL A., b. Oct. 22, 1836; *m.* Edna Smith, Nov. 15, 1876.
    3492 EDWIN OSCAR, b. March 16, 1840.
    3493 ALICE A., b. Nov. 22, 1842; *m.* John W. Pyatte.
    3494 MALVERTON H., b. Aug. 21, 1845; d. in 1864, in the war.
    3495 JOHN M., b. March 16, 1850; d. in 1872; not married.
    3496 LILLIE CAROLINE, b. May 3, 1853; *m.* Edwin G. Davis.

3488 ERASTUS BEEBE DENISON, (Wm. Horace[6], Beebe[5], Daniel[4], Daniel[3], John[2], George[1],) b. Nov. 1, 1830, was married to Nellie Wallace, March, 1866. They have:

    3497 WILLIE HORACE, b. March 12, 1867.

3489 ANDREW J. DENISON, (Wm. Horace[6], Beebe[5], Daniel[4], Daniel[3], John[2], George[1],) b. Feb. 1, 1833, was married to Charlotte L. Jones, Dec. 30, 1858. Lives at Clyde, N. Y. They have:

    3498 CHARLIE H., b. Feb. 19, 1866.

3493 ALICE AUGUSTA DENISON, (Wm. Horace[6], Beebe[5], Daniel[4], Daniel[3], John[2], George[1],) b. Nov. 22, 1842, was married to John W. Pyatte, Feb. 6, 1863. They have:

    3499 GEORGE HIRAM, b. Dec. 20, 1864.
    3500 WILLIE CARLTON, b. Jan. 27, 1873; d. Aug. 21, 1874.

3496 LILLIE CAROLINE DENISON, (Wm. Horace[6], Beebe[5], Daniel[4], Daniel[3], John[2], George[1],) b. May 3, 1853, *m.* Edwin G. Davis, May 24, 1868; died March 15, 1869. She had:

    3501 MILLIE CAROLINE, b. Feb. 24, 1869; d. May 15, 1869.

3468 KETURAH DENISON, (Beebe[5], Daniel[4], Daniel[3], John[2], George[1],) b. Sept. 20, 1787, was married to Dr. Enos Lewis of Norwich, Vt. He died Sept. 14, 1823. They had these children:

    3502 WILLIAM, b. April 14, 1814; d. April 18, 1814.
    3503 WILLIAM E., b. May 25, 1815; lives in Norwich, Vt.
    3504 DR. CHARLES D., b. June 6, 1817; lives at Dry Ridge, Ky.
    3505 ANN EMERSON, b. April 10, 1820; lives at Mystic Bridge, Conn.
    3506 LUCY MARY, b. Aug. 24, 1822; *m.* Benj. F. Holmes, Sept. 20, 1842; one child, Anna M., b. May 8, 1854; Mrs. Lucy Mary Holmes, d. Sept. 11, 1874.

3467 HANNAH DENISON, (Beebe[5], Daniel[4], Daniel[3], John[2], George[1],) b. in 1785, was married to Moses Root. They had these :

    3507 JEREMIAH.   **3511** DANIEL.
    3508 FREDERIC.   **3512** WILLIAM.
    3509 ENOS.   **3513** HENRY D.
    3510 CHARLES.

3469 NANCY DENISON, (Beebe[5], Daniel[4], Daniel[3], John[2], George[1],) b. in 1790, was married to Solomon White ; lived at Norwich, Vt., and had these :

    3514 JAMES.   **3517** HARRIET.
    3515 ENOS.   **3518** LUCRETIA.
    3516 HANNAH.   **3519** MARTHA.

3475 GILBERT PERRY DENISON, (Beebe[5], Daniel[4], Daniel[3], John[2], George[1],) b. July 24, 1813, was married to Betsey E. Andrews, Dec. 21, 1835. They live in Aurora, Kane Co., Illinois, and have had these three children :

    3520 SALMON SQUIRE, b. Aug. 26, 1836; m. Ann Gray.
    3521 HORACE ADELBERT, b. March 10, 1841; d. Jan. 21, 1864.
    3522 JOSEPHINE, b. Dec. 23, 1843; m. Gustavus Aucutt.

3520 SALMON SQUIRE DENISON, (Gilbert Perry[6], Beebe[5], Daniel[4], Daniel[3], John[2], George[1],) b. August 26, 1836, was married, Jan. 30, 1873, to Ann Gray. Their children are :

    3523 BETSY DANA, b. Jan. 27, 1874.
    3524 LOIS, b. July 7, 1875.
    3525 PERRY, b. Sept. 30, 1878.

3522 JOSEPHINE DENISON, (Gilbert Perry[6], Beebe[5], Daniel[4], Daniel[3], John[2], George[1],) b. Dec. 23, 1843, was married, Nov. 7, 1865, to Gustavus Aucutt. [The name, "Aucutt," is probably the same as Orcutt or Alcott.] Their children are :

    3526 FRANKLIN DENISON, b. June 25, 1867.
    3527 CORA MARY, b. April 3, 1869.
    3528 CHARLES MERRIMAN, b. Aug. 8, 1870.
    3529 GUSTAVUS CLARENCE, b. June 7, 1872.
    3530 PERLEYETT, b. Aug. 5, 1874.
    3531 JOSEPHINE RUTH, b. June 23, 1876.
    3532 HARRY, b. Oct. 31, 1878.

3473 JOHN DENISON, (Beebe[5], Daniel[4], Daniel[3], John[2], George[1],) b. April 6, 1799, was married, Oct. 11, 1837, to Jane Fairchild, who was born, Aug. 3, 1812. He was born in Stonington, Conn. He settled in Richmond, Michigan. His children were as follows :

No. 3549.

3533 JOHN H., b. Oct. 8, 1838; not married.
3534 HANNAH. b. Aug. 20, 1840; m. Charles Nichols.
3535 ORVIL W., b. Aug. 8, 1844; d. March 7, 1865.
3536 PAULINA J., b. Oct. 11, 1850; m. Wm. E. Pulvers.
3537 EMMA, b. Oct. 23, 1855.

3536 PAULINA J. DENISON, (John[6], Beebe[5], Daniel[4], Daniel[3], John[2], George[1],) b. Oct. 11, 1850, was married, Jan. 21, 1873, to William E. Pulvers of Sodus, N. Y., she being " of Lenox, Michigan." They live in Lenox, Mich., and have :

3538 CLARENCE ORVIL, b. Nov. 20, 1875.

3534 HANNAH DENISON, (John[6], Beebe[5], Daniel[4], Daniel[3], John[2], George[1],) b. Aug. 20, 1840, was married to Charles Nichols, Aug. 31, 1856. They live in Elk, (Peck P. O.) Sanilac County, Michigan, and have had these children :

3539 ORRIN, b. May 14, 1857; d. Feb. 1, 1866.
3540 JANE P., b. April 14, 1860; m. Wm. E. Ferguson.
3541 JOHN E., b. April 10. 1863.
3542 REUBEN V., b. May 30, 1865.
3543 HATTIE H., b. Aug. 8, 1872.
3544 WILLIE, b. Aug. 30, 1868.
3545 WILFRED, b. April 7, 1874.

2741 FREDERICK DENISON, (Daniel[4], Daniel[3], John[2], George[1],) b. Sept. 23, 1762, was married, Aug. 19, 1789, to Hannah Fish, lived in Stonington, Conn.; died there, Sept. 4, 1832. His children were as follows :

3546 FREDERICK, b. May 22, 1790; m. Desire Frink, Sept. 11, 1814; d. May 31, 1817; no child.
3547 ERASTUS, b. Dec. 22, 1791; m. Prudence Spicer.
3548 HANNAH, b. Oct. 10, 1793; d. Dec. 9, 1793.
3549 NATHAN F., b. Oct. 7. 1794; m. Mary E. Avery.
3550 SALLY, b. July 10, 1797; d. Feb. 20, 1799.
3551 BETSEY, b. July 4, 1799; m. Henry W. Avery.
3552 HANNAH, b. Nov. 21, 1801; d. Oct. 26, 1802.
3553 DELIA A., b. Dec. 13, 1803; m. Daniel Latham.
3554 ALFRED, b. Jan. 24, 1806; d. Oct. 18, 1807.
3555 CHARLES H., b. Feb. 21, 1811; d. June 30, 1829.
3556 DANIEL A., b. June 19, 1813; m. Delia Gardner, Oct. 27, 1836; no child.

3549 NATHAN F. DENISON, (Frederick[5], Daniel[4], Daniel[3], John[2], George[1],) b. Oct. 7, 1794, was married, Dec. 25, 1823, to Mary E. Avery. He lived at Mystic Bridge, Conn., and d. May 10, 1878. He has had these four daughters :

3557 MARY ELIZABETH, b. June 18, 1825; m. Erastus Avery.
3558 HANNAH FISH, b. Feb. 15, 1827; m. Hiram C. Holmes.
3559 EMILY AMANDA, b. Nov. 14, 1828; m. Gurdon Bill.
3560 LUCY GLOVER, b. June 30, 1831; m. Frederick Bill, at Groton, May 19, 1858. No children of Lucy G., wife of Frederick Bill are reported by her father. The other three had children, of whom I have his record.

3557 MARY ELIZABETH DENISON, (Nathan F.[6], Frederick[5], Daniel[4], Daniel[3], John[2], George[1],) b. June 18, 1825, was married, March 21, 1844, to Erastus Avery of Groton. She died Aug. 22, 1867. Children :

3561 CHARLES DENISON, b. Sept. 5, 1846.
3562 JAMES CARLTON, b. Feb. 19, 1849.
3563 MARIE ANNA, b. Sept. 10, 1853.
3564 DELIA WHEELER, b. Aug. 4, 1855.
3565 HENRY WILLIAM, b. Nov. 21, 1857; d. Dec. 8, 1871.

3558 HANNAH FISH DENISON, (Nathan F.[6], Frederick[5], Daniel[4], Daniel[3], John[2], George[1],) b. Feb. 15, 1827, was married, Jan. 30, 1850, to Hiram C. Holmes, of Mystic Bridge. They had :

3566 FREDERICK AVERY, b. Nov. 15, 1850; d. April 23, 1877.
3567 CHARLES CARROL, b. July 4, 1853; d. April 29, 1854.
3568 EVELYN, b. March 28, 1855.
3569 MARY ELIZABETH, b. Dec. 28, 1870.

3559 EMILY AMANDA DENISON, (Nathan F.[6], Frederick[5], Daniel[4], Daniel[3], John[2], George[1],) b. Nov. 14, 1828, was married to Gurdon Bill, of Springfield, Mass., May 12, 1853. Their children :

3570 NATHAN DENISON, b. Oct. 12, 1855.
3571 HATTIE ELIZA, b. Aug 21, 1857.
3572 MARY AVERY, b. Sept. 15, 1859.
3573 EDWARD EVERETT, b. Feb. 22, 1862.
3574 CHARLES, b. Feb. 13, 1870.

3547 REV. ERASTUS DENISON, (Frederick[6], Daniel[4], Daniel[3], John[2], George[1],) b. Dec. 22, 1791, was a Baptist preacher. He married Prudence Spicer, June 25, 1815, and had nine children ; but they all died in infancy. His wife Prudence died in Groton, May 21, 1864, aged 69 years. He died there, of cancer, Sept. 20, 1866, aged 74 years and nine months. All his children died unnamed.

3553 DELIA ANN DENISON, (Frederick[5], Daniel[4], Daniel[3], John[2], George[1],) b. Dec. 13, 1803, was married, Sept. 10,

Capt. John Denison's Descendants. 171

1826, to Daniel Latham. He died Jan. 12, 1879. The children:

3575 DANIEL DENISON, b. Aug. 3, 1827; m. Mary Ann Strickland.
3576 BETSEY ANN, b. Oct. 2, 1829; m. James Fitch, Jr., May 31, '48.
3577 DELIA, b. Oct. 25, 1832; m. Archibald T. Douglas, Dec. 21, 1850.
3578 ELLEN, b. July 28, 1839; m. E. Parker Clarke, Aug. 21, 1866.

3575 DANIEL DENISON LATHAM, (Delia Ann^6, Frederick^5, Daniel^4, Daniel^3, John^2, George^1,) b. Aug. 3, 1827, was married, May 30, 1859, to Mary Ann Strickland. They live in New London, Conn., and have:

3579 DANIEL, b. Nov. 3, 1859.

3551 BETSEY DENISON, (Frederick^5, Daniel^4, Daniel^3, John^2, George^1,) b. July 4, 1799, was married, Nov. 27, 1817, to Henry W. Avery. They lived in Groton, Conn., until late in life, when they emigrated to Illinois. She d. in Belvidere, Ill., May 11, 1866. The children:

3580 FREDERICK D., b. Oct. 30, 1818; a clergyman.
3581 HENRY W., b. May 31, 1825.

BORODELL DENISON'S DESCENDANTS.

SEE PAGE 14.

The following came to us too late to be printed in its proper place on page 14. Therefore we put it here.

165 SAMUEL STANTON, (son of 9 Borodell and Samuel Stanton,) b. June 16, 1683, was twice married; first, to Sarah Gardiner, May 20, 1711; second, to Lois Cobb, March 19, 1718. He d. July 3, 1736, aged 53 years. His children:

3591 BORODELL, b. March 28, 1712; m. Simeon Sparhawk.
3592 SARAH, b. Oct. 10, 1714, m. Joshua Thompson.
3593 MARY, b. Nov. 5, 1716; m. Samuel Frink, Jr.
3594 SAMUEL, b. March 14, 1719; m. Susanna Champlin.
3595 ANDREW, b. July 4, 1721; m. Sarah Noyes.
3596 LOIS, b. April 9, 1725; m. Edward Denison, 1750.
3597 EUNICE, b. July 1, 1728; m. John Denison, 1750.
3598 NATHAN, b. April 2, 1732; m. Elizabeth Billings.

3598 NATHAN STANTON, (son of 165 Samuel,) b. April 2, 1732, was married, and had these children :

    3599 LOIS.
    3600 ELIZABETH.
    3601 MARY.
    3602 EBENEZER.
    3603 SAMUEL.
    3604 EDWARD.
    3605 ANDREW.

3699 ELIZABETH STANTON, (dau. of 3568 Nathan,) was married to John Noyes, among whose ancestors was John Howland of the Mayflower. The children:

    3606 LYDIA.
    3607 EDWARD, twin.
    3608 SAMUEL, twin.
    3609 ELIZABETH.
    3610 MARY STANTON.
    3611 FANNY.
    3612 PRUDENCE.
    3613 PHEBE.
    3614 JOHN.
    3615 LOIS.

3610 MARY STANTON NOYES, (dau. of Elizabeth S. and John Noyes,) b. April 17, 1896, was married to Moses Bradford Butterfield, May 13, 1821. She died Sept. 3, 1836. Two children :

    3616 MARY SOPHRONIA, b. Jan. 6, 1827.
    3617 ELIZABETH STANTON, b. July 16, 1836.

3616 MARY SOPHRONIA BUTTERFIELD, (dau. of Mary Stanton and Moses B. Butterfield,) was married to Col. Champion Spalding Chase, of Omaha, Nebraska, May 1, 1848. They have :

    3618 CLEMENT CHAMPION, b. Feb. 25, 1860, at Racine, Wis.

3617 ELIZABETH STANTON BUTTERFIELD, (dau. of Mary Stanton and Moses B. Butterfield,) b. July 16, 1836, was married to Hon. James M. Woolworth, of Omaha, Nebraska, Aug. 3, 1871. The children :

    3619 MELIORA CLARKSON, b. Jan. 13, 1873.
    3620 ROBERT HARPER CLARKSON, b. Sept. 14, 1874.

DESCENDANTS OF

GEORGE DENISON, OF WESTERLY, R. I.,

SECOND SON OF

CAPT. GEORGE.

GEORGE DENISON'S DESCENDANTS.

I.

10 GEORGE DENISON, (George[1],) b. in 1653, was married to Mercy Gorham, daughter of Capt. John Gorham, whose wife was Desire Howland, daughter of John Howland of the Mayflower. She was born in Barnstable, Mass., Jan. 20, 1658, and died Sept. 24, 1725. They lived in Westerly, R. I., where he died Dec. 27, 1711, aged 58 years and more. His children:

    3651 EDWARD, bapt. Nov. 14, 1683; b. in 1678; twice married.
    3652 JOSEPH, bapt. Nov. 14, 1683; b. in 1681; *m.* Prudence Minor.
    3653 MERCY, bapt. March 1, 1685; b. in 1683; *m.* Mordecai Dunbar.
    3654 SAMUEL, bapt. Sept. 26, 1686; b. 1685; *m.* Mary Minor.
    3655 DESIRE, bapt. July 15, 1688; b. 1687; d. young.
    3656 ELIZABETH, bapt. Sept. 11, 1690; b. Sept. 11, 1689; *m.* Christopher Champlin, Jr.
    3657 DESIRE, bapt. April 16, 1693; b. in 1693; *m.* John Williams.
    3658 THANKFUL, bapt. April 1, 1695; b. in 1695; *m.* Thomas Stanton.
    3659 GEORGE, bapt. May 7, 1699; b. in 1698; twice married.

THE WILL OF 10 GEORGE DENISON.

I. GEORGE DENISON, of the town of Westerly, in the colony of R. I., and Providence Plantations, in N. England, in America, do give unto my well beloved wife, Mercy Denison, all my moveable estate, be it in what sort or kind so ever, and for the consideration thereof, I do order my said wife to pay all the just debts that I do owe, and I order her to receive all the debts that are due to me. And I also give unto my youngest son, George Denison, the house and land which I now live on, at his mother's decease; but so long as his mother lives, I give unto her the whole use and improvement of all my land which I now live on, during her life, and at her death, it is to be my son George Denison's. And I further order my wife, Mercy Denison, to pay to my two youngest daughters, viz: Desire and Thankful Denison, each of them 10 pound, and I leave it to my wife to give them what else she can spare. And as for my 3 elder sons, Edward, Joseph, [and] Samuel Denison, and my two elder daughters, viz: Mercy Dunbar and Elizabeth Champlin, I have given them already all that I can, and therefore I give them no more; and in witness that this is my last deed of gift, I have hereunto set my hand and seal this 24th day of December, 1711.

Witnesses: ISAAC THOMPSON,
      WM. STANTON,   GEORGE DENISON. [Seal.]
      EDWARD DENISON.

3656 ELIZABETH DENISON, (George^2, George^1,) b. Sept. 11, 1689, was married, Dec. 5, 1705, to Christopher Champlin, Jr., of Westerly, R. I. She died Nov. 22, 1749; he died Oct. 23, 1734, aged 50 years, 1 month; and he was b. Sept. 26, 1684. His estate was very large. He made a "planetary record" of his children's births. We print this record as he wrote it, except that we do not attempt to print the "planetary signs."

    3666 CHRISTOPHER, born, Nov. ye 30th, 32 min. past 7 in ye morning, 1707.
    3667 JOSEPH, born, Aug. ye 4th, 1709, at 8 o'clock in ye morning.
    3668 ELIJAH, born, July ye 26th, 1711; died Feb. ye 18th, 1712.
    3669 ANN, born, March ye 29th, 1714.
    3670 GEORGE, born, Feb. ye 15th, 1716.
    3671 ELIZABETH, born, Jan. ye 10th, 1719.
    3672 THANKFUL, born, March ye 27th, 1721; d. Oct. ye 22d, 1725.
    3673 LYDIA, born, Nov. ye 19th, 1723; d. Oct. ye 10th, 1725.
    3674 ELIJAH, born, Ma ye 23d, 1726; d. March ye 29th, 1729.
    3675 JABEZ, born, Aug. ye 31st, 1728, on ye 7th day of the week.
    3676 OLIVER, born, May ye 12th, 1730, on ye 3rd day of ye week.
    3677 MARY, born, June ye 29th, 1731, on ye 7th day of ye week, at 7 o'clock in ye morning.

3655 DESIRE DENISON, (George^2, George^1,) bapt. April 16, 1693, was married to John Williams, Feb. 19, 1712; lived in Stonington. She d. Aug. 13, 1737; he d. Dec. 30, 1761. The children:

    3678 JOHN, bapt. May 25, 1718; b. May 11, 1714.
    3679 WILLIAM,   "   " ; b. May 1, 1716.
    3680 DESIRE,   "   " ; b. Aug. 25, 1712.
    3681 THANKFUL, "   " ; b. Feb. 8, 1717.
    3682 MERCY, bapt. June 19, 1720; b. Nov. 7, 1719.
    3683 THOMAS, bapt. May 6, 1722; b. Sept. 20, 1721; killed at Fort Griswold, Sept. 6, 1781.
    3684 ROBERT, bapt. June 9, 1723; b. March 8, 1722.

3685 GEORGE, bapt. June 29, 1726; b. July 9, 1726; m. Eunice Avery.
3686 EDWARD; d. on board prison ship.
3687 DEBORAH; m. Nehemiah Williams.

3658 THANKFUL DENISON, (George², George¹,) bapt. April 1, 1695, was married to Thomas Stanton, son of Robert and Joanna, Dec. 31, 1713. They lived in Stonington, Conn., and had these children:

3688 ROBERT, b. Nov. 14, 1716; m. Anna Stanton, May 26, 1736.
3689 THANKFUL, b. July 21, 1718; m. Col. Elias Thompson.
3690 MARY, b. May 27, 1720; m. Col. Henry Babcock.
3691 ELIZABETH, b. June 10, 1722; m. Phineas Stanton.
3692 MERCY, b. June 14, 1724; m. Ebenezer Goddard.
3693 PRUDENCE, b. April 22, 1726; m. Col. Giles Russell.
3694 NATHAN, b. June 19, 1728; d. in infancy.
3695 THOMAS, b. Dec. 17, 1729; m. Sarah Chesebro', Jan. 10, 1751.
3696 ANNA, b. March 22, 1732; m. Nathan Chesebro', Dec. 6, 1752.
3697 DESIRE, b. April 22, 1734; m. Amos Hallum, Oct. 18, 1758.
3698 HANNAH, b. Sept. 29, 1736; m. Robert Potter, Esq., Aug. 28, 1754

3653 MERCY DENISON, (George², George¹,) bapt. March 1, 1685, was married to Mordecai Dunbar. Their children:

3699 THANKFUL, bapt. Oct. 5, 1712.
3699½ MARY, bapt. Oct. 5, 1712.
3700 ELIZABETH, bapt. April 28, 1717

II.

3651 EDWARD DENISON, (George², George¹,) b. in 1678, had two wives; first, Mercy ———, the mother of his children, who was alive Oct. 18, 1715, when she signed a legal document; second, his cousin, Ann, dau. of Capt. John Denison, and widow of Samuel Minor, to whom he was married, March 2, 1718. Edward Denison was drowned Dec. 9, 1726. He was tavern keeper in Westerly, R. I. His children:

3700½ EDWARD, b. in 1699; d. young.
3701 JOHN, b. in 1701; d. in 1776; had three wives.
3701½ ELISHA, b. in 1703; died Nov. 2, 1714; accidentally shot.
3702 MARY, b. in 1705; m. Benj. Billings, June 22, 1724.
3702½ DESIRE, m. Jabez Smith, Nov. 11, 1736.
3703 ABBY, m. Andrew Galloway.

3701 JOHN DENISON, (Edward³, George², George¹,) b. in 1701, was married, Nov. 9, 1720, to Anna Denison, dau. of William of North Stonington. She was drowned in a well, Sept. 15, 1721. He married, second, Mary Noyes, dau. of Dr. James Noyes, and had:

3704 ANN, by 1st wife, b. and d. in 1721.
3705 EDWARD, b. March 4, 1725; *m.* Lois Stanton.
3706 JOHN, b. Jan. 26, 1727; *m.* Eunice Stanton.
3707 ANN, twin, bapt. Sept. 4, 1737; *m.* Nathaniel Minor.
3708 JESSE, twin, bapt. Sept. 4, 1737; *m.* Mary Denison.
3709 ELISHA, bapt. April 15, 1739; died young.
3710 MARY, bapt. Jan. 24, 1742; *m.* Oliver Smith.

The wife Mary died, June 14, 1742; and, July 7, 1743, he was married to Rebecca Noyes, dau. of Capt. Thos. Noyes. They had:

3711 REBECCA, bapt. July 24, 1744; d. in infancy.
3712 REBECCA, bapt. Nov. 3, 1745; d. in infancy.
3713 REBECCA, bapt. Aug. 2, 1747; *m.* Paul Crandall.
3714 ELISHA, bapt. July 2, 1749; d. in infancy.
3715 ELISHA, bapt. Nov. 3, 1751; *m.* Elizabeth Noyes.
3716 MERCY, bapt. Feb. 24, 1754; *m.* Peleg Brown.

The wife Rebecca died, Sept. 11, 1754. Tradition says, he married, fourth, a Widow Billings. In the records, he is mentioned as "Capt. John Denison."

3706 JOHN DENISON, Jr.(John^4, Edward^3, George^2, George^1,) b. Jan. 26, 1727, was married, Dec. 19, 1750, to Eunice Stanton, dau. of Samuel and Sarah (Gardiner) Stanton. His brother Edward was married to her sister Lois, at the same time. They were grand daughters of Borodell Denison. Edward had no child. John had these:

3718 EUNICE, bapt. Aug. 30, 1752; *m.* James Noyes.
3719 EDWARD, bapt. March 3, 1754; died young.
3720 LOIS, bapt. Dec. 21, 1755; *m.* Jonathan Waldron.
3721 MARY, bapt. in May, 1757; d. Dec. 11, 1781.
3722 JOHN, b. June 3, 1759; twice married.

3718 EUNICE DENISON, (John, Jr.^{5}, John^4, Edward^3, George^2, George^1,) was married to James Noyes, Dec. 2, 1772; lived in Stonington; he d. Aug. 5, 1831; she d. April 25, 1801. The children:

3723 EDWARD D., b. Sept. 2, 1773.
3724 LOIS, b. May 1, 1776.
3725 JAMES, b. March 29, 1779.
3726 JESSE D., b. March 14, 1781.
3727 NATHANIEL M., b. Nov. 15, 1783.
3728 JOHN D., b. April 19, 1786.
3729 CHARLES B., b. Sept. 27, 1788.

3720 LOIS DENISON, (John, Jr.[5], John[4], Edward[3], George[2], George[1],) married Jonathan Waldron, May 10, 1781. He d. July 17, 1790. They lived in Stonington. Their children:

    3730 POLLY, b. Aug. 30, 1782; d. Aug. 31, 1783.
    3731 NATHANIEL, b. Oct. 17, 1782.
    3732 GEORGE, b. March 17, 1785.
    3733 JOSEPH, b. June 8, 1787.
    3734 JONATHAN, b. June 8, 1788.

3722 JOHN DENISON, 3D, (John Jr.[5], John[4], Edward[3], George[2], George[1],) was married, Sept. 24, 1786, to Ede Brown, daughter of Samuel Brown of Stonington. Their children:

    3735 MARY, b. Oct. 14, 1787; m. Isaac Champlin, Nov. 8, 1807.
    3736 LOIS, b. Dec. 16, 1789; m. 3979 Amos Denison, jr. See his record.
    3737 EDWARD, b. Oct., 1793; m.; no child; d. March 25, 1874.
    3738 JOHN, b. in 1795; twice married; d. Sept. 30, 1851.
    3739 SAMUEL, b. in 1797; lives in Paris, unmarried.

Mrs. Ede (Brown) Denison died Nov. 1, 1797, aged 31 years and 6 mos. John Denison, 3d, married 2nd, Esther Brown of Norwalk, Conn., and had these children:

    3740 EDE, b. Dec., 1801; d. May 10, 1805.
    3741 STEPHEN B., b. Feb. 2, 1807; d. March 8, 1834.
    3742 JESSE, b. Aug. 1809; d. in infancy.
    3743 ELIZABETH, b. May 15, 1812; m. Julius W. Adams.
    3744 EUNICE A., b. April 1, 1805; died unmarried, April 5, 1867.
    3745 ELISHA J., b. Feb. 23, 1815; lives in Brooklyn, N. Y.; unmarried.

Mrs. Esther (Brown) Denison d. March 29, 1828; Mr. John Denison, 3d, d. Nov. 21, 1848.

3735 MARY DENISON, (John, 3d[6], John, Jr.[5], John[4], Edward[3], George[2], George[1],) b. Oct. 14, 1787, was married, Nov. 8, 1807, to Isaac Champlin, of Westerly, R. I. He died Aug. 8, 1861; she died in Stonington, Jan. 30, 1862. They had these four children:

    3746 JOHN DENISON, b. Dec. 5, 1810; m. Sylvia Bostwick.
    3747 MARY ELIZABETH, b. Nov. 2, 1813; d. in infancy.
    3748 MARY, b. and d. Aug. 12, 1808.
    3749 WILLIAM, b. Oct. 3, 1809; d. Oct. 28, 1809.

3746 JOHN DENISON CHAMPLIN, (son of 3735 Mary and Isaac,) b. Dec. 5, 1810, was married, Sept. 12, 1831, to Sylvia Bostwick of New Preston, Conn., b. also Dec. 5, 1810. She d. March 5, 1856, at Lexington, Ky. Their children:

10 George Denison's Descendants.

3750 John Denison, Jr., b. Jan. 29, 1834, in Stonington, Conn.
3751 William Belden, b. July 15, 1836, in Stonington, Conn.
3752 Caroline Brown, b. Feb. 4, 1839, at Wetumpka, Ala.; d. in New Orleans, Feb. 22, 1862.
3753 Edward Elmore, b. June 13, 1841, in Dorchester, Mass.
3754 Isabella, b. Oct. 20, 1843, in Albany, N. Y.; d. Feb. 20, 1844.

3750 John Denison Champlin, Jr., (son of 3746 John Denison Champlin,) b. Jan. 29, 1824, is an author and editor, and lives in New York City. He was married, Oct. 8, 1873, at Litchfield, Conn., to Franka E. Colvocoresses, dau. of Capt. George M. Colvocoresses, U. S. N. They have one child:

3755 John Denison Champlin, 3rd, b. July 23, 1875.

3738 John Denison, 4th, (John, 3d[6], John, Jr.[5], John[4], Edward[3], George[2], George[1],) b. in 1795, was married, first, to Jane N. Mott, who had two children. She died, and he married, second, Elizabeth Nitchie; no other child. He d. Sept. 30, 1851. His children:

3756 Elizabeth, b. Jan. 13, 1829; m. Fred Smith; no child.
3757 John W., b. Nov. 5, 1831; m. Frances Stanton.

3757 John W. Denison, (son of 3738 John Denison, 4th,) b. Nov. 10, 1831, was married, Dec. 25, 1851, to Frances Stanton; lives in Stonington; has one child:

3758 John M., b. Oct. 17, 1852; m. Anna Smith, Feb. 18, 1876.

3743 Elizabeth Denison, (John, 3d[6], John, Jr.[5], John[4], Edward[3], George[2], George[1],) b. May 15, 1812, was married, Dec. 2, 1835, to Col. Julius W. Adams. They live in Brooklyn, N. Y. Eight children:

3759 Minnie, b. Oct. 18, 1836; d. April, 1840.
3760 Julius, b. April 3, 1840; d. Nov. 15, 1865.
3761 Stephen, b. June 7, 1843.
3762 Minnie, b. Oct. 18, 1844; d. Dec. 25, 1845.
3763 Kirkwood, b. Aug. 29, 1846; d. Nov. 23, 1867.
3764 Irving, b. Feb. 23, 1848; d. Sept. 22, 1875.
3765 William, b. Aug. 2, 1850; d. Dec. 22, 1868.
3766 Alice, b. Sept. 2, 1853.

3710 Mary Denison, (John[4], Edward[3], George[2], George[1], bapt. Jan. 24, 1742, was married to Oliver Smith, son of Mary (Denison) and Nathan Smith. They had:

3767 Edward, bapt. Sept. 9, 1764.
3768 Mary, bapt. Sept. 9, 1764.
3769 Elizabeth, bapt. Sept. 9, 1764.

3770 Nathan, bapt. Sept. 9, 1764.
3771 Oliver, bapt. May 3, 1767.
3772 John, bapt. Oct. 29, 1769.
3773 Denison, bapt. Oct. 29, 1769.
3774 Nathaniel, bapt. April 17, 1782.
3775 Coddington, bapt. April 17, 1782.
3776 Washington, bapt. April 17, 1782.
3777 Nancy, bapt. April 17, 1782.
3778 Sally, bapt. April 17, 1782.
3779 Fanny, bapt. April 17, 1782.
3780 Jesse, bapt. July 13, 1788.

3716 Mercy Denison, (John[4], Edward[4], George[2], George[1],) bapt. Feb. 24, 1754, was married to Peleg Brown, April 14, 1776. She d. Sept. 22, 1781; and Peleg Brown, (called "Capt." in the records,) was married, second, Oct. 24, 1782, to Anna Ingraham. Mercy (Denison) Brown had these three children:

3781 Mercy, b. Feb. 22, 1777; *m.* Nathaniel Palmer.
3782 Elizabeth, b. Jan. 29, 1781; *m.* Stiles Phelps.
3783 Peleg, b. March 16, 1779; d March 22, 1780.

3715 Elisha Denison, (John[4], Edward[3], George[2], George[1],) bapt. Nov. 3, 1751, was married to Elizabeth Noyes, April 26, 1772; she d. May 13, 1831; had these children:

3784 Elizabeth, b. Nov. 29, 1773; *m.* Nathaniel Ledyard.
3785 Mehitable, b. Sept. 5, 1776; *m.* Samuel Hurlburt.
3786 Phebe, b. April 22, 1782; *m.* W. J. Robinson.
3787 Elisha, b. May 2, 1779; d. March 4, 1803.

3708 Jesse Denison, (John[4], Edward[3], George[2], George[1],) bapt. Sept. 4, 1737, and was married, Jan. 24, 1759, to Mary Denison, dau. of Avery, and had:

3788 Mary, b. Feb. 8, 1765; d. unmarried.
3789 Elizabeth; *m.* a Mr. Drummond of Scotland.

Soon after his marriage, Jesse Denison removed to the island of St. Eustatia. He died there, and his widow was married to a Dr. Boscawen. She died in the island of Jamaica. See pp. 102-3.

3707 Ann Denison, (John[4], Edward[3], George[2], George[1],) bapt. Sept. 4, 1737, was married to Nathaniel Minor, Feb. 20, 1754, and had only this child:

3790 Abigail; *m.* John Denison, 5th, Sept. 6, 1772.

10 George Denison's Descendants.

3784 ELIZABETH DENISON,(Elisha[5], John[4], Edward[3], George[2], George[1],) b. Nov. 29, 1773, was married to Nathaniel Ledyard, Feb. 7, 1795, and lived in New London, Conn. He died Oct. 10, 1815, aged 47 years, 9 mos. She died in 1849. Their children:

    3791 ELIZABETH D., b. Jan. 10, 1796; d. July 28, 1848.
    3792 MARY L., b. Oct. 24, 1797; m. John Ledyard.
    3793 EBENEZER G. C., b. Sept. 20, 1802; d. in Mobile, in 1843.
    3794 FANNY P., b. Aug. 11, 1799; lives in New London, Conn.
    3795 ELISHA D., twin, b. Sept 11, 1805; m. Miss Falconer in Alabama.
    3796 EDWARD D., twin, b. Sept. 11, 1805: m. Elizabeth Wallace.
    3797 NATHANIEL L., b. Sept. 30, 1807; m. Miss Vaughn.
    3798 GEORGE W., b. Oct. 5, 1809; d. in California, July 12, 1850.
    3799 WILLIAM D., b. July 26, 1811; m. Fanny Worthington.

3785 MEHITABLE DENISON, (Elisha[5], John[4], Edward[3], George[2], George[1],) b. Sept. 5, 1776, was married to Samuel Hurlburt, June 2, 1796. They lived in New London, Conn. He d. July 27, 1845, in his 80th year. She d. Jan. 13, 1842. Their children were:

    3800 CHRISTOPHER, b. July 6, 1797; d. July 5, 1834, unmarried.
    3801 JOSEPH, (REV.) b. Aug. 22, 1799; m. Mary C. Hattrick, June 16, 1824; d. June 5, 1775. They lived at New London.
    2802 ELISHA D., b. Sept. 3, 1801; m. Martha Purser; d. Aug. 4, 1854.
    3803 RICHARD, b. July 24, 1803; d. in infancy.
    3804 SAMUEL, b. March 4, 1806; d. unmarried in 1850.
    3805 JOHN D., b. July 10, 1808; m. Edwinia Hicks.
    3806 WILLIAM W., b. March 29, 1813; m. Elizabeth Butler.
    3807 GEORGE, b. Aug. 19, 1815; m. Sarah Lewis; d. July 15, 1846.
    3808 MARY, b. May 27, 1820; d. July 20, 1820.
    3809 MATILDA, b. July 8, 1816; m. Ebenezer Learned, Aug. 12, 1834; d. in 1837.

3786 PHEBE DENISON, (Elisha[5], John[4], Edward[3], George[2], George[1],) b. April 22, 1782, was married to W. J. Robinson, March 23, 1802. They lived in Morristown, N. J. She died Dec. 31, 1853, aged 71 years and 8 mos. He d. Sept. 9, 1845. Their children:

    3810 MATILDA C., b. Dec. 9, 1802; d. unmarried.
    3811 ELISHA D., b. Feb. 9, 1814; d. unmarried, March 1, 1860.
    3812 ELIZABETH D., b. July 4, 1807; not married.
    3813 MARY M., b. Nov. 26, 1811; m. Edwin Hicks of Brooklyn, N. Y.
    3814 PHEBE D., b. Oct. 11, 1809.
    3815 WILLIAM D., b. Sept. 28, 1804; married; d. Oct. 20, 1839.
    3816 EMMA, b. Nov. 4, 1822.

3817 SAMUEL, b. July 23, 1817; d. Oct. 17, 1818.
3818 BOUND, b. in 1818.
3819 JULIA GORAM, b. Feb. 23, 1820; d. April 6, 1860.

3702 MARY DENISON, (Edward³, George², George¹,) b. in 1705, was married to Benjamin Billings, June 22, 1724. They lived in Westerly, R. I., where he succeeded Edward Denison, as "tavern-keeper," after 1726. Their children:

3820 DESIRE, b. June 5, 1726.
3821 BENJAMIN, b. Dec. 1, 1728.

3702½ DESIRE DENISON, (Edward³, George², George¹,) was married to Jabez Smith, of Groton, Conn., Nov. 11, 1736. They lived in Groton, where she died in 1740. Her children:

3826 DESIRE, b. July 31, 1737.
3827 PRISCILLA, b. in 1740.

Jabez Smith, *m.* 2nd, Amy Avery, May 26, 1742, and had eight more children, as follows:

3828 AMY, b. Jan. 18, 1747.
3829 EUNICE, b. Feb. 25, 1749.
3829½ JABEZ, b. Aug. 31, 1751.
3830 ANNA, b. Dec. 4, 1754.
3831 JOHN, b. April 11, 1757; d. young.
3832 MARY, b. Oct. 31, 1759.
3833 JOHN, b. April 10, 1762.
3834 PEREZ S., b. July 15, 1766.

3703 ABBY DENISON, (Edward³, George², George¹,) was married to Andrew Galloway, about 1738. Their children:

3835 MARY, b. April 5, 1739.
3836 PRUDENCE, b. June 1, 1742.
3837 ANDREW, b. Aug. 7, 1745.

3652 JOSEPH Denison, (George², George¹,) bapt. Nov. 14, 1683, was married Feb. 17, 1707, to Prudence Minor, dau. of Dr. Joseph Minor. He d. Feb. 18, 1725; his wife d. May 26, 1726, in her 38th year. He lived and d. in Stonington, Conn. His children:

3841 JOSEPH, b. Sept. 21, 1707; had three wives.
3842 PRUDENCE, b. Nov. 28, 1709; *m.* Benj. Sprague, Jan. 20, 1726; d. in 1726; no child.
3843 BORODELL, b. Feb. 14, 1712; *m.* Ezekiel Turner.
3844 AMOS, b. Feb. 18, 1714; *m.* Martha Gallup.
3845 NATHAN, b. Feb. 20, 1716; *m.* Ann Carey.
3846 ELIZABETH, b. Feb. 15, 1720; *m.* Samuel Minor.
3847 JOANNA, b. Jan. 28, 1718; *m.* Henry Hewitt.

3848 THANKFUL, bapt. April 7, 1723; *m.* Elisha Williams.
3849 ANNA, bapt. May 3, 1724; *m.* Amos Allen, 1739.

3843 BORODELL DENISON, (Joseph³, George², George¹,) b. Feb. 14, 1712, was married, May 12, 1729, to Ezekiel Turner. They lived in Groton, Conn., and had these children :

3850 THEODY, b. Aug. 14, 1730.
3851 PRUDENCE, b. March 8, 1732; *m.* Moses Palmer.
3852 EZEKIEL, b. Jan. 27, 1734.
3853 EUNICE, b. July 22, 1740.
3854 AMOS, b. Sept. 1, 1744.

3846 ELIZABETH DENISON, (Joseph³, George², George¹,) b. Feb. 15, 1720, was married to Samuel Minor, April 29, 1739, and died Dec. 9, 1742. He *m.* 2nd, Esther Gallup. The wife, Elizabeth Denison, had two children ,

3855 BRIDGET, b. Feb. 26, 1740; d. Nov. 7, 1742.
3856 ELIZABETH, b. May 13, 1742.

3847 JOANNA DENISON, (Joseph³, George², George¹,) b. Jan. 28, 1718, was married Dec. 24, 1735, to Henry Hewitt ; lived in Canterbury, Conn. Children :

3857 AMOS, b. Feb. 17, 1737; d. May 17, 1753.
3858 HENRY, b. Jan. 2, 1739.
3859 THOMAS, b. Sept. 29, 1740.
3860 JOANNA, b. July 3, 1742.
3861 CONTENT, b. May 1, 1748.
3862 HANNAH, b. May 23, 1750.
3863 STEPHEN, b. July 10, 1752; d. in childhood.
3864 ANNE, b. July 1, 1754.
3865 STEPHEN, b. June 7, 1757.

3841 JOSEPH DENISON, JR., (Joseph³, George², George¹,) b. Sept. 21, 1707, was married, Jan. 16, 1733, to Mrs. Content Russell, widow of Rev. E. Russell. She died childless, Sept. 20, 1749 ; and April 23, 1751, he was married, 2nd, to Mrs. Bridget Wheeler, dau. of Thomas Noyes. He was a deacon ; July 21, 1748, he was made a deacon of the first church in Stonington. He seems to have had a long life, for his name is signed to church records as late as March 30, 1789 ; and he appears to have had a third wife, for he had a wife, Elizabeth Hallum, admitted to the church, Oct. 3, 1773. He d. Feb. 15, 1795. His children, all by Mrs. Bridget (Noyes) Wheeler, the second wife, were as follows :

3866 Content, b. Jan. 29, 1752; *m.* John Williams.
3867 Peleg, b. Nov. 24, 1753; d. in 1754.
3868 Peleg, b. July 6, 1755; *m.* Mary Gray.
3869 Amos, b. March 18, 1757; *m.* Hannah Williams.
3870 Mary.
3871 Ezra, b. May 5, 1759; d. Sept. 28, 1760.
3872 Ephraim, twin, b. May 5, 1761; d. in 1761.
3873 Manasseh, twin, b. May 6, 1761; d. in 1761.
3874 Bridget, b. March 23, 1763; *m.* Nehemiah Mason, Nov. 6, 1782.
3875 Joseph, bapt. April 23, 1765; d. soon after college graduation, unmarried, Aug. 20, 1789.
3876 Elizabeth, bapt. April 26, 1767; died young.

3866 Content Denison, (Dea. Joseph[4], Joseph[3], George[2], George[1],) b. Jan. 29, 1752, was married, Jan. 18, 1770 to John Williams of Stonington, and had these:

3877 John, bapt. July 5, 1772; b. Nov. 20, 1771.
3878 Elihu, bapt. Jan. 11, 1773; b. Oct. 8, 1772.
3879 Lydia, bapt. Aug. 1774; b. May 23, 1774.
3880 Joseph, bapt. June 23, 1776; b. March 27, 1776.
3881 Bridget, bapt. Aug. 2, 1778; b. Jan. 10, 1778.
3882 Desire, bapt. Dec. 23, 1784; b. July 18, 1780.
3883 William, twin, bapt. Dec. 23, 1784; b. May 4, 1782.
3884 Stanton, twin, bapt. Dec. 23, 1784; b. May 4, 1782.
3885 George, bapt. Dec. 23, 1784; b. Oct. 3, 1784.

3874 Bridget Denison, (Dea. Joseph[4], Joseph[3], George[2], George[1],) b. March 23, 1763, was married to Nehemiah Mason, Nov. 6, 1782. They had these:

3886 Mary, b. June 5, 1783; *m.* Amos Minor.
3887 Mehetible, b. Sept. 19, 1784; *m.* Alex. Latham.
3888 Bridget, b. April 9, 1786.
3889 Andrew, b. June 2, 1788.
3890 Joseph, b. April 4, 1790.
3891 Daniel, b. July 23, 1792.
3892 Peleg, b. Aug. 30, 1794.
2893 Nehemiah, b. Nov. 14, 1800.

3868 Peleg Denison, (Dea. Joseph[4], Joseph[3], George[2], George[1],) b. July 6, 1755, was married, March 9, 1780, to Mary Gray; lived in Stonington; he d. May 21, 1800; she died at Albany, N. Y., July, 1837, aged 80. Their children:

3894 Noyes, b. Dec. 9, 1780; d. in 1814.
3895 Mary, b. Nov. 26, 1782; *m.* Nathan Stanton,
3896 Samuel M. G., b. June 15, 1784; d. June 2, 1796.
3897 Leonard, b. Jan. 1, 1792; *m.* Phebe A. Ely.
3898 Peleg, Jr., b. May 15, 1786; *m.* Harriet Eldridge.
3899 Joseph, b. March 11, 1788; d. in 1843.

3900 ELIZABETH, b. June 13, 1790; d. in 1836.
3901 SAMUEL, b. Oct. 7, 1793; d. Dec. 26, 1862.
3902 BRIDGET, b. May 28, 1794; m. Dea. Noyes Palmer.

3895 MARY DENISON, (Peleg[5], Dea. Joseph[4], Joseph[3], George[2], George[1],) b. Nov. 26, 1782, was married, June 4, 1804, to Nathan Stanton, of Stonington, Conn. They lived in Florida, N. Y.; she d. Dec. 25, 1846. Their children:

3903 MARY DENISON, b. June 4, 1806; m. John Blood; d. Nov. 26,'80.
3904 BENJAMIN F., b. Feb. 19, 1813.
3905 JOSEPH DENISON, b. Aug. 17, 1815.
3906 BRIDGET ELIZABETH, b. Oct. 13, 1818; d. in 1819.

3902 BRIDGET DENISON, (Peleg[5], Dea. Joseph[4], Joseph[3], George[2], George[1],) b. in 1794, was married, to Dea. Noyes Palmer, Jan. 4, 1816, and d. Jan. 6, 1818. One child:

3907 NOYES, b. Nov. 12, 1817, and d. Feb. 13, 1818.

3897 LEONARD DENISON, (Peleg[5], Dea. Joseph[4], Joseph[3], George[2], George[1],) b. Jan. 1, 1792, was married Feb. 15, 1819, to Phebe Augusta Ely, of Sackett's Harbor, N. Y. He settled at Sackett's Harbor, and become one of the most prominent and influential men in that region. With his brothers, he owned the first line of steamboats established on Lake Ontario. He was largely engaged in the carrying trade, with sailing vessels. During the war of 1812, he transported troops, cannon, supplies, etc., for the government. At one time, he was Collector of the port; and he held other public offices. Through his long life, he was noted for enterprize, and for high, unimpeachable character. He d. March 11, 1879, aged 87 years; his wife, born June 5, 1801, died July 26, 1878, aged 77 years. Their children:

3908 MARY AUGUSTA, b. Sept. 5, 1820; d. Aug. 1, 1821.
3909 ELISHA E., b. Nov. 24, 1822; not married; d. in 1863, being drowned near Baton Rouge, La., while in the U. S. service.
3910 AUGUSTA ELIZABETH, b. April 14, 1824; d. Oct. 6, 1824.
3911 AUGUSTA MINERVA, b. Dec. 13, 1825; twice married.
3912 AMELIA S., b. Jan. 5, 1828; m. Geo. Kingsbury.
3913 ELIZABETH C., b. Sept. 26, 1829; twice married.
3914 LEONARD S., b. March 8, 1833; m. Augenette Sigorney, July 4, 1855; was at Omaha in 1859; d. in May, 1877.
3915 CHARLES HENRY, b. Jan. 16, 1837; d. May 26, 1838.
3916 MARY LORD, b. June 27, 1839; d. May 2, 1855.
3917 GEORGE WILSON, b. Aug. 10, 1840; m. Dec., 1870.

3918 HENRIETTA M., b. March 11, 1842; twice married.
3919 ANNA CAROLINE, b. Aug. 14, 1843; d. July 10, 1845.

3911 AUGUSTA MINERVA DENISON, (Leonard⁶, Peleg⁵, Dea. Joseph⁴, Joseph³, George², George¹,) b. Dec. 13, 1825, was married, first, Dec. 21, 1847, to James A. Greenlee, of Morgantown, N. C.; 3 children. He died, and she was married, second, March 2, 1859, to Samuel Ellis; two children. She lives at Sauk Rapids, Minnesota. Her children, the first three being Greenlees, and the last two Ellises :

3920 AMELIA DENISON G., b. Dec. 24, 1848; m. E. F. Barnum, Oct., 1865; lives at Sauk Rapids, Minn., has children.
3921 ELIZABETH DENISON G., b. Sept. 22, 1850; m. Charles G. Wood, Sept. 22, 1869; lives at Sauk Rapids, Minn.; has children.
3922 WM. LUCIUS MCREE DENISON G., b. Dec. 15, 1853; d. Jan. 1,'60.
3923 SAMUEL A. E., b. Dec. 13, 1861.
3924 MARY MINERVA E., b. Sept. 20, 1864; d. March 2, 1865.

3912 AMELIA SOPHIA DENISON, (Leonard⁶, Peleg⁵, Dea. Joseph⁴, Joseph³, George², George¹,) b. Jan. 5, 1828, was married, Sept. 30, 1859, to Geo. Kingsbury, of St. Louis ; lives at Sackett's Harbor, N. Y.; one child :

3925 HENRY LAY, b. Nov. 28, 1860; d. Dec. 10, 1865.

3913 ELIZABETH CAMP DENISON, (Leonard⁶, Peleg⁵, Dea. Joseph⁴, Joseph³, George², George¹,) b. Sept. 26, 1829, was married, 1st, May 1, 1860, to Judge Orville Jennings of Little Rock, Ark, U. S. District Attorney ; and 2nd, to John Rutherford, of North Carolina, Aug., 1870. They lived at Bridgewater, N. C.; he d. March 13, 1880.

3917 GEORGE WILSON DENISON, (Leonard⁶, Peleg⁵, Dea. Joseph⁴, Joseph³, George², George¹,) b. Aug. 10, 1840, was married, Sept. 26, 1871, to Olivia C. Vandegrift, of McDonough, Delaware. They live at Sackett's Harbor, N. Y. In 1865, and after, he was Register of the Land Office at Little Rock, Ark. His children :

3926 LINA V., b. Dec. 1, 1872, at Little Rock.
3927 HETTY M., b. Jan. 28, 1875, at Little Rock.
3928 MAGGIE A., b. Jan. 14, 1877, at Sackett's Harbor.

3918 HENRIETTA MARIA DENISON, (Leonard⁶, Peleg⁵, Dea. Joseph⁴, Joseph³, George², George¹,) b. March 11, 1842, was married, first, Jan., 1869, to Henry Flynn ; and second, Oct.

10 George Denison's Descendants.

31, 1876, to Edward Halliday; lives in New York City, winters, and at Sackett's Harbor, summers.

3898 PELEG DENISON, (Peleg⁵, Dea. Joseph⁴, Joseph³, George², George¹,) b. in 1786, was married to Harriet Eldridge, in 1809. She died, March 4, 1825. He m. 2nd, Nancy Bolles and d. March 12, 1843. His children, all by 1st wife, were:

- **3936** HANNAH E., b. March 26, 1810; m. Geo. W. Noyes.
- **3937** HARRIET E., b. Dec. 13, 1811; d. June 30, 1832.
- **3938** PELEG, b. Dec. 16, 1816; m. Martha A. Suffern.
- **3939** MARY, b. April 13, 1814; m. Hiram DeW. Keyser.
- **3940** BRIDGET, b. Nov. 7, 1818; m. Pardon T. Kinney.
- **3941** DANIEL E., b. June 20, 1821; d. in 1831.
- **3942** CAROLINE ELIZABETH, b. Feb. 23, 1825; m. Rev. J. B. Gould.

3936 HANNAH E. DENISON, (Peleg⁶, Peleg⁵, Dea. Joseph⁴, Joseph³, George², George¹,) b. in 1810, was married, Sept. 2, 1827, to George W. Noyes, lived at Mystic Bridge, and died Sept. 5, 1829. She had:

- **3943** GEORGE D., b. March 23, 1829; d. March 4, 1854.

Geo. W. Noyes had two other wives. The 2nd was Prudence Dean Brown, who had seven children, and died, Jan. 22, 1854. The 3d was Emily F. Denison, dau. of 3207 Isaac and Lavina, to whom he was married, Jan. 16, 1856. She had but one child:

- **3944** FREDERICK, b. July 20, 1858.

Geo. W. Noyes died Feb. 26, 1866. His children by the second wife were:

- **3945** SARAH E., b. Nov. 24, 1835; d. March 5, 1836.
- **3946** HENRY B., b. Jan. 15, 1837; m. Ellen Holmes, Jan. 10, 1870.
- **3947** JOSEPH R., b. Nov. 26, 1838; d. July 30, 1859.
- **3948** WILLIAM H., b. April 4, 1841; d. Sept. 24, 1858.
- **3949** ELLEN E, b. July 27, 1843; m. John Gallup; Oct. 5, 1870.
- **3950** THEODORE F., b. Aug. 25, 1847; d. Oct. 27, 1848.
- **3951** EDWIN B., b. Jan. 27, 1850; m. Eliza Tift, Oct., 1873.

3939 MARY DENISON, (Peleg⁶, Peleg⁵, Dea. Joseph⁴, Joseph³, George², George¹,) b. April 13, 1814, was married to Hiram DeWitt Keyser, of Albany, N. Y, June 8, 1836. Her children:

- **3952** DEWITT, b. March 4, 1837; d. July 21, 1839.
- **3953** MARY ANN, b. Oct. 22, 1838.
- **3954** JOSEPH DENISON, b. Nov. 2, 1840; was in Andersonville prison; d. Aug. 14, 1875.

3955 DANIEL ELDRIDGE, b. Dec. 19, 1841; m. Carrie DuBois; is a lawyer.
3956 HARRIET DENISON, twin, b. March 5, 1845; d. March 15, 1845.
3957 CATHERINE, twin, b. March 5, 1845; d. July 27, 1852.
3958 CHARLOTTE ELIZABETH, b. Sept. 15, 1847; d. July 21, 1852.
3959 HIRAM, b. April 14, 1851; d. Aug. 21, 1851.
3960 JOHN B., b. March 18, 1849; d. June 15, 1850.
3961 AUGUSTA, twin, b. Sept. 6, 1852; d. March 17, 1854.
3962 CAROLINE, twin, b. Sept. 6, 1852; d. Dec. 1, 1852.

3938 PELEG DENISON, (Peleg^6, Peleg^5, Dea. Joseph^4, Joseph^3, George^2, George^1,) b. Dec. 15, 1816, was married to Martha Augusta Suffern, of Haverstraw, N. Y., Nov. 22, 1843. She was born July 20, 1820. She died, Jan. 6, 1867, at Morristown, N. J., having had six children. May 21, 1870, he m. Mrs. Martha V. Bryan. His children, all by the first wife, were as follows:

3963 CAROLINE AUGUSTA, b. Aug. 7, 1844; m. Nelson C. Tompkins.
3964 EDGAR, b. Feb. 19, 1846; married.
3965 SAMUEL, b. Jan. 4, 1848; d. Oct. 9, 1848.
3966 NANCY ADELIA, b. Feb. 5, 1849; d. Oct. 12, 1849.
3967 ANNA SUFFERN, b. April 12, 1854.
3968 FRANCIS MARION, b. June 25, 1862; d. Oct. 9, 1862.

3940 BRIDGET DENISON, (Peleg^6, Peleg^5, Dea. Joseph^4, Joseph^3; George^2, George^1,) b. Nov. 7, 1818, was married to Rev. Pardon T. Kinney, a Methodist preacher, May 29, 1837. She died, Aug. 10, 1862. Her children:

3969 HARRIET DENISON, b. June 24, 1839; d. Sept. 18, 1841.
3970 ACHSAH ANN, b. Jan. 30, 1843.
3971 SAMUEL DENISON, b. July 25, 1845; d. Dec. 18, 1845.
3972 ELIZABETH ELDRIDGE, b. Jan. 20, 1847.
3973 PARDON T., b. May 5, 1849; d. Sept. 25, 1850.
3974 CORNELIUS, b. June 24, 1852.
3975 ELLA MINNETTE, b. Sept. 5, 1856.
3976 CLINTON, b. Nov. 22, 1860.

3942 CAROLINE ELIZABETH DENISON, (Peleg^6, Peleg^5, Dea. Joseph^4, Joseph^3, George^2, George^1,) b. Feb. 23, 1825, was married to Rev. John B. Gould, April 21, 1847. They have but one child:

3977 JOHN MELVILLE, July 4, 1848; is a lawyer in Boston.

3869 AMOS DENISON, (Dea. Joseph^4, Joseph^3, George^2, George^1,) b. March 18, 1757, was married, Aug. 3, 1777, to

10 *George Denison's Descendants.*

Hannah Williams. He d. Oct., 1835; she d. Aug. 19, 1829. They lived in North Stonington, Conn. Their children:

 3978 CHARLES WHEELER, b. June 26, 1778; *m.* Eliza Stanton.
 3979 AMOS, b. Aug. 19, 1780; *m.* Lois Denison.
 3980 HANNAH, b. Aug. 23, 1782; d. May 4, 1785.
 3981 SARAH POTTER, b. Sept. 3, 1785; *m.* Luke Palmer.
 3982 EDWARD, b. Nov. 30, 1790; d. Dec. 5, 1818.
 3983 EZRA STILES, b. June 26, 1793; d Dec. 5, 1812.
 3984 MARTHA, b. March 17, 1796; *m.* Rev. Henry Sherman.
 3985 HANNAH ELIZA, b. June 11, 1799; *m.* Ephraim Williams.

3978 CAPT. CHARLES WHEELER DENISON, (Amos[5], Dea. Joseph[4], Joseph[3], George[2], George[1]) b. June 26, 1778, was married, Nov. 24, 1805, to Eliza Stanton, dau. of Zebulon. He d. Aug. 14, 1817. She d. Aug. 8, 1825, aged 42 years. His children:

 3986 ELIZA, b. Aug. 30, 1806; *m.* J. E. Culver, May 16, 1826.
 3987 Rev. CHARLES W., b. in 1808; twice married.
 3988 ELISHA, b. in 1810; d. young.
 3989 SARAH, b. in 1812; *m.* Nathan Storrs.
 3990 HARRIET, b. in 1814.

3987 REV. CHARLES W. DENISON, (Chas. Wheeler[6], Amos[5], Dea. Joseph[4], Joseph[3], George[2], George[1],) b. in 1806, was married, first, to Mary Palmer, who had three children, and died in 1846. Sept. 7, 1846, he *m.* 2nd, Mary Ann Andrews, of Cambridge, Mass.; no other child. He was first a Baptist preacher, and later an Episcopalian. He is a man of brilliant parts, who has made considerable use of his pen. His second wife, author of "That Husband of Mine," has won literary reputation. His children:

 3991 CHARLES WILBERFORCE, b. May, 1839.
 3992 GEORGE SHERMAN, b. Nov., 1844.
 3993 MARY PALMER, b. June, 1846.

3979 AMOS DENISON, JR., (Amos[5], Dea. Joseph[4], Joseph[3], George[2], George[1],) b. Aug. 19, 1780, was married, Nov., 1808, to Lois Denison, dau. of John and Ede; lived in Stonington. He died there; his wife died at Parma, Ohio, Feb. 6, 1875. Their children:

 3994 HARRIET E., b. Aug. 27, 1809; *m.* Frederic Cogswell.
 3995 AMOS E. W., b. Sept. 20, 1811; *m.* Mary Dexter.
 3996 MARY C., b. May 19, 1814; *m.* S. H. Green; no child.
 3997 CAROLINE EDITH, b. Nov. 11, 1816; *m.* Wm. C. Moss.

10 George Denison's Descendants.

3994 HARRIET E. DENISON, (Amos, Jr.⁶, Amos⁵, Dea. Joseph⁴, Joseph³, George², George¹,) b. Aug. 27, 1809, was married to Frederic Cogswell, May 5, 1833 ; they lived in Griswold, Conn., and had :

    3998 HARRIET E., b. March 13, 1834.
    3999 MARY G., b. March 14, 1837.
    4000 FREDERIC I , b. July 19, 1841.
    4001 EDWARD, b. June 12, 1843.
    4002 WILLIAM, b. April, 1846.
    4003 FRANK F., b. Jan., 1851.

3995 AMOS E. W. DENISON, (Amos, Jr.⁶, Amos⁵, Dea. Joseph⁴, Joseph³, George², George¹,) was married to Mary M. Dexter, April 12, 1838, and had these children :

    4004 JOHN, b. April 28, 1839; died young.
    4005 SARAH D., b. July 10, 1841 ; m. W. N. Stevens, Feb. 1868; died childless in 1874.
    4006 STEPHEN B., b. June 2, 1843; died young.
    4007 JOHN DEXTER. b. Dec. 2, 1845 ; m. Emma Whittaker in 1874, who d. in 1875.
    4008 AMOS, b. Oct. 11, 1849.
    4009 EPHRAIM W., b. Dec. 12, 1854; m. Lizzie C. Kontz, 1875 ; has :
        4010 AMOS A., b. May 11, 1876.

3997 CAROLINE EDITH DENISON, (Amos, Jr.⁶, Amos⁵, Dea. Joseph⁴, Joseph³, George², George¹,) b. Nov. 11, 1816, was married, Nov. 12, 1832, to Wm. C. Moss of Stonington. Her children are :

    4011 WILLIAM C., b. June 21, 1834.
    4012 AMOS D., b. Aug. 1, 1836.
    4013 CAROLINE E., b. July 18, 1838.
    4014 MARY D., b. Aug. 3, 1840 ; m. Charles A. Matthews, Mar. 15,'64.
    4015 ELLEN A., b. June 30, 1843 ; m. Benj. Ladd Cook, June 8, 1869.
    4016 JOHN KNOX, b. Aug. 16, 1845.
    4016½ HARRIET A., b. Dec. 16, 1847 ; d. Feb. 17, 1848.
    4017 SAMUEL H., b. Nov. 18, 1848.
    4018 ANNA LOUISA, b. March 4, 1852.
    4019 SARAH PALMER, b. May 7, 1854.

3981 SARAH P. DENISON, (Amos⁵, Dea. Joseph⁴, Joseph³, George², George¹,) b. Sept. 3, 1785, was married, March 11, 1804, to Luke Palmer; lived in Stonington. [See p. 13.] Children :

    4020 SALLY MARIA, b. Jan. 7, 1805; d. unmarried, Nov. 3, 1874.
    4021 BETSEY D., b. Nov. 28, 1806 ; m. Wm. Weed.
    4022 LUKE, b. Oct. 18, 1808; m. Mary C. Holbrook.

10 George Denison's Descendants.

4023 HANNAH W., b. Aug. 4, 1810; m. J. Noyes, no child.
4024 GRACE BILLINGS, b. Aug. 28, 1812; m. Daniel Carew.
4025 HARRIET NEWELL, b. August 31, 1814; m. Theodore Butler.

4321 BETSEY D. PALMER, (dau. of 3981 Sarah P. and Luke,) was married, Nov. 6, 1836, to Wm. Weed; lived in Buffalo, N. Y.; she d. July 12, 1843, at Stonington. Children :

4026 HANNAH PALMER, b. Oct. 6, 1837; m. Geo. Sheffield.
4027 WILLIAM PALMER, b. Oct. 14, 1839; lives at Pleasantville, Pa.
4028 LUKE PALMER, b. March 24, 1842; d. June 16, 1843.

4022 LUKE PALMER, Jr., (son of 3981 Sarah P. and Luke.) was married, Jan. 8, 1851, to Mary C. Holbrook; lives at Burlington, Iowa. Children :

4029 LUKE, b. Nov. 20, 1851.
4030 SARAH MARIA, b. Oct. 18, 1853.

3984 MARTHA DENISON, (Amos[5], Dea. Joseph[4], Joseph[3], George[2], George[1],) b. March 26, 1796, was married, first, to Rev. Henry Sherman; second, May 1, 1826, to Rev. Stephen Peet, of Euclid, Ohio. Mr. Peet d. March 21, 1855; she d. Nov. 13, 1877. Children :

4031 REBECCA AUSTIN SHERMAN; m. James W. Vail, of Buffalo; they now live in Wisconsin, and have six or seven children.
4032 MARTHA PEET, b. July 14, 1827; not married.
4033 HARRIET PEET, b. March 26, 1829; m. Hon. H. H. Gray of Darlington, Wis., and has these children : Harriet, Mattie, Addie, James, Emerson, Harry. Clara, Eunice.
4034 REV. STEPHEN DENISON PEET, b. Dec. 2, 1830; twice married.
4035 JOSEPH BURR PEET, b. Oct. 29, 1832; not married.
4036 EMERSON W. PEET, b. Oct. 16, 1834.

4034 REV. STEPHEN DENISON PEET, (Martha[6], Amos[5], Dea. Joseph[4], Joseph[3], George[2], George[1],) b. Dec. 2, 1830, was married first, Jan. 16, 1856, to Rachel Mosely who d. March 18, 1863; and second, July 5, 1866, to Olive Cutler of Elkhorn, Wis. He is a graduate of Amherst College, and of Andover Seminary. Mr. Peet is Secretary of the Ohio Archæological Society, and gives much attention to archæological studies. His children :

4036½ CARRIE ANNA, b. Dec. 16, 1856.
4037 STEPHEN THEODORE. b. April 16, 1859.
4038 FRANK DENISON, b. June 24, 1862.
4039 MARY ELIZA, b. Sept. 3, 1867.
4040 CHARLES EMERSON, b. April 9, 1869.
4041 HATTIE EMMA, b. Jan. 8, 1871.

4042 MINNIE WALWORTH, b. Sept. 16, 1872.
4043 FREDDIE WILLIAM, b. Oct. 30, 1874.
4044 KATY ANNA, b. Aug. 26, 1876.

3844 AMOS DENISON, (Joseph³, George², George¹,) b. Feb. 18, 1714, was married, May 20, 1742, to Martha Gallup; lived in Stonington; had six children, there being 14 years between the births of the fifth and sixth. Their children were:

4045 EUNICE, b. April 16, 1744; m. Gilbert Smith of Groton, Aug. 2, 1764.
4046 MARTHA, b. Dec. 30, 1746; m. Joshua Swan, Dec. 1, 1763.
4047 PRUDENCE, b. March 20, 1748; m. Stephen Babcock, Aug. 21, 1766.
4048 JOSEPH, b. March 20, 1750; m. Mary Smith of Norwich, June 13, 1771.
4049 AMOS, b. in 1752.
4050 CYNTHIA, bapt. June 15, 1766; m. James Rogers of Richmondton, R. I.

4045 EUNICE DENISON, (Amos⁴, Joseph³, George², George¹,) b. April 16, 1744, was married to Gilbert Smith of Groton, Aug. 2, 1764, and had these children:

4051 GILBERT, b. Sept. 25, 1766.
4052 EUNICE, b. Oct. 31, 1772.
4053 MARTHA, b. May 24, 1776.
4054 AMOS D., b. Nov. 14, 1778.

4046 MARTHA DENISON, (Amos⁴, Joseph³, George², George¹,) b. Dec. 30, 1746, was married Dec. 1, 1763, to Joshua Swan. They had these children:

4055 AMOS, b. May 13, 1764.
4056 JOSHUA, b. June 8, 1766.
4057 ADAM, b. June 29, 1768.
4058 PELEG, b. July 2, 1770.
4059 GILBERT, b. June 17, 1777.
4060 ISAAC, b. July 18, 1779.

4047 PRUDENCE DENISON, (Amos⁴, Joseph³, George², George¹,) b. March 20, 1748, was married, Aug. 21, 1766, to Stephen Babcock, a lawyer. They had:

4060½ AMOS, b. June 20, 1767.

4048 JOSEPH DENISON, (Amos⁴, Joseph³, George², George¹,) b. March 20 1750, was married, June 13, 1771, to Mary Smith of Norwich, b. April 27, 1753. In 1792, they emigrated to Galway, Saratoga Co., N. Y. He died there, March 17, 1833; she died there, March 7, 1831. Their children:

4061 MARTHA, b. May 13, 1772; m. Asahel Fitch.
4062 AMOS, b. Oct. 19, 1774; thrice married.
4063 CHARLES, b. Oct 30, 1776; m. Sarah Henderson.
4064 POLLY, b. Dec. 27, 1778; m. John Leavenworth.
4065 LEMUEL, b. 1781; d. unmarried in 1823.
4066 LUTHER, b. 1783; m. Betsey Morehouse.
4067 PRUDENCE, b. April 27, 1786; m. Levi Sherman.
4068 JOSEPH, b. Oct. 25, 1787; m. Deborah James.
4069 ISAAC, b. 1791; d. in 1791.
4070 ISAAC, b. 1794; m. Chloe Boyd.
4071 EUNICE, b. in 1796; d. young.

4061 MARTHA DENISON, (Joseph^5, Amos^4, Joseph^3, George^2, George^1,) b. May 13, 1772, was married to Asahel Fitch, in 1793; lived at Scipio, N. Y.; she d. Oct. 2, 1843; he d. Dec. 13, 1851, in his 80th year. They had 4 children :

4072 WILLIAM REED, b. Oct. 19, 1794; lived in West Groton, N. Y.
4073 ALVAH, b. June 7, 1797; lived in Venice, N. Y.
4074 CHARLES D., b. April 5, 1800; lived in Kansas.
4075 CYNTHIA D, b. Oct. 27, 1802.

4072 WILLIAM REED FITCH, (son of 4061 Martha Denison and Asahel Fitch,) b. Oct. 19, 1794, m. Aurilla Dunning; lived in West Groton, N. Y. He died April 7, 1875; she d. Sept. 27, 1863. Their children :

4076 DEWITT C., b. Feb. 26, 1819; m. Lucy Bothwell.
4077 CHARLES N., b. March 25, 1821; m. Olive F. Smith; lives in De Soto, Mo.
4078 MORTIMER D., b. Aug. 2, 1823; m. Louisa Helm.
4079 WILLIAM H., b. Nov. 23, 1825; m. Fannie A. Brown.

4073 ALVAH FITCH, (son of 4061 Martha Denison and Asahel Fitch,) b. June 7, 1797, m. Louisa U. Morse; lived at Venice, N. Y. One child :

4080 MARY, b. March 26, 1835.

4074 CHARLES D. FITCH, (son of 4061 Martha Denison and Asahal Fitch,) b. April 5, 1800, m. Elovsey Smith; lived in Kansas. One child :

4081 MORELL S.

4075 CYNTHIA D. FITCH, (dau. of 4061 Martha Denison and Asahel Fitch,) b. Oct. 26, 1802, m. Eli Smith. Their children :

4082 ELOVSEY; m. Dr. Hoxie of Auburn, N. Y.
4083 MARTHA, m. George Barnes of Scipio, N. Y.
4084 HELEN; m. John Aiken of Scipio, N. Y.

4062 AMOS DENISON, (Joseph[5], Amos[4], Joseph[3], George[2], George[1],) b. Oct. 19, 1774, was married, Jan. 26, 1804, to Polly Fitch, b. Nov. 27, 1781; lived at Greenfield, N. Y.; he d. Sept. 17, 1849; she d. Feb. 27, 1821. He. m., second, Jan. 13, 1822, Rebecca Sherman, who d. Oct. 27, 1827. He m., third, Nancy Paul, May 9, 1824. His children:

    4085 NATHAN F., b. Dec. 14, 1804; d. Nov. 28, 1843.
    4086 HIRAM, b. Aug. 22, 1807; m. Delia Salisbury.
    4087 ELMINA, b. Dec. 24, 1809.
    4088 MARY, b. Oct. 8, 1811; m. Orin Mosher.
    4089 LYDIA, b. Dec. 10, 1814; d. April 14, 1840.
    4090 BETSEY, b. March 1, 1818.
    4091 AMOS, b. Feb. 26, 1821; d. August, 1834.
    4092 PHEBE, b. June 19, 1824.

4086 HIRAM DENISON, (Amos[6], Joseph[5], Amos[4], Joseph[3], George[2], George[1],) was married to Delia Salisbury, Jan. 2, 1839; residence, Galway, N. Y. One child:

    4093 DELIA ANN; m. Charles H. Brockett, Sept. 15, 1864.

4088 MARY DENISON, (Amos[6], Joseph[5], Amos[4], Joseph[3], George[2], George[1],) was married, Jan. 19, 1836, to Orin Mosher; residence, Galway, N. Y.; he d. May 31, 1853. Children:

    4094 HORACE L., b. Feb. 23, 1837; d. July 14, 1843.
    4095 AMOS H., b. May 11, 1839; d. Nov. 27, 1840.
    4096 EMILY A., b. Sept. 16, 1841.
    4097 DEWITT C., b. Nov. 29, 1844; d. Dec. 14, 1863.
    4098 CHARLES F., b. July 19, 1847; d. Oct. 13, 1850.
    4099 CYNTHIA E., b. Nov. 17, 1849; d. Oct. 26, 1850.
    4100 JULIA M., b. Oct. 23, 1851.

4063 CHARLES DENISON, (Joseph[5], Amos[4], Joseph[3], George[2], George[1],) b. Oct. 30, 1776, was married, July 18, 1799, to Sarah Henderson. Residence, Genoa, N. Y.; he d. Aug. 4, 1851. Children:

    4101 MARY, b. Nov. 25, 1800; m. Freeman Strong, Feb. 11, 1819.
    4102 ANN, b. Nov. 16, 1802; m. Wm. Monahan, Feb. 6, 1817.
    4103 ALMOND, b. Jan 3, 1805; d. June 20, 1844.
    4104 ROXENA, b. May 10, 1807; P. O. Venice, N. Y.
    4105 ALEXANDER, b. Nov. 5, 1809; d. June 17, 1837.
    4106 MARTHA F., b. June 27, 1812; m. S. Bower, June 30, 1833.
    4107 PRUDENCE S., b. March 27, 1814; m. Joseph Bower, Dec. 29,'34.
    4108 SOPHIA, b. Sept. 24, 1816; d. June 27, 1819.
    4109 SARAH L., b. April 28, 1823; m. Wilson D. Devine of Venice, N.Y.

4064 POLLY DENISON, (Joseph[5], Amos[4], Joseph[3], George[2], George[1],) b. Dec. 27, 1778, was married, Sept. 10, 1795, to

John Leavenworth, who was born in Watertown, Conn. In 1801, they settled permanently in Genoa, N. Y., where they died. Their children :

4110 HIRAM, b. Aug. 25, 1797; twice married; 12 children.
4111 POLLY, b. Dec. 26, 1799; *m.* Heman Holden; 3 children.
4112 FANNY, b. Aug. 1, 1803; *m.* Wm. Manchester; 4 children.
4113 CLARA, b. June 28, 1808; *m.* Wm. P. Thornton; 2 children.
4114 OLIVIA, b. May 9, 1810; *m.* Alanson Ferris; 4 children.
4115 HORACE, b. July 8, 1817; *m.* Eliza Jane Henderson; 2 children.

4110 HIRAM LEAVENWORTH, (Polly[6], Joseph[5], Amos[4], Joseph[3], George[2], George[1],) b. Aug. 25, 1797, was married, first, July 4, 1819, to Lavina Holden, b. Nov. 4, 1800, and d. May 14, 1832 ; second, Oct. 20, 1834, to Lucy Emerson. He was editor of the Waterloo Gazette, the St. Catherines Journal, and of several other newspapers. His children :

4116 MATILDA, b. June 11, 1820; twice married; 2 sons.
4117 CLARINDA, b. Sept. 10, 1821; *m.* Smith D. Elliott; 6 children.
4118 EDWIN S., b. Sept. 21, 1823; thrice married; 7 children.
4119 JOHN H., b. March 4, 1826; d. at sea, March, 1847.
4120 HIRAM F., b. March 19, 1828; twice married.
4121 LAVINIA, b. Dec. 26, 1829; *m.* Harrison Roberts.
4122 GILBERT, b. Dec. 28, 1831; d. April, 1849.
4123 ELIZABETH, b. Oct. 24, 1835; d. Aug. 26, 1836.
4124 LUCY, b. June 26, 1839; *m.* Thomas Smith; 4 children.
4125 CLARA, b. Feb. 20, 1841; *m.* Morgan L. Jennings.
4126 FANNY, b. April 8, 1844; d. Nov. 2, 1846.
4127 MARY, b. March 17, 1846; *m.* Jas. McEdwards.

Edwin S. and Hiram F. live at St. Catherines, Canada.

4111 POLLY LEAVENWORTH, (Polly[6], Joseph[5], Amos[4], Joseph[3], George[2], George[1],) b. Dec. 26, 1799, was married, Oct. 5, 1819, to Heman Holden; lived at Reading, N. Y.; he died May 20, 1874; she died June 19, 1866. Children :

4128 OSCAR, b. Oct. 20, 1820; *m.* Sally Wilson.
4129 MARY, b. July 9, 1829; *m.* Norman Devine.
4130 JOHN H., b. Feb. 15, 1834.

4112 FANNY LEAVENWORTH, (Polly[6], Joseph[5], Amos[4], Joseph[3], George[2], George[1],) b. Aug. 1, 1803, was married to Wm. Manchester, in 1831. P. O. Venice, N. Y. Four children :

4131 CHARLES W., b. Nov. 16, 1832; *m.* Sarah M. Henderson.
4132 JOHN L., b. March 16, 1834; *m.* Martha Billings.
4133 JULIA W., twin, b. May 25, 1842; *m.* Wm. Jennings.
4134 FANNY L., twin, b. May 25, 1842; *m.* Byron Tifft.

4113 CLARA LEAVENWORTH, (Polly[6], Joseph[5], Amos[4], Joseph[3], George[2], George[1],) b. June 28, 1808, was married, Jan. 10, 1827, to Wm. P. Thornton. Two children :

 4135 STEPHEN, b. Feb. 22, 1828.
 4136 EDWIN S., b. March 30, 1837; m. Martha Knox ; 6 children :

4114 OLIVIA LEAVENWORTH, (Polly[6], Joseph[5], Amos[4], Joseph[3], George[2], George[1],) b. May 9, 1810, was married, March 4, 1840, to Alanson Ferris. Children :

 4137 HENRY, b. Aug. 17, 1841 ; d. July 30, 1847.
 4138 ADALINE, b. May 30, 1845 ; m. Oscar F. Smith ; 4 children.
 4139 HIRAM L., b. Feb. 9, 1849 ; m. Ida May St. John.
 4140 JOHN, b. Feb. 1, 1852 ; m. Rosa Paine.

4115 HORACE LEAVENWORTH, (Polly[6], Joseph[5], Amos[4], Joseph[3], George[2], George[1],) b. July 8, 1817, was married, Oct. 23, 1844, to Eliza Jane Henderson. P. O. East Geneva, N. Y. Children :

 4141 ALETHE, b. Nov. 9, 1849 ; d. Nov. 21, 1849.
 4142 ELMINA JOSEPHINE, b. July 3, 1851 ; m. Oscar Tifft.

4066 LUTHER DENISON, (Joseph[5], Amos[4], Joseph[3], George[2], George[1],) b. in 1783, was married in 1813, to Betsey Morehouse. He d. May, 1814 ; she d. Dec. 7, 1871, aged 77. They had one child :

 4143 CAROLINE E., b. Dec. 4, 1813 ; m. Francis E. Thornton, April 29, 1834. He d. March 22, 1872. Two children :
  4144 MARY F., b. May 19, 1840 ; m. Frank. Morey ; 3c.
  4145 CHARLES, b. June 16, 1849 ; m. Cleora Green ; 1c.

4068 JOSEPH DENISON, (Joseph[5], Amos[4], Joseph[3], George[2], George[1],) b. Sept. 25, 1787, was married Sept. 25, 1812, to Deborah James, b. in 1796, at Greenfield, N. Y. They lived in Hanover, N. Y.; he d. in 1879. His children :

 4146 SALLYETT, b. in 1814.
 4147 JOHN, b. Aug. 8, 1818 ; m. Eleanor M. Farnesworth.
 4148 EDWIN, b. May 5, 1828 ; m. Elizabeth A. Downer.

4047 JOHN DENISON, (Joseph[6], Joseph[5], Amos[4], Joseph[3], George[2], George[1],) was married, Sept. 9, 1850, to Eleanor M. Farnsworth, b. in 1827, at Alden, N. Y. They live at Dewitt, Iowa. Children :

 4149 FLORA E., b. June 25, 1852 ; m. C. E. Dinehart, Oct. 20, 1875 ; lives in Chicago ; has one child, Clarence, b, April 3, 1877.
 4150 WALTER P., b. July 14, 1856.

10 George Denison's Descendants.

4151 CHARLES, b. May 15, 1861; d. in 1864, aged 3 years, 7 mos.
4152 JOHN C., b. July 10, 1866.

4048 EDWIN DENISON, (Joseph[6], Joseph[5], Amos[4], Joseph[3], George[2], George[1],) b. May 5, 1828, was married. May 20, 1852, to Elizabeth Downer, b. March 1, 1833; P. O., Forestville, N. Y. Children:

4153 FLORENCE, b. Aug. 13, 1853.
4154 MINNIE, b. Jan. 8, 1857.
4155 CHARLES, b. May 30, 1858.
4156 LIZZIE, b. Oct. 13, 1862.
4157 JOHN, b. Aug. 18, 1865.

3845 NATHAN DENISON, (Joseph[3], George[2], George[1],) b. Feb. 20, 1716, was married in 1736, to Ann Carey, dau. of Eleazer Carey of Windham, Conn., and settled in Windham. His wife Ann died, May 16, 1776, aged 60. He married second, March 15, 1778, Hannah Fuller; and about the year 1800, he went to Kingston, Pa., where he died March 10, 1803, aged 88 years. His children, all by the first wife, were as follows:

4171 JOSEPH, b. Nov. 2, 1738; was a clergyman.
4172 COL. NATHAN, b. Jan 25, 1740; m. Elizabeth Sill.
4173 ANN, b. Nov. 19, 1742; m. Solomon Huntington.
4173½ ELEAZER, b. Dec. 24, 1744; m. Susanna Elderkin.
4174 LYDIA, b. April 27, 1747; m. Joshua B. Elderkin.
4175 AMOS, b. May 31, 1749; d. young.

4171 REV. JOSEPH DENISON, (Nathan[4], Joseph[3], George[2], George[1],) b. Nov. 2, 1738, was a graduate of Yale College in 1763. He became pastor of the Cong. Church in Middlefield, Ct., in 1765, where, in 1768, the society voted to give him 5 pr. cent on the grand levy, if he would never leave them, and give bonds to this effect. He died at Middlefield, Feb. 12, 1770.

4172 COL. NATHAN DENISON, (Nathan[4], Joseph[3], George[2], George[1],) b. Jan. 25, 1741, emigrated to Pennsylvania in 1769; and April 1, 1769, he was married, at Wilkesbarre, to Elizabeth Sill, eldest dau. of Jabez Sill. She was born Nov. 22, 1750. He commanded the left wing of the patriot forces, in the battle which preceded the "Wyoming Massacre," July 3, 1778. He was a man of strong ability and character, and stood among the foremost in the region where he lived. He died at Kingston, Pa., Jan. 25, 1809. His children:

4176 LAZARUS, b. Dec. 5, 1773; m. Elizabeth Carpenter.
4177 ELIZABETH S., b. March 7, 1777; m. Elijah Shoemaker.

Sally Abbott
Aug 20 1881
4182

4178 MARY, b. June 2, 1779; m. Thomas Patterson.
4179 ANN, b. Feb. 22, 1783; m. Daniel Turner.
4180 JOHN, b. June 20, 1787; m. Laura Fellows.
4181 GEORGE, b. Feb. 22, 1790; m. Caroline Bowman.
4182 SARAH, b. Feb. 8, 1794; m. 1st, Thos. Ferrier; 2nd, Stephen Abbott.

4176 LAZARUS DENISON, (Col. Nathan[5], Nathan[4], Joseph[3], George[2], George[1],) was married to Elizabeth Carpenter, of Orange Co., N. Y., Feb. 14, 1802. He lived at Kingston, Pa., and d. there, March 15, 1841. His children:

4183 HIRAM, b. Jan. 9, 1803; d. in 1868, unmarried.
4184 MARY, b. Sept. 22, 1804; m. Chauncey A. Reynolds.
4185 WAYMAN, b. April 21, 1806; d. in 1828.
4186 NATHAN, b. May 22., 1808; d. in 1831, unmarried.
4187 BENJAMIN C., b. July 22, 1810; m. Frances Johnson.
4188 ELIZABETH, b. April 29, 1812; m. Wm. Hancock.
4189 SARAH, b. March 12, 1814; m. Gilbert Reilay.
4190 CHARLES, b. Jan. 23, 1816; m. Ellen E. Hulings.

4190 CHARLES DENISON, (Larazus[6], Col. Nathan[5], Nathan[4], Joseph[3], George[2], George[1],) b. Jan. 23, 1818, was married to Ellen E. Hulings, of Norfolk, Va., May 7, 1845. He was a lawyer; lived at Wilksbarre, Pa; was a member of Congress from 1863, to his death, June 27, 1867. His children:

4191 CHARLES, b. April 12, 1846.
4192 GEORGE, b. Aug. 28, 1848; d. Aug. 28, 1850.
4193 ELIZABETH, b. Oct. 11, 1851.
4194 HENRY G., b. Jan. 28, 1854; d. April 6, 1856.
4195 MARIA P., b. Nov. 13, 1856.
4196 HIRAM, b. May 21, 1859; d. July 31, 1863.
4197 MARY H., b. May 20, 1861.

4184 MARY DENISON, (Lazarus[6], Col. Nathan[5], Nathan[4], Joseph[3], George[2], George[1],) b. in 1806, married Chauncey A. Reynolds, and had:

4198 LAZARUS D., b. July 1, 1833; was a lawyer; d. July 25, 1858, unmarried.

4187 BENJAMIN C. DENISON, (Lazarus[6], Col. Nathan[5], Nathan[4], Joseph[3], George[2], George[1],) b. in 1810, was married in 1850, to Frances Johnson. He was a printer; lived in Philadelphia, and died in 1853. He had:

4199 ELIZABETH; d. in childhood.

4188 ELIZABETH DENISON, (Lazarus[6], Col. Nathan[5], Nathan[4], Joseph[3], George[2], George[1],) b. April 29, 1812, was married to Wm. Hancock, in 1847, and died May, 1855. Her children :

 4200 HIRAM D., b. Feb. 9, 1850.
 4201 ELLEN E., b. June 30, 1851; *m*. O. M. Lance.
 4202 EMILY J., b. Jan. 12, 1853.

4201 ELLEN E. HANCOCK, (dau. of 4188 Elizabeth,) *m*. Oscar M. Lance, Jan. 9, 1873. The children :

 4203 OSCAR M., b. Oct. 3, 1873.
 4204 JOHN HANCOCK, b. Jan. 21, 1876.
 4205 ELIZABETH D., b. June 28, 1877.
 4206 CATHERINE B., b. Sept. 22, 1879.

4189 SARAH DENISON, (Lazarus^6, Col. Nathan^5, Nathan^4, Joseph^3, George^2, George^1.) b. in 1816, was married March 8, 1838, to Gilbert Reilay, of Troy, N. Y. They settled, first, at Starkey, N. Y.; afterwards went to Kingston, Pa. They had these children :

 4207 ELIZABETH, b. Feb. 12, 1839; *m*. Dr. J. S. Pfonts; one child: Gilbert Reila., b. March 15, 1864.
 4208 CHARLES D., b. July 12, 1842; killed in battle of the Wilderness, May 9, 1864.
 4209 CHAUNCY, b. Feb. 10, 1847; d. Aug. 22, 1848.
 4210 CATHERINE, b. Aug. 10, 1851.
 4211 RICHARD B., b. Nov. 10, 1853; *m*. Sarah Wilde.
 4212 ANNA D., b. July 22, 1856.

4177 ELIZABETH S. DENISON, (Col. Nathan^5, Nathan^4, Joseph^3, George^2, George^1,) b. March 7, 1777, was married, May 28, 1800, to Elijah Shoemaker, Jr., only son of Elijah Shoemaker, who was killed in the Wyoming massacre. He was elected Sheriff of Luzerne County, in 1815, for three years. He d. at Kingston, Pa., Oct. 15, 1831; she d. there, July 13, 1829. Their children :

 4213 CHARLES DENISON, b. July 9, 1802; twice married.
 4214 ELIZABETH, b. June 22, 1804; twice married.
 4215 JANE, b. April 8, 1806; *m*. John Passmore.
 4216 ELIJAH, b. March 25, 1808; *m*. Jane Hanover.
 4217 GEORGE, b. March 27, 1810; *m*. Rebecca W. Jones.
 4218 ROBERT MCDOWELL, b. Feb. 29, 1812; unmarried.
 4219 NATHAN, b. April 10, 1814; d. in 1832, unmarried.
 4220 CAROLINE, b. Feb. 8, 1816; *m*. Dr. Levi Ives.
 4221 LAZARUS D., b. Nov. 5, 1819; *m*. Esther Wadhams.

4213 CHARLES DENISON SHOEMAKER, (Elizabeth S.^{6}, Col. Nathan^5, Nathan^4, Joseph^3, George^2, George^1,) b. July 9, 1802, was married, first, Oct. 24, 1825, to Mary E. Denison, dau. of Austin Denison of New Haven, who was a descendant of Robert of Milford, Conn., (who was in Milford in 1645, and, after 1666, of Newark, N. J.) She d. Aug. 1, 1831; and May 18, 1835, he *m.* second, Stella (Mercer) Sprigg of New Orleans, who d. Nov. 3, 1875. He was a graduate of Yale College, was Associate Judge in Luzerne Co., and has held other offices of trust. His children:

4222 Austin D., b. Aug., 1826; educated at Lafayette Col., graduated in the Medical School at New Haven in 1850; practiced at Wilkesbarre; visited Europe and the West Indies; is said to be a practicing physician at Honolulu.
4223 Martha Ann, b. Dec. 14, 1828; d. July 1, 1844.
4224 Robert C., b. April 14, 1836; *m.* Helen (Lea) Lonsdale.
4225 Frederic M., b. Oct. 19, 1837; *m.* Caroline Shoemaker.
4226 William M., b. June 20, 1840; was adjutant of the 9th Pa. Reg. in the war; is now in the insurance business; *m.* Ella Hunt, Feb. 6, 1879.
4227 Frank L., b. Oct. 30, 1842; *m.* Fanny Bell Mills, Oct. 10, 1870; is a graduate of West Point, and a Captain in the 4th Cavalry.

4224 Robert C. Shoemaker, (son of 4213 Charles D.,) b. April 4, 1836, graduated at Yale College in the class of 1855, and studied law; *m.* Helen (Lea) Lonsdale, Nov. 22, 1876; and has:

4227½ Stella Mercer, b. Sept. 7, 1877.
4228 Grace Lea, b. Sept. 4, 1879.

4225 Frederick M. Shoemaker, (son of 4213 Charles D.) b. Oct. 19, 1837, *m.* Caroline Shoemaker, Oct. 19, 1864. He served in the war of the rebellion as adjutant of the 143d Pa. regiment; is now superintendent of a Coal Co. He has:

4229 Charles D., b. Oct. 10, 1866.

4214 Elizabeth Shoemaker, (Elizabeth S.[6], Col. Nathan[5], Nathan[4], Joseph[3], George[2], George[1],) b. June 22, 1804, was married to John Donley, Aug. 14, 1823; and, second, June 1, 1845, to Dr. Henry Spence. There were three children by John Donley, as follows:

4230 James, b. Oct. 25, 1825; d. at Fond du Lac, Wis.
4231 Augusta, b. Dec. 5, 1826; *m.* Wm. R. Mercer.
4232 Elizabeth, *m.* Henry Hanover, Dec. 15, 1853.

4231 Augusta Donley, (dau. of 4214 Elizabeth and John Donley,) was married, to Wm. R. Mercer, Sept. 10, 1847; lived at La Crosse, Wis. Children:

4233 STELLA R.
4234 WILLIAM R.
4235 JAMES.
4236 GEORGE.
4237 MARY.
4238 LEVI.

4232 ELIZABETH DONLEY, (dau. of 4214 Elizabeth and John Donley,) was married to Henry Hanover, Dec. 15, 1853. Three children:

4239 LEVI, b. Nov. 17, 1855; is a machinist.
4240 CAROLINE, b. Nov. 17, 1856.
4241 CHARLES, b. July 25, 1858; is a clerk.

4216 ELIJAH SHOEMAKER, JR., (Elizabeth S.[6], Col. Nathan[5], Nathan[4], Joseph[3], George[2], George[1],) b. March 25, 1808, was married, Feb. 9, 1842, to Jane Hanover. Lived in Kingston, Pa.; was a farmer; d. Jan 13, 1863. The children:

4242 MARTHA A., b. Sept. 22, 1848; d. Dec. 21, 1860.
4243 ELIJAH McDOWELL, b. Dec. 26, 1857.
4244 SUSAN A., b. Aug. 18, 1860.

4217 GEORGE SHOEMAKER, (Elizabeth S.[6], Col. Nathan[5], Nathan[4], Joseph[3], George[2], George[1],) b. March 27, 1810, was married, Jan. 14, 1825, to Rebecca W. Jones. He was a farmer and merchant at Kingston, Pa; d. Oct. 6, 1849. Children:

4245 NATHAN, b. Dec. 5, 1835; was educated at Lafayette College; m. Emma Shoemaker, June 10, 1860; d. July 6, 1862.
4246 CAROLINE, b. June 1, 1837; m. Eugene La Bar.
4247 MARY, b. July 13, 1839.
4248 GEORGE, b June 28, 1844; m. Lillie Hoyt, Oct. 10, 1872.
4249 CHARLES D., b. Dec. 5, 1847.

4246 CAROLINE SHOEMAKER, (dau. of 4217 George.) b. June 1, 1837, was married to Eugene La Bar, Sept. 9, 1863; lives at Chicago, Ill. Children:

4250 GEORGE S., b. July 10, 1869.
4251 EUGENE E., b. July 29, 1873.

4221 LAZARUS D. SHOEMAKER, (Elizabeth S.[6], Col. Nathan[5], Nathan[4], Joseph[3], George[2], George[1],) b. Nov. 5, 1819, was educated at Kenyon College, Ohio, and was graduated from Yale College in the class of 1840. He was a member of the Pennsylvania Senate three years from 1867; and he represented the twelfth district of his state in the 42d and 43d Congresses. At present he is practicing law in Wilkesbarre. Oct. 10, 1848, he was married to Esther W. Wadhams. His children:

4252 CLORINDA W., b. Aug. 5, 1849; m. Irving W. Stearns.
4253 SAMUEL W., b. Sept. 15, 1851; d. Sept. 20, 1877, unmarried.

4254 STELLA M., b. Dec. 10, 1853; d. March 9, 1859.
4255 ELIZABETH S., b. Feb. 11, 1856.
4256 CAROLINE L., b. April 25, 1857; m. Wm. G. Phelps, Nov. 17, 1880.
4257 LEVI I., b. Sept. 28, 1859; a Junior in Yale College.
4258 JANE A., b. Oct. 30, 1861.
4259 ESTHER W., b. Nov. 9, 1863.
4260 ANNA D., b. Oct. 15, 1866; d. June 16, 1874.

4253 CLORINDA W. SHOEMAKER, (dau. of 4221 Lazarus D.) was married, Nov. 20, 1872, to Irving W. Stearns of Wilkesbarre. The children:

4261 LAZARUS DENISON, b. Dec. 27, 1875.
4262 IRVING A., b. July 15, 1877.

4220 CAROLINE SHOEMAKER, (Elizabeth S.[6], Col. Nathan[5], Nathan[4], Joseph[3], George[2], George[1],) b. Feb. 8, 1816, was married, June 7, 1841, to Dr. Levi Ives, of New Haven, Conn. One child:

4263 ROBERT S., b. in New Haven, April 28, 1842.

4263 ROBERT S. IVES, (son of 4220 Caroline and Dr. Levi Ives,) b. April 28, 1842, was duly educated and became a practicing physician in New Haven. He m. Maria Stille, Oct. 17, 1866. The children:

4264 CAROLINE STILLE, b. Feb. 8, 1868.
4265 ALFRED STILLE, b. July 6, 1870.

4178 MARY DENISON, (Col. Nathan[5], Nathan[4], Joseph[3], George[2], George[1],) b. Jan. 2, 1779, was married about 1802, to Thomas Patterson, who was born in Ireland, July 7, 1775. They lived in Huntington, Luzerne Co., Pa. He was a farmer and teacher. He died April 29, 1844; she died June 1, 1858. Their children:

4266 NATHAN, b. May 5, 1803; m. Susan Letchworth.
4267 THOMAS, b. Feb. 15, 1806; m. Ann M. Haff.
4268 ELIZABETH S., b. March 17, 1808; m. D. A. Bowman.
4269 EZEKIEL M., b. May 6, 1810; m. Henrietta Deeth.
4270 MARY ANN, b. Jan. 22, 1812; m. Dr. John D. Thompson.
4271 ROBERT S., b. May 22, 1816; m. Minerva T. Trescott.
4272 SARAH D., b. June 27, 1819; m. Richard Sharpe.
4273 JOHN D., b. Dec. 23, 1821; twice married.

4266 NATHAN PATTERSON, (son of 4178 Mary and Thomas,) b. Sept. 5, 1803, was married, Feb. 10, 1823, to Susan Letchworth. He lives, (Sept. 1880,) at Summit Hill, Pa., and is a coal merchant. His wife d. Jan. 26, 1872. Three children:

4274 THOMAS NATHAN, b. Dec. 1, 1830.
4275 SAMUEL, b. April 5, 1832.
4276 WM. LETCHWORTH, b. Sept. 27, 1834.

4274 THOMAS NATHAN PATTERSON, (son of 4266 Nathan,) b. Dec. 1, 1830, was married to Rachel Spencer, June 19, 1860, and died at Mahony City, Pa., July 21, 1880. His children:

4277 GEORGE SPENCER, b June 24, 1861.
4278 SAMUEL WHITE, b. Sept. 24, 1863.
4279 THOMAS LINCOLN, b. June 24, 1865.
4280 SUSAN L., b. March 8, 1867.
4281 WM. TAYLOR, b. Dec. 10, 1868.

4275 SAMUEL PATTERSON, (son of 4266 Nathan,) b. April 5, 1832, was married Nov. 1, 1871, to Gertrude P. Pollock, of Como, Ill., settled at Sterling, Ill., and engaged in the milling business in partnership with B. C. Church. One child:

4282 CLARA M., b. Aug. 9, 1872.

4276 WM. LETCHWORTH PATTERSON, (son of 4266 Nathan,) b. Sept. 27, 1834, is a civil engineer. He was married to Mary I. Wallace, dau. of Hugh Wallace of Sterling, Ill., March 20, 1860. He had a contract for building a portion of the Union Pacific Railroad, on the completion of which, he settled at Sterling, Ill. His children:

4283 NATHAN DENISON, b. Jan. 2, 1861.
4284 MARY, b. Feb. 17, 1863.
4285 SUSAN LETCHWORTH, b. Nov. 9, 1864.
4286 HUGH WALLACE, b. May 6, 1868.
4287 STELLA, b. June 4, 1871.
4288 LILLIAN, b. Nov. 22, 1872.
4289 ISABELLA, b. March 22, 1875.

4267 THOMAS PATTERSON, JR., (son of 4178 Mary and Thomas,) b. Feb. 15, 1806, was married, Feb. 12, 1833, to Mary Ann Haff. She d. at Mauch Chunk, Feb. 25, 1845. He d. Aug. 19, 1874, at Huntington, Pa. All their children died young.

4268 ELIZABETH D. PATTERSON, (dau. of 4178 Mary and Thomas,) b. March 17, 1808, was married, Jan. 27, 1831, to Derrick A. Bowman. She died Nov. 28, 1843. Her children:

4290 CAROLINE E., b. in 1833; lives at Sterling, Ill.
4291 EZEKIEL E., b. in 1835; d. in 1865.
4292 JESSE G., b. in 1837; d. in 1875.

4291 EZEKIEL E. BOWMAN, (son of 4268 Elizabeth D.,) b. in 1833, was married in 1859, to Mary Butler, and d. at Mauch Chunk, in 1865. Two children:

 4293 THOMAS P., b. in 1860; lives in Illinois.
 4294 WILLIAM B., b. in 1863; Naval Cadet at Annapolis.

4269 EZEKIEL M. PATTERSON, (son of 4178 Mary and Thomas,) b. May 6, 1810, was married, Nov. 20th, 1855, to Henrietta Deeth. He is a capitalist, and a director in the Easton and Amboy R. R. Co. The children:

 4296 MARY D., b. in 1859.
 4297 THOMAS; d. when two years old.
 4298 JOHN E., b. in 1867.

4270 MARY ANN PATTERSON, (dau. of 4178 Mary and Thomas,) b. Jan. 22, 1812, was married, Feb. 17, 1841, to Dr. John D. Thompson, who died at Mauch Chunk, of cholera, Aug. 19, 1854. The children:

 4299 ELIZABETH D., b. in 1841.
 4300 CAROLINE L., b. in 1845.
 4301 ROBERT I., b. in 1852; d. in 1868.
 4302 SALLIE P., b. in 1855; d. in 1857.

4271 ROBERT S. PATTERSON, (son of 4178 Mary and Thomas,) b. May 22, 1816, was married, in 1857, to Minerva T. Trescott, and d. March 28, 1871. Children:

 4303 SUSAN A., b. July 25, 1858.
 4304 THOMAS L., b. April 14, 1860.
 4305 MARY A., b. June 27, 1862.
 4306 SALLIE E., b. Oct. 16, 1864.
 4307 RICHARD S., b. Sept 8, 1867.

4272 SARAH D. PATTERSON, (dau. of 4178 Mary and Thomas,) b. June 27, 1819, was married to Richard Sharpe, Sept. 22, 1847; lives at Wilkesbarre, Pa. He was born in England, April 10, 1813. The children:

 4308 MARY ANN, b. July 21, 1849.
 4309 ELIZABETH M., b. Sept. 26, 1850.
 4310 RICHARD, b, June 3, 1852.
 4311 EMILY, b. Jan. 24, 1854.
 4312 SALLIE, b. Sept. 29, 1855; d. Jan 30, 1870.
 4313 MARTHA, b. June 17, 1860.

4273 JOHN D. PATTERSON, (son of 4178 Mary and Thomas,) b. Dec. 23, 1821, was married, first, Feb. 11, 1852, to Margaret Reilay, who d. June 30, 1853; and, second, Sept. 29, 1855, to Charlotte Shotwell. Children:

 4314 CHESTER PATTERSON, b. in 1853; d. in 1853.
 4315 LILLIE G. PATTERSON, b. in 1856, was married in 1879, to David Nevin, of Easton, Pa., a lawyer, and has:
  4316 JOHN DENISON NEVIN, b. in 1880.

4179 ANN DENISON, (Col. Nathan[5], Nathan[4], Joseph George[2], George[1],) b. Feb. 22, 1783, was married to Daniel Turner. She d. in Kingston, Pa., June 4, 1823. He d. Nov. 5, 1863. Only one child:

 4317 GEORGE D., b. Dec. 27, 1809; is a merchant at Hope, N. J.

4317 GEORGE D. TURNER, (Ann[6], Col. Nathan[5], Nathan[4], Joseph[3], George[2], George[1],) b. Dec. 27, 1809, was married, April 18, 1837, to Dorinda B. Hunt, b. March 5, 1818, and died June 5, 1879. He is a merchant at Hope, N. J. His children:

 4318 MARGARET ANN, b. Jan. 5, 1838.
 4319 EDWIN, b. March 2, 1839.
 4320 THEOPHILUS H., b. July 1, 1841; d. July 27, 1869, in Kansas.
 4321 LEONORA, b. Oct. 1, 1843.
 4322 DANIEL, b. Dec. 19, 1845; d. Sept. 10, 1879, in Kansas.
 4323 GEORGE D., Jr., b. Jan. 7, 1848; d. May 15, 1855.
 4324 FLETCHER, b. Jan. 1, 1852.
 4325 MARY, b. March 26, 1856.
 4326 WILLIAM, b. Feb. 9, 1859.

All unmarried, Oct., 1880, except Margaret Ann.

4318 MARGARET ANN TURNER, (dau. of 4317 George D.,) b. Jan. 5, 1838, was married, Sept. 20, 1864, to J. Seward Wills of Stanhope, N. J. Children:

 4327 SAMUEL SAYRE, b. Sept. 10, 1865.
 4328 MARY LEONORA, b. Sept. 13, 1867.
 4329 JOHN, b. Jan. 1, 1871.
 4330 GEORGE TURNER, twin, b. Oct. 30, 1873; d. July 18, 1875.
 4331 FREDERICK SEWARD, twin, b. Oct. 30, 1873.
 4332 EDWIN TURNER, b. Jan. 16, 1876.

4180 JOHN DENISON, (Col. Nathan[5], Nathan[4], Joseph[3], George[2], George[1],) b. June 20, 1787, was married, first, to Laura Fellows, who d. Feb. 20, 1824, aged 37 years; and second, to Mary Watkins of New Jersey, who d. Nov. 22, 1850. He d. in Licking Co., Ohio, July 27, 1840. His children:

4333 STANLEY, b. in Pa., Jan. 13, 1813, m. Jane Haughn in Franklin Co., Ohio, Sept. 12, 1840; has one dau. and two sons, Homer and Alvah. The dau. m. a Mr. Ketchum, and has children. Homer has a wife; Alvah is single. They all live in Missouri.

4334 ELIZABETH, b. in Licking Co., Ohio, June 12, 1816; m. Wm. A. McGriffie, in Iowa, May 27, 1841; had 4 sons and 3 daughters. Died in 1860.

4335 AMANDA, b. in Licking Co., Ohio, Aug. 16, 1817, m. Rev. Isaac Swisher, in Licking Co., Ohio, Aug. 1, 1839; has 8 children, 3 sons and 5 daus., all married; and all (parents and children) live in Daviess Co., Mo.

4336 WESLEY, b. in Licking Co., O., Dec. 6, 1818, m. Ann M. Loomis.

4337 SAMANTHE, b. Sept. 26, 1820; d. unmarried, Dec. 6, 1839.

4338 ORVILLE, b. Aug. 4, 1822, m. Marinda Haltsman; had 2 sons and 2 daus.; Dorcy B., the oldest son is in California; the other, Alvah D., d. in the Union Army; and Orville Denison himself, after serving in the Union Army, was murdered by rebels in Missouri, in 1864.

4339 HOWTON, b. Jan. 22, 1824; d. young.

4340 EMILY, twin, b. Jan. 1, 1825; m. John Thorp; 6 children.

4341 LAURA, twin, b. Jan. 1, 1825; m. J. P. Ninan; 3 children.

4342 HENRY, b. Jan. 2, 1827; m ; d. April 5, 1856, in Iowa; no child.

4343 ASA C., b. Oct. 11, 1829; d. in Oregon, Aug. 15, 1854.

4336 WESLEY DENISON, (John[6], Col. Nathan[5], Nathan[4], Joseph[3], George[2], George[1],) b. in Licking Co., Ohio, Dec. 6, 1818, was married there, Aug. 25, 1842, to Ann M. Loomis. His children:

4344 LAURA V., b. March 3, 1844; m. D. Young, had 4 children; d. Nov. 13, 1873.

4345 HENRY H., b. Nov. 14, 1845; d. in infancy.

4346 LEWIS B., b. April 1, 1848; m. Emma M. Westervelt, Oct. 21, 1874; 2 children.

4347 CYRUS H., b. Sept. 2, 1850; d. young.

4348 LEONARD L., b. Jan. 9, 1853; lives in Delaware, O.

4349 JOHN F., b. April 30, 1855; lives in Carlinsville, Ill.

4350 WILLIAM C., b. Oct. 19, 1858; lives in Delaware, O.

4181 GEORGE DENISON, (Col. Nathan[5], Nathan[4], Joseph[3], George[2], George[1],) b. Feb. 22, 1790, was married in 1814, at Wilkesbarre, Pa., to Caroline Bowman, dau. of Ebenezer. He was a member of Congress from 1819 to 1823; and, before as well as after this, he was frequently returned to the legislature. For many years he was Register and Recorder of Luzerne County, Pa. He d. Aug. 20, 1831; his wife d. July 1, 1833. The children:

4351 CHARLES, b. 1816.

4352 HARRIET, b. 1818.
4353 GEORGE, b. July 27, 1820; was a graduate of Dickinson College, in 1841; d. unmarried, May 11, 1843.
4254 HENRY M., b. Aug. 1, 1822; was a clergyman.
4355 MARY W., b. July 2, 1824; d. unmarried, Aug. 19, 1843.

4354 HENRY M. DENISON, (George⁶, Col. Nathan⁵, Nathan⁴, Joseph³, George², George¹,) b. Aug. 1, 1822, was an Episcopal clergyman. He was married, "about 1850," to Alice Tyler, dau. of President John Tyler. She d. in Louisville, while he was Rector there. He went to Charleston, S. C., where he d. Sept., 1859, of yellow fever. One child:

4356 ELIZABETH, b. in 1851.

4173 ELEAZER DENISON, (Nathan⁴, Joseph³, George², George¹,) b. in 1744, was married in 1769, to Susanna Elderkin of Windham, Conn. He died in Windham, in 1784, aged 40. His inventory was £348, 10s., 4d. His children:

4357 ELEAZER, b. Jan. 10, 1770.
4358 SUSANNA, twin, b. Dec. 27, 1771; m. Jonathan Lincoln.
4359 PRUDENCE, twin, b. Dec. 27, 1771; m. Thomas Davis.
4360 CHARLOTTE, b. April 20, 1773; Daniel Sawyer.
4361 ANN, b. Dec. 25, 1774; m. Alvah Canada.
4362 REBECCA, b. Feb. 25, 1776; m. Peter Simpson.
4363 GEORGE W., twin, b. Dec. 21, 1777.
4364 CHARLES LEE, twin, b. Dec. 21, 1777; m. Sally Bates.
4365 FERNANDUS, b. 1779.
4366 JOSEPH, b. 1781; m. Catherine Buck.
4367 MARY, b. 1784; m. George Bingham.

4366 JOSEPH DENISON, (Eleazer⁵, Nathan⁴, Joseph³, George², George¹,) b. in 1781, was married in 1803, at Windham, Conn., to Catherine Buck, and died in 1813; his wife died in 1838. Children:

4368 WILLIAM, b. 1804; m. Emeline Bills.
4369 EMELINE, b. 1806.
4370 LUCIUS, b. 1813; m. Lydia Bibbing.

IV.

3654 SAMUEL DENISON, (George², George¹,) bapt. Sept. 26, 1686, was married to Mary Minor. They lived in Stonington; but, July 4, 1716, he bought a homestead on Oyster

10 George Denison's Descendants.

River, in Saybrook, Conn., and immediately occupied it. His first four children were born in Stonington; the others in Saybrook:

4391 SARAH, b. Jan. 6, 1710; m. Wm. Babcock.
4392 SAMUEL, b. Oct., 23, 1711; m. Abigail Conkling.
4393 MERCY, b. 1713; m. Nathaniel Chapman.
4394 ELIZABETH, bapt. June 6, 1714.
4395 JOANNA, b. Dec. 13, 1716; m. Moses Tyler.
4396 MARY, twin, b. Jan. 6, 1718.
4397 GEORGE, twin, b. Jan. 6, 1718; m. Jemima Post.
4398 CHRISTOPHER, b. 1720; m. Elizabeth Kelley.
4399 GIDEON, b. 1724.
4400 STEPHEN, b. Feb. 6, 1725.

4391 SARAH DENISON, (Samuel[3], George[2], George[1],) b. Jan. 16, 1709, was married to William Babcock, of Westerly, R. I., Aug. 11, 1730. They lived in Westerly, where he was Town Clerk for many years. Their children:

4401 WILLIAM, b. May 19, 1731; d. Feb. 6, 1750.
4402 JOSHUA, b. Dec. 2, 1732.
4403 CHRISTOPHER, b. Sept. 12, 1734.
4404 SARAH, b. Oct. 17, 1736.
4405 ELIJAH, b. July 19, 1738; d. young.
4406 ELIAS, b. July 28, 1740.
4407 MERCY, b. July 14, 1745.
4408 PHINEAS, b. Sept. 28, 1742.
4409 SAMUEL, b. Sept. 4, 1747.

4392 SAMUEL DENISON, (Samuel[3], George[2], George[1],) b. Oct. 23, 1711, was married to Abigail Conkling of Saybrook, in 1736. Their children:

4410 SAMUEL, b. May 4, 1738; m. Temperance Post; 4 children.
4411 MARY, b. Jan. 9, 1742; m. Joseph Post, March 21, 1765.
4412 ABIGAIL, b. April 14, 1744.
4413 SARAH, b. April 20, 1747; m. Aaron Ely, Nov. 9, 1769.

4410 SAMUEL DENISON, (Samuel[4], Samuel[3], George[2], George[1],) b. May 4, 1738, was married to Temperance Post in *april ?* 1762. They had:

4414 SAMUEL, b. Feb. 17, 1763.
4415 ASA, twin, b. Aug 10, 1764.
4416 ABIGAIL, twin, b. Aug. 10, 1764; m. 4701 Jedediah Denison, April 19, 1783; had ten children. See his record.
4417 DANIEL.

4395 JOANNA DENISON, (Samuel[3], George[2], George[1],) b. Dec. 13, 1715, was married to Moses Tyler of Preston, Conn. Nov. 11, 1742. Children:

4418 ELIJAH, b. Dec. 1743; d. in 1746.
4419 THANKFUL, b. Sept. 1745; d. in 1746.
4420 DANIEL, b. in 1747.
4421 LUCRETIA, b. in 1749.
4422 JAMES, b. in 1751.

4393 MERCY DENISON, (Samuel³, George², George¹,) b. in 1713, was married, Feb., 1737, to Nathaniel Chapman of Saybrook. They lived on the farm, in Saybrook, now occupied by his grandson, Gideon Chapman, of the 7th Chapman generation. Children:

4423 MERCY, b. Nov. 23, 1737; d. March 27, 1739.
4424 MARY, b. Sept. 18, 1739; d. in 1739.
4425 NATHANIEL, b. Sept. 18, 1740; d. in 1770, unmarried.
4426 MERCY, b. Dec. 27, 1742.
4427 TITUS, b. Sept. 30, 1744.
4428 GIDEON, b. Dec. 22, 1746; d. in 1769, unmarried.
4429 ABISHA, b. Nov. 26, 1748.
4430 LEBBEUS, b. Jan. 1, 1751; d. in 1751.
4431 LEBBEUS, b. Nov. 21, 1752.
4432 MARY, b Dec. 21, 1754.

4397 GEORGE DENISON, (Samuel³, George², George¹,) b. Jan. 6, 1718, was married to Jemima Post of Saybrook, Conn. in 1740; lived at Saybrook. They had:

4441 GEORGE, b. May 13, 1742.
4442 JOSEPH, b. Oct. 13, 1744; m. Anna Lay.
4443 STEPHEN, b. Oct. 12, 1746; m. Juliana Chapman.
4444 EZEKIEL, b. March 21, 1750.
4445 EDMUND, b. Aug. 10, 1753.
4446 JEMIMA, b. Nov. 12, 1755.
4447 HANNAH, b. Oct. 25, 1758; m. Ethiel Plant, Nov. 20, 1783.
4448 MERCY, b. May 25, 1761; m. Samuel Jones.
4449 SABA, bapt. July 22, 1764; m. William Murdock.

4442 JOSEPH DENISON, (George⁴, Samuel³, George², George¹,) b. Oct. 13, 1744, was married, May 5, 1771, to Anna Lay; lived in Westbrook, Conn.; she d. Aug. 19, 1830, aged 77; he d. Oct. 11, 1830. Children:

4450 JOSEPH, bapt. Aug. 2, 1772; m. Irene Clark.
4451 ANN, b. Dec. 24. 1773; m. Elisha Platts.
4452 HENRY, b. in 1775; m. Olivia Hill.
4453 POLLY, bapt. May 26, 1776; m. David Butler.
4454 EZEKIEL, bapt. May 9, 1779; m. Hannah Hotchkiss; no ch.
4455 JEMIMA, bapt. June 24, 1781; m. Enoch L'Homidieu: no ch.
4456 EDMUND, bapt. Nov. 28, 1784; d. in infancy.
4457 EDMUND, bapt. June 22, 1788; m. Rachel Chittenden.

4458 ZINA, bapt. Jan. 16, 1791; d. in infancy.
4459 ZINA, bapt. March 2, 1800; m. Lucy Spencer.

4450 JOSEPH DENISON, JR., (Joseph[5], George[4], Samuel[3], George[2], George[1],) b. in 1772, was married, in 1805, to Irene Clark; she d. Nov. 30, 1835, aged 50; he d. July 27, 1858, aged 86. Children:

4460 SYLVIA, b. in 1805; d. young.
4461 LOUISA, b. Jan. 9, 1806.
4462 CHARLES, b. Aug. 30, 1807; m. Azubah Towner.
4463 SYLVIA, b. Nov. 9, 1818; m. Timothy Stannard.
4464 MARY, b. March 15, 1820; twice married.

4462 CHARLES DENISON, (son of 4450 Joseph, Jr.) b. Aug. 30, 1807, m. Azubah Towner, Oct. 15, 1834, in Westbrook, Conn.; lives in Clinton, Conn. Children:

4465 CHARLES M., b. Sept. 15, 1836; m. Anna Ellis.
4466 ENFIELD T., b. Jan. 29, 1841.
4467 JOSEPH W., b. Aug. 13, 1843.
4468 ELLEN E., b. Sept 22, 1845.

4452 HENRY DENISON, (son of 4452 Joseph,) b. in 1775, m. Olivia Hill. Children:

4469 SUSAN ELIZABETH, bapt. Nov. 15, 1812.
4470 HENRY SANFORD, bapt. Oct. 30, 1814.

4451 ANN DENISON, (Joseph[5], George[4], Samuel[3], George[2], George[1],) b. Dec. 24, 1773, m. Elisha Platts, December, 1795. He d. June 10, 1852, aged 78; she d. Sept. 10, 1860. Five children:

4471 ANNA, b. June 10, 1799; m. Alfred Chittenden; 5 children.
4472 ELISHA, b. July 31, 1802.
4473 AARON, b. July 25, 1807.
4474 Two others, d. young.

4457 EDMUND DENISON, (Joseph[5], George[4], Samuel[3], George[2], George[1],) b. in 1788, m. first, Rachel Chittenden, who d. at Silver Lake, Pa., July 16, 1816, aged 24; second, Mary Ann Buell, who d. Nov. 22, 1822, aged 26; third, Betsey Miner. Dates of the marriages not found. Children:

4475 CYNTHIA; m. Washington Wright of Middletown, Conn.
4476 EDMUND AMBROSE, bap. July 4, 1813; d. Feb. 11, 1838 at Mobile.
4477 RACHEL; m. Hamilton Stevens of Guilford, Conn.
4478 ONE, d. unnamed.
4479 WILLIAM HENRY, b. Feb. 7, 1819; twice married.
4480 GEORGE, b. Feb. 10, 1822; d. Oct. 10, 1822.

4481 MARY ANN, b. March 11, 1826; *m.* Edwin A. Hamlin.
4482 GEORGE, d. in 1856, at Benicia, Cal., aged 25.

4479 WILLIAM HENRY DENISON, (Edmund[6], Joseph[5], George[4], Samuel[3], George[2], George[1],) b. Feb. 7, 1819, *m.* first, Caroline M. Wright, who d. March 24, 1858, aged 37 ; second, Maria Stoddard of Michigan. He lives at Gibralter, Wayne Co., N. Y. Children :

4483 LOUISA, b. Oct. 1, 1843; *m.* Harris T. Smith of Westbrook, Conn.
4484 EDMUND.

4481 MARY ANN DENISON, (Edmund[6], Joseph[5], George[4], Samuel[3], George[2], George[1],) b. March 11, 1826, was married to Edwin A. Hamlin, May 7, 1854. They live at Naples, N. Y. Children :

4485 MARY ANN, b. Nov. 25. 1856.
4486 GEORGE DENISON, b. Nov. 5, 1858.
4487 CHARLES EDWIN, b. Nov. 13, 1863.
4488 FRED. ERASTUS, b. Jan. 8, 1866.

4459 ZINA DENISON, (Joseph[5], George[4], Samuel[3], George[2], George[1],) b. in 1800, and bapt. March 2, 1800, was married to Lucy Spencer. Children :

4489 CHARLES CARROLL, bapt. Sept. 22, 1833, *m.* Mary Tuttle of Fair Haven, Conn.
4490 GEORGE.
4491 HENRY E.

4443 STEPHEN DENISON, (George[4], Samuel[3], George[2], George[1],) b. Oct. 12, 1746, was married Nov. 22, 1774, to Julianna Chapman, dau. of Caleb Chapman of Westbrook, Conn. b. Oct. 16, 1753. Children :

4492 JEMIMA, bapt. March 17, 1776; d. young.
4493 DEBORAH, bapt. Sept. 21, 1777; d. young.
4494 JEMIMA. bapt. Dec. 9, 1779.
4495 DEBBY, bapt. June 22, 1783.
4496 GEORGE, bapt. May 28, 1786.
4497 JULIA, bapt. May 5, 1792.

4448 MERCY DENISON, (George[4], Samuel[3], George[2], George[1],) b. May 25, 1761, was married, Oct. 4, 1781, to Samuel Jones ; lived at Westbrook, Conn. Children :

4498 JEMMY, bapt. Aug. 21, 1783.
4499 EZEKIEL, bapt. May 2, 1791.

4449 SABA DENISON, (George[4], Samuel[3], George[2], George[1],) bapt. July 22, 1764, was married to William Murdock ; lived in Westbrook, Conn. Children :

4500 SABA, bapt. July 20, 1785.
4501 ELISHA, bapt. Aug. 18, 1787.
4502 ELISHA. bapt. May 9, 1790.
4503 RUSHA, bapt. Sept. 16, 1798.

4398 CHRISTOPHER DENISON, (Samuel³, George², George¹,) b. in 1720, was married, March, 1742, to Elizabeth Kelly, at Saybrook, Conn. They lived in Saybrook. Children:

4504 CHRISTOPHER, JR., b. 1743; m. Cecilia Dudley.
4505 JOHN, b. Nov. 22, 1744; m. Lydia Pratt.
4506 ELIZABETH, b. 1747.
4507 MARY, b. May 28, 1758.

And others probably.

4504 CHRISTOPHER DENISON, JR., (Christopher⁴, Samuel³, George², George¹,) b. in 1743, was married about 1775, to Cecilia Dudley. The testimony of his descendants is, that he was born in Saybrook, Conn., was married there, and immediately emigrated to Hudson, N. Y., where his children were born. He served in the war of the Revolution, and, in his later years, received a pension. He d. in 1839, aged 96. His children :

4508 CHRISTOPHER, 3d., b. 1776; d. May, 1840, aged 64.
4509 JAMES; m. Dorcas Clark, of Waltham, Vt.
4510 GEORGE; d. when five years old.
4511 ZINA; m. Elizabeth Pierce of Troy, N. Y.
4512 ELIZABETH; m. James Wilcox, New Haven, Vt.
4513 ABIGAIL; m. Hiram Scott, New Haven, Vt.
4514 CLORINDA; m. William Scott, New Haven, Vt.

4508 CHRISTOPHER DENISON, 3RD, (Christopher, Jr.⁵, Christopher⁴, Samuel³, George ², George¹,) b. in 1776, was married in 1801, to Dovecine Humphrey, of Simsbury, Conn. Lived at New Haven, Vt. Children :

4514½ AMANDA, b. 1802; d. Sept. 1, 1855.
4515 HARVEY HUMPHREY, b. June 10, 1803; m. 1st. Maria Palmer; and 2d. Maria Messler, Oct. 11, 1840; one child. He was killed in Genesee Co., N. Y., Nov. 2, 1849.
4516 EMILY M., b. June 3, 1806; m. Lyman Huested, March 19, 1826; d. Dec. 22, 1855.
4517 MARY ANN, b. Oct. 31, 1809; m. Jason Hawkins, March 18, 1828; d. May 8, 1839.
4518 ELIZA A., b. June 7, 1813; m. Henry Cram, March 4, 1833.
4519 HARRY CHRISTOPHER, b. Oct. 1, 1816.

10 George Denison's Descendants.

4519 HARRY CHRISTOPHER DENISON, (Christopher[6], Christopher, Jr.[5], Christopher[4], Samuel[3], George[2], George[1],) b. Oct. 1, 1816, was married in 1839, to Maria P. Wesler, of Niagara Co., N. Y. He lived in Jackson, Mich., and had eight children by his wife Maria P. She d. April 22, 1863. He m. second, Jan., 1864, Mrs. C. W. Bailes, who had one child. He d. Sept. 25, 1867. The children :

    4520 FRIEND T., b. Aug. 22, 1841; lives in Muir, Mich.; m. Delia Hilton of N. Y., Jan. 14. 1872; no child.
    4521 EMILY M., b. Oct. 28, 1843; m. J. B. Estelle; lives in Michigan City, Indiana.
    4522 JEROME P., b. Oct. 19, 1845; P. O. Henrietta, Mich.
    4523 MARY, b. March 21, 1849.
    4524 CHARLES H., b. Oct. 7, 1851; m.; lives in Gowen, Mich.
    4525 EDWARD L., b. Aug. 28, 1853; d. Sept. 29, 18.5.
    4526 FRANK E., b. Sept. 13, 1856.
    4527 FREDERIC W., b. Dec. 25, 1859.
    4528 JOHN D., b. Dec. 18, 1864.

4523 MARY DENISON, (dau. of 4519 Harry Christopher,) m. J. W. Lickens, Feb. 7, 1877. They live in Owasso, Mich., and have :

    4529 FRED RUPERT, b. Jan. 9, 1878.

4524 CHARLES H. DENISON, (son of 4519 Harry Christopher,) b. Oct. 7, 1851, was married, Dec. 1, 1878, to Julia M. Hilton; lives in Gowen, Mich., and has :

    4530 RUBY E., b. Jan. 24, 1880.

4521 EMILY MARIA DENISON, (dau. of 4519 Harry Christopher,) b. Oct. 28, 1843, was married Dec. 13, 1863, to John Byron Estelle, b. Jan. 31, 1839. They live in Michigan City, Ind., and have these children :

    4531 HARRY, b. Jan. 2, 1867.
    4532 BERTHA, b. Sept. 19, 1868.
    4533 JESSIE, b. Feb. 11, 1872; d. Aug. 8, 1872.
    4534 CLARENCE, b. Dec. 12, 1874; d. Sept. 10, 1875.
    4535 HOWARD, b. June 9, 1877.
    4536 HERBERT, b. Jan. 9, 1880; d. June 28, 1880.

4505 JOHN DENISON, (Christopher[4], Samuel[3], George[2], George[1],) b. Dec. 2, 1744, was married to Lydia Pratt, in 1766. He was with Gen. Wolfe's army at the capture of Quebec, Sept. 13, 1759. He died in Chenango Co., N. Y., April 25, 1825 ; his wife d. Sept. 15, 1787, aged 43. Their children :

4537 JOHN, b. Nov. 5, 1767; m. Sally Cowles.
4538 WILLIAM, b. Feb. 11, 1770; m. Elizabeth Lester.
4539 BAINAI, b. April 23, 1773; m. Lydia Silliman.
4540 JESSE, b. Sept. 11, 1776; m. Phebe Wyness.
4541 BECKWITH, b. Nov. 22, 1780; m. Julia Chittenden.
4542 LYDIA, b. 1784; m. James Burr, of Haddam.

4537 JOHN DENISON, JR., (John[5], Christopher[4], Samuel[3], George[2], George[1],) b. Nov. 5, 1767, was married, Dec. 29th, 1791, to Sally Cowles. Before he was 18 years old, he emigrated from Saybrook, with eight others, to Durham, Greene Co., N. Y., when that region was a wilderness. They went up Catskill Creek with an ox team, cutting their way through the forest to the mouth of one of its branches, which they named Saybrook Creek, a name it still bears. This was in 1785. In February, 1817, he removed from Durham to Guilford, Chenango Co., N. Y., having then five sons and two daughters. He d. Aug. 5, 1836; his wife Sally d. Feb. 8, 1836, aged 70. Their children :

4543 JOHN, 3d., b. Sept. 20, 1792; m. Betsey Palmer.
4544 LYDIA, b. June 19, 1794; m. Abel Stockwell.
4545 BAINAI, b. June 4, 1796; m. Deborah Palmer.
4546 HIRAM, b. April 6, 1800; m. Patience Smith.
4547 SALLY, b. May 17, 1804; m. Elias H. Rice.
4548 EBER C., b. Oct. 30, 1809; m. Charlotte Mills.
4549 ALFORD, b. Oct. 5, 1811; d. Oct. 12, 1833, unmarried.

4538 WILLIAM DENISON, (John[5], Christopher[4], Samuel[3], George[2], George[1],) b. Feb. 11, 1770, was married to Elizabeth Lester, Sept. 29, 1793; lived in Saybrook, Conn.; died Sept. 2, 1859; his wife died in March, 1846. Their children were:

4550 SARAH, b. April 7, 1797; d. March 21, 1800.
4551 JOHN, b. March 5, 1799.
4552 LESTER E., b. Aug. 10, 1801.
4553 MARY, b. Jan. 14, 1804; m. John Harris; 6 children.
4554 REV. WILLIAM, b. June 2, 1806.
4555 ELIZA, b. Aug. 30, 1808; m. Isaac Bailey; one child.
4556 REV. ALBERT E.; m. Lucy Ann Mason, June 6, 1844.

4551 JOHN DENISON, (William[6], John[5], Christopher[4], Samuel[3], George[2], George[1],) b. March 5, 1799, was married to Temperance A. Platts, June 1, 1835, and died Aug. 25, 1876. He lived in Winthrop, Conn., and had :

4557 AMELIA P., b. Dec. 4, 1839; m. Albert C. Clark in 1862; d. Nov. 12, 1864; had a dau.

4558 CLARA P., b. May 5, 1843; *m.* Wilbur F. Arnold, Aug. 29, 1866; lives in New Britain, Conn.; has had:
 4559 CARLTON W., b. Aug. 17, 1867; d. Feb., 1871.

4552 LESTER E. DENISON, (William⁶, John⁵, Christopher⁴, Samuel³, George², George¹,) b. Aug. 10, 1801, was married to Maria Watrous; lived in Winthrop, Conn.; died Oct. 6, 1866. He had this one child:
 4560 HENRY, b. Aug. 30, 1845; *m.* M. Stannard in 1866; lives in Winthrop, Conn.; has but one child:
  4561 LEWIS L, b. Oct. 28, 1867.

4553 MARY DENISON, (William⁶, John², Christopher⁴, Samuel³, George², George¹,) b. Jan. 14, 1804, was married to John Harris of Winthrop, Conn., Aug. 18, 1828. She d. Nov. 6, 1842; he d. Oct. 9, 1857, aged 57. Children:
 4562 ELIZA, b. Aug. 6, 1829; *m.* Gideon Hull; 3 children.
 4563 WILLIAM, b. July 18, 1831; lives in Killingworth, Conn.
 4564 MARY M., b. April 8, 1833; d. in Winthrop.
 4565 EDGAR, b. Dec. 18, 1835; lives in Killingworth, Conn.
 4566 JEDEDIAH, b. Feb. 6, 1838; *m.* Eliza Platts; d. in Winthrop.
 4567 CHAUNCY, b. Dec. 26, 1840; lives in Suffield, Conn.

4554 REV. WILLIAM DENISON, (William⁶, John⁵, Christopher⁴, Samuel³, George², George¹,) b. June 2, 1806, was married to Sally Loomis of Franklin, Conn., March 19, 1833. They had one child:
 4568 SARAH A., b. Aug. 28, 1837; *m.* Gilbert Denison, Dec. 14, 1865; no child. This Gilbert Denison got the name by adoption. He was a son of Elihu Wright of Westbrook.

4555 ELIZA DENISON, (William⁶, John⁵, Christopher⁴, Samuel³, George², George¹,) b. Aug. 30, 1808, was married to Isaac Bailey, Jan. 29, 1837, at Winthrop, Conn., and had:
 4569 CHARLOTTE E., b. May 28, 1840; *m.* Hezekiah C. Post, Nov., 1863; one child, Frank W.

4556 REV. ALBERT E. DENISON, (William⁶, John⁵, Christopher⁴, Samuel³, George², George¹,) was married to Lucy Ann Mason, at Plainville, Conn., June 6, 1844. Their children:
 4570 WILLIAM A., b. May 9, 1845; *m.* Margaret A. Hurd.
 4571 JOHN L., b. July 28, 1848; d. Oct. 14, 1857.
 4572 MARY E., b. June 13, 1851; d. Sept. 13, 1851.
 4573 HATTIE M., b. Nov. 1, 1854.

4570 WILLIAM A. DENISON, (son of 4556 Rev. Albert E.,) b. May 9, 1845, was married to Margaret A. Hurd, New Haven, Conn., in 1867. They have:
 4574 CHARLES A., b. Feb. 7, 1868.

4539 Bainai Denison, (John[5], Christopher[4], Samuel[3], George[2], George[1],) b. April 23, 1773, was married, Jan. 1, 1805, to Lydia Silliman. He died Dec. 18, 1842; she died Aug. 13, 1834, aged 54 years. Their children were:

    4575 Socrates, b. Nov. 12, 1805; m. Ann M. Kirtland, Jan. 1, 1845.
    4576 Lydia A., b. Jan. 18, 1809; m. Hezekiah C. Kirtland, Sept. 21, 1835.
    4577 Erastus B., b. Feb. 5, 1811; m. Mary Bushnell of Saybrook.
    4578 Sarah S., b. Aug. 23, 1813; not married; lives with John T.
    4579 Daniel S., b. Dec. 23, 1815; d. at Eutaw, Ala., Oct. 1849, unm.
    4580 Eunice P., b. April 2, 1818; not married; lives with John T.
    4581 John T., b. Aug. 7, 1820; not married; lives at Middletown, Ct.
    4582 Mary E., b. July 9, 1822; d. July 29, 1844, in Ohio, unmarried.
    4583 Huldah A., b. April 16, 1825; not married; lives with John T.

4575 Socrates Denison, (Bainai[6], John[5], Christopher[4], Samuel[3], George[2], George[1],) married Ann M. Kirtland, Jan. 1, 1845, and had:

    4584 Fannie R., b. Nov. 2, 1845.
    4585 Salome C., b. July 2, 1847; m. Washington F. Wilcox, Jan. 1, 1868.
    4586 Joseph K., b. July 15, 1850.

4577 Erastus B. Denison, (Bainai[6], John[5], Christopher[4], Samuel[3], George[2], George[1],) m. Mary Bushnell of Saybrook, April 27, 1835. He died in Ohio, Sept. 25, 1842; she died Oct. 29, 1846. They had but one child:

    4587 Frederick H.; lives in Idaho; mining.

4576 Lydia A. Denison, (Bainai[6], John[5], Christopher[4], Samuel[3], George[2], George[1],) m. Hezekiah C. Kirtland, Sept. 21, 1835, and had:

    4588 Frederick B., b. Jan. 1, 1838; m. Adaline A. Miller.
    4589 Saloma L., b. May 18, 1840.
    4590 Mary E., b. Dec. 9, 1843; m. Dexter D. Gilman, April 20, 1876.
    4591 Denison C., b. Sept.4, 1846; m. Mary E. Austin, Sept. 4, 1873.

4543 John Denison, (John[6], John[5], Christopher[4], Samuel[3], George[2], George[1],) b. Sept. 20, 1792, m. Betsey Palmer of Guilford, Chenango Co., N. Y., Feb. 1, 1816. Residence, Ketchumville, Tioga Co., N. Y. His children:

    4592 Daniel P.
    4593 Dianthe.
    4594 Delaverge.

4544 LYDIA DENISON, (John⁶, John⁵, Christopher⁴, Samuel³, George², George¹,) b. June 19, 1794, *m.* Abel Stockwell, Dec. 13, 1821. Lived at Port Huron, Mich. Her children:

    4595 CYRUS M., b. June 20, 1823; is a physician; *m.*; 5 ch.
    4596 SARAH H., b. May 7, 1828; d. April 16, 1861.

Abel Stockwell was a deacon. He died Aug. 27, 1863; his wife then lived with her son, Cyrus M., at Port Huron, Mich., where she died, April 21, 1868. Their son, Cyrus M., is a distinguished physician, and author of several medical works. He lives at Port Huron, Mich., and has five children.

4545 BAINAI DENISON, (John⁶, John⁵, Christopher⁴, Samuel³, George², George¹,) b. June 4, 1796, *m.* Deborah Palmer, of Guilford, Chenango Co., N. Y., Sept. 7, 1820. He d. Aug. 23, 1868. His children:

    4597 ADELIA.
    4598 LUCINA.
    4599 WILLIAM.
    4600 EBER; d. in the war of the rebellion.

4548 DEA. EBER C. DENISON, (John⁶, John⁵, Christopher⁴, Samuel³, George², George¹,) b. Oct. 30, 1809, *m.* Charlotte Mills, of Guilford, N. Y., Oct. 23, 1834; lives in Chesterfield, Mich.; is a Deacon of the Cong. Church, and a prominent man. His children:

    4601 ALFORD M., b. July 20, 1835; *m.* in 1874.
    4602 SAMUEL H., b. Feb. 2, 1840; d. Sept. 5, 1871.

4601 ALFORD M. DENISON, (son of 4548 Dea. Eber C.,) b. July 20, 1835, was married Sept. 24, 1874, to Ann B. Milton, b. July 19, 1853, in Somersetshire, England. They live at Milton, Mich. They have:

    4603 EBER WILLIAM, b. July 2, 1875.

4546 HIRAM DENISON, (John⁶, John⁵, Christopher⁴, Samuel³, George², George¹,) b. April 6, 1800, *m.* Patience Smith of Bainbridge, N. Y., Oct. 31, 1820. In 1846, he emigrated from Castle Creek, N. Y., to Chesterfield, Macomb Co., Mich. He has been Town Clerk, Justice of the Peace, and Elder in the Presbyterian Church. His children:

    4604 LEANDER C., b. July 28, 1821; d. Dec. 25, 1840.
    4605 FESTUS E., b. Aug. 18, 1823; *m.* Caroline Carey, April 13, 1845; no child.

10 George Denison's Descendants.

4606 ELVIRA E., b. May 6, 1826; m. Daniel M. Mills, Nov. 11, 1846.
4607 SIMEON S., b. Dec. 19, 1833; m. Lydia West, April 8, 1860; d. Nov. 13, 1866.
4608 ANTOINETTE, b. Jan. 30, and d. July 17, 1832.

4606 ELVIRA E. DENISON, (dau. of 4546 Hiram and Patience,) b. May 6, 1826, m. Daniel M. Mills, Nov. 11, 1846. They live at New Baltimore, Mich. Their children:

4609 HIRAM E., b. Feb. 18, 1848.
4610 SAMUEL E., b. June 30, 1850.
4611 CAROLINE A., b. Feb. 3, 1855.
4612 HARVEY O., b. March 14, 1858.
4613 SUSAN A., b. Dec. 4, 1860.
4614 FESTUS E., b. Sept. 3, 1863.
4615 JENNIE E., b. Feb. 24, 1868.

4607 SIMEON S. DENISON, (son of 4546 Hiram and Patience,) m. Lydia West, April 8, 1860; and d. in 1866. He had:

4616 IRVING, b. Jan. 21, 1862.
4617 ALFRED L., b. Aug. 2, 1864; d. April 8, 1867.

4547 SALLY DENISON, (John[6], John[5], Christopher[4], Samuel[3], George[2], George[1],) m. Elias H. Rice, May 23, 1825, and had:

4618 IRA A., b. Sept. 17, 1828; P. O. Millburn, Ill.
4619 ROSETTA, b. April 10, 1832; d. Nov. 2, 1858.
4620 AMELIA S., b. Feb. 19, 1834; m.; lives in Nebraska.
4621 ALFORD D., b. Jan 26, 1836; m. Cleanthe Storms; 3 ch.
4622 CHAUNCY E., b. Aug. 22, 1838; d. Oct. 4, 1874.

4541 BECKWITH DENISON, (John[5], Christopher[4], Samuel[3], George[2], George[1],) b. Nov. 22, 1780, was married, 1st, to Julia Chittenden, July 13, 1805; 2nd, to Mary Hurd, June 5, 1816; 3rd, to Desire Wixom, Oct. 10, 1826. The 1st wife d. June 18, 1815; the 2nd, March 10, 1826; the 3rd, Oct. 15, 1859. He lived in Seneca Co., N. Y. He d. Sept. 15, 1859. His children:

4623 UNA, b. Oct. 22, 1806; d. July, 1848, unmarried.
4624 JULIA M., b. April 21, 1809; d. Nov., 1810.
4625 JAMES H. H., b. June 3, 1817.
4626 MARY C., b. Oct. 11, 1822; m. Ira H. Cole.
4627 LAURA A., b. May 22, 1825; d. May 19, 1875, unmarried.
4628 GEORGE B., b. July 18, 1827; m. Susan King.

4628 GEORGE B. DENISON, (Beckwith[6], John[5], Christopher[4], Samuel[3], George[2], George[1],) b. July 18, 1827, m. Susan King,

Dec. 4, 1851; was of Covert, Seneca Co., N. Y. His children:

    4629 CHARLES W., b. Sept. 3, 1852.
    4630 SYLVESTER B., b. March 17, 1855.
    4631 ALFRED S., b. April 10, 1867; d. Sept. 20, 1874.

4625 JAMES H. H. DENISON, (Beckwith[6], John[5], Christopher[4], Samuel[3], George[2], George[1],) b. Jan. 3, 1817, was married to Louisa Cole, Sept. 2, 1846; lives at Sheboygan Falls, Wis. His children:

    4632 MARY, b. Aug. 2, 1847; m. Frederick A. Leavens.
    4633 GERTRUDE, b. Aug. 28, 1849; m. Frank T. Bemis.
    4634 GEORGE, b. Dec. 17, 1853; d. Feb. 12, 1861.
    4635 CHARLES B. b. July 27, 1855; d. Feb. 23, 1861.
    4636 FRANK H., b. Feb. 8, 1862.
    4637 JAMES F., b. Dec. 12, 1866.

4632 MARY DENISON, (dau. of 4625 James H. H.,) m. Fred. A. Leavens, Jan. 11, 1872, and has:

    4638 LETTIE, b. Sept. 6, 1873.
    4639 FREDERICK D., b. March 29, 1875.

4633 GERTRUDE DENISON, (dau. of 4625 James H. H.,) m. Frank T. Bemis, May 27, 1872, and has:

    4640 MARY LUELLA, b. Sept. 22, 1873.
    4640½ ALBERT D., b. June 28, 1877.

4626 MARY C. DENISON, (Beckwith[6], John[5], Christopher[4], Samuel[3], George[2], George[1],) m. Ira H. Cole, Jan. 3, 1849; lives at Farmer's Village, N. Y.; has:

    4641 GEORGE HERBERT. b. Jan. 30, 1850.
    4642 ADDIE, b. July 25, 1851.
    4643 WILLIAM D., b. March 30, 1853.
    4644 SARAH LOUISA, b. April 14, 1855.
    4645 FREMONT, b. Sept. 18, 1856.
    4646 IRVING, b. Sept. 21, 1859.
    4647 HERVEY, b. Aug. 25, 1861.
    4648 WIRT, b. June 3, 1863; d. Feb. 7, 1865.
    4649 ELBERT, b. Sept. 19, 1865.

4542 LYDIA DENISON, (John[5], Christopher[4], Samuel[3], George[2], George[1],) was married to James Burr, of Haddam, Conn., in 1804. Two children:

    4650 ELIZA S., b. July, 1805; m. Eleazer Bailey.
    4651 LYDIA, b. July, 1807; m. Daniel P. Lane.

4650 ELIZA L. BURR, (dau. of 4542 Lydia and James,) was married in 1822, to Eleazer Bailey. They lived in Higganum, Conn. He d. Dec., 1870. Children:

    4652 RICHARD M., b. Nov. 1823; m. Maria Bailey.
    4653 LYDIA M., b. July, 1825; m. Porter Smith.
    4654 SARAH S., b. Jan. 1827; m. Joseph Clark.
    4655 JAMES B., b. Jan., 1829; m. Nancy Belden.
    4656 BENNI D., b. Nov., 1830; d. in 1865.
    4657 ELSIE, twin, b. in 1832; d. in 1832.
    4658 JEMIMA, twin, b. in 1832; d. in 1832.
    4659 ELIZA E., b. Feb. 1834; d. Nov., 1856.
    4660 MATILDA M., b. May, 1837; m. Jared Lewis.
    4661 DANIEL B., b. in 1839; d. young.

4651 LYDIA BURR, (dau. of 4542 Lydia and James,) was married, Nov. 1829, to Daniel P. Lane, of Haddam, Conn. He d. Nov. 25, 1869. Children:

    4662 JOHN D., b. Jan. 8, 1831; m. Nancy Vanmeter.
    4663 JAMES B., b. May 11. 1834; m. Hannah Knapp.
    4664 ELIZA, b. Feb. 11, 1833; d. March 15, 1833.
    4665 CHARLES W., b. Aug. 10, 1836; d. March 23, 1863.
    4666 ANNA, b. Feb., 1839; d. Oct. 20, 1840.

John D. Lane lived in Cromwell, Conn.; James B. lives at Elmira, N. Y.

4540 JESSE DENISON, (John[5], Christopher[4], Samuel[3], George[2], George[1],) b. Sept. 11, 1776, was married, Oct. 28, 1802, to Phebe Wyness, b. May 29, 1784, at Rensalaerville, N. Y. He emigrated to New Durham, N. Y. After his marriage, he settled at Covert, Seneca Co., N. Y. Later in life, he removed to Saidburg, Pa. He d. April 21, 1858; his wife d. Dec. 18, 1848. Children:

    4667 WILLIAM, b. Aug. 16, 1804; m. Jane Goady.
    4668 ACHSAH, b. June 27, 1806; d. Sept. 23, 1863; unmarried.
    4669 LODEMIA, b. Aug. 19, 1808; m. Michael Remington.
    4670 ANSEL, b. Feb. 3, 1811; m. Sarah H. Bonnel.
    4671 LEWIS, b. Aug. 23, 1813; m. ; has dau. Rebecca F.
    4672 ELNATHAN, b. May 12, 1816; lives at Clear Creek, Iowa.
    4673 OLIVER C., b. July 18, 1820; m. Sarah Jane Quigley.
    3674 LYDIA, b. Feb. 17, 1825; twice married; no child.

4667 WILLIAM DENISON, (Jesse[6], John[5], Christopher[4], Samuel[3], George[2], George[1],) b. Aug. 16, 1804, was married to Jane Goady, in 1833; lives at Willowdale, Ida Co., Iowa. Children:

10 George Denison's Descendants.

4675 SAMUEL G., b. May 3, 1835.
4676 ELIZA JANE, b. Aug. 7, 1836; m. Andrew Spence.
4677 AUGUSTUS, b. April 17, 1838.
4678 MARY ANN, b. Sept. 19, 1841.
4679 LEWIS, b. Jan. 19, 1844.
4680 NANCY PATTALINE; b. June 16, 1846.
4681 WINFIELD SCOTT, b. Feb. 7, 1852.

4669 LODEMIA DENISON, (Jesse[6], John[5], Christopher[4], Samuel[3], George[2], George[1],) b. Aug. 19, 1808, was married, May 13, 1829, to Michael Remington, b. in 1802, in Broome Co., N. Y. They live at Pilot Knob, Ind. Children:

4682 MARY ANN, b. Sept 18, 1830; m. Libeus Welman; 2 children.
4683 RILEY, b. July 10, 1832.
4684 BECKWITH, b. April 8, 1834; d. April 8, 1841.
4685 UNNAMED DAU., b. June 2, 1836; d. June 16, 1836.
4686 SARAH, b. March 8, 1842.
4687 SOPHIA, b. June 22, 1844; d. March 23, 1855.
4688 CATHERINE, b. Jan. 17, 1851; d. Dec. 14, 1855.
4689 PHEBE, b. May 28, 1853; d. Oct. 20, 1853.

4670 ANSEL DENISON, (Jesse[6], John[5], Christopher[4], Samuel[3], George[2], George[1],) b. Feb. 3, 1811, was married, Feb. 21, 1836, to Sarah H. Bonnel; lives at Summit, Crawford Co., Pa. Children:

4690 WILLIAM H., b. March 22, 1841; m. Sarah C. Teater, June 8, 1876; she was b. March 1, 1851; they live at Summit, Pa.
4691 PHEBE R., b. Jan. 24, 1846; d. April 13, 1876.

4673 OLIVER C. DENISON, (Jesse[6], John[5], Christopher[4], Samuel[3], George[2], George[1],) b. July 18, 1820, was married, July 3, 1857, to Sarah Jane Quigley, b. Jan. 1, 1828; lives at Linesville, Pa. Children:

4692 WALTER, b. Sept. 6, 1858.
4693 A SON, b. and d. in April, 1863.
4694 JESSE, b. April 13, 1867.

4399 GIDEON DENISON, (Samuel[3], George[2], George[1],) b. in 1724, was married to Elizabeth ——, May, 1752, and lived at Saybrook, Conn., in 1752. They had:

4695 GIDEON, b. in 1753; m. Jerusha Butler.
4696 DESIRE, b. May 5, 1755; m. Wm. Willard.
4697 ELIZABETH, b. Aug. 21, 1756.
4698 CLARISSA, bapt. Aug. 26, 1770; d. unmarried, Feb. 14, 1858.
4699 HETTY, bapt. Nov. 3, 1765; m. Simeon Lay.
4700 EZRA, bapt. April 22, 1764; no family.
4701 JEDEDIAH, b. Dec. 23, 1759; m. Abigail Denison.

4702 JEREMIAH, bapt. April 12, 1761.
4703 MOLLY, bapt. July 2, 1768.

4695 GIDEON DENISON, JR., (Gideon^4, Samuel^3, George^2, George^1,) b. in 1753, was married to Jerusha Butler, May 28, 1780, at Norwich, Conn. Their children :

4704 AN INFANT DAUGHTER, b. and d. in 1781, atNorwich, Conn.
4705 HENRY, b. July 16, 1782.
4706 MINERVA, b. 1784 ; *m.* Commodore John Rogers.
4707 LOUISA, b. 1786, at Havre de Grace, Md.
4708 ELIZABLTH. b. 1788; at Havre de Grace. Md.

4706 MINERVA DENISON, (Gideon, Jr.^{5}, Gideon^4, Samuel^3 George^2, George^1,) b. in 1784, was married to Commodore John Rogers, U. S. N. She died at Rock Island, Ill., Feb. 17, 1877, aged over 92 years. Among her children were these :

4709 JOHN ; Rear Admiral U. S. Navy.
4710 HENRY; Lieut. U. S. Navy; lost in the Albany.
4711 LOUISA ; *m.* Gen. Montgomery C. Meigs. U. S. A.
4712 ANNE; *m.* John N. McComb, U. S. A. He was on Gen. Mc-Clellan's staff.

4707 LOUISA DENISON, (Gideon, Jr.^{5}, Gideon^4, Samuel^3, George^2, George^1,) b. in 1786, *m.* Capt. Alexander Wadsworth, U. S. N. They had :

4713 LOUISA D.; *m.* Chas. G. Baylor of Baltimore, Jan. 6, 1853.
4714 ANNE.
4715 ALEXANDER.

4489 ELIZABETH DENISON, (Gideon, Jr.^{5}, Gideon^4, Samuel^3. George^2, George^1,) b. in 1788, was married to Com. John D. Henley, U. S. Navy, who fought with McDonough on Lake Champlain, and served otherwise with distinction. They had :

4716 FRANCES; *m.* Rev. Edward Y. Higbee, D.D, (Episcopal) N. Y.
4717 HENRIETTA; *m.* J. B. H. Smith, a Washington lawyer.
4718 ELIZA ; *m.* Lieut. Stephen B. Luce, U. S. N.

4699 HETTY DENISON, (Gideon^4,Samuel^3,George^2,George^1,) b. Nov. 3, 1765, was married, May 24, 1786, to Simeon Lay, of Saybrook, Conn. They lived at Westbrook, Conn.; he d. Aug. 10, 1808, in his 60th year ; she d. March 1, 1841, in Hartland, N. Y.; both are buried in the Old Cemetery at Westbrook, Conn. Their children :

4719 SYLVIA, b. Nov. 29, 1787.
4720 WM. HENRY, b. April 21, 1789.
4721 JERUSHA, b. Feb. 5, 1791.

10 *George Denison's Descendants.*

4722 EZRA DENISON, b. April 21, 1793; d. Aug. 16, 1807.
4723 SIMEON, b. April 26, 1795.
4724 MINERVA, b. Nov. 30, 1798.
4725 ELIZABETH, b. Oct. 21, 1800.

4701 JEDEDIAH DENISON, (Gideon[4], Samuel[3], George[2], George[1],) b. Dec. 23, 1759, was married, April 19, 1783, to Abigail Denison, dau of 4410 Samuel and Temperance (Post) Denison; lived in Saybrook, Conn. He died Nov. 30, 1833, aged 74; she d. Dec. 17, 1834, aged 69. Children:

4726 CHARLES, b. Jan. 22, 1786; *m.* Elizabeth Chalker.
4727 JEDEDIAH, b. Dec. 1, 1788; *m.* Anna Doane.
4728 JEREMIAH C., b. Jan. 18, 1790; *m.* Chloe B. Clark.
4729 ABIGAIL, b. July 19, 1793; *m.* Edward Potter.
4730 WILLIAM, b. June 23, 1795; untraced wanderer after 1818.
4731 GIDEON. b. Feb. 20, 1798: d. at New Orleans in 1833.
4732 EZRA, b. March 6, 1800; *m.* Ann Doane; P. O., N. Y. City.
4733 RICHARD A., b. Jan. 27, 1802; d. Oct. 20, 1849.
4734 REV. GEORGE H., b. May 6, 1804; a Methodist preacher; was drowned in attempting to cross Brazos River, Sept., 1841.
4735 EDWARD, b. May 30, 1806; d. unmarried, Nov. 12, 1836.

4726 CHARLES DENISON, (Jedediah[5], Gideon[4], Samuel[3], George[2], George[1],) b. Jan. 22, 1786, was married, Nov. 8, 1810, to Elizabeth Chalker. Two children:

4736 CHARLES STEWART, b. July 24, 1815; *m.* Amelia E. Williams.
4737 ELIZABETH CHALKER, b. April 2, 1817; *m.* Lorenzo Redfield.

4636 CHARLES STEWART DENISON, (Charles[6], Jedediah[5], Gideon[4], Samuel[3], George[2], George[1],) b. July 24, 1815, was married, Oct. 6, 1839, to Amelia E. Williams; lived at West Meriden, Conn.; he d. Dec. 14, 1871. Three children;

4738 JANE, b. in 1842.   **4738½** CHARLES.   **4538¾** ERASTUS.

4737 ELIZABETH C. DENISON, (Charles[6], Jedediah[5], Gideon[4], Samuel[3], George[2], George[1],) b. April 2, 1817, was married Nov. 20, 1836, to Lorenzo Redfield; lived at Saybrook; he d. Aug. 31, 1875; she d. June 3, 1875. Children:

4739 HERBERT D., b. Sept, 26, 1838.
4740 MARY E., b. May 3, 1841; d. June 27, 1843.
4741 MARY FRANCES, b. June 1, 1845,
4742 ALICE E., b. Oct. 18, 1847; d. Oct. 4, 1852.
4743 ANGENETTE A., b. March 17, 1849; *m.* Wm. Bushnell, Saybrook.
4744 AGNES A., b. April 3, 1855.
4745 EMMA D., b. Dec. 13, 1857.

4727 JEDEDIAH DENISON, (Jedediah[5], Gideon[4], Samuel[3], George[2], George[1],) b. Dec. 1, 1788, was married, June 16

1808, to Anna Doane; he d. July 3, 1842; she d. July 3, 1837. Children:

    4746 ERASTUS, b. June 24, 1812; d. unmarried, Feb. 6, 1838.
    4747 MARY A., b. Jan. 8, 1815; d. Feb. 29, 1816.
    4748 JULIETTA, b. Jan. 12, 1817; d. July 3, 1837.
    4749 ELIZABETH, b. July, 1820; d. Feb. 3, 1821.
    4750 WILLIAM W., b. April 20, 1822; d. in the war.

4728 JEREMIAH C. DENISON, (Jedediah[5], Gideon[4], Samuel[3], George[2], George[1],) b. Jan. 18, 1790, was married, March 7, 1812, to Chloe B. Clark, dau. of Rufus; lived at Saybrook. He d. Aug. 13, 1854; his wife d. May 16, 1873. Their children:

    4751 RUFUS C., b. Oct. 30, 1812; m. Catherine Bushnell.
    4752 MARIA LOUISA, b. April 24, 1815; d. April 28, 1817.
    4753 MARIA LOUISA, b. Dec. 19, 1817; m. Azariah Whittlesey.
    4753½ CLARISSA, b. Dec. 30, 1819; d. Sept. 6, 1820.
    4754 MARY AUGUSTA, b. Feb. 23, 1826; d. May 2, 1837.

4751 RUFUS C. DENISON, (son of 4728 Jeremiah C.,) b. Oct. 20, 1812, was married, Sept. 18, 1838, to Catherine Bushnell, of Saybrook. Two children:

    4755 GEORGE WM., b. Oct. 5, 1839; m. E. Overman.
    4756 MARY A. NEWELL, b. Aug 21, 1843; d. May 3, 1870.

4755 GEORGE WM. DENISON, (son of 4751 Rufus C.,) b. Oct. 5, 1839, was married Oct. 18, 1870, to Emma Overman, dau. of Benjamin of Florida; lives at Saybrook. Children:

    4757 WILLIAM B., b. Aug. 24, 1871.
    4758 MARGARET L., b. May 30, 1873.
    4759 CATHERINE NEWELL, b. Nov. 18, 1875.

4753 MARIA LOUISA DENISON, (dau. of 4728 Jeremiah C.,) b. Dec. 19, 1817, was married, Sept. 20, 1836, to Azariah Whittlesey, of Saybrook. He d. Dec. 27, 1856, aged 49. The children:

    4760 MARY D., b. Sept. 4, 1840: m. Peter DuVernett of N. Y.
    4761 MADISON, b. April 7, 1843; d. May 7, 1867.
    4762 CHLOE C., b. June 10, 1845.
    4763 AZARIAH, b. Dec. 24, 1846.

V.

3659 GEORGE DENISON, (George[2], George[1],) b. in 1699, was married, first, Sept. 28, 1721, to Sarah Minor, dau. of Dr.

Joseph and Sarah (Tracy) Minor. She d. Sept. 27, 1724, in the 25th year of her age. He was married, second, May 10, 1727, to Joanna Hinckley, dau. of Samuel and Martha (Lathrop) Hinckley. He was a shipwright, and lived on his father's homestead farm, in Westerly, R. I. He d. Jan. 16, 1737. His children:

    4764 JOSEPH, b. Jan. 26, 1723; m. Lucy Chesebro'.
    4765 MARY, b. Sept., 1724.
    4766 ELIJAH, b. July 6, 1728; d. in 1736.
    4767 GEORGE, b. April 14. 1730; d. in June, 1730.
    4768 SARAH, b. Sept. 7, 1733; m. Ezra Kinney.

4764 JOSEPH DENISON, (George^3, George^2, George^1,) b. Jan. 26, 1723, was married in 1748, to Lucy Chesebro'; lived in Stonington. Children:

    4769 NATHANIEL, b. in 1748.
    4770 GEORGE, b. in 1750.
    4771 LUCY, b. in 1752.
    4772 SARAH, b in 1754.
    4773 ANN, b. in 1756.
    4774 HANNAH, b. in 1758.
    4775 THANKFUL, b. in 1760.

4769 NATHANIEL DENISON, (Joseph^4, George^3, George^2, George^1,) b. in 1748, was married about 1767. He was a soldier of the Revolutionary War. His grandson, Dudley F. Denison, had a gun he carried in that war, with his name carved on it. He was lost at sea about 1795. His will is in the Stonington Probate office. His children

    4776 BENADAM, b. in 1772; m. Rhoda Randall.
    4777 BETSEY PRUDENCE, b. in 1780; m. Charles Palmer.
    4778 HANNAH; m. Henry Palmer.
    4779 DESIRE; m. Robert Bentley.
    4780 ESTHER, b. in 1768; m. Joseph Davis.
    4781 MARY; m. a Taylor.

4776 BENADAM DENISON, (Nathaniel^5, Joseph^4, George^3, George^2, George^1,) b. in 1772, was married in 1794, to Rhoda Randall. (In the Randall Genealogies he is called "Adam" Denison.) She was born in Stonington, Conn., in 1773, and d. at Halifax, Vt., in 1857. He emigrated from Stonington to Halifax, Vt., about 1804, and d. there in 1840. His first five children were born in Stonington, the others in Halifax, as follows:

4782 BENADAM, b. in 1795; m. Lydia Boardman.
4783 RHODA, b. in 1797; m. Elisha Frink.
4784 PRUDENCE C., b. Dec. 15, 1799; m. George W. Terrett.
4785 ESTHER, b. in 1801; m. George Preston.
4786 BETSEY, b. in 1803; m. Willard Holman.
4787 CHARLES, b. in 1805; d. in Conn.
4788 DUDLEY F., b. March 31, 1808; m. Olive M. Wood.
4789 HANNAH, b. in 1810; m. Warren Everett.
4790 EUNICE, b. in 1812; m. Edward Fish.
4791 ANNIS F., b. in 1815; m. Benj. Woodward.

4784 PRUDENCE C. DENISON, (Benadam^6, Nathaniel^5, Joseph^4, George^3, George^2, George^1,) b. Dec. 15, 1799, married George W. Terrett, Dec. 3, 1822; lived in West Granville, Mass. Children:

4792 GEORGE W., Jr., b. Sept. 5, 1823; d. Jan. 6, 1873.
4793 MARY ANN, twin, b. May 15, 1825.
4794 ANN MARY, twin, b. May 15, 1825.
4795 MELVINA P., b. July 18, 1827.
4796 HANNAH E., b. Aug. 15, 1829.
4797 ADELINE P., b. Jan. 29, 1831.
4798 BENJAMIN F., b. July 31, 1833.
4799 WILLIAM D., b. Feb. 26, 1836; d. Sept. 5, 1837.
4800 CHARLES W., b. March 19, 1839.
4801 CATHERINE E., b. June 29, 1841.

4788 DUDLEY F. DENISON, (Benadam^6, Nathaniel^5, Joseph^4, George^3, George^2, George^1,) b. March 31, 1808, was married, Jan. 22, 1835, to Olive M. Wood; b. Oct. 4, 1813; P. O. address, Baraboo, Wisconsin. Their children:

4902 HENRIETTA M., b. Sept. 22, 1836; d. Jan. 13, 1837.
4803 OLIVE MARIA, b. Jan. 17, 1838.
4804 HARRIET GERTRUDE, b. Jan. 28, 1845.
4805 IMOGENE H., b. Oct. 27, 1849; d. May 20, 1855.

4783 RHODA DENISON, (Benadam^6, Nathaniel^5, Joseph^4, George^3, George^2, George^1,) b. in 1797, married Elisha Frink, being his second wife. They lived in Tolland, Mass.; she d. in Granville, Mass., in 1845; had one child:

4805 ANGELINE, who lived only three years.

There was one child by the first wife, Betsy M. Frink. Elisha Frink died, and in 1846, his dau. Betsey M., married Amos H. Fowler, and had three children:

4806½ ALFRED A., b. Jan. 18, 1847.
4807 ELLEN M., b. Nov. 13, 1850.
4808 ELBERT E., b. March 15, 1854.

4777 BETSEY P. DENISON, (Nathaniel⁵, Joseph⁴, George³, George², George¹,) b. in 1782, was married, Jan. 10, 1802, to Charles Palmer. They lived in Stonington; but "emigrated to New Marlboro, Mass., with Henry Palmer and the Taylors." Their children are on the Stonington records as follows:

    4809 ELIZA H., b. Aug. 16, 1803.
    4810 EDWARD D., b. March 19, 1805.
    4811 JENNETT A., b. Sept. 21, 1809.
    4812 FRANCES A., b. Dec. 9, 1812.
    4813 CHARLES L., b. June 27, 1815.
    4814 PHEBE E., b. Oct. 22, 1817.
    4815 LUCY C., b. July 15, 1819.
    4816 LUCRETIA C., b. June 3, 1821.

4780 ESTHER DENISON, (Nathaniel⁵, Joseph⁴, George³, George², George¹,) was married to Joseph Davis of Stonington, March 2, 1785. Children:

    4817 ESTHER, b. Oct. 22, 1785.
    4818 THANKFUL, b. Sept. 17, 1787.
    4819 JOSEPH, b. April 2, 1789.
    4820 LUCRETIA, b. May 29, 1790.
    4821 DESIRE, b. Nov. 21, 1791.

4768 SARAH DENISON, (George³, George², George¹,) b. Sept. 7, 1733, was married to Ezra Kinney, in 1748; lived in Preston; had these:

    4822 JOANNA, b. June 25, 1749.
    4823 MERCY, b. July 12, 1851.
    4824 JEMIMA, b. May 3, 1753.
    4825 SARAH, b. Aug. 1, 1755; d. young.
    4826 PEABODY, b. July 20, 1757.
    4827 SARAH, b. Oct. 22, 1760.
    4828 CYNTHIA, b. May 26, 1763; *m.* Nathan Stanton, in 1781. Nathan and Cynthia (Kinney) Stanton had a daughter Sarah, who married Rufus Prentice of Preston, Conn., and was mother of GEO. D. PRENTICE, the poet and journalist.
    4829 DENISON, b. Jan. 5, 1766.
    4830 LUCRETIA, b. May 13, 1770.
    4831 EZRA b. Feb. 18, 1773.

DESCENDANTS OF

WILLIAM DENISON, OF STONINGTON, CONN.

THIRD SON OF

CAPT. GEORGE.

WILLIAM DENISON'S DESCENDANTS.

I.

11 WILLIAM DENISON'S WILL, ETC.

11 WILLIAM DENISON, (George[1],) b. in 1655, was married to Sarah Stanton, (dau. of the first Thomas, and widow of Thomas Prentice.) They lived in Stonington, Conn. Wm. Denison d. March 2), 1715; she d. Aug. 7, 1713. Their children:

 4901 WILLIAM, b. March 24, 1687; *m.* Mercy Gallup.
 4902 SARAH, b. April 14, 1789; *m.* Benj. Avery.
 4903 GEORGE, b. Feb. 28, 1692; *m.* Lucy Gallup.

11 WILLIAM DENISON'S WILL. 1715.

IN THE NAME OF GOD, AMEN, The 5 day of February, in the year 1715. I, William Denison of Stonington, in the county of New London, in his majesty's colony of Connecticut, in N. England, gentleman, being sick and weak in body, but of perfect mind and memory, thanks be given to God therefor, calling to mind the mortality of my body, do make and ordaine this my last will and testament; That is to say, first of all, I give and recommend my soul unto the hand of God that gave it, and my body I commit to the earth to be decently buried at the discretion of my executors hereafter named; and as touching such worldly estate wherewith it hath pleased God to bless me, I give, devise, and dispose of as followeth: That is to say, First, I will that all those debts and duties as I owe to any person or persons whomsoever, shall be well and truly paid by my executors hereafter named, in some convenient time after my decease. Item—I give and bequeath unto my well-beloved son, Wm. Denison, all that tract or parcel of land and meadow, which I bought of the executors of Mr. Jno. Hallam, and the highway or out lot I bought with it, and also all that tract of land lying on the east side of Mistuxett Brook, southward and eastward of Gallup's line, except 40 acres on the east side of said brook, beginning where Gallup's line crosseth Mistucsett brook—and so down stream ten rods, to a mear stone; thence 20 rods a paralell line with Gallup's line to a stone marked; thence south east noreast to a walnut tree northward of the bars, thence to run a paralell line with the stone wall of the paster, to the east end of said paster. Also, I give to my son William a certain tract or parcel of swampy or low land on the west side of said brook, northward of Elnathan Miner's house (at Mistucsett) and eastward of a great ledge of rocks, and so from the northermost of the ledge of rocks an east line to Mistuxett brook, and so by the brook to the south side of said land. Also, I give to my son William aforesaid, that tract or parcel of land, which was Mr. Nathaniel Beebe's, whereon Henry Jones now dwells, with the buildings now upon it. Also, I give to my well-beloved son, George Denison, my dwelling house and farm whereon I now live, with the orchards and out-houses now upon it, excepting that swampy land east of the ledge of rocks (given to William.) And also to George I give 40 acres, excepted out of William's part on the east side Mistucsett brook. Also, I give to George 5 twelve acre lots lying at a place called Edward's orchard, only my will is that my son Wm. shall have the whole benefit of said orchard for the term of twelve years from the time of my decease. I also give to Geo. 250 acres of land lying northward of a place called Ashaway in Sd. Stonington, and $3\frac{1}{2}$ acres of saltmarsh upon six-penny island. Item—I give and bequeath unto my well beloved sons William and Geo. above-named, all other my out lands and grants in lands, now or of right hereafter, belonging to me in any plantation or government wheresoever, to be equally divided between them. Item—I give and bequeath to my loving daughter Sarah Avery, the sum of one hundred pounds in current money, or in other pay at money price, to be paid to her by my executors hereafter named, each of them an equal part thereof, within 12 months after my decease; also my said daughter to have the bed which was her mother's, and the furniture belonging to it, and the large silver cup, one chest, one box and 4 pewter platters. Item—I give also to my son William my silver headed cane, and my best sute of wearing appa el. Item—I give to my son George the long table and chest of drawers, and one feather bed and furniture of the great room. Item—I give to my son George, my two Indian boys, Ned and Kindne s, and the Indian gearl named Juda, and my four oxen, and my cart, and plow, yoke, and chains. Item—I give to Mrs. Mary Wells, widow, of Coulchester, the sum of ten pounds current money to be paid by my executors, hereafter named, within one month after my decease. Item

—I give and bequeath to my brother George's son George, the sum of five pounds, when he shall attain the age of 21 years, to be paid by my executors hereafter named. Item—I order my executors to take especial care of Mr. Nathaniel Beebe during his natural life, and to allow him a christian burial at his death. Item—I give and bequeath all the remainder of my estate to be equally divided between my two sons Wm. and Geo; and further my will is, that if either of my sons shall hereafter meet trouble with respect to the title of any of their lands, and lose any part thereof, the other brother shall make good to the losing brother, one half of the value of the land so lost, to be set out to him in land by suitable men appointed by the court of Probate, and also pay one-half of the charge that may arise in defending said land; and I do hereby constitute, mark and ordain my trusty and beloved sons, William and George Denison, to be my sole executors of this my last will and testament, and I do hereby utterly disallow, revoke and make void, all other and former wills and testaments by me made before this time, ratifying and confirming this, and no other, to be my last will and testament. In witness whereof I hereunto set my hand and seal.

Witnesses—   WILLIAM DENISON. [Seal.]
NATHANIEL CHESEBROUGH.
ELNATHAN MINOR.
JAMES STEVENSON.

4902 SARAH DENISON, (William[2], George[1],) b. April 14, 1689, was married to Benjamin Avery of Groton, Conn., in 1713. He was son of the first John Avery. They lived in Groton, and had these children:

    4904 SARAH, born in 1714; m, 1st, Beebe Denison and 2d Benadam Denison.
    4905 BENJAMIN, b. in 1715; m. Mary Morgan.
    4906 GEORGE, b. in 1716; m. Lydia Gardiner.
    4907 WILLIAM, b. in 1717; m. Phebe Denison, dau. of 104 Daniel.
    4908 ABIGAIL, b. in 1718; m. —— Avery.
    4909 DAVID, b. in 1719; m. Hannah Meach.
    4910 MARY, b. in 1721; m. John Morgan.
    4911 LUCY, b. in 1723.
    4912 THANKFUL; m. Benjamin Avery.
    4913 DANIEL, b. in 1725.
    4914 JOHN, b. in 1727.

II.

4901 WILLIAM DENISON, Jr., (William[2], George[1],) b. Mar. 24, 1687, was married to Mercy Gallup, May 10, 1710. They lived in Stonington. He d. Feb. 24, 1724, aged 37; she d. March 2, 1724, aged 35. His estate was inventoried at £2479 —18s—6d. Their children:

    4915 MERCY, b. June 25, 1711; *m.* Hubbard Burrows.
    4916 SARAH, b. July 2, 1713; *m.* Elisha Niles.
    4917 ESTHER, b. Feb. 6, 1715, *m.* Jonathan Wheeler.
    4918 WILLIAM, b. Dec. 9, 1716; *m.* Prudence Denison.
    4919 HANNAH, b. April 19, 1719; d. March 21, 1721.
    4920 BENADAM, b Feb. 6, 1721; twice married.
    4921 JONATHAN, b. May 12, 1722; *m.* Martha Williams; no child.
    4922 NATHAN, b. Feb. 11, 1724.

4918 WILLIAM DENISON, 3d, (William[3], William[2], George[1],) b. Dec. 9, 1716, was married June 23, 1737, to Prudence Denison, dau. of 104 Daniel. They lived in Stonington, Conn., and had children as follows:

    4923 WILLIAM, bapt. Oct. 15, 1738.
    4924 PRUDENCE, b. Nov. 27, 1740; *m.* James Minor.
    4925 ANDREW, b. Nov. 30, 1742.
    4926 BEEBE, b. Jan. 1, 1744; *m.* Prudence Holmes.
    4927 DARIUS, b. March 11, 1747; *m.* Mary Billings.
    4928 MERCY, b. July 19, 1749; *m.* Daniel Minor.
    4929 ALICE, b. Nov. 27, 1753; *m.* Robert Denison.

William Denison, 3rd, d. July 7, 1779. His widow married Thomas Prentice, Dec. 9, 1779, and d. Feb. 11, 1812.

4915 MERCY DENISON, (William[3], William[2], George[1],) b. June 25, 1711, was married, May 28, 1730, to Hubbard Burrows. They lived in Groton, Conn. Their children:

    4931 ESTHER, b. Sept. 28, 1731.
    4932 HANNAH, b. Nov. 21, 1733; *m.* Daniel Packer.
    4933 HUBBARD, b. June 26, 1739; *m.* Priscilla Baldwin, dau. of Capt. John and Eunice (Spalding) Baldwin of Stonington; was killed in Fort Griswold, Sept. 6, 1781.
    4934 ELISHA, b. Nov. 27, 1744.
    4935 SARAH, b. Aug. 16, 1747; *m.* Elisha Niles.
    4936 MARY, b. Oct. 7, 1749.
    4937 JONATHAN, b. May 13, 1752; *m.* Lucy Avery.

11 William Denison's Descendants.

4931 ESTHER DENISON, (William[3], William[2], George[1],) b Feb. 6, 1715, was married to Jonathan Wheeler, March 1, 1732. They lived in Stonington, Conn. Their children :

- **4938** ESTHER, b. Dec. 27, 1732.
- **4939** PRUDENCE, b. Dec. 20, 1734.
- **4940** JONATHAN, b. Jan. 12, 1737.
- **4941** RICHARD, b. Jan. 16, 1739.
- **4942** THANKFUL, b. Jan. 31, 1741.
- **4943** JOHN, b. Aug. 6, 1744; m. Mary Minor.
- **4944** DAVID, b. Jan. 13, 1746.
- **4945** CONTENT, b. Aug. 30, 1749.
- **4946** ZERVIAH, b. Oct. 3, 1752; m. Allen Yorke.
- **4947** PATIENCE, b. Feb. 6, 1756; m. Joseph Page.
- **4948** JOSHUA, b. Dec. 13, 1761; m. Mary Turner.

4926 BEEBE DENISON, (William[4], William[3], William[2], George[1],) b. Jan. 1, 1744, was married to Prudence Holmes, Oct. 13, 1774. He d. Feb. 10, 1823; she d. Aug. 2, 1844, aged 89. They lived in Stonington, Conn., and had these:

- **4949** MERCY, b. March 9, and d. in June, 1776.
- **4950** CONTENT, b. June 4, 1777; m. Samuel Remington.
- **4951** ABIGAIL, b. Oct. 9, 1779; d. March, 1865, unmarried.
- **4952** ANDREW, b. April 15, 1781; m. Mary Middleton; 2nd, Wid. Mary Ann Eccleston.
- **4953** PRENTICE, b. June 16, 1783.
- **4954** BEEBE, b. March 13, 1785; m. Eunice Parke.
- **4955** PRUDENCE, b. Nov. 25, 1787.
- **4956** RUSSELL, b. June 16, 1789; d. unmarried.
- **4957** EUNICE, b. July 21, 1791; m. Illustrious Remington.
- **4958** HENRY, b. April 8, 1793; m. Lucy Smith.
- **4959** POLLY, b. Jan. 18, 1795.
- **4960** NANCY, b. Aug. 17, 1798; m. David Kellogg.

4924 PRUDENCE DENISON, (William[4], William[3], William[2], George[1],) b. Nov. 27, 1740, was married to James Minor, April 6, 1761. She d. Sept. 13, 1777. They had :

- **4961** PHEBE, b. Jan. 30, 1762.
- **4962** JAMES, b. Oct. 4, 1764.
- **4963** ANDREW, b. Sept. 8, 1766.
- **4964** PRUDENCE, b. July 8, 1768.
- **4965** LOIS, b. March 30, 1772.
- **4966** EUNICE, b. Feb. 18, 1775.
- **4967** DENISON, b. Aug. 28, 1777.

4954 BEEBE DENISON, JR., (Beebe[5], William[4], William[3], William[2], George[1],) b. March 13, 1785, m. Eunice Parke, Feb. 9, 1806. Eunice (Parke) D. died in 1816. He m. 2d, Fanny

Allen, Dec. 24, 1819. He d. Sept. 27, 1840 ; the wife, Fanny, d. Nov. 25, 1865. He lived in Stonington, Conn., and had these :

 4968 ABIGAIL, b. June 21, 1811; m Rev. Jesse B. Denison. See his record.
 4969 ELIZA, b. Sept. 19, 1814; d. Sept. 6, 1334; not married.
 4970 MARY, b. Nov. 6, 1808; m. Elisha Willcox.
 4971 RUSSELL A., b. Jan. 6, 1822; m. Susan E. Balcom, July 27, 1859; no child.
 4972 CHARLES H., b. March 14, 1824; m. Alice Adams in 1852.

4970 MARY DENISON, (Beebe, Jr.[6], Beebe[5], William[4], William[3], William[2], George,) b. Nov. 6, 1808, was married to Elisha Willcox ; lived in Stonington, Conn., and had these :

 4973 EUNICE; m.
 4974 JESSE; d.
 4975 HANNAH; d.
 4976 ELISHA; m.

4958 HENRY DENISON, (Beebe[5], William[4], William[3], William[2], George[1],) b. April 8, 1793, was married to Lucy Smith, April 21, 1817, who d. in 1872, aged 74. He lived at the Head of Mystic, Conn., and had these children :

 4977 LUCY A., b. Jan. 27, 1818; m. Amos Gay, Sept. 10, 1835; one ch.
 4978 HANNAH L., b. Sept. 27, 1820; m. Elias Wilcox.
 4979 EUNICE, b. Oct. 30, 1822; m. James Standish.
 4980 JULIA, b. Feb. 22, 1825; m. Elnathan Wilcox.
 4981 WILLIAM H., b. Feb. 18, 1828; m. Caroline Dow.
 4982 HARRIET DELIA, b. Jan. 5, 1831; m. Aldridge Kenyon.
 4983 ROWLAND S., b. Oct. 25, 1832; m. Eliza Bushnell, May 6, 1849.
 4984 EMILY, b. Jan. 16, 1836; m. Horace Spencer.
 4985 JEROME, twin, b. Sept. 5, 1838; m. 1st, Ann A. Williams; 2nd, Mary J. Gibson.
 4986 JANE, twin, b. Sept. 5, 1838; m. Charles Sabin, Jan. 4. 1872.

4977 LUCY A. DENISON, (Henry[6], Beebe[5], William[4], William[3], William[2], George[1],) b. Jan. 27, 1818, m. Amos Gay, lived at Mystic, Conn., and had :

 4987 AMOS H., b. June 22, 1836; m. Nancy E. Morgan in 1860; 1 ch.

4978 HANNAH L. DENISON, (Henry[6], Beebe[5], William[4], William[3], William[2], George[1],) b. Sept. 27, 1820, was married to Elias Wilcox, April 23, 1843. They live in Stonington, Conn., and have had :

 4988 HANNAH A., b. April 2, 1855; d. Oct. 9, 1857.
 4989 LEANDER, b. April 30, 1844.

4990 ELLEN, b. Aug. 27, 1846.
4991 ALMEDA, b. Sept. 7, 1848.
4992 ELIAS T., b. Oct. 6, 1850.
4993 STEPHEN R., b. Aug. 26, 1852.
4994 ROWLAND H., b. Jan. 26, 1858.
4995 AN INFANT DAUGHTER, b. March 23, and d. June 1, 1860.
4996 ORREN A., b. Sept. 16, 1861.
4997 CORA L., b. May 30, 1864.

4979 EUNICE DENISON, (Henry[6], Beebe[5], William[4], William[3], William[2], George[1],) b. Oct. 30, 1822, was married to James L. Standish, of West Chester, Conn., July 4, 1845, and had :

4998 LUCIE E., b. Aug. 1, 1846.
4999 ABBIE S., b. Aug. 23, 1847; *m.* Jesse H. Wilcox, March 4, 1873.
5000 ARTHUR C., b. Aug. 17, 1849; *m.* Nettie E. Clark, Mar. 31, 1875.
5001 HENRY E., b. Dec. 8, 1851; d. Aug. 1, 1852.
5002 SARAH S., b. Sept. 28, 1853.
5003 JENNIE E., b. Dec. 8, 1856.
5004 LILLIE E., b. Feb. 10, 1860.
5005 BELLE E., b. Feb. 25, 1863.
5006 MILES L., b. Jan. 22, 1866.

4980 JULIA DENISON, (Henry[6], Beebe[5], William[4], William[3], William[2], George[1],) b. Feb. 22, 1825, was married to Elnathan Wilcox, May 9, 1847 ; lives in Stonington, Conn.; has had :

5007 AN INFANT SON, b. and d. Feb. 18, 1848.
5008 JULIA H., b. Jan. 1, 1849; *m.* Denison Palmer, May 5, 1869.
5009 JESSE HENRY, b. Aug. 10, 1852; *m.* Abbie S. Standish, Mar. 4, 1873.
5010 LUCY EMILY, b. Oct. 8, 1854; *m.* Nathan Strickland, Apr. 13, '71.
5011 MOSES HAVENS, b. Aug. 15, 1858.
5012 DENISON E., b. July 20, 1861.
5013 GEORGE W., b. Aug. 15, 1864.
5014 JENNIE D., b. May 31, 1867.

4981 WILLIAM H. DENISON, (Henry[6], Beebe[5], William[4], William[3], William[2], George[1],) b. Feb. 18, 1828, was married to Caroline S. Dow, May 9, 1852. Children :

5015 GILBERT H., b. Feb. 21, 1853.
5016 CHARLES S , b. Sept. 1, 1854.
5017 WILLIAM B., b. Oct. 1, 1859.
5018 GEORGE E., b. March 18, 1866.

5015 GILBERT H. DENISON, (William H.[7], Henry[6], Beebe[5], William[4], William[3], William[2], George[1],) b. Feb. 21, 1853, was married May 6, 1874, to Hattie Perry ; lives in Colchester, Conn. Children :

12 William Denison's Descendants.

5019 GILBERT H., b. March 14, 1875; d. Aug. 5, 1875.
5020 CARRIE, b. Aug. 2, 1876.

4982 HARRIET ADELIA DENISON, (Henry[6], Beebe[4], William[4], William[3], William[2], George[1],) b. Jan. 5, 1831, was married to Aldridge Kenyon, Nov. 29, 1855, and had these:

5021 HENRY A., b. Jan. 14, 1857.
5022 GEORGE S., b. Jan. 4, 1859.
5023 JENNIE L., b. July 10, 1866.
5024 LELIA MAY, b. Jan. 16, 1871.

In 1875, she was divorced from Aldridge Kenyon. May 11, 1875, she married Louis C. Bennet.

4983 ROWLAND S. DENISON, (Henry[6], Beebe[5], William[4], William[3], William[2], George[1],) b. Oct. 25, 1832, was married to Eliza Bushnell of Lisbon, Conn., May 3, 1859; lives in Norwich, Conn., and has had:

5025 LIZZIE M., b. June 23, 1861.
5026 FREDERIC, b. July 12, 1862; d. Aug. 13, 1862.
5027 HELEN A., b. Aug. 6, 1863; d. Oct. 12, 1864.
5028 ANNIE A., b. June 16, 1865; d. Nov. 30, 1869.
5029 LILLIAN H., b. Jan. 26, 1868.
5030 WILLIAM H., b. June 14, 1870.
5031 LUCY S., b. May 14, 1873.
5032 FRANK R., b. Sept. 14, 1875.

4984 EMILY DENISON, (Henry[6], Beebe[5], William[4], William[3], William[2], George[1],) b. Jan. 16, 1836, was married to Horace Spencer, Dec. 10, 1854; lives at Mystic, Conn., and has had:

5033 CHARLES H., b. Nov. 29, 1855.
5034 WILLIAM S., b. Jan. 14, 1859.
5035 EMMA J., b. July 16, 1863.
5036 ANNA G., b. May 16, 1867.
5037 HENRY JEROME, b. Sept. 17, 1870.
5038 SABIN E., b. Oct. 31, 1872; d. April 25, 1873.

4985 JEROME DENISON, (Henry[6], Beebe[5], William[4], William[3], William[2], George[1],) b. Sept. 5, 1838, was married, 1st, to Ann A. Williams. She died, Aug. 28, 1865. He married 2d, Mary Jane Gibson, March 17, 1869. He lives in Norwich, Conn., and has:

5039 ELOISE, (by 1st wife,) b. Jan. 7, 1864.
5040 LIZZIE, (by 2d wife,) b. July 16, 1875.

4928 MERCY DENISON, (William[4], William[3], William[2], George[1],) b. July 19, 1749, was married to Daniel Minor, Feb. 19, 1769. Their children:

11 William Denison's Descendants.

5041 MERCY, b. Jan. 30, 1770.
5042 ELSA, b. May 5, 1772.
5043 MARTHA, b. Sept. 27, 1774; d. June 25, 1775.
5044 PRUDENCE, b. Oct. 18, 1778.
5045 DANIEL, b. Oct. 30, 1780.
5046 WHEELER, b. Jan. 26, 1783,
5047 DARIUS, b. July 1, 1785.
5048 LUTHER, b. March 27, 1788.
5049 ANNA, b. Sept. 20, 1790.

4927 DARIUS DENISON, (William[4], William[3], William[2], George[1],) b. March 11, 1747, was married to Mary Billings, April 25, 1771. He d. Aug. 18, 1829; she d. June 15, 1823, aged 72. They lived in Stonington, Conn., and had these :

5050 PRUDENCE, b. March 21, 1772; m. Christopher Dean.
5051 POLLY, b. Nov. 10, 1774; twice married; 1st, to Obediah Stanton; 2d, to Henry Vanderpool.
5052 WILLIAM, b. Oct. 13, 1776; m. Phebe Irish.
5053 MERCY, b. May 10, 1779; m. Amos Grinnell.
5054 DARIUS, b. Dec. 28, 1783; m. Nancy Hyde.
5055 NANCY, b. Oct. 3, 1781; m. Joseph Lawton.
5056 AMOS B., b. Feb. 21, 1786; d. unmarried.
5057 LODOWICK, b. July 27, 1790; m. Elizabeth Irish.
5058 FANNY, b. Jan. 18, 1793; m. Hazard Holmes.

5050 PRUDENCE DENISON, (Darius[5], William[4], William[3], William[2], George[1],) b. March 21, 1772, was married to Christopher Dean, Jan. 5, 1794, being his second wife. They lived in Coleraine, Mass., and had :

5059 DARIUS, b. Jan 11, 1795; d. Jan. 22, 1872, at Durhamville, N. Y.
5060 REBECCA, b. April 8, 1797.
5060½ JABEZ, b. Dec. 10, 1798; d. Sept. 3, 1803.
5061 JAMES, b. Feb. 24, 1801; d. at Greenfield, Mass., June 8, 1858.
5062 NATHAN D., b. Dec. 11, 1802; d. April 13, 1815.
5063 JABEZ, b. June 18, 1805; d. in Texas, April 4, 1856, (or in 1860, as another report says,) leaving several children.
5064 MARY ANN, b. June 7, 1808; d May 6, 1815.
5065 SARAH ANN, d. Feb. 24, 1875.
5066 PRUDENCE, b. Dec. 20, 1817; m. David Avery of Charlemont, Ms.

5053 MERCY DENISON, (Darius[5], William[4], William[3], William[2], George[1],) b. May 10, 1779, was married, Aug., 1800, to Amos Grinnell. She had 4 children and died. Her children :

5067 JOANNA, b. Aug., 1801.
5068 BENJAMIN, b. 1805.
5069 MARY, b. March 24, 1807; m. Samuel W. Denison.
5070 MERCY, b. 1809.

He m. 2nd, Hannah Leeds, and had 7 more children.

11 William Denison's Descendants.

5054 DARIUS DENISON, (Darius[5], William[4], William[3], William[2], George[1],) b. Dec. 28, 1783 ; m. Nancy Hyde, 1807, and died Nov. 12, 1815. His children :

    5071 ALBERT, b. Oct. 25, 1807.
    5072 MARY, b. Aug. 31, 1811; m. Wm. R. Taugee; no child.
    5073 HARRIET, b. 1813; d. young.
    5074 ELIZA, b. Feb. 25, 1814; m. James Noyes, Dec. 24, 1837, who d. Oct. 27, 1843. They had :
        5075 MARY D., b. Sept. 18, 1838; d. Oct. 24, 1867.
        5076 JOHN JAMES, b. and d. in 1840.
    Mrs. Eliza (D.) Noyes m. 2nd, Christopher Pearce, Feb. 25, 1855.

5071 ALBERT DENISON, (Darius[6], Darius[5], William[4], William[3], William[2], George[1],) b. Oct. 25, 1807, m. first, Margaret Heath, March 15, 1827, who had five children, and d. May 19, 1859. He m. second, Mary W. Bentley, Nov. 26, 1861, who had two children, and d. Nov. 5, 1871. He m. third, Sept. 17, 1876, Mrs. Marcia Kilton of Omaha, Neb.; no child. His children :

    5077 MARY ELLEN, b. Jan. 23, 1830, in Groton, Conn.
    5078 HORACE, b. March 10, 1834; d. July 30, 1837.
    5079 CHARLES H., b. Jan 27, 1836; d. Jan. 5, 1858.
    5080 ALBERT E., b. Sept. 24, 1844, at Manchester, Conn.
    5081 FREDERICK E., b. Aug. 24, 1851, at Warehouse Point, Conn.; d. Dec. 26, 1877.
    5082 GEORGE, b. May 2, 1870; d. Aug. 3, 1870.
    5083 LAURA ALBERTINA, b. Oct. 25, 1871.

5077 MARY ELLEN DENISON, (dau. of 5071 Albert,) b. Jan. 23, 1830, was married, Oct. 24, 1853, to Nelson K. Benton ; they live at Warehouse Point, Conn. Children :

    5084 THOMAS KINGSBURY, b. Sept. 30, 1855.
    5085 ALBERT DENISON, b. May 7, 1857.

5080 ALBERT E. DENISON, (son of 5071 Albert,) b. Sept. 24, 1844, was married, Sept. 28, 1867, to Louisa H. Rensehousen, b. May 6, 1846; lives at Pittsfield, Mass. Children :

    5086 CHARLES HENRY, b. Oct. 22, 1868.
    5087 JESSIE HANNAH, b. March 15, 1873.
    5088 GEORGE, b. Aug. 23, 1875.

5057 LODOWICK DENISON, (Darius[5], William[4], William[3], William[2], George[1],) b. July 27, 1790, was married to Elizabeth Irish, and had eight children. In 1834, he, with his brother William, who married Phebe Irish, emigrated from Stonington,

11 William Denison's Descendants. 241

Conn., to Freedom, Portage Co., Ohio; and in 1855, he died in Cleveland, Ohio, of cholera. His wife died at Aberdeen, Miss., March 22, 1854. His children, all born in Stonington, Conn.:

5089 SILAS, b. in 1814; lost at sea in 1834, unmarried.
5090 WILLIAM V., b. in 1816; d. at Aberdeen, Miss., Dec., 1867.
5091 STILLMAN A., b. in 1818; d. in Florida, in 1843, unmarried.
5092 GUY, b. in 1820; d. in Alabama, in 1842, unmarried.
5093 DARIUS, b. April 8, 1824; d. in Ohio, unmarried, in 1850.
5094 CHARLES H., b. Jan. 8, 1828; d. in Texas, May 7, 1878.
5095 FRANK L., b. April 7, 1831; lives at Belton, Texas.
5096 MARY E., b. June, 1833; d. in Texas, Feb. 1866.

5095 FRANK L. DENISON, (Lodowick[6], Darius[5], William[4], William[3], William[2], George[1],) b. April 7, 1831, was married, first, Oct. 9, 1856, to Ann C. Evans, at Waco, Texas, where she died, June 19, 1857; and, second, Aug. 11, 1859, to Hannah G. Lambdin, at Waco, Texas, by whom he has nine children. In 1847, he emigrated from Ohio to Mississippi. In 1854, he went to Texas, where he practiced law many years, and, for a time, was State Prosecuting Attorney. Ill health compelled him to leave his law-practice. His present P. O. address is Belton, Bell Co., Texas. His children:

5097 BENJAMIN COOPER, b. July 7, 1860; d. Oct. 8, 1864.
5098 ELIZABETH A., b. June 28, 1862; m. Wm. H. Ross, Jan. 24, 1881.
5099 SUSAN A., b. Aug. 19, 1864.
5100 MARY L., b. July 17, 1866.
5101 FRANK L. Jr., b. Nov. 26, 1868.
5102 GIPPIE P., b. June 12, 1872; d. April 25, 1873.
5103 PHEBE L., b. March 12, 1874; d. Feb. 7, 1877.
5104 JOSEPHINE, b. Jan. 11, 1878.
5105 CHARLES G., b. Aug. 6, 1880.

Only three of Lodowick Denison's children, besides Frank L., were married, namely: William V., Charles H., and Mary E.

5090 WILLIAM V. DENISON, (son of 5057 Lodowick,) b. Jan., 1816, was married, first, to Louisa Burnett, who died at Aberdeen, Miss., June, 1851, leaving four children; and second, in 1858, to Mary Evans who had three children. He d. in 1867. All his children, except the oldest who is dead, are now living in Texas. He had:

5106 WILLIAM; d. in Memphis, Tenn., in 1878, leaving a widow and one child who are still living in that city.

5107 MARY, *m.* Edwin C. Evans; four children.
5108 CLARKE, *m.* Mattie Mangum in 1874; one child.
5109 FRANK, *m.* Emma Carroll, in 1878.
5110 LOUANNA.
5111 HELEN, *m.* Enos Reynolds, in 1880.
5112 HINDA, b. in 1863 or 1864.

5094 CHARLES H. DENISON, (son of 5057 Lodowick,) b. Jan. 8, 1828, was married, in 1853, to Ellen Catley, who died at Waco, Texas, in 1857. He died at Bryan, Texas, May 7, 1878. They had one child that died in infancy.

5096 MARY E. DENISON, (dau. of 5057 Lodowick,) b. June, 1833, was married twice; first, June 25, 1850, to George R. Hillyer, and second, to James Isles. She died at Richmond, Texas, Feb., 1866; no child.

5052 WILLIAM DENISON, (Darius^5, William^4, William^3, William^2, George^1,) b. Oct. 13, 1776, was married to Phebe Irish, lived first in Stonington, Conn., and had six children born there. In 1834, with his brother Lodowick, who married Elizabeth Irish, he emigrated to Freedom, Portage Co., Ohio. He died in 1852, while on his return from a visit to his son at La Crosse, Wis. His wife, Phebe, d. in September, 1845. Their children:

5113 ELIAS, b. in 1803; thrice married, but we have learned the names of only two of his children: Burton and Newton. He lives at Ravenna, Ohio.

5114 JOHN, b. in 1805; d. in 1843, at Freedom, Ohio, leaving a widow, and two children who died unmarried.

5115 PHEBE, b. in 1808; *m.* Ira Burroughs in 1835; d. at La Crosse, Wis., leaving two children: William Sydney, now a fine lawyer, and Charles.

5116 PRUDENCE, b. in 1810; *m.* George Tod, brother of Gov. Tod of Ohio; lived at Waukesha, Wis.; d. there in 1849; had two sons.

5117 HARRIET, b. in 1814; was married in 1880, when 66 years old; lives in Chicago, Ill. Her Texas cousin says: "I have never learned the name of her husband; but in early life, she formed a resolution never to marry any but a rich man. She 'held out faithful,' and gained her point. We may admire her firmness, and question her judgement."

5118 WILLIAM, Jr., b. April 8, 1821, studied law, began practice at La Crosse, Wis., and *m.* Miranda E. West. He was rising rapidly in his profession, when he was brutally murdered by "a Dutch gang," while out on a fishing excursion.

11 William Denison's Descendants.

5058 FANNY DENISON, (Darius[5], William[4], William[3], William[2], George[1],) b. Jan. 18, 1793, was married, April 20, 1817, to Hazard Holmes of Stonington, and had these children :

    5119 HAZARD, b. Jan. 23, 1818.
    5120 FRANCIS ELIAS, b. Aug. 10, 1820.
    5121 ALONZO, b. Sept. 24, 1822.
    5122 GEORGE W., b. Aug. 25, 1824.
    5123 MARY E., b. March 24, 1827.
    5124 MASON, b. July 30, 1828.
    5125 HARRIET, b. July 24, 1830.
    5126 ELLEN M., b. July 18, 1832.
    5127 EMELINE D. b. May 4, 1835.

4920 BENADAM DENISON, (William[3], William[2], George[1],) b. Feb. 6, 1721, was married, Nov. 3, 1742, to Anna Swan. He lived in Stonington, Conn., and had children as follows :

    5128 LUCY, b. Jan. 8, 1744; *m.* William Gallup.
    5129 JAMES, b. Aug. 25, 1745; *m.* Eunice Stanton.
    5130 BENADAM, b. July 9, 1747; *m.* Dimis Reed.
    5131 ROBERT, b. Sept. 28, 1749; *m.* 1st, Alice Denison; 2d, Deborah Dewey.
    5132 GEORGE, b. Oct. 8, 1751; *m.* Theody Brown.

Mrs. Anna (Swan) Denison died Nov. 29, 1751. Oct. 18, 1752, he *m.* 2nd, Mrs. Sarah (Avery) Denison, widow of 2503 Beebe. No other child. He d. in 1757.

5128 LUCY DENISON, (Benadam[4], William[3], William[2], George[1],) b. Jan. 8, 1744, married Wm. Gallup, July 2, 1761, and had :

    5135 OLIVER, b. Oct. 29, 1763.
    5136 PERCIS, b. April 22, 1765.
    5137 WILLIAM, b. May 9, 1767.
    5138 JOADAM, b. May 31, 1769.
    5139 LUCY, b. Oct. 31, 1772.
    5140 ANNE, b. April 4, 1775.

5129 JAMES DENISON, (Benadam[4], William[3], William[2], George[1],) b. Aug. 25, 1745, *m.* Eunice Stanton, dau. of Joseph, Jr., Sept. 29, 1773. He died April 26, 1813 ; she died, April 19, 1813. Their children were :

    5141 JOSEPH ADAM, b. Dec. 22, 1774; *m.* Rachel Chase.
    5142 ANNA, b. Dec. 1, 1780; Nathan Gere.
    5143 DIMIS, b. Feb. 3, 1783; *m.* Stephen Paine.
    5144 EUNICE, b. June 19, 1785; *m.* Tim. P. Fay.
    5145 LUCY, b. Aug. 4, 1788; d. unmarried.
    5146 JAMES, b. Oct. 24, 1791; twice married.
    5147 GEORGE, b. June 21, 1794; d. July 25, 1796.

11 William Denison's Descendants.

5141 JOSEPH ADAM DENISON, (James[5], Benadam[4], William[3], William[2], George[1],) b. Dec. 22, 1774, was married, June 9, 1802, at Cornish, N. H., to Rachel Chase. He had emigrated from Stonington, Conn., to Royalton, Vt. He d. Sept. 4, 1855, in his 81st year; his wife d. Aug. 23, 1858, aged 84. Their children :

5148 EUNICE STANTON, b. June 3, 1803; d. Sept. 2, 1804.
5149 JOSEPH ADAM, Jr., b. March 23, 1805; m. Eliza Skinner.
5150 EUNICE STANTON, b. Oct. 22, 1806; d. Feb. 23, 1809.
5151 GEORGE, (Rev.) b. April 24, 1809; m. Jeannette B. Ralston.
5152 RACHEL CHASE, b. Oct. 5, 1810; d. Aug. 29, 1812.
5153 JAMES, b. March 3, 1812; m. Wid. E. A. Royall.
5154 ALICE DUDLEY, b. April 30, 1814; m. D. W. Grant.
5155 RACHEL CHASE, b. Nov. 15, 1816; unmarried.
5156 DUDLEY CHASE, b. Sept. 13, 1819; m. Eunice Dunbar.

5149 DR. JOSEPH ADAM DENISON, JR., (Joseph Adam[6], James[5], Benadam[4], William[3], William[2], George[1],) b. March 23, 1805, was married, Dec. 24, 1829, to Eliza Skinner. He was a noted practicing physician at Royalton, Vt. He d. July 30, 1848; his wife d. in 1869, aged 61. His children :

5157 ELIZA, b. Nov. 26, 1830; m. John A. Jameson.
5158 PHILANDER CHASE, b. Jan. 8, 1832; d. March 2, 1832.
5159 GEORGE STANTON, b. Aug. 15, 1833; m. Wid. C. Forsyth.
5160 ELEANOR PORTER, b. June 17, 1835; d. April 26, 1841.
5161 JAMES, b. Jan. 9, 1837; m. Lizzie Lindsay.
5162 ALICE, b. Nov. 10, 1838.
5163 FRANKLIN, b. Feb. 6, 1842; a lawyer, unmarried.
5164 LUCY, b. May 15, 1843; d. unmarried, Dec. 25, 1866.
5165 CLARA, b. Dec. 2, 1844; m. J. D. Garfield.
5166 DR. CHARLES, b. Nov. 1, 1845; is at Denver, Col.; m. Ella H. Strong, dau. of Gen. Henry Strong of Chicago, Dec. 26, 1878; has Edith S., b. Oct. 6, 1879.
5167 SUSAN, b. Jan. 24, 1847; m. E. M. Gallaudet.
5168 FANNY, b. Dec. 18, 1848; d. Aug. 3, 1859.

5157 ELIZA DENISON, (dau. of 5149 Dr. Joseph Adam,) b. Nov. 26, 1830, was married, Oct. 11, 1855, to John A. Jameson; lived at Royalton, Vt. Children :

5169 MARY, b. Dec. 20, 1857.
5170 ELEANOR, b. May 15, 1864; d. Sept. 14, 1865.
5171 ELIZA, b. Nov. 24, 1865.
5172 JOHN ALEX., b. Sept. 12, 1868.
5173 REBECCA, b. May 9, 1870.

5159 GEORGE STANTON DENISON, (son of 5149 Dr. Joseph Adam,) b. Aug. 15, 1833, was married, Feb. 24, 1857, to Wid.

Cordelia Forsyth, at Pensacola, Florida ; and d. at sea, Aug. 24, 1866. One child:

 5174 WILLIAM, b. Dec. 26, 1857.

5161 JAMES DENISON, (son of 5149, Dr. Joseph Adam,) b. Jan. 9, 1837, was married, Dec. 26, 1859, to Lizzie Lindsay of Salem, Mass.; lives at Kendall Green, Washington, D. C. His children :

 5175 GEORGE STANTON, b. Oct. 9, 1860; d. Sept. 12, 1861.
 5176 LIZZIE L., b. Jan. 19, 1862; d. June 2, 1862.
 5177 EDWARD T., b. Oct. 27, 1864; d. Sept. 14, 1866.
 5178 RICHARD L., b. Sept. 23, 1871; d. June 23, 1872.
 5179 LINDSAY, b. March 23, 1873.
 5180 RAYMOND CHASE, b. Oct. 3, 1876.

5165 CLARA DENISON, (dau. of 5149 Dr. Joseph Adam,) b. Dec. 2, 1844, was married, Sept. 8, 1870, to Isaac D. Garfield, at Royalton, Vt., and has :

 5181 CLARA LOUISA, b. July 15, 1872.

The first husband died. She m. 2nd, Hon. Robert McLelland, and lives in Galena, Ill.

5167 SUSAN DENISON, (dau. of 5149 Dr. Joseph Adam,) b. Jan. 24, 1847, was married, Dec. 22, 1868, to Edward Minor Gallaudet, Principal of the Institution for the Deaf and Dumb at Washington, D. C. They live at Kendall Green, Washington. Children :

 5182 DENISON, b. April 1, 1870.
 5183 EDSON FESSENDEN, b. April 21, 1871.
 5184 ELIZA, b. June 28, 1874; d. Aug. 26, 1875.
 5185 HERBERT DRAPER, b. Oct. 12, 1876.

5151 REV. GEORGE DENISON, (Joseph Adam[6], James[5], Benadam[4], William[3], William[2], George[1],) b. April 24, 1809, was married, Sept. 16, 1832, at Lockport, N.Y., to Jeanette B. Ralston. He was an Episcopal clergyman; lived at Lockport, N. Y., and at several places in the West ; d. at Keokuk, Iowa, June 3, 1861. Children :

 5186 FRANCES R., b. Aug. 7, 1833; d. July 4, 1834.
 5187 GEORGE, b. March 19, 1835; d. Dec. 27, 1836.
 5188 HENRY HEBER, b. Oct. 28, 1837; m. Lucia Skinner.
 5189 GEO. DUDLEY, b. March 13, 1841; d. unmarried, May 2, 1864.
 5190 MARY HOSMER, b. April 26, 1843; d. Sept. 22, 1843.
 5191 ALICE CHASE, b. Nov. 14, 1846; lives at Royalton, Vt.
 5192 CHARLES SIMEON, b. July 12, 1849; of Michigan University.

Rev. George Denison entered Dartmouth college in 1825. In the spring of 1827 he went to Ohio, and entered Kenyon college, which was organized under the presidency of his uncle, Bishop Chase of the Diocese of Ohio. He graduated at Kenyon in 1829; then took a scientific and mathematical course at Yale college. About 1830, he was elected professor of mathematics and natural philosophy in Kenyon college. In 1832, he was ordained to the ministry of the Protestant Episcopal church. About 1833, he resigned the professorship and took charge of Trinity church, Newark, Ohio, where he remained until 1837; when he was called to the charge of Grace church, Lockport, New York. Here he remained until the spring of 1842, when he resumed the charge of Trinity church, Newark, Ohio, and remained until 1848, when he was a second time elected to the professorship of mathematics and natural philosophy in Kenyon college. He occupied this chair until the fall of 1853, when he was called to the charge of St. John's church, Keokuk, Iowa, where he resided and labored until his death. Mr. Denison was invariably successful in building up large and flourishing parishes, and continually added to his labors by incessant missionary work in his vicinage.

Mr. Denison's attainments as a scientist and mathematician were of a very high order, and at the time of his death, a leading church journal pronounced him one of the most gifted of the clergy in the west. He was an industrious and voluminous writer upon scientific and theological subjects in the press, but none of his writings have ever been collected in book form. He left almost no manuscripts, his sermons consisting merely of outlines and brief notes, upon which his extemporaneous discourses were framed.

5188 Henry Heber Denison, (son of 5151 Rev. George,) b. Oct. 28, 1837, was married Oct. 16, 1865, at Royalton, Vt., to Lucia Skinner, who d. May 5, 1876. He lives in St. Louis, Mo. Children:

5193 Dudley Chase, b. Jan. 30, 1868.
5194 Grace Maria, b. Oct. 27, 1872.

Henry H. Denison graduated at Kenyon college, Ohio, in 1857; was professor of ancient languages in St. Paul's college, Missouri, in 1858–9; was connected with a Vermont regiment in the war for the suppression of the rebellion; served in various states of the south, and always on detached service; was mustered out of service in July, 1865, and resumed the practice of law; was a member of the legislature of Vermont in 1867–8; and in the spring of 1870, removed to St. Louis, Missouri, where he has since been engaged in the practise of the law.

5153 JAMES DENISON, (Joseph Adam[6], James[5], Benadam[4], William[3], William[2], George[1],) b. March 3, 1812, was married at Matagorda, Texas, April 2, 1848, to Wid. E. A. Royall. He was a graduate of Kenyon College; was a lawyer distinguished in his profession; at one time was law partner of Hon. Salmon P. Chase. In 1870, he was a judge of the Supreme Court of Texas. He d. at San Antonio, Texas, Feb. 16, 1873. Children:

    5195 ALICE DUDLEY, b. Jan. 9, 1849.
    5196 MARY CHASE, b. Aug. 1, 1851; d. June 1, 1852.
    5197 JOSEPH ADAM, b. Jan. 9, 1856.

5195 ALICE DUDLEY DENISON, (dau. of 5153 James,) b. Jan. 9, 1849, was married at Rockford, Ill., July 1, 1868, to Elijah S. Hewitt. They live in Ill. Children:

    5198 MAUD ELIZABETH, b. Nov. 9, 1872, at Rockford, Ill.
    5199 RALPH DUDLEY, b. Dec. 2, 1873, at Elgin, Ill.

5154 ALICE DUDLEY DENISON, (Joseph Adam[6], James[5], Benadam[4], William[3], William[2], George[1],) b. April 30, 1814, was married, Oct. 1, 1832, to David Wadsworth Grant, of Bloomfield, Conn., where he lived and died. He was widely known as an enterprising and respected citizen. He d. Sept. 7, 1862; she d. Dec. 22, 1853. Children:

    5200 A DAUGHTER, b. and d., April 9, 1839.
    5201 DAVID DENISON, b. Jan. 2, 1841; d. Feb. 26, 1841.
    5202 DAVID DENISON, b. April 1, 1843; m. Mary E. Caswall.
    5203 JOSEPH W., b. Nov. 14, 1845; m. Myra B. Fay.
    5204 GEORGE D., b. Sept. 8, 1848; d. Nov. 4, 1851.
    5205 ALICE DUDLEY, b. Oct. 18, 1851; unmarried.

The son, David Denison Grant, is now, (1878,) postmaster at Franklin, Venango Co., Pa. His brother, Joseph Wadsworth Grant, has the same P. O. address. David Denison Grant was married in Boston, Mass. His wife is a daughter of Rev. Henry Caswall, D. D. He has a son:

    5205½ DAVID CASWALL GRANT, b. Oct. 12, 1869.

5156 Hon. Dudley Chase Denison, (Joseph Adam[6], James[5], Benadam[4], William[3], William[2], George[1],) b. Sept. 13, 1819, was married, Dec. 22, 1846, to Eunice Dunbar. He lives in Vermont; is a lawyer; and is now, (Jan. 1877,) a member of Congress. He has had seven children, as follows:

    5206 Joseph Dudley, b. Nov. 1, 1847; *m.* Elizabeth A. Rix.
    5207 Catherine Amanda, b. March 25, 1850.
    5208 Elizabeth, b. Feb. 13, 1852; d. June 5, 1853.
    5209 John Henry, b. July 15, 1855.
    5210 Gertrude May, b. Sept. 22, 1857.
    5211 Edward Dunbar, b. Feb. 3, 1860; d. Dec. 6, 1860.
    5212 Lucy Dunbar, b. Jan. 9, 1867.

5206 Joseph Dudley Denison, (son of 5156 Hon. Dudley C.,) b. Nov. 1, 1847, was married, Sept. 10, 1874, to Elizabeth Abigail Rix, at Royalton, Vt., and has:

    5213 Eunice Dunbar, b. Oct. 6, 1875.

5130 Benadam Denison, (Benadam[4], William[3], William[2], George[1],) b. July 9, 1747, was married to Dimis Reed, in 1770, and settled in Norwich, Conn. He d. in 1811; his wife Dimis, d. in 1821. His children were:

    5214 James, b. 1771; d. in 1776.
    5215 Ann, b. 1773; d. in 1781.
    5216 James, b. 1778; d. Jan. 7, 1801; not married.
    5217 George, b. 1781; d. Dec. 19, 1828.
    5218 Charles, b. 1783; d. Dec. 16, 1814.
    5219 Ann, b. 1785; *m.* Hon. Roger Huntington.
    5220 Harriet, b. 1787; d. in 1808.
    5221 Lucy, b. 1789; *m.* Joseph Kingsley, of Norwich, in 1814.

5219 Ann Denison, (Benadam, Jr.[5], Benadam[4], William[3], William[2], George[1],) b. in 1785, was married, Jan. 30, 1814, to Hon. Roger Huntington, of Norwich, had 3 children, and died in 1819. Her children were:

    5222 Harriet D., b. Jan. 9, 1815.
    5223 James D., b. Jan. 25, 1817.
    5224 Mary Ann, b. March 30, 1819.

Roger Huntington *m.* 2nd, Amelia M. Lambert, and had five more children. He held various important public offices. He died June 27, 1852.

5221 Lucy Denison, (Benadam, Jr.[5], Benadam[4], William[3], William[2], George[1],) b. in 1789, *m.* Joseph Kingsley in 1814;

11 William Denison's Descendants.

lived in Norwich, Conn.; he d. in 1838, aged 49 ; she d. in 1865, aged 76. Children :

5225 HARRIET ANN, b. in 1815.
5226 LUCY, b. 1816; d. in 1837.
5227 ABBY, b. 1821.
5228 DENISON, b. in 1823.
5229 CHESTER, b. 1825.
5230 JOSEPH, b. 1827.
5231 GERRETT, b. 1838.

5131 ROBERT DENISON, (Benadam[4], William[3], William[2], George[1],) b. Sept. 28, 1749, was married, 1st, to Alice Denison, and had these :

5232 ROBERT, b. Sept. 2, 1774; m. Betsey Baker; no child.
5233 MARTHA, b. Sept. 2, 1777; m. Cary Ingraham.
5234 BENADAM, b. April 12, 1783; m. Harriet Babcock.
5235 JONATHAN, b. Feb. 2, 1780; m. Catherine Brown.
5236 JAMES, b. July 1, 1785; m. Cynthia Babcock.
5237 EDWARD, b. Feb. 6, 1788; d. Oct. 8, 1794.
5238 ALICE, b. June 4, 1790; m. William Dewey.
5239 ELIAS, b. June 15, 1794; d. Sept. 10, 1794.

Mrs. Alice Denison died Sept. 24, 1794. She was married to Robert Denison, Sept. 19, 1773. He m. 2nd, Deborah Dewey, Nov. 2, 1796, and had these :

5240 DEBORAH, b. 1797; m. Dea. Charles Lewis.
5241 JOSEPH S., b. March 8, 1798; twice married.
5242 LUCY ANN, b. 1800.
5243 WILLIAM E., b. Oct. 7, 1802; m. Mary L. Allen.
5244 NOYES P., b. 1804.
5245 ALLEN, b. 1807; m. Eliza Parke.
5246 GEORGE W., b. 1809; m. Amira Chesebro'.
5247 EMELINE, b. Oct. 13, 1811; m. Frank Miner.
5248 ELIZA, b. May 8, 1815; m. Thomas Miner.

Mr. Robert Denison died Feb. 9, 1820. He lived and died in Stonington.

5234 BENADAM DENISON, (Robert[5], Benadam[4], William[3], William[2], George[1],) b. April 12, 1783, was married to Harriet Babcock, May 3, 1818, and died June 29, 1828. His children were :

5248½ EBER, b. Sept. 26, 1824; m. Elizabeth Smith.
5249 DEBORAH, b. July 19, 1819; m. Wm. Glaspie.
5250 BENADAM, b. Aug. 5, 1822.

5248½ EBER DENISON, (Benadam[6], Robert[5], Benadam[4], William[3], William[2], George[1],) b. Sept. 26, 1824, was married to

250   *11 William Denison's Descendants.*

Elizabeth Smith, March 11, 1848 ; lives in Oxford, Mich., and has :

 5251 HARRIET E., b. Feb. 21, 1849; d. Aug. 14, 1867.
 5252 MARY ALICE, b. Oct. 6, 1850; m. Daniel S. McKenzie.
 5253 WILLIAM, b. Nov. 24, 1852.
 5254 EBER J., b. June 5, 1856.

5249 DEBORAH DENISON,) Benadam[6], Robert[5], Benadam[4], William[3], William[2], George[1],) b. July 19, 1819, m. William Glaspie, July 7, 1835, in Oxford, Michigan. Their children are :

 5256 HARRIET A., b. Sept. 7, 1839; m. W. G. Hinman.
 5257 LUCY ANN, b. Feb. 7, 1842; m. Lewis Parker.
 5258 S. ELIZABETH, b. July 4, 1846; m. Silas P. Hovey.
 5259 W. DENISON, b. July 30, 1848; m. Eva Gordon.
 5260 CHARLES H., b. March 12, 1851; m. Minnie Snyder.
 5261 MARY E., b. June 22, 1853; m. Norman Goodrich.
 5262 EBER D., b. Dec. 21, 1855.

5235 JONATHAN DENISON, (Robert[5], Benadam[4], William[3], William[2], George[1],) b. Feb. 2, 1780, was married to Catherine Brown, in 1802. They lived in Stonington. He died, May 16, 1828 ; she died April 27, 1863. Their children were as follows :

 5263 DUDLEY, b. May 16, 1803; m. Amanda Spaulding.
 5264 HENRY, b. Feb. 12, 1805; m. Emily L. Allen.
 5265 REV. JESSE B., b. Aug. 14, 1808; m. Abby Denison.
 5266 ZELIDA, b. Aug. 30, 1810; m. Charles Griffing.
 5267 ANN B., b. Sept. 13, 1812; m. Thomas Yorke.
 5268 BETSEY P., b. Dec. 29, 1814; m. Galusha Owen.
 5269 SARAH, b. April 3, 1817; m. S. B. Woodmancy.
 5270 ROBERT S., b. Feb. 27, 1819; m. Susan Eggleston.
 5271 JOHN W., b. March 29, 1821; m. Naomi Lankton.
 5272 JAMES E., b. June 4, 1825; m. Nancy Lankton.
 5273 MIRANDA S., b. Sept. 15, 1826; m. Peleg Peckham, Oct. 26, 1844.

5263 DUDLEY DENISON, (Jonathan[6], Robert[5], Benadam[4], William[3], William[2], George[1],) b. May 16, 1803, was married to Amanda Spaulding, Dec. 28, 1826 ; lives at Mystic River. Has :

 5274 ERASTUS W., b. Jan. 1, 1828.
 5275 MARY E., b. Sept. 13, 1829; d. April 7, 1838.
 5276 ANN B., b. Aug. 31, 1832; d. in 1838.
 5277 LUCY E., b. Aug. 31, 1835; d. April 8, 1838.
 5278 DUDLEY A., b. Aug. 27, 1840; m. Hattie G. Owen.
 5279 MARY LEE, b. Aug. 28, 1842; m. Wm. L. Maples.

11 William Denison's Descendants.

5278 DUDLEY A. DENISON, (son of 5263 Dudley,) b. Aug. 27, 1840, *m.* Hattie G. Owen, Nov. 2, 1864, and has :

    5280 EDGAR R., b. June 18, 1866; d. April 21, 1869.
    5281 JENNIE O., b. Oct. 11, 1869.
    5282 DUDLEY, b. Oct. 6, 1871; d. Feb. 27, 1875.
    5282½ HARRIET ALBERTA. b. Feb. 16, 1878.

5279 MARY L. DENISON, (dau. of 5263 Dudley,) b. Aug. 28, 1842, *m.* William L. Maples, Feb. 16, 1864, and has :

    5283 MINNIE, b. June 10, 1865, at Mystic River, Conn.
    5284 KATE ISABEL, b. Nov. 6, 1869, at Mystic River, Conn.

5266 ZELIDA DENISON, (Jonathan[6], Robert[5], Benadam[4], William[3], William[2], George[1],) b. Aug. 30, 1810, was married in 1833, to Charles T. Griffing. They live in Boonville, Mo. Their children :

    5285 CHARLES R., b. March 22, 1834.
    5286 JULIA A., b. March 15, 1836; *m.* W. L. Taylor, Westfield, N. Y.
    5287 WILLIAM H., b. Nov., 1837; lives in Iowa.
    5288 DENISON JAMES, b. 1840; lives in Rochester, Minn.
    5289 CATHERINE ZELIDA, b. 1843; *m.* a Lawrence, of Iowa.
    5290 JOSEPH DUDLEY, b. 1846; lives at Rochester, Minn.
    5291 NETTIE, b. March 6, 1849; *m.* Mr. Matthews of Iowa.

5265 REV. JESSE B. DENISON, (Jonathan[6], Robert[5], Benadam[4], William[3], William[2], George[1],) b. Aug. 14, 1808, was married Jan. 28, 1835, to 4968 Abigail Denison. He was licensed to preach in 1834; was ordained at Warren, R. I., in 1843 ; lives now in Hartford, Conn. His children :

    5292 ABIGAIL E., b. April 15, 1836; d. April 29, 1838.
    5293 JESSE L., b. May 14, 1839; d. July 11, 1840.
    5294 MARY E., b. May 26, 1841; d. Sept., 1842.
    5295 CHARLES H., b. Sept. 7, 1844; d. July 19, 1846.
    5296 CHARLES, b. Oct. 20, 1847; *m.* Edith L. Stannard, Oct. 2, 1873.
    5297 DWIGHT, b. Feb. 21, 1851; d. in 1853.

5269 SARAH DENISON, (Jonathan[6], Robert[5], Benadam[4], William[3], William[2], George[1],) b. April 3, 1817, was married to Sylvester B. Woodmancy, of Lisbon, Conn., in 1839. He died in 1870, at Lisbon ; she died in Hartford, Conn., Jan. 3, 1878. Their children :

    5298 SARAH R., b. 1840; *m.* Enoch Bolles, in 1866.
    5299 MARY E., b. 1843; *m.* James B. Struthers, Hartford, Conn., 1867.
    5300 FRANCES M., b. 1845 ; *m.* John McAuliffe, in 1868.
    5301 CHARLES S., b. 1847.
    5302 GEORGIANA, b. 1849; *m.* Wm. G. Hooker, of New Haven.

5270 ROBERT S. DENISON, (Jonathan⁶, Robert⁵, Benadam⁴, William³, William², George¹,) b. Feb. 27, 1819, was married to Susan Eccleston, April 1, 1849; lives in Groton, Conn.; has had these:

    5303 SUSAN C., b, Jan. 31, 1850; d. Jan. 1, 1862.
    5304 WALTER R., b. Nov. 28, 1851; m. Sarah Gove, of Nahant, Mass., Sept. 10, 1879.
    5305 JAMES D., b. April 8, 1853; m.; lives in Kansas.
    5306 CHARLES F., b. Aug. 13, 1856.
    5307 CLARA M., b. Feb. 9, 1859; m. Frank Chapman of Gales Ferry, Conn., Nov. 26, 1879.
    5308 FRANK, b. Jan. 8, 1861.
    5309 MARY L., b. Jan. 1, 1864.
    5310 MARTHA R., b. April 16, 1866.
    5311 WILLIAM H., b. April 8, 1868.

5264 HENRY DENISON, (Jonathan⁶, Robert⁵, Benadam⁴, William³, William², George¹,) b. Feb. 12, 1805, m. Emily L. Allen. He d. May 8, 1864; she d. Sept. 28, 1876. Their children:

    5312 SARAH M., m. Selden Porter; is dead; three children.
    5313 MARY JANE, m. George Botton; has son George.
    5314 HENRY.
    5315 EMMA B.
    5316 CHARLES.

5272 JAMES ELLIOT DENISON, (Jonathan⁶, Robert⁵, Benadam⁴, William³, William², George¹,) b. Jan. 4, 1825, was married, Dec. 30, 1846, to Nancy Lankton, who was born Dec. 19, 1827. They have had eleven children, all born in Hartford, Conn.:

    5317 MARY A., b. Oct. 20, 1847; d. April 1, 1849.
    5318 ORPHA L., b. June 29, 1849.
    5319 JAMES EBER, b. April 16, 1851.
    5320 ABBIE A., b. March 14, 1853.
    5321 DUDLEY C., b. Oct. 8, 1855; d. Feb. 20, 1856.
    5322 ROBERT D., b. Feb. 12, 1857.
    5323 MARY IRISTA, b. Dec. 7, 1858.
    5324 FRANK A., b. Aug. 15, 1862; d. Aug. 12, 1866.
    5325 HATTIE OWEN, b. Nov. 27, 1864; d. Sept. 7, 1866.
    5326 KATIE E., b. June 10, 1867; d. Dec. 10, 1868.
    5327 JESSIE KITTIE, b. March 15, 1871.

5318 ORPHA L. DENISON, (dau. of James E.,) b. June 29, 1849, m. Alphonso Coon, Sept. 20, 1872. He d. Nov. 2, 1875. They had one child:

    5328 MABEL, b. Jan. 2, 1875.

11 William Denison's Descendants.

5267 ANN B. DENISON, (Jonathan[6], Robert[5], Benadam[4], William[3], William[2], George[1],) b. Sept. 13, 1812, was married June 21, 1832, to Thomas York. Their children :

    5329 DELOS PALMER, b. Sept. 22, 1833; *m.* Laura Lewis; 3 child.
    5330 HARRIET ZELIDA, b. July 8, 1835; *m.* G. W. Messick; 7 ch.
    5331 MERCY ANTOINETTE, b. June 26, 1836; *m.* Wm. L. Spooner; 1c.
    5332 FRANK DENISON, b. Sept. 14, 1852.

5271 JOHN W. DENISON, (Jonathan[6], Robert[5], Benadam[4], William[3], William[3], George[1],) b. March 24, 1821, *m.* Naomi Lankton, in 1844. She was born April 23, 1825. He died Feb. 24, 1850, on his way to Oregon. They had four children :

    5333 DR. JAMES SMITH, b. July 21, 1845; lives in Oregon.
    5334 SARAH NAOMI, b. Aug. 29, 1846; *m.* Eli I. Walker; 7 ch.
    5335 CATHERINE L., b. Feb. 24, 1848; *m.* John W. Asbury; 3 ch.
    5336 JOHN NATHAN, b. Dec. 25, 1849; is a Methodist preacher.

Mrs. Naomi (Lankton) Denison *m.* 2nd, Thomas Smith Mills, in 1853, and has had five more children. She lives in Brownville, Linn Co., Oregon.

5268 BETSEY P. DENISON, (Jonathan[6], Robert[5], Benadam[4], William[3], William[2], George[1],) b. Dec. 29, 1814, *m.* Galusha Owen, Dec. 26, 1841. They had :

    5337 JENNIE AMELIA, b. Feb. 18, 1844; *m.* DeB. R. Keim, June 25, 1872.
    5338 FREDERIC DENISON, b. Jan. 19, 1854.
    5339 CHARLES SUMNER HERBERT, b. May 7, 1858.

5273 MIRANDA S. DENISON, (Jonathan[6], Robert[5], Benadam[4], William[3], William[2], George[1],) b. Sept. 15, 1826, was married in 1847, to Peleg Peckham, b. in Hopkinton, R. I., June 26, 1818; lived in St. Louis; d. June 21, 1851. One child :

    5340 CHARLES CLARK, b. March 14, 1848.

5337 JENNIE AMELIA OWEN, (dau of 5268 Betsey P. Denison and Galusha Owen,) b. Feb. 18, 1844, in Hartford, Conn., was married, June 25, 1872, to DeB. Randolph Keim, of Reading, Pa., author and journalist. In the war of the rebellion, Mr. Keim was, from 1861 to 1864, war correspondent of the New York Herald, at the head-quarters of Generals Grant and McPherson. In the winter of '64-5, he was on the editorial staff of the Herald. Next he was appointed the Herald's foreign correspondent in Africa, Asia, and Australia. In 1870,

11 William Denison's Descendants.

President Grant made him agent of the U. S., to inspect consulates in all parts of the world. He has since resided in Washington, as correspondent of leading papers in Philadelphia, St. Louis, etc. The children:

    5341 ELIZABETH RANDOLPH, b. Aug. 1, 1873, at Martha's Vineyard, Mass.
    5342 HARRIET VIRGINIA, b. July 9, 1875, at Martha's Vineyard, Ms.
    5343 DE BENNEVILLE, b. June 13, 1880, at Reading, Pa.

5334 SARAH NAOMI DENISON, (dau. of 5271 John W.)—(John W[7], Jonathan[6], Robert[5], Benadam[4], William[3], William[2], George[1],) b. Aug. 29, 1846, was married, Feb. 1864, to Eli J. Walker. They live at Fort Kalamath Reservation, Oregon. Children:

    5344 ULYSSES SHERIDAN, b. in 1864.
    5345 PHILIP H. GRANT, b. in 1866.
    5346 JOHN W. DENISON, b. in 1868.
    5347 IRA ELLIS, b. in 1869.
    5348 JEREMIAH THOMAS, b. in 1871.
    5349 WILLIAM, b. in 1873.
    5350 NETTIE NAOMI, b. 1876.

5335 CATHARINE L. DENISON, (John W.[7], Jonathan[6], Robert[5], Benadam[4], William[3], William[2], George[1],) b. Feb. 21, 1848, was married Dec., 1863, to John W. Asbury Belien. They live at Fort Kalamath Reservation, Jackson Co., Oregon. Children:

    5351 ALICE, b. in 1864.
    5352 JESSE GREEN, b. in 1868.
    5353 EVA, b. in 1869.

5236 JAMES DENISON, (Robert[5], Benadam[4], William[3], William[2], George[1], b. July 1, 1785, was married, Nov. 16, 1817, to Cynthia Babcock. He lived in Brookfield, N. Y., and died there, July 4, 1857. He had these children:

    5354 ORRIN B , b. Oct. 8, 1825; m. Carolina A. Langworth, Jan. 3, 1861; no child.
    5355 HARRIET, b. March 22, 1819; twice married.
    5356 FIDELIA, b. March 12, 1821; m. L. P. Clark.
    5357 OLIVIA, b. Sept. 4, 1822; m. Allen Green.
    5358 VASHTI L., b. June 5, 1827; twice married.
    5359 ANN JANETTE, b. March 15, 1828; m. J. T. Stillman.
    5360 JAMES RAY, b. Oct. 18, 1835; m. Mary Elliott, Aug. 30, 1855; has Addie, b. Jan. 10, 1866.

11 William Denison's Descendants.

5357 OLIVIA DENISON, (James[6], Robert[5], Benadam[4], William[3], William[2], George[1],) b. Sept. 4, 1822, was married to Allen Green, Oct. 15, 1841; lived in Hampton, Iowa; d. Oct. 8, 1868. She had:

    5361 HATTIE A., b. Jan. 5, 1847; d. Dec. 24, 1856.

5359 ANN JANETTE DENISON, (James[6], Robert[5], Benadam[4], William[3], William[2], George[1],) b. March 15, 1828, was married to J. T. Stillman, Sept. 9, 1850. Their children:

    5362 CLARA, b. June 2, 1854.
    5363 NELLIE, b. June 22, 1857.
    5364 HATTIE, b. Oct. 29, 1859.
    5365 JOHN, b. Feb. 15, 1872.

5356 FIDELIA DENISON, (James[6], Robert[5], Benadam[4], William[3], William[2], George[1],) b. March 12, 1821, was married to Lucius P. Clark, a lawyer, May 4, 1842; lives at Morrisville, N. Y.; has but one child:

    5366 EDWARD PAYSON, b. Sept. 21, 1863.

5238 ALICE DENISON, (Robert[5], Benadam[4], William[3], William[2], George[1],) b. June 4, 1790, was married to Wm. E. Dewey, Sept. 25, 1809. She d. Feb. 10, 1856. He d. April 10, 1858. Their children:

    5367 WILLIAM M., b. Jan 22, 1811; m. Eliza Brown.
    5368 MARY ANN, b. April 25, 1813; four times married.
    5369 RICHARD W., b. 1816; d. in 1837; not married.
    5370 JOSEPH N., b. July 20, 1819; m. Sarah Brown; d. Oct. 29, 1860.
    5371 ISRAEL R., b. July 16, 1823; m. Abby Eldredge.
    5372 PHEBE ESTHER, b. June 17, 1826; m. Gurdon M. Lamphere.
    4373 EMELINE, b. April 3, 1831; m. Rev. Wm. A. Taylor.

5240 DEBORAH DENISON, (Robert[5], Benadam[4], William[3], William[2], George[1],) b. in 1797, was married, Oct. 22, 1820, to Dea. Charles Lewis; lived in Sherburne, N. Y.; d. Sept. 1, 1872. Her children:

    5374 AN UNNAMED INFANT.
    5375 HARRIET, b. Jan. 20, 1829; m. Lucius Newton; had Helen and Bell; d. in 1869.
    5376 JANE, b. Nov. 3, 1831; d. Nov. 20, 1843.
    5377 CHARLES W., b. Aug. 4, 1830.

5241 JOSEPH S. DENISON, (Robert[5], Benadam[4], William[3], William[2], George[1],) b. March 8, 1798, was married, 1st, to Martha Gallup. In 1826, he m. 2nd, Maria Babcock, by whom he had these:

5378 HORACE P., b. Sept. 6, 1828.
5379 NOYES W., b. July 10, 1836.
5380 ALLEN EUGENE, b. June 1, 1842; d. in the war; not married.

Joseph S. Denison lived in Brookfield, N. Y. He m. 3d, Graty Smith; he d. Jan. 25, 1868.

5378 HORACE P. DENISON, (Joseph S.[6], Robert[5], Benadam[4], William[3], William[2], George[1],) b. Sept. 6, 1828, was married in 1851, to M. B. Smith; lives in Saginaw, Mich.; has had these :

5381 DEVILLE E., b. Sept. 16, 1852; m. Jennie S. Bloor, Jan. 19, '76, and had : Janet Irvin. b. May 10, '79.
5382 IDA M., b. July 13, 1855.
5383 CHARLES H., b. March 10, 1858.
5384 FRANK E., b. Jan. 15, 1860; d. March 25, 1871.
5385 HARRIET G., b. Dec. 20, 1872.

5379 NOYES W. DENISON, (Joseph S.[6], Robert[5], Benadam[4], William[3], William[2], George[1],) b. July 10, 1836, was married, June 27, 1860, to Z. DeEtta Ellison; lives in Saginaw, Mich.; has had these :

5386 ROSA MAY, b. May 27, 1861.
5387 ETTIE MARIA, b. Jan. 26, 1865.
5388 WILLIAM E., b. Feb. 17, 1869; d. May 18, 1873.
5389 ADELINE M., b. Oct. 30, 1873.
5390 EUGENE, b. March 28, 1875; d Dec. 30, 1875.

5242 LUCY ANN DENISON, (Robert[5], Benadam[4], William[3], William[2], George[1],) b. in 1800, was married, 1st, to Nathaniel Lewis, July 7, 1822 ; and 2nd, to Capt. Henry Crary.

5391 ELIZABETH; m. Alfred West of Eureka, Cal.
5392 JANE; m. Capt. Hall of Westerly, R. I.; no child :

5243 WILLIAM E. DENISON, (Robert[5], Benadam[4], William[3], William[2], George[1],) b. Oct. 7, 1802, was married to Mary L. Allen, March 7, 1827 ; lived at Nepaug, Conn, and had :

5393 MARY ANN, b. Dec. 21, 1827; m. Warren N. Jones, 1848.
5394 WILLIAM A., b. Sept. 27, 1830; m. Lucy L. Wright.
5395 ELIZA A., b. Nov. 26, 1835; m. Edwin R. Merrill.
5396 DEBORAH ANN, b. June 21, 1840; m. Edward Ackart.

5393 MARY ANN DENISON, (dau. of 5243 Wm. E.,) b. Dec. 21, 1827, m. W. N. Jones, and had :

5397 MARY L., b. June 25, 1849; m. Charles Wilson in 1869.

5394 WILLIAM A. DENISON, (William E.[6], Robert[5], Benadam[4], William[3], William[2], George[1],) b. Sept. 27, 1830, was married to Lucy L. Wright, Oct. 20, 1856, at Nepaug, Conn. They have had:

 5398 MARY L., b. Aug. 20, 1857; m. Wm. Butler, Oct., 1876.
 5399 WILLIAM N., b. Aug. 7, 1858.
 5400 ADDIE E., b. Sept. 17, 1859.
 5401 BELLE E., b. Sept. 27, 1863.

5395 ELIZA A. DENISON, (William E.[6], Robert[5], Benadam[4], William[3], William[2], George[1],) b. Nov. 26, 1835, was married, Oct. 20, 1854, to Edwin R. Merrill; live at Nepaug, Conn. Children:

 5402 ELLA J., b. Jan. 9, 1856; m. B. L. Belden, July 1, 1876.
 5403 FRANK D., b. April 1, 1860.
 5404 CHARLES L., b. July 23, 1863.
 5405 BURTON A., b. Aug. 17, 1867.

5396 DEBORAH A. DENISON, (William E.[6], Robert[5], Benadam[4], William[3], William[2], George[1],) b. June 21, 1840, was married, Nov. 21, 1860, to Edward Ackart; lives at Collinsville, Conn. One child:

 5406 IDA ELIZA, b. Oct. 22, 1861; d. Dec. 3, 1861.

5244 NOYES P. DENISON, (Robert[5], Benadam[4], William[3], William[2], George[1],) b. in 1804, m. Harriet L. Smith. He d. in Virginia, in 1875. He had children; among them was:

 5407 NOYES R. DENISON, who m. Mary A. Miner, Feb. 17, 1861. He lived in Groton, Conn.; died July 4, 1876. Children:
  5408 GEORGE E., b. May 8, 1862.
  5409 MARY E., b. Feb. 6, 1865.
  5410 EMILY M., b. June 13, 1866.
  5411 RALPH H., b. Oct. 4, 1871.
  5412 ISABEL N., b. July 12, 1875.

3245 ALLEN DENISON, (Robert[5], Benadam[5], William[3], William[2], George[1],) b. in 1807, m. Eliza Parke, Dec. 9, 1832, lived at Noank, Conn., and had:

 5413 GEORGE P., b. May 8, 1834; lost at sea in 1850.
 5414 CYRUS A., b. Sept. 12, 1840; d. Sept. 16, 1869.
 5415 ELIZABETH, b. Nov. 27, 1843; m. Elias Brown, Dec. 6, 1865; no child.

5246 GEORGE WARREN DENISON, (Robert[6], Benadam[4], William[3], William[2], George[1],) b. in 1809, was married to Amira Chesebro', Aug. 19, 1838; lives at Noank, Conn., and has had these:

 5416 FRANCIS W., b. June 17, 1840; d. Aug. 14, 1841.
 5417 FANNY E., b. Oct. 7, 1844; d. March 30, 1846.

11 William Denison's Descendants.

5418 ROBERT W., b. June 23, 1842; d. Jan. 23, 1847.
5419 MARY, b. Feb. 17, 1852; d. May 14, 1853.
5420 H. AMIRA, b. Oct. 2, 1847; m. John F. Murphy, July 16, 1865, and has:
    5421 WARREN D., b. Feb. 5, 1870.
    5422 WILLIAM P., b. July 10, 1871.

5247 EMELINE DENISON, (Robert⁵, Benadam⁴, William³, William², George¹,) b. Oct. 13, 1811, was married to Francis W. Minor, June 7, 1835. He went to sea with his son William E., Feb. 18, 1865, and was never again heard from. They had:

5423 FRANCIS E., b. July 15, 1837; d. Dec. 13, 1839.
5424 FRANCIS W., b. May 23, 1843.
5425 CHARLES A., b. Aug. 31, 1847.
5426 EMELINE, b. Feb. 23, 1844; m. Samuel B. Allen, Sept. 3, 1874.
5427 WILLIAM EDWIN, b. March 5, 1845; lost at sea in 1865.
5428 ALONZO S., b. June 25, 1849; d. March 27, 1858.

5248 ELIZA A. DENISON, (Robert⁵, Benadam⁴, William³, William², George¹,) b. May 8, 1815, m. Thomas Minor, Aug. 25, 1835. She d. Feb. 15, 1845; he d. April 2, 1847. Their children:

5429 GEORGE WARREN, b. June 16, 1836; d. Jan. 28, 1858; not mar.
5430 CHARLES HENRY, b. July 1, 1837; d. April 26, 1842.
5431 ELIZA, b. July 21, 1841; m. 3230 Hiram C. Denison.

All the deaths in this family were from consumption.

5132 GEORGE DENISON, (Benadam⁴, William³, William², George¹,) b. Oct. 8, 1751, was married in Stonington, Conn., to Theody Brown, Jan. 9, 1772, and afterwards went to Hartland, Vt., where he was a very prominent man, known as "Col. George Denison." He had these children recorded in Stonington and Vermont:

5432 BENADAM, b. March 31, 1773; d. Jan. 8, 1837.
5433 JONATHAN, b. April 26, 1775; d. Oct. 22, 1779.
5434 SARAH, b. May 3, 1777; m. Charles Geer.
5435 GEORGE W., M. D., b. Oct. 16, 1779; lived at Burke, Vt.
5436 AMOS, b. April 27, 1782; d. March 28, 1834.
5436½ THEODY, b. June 27, 1784; d. Oct. 2, 1784.
5437 ANN BORODELL, b. Dec. 2, 1785; m. Wm. Barrett; d. Feb. 3,'55.
5438 MASON, b. March 18, 1788; d. Sept. 27, 1838.
5439 LUCY, b. June 15, 1790; m. Dr. John S. Jenks.
5440 DANIEL, b. May 15, 1794; m. Pamelia L. Head.

Mrs. Theody (Brown) Denison d. April 25, 1800. He m. 2nd, Submit Lyman, Feb. 12, 1804. He died Jan. 19, 1829.

11 William Denison's Descendants. 259

5434 SARAH DENISON, (George[5], Benadam[4], William[3], William[2], George[1],) b. May 3, 1777, was married in Hartland, Vt., Dec. 17, 1799, to Charles Geer. They lived in Brooklyn, Pa. She died March 16, 1841 ; he died Feb. 5, 1842. Their children :

    5441 SARAH DENISON, b. Feb. 12, 1801.
    5442 LUCY F., b. Oct. 16, 1802.
    5443 CHARLES D., b. Oct. 29, 1805.
    5444 ROBERT W., b. April 17, 1808.
    5445 JULIA A., b. May 11, 1815.

5440 DANIEL DENISON, (George[5], Benadam[4], William[3], William[2], George[1],) b. May 15, 1794, was married to Pamelia Lathrop Head, April 18, 1827. She was born Jan. 22, 1801, and d. Aug. 21, 1863. He d. Jan. 21, 1861. They lived on his father's homestead in Hartland, Vt. Their children :

    5446 DANIEL BORODEL, b. Jan. 1, 1828. See Appendix.
    5447 PAMELIA SUBMIT, b. March 19, 1830. See Appendix.
    5448 GEORGE, b. Nov. 24, 1831.
    5449 JOHN HEAD, b. Aug. 29, 1833; *m.* Louisa A. Porter, Queechy, Vt.
    5450 MARY ANN, b. April 30, 1835 ; d. March 16, 1838.
    5451 HELEN JANE, b. April 18, 1837; *m.* Hosea Q. Thompson.
    5452 HENRY CLAY, b. May 18, 1841. See Appendix.

5448 GEORGE DENISON, (Daniel[6], George[5], Benadam[4], William[3], William[2], George[1],) b. Nov. 24, 1831, was married to Emma Abbott Webster, of St. Louis, Mo., Feb. 3, 1864. She was b. Jan. 8, 1843. They live in St Louis. Children :

    5453 HENRY WEBSTER, b. Nov. 22, 1864.
    5454 ROBERT CHARLES, b. July 22, 1868.
    5455 GEO. BORODEL, b. Feb. 3, 1871.
    5456 HELEN ABBOTT, b. Jan. 31, 1873.

5451 HELEN JANE DENISON, (Daniel[6], George[5], Benadam[4], William[3], William[2], George[1],) b. April 30, 1835, was married, May 15, 1855, to Hosea Q. Thompson. They live in Stoneham, Mass. Children :

    5457 HOSEA, b. March 20, 1856; d. March 26, 1866.
    5458 ADDIE LOUISE, b. April 9, 1858.
    5459 JESSIE ELLENWOOD, b. July 27, 1860.
    5460 JAMES MADISON, b. July 31, 1876.

5432 BENADAM DENISON, (George[5], Benadam[4], William[3], William[2], George[1],) b. March 31, 1773, was married, first, April 11, 1802, to Polly Morse ; and second, to Eunice Wil-

11 William Denison's Descendants.

liams, Dec. 10, 1817. He lived at Montrose, Pa., and d. there, Feb. 8, 1837. His second wife d. Oct. 12, 1872. His children :

5461 BENADAM, Jr., b. May 10, 1810; m. Adeline B. Blair.
5462 POLLY, b. Aug. 24, 1805; m. Sloan Hamilton; she, her husband, and their children, are all dead.
5463 OLIVER b July 16, 1807; is a printer.
5464 JOHN W., b. Sept. 4, 1818; twice married.
5465 ELIZABETH, b. March 11, 1821; m. R. T. Stevens.
5466 GEORGE M., b. Nov. 22, 1823; m. Sallie M. Crickers.
5467 EUNICE, b Dec. 13, 1825; m. R. T. Stevens.
5468 CHARLES G., b. May 23, 1828; m. Martha A. Laud.
5469 FREDERIC. b. May 7, 1830; m.; lives at Mahopany, Pa.
5470 LEWIS B., b. Aug. 4, 1832; d. Sept. 6, 1850.
5471 ANN M., b. Dec. 8, 1834; d. Oct. 27, 1836.
5472 ADAM B., b. March 9, 1837; m.; P. O., Shaucks, O.

5461 BENADAM DENISON, JR., (Benadam[6], George[5], Benadam[4], William[3], William[2], George[1],) b. May 10, 1810, was married, first, March 25, 1843, to Adeline B. Blair, who d. Feb. 23, 1857; and second, Sept. 9, 1859, to Ruth Ann Graves, b. March 24, 1840. He lives at Binghampton, N. Y. His children :

5473 ALFRED B., b. April 17, 1844; m. Louise Bartholomew.
5474 JOSEPH M., b. Sept. 4, 1845; m. Millie Willis.
5475 IMOGENE, b. Dec. 27, 1848; m. Eugene Piper.
5476 VIRGIE, b. Dec. 17, 1852; m. Herbert Willis.
5477 IDA, b. Aug. 4, 1854.
5478 BELLE. b. Jan. 13, 1861.
5479 LOUISE, b. Sept. 2, 1866.

5476 VIRGIE DENISON, (dau. of 5461 Benadam, Jr.,) m. Herbert Willis, April 26, 1876, and has :

5480 LENA, b. May 11, 1877.

5473 ALFRED B. DENISON, (son of 5461 Benadam, Jr.,) b. April 17, 1844, was married, Sept. 18, 1866, to Louise Bartholomew, lives in Binghampton, N. Y. Children :

5481 WILLIAM, b. Oct. 9, 1867.
5482 MAY, b. Sept. 26, 1871.

5463 OLIVER DENISON, (Benadam[6], George[5], Benadam[4], William[3], William[2], George[1],) b. July 16, 1807, m. Laura Booth, Nov. 3, 1830. She was born, Aug. 14, 1814. They live in Dundee, Yates Co., N. Y. Their children :

5483 WILLIAM O., b. March 14, 1832; m.; lives in Washington, D.C. No child.

11 William Denison's Descendants.

5484 Charles E., b. March 2, 1836; m. Lydia Caddock. Children: Lucy, b. Sept. 2, 1858; William, b. April 5, 1860. Charles E. Denison was killed in battle at Dallas, Ga.

5485 Mary, b. May 10, 1839; d. 1842.

5486 Edward A., March 2, 1841; m. Caroline A. Prosser, Nov. 19, 1859; lives at Hall's Corners, Ontario Co., N. Y. Their children: Lodema, b. in 1861; Clara, b. in 1865; Oliver, b. in 1867; Mary, b. in 1869; Warren, b. in 1872.

5487 Benadam Denison, b. Sept. 11, 1844; m. MaryWoodyard of Va.; lives at Hall's Corners, Ontario Co., N. Y. Children: William, b. in 1872; Elmer, in 1874; Minnie in 1876.

5488 Helen Denison, b. March 27, 1847; m. Jesse Caddock; lives at Dundee, N. Y. Children: Franklin, b. Dec. 30, 1863; Elmer, b. April 10, 186 .

5489 Clara, b. Feb. 27, 1850; m. Geo. W. Sheffield, Oct. 25, 1869; lives at Dundee, N. Y. Children: Nettie, b. July 23, 1871; Arthur, b. Jan. 1, 1874.

5490 George, b. Dec. 25, 1852; m. Ella Weaver, March 8, 1874; lives at Dundee, N, Y. Children: William, b. Sept. 14, 1876; Rufus, b. March 12, 1878; Emma, b. Aug. 18, 1879.

5491 Lida, b. Aug. 30, 1855; m. Rufus Alderman, Oct. 25, 1869; lives at Dundee, N. Y. Children: Maud, b. Dec. 14, 1871; Henry, b. Feb. 5, 1874; Edith, b. Jan. 13, 1876; Zadie, b. March 8, 1879.

5464 John W. Denison, M. D., (Benadam[6], George[5], Benadam[4], William[3], William[2], George[1],) b. Sept. 4, 1818, was married, first, Sept. 23, 1843, to C. M. Fopett, who d. July 18, 1854; and second, Jan. 10, 1856, to C. C. Whitcomb. He lives at Carney, Pa. Children:

5492 George E., b. in 1844; d. Feb. 4, 1847.
5493 Ann E., b. in 1846; d. Jan. 25, 1851.
5494 Emeline M., b. Dec. 21, 1847; m. Geo. McCabe.
5495 Lucia M., b. March 15, 1852.
5495½ Sarah H., b. Jan. 24, 1857; d. Feb. 1, 1857.

5465 Elizabeth Denison, (Benadam[6], George[5], Benadam[4], William[3], William[2], George[1],) b. March 11, 1821, was married, May 2, 1843, to Reuben T. Stevens; lived at Great Bend, Pa.; d. there after 1860. Her children:

5496 Mary E., b. Feb. 20, 1849.
5497 Cornelia J., b. July 28, 1850.
5498 George W., b. Nov. 1, 1852.
5499 Philander, b. Jan. 28, 1856.
5500 Charles, b. Dec. 18, 1860.

5467 Eunice Denison, (Benadam[6], George[5], Benadam[4], William[3], William[2], George[1],) was the second wife of Reuben

T. Stevens, (whose first wife was her sister Elizabeth,) to whom she was married, March 13, 1866. Her children:

    5501 LIBBIE, b. Oct. 28, 1868; d. Feb. 22, 1869.
    5502 CARRIE, b. Jan. 21, 1870.

5466 GEORGE M. DENISON, (Benadam[6], George[5], Benadam[4], William[3], William[2], George[1],) b. Nov. 22, 1823, was married, May 31, 1852, to Sallie M. Cricker, b. June 16, 1832. He lived at Dimock, Pa., and d. there Jan. 12, 1867. His children:

    5503 CHARLES H., b. May 15, 1853.
    5504 KATE LOUISE, b. June 18, 1855.
    5505 ANNA MARIA, b. April 23, 1857.
    5506 THOMAS JEFFERSON, b. March 27, 1859.
    5507 GEORGE M., b. March 29, 1861.
    5507½ MARTHA ELIZABETH, b. Oct. 23, 1864.

5468 CHARLES G. DENISON, (Benadam[6], George[5], Benadam[4], William[3], William[2], George[1],) b. May 23, 1828, is a highly respectable merchant of Corning, N. Y., where he has lived since 1848. He has been four times elected mayor of the city, and has held other important public positions. He m. Martha A. Laud, April 10, 1855. She d. at Corning, May 11, 1880, aged 46, a greatly beloved wife and mother, and a bright and shining light in the church. The children:

    5508 M. ELLA, b. Feb. 27, 1856.
    5509 CARRIE E., b. June 29, 1861.
    5510 CHARLES L. b. July 1, 1866.

5435 DR. GEORGE WASHINGTON DENISON, (George[5], Benadam[4], William[3], William[2], George[1],) b. Oct. 16, 1779, was married to Sally Jenks, and lived at Burke, Vt. He d. March 4, 1857; she d. Jan. 25, 1843, aged 53. Their children:

    5511 GEORGE JENKS, b. June 7, 1814; m. Ann Bundy.
    5512 DANIEL BROWN, b. Aug. 4, 1815; lives at Port Perry, C. W.
    5513 EMELINE, b. Sept. 20, 1816; m. Dr. Selim Newell.
    5514 WILLIAM GALLUP, b. March 2, 1818; m. Harriet Sanderson.
    5515 BENJ. FRANKLIN, b. June 2, 1820; m. Susan B. Gillespie.
    5516 CHARLES OTIS, b. June 7, 1822; m. Martha McGaffey.
    5517 LAFAYETTE, b. May 26, 1825; m. Mary J. ——.
    5518 DEWITT CLINTON, b. May 3, 1830; m. Anne A. Dyer.

5511 GEORGE JENKS DENISON, (son of 5435 Dr. George W.,) b. June 7, 1814, was married, Dec. 23, 1838, to Ann

11 William Denison's Descendants.

Bundy, who d. Nov. 29, 1877 ; lived in Burke, Vt. Two children :

    5519 Ann Maria. b. March 31, 1845 ; *m.* Henry Bickford, M. D.
    5520 Mary Eunice, b. July 10, 1856.

5513 Emeline Denison, (dau. of 5435 Dr. George W.,) b. Sept. 20, 1816, was married, in 1835, to Dr. Selim Newell, who d. in 1871 ; lived in St. Johnsbury, Vt. Children :

    5521 Henry Clay, b. Oct. 19, 1835; *m.* H. Maria Hazen, in 1866.
    5522 Geo. Washington, b. Aug. 3, 1837; d. in 1851.
    5523 Ellen Amanda. b. June 5, 1843; *m.* Geo. H. Bradford, 1875.
    5524 Charles Denison, b. Oct. 17, 1846; *m.* Elizabeth Kilbourne, 1876.
    5525 Addie Estelle, b. March 4, 1848; *m.* Henry G. Ely, 1867.
    5526 Mary Emeline. b. Sept. 24, 1850; *m.* Robert McKunion, 1873.
    5527 Etta Mattocks, b. Sept. 16, 1853,

5514 William Gallup Denison, (son of 5435 Dr. George W.,) b. March 2, 1818, was married, Sept. 2, 1839, to Harriet Sanderson ; lives in Enfield, N. H. Five children :

    5528 William H. H., b. Nov. 25, 1840; lives at Derby line. Vt.
    5529 Benjamin F., b. April 1, 1843; lives at Enfield, N. H,
    5530 Jane Amelia. b. Jan. 27, 1849; lives in Chicago, Ill.
    5531 Wesley Clarence, b. May 29, 1855; lives at Enfield, N. H.
    5532 Arthur Adelbert, b. May 16, 1858; d. Aug. 1, 1864.

5515 Benj. Franklin Denison, (son of 5435 Dr. George W.,) b. June 2, 1820, was married in 1857, to Susan B. Gillespie, of L. I.; lives at Port Townsend, Washington Territory ; no child.

5516 Charles Otis Denison, M. D., (son of 5435 Dr. George W.,) b. June 7, 1822, was married, Oct. 10, 1849, to Martha McGaffey ; lived in Lyndon, Vt.; d. May 1, 1860. Two children :

    5533 Sarah A. b. Oct. 27, 1855; *m.* Charles M. Mower.
    5534 Charles O., b. Sept. 6, 1860.

5517 Dr. Lafayette Denison, (son of 5435 Dr. George W.,) b. May 26, 1825, was married to Mary J. ——— ; lived at Fidelity, Ill.; d. March 23, 1863. Two children :

    5535 Theodore M., b. Aug. 4, 1862; d. June 27, 1863.
    5536 Emeline, b. Feb. 20, 1861.

5518 DeWitt Clinton Denison, (son of 5435 Dr. George W.,) b. May 3, 1830, *m.* Anne Abbott Dyer, of Calais, Me., May 3, 1864 ; lives at LaConner, Washington Ter. Children :

11 William Denison's Descendants.

5537 HARRIET DYER, b. Nov. 23, 1865.
5538 BENJ. FRANKLIN, b. Jan. 5, 1869.
5539 MILLE AUSTIN, b. Nov. 2, 1879.
5540 GEO. WILLIAM, b. Feb. 15, 1875.
5541 CHARLES EDWARD, b. Aug 19, 1877.

5438 DR. MASON DENISON, (George[5], Benadam[4], William[3], William[2], George[1],) b. March 18, 1788, was married, Dec. 18, 1814, to Wealthy Lathrop; lived and d. at Montrose, Pa.; d. Sept. 27, 1838. His children:

5542 GEORGIANA S., b. Sept. 7, 1820; d. March 23, 1837.
5543 GEORGE, b. April 8, 1815; d. Feb. 10, 1819.
5544 JANE ANTOINETTE, b. June 16, 1823.
5545 WILLIAM D., b. May 28, 1827.
5546 DANIEL MASON, b. June 28, 1825.

5544 JANE ANTOINETTE DENISON, (dau. of 5438 Dr. Mason,) b. June 16, 1823, was married Oct. 1, 1849, to Edmund Baldwin; lives at Montrose, Pa. Children:

5547 BENJAMIN L., b. July 2, 1850; m. Lucy E. Howell.
5548 HARRY D., b. Sept. 27, 1852.
5549 WILLIAM B., b. Dec. 14, 1858.
5550 GEORGE S., b Jan. 11, 1855; m. Lizzie L. Frink.

5446 DANIEL M. DENISON, (son of 5438 Dr. Mason,) b. June 28, 1825, was married, Sept., 1859, to Isabella Stryker, of Binghampton, N. Y., who d. Aug. 14, 1871. He lives at Augusta, Ga. Children:

5551 ROSA ANTOINETTE, b. Oct. 6, 1862.
5552 GEORGIANA KATE, b. Nov. 30, 1864.
5553 ELLA BELLE, b. Aug. 21, 1866; d. Sept. 4, 1867.
5554 ELLA STRYKER, b. Sept. 5, 1869.

5545 WILLIAM D. DENISON, (son of 5438 Dr. Mason,) b. May 28, 1827, died at Gainesville, Florida, in 1859, and left two children:

5555 MASON.
5556 GEORGIA.

5439 LUCY DENISON, (George[5], Benadam[4], William[3], William[2], George[1],) b. June 15, 1790, was married, Jan. 14, 1816, to Dr. John S. Jenks, b. Aug. 25, 1785. They lived at Burke, Vt.; she d. May 8, 1837; he d. Jan 2, 1875. Their children:

5557 DR. NATHANIEL, b. Oct. 14, 1818.
5558 DANIEL D., b. Aug. 11, 1822; d. April 24, 1825.
5559 THEODA BROWN, b. Sept. 30, 1824; d. Dec. 13, 1842.
5560 LUCY D., b. Nov. 27, 1830; twice married; 3 children.

5557 Dr. Nathaniel Jenks, (son of 5439 Lucy and Dr. John S.,) b. Oct. 14, 1818, was married, Aug. 29, 1847, to Lucy Thornton, b. April 2, 1826. They live at Barnston, Province of Quebec. Children:

    5561 John Nathaniel, b. July 18, 1848.
    5562 Leslie H., b. Dec. 28, 1849.
    5563 Lucy Denison, b. July 15, 1855; d. March 24, 1862.
    5564 Minnie Gertrude, b. Oct. 26, 1860.

III.

4903 George Denison, (William[2], George[1],) b. Feb. 28, 1692, was married, June 6, 1717, to Lucy Gallup. They lived on the old homestead farm in Stonington, Conn., and had these children:

    5565 Ann, b. Aug. 6, 1718; d. April 25, 1725.
    5566 A. Daughter, b. and d. in September, 1720.
    5567 Lucy, b. Oct. 13, 1721; d. April 14, 1725.
    5568 Mary, b. Nov. 27, 1723; d. July 14, 1724.
    5569 George, b. Jul. 3, 1725; m. Jane Smith.
    5570 William, b. June 14, 1727; m. Priscilla Fellows.
    5571 Mercy, b. Feb. 24, 1729; m. Elisha Gallup.
    5572 Esther, b. Sept. 16, 1732; d. Nov. 14, 1754.
    5573 Samuel, b. Feb. 18, 1735; d Sept. 10, 1754.
    5574 David, b. Jan. 20, 1736; m. Keziah Smith.

5569 George Denison, Jr., (George[3], William[2], George[1],) b. July 3, 1725, was married to Jane Smith, (dau. of 2501 Mary (Denison) Smith,) Feb. 23, 1748. They lived in Stonington, on the old homestead, and had:

    5575 Lucy, b. Feb. 9, 1750; m. Elisha Williams; had a large family.
    5576 George, b. Sept. 16, 1753; m. Abby Palmer.
    5577 Dorothy, twin, b. April 8, 1756; m. Daniel Denison, son of 2503 Beebe.
    5578 William, twin, b. April 8, 1756; m. Anna Slack.
    5579 Oliver, b. March 2, 1758; m. Martha Williams.
    5580 Nathan, b. April 8, 1760; m.; settled in Coleraine, Mass.
    5581 Gilbert, b. Sept. 18, 1762; m. Huldah Palmer.
    5582 Elisha, b. Oct. 12, 1764; died on the Jersey prison ship, in Rev.
    5583 Dudley, (Dr.) b. July 25, 1767; m. Nancy Latimer in 1795; d. Oct. 1, 1797, aged 29 years; no child.
    5584 Esther, b. Nov. 16, 1769; m. Enoch Burrows.
    5585 Jane, b. Sept. 16, 1772; d. when 7 years old.

11 William Denison's Descendants.

5571 MERCY DENISON, (George³, William², George¹,) b. Feb. 24, 1730, was married to Elisha Gallup, Jan. 28, 1747. Their children:

    5586 ANN, b. June 3, 1748.
    5587 ESTHER, b. Oct. 15, 1750.
    5588 MERCY, b. July 11, 1753.
    5589 ELISHA, b. Oct. 16, 1755; d. Nov. 16, 1762.
    5590 EUNICE, b. April 1, 1758.
    5591 JOSEPH, b. Oct. 18, 1760.
    5592 MARTHA, b. March 30, 1763.
    5593 ELISHA, b. April 30, 1766.
    5594 EDWARD, b. Dec. 31, 1768.
    5595 DENISON, b. Aug. 30, 1776.

5576 GEORGE DENISON, (George⁴, George³, William², George¹,) b. Sept. 16, 1753, was married to Abby Palmer, in 1778, and d. in 1835. Children:

    5596 GEORGE, b. 1780; m. Hannah Latham.
    5597 WILLIAM G., b. April 26, 1788; lived in Vermont.
    5598 HENRY, b. 1784; d. in Kentucky.
    5599 JULIA, b. May 20, 1798; m. John Phillips of Somers, Ct.

5580 NATHAN DENISON, (George⁴, George³, William², George¹,) b. April 8, 1760, m. Thankful Dean, in 1787; lived in Coleraine, Mass.; d. in 1803; she d. in 1814. His children:

    5600 NATHAN, b. in 1789; m. Acsah Hendee.
    5601 PRUDENCE, b. in 1791; m. John D. Gallup.
    5602 THANKFUL, b. Aug. 1, 1794; m. Calvin Tyler, of Norwich, Ct.

5597 WILLIAM G. DENISON, (George⁵, George⁴, George³, William², George¹,) b. April 26, 1788, was married, Feb. 24, 1813, to Esther Strickland, b. Oct. 19, 1789; lived in Vermont. He d. at Stafford, Conn., May 23, 1826; she d. at Palmer, Mass., July 16, 1869. Children:

    5603 HARRIET A., b. Aug. 20, 1815; m. Rev. B. R. Harrington; no ch.
    5604 FRANCES A., b. May 28, 1817; m. a Mr. Alden.
    5605 MARTHA J., b. Aug. 14, 1818; m. Geo. Mooers.
    5606 ESTHER, b. Dec. 8, 1819; m. A. M. Butterfield.
    5607 BETSEY S., b. Feb. 23, 1821.
    5608 CHARLOTTE A., b. Oct. 12, 1822; m. Barden Bennett.
    5609 WILLIAM G., b. July 31, 1824; thrice married.
    5610 JULIA ANN, b. Feb. 19, 1826; m. Morris P. McClintock.

5604 FRANCES A. DENISON, (dau. of 5597 William G.,) b. May 28, 1817, m. Edmund B. Alden, Jan., 1847. They live at Thompsonville, Conn., and have:

5610½ Henry Denison, b. Oct. 7, 1850.
5611 Julia Esther, b. May 20, 1853.
5611½ Martha Jane, b. Dec. 25, 1863.

5605 Martha J. Denison, (dau. of 5597 Wm. G.,) b. Aug. 14, 1818, was married, Oct. 10, 1839, to Geo. Mooers, at Palmer, Mass.; lives at Thorndike, Mass. Children :
5612 George Denison, b. Oct. 29, 1841; m. Lizzie Breard.
5612½ Frank Gardner, b. March 12, 1845; d. Jan. 8, 1867.

5606 Esther Denison, (dau. of 5597 Wm. G.,) b. Dec. 8, 1819, was married, in 1838, to A. M. Butterfield, of Waterford, Vt. He d. in 1863. Children :
5613 Martha Jane, b. Aug., 1839; d. Aug., 1849.
5614 Margaret Ann, b. April, 1843; d. Feb., 1846.
5615 Agnes May, b. Aug., 1850; d. April, 1871.

5608 Charlotte A. Denison, (dau. of 5597 Wm. G.,) b. Oct. 12, 1822, was married, Nov. 20, 1855, at Palmer, Mass., to Barden Bennett, b. Jan. 25, 1814. P. O. Lamartine, Wis. Children :
5616 Morris D., b. Nov. 15, 1858; d. March 28, 1860.
5617 Homer W., b. Sept. 16, 1861.

5609 Wm. G. Denison, Jr., (son of 5597 Wm. G.,) b. July 31st, 1824, was married, first, May, 1847, to Esther Franklin, who d. in 1850 ; second, to Emma Barnes, who d. Sept., 1853 ; third, June, 1864, to Emma Taggart. He d. Aug. 17, 1873, at Denver, Col. His third wife d. there, Sept. 4, 1874. Children :
5618 Frank, b. July 26, 1853; killed by cars, Nov. 15, 1865.
5619 Alice Taggart, b. in 1865.

5610 Julia Ann Denison, (dau. of 5597 Wm. G.,) b. Feb. 19, 1826, was married May 12, 1846, to Morris P. McClintock, b. Oct. 6, 1825 ; and he d. May 16, 1863. Children :
5620 Jennette, b. Jan. 17, 1851; d. July 15, 1853.
5621 Frederick D., b. June 26, 1853.
5622 Annie, b. Sept. 19, 1863.

5596 George Denison, (George[5], George[4], George[3], William[2], George[1],) b. in 1780, was married to Hannah Latham ; lived in Warren, Pa.; d. Jan. 2, 1864. His children :
5623 Abby Ann, b. Nov. 15, 1807; m. Joseph Gallup.
5624 George; twice married.
5625 Julia Ann, b. Aug. 15, 1812; m. Earl Howe.

5626 ANGELINE M., b. Jan. 2, 1820; m. Morris E. Brown.
5627 HENRY; m. Caroline Burrows.
5628 ADELINE; d. young.
5629 JOSEPH; m. Lura Burrows.
5630 CHARLOTTE A., b. Oct. 2, 1825; m. Wm. Batty.
5631 ERASTUS, b. June 7, 1829; m. Helen Packer.

5624 GEORGE DENISON, JR., (George[6], George[5], George[4], George[3], William[2], George[1],) m. 1st, Cynthia Buck, Sept. 1, 1836, who d. Dec. 15, 1841. He married, 2d, Sarah A. Buck, Nov. 1, 1843. His children :

5632 ADELINE, b. Sept. 13, 1837; m. Wm. Aumac, May 12, 1857, and d. Feb. 10, 1858.
5633 MARY A., b. April 20, 1839; m. E. Wheeler.
5634 CYNTHIA L., b. Feb. 14, 1841; m. C. Smith, March 10, 1860.
5635 FRANCES F., b. Dec. 12, 1844; m. Wm. Flett.
5636 HENRY, b. June 10, 1847; m. Sarah Cokelet, Dec. 25, 1873.
5637 CHARLOTTE, b. Oct. 2, 1850; d. Jan. 13, 1860.
5638 CAROLINE E., b. June 2, 1855; m. Charles Blauvelt, Jan. 23, '76.

5623 ABBY ANN DENISON, (George[6], George[5], George[4], George[3], William[2], George[1],) b. Nov. 15, 1807, was married to Joseph Gallup, of Cuba, N. Y., Nov. 3, 1825. Their children :

5639 JOSEPH OSCAR, b. Aug. 30, 1828; m. Isabel Carpenter.
5640 ABBY ELLEN, b. March 25, 1831; m. Robert Wasson.
5641 FRANCES ADELINE, b. Oct. 24, 1833; m. Jefferson Halsted.
5642 GURDON, b. Feb. 18, 1836; m. Hannah Nash.
5643 CHARLOTTE A., b. Aug. 2, 1838; m. James Carpenter.
5644 ELIZABETH, b. Feb. 16, 1841; m. Henry Chesebro'.
5645 GILES F., b. April 21, 1843; m. Mary E. Green.
5646 EMMA, b. March 25, 1845; m. James Chesebro'.
5647 CHARLES A., b. Dec. 20, 1848; d. July 28, 1864.

5625 JULIA ANN DENISON, (George[6], George[5], George[4], George[3], William[2], George[1],) b. Aug. 15, 1812, was married to Earl Howe, of Orwell, Pa., Jan. 27, 1829. Their children :

5648 CHARLOTTE E., b. Dec. 5, 1829; m. E. M. Farrar; 2 ch.
5649 PHEBE, b. Dec. 2, 1831; d. Dec. 15, 1842.
5650 HENRY, b. Aug. 11, 1834; m. Jane Russell; 4 ch.
5651 WILLIAM, b. Sept. 2, 1836; m. Cynthia Congdon; 5 ch.
5652 PHILANDER, b. Feb. 26, 1838; d. Dec. 16, 1842.
5653 HELEN M., b. Dec. 23, 1840; d. Dec. 15, 1842.
5654 MARY H., b. Oct. 3, 1843.
5655 GEORGE H., b. Oct., 1846; d. Jan. 1850.
5656 JOSEPH, b. Aug. 1848; d. Feb. 1850.

By a second marriage, Earl Howe had: Rosie, b. July 4, 1853.

11 William Denison's Descendants.

5627 HENRY DENISON, (George[6], George[5], George[4], George[3], William[2], George[1],) *m.* Caroline Burrows, Aug. 29, 1841, and died, Jan. 29, 1847. He had two children :

> **5657** HENRY, b. June 27, 1842; d. May 29, 1864, unmarried.
> **5658** EDWARD, b. Oct. 20, 1844; was adopted by John Conner of Brooklyn, N. Y., took his name and inherited his property; *m*; has children.

5629 JOSEPH DENISON, (George[6], George[5], George[4], George[3], William[2], George[1],) *m.* Lura Burrows, Feb. 27, 1845, and lives at Mystic River. His children :

> **5659** JOSEPH L., b. Dec. 21, 1845 ; d. July 29, 1867.
> **5660** DANIEL B., b. July 17, 1849; *m.* Mary Park, Oct. 24, 1876.
> **5661** GEORGE W., b. Feb. 15, 1854; d. Feb. 16, 1880.
> **5662** FRANK, b. Nov. 13, 1856.

5631 ERASTUS DENISON, (George[6], George[5], George[4], George[3], William[2], George[1],) b. June 7, 1829, was married to Helen Packer, Jan. 2, 1862 ; lives at Mystic River ; has these :

> **5663** EUGENE, b. May 24, 1865.
> **5664** ANNA, b. Oct. 19, 1866.
> **5665** FREDERICK, b. April 4, 1869.
> **5666** M. JANE, b. June 4, 1871.
> **5667** ANGELINE, b. Sept. 5, 1873.

5630 CHARLOTTE A. DENISON, (George[6], George[5], George[4], George[3], William[2], George[1],) was married to William E. Batty ; lives at Cedar Keys, Fla. Their children :

> **5668** WILLIAM H., b. March 26, 1846.
> **5669** EUGENE, b. Oct. 10, 1848.
> **5670** ELIZABETH, b. Sept. 23, 1856.
> **5671** ELLA, b. July 3, 1851; d. Oct. 8, 1854.
> **5672** FRANK, b. Sept. 8, 1853; d. Oct. 13, 1854.

5627 ANGELINE M. DENISON, (George[6], George[5], George[4], George[3], William[2], George[1],) b. Jan. 2, 1820, *m.* Morris E. Brown, Nov. 16, 1837. Their children :

> **5673** ELIZABETH M., b. Nov. 18, 1838.
> **5674** PETER D., b. Jan. 27, 1842.
> **5675** FRANCIS D., b. April 2, 1846.
> **5676** MARY JANE, b. Oct. 3, 1856.
> **5677** WALTER, b. Oct. 6, 1859.

5633 MARY A. DENISON, (George[7], George[6], George[5], George[4], George[3], William[2], George[1],) b. April 20, 1839, *m.* Edward H. Wheeler, July 3, 1857 ; lives at Keyport, N. J. Their children :

11 William Denison's Descendants.

5678 WALTER D., b. Nov. 6, 1859.
5679 EDWIN H., b. Aug 2, 1862.
5680 GEORGE D., b. June 29, 1864.
5681 MARY A., b. Jan. 20, 1868.
5682 SHIRLEY M., b. Aug. 10, 1870; d. Aug. 26, 1875.
5683 CLARENCE L., b. June 29, 1873.
5684 FREDERICK L , b. Oct. 13, 1875.

5635 FRANCES F. DENISON, (George[7], George[6], George[5], George[4], George[3], William[2], George[1],) b. Dec. 12, 1844, was married, March 14, 1864, to William Flett of Red Bank, N. J. Children :

5685 IDA SARAH, b. Dec. 24, 1864.
5686 HARRY DENISON, b. Oct. 23, 1867.

5578 WILLIAM DENISON, (George[4], George[3], William[2], George[1],) b. April 8, 1756, was married to Anna Slack, April 19, 1780. They went to Zanesville, Ohio, and lived in other places. He d. July 21, 1820 ; she d. June 19, 1841, aged 87. Their children :

5687 GURDON, b. May 3, 1781; twice married.
5688 NANCY, b. Oct. 10, 1782; d. July 23, 1803.
5689 LUCY, b. Aug 28, 1785; m. Jesse Williams.
5690 WARREN, b. Feb. 7, 1788; m. Mary Passmore.
5691 MATILDA, b. March 27, 1790; twice married.
5692 GEORGE, b. July 4, 1792; d July 23, 1803.
5693 WILLIAM S., b. Nov. 13, 1794; m. Mary O. Fisher.
5694 ELIZABETH, b. Aug. 16, 1797; twice married.

5687 GURDON DENISON, (William[5], George[4], George[3], William[2], George[1],) was married, first, May 24, 1812, to Etherlinda Slack, of Mansfield, Conn., who d. July 21, 1822, aged 34 ; second, January, 1823, to Elizabeth Krusan, who d. in 1874, at Springfield, Ohio. He d. February, 1845. Children :

5695 ALONZO C., b. in 1813; m. Maria Shepardson; lives in Iowa City; one child, named Gurdon S.; the wife d. in 1852.
5696 GEORGE S., b. April 21, 1814; m. Susan Headly.
5697 JOSEPH, b. in 1816; lives in Iowa; has 6 children.
5698 CHARLES R., b. July 31, 1818.
5699 ETHERLINDA, b. in 1821; d. September, 1822.
5700 MARIA, b. in 1822; m. Samuel Hibbs; lives at Hopewell, Ohio; 4 children: Shelby, Easton, Denison, and James.

5696 GEORGE S. DENISON, (Gurdon[6], William[5], George[4], George[3], William[2], George[1],) b. April 21, 1814, was married Feb. 14, 1839, to Susan Headly, b. Sept. 3, 1817, in Luzerne Co., Pa.; lives in Tiffin, Johnson Co., Iowa. Children :

11 William Denison's Descendants.

5701 ETHERLINDA, b. Sept. 19, 1841; m. John K. Smith, Oct. 23, '63.
5702 CHARLES H., b. March 31, 1840; d. at siege of Vicksburg in '63.
5703 LAFAYETTE, b. Sept. 27, 1846; d. July 10, 1847.
5704 ELMIRA J., b. Oct. 17, 1850; m. Hugh L. Snyder, of Iowa.
5705 CAPT. RILEY, b. Aug. 17, 1853; lives in Iowa, unmarried.
5706 SINA A., b. Jan 21, 1856; m. Bowen Booker, Feb. 27, 1878.

5698 CHARLES R. DENISON, (Gurdon[6], William[5], George[4], George[3], William[2], George[1],) was married, Nov. 12, 1848, to Sarah J. Peterson, b. May 30, 1830; lives at Kossuth, Des Moines Co., Iowa. Four children:

5707 WINFIELD SCOTT, b. July 21, 1849; m. Sarah E. Blair, Feb. 22, 1878.
5708 ALONZO J., b. July 2, 1851.
5709 CORDELIA E., b. March 21, 1855; m. James L. Davis of Nebraska, Oct. 22, 1872.
5710 EUNICE C., b. Dec. 18, 1859.

5689 LUCY DENISON, (William[5], George[4], George[3], William[2], George[1],) b. Aug. 28, 1785, was married, Sept. 22, 1810, to Jesse Williams; lived in Zanesville, Ohio; d. Sept. 5, 1840. Children:

5711 GURDON, b. in 1811; m. Charlotte Williams.
5712 LUCY, b. in 1813; twice married; 5 children.
5713 NANCY, b in 1814; m. Thomas Leggett, of Zanesville, O.
5714 WILLIAM, b. in 1816; m. Mary Williams; lives in Salem, Ohio.
5715 W. H. HARRISON, b. in 1818; d. September, 1840.
5716 JULIA, b. in 1821; d. September, 1840.
5717 WASHINGTON, b. in 1823; lives in Sangamon, Ill.
5718 LAFAYETTE, b. in 1825; lives at Sangamon, Ill.
5719 DENISON, b. in 1837; lives in Sangamon, Ill.
5720 ELIZABETH, b. in 1830; m. Dr. Dupler; 3 children.

5690 WARREN DENISON, (William[5], George[4], George[3], William[2], George[1],) b. Feb. 7, 1788, was married July 5, 1815, to Mary Passmore; he d. Sept. 7, 1820, at Salem, O. Children:

5721 WASHINGTON, twin, b. in 1816; m. a Callahan; lives in Ohio.
5722 MADISON, twin, b. in 1816; m. a Whitcraft; lives in Ohio.
5723 WARREN, b. in 1819; a wanderer, not traced.

5691 MATILDA DENISON, (William[5], George[4], George[3], William[2], George[1],) b. March 27, 1790, was married, first, Aug. 2, 1812, to Jared Shepardson; and second, to Joseph Shepardson, brother of her first husband. She died March, 1868, at Iowa City, Ia. Her children, all by the first husband, were as follows:

5724 MARIA; *m.* Alonzo Denison; 1 child.
5725 MATILDA; *m.* Morris Heady; lives in Iowa City.
5726 SOPHIA; lives with her uncle near Albany, N. Y.
5727 LOUISIANA; *m.* Thomas King; lives at Mount Pleasant, Iowa.
5728 NAPOLEON BONAPARTE; lives near Iowa City.
5729 JOSEPH BONAPARTE; lives near Iowa City.

5693 WILLIAM S. DENISON, (William^5, George^4, George^3, William^2, George^1,) b. Nov. 13, 1794, was married, May 31, 1860, to Mary O. Fisher. He was a very wealthy farmer who lived to be 66 years old before he married. He endowed the "Denison University," at Granville, Ohio, and gave $30,000 for other educational purposes. He was still living, in 1878, at Salem, Ohio, where he had 1500 acres of the finest farming land. He was educated at the "Ohio University," at Athens. The letter which gives this account of him, says, "his three children are healthy and robust scions of the old stock," but fails to give the dates of their birth. Their names are as follows:

5730 ANNA EVALINA.
5731 JOSEPH WILLIAM.
5732 CHARLES DUNLAP.

5694 ELIZABETH DENISON, (William^5, George^4, George^3, William^2, George^1,) b. Aug. 16, 1797, was married, first, Jan. 31, 1822, to James Van Zant, of Zanesville, O., who d. Aug. 30, 1830; and, second, December, 1832, to James Kitchen, of Springfield, O. Four children by the first husband, and two by the second:

5733 WILLIAM D., (Van Zant,) *m.* Phebe Merriam; d. in 1875; six children: Eldon, Charles, Cyrus, Theodore, Edward, Lucy C.
5734 ELIZA, (Van Zant,) d. at the age of four years,
5735 LUCY ANN, (Van Zant,) *m.* Thomas J. Cox of Zanesville; 3 ch.: William Van Zant, Elizabeth Maria, James Buckingham.
5736 JAMES MONROE, (Van Zant,) *m.* Mary Grable; lives at Winona, O.; 3 children: Lewis K., Frank, Harmon.
5737 SARAH JANE, (Kitchen,) *m.* Geo. Merriam; lived at Zanesville, O.; left two daughters: Elizabeth K., and Martha T.
5738 LEWIS SPRINGER, (Kitchen,) *m.* Mary Jones; lived at Zanesville; 6 children: Frances Elizabeth, James, William, Thomas Cox, Mary, Benj. Jones.

5579 OLIVER DENISON, (George^4, George^3, William^2, George^1,) b. March 2, 1758, was married, Jan. 1, 1786, to Martha Williams. He died Feb. 14, 1817; his wife, Martha, died Aug. 20, 1855, aged 93. They had:

11 William Denison's Descendants.

5739 OLIVER, b. Jan. 2, 1787; m. 1st, to Nancy Graves; 2d, to Nancy D. Noyes.
5740 JUSTIN W., b. March, 1789; m. Maria Collins; d. Oct. 13, 1839.
5741 MARCIA P., b. 1791; m. Warren Palmer; one child: Warren.
5742 MARTHA, b. 1793; m. Denison Chesebro'.
5743 ELAM W., b. 1794; m. Clara Palmer.
5744 GRACE B., b. Aug. 24, 1799; m. Joseph Noyes.
5745 LUKE P., b. 1797; d. July 3, 1833, by suicide.
5746 EUNICE W., b. Oct. 24, 1801; m. Thomas Noyes.
5747 THOMAS L., b. May 30, 1804; d. Oct. 13, 1823.

5739 OLIVER DENISON, JR. (Oliver[5], George[4], George[3], William[2], George[1],) b. Jan. 2, 1787, was married, first, March 3, 1811, to Nancy Graves. They had one child:

5748 MARTHA ANN B., b. Dec. 23, 1811; m. Nathaniel Clift.

The wife, Nancy Graves, died Feb. 24, 1825; and Oliver Denison, Jr., was married, second, Nov. 24, 1825, to Nancy D. Noyes. He died Sept. 8, 1873; Nancy D. Noyes, his second wife, died June 10, 1870. They had these children:

5749 EMMA J., b. Oct. 24, 1826; m. Asa F. Kendrick.
5750 OLIVER, b. April 18, 1828; m. Harriet W. Wilcox.
5751 MARCIA P., b. April 8, 1830; m. Paul B. Stanton.
5752 EDGAR, b. Jan. 20, 1833; m. Margaret E. Mandeville.
5753 SARAH E., b. March 29, 1835; not married.
5754 NATHAN N., b. Jan. 9, 1838; m. Sarah A. Green.
5755 PHEBE M., b. May 30, 1840; not married.

5743 ELAM W. DENISON, (Oliver[5], George[4], George[3], William[2], George[1],) b. in 1794, was married to Clara Palmer, and had these:

5756 CLARISSA, m. John Green.
5757 ELAM, b. 1822; d. Jan. 21, 1824.

5742 MARTHA DENISON, (Oliver[5], George[4], George[3], William[3], George[1],) b. in 1793, was married to Denison Chesebro', son of Elder Elihu, Nov. 15, 1818; lived at Stonington, Conn. Children:

5758 OLIVER D., b. Jan. 2, 1820; m. Frances Hancox.
5759 JAMES, b. Aug. 2, 1821; m. Frances ——; 2 children.
5760 BENJ. F., b. Nov. 22, 1825; d. unmarried, in Cal.
5761 EMILY, b. Oct. 18, 1831; m. John Brown; 3 children.

5750 OLIVER DENISON, (Oliver, Jr.[6], Oliver[5], George[4], George[3], William[2], George[1],) b. April 18, 1828, was married, Jan. 5, 1863, to Harriet W. Wilcox; lives at Mystic Bridge, Conn. Children:

5762 NANCY, b. March 14, 1864.
5763 PHEBE M., b. Sept. 30, 1865.
5764 GEORGIANA, b. March 20, 1868.
5765 OLIVER, b. April 18, 1870.
5766 JUSTIN W., b. Dec. 27, 1872.

5752 EDGAR DENISON, (Oliver, Jr.^{6}, Oliver^5, George^4, George^3, William^2, George^1,) b. Jan. 20, 1833, was married to Margaret E. Mandeville, March 2, 1860; she d. May 7, 1871; their children:

5767 LYDIA M., b. April 3, 1862: d. Feb. 13, 1870.
5768 ANN B., b. Feb. 7, 1866.

5754 NATHAN N. DENISON, (Oliver, Jr.^{6}, Oliver^5, George^4, George^3, William^2, George^1,) b. Jan. 9, 1838, was married to Sarah A. Green, March 20, 1867, and has had these:

5769 CLARA JANE, b. April 28, 1868; d. Jan. 28, 1869.
5770 PAUL S., b. Jan. 16, 1870.
5771 JOHN G., b. Dec. 20, 1871.
5772 ELAM W., b. Jan. 4, 1874.

5748 MARTHA ANN B. DENISON, (Oliver, Jr.^{6}, Oliver^5, George^4, George^3, William^2, George^1,) was married, May 11, 1837, to Nathaniel Clift, son of Nathaniel and Eunice; he d. in 1841. The children:

5773 HIRAM, b. March 8, 1838.
5774 NATHANIEL, b. June 29, 1841.

5749 EMMA JANE DENISON, (Oliver, Jr.^{6}, Oliver^5, George^4, George^3, William^2, George^1,) b. Oct. 24, 1826, was married, Nov. 22, 1847, to Asa F. Kendrick. They live at Buckland, Mass., and have had these children:

5775 EMMA J., b. March 27, 1850.
5776 FRANK D., b. May 21, 1855.
5777 ANNIE E., b. June 21, 1858; d. Aug. 16, 1859.
5778 GEORGE O., b. April 30, 1861; d. March 15, 1866.
5779 SUSAN L., b. May 29, 1862; d. Aug. 12, 1864.

5744 GRACE B. DENISON, (Oliver^5, George^4, George^3, William^2, George^1,) b. Aug. 24, 1799, was married to Joseph Noyes, Nov. 19, 1818; he d. June 12, 1872. They had:

5780 PHEBE, b. April 24, 1820; d. Aug. 22, 1823.
5781 CYRUS W., b. Jane 27, 1822; *m.* Jane Harding; d. July 2, 1853; no child.
5782 DENISON, b. Jan. 11, 1824; d. Dec. 13, 1859.
5783 EDMUND S. b. Jan. 9, 1826; d. May 4, 1836.
5784 LUCY A., b. Dec. 21, 1827; *m.* Richard A. Wheeler, Nov. 5, '56.

5785 HANNAH D., b. Dec. 31, 1829; d. Sept. 16, 1873.
5786 IRA H., b. Jan. 9, 1832; d. Sept. 28, 1872.
5787 CHARLES S., b. April 5, 1834.
5788 EDMUND S., b. May 24, 1836; m. Eliza P. Brown, Feb. 5, 1867.
5789 JOSEPH, b. July 31, 1839; d. July 17, 1858.
5790 AVERY W., b. April 27, 1842.

5746 EUNICE W. DENISON, (Oliver[5], George[4], George[3], William[2], George[1],) b. Oct. 24, 1801, was married to Thomas Noyes, Feb. 1, 1825; lives at Mystic Bridge, Conn. Children:

5791 MARTHA, b. Feb. 11, 1826; m. Noyes P. Brown.
5792 MARY, b. Nov. 4, 1828; m. Jesse D. Noyes.
5793 THOMAS W., b. Sept. 23, 1830; m. Phebe J. Kemp.
5794 PHEBE, b. May 6, 1834; m. Enoch F. Chapman.
5795 WILLIAM, b. May 6, 1836; m. Hannah Palmer.
5796 ELIZA P., b. May 7, 1839; m. Seth Williams.
5797 JANE B., b. Feb. 3, 1843.

5740 JUSTIN W. DENISON, (Oliver[5], George[4], George[3], William[2], George[1],) b. March, 1789, was married to Maria Collins, March 11, 1811. He died Oct. 13, 1839; his wife died Aug. 2, 1839, Aged 45. Their children were:

5798 JUSTIN W., Jr., b. Jan. 1, 1813; d. July, 1836, at New Orleans, of yellow fever; not married.
5799 OLIVER, b. Aug. 28, 1815; d. Nov. 9, 1840; m. Charlotte Sawyer.
5800 ELISHA P., b. July 31, 1817; m. Mary Dickinson; lost at sea in 1841; no child.
5801 MARIA, b. May 30, 1819; m. James Fish.
5802 ANN E., b. Jan. 10, 1821; m. Stephen Denison. See his record.
5803 MERCY A, b. Feb. 2, 1823; m. Fred. W. Funch.
5804 THOMAS L., b. July 25, 1825; d. Aug. 13, 1837.
5805 ELIAS W., b. June 18, 1827; m Phebe A. Stoddard.
5806 ANDREW I., b. Nov. 4, 1829; d. June 13, 1850, in California; unmarried.

5799 OLIVER DENISON, (Justin W.[6], Oliver[5], George[4], George[3], William[2], George[1],) b. Aug. 28, 1815; m. Charlotte Sawyer, May 9, 1833. He was shot dead, Nov. 9, 1840, at Garden Keyes, Fla. He had but one child:

5807 ELIZA, b. April 16, 1840.

5801 MARIA DENISON, (Justin W.[6], Oliver[5], George[4], George[3], William[2], George[1],) b. May 30, 1819, m. James Fish, Aug. 5, 1839. She died, Aug. 12, 1841, having had one child:

5808 GEORGE A., b. April 12, 1840.

5803 MERCY A. DENISON, (Justin W.[6], Oliver[5], George[4], George[3], William[2], George[1],) b. Feb. 2, 1823, was married,

Oct. 29, 1843, to Frederick W. Funch. They live at Mystic River, and have these :

- **5809** MARIA E., b. Oct. 25, 1847; d. Oct. 9, 1848.
- **5810** FREDERICK W., b. Sept. 20, 1849; *m.* Rachel M. Johnson, Dec. 19, 1873.
- **5811** JOHN M., b. 1854; d. April 2, 1855.
- **5812** CAROLINE J., b. Jan. 7, 1856; *m.* Henry Howell, Feb. 22, 1876.
- **5813** MARY A., b. April 7, 1858; d. May 18, 1860.
- **5814** EMMA J., b. Oct. 17, 1861.

5805 ELIAS W. DENISON, (Justin W.^{6}, Oliver^5, George^4, George^3, William^2, George^1,) b, June 18, 1827, was married to Phebe A. Stoddard, Oct. 21, 1850. She was born Oct. 2, 1831. They live at Wequetequock, Stonington, Conn., and have had these children :

- **5815** ESTELLE A., b. April 12, 1852; d. Jan. 13, 1856.
- **5816** SIDNEY J., b. Sept. 13, 1854; d. Jan. 11, 1856.
- **5817** PHEBE E., b. Sept. 25, 1856.
- **5818** ELIAS SYDNEY, b. Sept. 14, 1858.
- **5819** GEORGE L., b. July 4, 1861.
- **5820** FRANKLIN P., b. Dec. 27, 1867.
- **5821** JOSIE B , b. Aug. 10, 1871.

5581 GILBERT DENISON, (George^4, George^3, William^2, George^1,) b. Sept. 18, 1762, was married to Huldah Palmer, Dec. 26, 1884. They lived in Vermont. Their children :

- **5822** GILBERT, b. 1786; *m.* Sophia Culver.
- **5823** HULDAH, b. 1788; *m.* Phineas Stewart.
- **5824** SOPHIA, b. 1790; *m.* Henry Clark.
- **5825** ELISHA, b. 1792; had a family.
- **5826** HENRY, b. 1794; d. unmarried. He was b. in Guilford, Vt.; studied at Vermont University and at Williams College; went to Georgia in 1816; began publishing a newspaper at Milledgeville in 1818, and d. there, Oct. 31, 1819.

5822 GILBERT DENISON, (Gilbert^5, George^4, George^3, William^2, George^1,) b. in 1786, was married to Sophia Culver in 1808; lived at the Head of Mystic, Conn.; he died ; she died at Cleveland, Ohio, April 2, 1871, aged 83. Children :

- **5827** GILBERT P., b. Oct. 31, 1810; d. Dec. 20, 1830.
- **5828** HENRY C., b. May 27, 1812; d. Jan. 8, 1838.
- **5829** MARY, b. April 2, 1814; *m.* Benj. F. Collins.
- **5830** ANN MARIA, b. 1816; *m.* Dr. Ezra Vincent.
- **5831** CHARLES P., b. Sept. 20, 1818; d. March 20, 1821.
- **5832** CHARLES H., b. 1821; *m.* Mary A. Cottrell.
- **5833** JANE B., b. 1823; *m.* Rev. Pliny S. Warner.
- **5834** LOUISA, b. March 28, 1825; d. Sept. 28, 1827.

11 William Denison's Descendants.

5823 HULDAH DENISON, (Gilbert[5], George[4], George[3], William[2], George[1],) b. in 1788, was married to Phineas Stewart, in 1808. He d. Feb., 1872. Children:

    5835 JOHN G., b. July 29, 1814; lives at Coshocton, O.
    5836 SOPHIA D., b. Nov. 15; m. a Brown of Malone, N. Y.
    5837 LUCIEN E., b. Jan. 17, 1817; lives unmarried in New Mexico.
    5838 CHARLES C., b. Sept. 15, 1818.

5829 MARY DENISON, (Gilbert, Jr.[6], Gilbert[5], George[4], George[3], William[2], George[1],) b. in 1814, was married, Oct. 1, 1835, to Benjamin F. Collins; they lived at Norwalk, Ohio; he died Aug. 14, 1867, aged 60. Children:

    5839 GILBERT DENISON, b. June 15, 1837; d. July 17, 1837.
    5840 ANNA LOUISA, b. Dec. 25, 1838; d. Aug. 25, 1840.
    5841 HENRY, b. Jan. 19, 1841; d. July 19, 1843.
    5842 CHARLES D., b. June 22, 1843; m. Emma L. Huntington.
    5843 ELLA VINCENT, b. July 17, 1845; m. E. H. Draper.
    5844 FRANK STILLMAN, b. Dec. 31, 1847.
    5845 ANNIE DENISON, b. Dec. 5, 1849; d. Aug. 1, 1855.
    5846 WALTER BOWMAN, b. April 5, 1853; d. Aug. 10, 1855.
    5847 JENNIE DENISON, b. Jan. 22, 1856.

5830 ANN MARIA DENISON, (Gilbert, Jr.[6], Gilbert[5], George[4], George[3], William[2], George[1],) b. in 1816, was married, May 11, 1844, to Dr. Ezra Vincent. She d. Oct. 27, 1848. One child:

    5848 WALTER BORODELL, b. Aug. 6, 1845, in Providence, R. I.

5832 CHARLES H. DENISON, (Gilbert, Jr.[6], Gilbert[5], George[4], George[3], William[2], George[1],) b. in 1821, was married, May 24, 1848, to Mary A. Cotrell. They have no child. He lived at Mystic, Conn., and was Railroad Commissioner for Connecticut; but he now lives at Oakland, Cal., and has an insurance office in San Francisco.

5833 JANE B. DENISON, (Gilbert, Jr.[6], Gilbert[5], George[4], George[3], William[2], George[1],) b. in 1823, was married, April 27, 1863, to Rev. Pliny F. Warner; no child. Mr. Warner was pastor of the first Congregational Church in Stonington, Conn. from Oct. 31, 1860, to Feb. 24, 1863. He has since lived in the Western States, and was for several years at Fort Scott, Kansas.

5584 ESTHER DENISON, (George[4], George[3], William[2], George[1],) b. Nov. 16, 1769, was married in 1790, to Enoch Burrows, a descendant of John Burrows of New London,

Conn., one of the first settlers and largest landholders. Their children:
    5849 LUCY, b. Jan. 8, 1791; m. John Hyde.
    5850 MARY, b. in 1793.
    5851 SILAS, b. in 1795.

5849 LUCY BURROWS, (dau. of 5584 Esther and Enoch,) b. in 1791, was married, Feb. 21, 1808, to John Hyde, b. at Poquetanock, Conn., June 1783, eldest son of Dr. Phineas Hyde, and a descendant of William Hyde, one of the first settlers of Norwich, Conn. He settled at the Head of Mystic, and was a cotton manufacturer. Their children:
    5852 JOSHUA BURROWS, b. June 28, 1809.
    5853 JOHN J., b. Feb. 15, 1811.
    5854 LUCY ESTHER, b. Dec. 26, 1812.
    5855 ENOCH B., b. Jan. 20, 1815; d. May 4, 1880.
    5856 SILAS B., b. Sept. 27, 1816; d. Aug. 7, 1843.
    5857 JAMES WILLIAMS, b. 1818; d. in infancy.
    5858 HARRIET E., b. May 27, 1820.
    5859 GEO. DENISON, b. April 13, 1822; unmarried.
    5860 THEOPHILUS R., b. May 20, 1824.
    5861 CHARLES CAROL. ! , Feb. 1, 1826; unmarried.
    5862 WILLIAM P., b. Feb. 15, 1823.
    5863 JOSEPH A. b. Sept. 26, 1826; d. Oct. 31, 1831.
    5864 HELEN A., b. Dec. 19, 1832; m. Enoch B. Brown, Sept. 17, 1872; P. O., Mystic, Conn.
    5865 EDWARD L., b. May 21, 1835.

5852 JOSHUA BURROWS HYDE, (son of 5849 Lucy and John,) m. Anna Maria Bamman; lives in Brooklyn, N. Y. Their children:
    5866 ANNA MARIA.
    5867 KATHERINE.
    5868 WALTER LAWRENCE.

5854 LUCY ESTHER HYDE, (dau. of 5849 Lucy and John,) was married, Sept., 1835, to Rev. James McDonald, son of Gen. John and Lydia Wiley McDonald, of Limerick, Me. He was graduated at Union College in 1832, received D. D. there, and was pastor of the first Presbyterian church in Princeton, N. J., in which place he died, April 19, 1876. The children:
    5869 JOHN JAMES.
    5870 ISABELLA.
    5871 MALCOM.
    5872 AUGUSTUS.
    5873 GEORGE.
    5874 DR. ARTHUR K., m. Estelle Scrymer, Jan. 25, 1881.

11 William Denison's Descendants.

5858 HARRIET ELIZABETH HYDE, (dau. of 5849 Lucy and John,) was married, Nov. 10, 1846, to Lucien Bonaparte Hanks, son of Freeman and Rebecca Hanks of Hartford, Conn. Children:

5875 ALEXANDER P. R.; an officer in the U. S. Revenue service.
5876 WILLIAM H. F.

5865 REV. EDWARD LAWRENCE HYDE, (son of 5349 Lucy and John,) b. May 21, 1835, was married, March 25, 1874, at Plainfield, N. J., to Imogene Adell Clark, dau. of Ephraim Clark, b. at Friendship, N. Y., May 1, 1847. He joined the Providence Conference of the Methodist Episcopal Church, March, 1869. His children:

5877 WILLIAM FRANCIS, b. Oct. 17, 1875.
5878 HELEN MANDANE, b. Dec. 8, 1876.

5862 REV. WILLIAM P. HYDE, (son of 5849 Lucy and John,) was married, June 6, 1859, to Seraphine S. Carr, dau. of Wm. Carr, of Warren, R. I., a descendent of Gov. Caleb Carr, of Newport, R. I. He joined the Providence Conference of the Methodist Episcopal church, March, 1865. His children:

5879 WM. FLETCHER, b. Sept. 23, 1860.
5880 ANNIE L., b. May 17, 1862; d. Dec. 20, 1869.
5881 BESSIE CARR, b. June 5, 1864.
5882 LAURA, b. Feb. 21, 1866.
5883 EDWARD, b. Oct. 2, 1867.
5884 Enoch B., b. May 12, 1869; d. May 14, 1869.
5885 MARY ELIZABETH, b. April 20, 1870.
5886 JOHN HYDE, b. March 1, 1872; d. March 25, 1872.
5887 JAMES MCDONALD. b. June 25, 1873.
5888 LILLIAN SERAPHINE, b. Aug. 13, 1875.
5889 JENNIE WHEATON, b. Jan. 4, 1877.

5860 THEOPHILUS ROGERS HYDE, (son of 5849 Lucy and John,) was married, April 30, 1850, to Fanny Hazard Brown. They lived at Stillmanville, Ct., 1880. Children.

5890 ORTEMUS STILLMAN, b. April 5, 1853; m. H. W. Covill; lived in Waterbury, Ct., 1880. Two children: Margaret and Jeannette.
5891 THEOPHILUS ROGERS HYDE, b. Dec. 18, 1855; m. Jane Pelton Burdon; lives at Waterbury, Ct., in 1880.
5892 CHARLES CARROLL, b. Oct. 11, 1859; d. May 11, 1860.
5893 FRANCIS HAZARD STILLMAN, b. June 19, 1863.
5894 FANNY HAZARD, b. June 15, 1866.
5895 EDWARD ADDISON, b. Oct. 29, 1868.

5570 WILLIAM DENISON, (George[3], William[2], George[1],) b. June 14, 1727, was a physician. He was married Nov. 29, 1749, to Priscilla Fellows, of Plainfield, Conn., had two children, and died Sept. 20, 1754. His children were:

    5896 MARY, b. Dec. 12, 1750, twice married.
    5897 PRISCILLA, b. Aug. 19, 1754; *m.* William Dixon.

The daughter Priscilla was adopted and brought up in Stonington by her uncle George Denison and his wife Jane. She was married to William Dixon, of Westerly, R. I. Her son, Nathan F. Dixon, was U. S. Senator, from R. I., and her grandson, Nathan F. Dixon, of Westerly, was member of Congress, from R. I., from March 4, 1863 to March 4, 1869. Two of her granddaughters were married to Jesse L. Moss, of Stonington. See the next records.

5896 MARY DENISON, (Dr. William[4], George[3], William[2], George[1],) b. Dec. 12, 1750, was married 1st, to Appleton W. Rosseter, Jan 31, 1770 ; 2nd, to Jonathan Culver, in 1785. She died in 1810, aged 60. Jonathan Culver died in 1807, aged 62. Her children:

    5898 ESTHER D.
    5899 DUDLEY D.
    5900 JONATHAN.

5897 PRISCILLA DENISON, (Dr. William[4], George[3], William[2], George[1],) b. Aug. 19, 1754, was married to William Dixon, Sept. 10, 1772. She died in Westerly, R. I., Sept. 24, 1842. Their children:

    5901 NATHAN F., b. Dec. 13, 1774; *m.* Betsey Palmer.
    5902 PRISCILLA, b. Sept. 17, 1776; *m.* —— Wiley.
    5903 WILLIAM, b. Nov. 6, 1780; not married.
    5904 GEORGE, b. June 16, 1783; *m.* M. —— Angell.
    5905 SAMUEL D., b. Nov. 5, 1785; *m.* —— Rhodes.

5901 HON. NATHAN F. DIXON, (son of Wm. and Priscilla (Denison) Dixon,) b. Dec. 13, 1774, was married Jan. 14, 1804, to Betsey Palmer; lived at Westerly, R. I.; was U. S. Senator. Children :

    5906 WILLIAM P., b. Nov. 7, 1804.
    5907 A DAUGHTER, b. April 5, 1807; d. April 10, 1807.
    5908 ELIZA P., b. April 18, 1808; *m.* Rev. Mark Tucker.
    5909 FRANCES S., b Feb. 20, 1810; *m.* Jesse L. Moss.
    5910 NATHAN F., b. May 1, 1812; *m.* Harriet Swan.
    5911 PRISCILLA, b. June 17, 1815; *m.* Capt. Alex. S. Palmer.

11 William Denison's Descendants. 281

5912 COURTLAND P., b. March 19, 1820; m. Elizabeth Williams.
5913 SALLY R., b. Oct. 12, 1818; m. Jesse L. Moss; 2nd wife.

5910 HON. NATHAN F. DIXON, JR., (son of Hon. Nathan F. and Betsey,) b. May 1, 1812, was married, June 28, 1843, to Harriet Swan; lives in R. I., was member of Congress from 1863 to 1869. He d. April 11, 1881. Children:

5914 NATHAN F., b. June 10, 1845; d. in infancy.
5915 NATHAN F., b. Aug. 25, 1847.
5916 EDWARD H., b. Oct. 4, 1849.
5917 PHEBE ANN S., b. Feb. 19, 1852.
5918 WALTER P., b. Dec. 8, 1855.
5919 HARRIET S., b. Feb. 24, 1859.

5909 FRANCES S. DIXON, (dau. of 5901 Hon. Nathan F.,) b. Feb. 20, 1810, m. Jesse L. Moss, Oct. 8, 1828; lived at Westerly, R. I.; d. Dec. 11, 1850. The children:

WILLIAM, b. Aug. 25, 1830.
ESTHER CHESEBRO', b. March 22, 1833; d. Sept. 27, 1834.
COURTLAND, b. Jan., 1835.
NATHAN F., b. Sept. 16, 1338.
JESSE, b. Nov. 12, 1847.

5913 SALLY R. DIXON, (dau. of 5901 Hon. Nathan F.,) b. Oct. 12, 1818, m. Jesse L. Moss, and d. May 26, 1873. The children:

FANNY D., b. Feb. 6, 1857.
ROUSE BABCOCK, b. Oct. 15, 1862.

5574 DAVID DENISON, (George^3, William^2, George^1,) b. Jan. 29, 1736, was married Dec. 30, 1756, to Keziah Smith, of Groton, Ct., lived first in Stonington, and next in New London. He served in the revolutionary army, as an officer, and lost most of his property when Arnold, the traitor, burned New London. In 1785, he emigrated to Rindge, N. H., and then to Guilford, Vt., when the country was new. He d. Jan. 24, 1808; his wife d. June 28, 1815, aged 78 years. Their children:

5020 SAMUEL, b. Aug. 25, 1757; d. Jan. 16, 1761.
5921 JABEZ, b. May 4, 1759; m. Mary Briggs.
5922 DAVID, b. March 16, 1761; m. Mary Babcock.
5923 SAMUEL, b. March 17, 1763; m. Eunice Haughton.
5924 EDWARD, b. Oct. 4, 1765; m. Ruey Babcock.
5925 WEALTHY, b. Nov. 29, 1767; d. young.
5926 GEORGE, b. in 1769; m. Lucy Babcock.
5927 JOHN, b. in 1771; m. Mary Avery.

5928 DESIRE, b. in 1773; d. old, unmarried.
5929 AMY, b. in 1775; m. Nathaniel Avery, in 1800; no ch.
5930 EMMA, b. in 1777; m. Wm. Fox, of Fabius, N. Y.; no ch.

5921 JABEZ DENISON, (David⁴, George³, William², George¹,) b. May 17, 1759, was married, November, 1794, to Mary Briggs, b. June 9, 1766, and d. Feb. 23, 1842; lived in Guilford, Vt. Children:

5931 MARY, b. June 5, 1796; m. Jos. Wetherh'd; 2 ch.; Noyes and Oscar; lived in Coleraine, Mass.
5932 PHEBE, b. June 2, 1798; m. Wm. Stevens; 7 ch; d. April 23, 1878, in Guilford, Vt.; lived at Green River, Vt.
5933 PRUDENCE, b. July 24, 1800; m. Caleb Green; lived in Greenfield, Mass.; 4 children: Maria, Ellen, Caleb, Ann.
5934 BELINDA, b. Sept. 9, 1804; d. unmarried, March 12, 1875.
5935 JABEZ, b. Oct. 10, 1807; m. Bethany Brown.

5935 JABEZ DENISON, JR., (Jabez⁵, David⁴, George³, William², George¹,) b. Oct. 10, 1807, was married, in 1838, to Bethany Brown; lived in Guilford, Vt. Children:

5936 CELIA B., b. Jan. 4, 1840; m. Geo. E. Richardson.
5937 MARY B., b. Jan. 17, 1843; a teacher in Vermont; she has a ring that belonged to the original Ann Borodell.
5938 ALICE, b. Feb. 19, 1845; m. Elias P. Johnson.
5939 ANN BORODELL, b. May 5, 1847; d. Oct. 27, 1867.

5936 CELIA B. DENISON, (Jabez⁶, Jabez⁵, David⁴, George³, William², George¹,) b. Jan. 4, 1840, in Guilford, Vt., was married, April 5, 1855, to George E. Richardson, who was born in Claremont, N. H., Jan. 31, 1826. She d. July 25, 1872. They lived chiefly in Guilford, Vt. The children.

5940 JOSEPH D., b. Feb. 29, 1856; d. July 31, 1872.
5941 GEORGE F., b. March 4, 1857; d. Aug. 15, 1864.
5942 CELIA INANTHE, b. Oct. 27, 1859.
5943 WILLIAM A., b. July 20, 1861; d. Jan. 31, 1879.
5944 GEORGE W., b. June 30, 1865.
5945 MARY A., b. Nov. 6, 1867.
5946 ELLEN S., b. May, 1870.
5947 HORACE G., b. April 10, 1872; d. Aug. 13, 1872.

5938 ALICE DENISON, (Jabez⁶, Jabez⁵, David⁴, George³, William², George¹,) b. Feb. 19, 1845, was married, April 25, 1866, to Elias P. Johnson; residence, Vernon, Vt. Children:

5948 JOSIE A., b. June 22, 1871.
5949 EVA M., b. March 3, 1874.
5950 JAY E., b. April 8, 1877.

11 William Denison's Descendants.

5922 DAVID DENISON, (David[4], George[3], William[2], George[1],) b. March 16, 1761, was married to Mary Babcock; lived in Leyden, Mass. She d. Feb. 5, 1817, aged 56; he d. Feb. 22, 1839. Children:

- **5951** DAVID, b. April 5, 1780; thrice married.
- **5952** MARY, b. June 30, 1782; m. Ezra Conable.
- **7953** CLARISSA, b. Jan. 23, 1784.
- **5954** CHARLES H., b. March 5, 1786; m. Sarah Billings.
- **5955** NANCY, b. April 29, 1789; d. young.
- **5956** DESIRE, b. April 14, 1791; d Oct, 1847.
- **5957** ELIZABETH, b. July 23, 1794; twice married.
- **5958** JOSEPH B., b. Dec. 23, 1796.
- **5959** SOPHRONIA, b. March 23, 1799; m. Jonathan Budington.

5951 DAVID DENISON, (David[5], David[4], George[3], William[2], George[1],) b. April 5, 1780, was married, first, in 1802, to Huldah Crandall, who had two children, and d. Aug. 20, 1805; second, in 1807, to Lucy Avery, who bore ten children, and d. Jan. 13, 1830; and, third, to Lucy Burt Cooley, who d. Oct. 31, 1869, aged 82. He lived in Coleraine, Mass., and died there, May 4, 1847. His children:

- **5960** HULDAH C., b. Sept. 23, 1803; d. unmarried.
- **5961** LOUISA L., b. Aug. 6, 1805; m. Rufus Chandler.
- **5962** NANCY E., b. Dec. 15, 1808; m. David Cheney.
- **5963** EMELINE H., b. Oct. 14, 1810; m. Rev. Robert Allyn.
- **5964** ELLEN D., b. May 19, 1812; m. Isaac T. Goodenow; no child; lives at Manhattan, Kansas.
- **5965** DAVID A., b. Sept. 23, 1813; m. Emeline A. Cone; no ch.; d. Aug. 7, 1865.
- **5966** REV. JOSEPH, b. Oct. 1, 1815.
- **5967** CHARLES G., b. Sept. 21, 1817; drowned Oct. 7, 1819.
- **5968** HENRY S., twin, b. Feb. 27, 1820; d. Jan. 10, 1840.
- **5969** HIRAM S., twin, b. Feb. 27, 1820; lives in Kansas, unmarried.
- **5970** GEORGE, b. July 1, 1822; m. Kate Russell; no child; d. Feb. 15, 1876.
- **5971** DARIUS C., b. April 19, 1825; d. unmarried, Oct. 23, 1850.

5961 LOUISA L. DENISON, (David[6], David[5], David[4], George[3], William[2], George[1],) b. Aug. 6, 1805, was married, May 10, 1826, to Rufus Chandler, and d. Oct. 29, 1834; he d. Jan. 17, 1841. Children.

- **5972** LOUISA M., b. May 14, 1827; m. Albert Plumb; 3 ch.
- **5973** RUFUS K., b. July 1, 1829; d. April 22, 1875; wife and 3 ch.
- **5974** ABBIE F., b. June 26, 1832; m. Jos. I. Smith; one child; d. in 1867.
- **5975** DAVID D., b. Sept. 14, 1834; has wife and 1 child, at Cedar Rapids, Ia.

5963 EMELINE H. DENISON, (David[6], David[5], David[4], George[3], William[2], George[1],) b. Oct. 14, 1810, was married to Rev. Robert Allyn. He is President of the State Normal University, at Carbondale, Ill. She d. April 24, 1844. Her children:

    5976 CHARLES, b. Sept. 5, 1842.
    5977 EMELINE LUCY, b. April 12, 1844.
    Rev. Robert Allyn m. 2nd, Mary B. Budington. See her record.

5976 CHARLES ALLYN, (son of Rev. Robert,) b. Sept. 5, 1842, was married, Nov. 18, 1867, to Helen Starr. He has a book store in New London, Ct. The children:

    5978 CHARLES, JR., b. June 1, 1869.
    5979 LOUISA HURLBERT, b. Oct. 2, 1870.
    5980 ROBERT ALLYN, b. Nov. 27, 1875.

5977 EMELINE LUCY ALLYN, (dau. of Rev. Robert,) b. April 12, 1844, was married, Dec. 20, 1877, to William Hypes, of Lebanon, Ill. She had been Prof. in Jacksonville (Ill.,) Female College. One child:

    5981 ANNA CORNELIA, b Nov. 1, 1878.

5962 NANCY E. DENISON, (David[6], David[5], David[4], George[3], Wiliam[2], George[1],) b. Dec. 15, 1808, was married, Aug. 19, 1835, to David Cheney, b. Oct. 17, 1803. He d. March 1, 1863. They lived at Xenia, Ohio. Children:

    5982 EMELINE, b. July 7, 1838.
    5983 LUCY ELLEN, b. March 10, 1841.
    5984 DAVID D., b. Oct. 29, 1843; lives at Fletcher, Ohio.
    5985 HENRY W., b. June 26, 1848; lives in Chicago, Ill.
    5986 GEORGE W., b. Aug. 29, 1850.

5966 REV. JOSEPH DENISON, (David[6], David[5], David[4], George[3], William[2], George[1].) b. Oct. 1, 1815, was married, first, July 8, 1845, to Sarah J. Woodruff, who had seven children, and died Aug. 1, 1859; and, second, Nov. 21, 1859, to Frances A. Dennis. He was President of the Kansas Agricultural College, ten years, and is now president of Baker University, at Baldwin City, Kansas. His children:

    5987 HENRY L., b. May 16, 1846; m. Mary L. Leland.
    5988 ISAAC G., b. May 21, 1848; d. April 18, 1849.
    5989 ELLEN F., b. Feb. 15, 1850; m. Charles O. Whedon.
    5990 EMMA J., b. March 10, 1852; m. Maj. Fred. E. Miller.
    5991 CHARLES S., b. March 2, 1854; d. April 6, 1855.
    5992 GEORGE, twin, b. Nov. 23, 1856; lives in New Mexico.

11 William Denison's Descendants.

5993 GEORGIANA, twin, b. Nov. 28, 1856; d. Oct. 16, 1859.
5994 FANNIE K., b. Aug. 28, 1860.

5987 HENRY L. DENISON, (Rev. Joseph[7], David[6], David[5], David[4], George[3], William[2], George[1],) b. May 16, 1846, was married, June 13, 1872, to Mary L. Leland; lives in Denver, Col. Children:

5995 NELLY, b. July 5, 1873.
5996 FRANK, b. Dec. 13, 1875.
5997 IRELAND, b. Jan. 28, 1880.

5989 ELLEN F. DENISON, (Rev. Joseph[7], David[6], David[5], David[4], George[3], William[2], George[1],) b. Feb. 15, 1850, was married, Sept. 27, 1875, to Charles O. Whedon; lives in Lincoln, Nebraska. Their children:

5998 CHARLOTTE EMMA, b. Sept. 30, 1876.
5999 BURT DENISON, b. Feb. 27, 1878.
5999½ MAGGIE ELLA, b. April 8, 1880.

5990 EMMA JANE DENISON, (Rev. Joseph[7], David[6], David[5], David[4], George[3], William[2], George[1],) b. March 10, 1852, was married, March 12, 1873, to Maj. Fred. E. Miller; lives at Frankfort, Kansas. Children:

6000 FREDERICK OLIVER, b. May 9, 1874.
6001 AUGUST CENTENNIAL, b. Aug. 8, 1876.

5970 GEORGE DENISON, (David[6], David[5], David[4], George[3], William[2], George[1],) b. July 1, 1822, was married to Anna Catherine Russell, dau. of John Russell, of Greenfield, Mass. They had no child. He was a lawyer, and was Naval Officer of the port of New York, under President Lincoln. In connection with August Belmont, Francis Skiddy, and six other gentlemen, he built and owned the Missouri, Kansas and Texas Railroad, which is 786 miles long, and cost $31,000,000. He died of heart disease, Feb. 14, 1876, being suddenly stricken down, on the street, in Washington, D. C., and living afterwards but half an hour.

5952 MARY DENISON, (David[5], David[4], George[3], William[2], George[1],) b. Jan. 30, 1782, was married, in 1813, to Ezra Conable, of Bernardstown, Mass., being his second wife. The first wife, Abigail Stevens, had two children; Caroline A., b. Jan. 5, 1810, and Albert Lee, b. Aug. 10, 1811. MARY DENISON, the second wife, d. Nov. 7, 1836. Her children:

11 William Denison's Descendants.

6002 CHARLES D., b. March 1, 1815; d. Aug. 21. 1818.
6003 MARY ANN D., b. May 26, 1817; d. Oct. 20, 1843.
6004 ELIZABETH FRANCES, b. April 27, 1819; m. N. Hornaday.
6005 SOPHRONIA A., b. Oct. 7, 1822; lives at Des Moines, Iowa.
6006 SAMUEL C., b. Jan. 23, 1826; m. Eunice A. Brook, 8 ch.

6006 SAMUEL CHARLES CONABLE, (son of 5952 Mary and Ezra,) was married Oct. 6, 1848, to Eunice A. Brook; lives in Bernardstown, Mass. Eight children:

6007 HOLLIS EZRA, b. Aug 19, 1849; d. Aug. 7, 1851.
6008 HOLLIS EZRA, b. Aug 6, 1852; m. Emma I. Osgood.
6009 DANIEL BROOKS, b. May 27, 1854; d. July 24, 1859.
6010 MARY DENISON, b. May 23, 1861; d. Dec. 28. 1861.
6011 KATIE ALLEN, b. Dec. 29, 1862; d. April 15, 1864.
6012 SAMUEL WRIGHT, b. Dec. 6, 1864.
6013 WILLIE SEVERANCE, b. Oct. 20, 1867.
6014 CHARLES DENISON, b. July 25, 1872; d. Aug. 15, 1872.

5954 CHARLES H. DENISON, (David[5], David[4], George[3], William[2], George[1],) b. March 5, 1786, was married to Sarah Billings about 1819; lived at Whitingham, Vt.; d. in 1839. His children:

6015 CHARLES H., JR., b. March, 1820.
6016 AMOS B, b. Dec. 13, 1821; served in the war.
6017 SARAH A., d. March 18, 1845, aged 22.
6018 MINERVA, d. Oct. 2, 1844, aged 20.
6019 MARY, d. Aug. 18, 1845, aged 20.
6020 FANNIE S., b. March 12, 1830; m. Phineas R. Whittle.

6016 AMOS B. DENISON, (Charles H.[6], David[5], David[4], George[3], William[2], George[1],) b. Dec. 13, 1820, was married to Mrs. Mary A. Richmond, of Leyden, Mass., April 26, 1870; lives at Keene, N. H.; served in the war of rebellion, from April, '61, to July, '64. One child.

6021 JOHN A., b. Oct. 24, 1871.

6020 FANNIE SOPHRONIA DENISON, (dau. of 5954 Charles H.,) b. March 12, 1830, was married, June, 1850, to Phineas R. Whittle, of Keene, N. H.

6022 MARY ALICE, b. May 26, 1851.
6023 WILLIE LAWRENCE, b. March 1, 1854; d. May 8, 1872.

6022 MARY ALICE WHITTLE, (dau. of 6020 Fannie Sophronia,) b. May 26, 1851, was married, Oct. 7, 1874, to John F. Hoyt, of Shelburne, Falls, Mass. Their children:

6024 CHARLENA DENISON, b. July 31, 1875.
6025 HELEN M., b. Jan. 17, 1878.
6026 HAROLD G., b. Nov. 5, 1880.

11 William Denison's Descendants.

6915 CHARLES H. DENISON, Jr., (son of 5954 CHARLES H.,) b. March 1, 1820, was twice married; first, March 1, 1846, to Mary C. Brackett, of Guilford, Vt., who bore three children, and d. in 1855; second, May 14, 1858, to Lucy A. Thomas, of Marlboro, Vt., who has one child. He lives in Springfield, Mass. The children:

    6027 CHARLES FRANCIS, b. Jan. 12, 1847; m. Addie Tyler.
    6028 WILLIAM CURTIS; b. Aug. 31, 1848.
    6029 MARY ISABELLA, b. July 10, 1852.
    6030 LOTTIE LOUISE, b. Aug. 28, 1864.

Charles H. Denison, Jr., is an inventor and manufacturer of machinery. The following patents have been issued to him by the United States Patent Office: 1, Felloe-rounding machine for carriage wheels; 2, on the same; 3, Wood Planing Machine, for which a gold medal was awarded by the American Institute Fair; 4, Fastening for wheels and axles; 5, machinery for reinforcing button holes for paper collars; 6, 7 and 8, paper collar machines, which will make 150 finished collars per minute; 9, Cutting Press for collars, etc.; 10, Improvement on machine for uniting cloth and paper; 11, cuff machine.

6027 CHARLES FRANCIS DENISON, (son of 6015 Charles H., Jr.,) b. Jan 12, 1847, was married, Jan. 1, 1867, to Addie Tyler; lives in Springfield, Mass. They have:

    6031 CHARLES H., b. Oct. 14, 1875.

5957 ELIZABETH DENISON, (David⁵, David⁴, George³, William², George¹,) b. July 23, 1794, was married, first, Sept., 1821, to Rev. George Richardson, of North Charlestown, N. H., who died in March, 1828; and, second, Nov. 1835, to Ralph Cushman, of Bernardstown, Mass., who died Feb. 22, 1873. Her children:

    6032 ELIZABETH D., b. June 22, 1822; lives at Greenfield, Mass., unmarried.
    6033 GEORGE E., b. Jan. 31, 1826; lives at Fayetteville, Vt.
    6034 HENRY C., b. Aug. 20, 1836; lives in Bernardston, Mass.

6034 HENRY CLAY CUSHMAN, (son of 5957 Elizabeth Denison,) b. Aug. 20, 1836, was married, Jan. 16, 1861, to Louisa Keep Brown, who was born Jan. 16, 1841; both of Bernardston, Mass. They have six children:

6035 HOPE ELIZABETH, b. Feb. 14, 1862.
6036 RALPH HENRY, b. Sept. 30, 1865.
6037 EMMA LAURA, b. April 3, 1867.
6038 ALFRED BROWN, b. Aug. 28, 1870.
6039 LUCY BARTON, b. Dec. 13, 1872.
6040 CHARLOTTE NELLIE, b. June 30, 1879.

5958 JOSEPH B. DENISON, (son of 5922 David,) b. Dec. 23, 1796, was married, about 1833, to Melinda Farwell, who was born in 1810, and died in 1848, aged 38. He d. July 30, 1871. She was of North Charlestown, N. H. They had one child:

6041 ANDREW J, b. in 1835.

6041 ANDREW J. DENISON, (son of 5958 Joseph B.,) born in 1835, was married in 1859, to Margaret Hickey, of Chicago, Illinois. He lives at Waukegan, Ill. The children:

6042 MARY MELINDA, b. 1860; d. in 1863.
6043 FANNY D., b. 1861.
6044 JOSEPH B., b. 1863.
6045 ANDREW J., b. 1865.
6046 MARGARET, b. 1868.
6047 ANNA H., b. 1870.

5959 SOPHRONIA DENISON, (David[5], David[4], George[3], William[2], George[1],) b. March 23, 1799, was married, Feb., 1822, to Jonathan Budington, of Leyden, Mass., who was born Feb. 17, 1800; lived in Leyden; she d. July 21, 1843; he d. Aug. 10, 1880. Their children:

6048 MARY BUCKLAND, b. June 23, 1823; m. Rev. Robert Allyn.
6049 ELLEN PRISCILLA, b. April 3, 1826; m. Rev. Cyrus L. Eastman, Aug. 29, 1854; no child; d. July 17, 1864.
6050 STEPHEN BUCKLAND, b. March 12, 1830.
6051 CHARLES OLMSTEAD, b. Dec. 2, 1832; d. Aug. 30, 1860.
6052 JONATHAN, JR., b. Dec. 17, 1837; unmarried.

6048 MARY BUCKLAND BUDINGTON, (dau. of Sophronia and Jonathan,) b. June 28, 1823, was married, June 24, 1845, to Rev. Robert Allyn, President of the State Normal University, at Carbondale, Ill.; his second wife. See page 284. She d. October, 1879. Four children:

6053 ROBERT, JR., b. July 11, 1846; d. Sept. 7, 1849.
6054 JOSEPH GOODNOW, b. April 1, 1849.
6055 ELLEN SOPHRONIA, b. June 5, 1852.
6056 HATTIE AMANDA, b. Nov. 14, 1859.

11 William Denison's Descendants.

6050 STEPHEN BUCKLAND BUDINGTON, (son of Sophronia and Jonathan,) b. March 12, 1830, was married, at Beardstown, Ill., June 15, 1857, to Frances Caroline Hitchcock, who was b. at Bangor, Me., Jan. 1, 1840. She had two children born at Beardstown, Ill., and d. at Leyden, Mass., Dec. 11, 1865. He was married, second, Dec. 15, 1868, to Ereda Baker, of Hawley, Mass., who was born Jan. 4, 1841. They live at Leyden, Mass., and she has three children. His children by the two wives are as follows:

    6057 CHARLES NORMAN, b. Nov. 8, 1858; d. Nov. 24, 1861.
    6058 CARRIE FRANCES, b. May 21, 1863; d. Aug. 5, 1865.
    6059 ELLEN MAY, b. May 26, 1870.
    6060 ROBERT ALLYN, b. Oct. 22, 1872.
    6061 ETHEL HELENA, b. Dec. 19, 1877.

5924 CAPT. EDWARD DENISON, (David[4], George[3], William[2], George[1],) b. Oct. 4, 1765, was married, in 1793, to widow Ruey Burdick (born Babcock) of Stonington, Ct.; lived in Leyden, Mass. He d. June 14, 1843, aged 77 yrs., 8 mos.; she d. Nov. 3, 1837, aged 73. The children;

    6062 EMMA, b. Sept. 1, 1794; m. Philemon Stedman, Sept. 13, 1814; 7 children: Louisa, Rebecca, Gilbert, Henry, Willard, Charles and Alonzo. She d. June 3, 1867, aged 72.
    6063 EUNICE, b. March 6, 1796; m. Samuel Cole, June 1, 1819; 3 children: Samuel D., Cynthia C., and Mary C. She d. Oct. 3, 1869.
    6064 RUEY, b. March 11, 1798; m. Wheaton Talbot, Nov. 30, 1816; 4 children: Edward D., Maria F., Henry W., and Mary E. She d. Jan. 29, 1832.
    6065 EDWARD, b. Jan. 31, 1800; m. Elizabeth H. Hapgood.
    6066 DESIRE, b. Oct. 11, 1802; m. Dr. R. S. Smith; 2 ch.
    6067 ALMIRA, b. Nov. 27, 1804; unmarried.
    6068 DR. GEORGE W., b. Feb. 23, 1810; m. Elvira Hancock.

6065 CAPT. EDWARD DENISON, JR., (Edward[5], David[4], George[3], William[2], George[1],) b. Jan. 31, 1800, was married, Jan. 31, 1837, to Elizabeth C. Hapgood, of Marlboro', Mass.; lived in Leyden, Mass. He d. Feb. 12, 1879, aged 79 years. The children:

    6069 FRANCES E., b. Sept. 8, 1839; m. J. H. Newcomb.
    6070 MARIA R., b. Aug. 15, 1841; m. Henry C. Howe, of Gill.
    6071 EDWARD H., b. June 9, 1843; m. Celestina Dorrell.
    6072 ELLEN L., b. Aug. 3, 1845; m. C F. Sawyer, of Fitchburg.
    6073 MARION H., b. June 17, 1848.

6074 Eva J., b. Oct. 23, 1851; m. Clinton A. Ware.
6075 George H., b. Aug. 4, 1855.
6076 Carrie J., b. April 26, 18.7; m. Albert B. Warner, of Bernardston, Mass., Dec. 11, 1879.

6068 Dr. George W. Denison, (Edward[5], David[4], George[3], William[2], George[1],) b. Feb. 23, 1810; m. Elvira Hancock, practiced medicine, in Chicopee, Mass., 35 years; d. Aug. 29, 1875. Only one child:

6077 Lizzie E.; m. Dr. Francis Parker.

6069 Frances E. Denison, (dau. of 6065 Capt. Edward, Jr.,) b. Sept. 8, 1839, was married, to John H. Newcomb. Their children:

6078 Belle E., b. Feb. 24, 186.; m. Wm. H. Tyler, of Guilford, Vt., Jan. 11, 1881.
6079 Lizzie M., b. Dec. 7, 1862.
6080 Jessie M., b. Feb. 11, 1864.
6081 Alice L., b. April 27, 1865.
6082 Edward D., b. April 7, 1867.
6083 John H., b. Nov. 22, 18 1.
6084 Dwight C., b. Feb. 17, 1873.
6085 Julia L., b. May 4, 1875.
6086 Foneta A., b. July 20, 1877.

6071 Edward Hapgood Denison, (son of 6065 Capt. Edward, Jr.,) b. June 9, 1843, was married to Celestina Dorrell. Their children:

6087 Maud Mabel, b. Nov. 3, 1872.
6088 Nellie Agnes, b. July 6, 1876.
6089 Dona Edna, b. Feb. 11, 1878.

6074 Eva J. Denison, (dau. of 6065 Capt. Edward, Jr.,) b. Oct. 23, 1851, was married, Dec. 3, 1874, to Clinton A. Ware, of Northfield. One child:

6090 Burton A., b. Feb. 20, 1876.

6070 Maria R. Denison, (dau. of 6065 Capt. Edward, Jr.,) b. Aug. 15, 1841, was married, to Henry C. Howe, of Gill, Mass. One child:

6091 Mary Denison, b. Jan. 4, 1877.

6072 Ellen L. Denison, (dau. of 6065 Capt. Edward, Jr.,) b. Aug. 3, 1845, was married to C. F. Sawyer, of Fitchburg, Mass. They have:

6092 Clare Denison, b. Oct. 4, 1879.

5926 GEORGE DENISON, (David[4], George[3], William[2], George[1],) b. in 1769, was married to Lucy Babcock, dau. of Peleg Babcock, and emigrated to Fabius, N. Y. His wife d. in 1808; he m. 2d in 1809, Phebe Briggs, of Leyden, Mass.; he d. in 1813. His children:

    6093 GEORGE, d. when about 22 years old.
    6094 AMY, b. Feb. 24, 1801; m. Charles Kenyon.
    6095 OLIVE; m. Raymond P. Babcock.
    6096 ARAD JOSEPH, b. March 28, 1807.
    6097 JABEZ S., by the second wife, Phebe Briggs.

6094 AMY DENISON, (dau. of 5926 George,) b. Feb. 24, 1801, was married to Charles Kenyon, and emigrated with him to Scott, N. Y. She d. May 25, 1856; he d. Dec. 20, 1863, aged 73 years. Their children:

    6098 C. WARREN, b. Dec., 1827; m. Jane Price.
    6099 ELLEN O., b. June 22, 1835; m. Willard Morgan, of Scott, N. Y., and d. Feb. 2, 1856, aged 20 yrs, 7 mos., 8 da.

6095 OLIVE DENISON, (dau. of 5926 George,) was married to Raymond P. Babcock, emigrated with him to Scott, N. Y.; had six children, and d. in 1845. The children:

    6100 LUCY.   **6103** HERBERT.
    6101 ANDREW.   **6104** DELIA.
    6102 GEORGE.   **6105** OLIVE.

6096 ARAD JOSEPH DENISON, (son of 5926 George,) b. March 28, 1807, in Fabius, N. Y., was married, April 12, 1827, to Prudence M. Burrows, who was born July 6, 1807, in Guilford, Vt. She d. April 9, 1872; he d. April 10, 1876. Their children:

    6106 WILLARD ARAD, b. Feb. 2, 1828.
    6107 AVERY JOSIAH, b. Nov. 24, 1829.
    6108 JOSEPH B., b. March 26, 1831; d. June, 1831.
    6109 AMY SOPHIA, b. March 4, 1833.
    6110 LYDIA LOUISA, b. Sept. 9, 1834.
    6111 GEORGE WASHINGTON, b. Jan. 30, 1837.
    6112 CHARLES KENYON, b. Feb. 2, 1842; d. Nov. 12, 1874.
    6113 ANDREW RICHARD, b. May 6, 1843.
    6114 ADELAIDE LUCY, b. Oct. 6, 1847.

6106 WILLARD ARAD DENISON, (son of 6096 Arad Joseph,) b. Feb. 2, 1828, was married, March 12, 1848, to Belinda Worden, of Halifax, Vt. The children:

    6115 WILLARD, b. April, 1849.

6116 ALBERT, b. in 1851; d. June, 1860.
6117 FRANK, b. in 1853; d. in infancy.
6118 FRANK AVERY, b. in 1855, d. June, 1860.

6107 AVERY JOSIAH DENISON, (son of 6096 Arad Joseph,) b. Nov. 24, 1829, was married, first, May 4, 1859, to Emma Sophia Stewart, who d. April 2, 1861; and second, June 7, 1869, to Hattie Frances Minor, b. Oct. 12, 1842. The children:
6119 CARROLL AVERY, b. June 9, 1870.
6120 HELEN CARLETTA, b. July 16, 1875.

6109 AMY SOPHIA DENISON, (dau. of 6096 Arad Joseph,) b. March 4, 1833, was married, Dec. 1854, to Ezra W. Plum. Their children:
6121 AUGUSTA, b. Oct., 1856; d. young.
6122 AUGUSTA, b. 1859; d. June, 1865.
6123 ERNEST EZRA, b. Sept., 1869.

6110 LYDIA LOUISA DENISON, (dau. of 6096 Arad Joseph,) b. Sept. 9, 1834, was married, May, 1851, to Eri G. Baldwin. Their children:
6124 EMMA JANE, b. April, 1852; d. Oct., 1854.
6125 EFFIE S., b. 1856.
6126 CHARLES HENRY, b. 1858.

6111 GEORGE WASHINGTON DENISON, (son of 6096 Arad Joseph,) b. Jan. 30, 1837, was married, Nov. 1859, to Emily Whitting. Their children:
6127 CHARLES HENRY, b. Oct., 1860.
6128 EVA ELIZA, b. Aug. 6, 1862.
6129 LORETTA PRUDENCE, b. July, 1865.

6113 ANDREW RICHARD DENISON, (son of 6096 Arad Joseph,) b. May 6, 1843, was twice married; first, in Aug., 1869, to Sarah E. Martin, who d. the same day; second, Oct. 8, 1873, to Netta Laura Miller. One child:
6130 BERTIE RUSSELL, b. Jan. 7, 1875; d. Sept. 8, 1875.

6114 ADELAIDE LUCY DENISON, (dau. of 6096 Arad Joseph,) b. Oct. 6, 1847, was married Aug. 4, 1874, to Otis J. Laselle. Children:
6131 FREEMAN EDDIE, b. Nov., 1877.
6132 EVELYNE, b. Oct., 1880.

6097 JABE S. DENISON, (son of 5926 George, by the second wife,) was married to Louisa Kenyon, of Leyden, Mass., and emigrated to Ovid, Clinton, Co., Michigan. Three children:

6133 JARED; has a large family, mostly daughters.
6134 LOVILLA; *m.* George Simpson.
6135 CHARLOTTE.

5927 JOHN DENISON, (David⁴, George³, William², George¹,) born in 1771, was married to Mary Avery, of Groton, Ct., dau. of Thomas Avery, (son of Christopher,) and gr-gr-gr-grand daughter of the second James Avery. She was born Jan. 26, 1786. They lived in Coleraine, Mass. She died in 1852. Their children:

6136 MARY LOUISA, b. Oct. 1. 1810; d. unmarried, Dec. 22, 1859.
6137 JOHN AVERY, b. April 25, 1812; unmarried.
6138 HANNAH SMITH, b. May 5, 1814; *m.* Robert G. Marsh.
6139 GILBERT, b. in 1816; d. in infancy.
6140 THOMAS AVERY, b. Jan. 5, 1818; *m.* Clara Danforth.
6141 EUNICE; d. in infancy.
6142 JANE; d. in infancy.
6143 SOPHRONIA AUGUSTA, b. Aug. 8, 1824; *m.* Horatio N. Pratt.
6144 ANN BORODELL, b. June, 1827; *m.* John H. White.

6140 THOMAS AVERY DENISON, (John⁵, David⁴, George³, William², George¹,) b. Jan. 5, 1818, was married, May 18, 1844, to Clara Danforth of Portsmouth, N. H. He lived in Chicopee, Mass.; d. Sept. 13, 1873. His children:

6145 REV. GEORGE AVERY, b. Oct. 27, 1845; *m.* Elizabeth M. Chapin.
6146 CLARA JANE, b. Sept. 22, 1847; *m.* Oliver M. Hamilton.
6147 WILLIAM M., b. Sept. 1, 1850; d. in Central America, in 1874, unmarried.
6148 JOHN, b. Oct. 27, 1859; d. April 25, 1862.

6145 REV. GEORGE AVERY DENISON, (son of 6140 Thomas Avery,) b. Oct. 27, 1845, was married to Elizabeth M. Chapin, April 6, 1871. One child:

6149 JOHN AVERY, b. Aug. 17, 1876.

6146 CLARA JANE DENISON, (dau. of 6140 Thomas Avery,) b. Sept. 22, 1847, was married to Oliver M. Hamilton, May 14, 1872. They live in Springfield, Mass. Two children:

6150 BEATRICE, b. July, 1874.
6151 PHILIP.

6138 HANNAH SMITH DENISON, (John⁵, David⁴, George³, William², George¹,) b. May 5, 1814, was married, Nov. 13, 1834, at Chicopee Falls, Mass., to Robert G. Marsh. He d. at Holyoke. Four children:

11 William Denison's Descendants.

6152 ALBERT EDWARD, b. Dec. 31, 1836; twice married.
6153 WM. HENRY HARRISON, b. Sept. 8, 1841; twice married.

6143 SOPHRONIA AUGUSTA DENISON, (John[5], David[4], George[3], William[2], George[1],) b. Aug. 8, 1824, was married at Chicopee, Sept., 1847, to Horatio N. Pratt. They live in Nashville, Tenn. One child.

6154 DAISY E.

6144 ANN BORODELL DENISON, (John[5], David[4], George[3], William[2], George[1],) b. June, 1827, was married in June, 1850, to John H. White, of Hartford. He lives in Chicopee, Mass.; she d. The children :

6155 JOHN DENISON.
6156 MINNIE, d. May 18, 1871.

5923 SAMUEL DENISON, (David[4], George[3], William[2], George[1],) b. March 17, 1763, was married to Eunice Haughton, and emigrated to Ohio. We have failed to get a full record of his family. He had seven children. We know the names of all but the youngest, but have no dates. They are as follows :

6157 SAMUEL, JR.,   **6160** DAVID,
6158 HENRY,   **6161** EUNICE,
6159 JOHN,   **6162** MATILDA.

Appendix.

APPENDIX.

CAPT. GEORGE DENISON.

Capt. George Denison, emigrant, the head of the clan whose family records are given in this genealogy, came over to this country in the good ship Lion, with his father, William Denison, his brothers Daniel and Edward, and Rev. John Eliot, the apostle to the Indians. George was at this time thirteen years of age, and doubtless received much of his mental and moral training from Mr. Eliot, who was tutor in his father's family. William Denison was a merchant, and from the fact that he employed a tutor in his family, it is inferred that he must have been a man of considerable means. He was a deacon in the 1st Church in Roxbury, a man of liberal education, and of large influence in the colony. His wife did not come to this country until 1632, and did not unite with the church until some years later. William Denison built a house in Roxbury, and it remains until this day in good preservation. He died there, Jan. 25, 1653, an old man. She died there Feb. 23, 1645.

George Denison began his adult life in Roxbury, and at the age of 22, married Bridget Thompson in 1640. She was the daughter of John Thompson, gent., of Preston, Northamptonshire, England, whose widow, Alice, had come to America, and was living in Roxbury. We find quite widely distributed among the descendants, a courtship letter in verse, addressed by our ancestor to Miss Bridget Thompson, who seems to have been his first flame. We make room for it, not only as an interesting relic of the olden time, and a sample of the methods of courtship in 1640, but to correct a little romance invented by one of his descendants, which alleges that he was betrothed to Ann Borodell before he came to this country, and hastened back to her immediately upon the death of his first wife. There is no evidence of this, but much to the contrary. He was but thirteen when he emigrated, and probably never heard of Ann Borodell until he was carried a wounded soldier to her father's house, John Borodell of Cork, Ireland, (who was then living in England,) where Ann became his nurse, and afterward his wife. Whatever we may think of the literary merit of these verses, they seem to have prevailed with Miss Bridget:

CAPT. GEORGE DENISON'S COURTSHIP LETTER TO BRIDGET THOMPSON.

It is an ordinance, my dear, divine,
Which God unto the sons of men makes shine,
Even marriage, to that whereof I speak,
And unto you therein my mind I break.

In Paradise, oft Adam God did tell,
To be alone for man would not be well—
He in His wisdom, therefore, thought it right
To bring a woman into Adam's sight;

A helper that for him might be most meet,
To comfort him by her doing discreet.
I of that stock am sprung—I mean from him—
And also of that tree I am a limb.

A branch, tho' young, yet I do think it good
That God's great vow by man be not withstood;
Alone I am, a helper I would find,
That might give satisfaction to my mind.

The party that doth satisfy the same
Is Miss Bridget Thompson by her name;
God having drawn my affections unto thee,
My heart's desire is—that thine may be to me.

This with my blottings, tho' they trouble you,
Yet pass them by, because I know not how—
Though they at this time should much better be,
For love it is, that first has been to thee.

And I would wish that they much better were,
Therefore, I pray, accept them as they are,
So hoping my desire I shall obtain,
Your own true love,

A. D. 1040.   GEORGE DENISON, by name.

Appendix. 299

After three years of wedded life, Bridget died, leaving two daughters, Sarah and Hannah, who lived to be the heads of families in Stonington. Very soon after her death, he returned to England, enlisted under Cromwell in the army of the Parliament, won distinction, was wounded at Naseby, was nursed at the house of John Borodell by his daughter Ann, which led to his marriage with her, and his early return to Roxbury, where he was chosen Captain, and was called, " a young soldier lately come out of the wars in England." He is said to have had one son, John, born July 14, 1646, when he came to Roxbury the second time, which would make his absence about three years.

He did not long content himself with the quiet life in Roxbury. His daughter Ann had been born to him in that place, May 20, 1649. In 1651, he left Roxbury with his wife and four children for the Pequot settlement upon the west bank of the Thames, now New London. Here he had a house lot given to him by the town which he occupied until 1654, when he sold out, went to Stonington, and settled on the land, a part of which has been in the possession of his descendants until the present generation ; a tract of some five hundred acres in all, lying east of Pequotsop brook. His homestead place was bounded on the West by John Stanton's farm, now mainly owned by Joseph S. Williams, on the south by the Mason highway, which, with slight variations, is the road from Mystic Bridge to the Road church, eastward to Palmer hill, and then by Amos Richardson's land, easterly by Richardson's land and the town lots, and westerly by said lots and lands of Capt. John Gallup.

The first house was probably a log house, which only served a temporary purpose, and was removed in Captain Denison's life time to make room for his mansion house. This was located in the north west corner of his tract, a few feet west of the present dwelling of the Misses Sarah and Phebe M. Denison. The spot was undoutedly selected, with the eye of a military leader, for the purpose of defence against Indians, who were then numerous, and disputed possession of the country with the English. There is no other spot so eligible for the purpose of defence in the neighborhood. The house stood upon the southern slope of a narrow plot of ground about twenty-five rods long, buttressed with steep ledges on every side. This acre of ground, more or less, elevated from twenty to thirty feet above the surrounding ravines, and stockaded, was impregnable against any force the Indians could muster. There was a stone fort inside of the stockade near the house, and the remains of the old wall are still pointed out. It was removed about a hundred years ago by those who had slight appreciation of the value of historical monuments. The stones are still visible in the walls near the house. The location is a pleasant one, standing high above the adjacent fields and looking out southward over a broad tract of intervale, once probably cultivated by the aborigines, and now lying in meadow, the best part of the neighboring farms. In this direction you get glimpses of the Mystic River and the Sound, with Fisher's Island and Long Island in the distance. To the west lies Pequod hill, once crowned with an Indian fort, and the scene of the terrible slaughter under Capt. John Mason. To the north lies Quocataug with the Mystic valley on the left, stretching away toward Lantern hill; a scene of rural beauty not easily matched in the county. The land has many ledges, with loose well rounded boulders upon the top, left in the ice period, geologists tell us, and ground into their present form by the moving glaciers. It is still hard land, even for Stonington, with rough pastures which the plow has never broken and probably never will. There are however, smooth fertile acres between. Emigrants had been here five years before Captain Denison, to spy out the land, and the best locations had already been appropriated.

The mansion house which he erected could not have been a very imposing or substantial structure, for it was removed by his grandson George, son of William, about the year 1724. Tradition affirms that George, eldest son of George and Lucy Gallup Denison, was the first child born in the new house. The records fix the date of his birth, July 9, 1725, and that of his next older sister, Mary, July 14, 1724. This would make the age of the present structure 157 years, in the present year

Appendix. 301

1831. Upon this spot seven generations of the Denison family have been born. William[2] was probably born in the log house ; his son, George[3], born in the mansion house ; his son George[4], Oliver[5], Oliver[6], Edgar[7] and his children. The present farm of 250 acres, remained undivided from George[3] until the death of the sixth owner, Oliver[6], in the year 1873, a period of two hundred and twenty years from the settlement. About 50 acres, including the house and outbuildings were deeded to his daughters, Sarah and Phebe, and the rest of the land divided among the other heirs. It is quite rare in this country to find a farm that has been held in the same family by inheritance for seven generations.

Perched on this ledge of rocks, like a baron in his castle, Captain Denison had a commanding influence among his townsmen for forty years, was their trusted military leader in forays against the Indians, and their frequent representative at the General Court at Hartford. He had great executive ability, and managed well the public trusts committed to him, and his own private affairs. He not only lived and raised a numerous family from these rude acres, but accumulated, for those times, a large estate. Numerous tracts of land were given to him by the authorities, for his military services principally, so that at the time of his death he owned several thousand acres of land in Stonington, in Norwich and Windham, and in the State of Rhode Island. This laid the foundation of comfortable homes for his children and their descendants for several generations, and retained nearly all of them within easy reach of the ancestral homestead for a hundred years after his death. His sons and his daughters, with the exception of Margaret, who went to Swanzey, Mass., all remained in Stonington, or in adjoining towns. Of his eleven grandsons, four remained in Stonington, two in Westerly, R. I., one in North Stonington, one in Montville, one in New London, and two in Saybrook. Nearly all were quite large landholders and men of influence in their respective towns.

It is a little remarkable that none of the sons or grandsons, with a single exception, obtained the good old age of the emigrants. Capt. Denison died at the age of 76, and his wife Ann

Borodell, at 97, which shows that our emigrant ancestors were favored with unusual physical vigor. Of their three sons, John died at 52, and George and William at 59. William only survived his mother a year and a half. The grandsons died at the ages of 30, 37, 38, 38, 40, 43, 46, 55, 64, 67, 86. This last was George, the son of William, who lived at Pequot-Sop, and removed the mansion house to make room for the present more spacious dwelling. The hardships of the wilderness will hardly account for this diminution of vital force in the second and third generations. They were almost all cut off in the midst of life; and they had fewer difficulties and less exposure than the emigrants. It is not improbable that the products of the orchards they planted and the barley they harvested, when manufactured into alcoholic beverages, proved more perilous to life than struggles with the primitive forest, and the Indians. Later generations seem to have recovered the vigor of the founders of the clan, and give us a long list of persons who passed their three score years and ten. There is food for profitable reflection in these statistics.

There is a solitary entry upon the records of the First Church of Stonington, under date of Aug. 24, 1684, "Capt. Denison was took into full communion," which shows that his mind had not been much occupied with religious things until late in life. The name of his wife appears among the communicants at the organization of the church ten years earlier. His active military life, and the clearing of the wilderness, had not favored religious culture. His will, made ten years later, shows a very positive religious character, and a warm appreciation of his pastor, Rev. James Noyes, and of "the well bringing up and educating his grand children in religion and good learning."

The selection of the youngest son to be the principal heir, and to take the homestead, is probably a practical protest against the aristocratic usage of the mother country, which makes the eldest the favorite. William, the youngest son of Capt. Denison, takes the homestead and cares for his widowed mother. The youngest sons of John, George and William, also inherit the homestead of their respective fathers.

Appendix.

The descendants of Capt. Denison began to swarm from the hive in the fourth generation, and are now to be found in almost all states of the Union, and in Nova Scotia and Canada. Capt. Robert Denison, son of Robert of Mohegan, was of the fourth generation, settled in Nova Scotia, and has a numerous and highly respectable posterity in that province.

Robert Denison of the fifth generation, son of Daniel, emigrated to Knox, N. Y., and from there two of his sons and three of his daughters went to Napanee, Ontario, Canada, and became the founders of the Canada branch of the family. There was a large emigration, quite early, to Vermont and border towns in Massachusetts; and about the same time or a little later to New York and Pennsylvania. Thence they have spread westward, to Ohio, and the Northwestern states, across the continent to California and Oregon. Only a few have reported from the Southern states.

The intermarriage of Capt. Denison's daughters and granddaughters with the Palmers, Cheseboros, Stantons, Williamses, Billingses, Browns and Babcocks, gives him a very numerous posterity in Stonington and vicinity. Nearly half the people of the town can trace their lineage back to Capt. Denison. It is only incidentally that we have traced the descendants of the Denison women beyond their own children. If this were to be done, down to the present generation, it would make another volume as large as the present. If this should ever happen, it will be undertaken by some person who has faint conception of the patience and labor it involves.

Of his wife, Ann Borodell daughter of John Borodell of Cork, Ireland, it is agreed by all the traditions that have come down to us in the several branches of her descendants, that she was remarkable for her fine personal appearance and ladylike manners. On account of these qualities she was commonly called Lady Ann, which was a much higher compliment than to have inherited the title. This has been claimed for her but without authority. In some branches of the family, there are fine samples of embroidery which show her skill in needlework. The widow of the late Isaac D. Miner of Mystic Bridge, Conn., has one of these samples with an authentic record handed down through seven generations. It is still in good preservation. Mrs. Charles T. Stanton of Stonington, has a case of drawers, once her property and given by her to her daughter, Borodell, who married Samuel Stanton. There are other relics of Lady Ann at the old homestead where she once ruled. She had a brother John Borodell, who came to this country and settled, also a sister Margaret, who married a Shepherd, and for whom her daughter Margaret was probably named. This sister had descendants, one of whom married a Wheeler; and Joseph Noyes, who married Zurviah Wheeler, has a descendant of Margaret Borodell Shepherd for his wife. Ann Borodell must have been well born, for she lived amid the hardships of pioneer life to the remarkable age of 97. The remains were disinterred some twenty years ago, and removed from the old burying ground, at the foot of Denison street, to the Denison plat in the Elm Grove Cemetery. Here a substantial granite monument was erected to the memory of her husband about thirty years ago by contributions from his descendants. Deacon Ebenezer Denison, senior, was the principal mover in this filial work, and it was among the last of the many good deeds of his life.

The following account of the main incidents of his life is given by Richard A. Wheeler, in his history of the First Church of Stonington:

"Captain Denison took an active and decided part in 1656, in favor of having 'Mystic and Pawcatuck' set off, and a new township with a ministry of its own established. By this course he incurred the displeasure of the leading men of Pequot, and by favoring the claims of Massachusetts to the jurisdiction of the place, he drew upon himself the censure of the General Court, and when Southerton was incorporated and annexed to Suffolk County, he was appointed first townsman, commissioner, and 'clerk of the writs.' He was active and influential in securing the favor of the Massachusetts Court, and aided in securing large grants of land here, to parties there, which overlapped grants made to Cheseborough, Stanton, Palmer and others, by the General Court of Connecticut. This alienated some of his friends. But the re-union of the

Appendix.

settlement by means of the new charter had the effect of extinguishing these Massachusetts claims, and the Connecticut grants were left undisturbed.

" When Mr. Cheseborough, in 1664, asked the General Court of Connecticut for amnesty for the planters who had favored the claim of Massachusetts to this place, it was readily granted for all except Capt. Denison. Two years later it was extended to him, and ever afterward, he was regarded with favor by the General Court. From 1671 to 1694 he represented Stonington for fifteen sessions of the General Court. He was appointed magistrate, selectman, and held almost every office in town.

" While Captain Denison was prominent and active in civil affairs, he was more distinguished in military matters. With the exception of Capt. John Mason he was the most conspicuous and daring soldier of New London county, a natural military leader, and, though holding the rank of captain, he often commanded expeditions against the Indians, and was always most successful when commander-in-chief. He participated in the Narragansett swamp fight in 1675, and performed prodegies of valor. As early as February following that event, a series of forays were commenced against the Narragansett Indians. They were commanded by Capt. Denison and Capt. James Avery. These partisan bands were composed of volunteers, regular soldiers, Pequots, Mohegans and Niantics. It was the third of these roving excursions, begun in March and ended April 10th, 1676, in which the celebrated Narragansett chieftain, Canochet, was taken prisoner. He was brought to Stonington, and put to death at Anguilla, near where Gideon P. Chesebro' now resides. A council of war was held, during which his life was promised him if he would use his influence with the Indians to put a stop to the war, but he indignantly refused, saying that the Indians would not yield on any terms. He was told of his breach of faith in not keeping the treaties which he had made with the English, and of the men, women and children he had massacred, and how he had threatened to burn the English in their houses ; to all of which he haughtily and briefly replied, 'that he was now in their hands and they could do with him as they pleased.' He was importuned and urged to let a councillor of his go and treat with his people, but he haughtily refused, whereupon the council of war voted for his immediate execution. When Canochet was told that he must die, he seemed not at all moved, but said, 'that he liked it well, and that he should die before his heart had grown soft, or he had said anything unworthy of himself.' He was shot by Oneco, son of Uncas, and by Cassasinnamon and Herman Garrett two Pequot sachems. The Mohegans quartered him, and the Niantics built a fire and burnt his remains. His head was sent, as ' a token of love,' to the Council at Hartford.

"In June following, Captain Denison, commanded a company raised in New London county, for Major Talcott's expedition against the Indians in Massachusetts. They went as far north as Northampton, and returned after having scoured the country far up the Connecticut river, but met with a very few of the Indians. After a few days rest the army went again in pursuit of the Indians. This time they went first to the northwest of Providence, then south to Point Judith, then home through Westerly and Stonington to New London. After a short respite, they started again, July 18, 1676, and made their way this time into Plymouth Colony. They went to Taunton, from whence they returned homeward, but hearing that a large number of Indians were working their way westward, making depredations as they went, they pursued and overtook them, and had a sharp and final struggle with them beyond the Housatonic, after which they returned, and the men were disbanded.

"There were ten of these expeditions, including the volunteer forays, under Denison and Avery. They inflicted speedy vengeance upon the Indians, and broke their power forever. The remnants of the Indian tribes were gathered together, and located wherever the English desired. In all these military expeditions Captain Denison bore a conspicuous part, and won for himself undying fame."

THE WILL OF CAPT. GEORGE DENISON.

STONINGTON, Nov. 20, 1693.

I, George Denison of Stonington, in the county of New London, and Colony of Connecticut in New England, being aged and crazy in body, but sound in mind and memory, and being desirous to make preparation for death, and to set my house in order before I die, I do, therefore, as it becometh a Christian, first, freely and from my heart, resign my soul, through Christ, into the hands of God who gave it me, and my body to the earth from whence it came, and to be buried in decent manner by my executor and friends, in the hope of a joyful and glorious resurrection, through the perfect merits and mediation of Jesus Christ my strong Redeemer.

And as concerning my outward estate, which the Lord hath still entrusted me with, after all my just debts are paid, I give and dispose of as followeth:

First, I give and bequeath unto my dear and loving wife, Ann Denison, my new mansion place, to wit. the house we live in, the barns and buildings, the orchards, and the whole tract of land and improvements thereon, as far as Mistuxet eastward, and as it is bounded upon record, south, west, and north, except only thirty acres given to my son. John Denison, which is to lie on the south side next to Capt. Mason's, east of our field, and also one hundred pounds in stock, prized at the county price, all which is and hath been under our son William Denison's improvement and management for these several years, to mutual comfort and content, which I do will and bequeath unto my said wife for her comfortable supply during her natural life.

And I give unto my said wife, all the household stuff that was and is properly belonging unto us, before my son William took the charge of the family, to be wholly at her disposal, to bequeath to whom she pleaseth at her death.

Unto my eldest son, John Denison, I have already given his portion, and secured to him by a deed or deeds, and I do also give unto him, his heirs or assigns, forever, a county grant of two hundred acres of land, or two hundred pounds in silver money, which grant may be found on the General Court Records.

Also, I give unto him, my great sword and the gauntlet which I wore in the wars of England, and a silver spoon of ten shillings, marked G. & A.

Unto my son, George Denison, I have formerly given a farm, lying and being at the northwest angle of Stonington bounds, and adjoining the ten mile tree of the said bounds, which farm containeth one hundred and fifty acres, more or less, as also, the one half of a thousand acres of land, lying to the northward or northwest of Norwich, given to me as a legacy by Joshua the son of Uncas, the same time Mohegan sachem, the said land to be divided as may more fully appear in the deed, which I then gave him of both those tracts in one deed, signed and sealed with both my own and my wife's hand, and delivered to him and witnessed, and I have several times tendered to him to acknowledge it before authority, that so it might have been recorded according to the formality of law, the which he had wholly neglected or refused, and will not comply with me therein, and yet hath sold both those parcels of land and received pay for them; what his motive may be I cannot certainly divine, but have it to fear they are not good, nor tending to peace after my decease.

Wherefore to prevent further trouble, I see cause herein to acknowledge said deed, and to confirm those said parcels of land unto him, according to the date of said deed, and the conditions therein expressed, but do hereby renounce any other deed not herein expressed, the which two tracts of land before mentioned, with two Ind'an servants, to wit., an Indian youth or young man, and a woman, together with a considerable stock of neat cattle, horses, sheep and swine I then gave him, and permitted him to have and carry with him, I do now confirm to him, the which was and is to be, the whole of his portion, I either have or do see cause to give him, only I give unto him twenty shillings in silver, or a cutlas or rapier, the which I leave to the discretion of my executor, to choose which of them to do.

Unto my son, William Denison, I have formerly given him, one hundred and thirty acres of land, be it more or less, to wit., all of the land to the eastward of Mistuxet brook which did originally belong unto my new mansion place, and is part of three hundred acres granted unto me by New London, as may appear upon record, and three hundred acres of land, lying and cutting upon the North boundary of Stonington, as may more fully appear upon record in Stonington, and the native right thereof, with some addition, confirmed to me by Oneco, as may more fully appear by a deed under his hand and seal, acknowledged before Capt. Mason, and recorded in Stonington. Also, I then gave him two Indian servants, viz., John whom I bought of the county, and his son Job, which was born in our house, together with one third part of stock, which we have together, all which as aforesaid we formerly gave unto my son William Denison by a former deed, under our hands and seals, and I see just reason to confirm the same unto my son William, in this my last will, that so I may take off all scruple or doubt respecting the said deed. Moreover I give unto my son William Denison, fifty acres of land, as it was laid out and bounded unto me by Stonington surveyors, and joins upon the before-mentioned three hundred acres, on south side thereof, cuts also upon lands belonging to my son John Denison, to be to him my said son William Denison and his heirs forever. Also, I give unto my son William Denison, and his heirs forever, the one half of my allotment at Windham, to wit, five hundred acres of land, which is part of a legacy given me by Joshua, the son of Uncas, the same time sachem of Mohegan, as may more fully appear upon the Court Records at New London, as also, upon that former experience we have had of his great industry and child-like duty in the management of all our concern, for our comfort and comfortable supply, &c., it is therefore my will, and in confidence of his love, duty, and wonted care of his loving mother. my dear wife, after my decease, I say I do still continue him in the possession and improvement of my new mansion place, with the stock mentioned herein in my deed to my loving wife, he taking care of his said mother for her comfortable supply, with what may be necessary for her comfort during her natural life, and do, or cause to be paid to his said mother, forty shillings in silver money yearly, or half-yearly, while she shall live, and at her decease, I fully and absolutely give and bequeath that my aforesaid mansion place, together with the stock mentioned before, unto my said son, William Denison and his heirs forever. Also, I give unto my son William Denison, my rapier, and broad buff belt, and tin cartridge box, which I used in the Indian wars, together with my long carbine, which belt and sword I used in the same service.

Unto my eldest daughter Sarah Stanton, as I have given her formerly her portion as I was then able, so I do now give unto her ten pounds out of the stock as pay, and one silver spoon of ten shillings price, marked G. & A.

Unto my daughter Hannah Saxton, as I have given unto her, also, her portion as I was then able, so I do now give unto her ten pounds out of the stock, as pay.

Unto my daughter Ann Palmer, besides that I have formerly given her, I do now give her ten pounds out of the stock as pay.

Unto my daughter Margaret Brown, I have given already her portion, and give her ten pounds out of the stock as pay.

Unto my daughter Borrodel Stanton, I have formerly given, and do now give her five pounds out of the stock as pay, and command it to my beloved wife, that at or before her death, she would give her silver cup, which was sent us from England, with brother Borrodel's name, J. B., under the head, to her.

Unto my grandson, George Denison, the son of my oldest son John Denison, I give my black-fringed shoulder belt, and twenty shillings in silver money, toward the purchase of a handsome rapier to wear with it.

Unto my grandson, George Palmer, I give the grant of one hundred acres of land, which was granted unto me by the town of Stonington, not yet laid out, or forty shillings out of my stock, as pay, at the discretion of my executor to choose which. And whereas there is considerable rent due me for a house of my wife in Cork, in Ireland, which was given unto her as a legacy by her father, John Borodell, at his death, and no doubt may appear upon record in Cork, the which house stands upon lands which they call Bishop's land, and was built by our said father, he to have lived in the same, whereof my said wife was next to himself, as may also appear there upon record; and whereas I have a right to land in the Narragansett country, which is mine by deed of the native right from the true proprietors thereof, as may appear upon record in Boston, and in the records of Stonington, the which, my rights, have been and are under the possession and improvement of those who have no just right to them, to which by reason of the many troubles, woes and difficulties which have arisen, together with our remoteness, we have not been able to vindicate our just rights, but have been great sufferers thereby; but if it please God to send peaceable times, and our rights be recordable in law, I do by this my last will, give and bequeath my said right unto my sons John Denison and George Denison, to be equally divided betwix them, provided that they each one bear their equal share in the trouble and recovery of the same. Provided, also, that my son George Denison, do relinquish and deliver up any right he may pretend unto by a former deed which I gave him of the one half of Achagromeconsist, according as I formerly obliged him to do in a deed I gave him of the other farm, and gave him upon that consideration.

And in reference with Nathaniel Beebe, who hath been a retainer and boarder in our family between thirty and forty years; and for his board at our last reckoning, which was March 20th, 1680, he was indebted to me forty-six pounds six shillings and three pence, I say £46, 6s & 3d, as may appear under his hand to said account in my book, since which time he hath boarded in the family near upon fourteen years, which at four shillings and sixpence the week, amounts to one hundred and sixty-three pounds, sixteen shillings, out of which I do give unto Nathaniel Beebe, fifty pounds, in way of gratification and satisfaction for his love to me and my children, and offices of love shown unto myself and any of them, in mine or their sickness or weakness, which fifty pounds must be deducted from the one hundred and sixty three pounds, sixteen shillings, and the remainder will be one hundred thirteen pounds, which one hundred and thirteen pounds, sixteen shillings, together with the forty-six pounds, six shillings and three pence due upon book, under his hand, at our last reckoning as aforesaid, being added unto one hundred and thirteen pounds, sixteen shillings, the whole will be £160, 2s, 3d, the which I give unto my son William Denison, and his heirs forever, for him or them or any of them, or if they see cause to demand, receive and improve as their own proper estate. Also, I give unto my son William Denison, all and singular, whatsoever that belongeth unto me, not already disposed of, to be to him and his heirs forever, whom also I do hereby constitute, appoint, and make my sole executor, to pay all just debts, if any shall appear of which I know not any, and to receive all dues which either are or shall be due to me, and to pay all legacies according to this my will, within twelve months after my wife's decease, and to take care for my decent burial. But in case my son William Denison shall decease before he hath performed this my will, or before his children are of age, then my will is that the whole estate be under the improvement of his wife, our daughter-in law Sarah Denison, during the time of her widowhood, for her comfortable supply, and the well educating and bringing up of their children in religion and good learning; all which she shall do by the advice of the Reverend and my loving friend, Mr. James Noyes, my son John Denison and my son-in-law, Gershom Palmer, them or any two of them, if three cannot be obtained; but without advice she may not act, which three my dear friends, I do earnestly desire and hereby appoint as overseers for the children, and to take effectual care that this my will may be performed according to the true intent thereof; but if my said daughter-in-law shall marry again, then this whole estate to fall into the hands of those my overseers, and by them to be secured for my son William Denison's children, to wit, William Denison, George Denison and Sarah Denison, and by those overseers to be improved for their well bringing up as aforesaid, and faithfully to be delivered unto the children as they shall come of age, to wit: the males at twenty-one years of age, and the females at eighteen; and if any of the said children should die before they come of age, the survivors shall inherit the same, and if they should all die before of age, (the which God forbid, but we are all mortal,) then it is my declared mind and true interest of this my will that my grandson George Denison, the son of my eldest son John Denison, shall be the sole heir of that estate, out of which he shall pay unto his four brothers, to wit, John Denison, Robert Denison, William Denison, and Daniel Denison, ten pounds apiece in current pay, and also ten pounds in current pay unto his cousin Edward Denison, the son of my son George Denison; and in token that this is my last will and testament, I have hereunto set my hand and seal this 24th day of January, in the year of our Lord one thousand six hundred and ninety three-four.

GEORGE DENISON. [SEAL.]

Appendix. 311

CAPT. JOHN DENISON.

It seems strange that so little should be known among his descendants, of a man so conspicuous in his time as Capt. John Denison. He was the first-born of Capt. George Denison and his wife Ann Borodell, married to Phebe Lay, Nov. 26, 1657, at the age of 21, after each party had been duly apportioned by their fathers in a legal contract recorded at Saybrook. They were blest with nine children, six sons and three daughters, of whom one died in infancy. All the rest lived to be married, and with a single exception, had large families and a numerous posterity. Large tracts of land were given to each of the sons, generally during the father's life-time. And yet there were no stones for his grave, or that of his wife, and it was a long time before we found the place of their burial. A genealogy of the Chesebro' and Denison families, kept by Daniel Chesebro', who lived near the Head of the River, incidentally states, that they were buried in the burying ground at the foot of Denison street, in the village of Mystic Bridge. We had looked diligently for these graves in Saybrook, near the village of Essex, where his eldest son John settled upon the farm given to them by Robert Lay, but no trace of a grave or stone was to be found there, nor of his son John, nor of his grandsons Daniel and John who died there. There is a stone at the grave of his grandson James, who died before marriage, and of his grandson Jabez who had a large family, and died at the age of 90. In those early times gravestones were brought from England, and the building of monuments was so expensive, that many of the early settlers' graves were marked by no head stones that had inscriptions.

His five sons were all men of influence and left families. His descendants numbered in the book are 3,374. Those of his brothers William and George combined, only number 2,405 so far as they are recorded. His son John died at the early age of 30, soon after his settlement in Saybrook, leaving five children, the youngest Jabez being but six months old. The second son George, received a liberal education at Harvard College, was settled as a lawyer at New London, and was for a time clerk of the County Court. Robert settled in Mohegan, near Gardner's lake, now Montville, was a large land holder by purchase from the Indians, was among the founders of the church there, was twice married, and had twelve children by the first wife and two by the second.

William, the fourth son, settled in the northwest corner of Stonington, now North Stonington, upon land owned by his grandfather, Capt. George, and inherited from his father. It remained in the family several generations. He had twelve children, and was the progenitor of one of the most prolific and enterprising branches of the family. Descendants are still very numerous in Stonington, though the homestead has passed out of the family. Still more are found in New York state, in Vermont and in Maine. Daniel, the youngest son, remained upon the homestead in what is now the village of Mystic Bridge, and reared a numerous family. The old Denison house was probably built by Capt. John. It is mentioned in the diary of Thomas Miner, a co-temporary, as being moved a short time before his death. How long it had stood before the moving we have no means of knowing. It is a venerable pile, probably the oldest house in town; nearly or quite two hundred years old. The farm originally embraced all the land lying south of the Westerly road and west of Pequotsop brook, extending to the river on the west and south. In this old house six generations of Capt. John's descendants, have been born and brought up. The shingles upon the east side are said to be as old as the building. It is now quite out of repair and used as a tenement house. The timbers in it are large and sound, and might last many years, if the building were kept in repair.

The items from the inventory which accompany the will are interesting, as they show the state of society, and the simplicity of the early days. The wearing apparel of the lady of the house is appraised at £15, which though it may seem small now, represented then a goodly display of "woman's clothes,"

Appendix.

on Sunday at the Road Meeting House, the only church building in town. Meagre as this is, £6 is still smaller allowance for the " wearing clothes " of Capt. Denison. Their mode of travel is indicated by the generous supply of horse flesh: " 2 horses, 2 mares and 4 3-years old colts." There were no carriages or four-wheeled vehicles of any kind in those days for pleasure rides. The ambition of the thrifty settlers was to have a horse or colt for each son and daughter to ride, as they grew up. The roads were rough and hardly suitable for modern vehicles. There was comparatively little travel between Sundays, and most of the people, indoors and out, were busy with the hard problem of sustaining life. It was the age of homespun, and the women had their hands full in carding, spinning, weaving and bleaching every yard of cloth that was to be manufactured into clothing for the family. Sunday was the great day of the week for the family display, as well as for worship. The descendants of Capt. John, who have a lively imagination, can picture the scene as the seven steeds, saddled and bridled, were brought up to the horse block on Sunday morning, and one after another the parents and children mounted and took the east road over the hills toward the meeting house, to hear a discourse from that learned and godly man, Rev. James Noyes. The sanctuary was the chief place of concourse, the centre of news, and had to answer most of the ends of the newspapers and magazines of various sorts. The amount of time devoted to reading in the family, can readily be guessed, from that item in the inventory, " a bible and other books and a brush, 10 shillings." This very small sum covered all the accumulations of reading matter in a married life of thirty years. The gold ring, £2, 12s, was five times more valuable than all the books in the house. This ring possibly was the gift of Phebe to Capt. John when he went wooing in the early days to Saybrook. It ought to be in existence at this day, among some of his descendants. Who will produce it?

THE LAST WILL AND TESTAMENT OF JOHN DENISON OF STONINGTON.

In the name of God amen. I make this my last will in manner and form as followeth : I being now sick and weak in body, yet in good memory, yet not knowing but the time of my dissolution may be near, I give my soul unto God that gave it, and my body to Christian and decent burial at the discretion of my executor hereafter named. And, after my funeral expenses and just debts first being paid: as to my estate, I have and do dispose of it. Item, viz. : To my eldest son, John, I have formerly given him as may appear under my hand, the house and land where he now liveth, with stock, which is in full of his portion. Item : Unto my second son George, I have given a grant of two hundred acres of land, and sheep, and beding, and in convenient time my will is, that my executor pay out of my estate unto my said son George the sum of thirty pounds, and that with what I have done for him, to be in full for his portion. Item : Unto my third son, Robert, I have given lands and housing as may more fully appear by deed under my hand, he paying and performing the conditions therein expressed ; and also I give my said son the one half of thirty acres, which I had of my honored father, joining to the land given my brother William.

Item : Unto my fourth son, William, I give in Stonington as it was laid out 300 acres of land, and my right to a 12 acre lot in Stonington, and 2 three year old steers, and forty shillings to pay for boards and for nails, thirty shillings money, and this to be in full of his portion. Item : Unto my youngest son, Daniel, I give and bequeath the remaining part of my farm where I now live, with the other part of my thirty acres I had of my honored father as above said, with a twelve acre lot which I had of the town ; and to my above-named sons Robert and Daniel, the third part of a tract of land at a place called Chagomequansit, which was given me by my honored father, deceased. Also, I nominate my two sons, Robert and Daniel, my executors of this my last will. Item : Robert for to pay fifty pounds as above expressed, as may appear by deed of gift under my hand, unto my daughter Ann. And to my daughter Phebe, out of my estate, fifty pounds. And to my daughter Sarah, fifty pounds ; to each of my daughters, if they attain to the age of eighteen years, or at the time of their marriage, whichever shall first happen.

And my household goods, my will is, it be equally divided between my three daughters, Ann, Phebe and Sarah, only the beell meetell bool which is at my son John's, for to be my daughter Ann's, given by her mother. Also, my will is that my executors do take the care of my wife, and do in that case as the law doth direct. And having thus declared my mind, I make this for to be my last will and testament, revoking all other wills whatsoever.

This dated at Stonington, April 26, 1698.

This signed and sealed in   JOHN DENISON. [SEAL.]
presence of
GERSHOM PALMER and SAMUEL STANTON.

ITEMS FROM INVENTORY. Woman's clothes, £15 ; his wearing clothes, £6 ; a silver spoon, 12 shillings ; gold ring, £2, 12s ; a bible and other books and a brush, 10 shillings; house and lands he lived on, £150; 2 oxen, 9 cows, 11 3-yr. olds, 4 2-yr. olds, 12 yearlings, 1 bull, 32 sheep, 14 lambs, 2 horses, 2 mares, 4 3-yr. old colts.

The whole inventory, £509, 12s, 10d.

APPRAISERS. Nehemiah Palmer, Henry Stephens, Joseph Sexton, Adam Gallup,—Selectmen.

MAJOR GENERAL DANIEL DENISON.

For one who was so conspicuous in the early history of the colony of Massachusetts Bay as Major General Daniel Denison, there is little left upon record. We glean the following from an article in the Genealogical Register of New England, by Dr. Daniel Denison Slade of Boston, published in 1869:

"There is much uncertainty as to the origin of the family name. It is variously spelt Denison, Dennison, Denyson, Dennistown. It is unquestionably of ancient and probably of Norman origin. In the Patronymia Britannica is the following notice: 'The Dennistowns' of that ilk have an extraordinary way of accounting for their surname. One *Danziel, or Daniel (say they,) probably of Norman extraction, settled in Renfrewshire, and calling the estate Danzielstown, assumed therefrom his surname. The family are unquestionably ancient, the name appearing in the Charter of King Malcom I., who died in 1165, but the Norman Danziel is probably a fiction. The English Denisons are said to have sprung from a cadet of this ancient house, who went from Scotland in the time of Charles I., who fought at Marston Moor."

Daniel, the oldest son of William and Margaret Denison, was born in England in 1612, and came to this country proba-

---

* Burke's "Book of the landed Gentry of Great Britain," gives this as true, and says the Norman's name was "Danziel." He called his place "Danzielstoun," and from this came Denison. He was a full blooded Norman.

bly in the ship Lion in 1631, with his father, and brothers, Edward and George, the Winthrops, and Rev. John Eliot being his fellow voyagers. Daniel was then nineteen years old. The following year, 1632, he removed from Roxbury to Newtown, (Cambridge,) his name being on the list of first settlers and church members. He there married Patience, the daughter of Gov. Thomas Dudley, who was at this time a resident of the place. At a general court holden " att Newtown, March 4, 1634," Mr. Denison was appointed to assist in setting out " the bounds of ground betweene Newtowne and Rocksberry." He took the oath of freeman, April 1st, 1634; and under the same date, the court grant him two hundred acres, " all lying and being about the ffalls, easterly side of Charles River."

With eight others, he is authorized by a general Court at Newtowne, Sept. 3, 1634, to " sett out the bounds of all towns not yet sett out, and to settle all differences between any towns." He is also, with N. Easton, to have charge of powder at Ipswich, which is the first allusion we find to his military predilections.

In the following year, land was assigned to him in Ipswich, with " a house lot of about two acres, which he hath paled in, and built a house upon." To this plantation he at once removed, and with its history his name is closely united during the remainder of his days. It is difficult to conceive why, after having connected himself with the church and town affairs of Cambridge, he should so soon have quitted them for another abode. The probability however is, that the uncertainties which attended the project of establishing the capitol at Newtowne, and the differences which in this matter sprung up between Gov. Winthrop and his father-in-law, Mr. Dudley, whose cause he would naturally espouse, and who removed to Ipswich in 1635, decided him to take this step. Whatever may have been the reasons for the course pursued Mr. Denison at once commenced his public career of usefulness and honor in his new home. During the first year of his residence in Ipswich, he was returned as deputy, in which capacity he served for three consecutive years from 1635 to 1638. He was again elected in 1640, 44, 48, 49, 51 and 52. As a member of the memora-

Appendix. 317

ble court of November, 1637, he ordered those who had sympathised with Mrs. Hutchinson and Mr. Wheelright, to be disarmed, and among these, were his father and brother, " their arms to be delivered to Gov. Johnson."

In 1636, he was made town clerk of Ipswich, " to have sixpence for every entrance of land." In the same year, by the General Court he is chosen captain of Ipswich; with twelve others, he is deputed to assign the amount due from each town toward a sum to be levied for public uses. A quarterly Court having in 1636, been ordered to sit in Ipswich, Capt. Daniel Denison and Mr. Sam'l Apleton were chosen to assist in these courts. Thus within the space of two years, after becoming a resident of Ipswich, we find Mr. Denison serving his countrymen, in offices pertaining to town affairs, and to those of the colony, as well as in a military capacity.

Sept. 6, 1638, Capt. Denison with Mr. Bradstreet, and ten others, was allowed upon their petition, " to begin a plantation at Merrimack," and to have " liberty to associate to them such others as they can agree upon." At the same session of the court he was appointed with 15 others, " to consider of the manner and time of payment of a rate of £1200, and to lay it upon every towne pportionably," to be paid " at two months."

In 1641, he was one of a committee for furthering the trade of Ipswich. They were " to set up buoys, beacons, provide salt, cotton, sowing hempseed, flax seed, and card wire." The town granted him in 1643, 200 acres of land, " for his better encouragement to settle among us."

Great alarm having spread through the colonies, from a report that a general conspiracy existed among the native tribes, of which Miantonomo, the chief of the Narragansetts was a principal instigator, a general training of troops and provision of arms were ordered, and Capt. Denison with five others, was authorized at a session of the General Court, May 10, 1643, to put the country into a posture of war, and to see to fortifications.

On petition, several gentlemen of Ipswich, Beverly, and the adjoining towns, among whom was Capt. Denison, "out of care for the safety of the public weal, by the advancement of the military art and exercise of arms," were incorporated as a military company. The inhabitants of Ipswich agree to pay him £24, 7s. annually, as their military leader. In the year preceding, he had been chosen sergeant major, which office he held until his election as Major General. Johnson in his "*Wonder-working Providence*," thus speaks of him: "The two counties of Essex and Norfolk, are for present joyned in one regiment; their first major who now commandeth this regiment is the proper and valient Major General Daniel Denison, a good soldier and of a quick capacity, not inferiour to any of these other chief officers; his own company are well instructed in feats of warlike activity."

The house of representatives conferred the honor of speakership upon him during the two sessions of 1649, and again in the years 1651 and 1652. Mindful of the great importance of education and of the interests of his town, Major Denison was instrumental in establishing the grammer school of Ipswich, and was made one of the ffeoffers in 1651. He afterwards gave freely for its maintenance. In 1651 he petitioned the General Court to confirm a grant of 267 acres, which had been assigned to his father, " and in consideration of the said grant and their favor to mee, they be pleased to grant to mee, and my heirs forever, 600 acres of land where it may be found, according to law." After several years the court granted his request, but the land was not laid out until July, 1662.

In the following year he was ordered to supply the place of Gen. Robert Sedgewick, who was absent. To the office of Major General he was appointed in 1653, and held it at different times until 1680. In this year he was chosen an Assistant and thenceforwards to his decease. In September, he was elected Secretary of the Colony, in the absence of Edward Rawson. In May, General Denison was appointed by the Court one of a committee to join with the commissioners of the united colonies to draw up the case respecting " the Dutch and Indians." A few years previous he had been placed on a committee with the Governor and two others, " for the purpose of ending differences, settling trade, &c., with the Dutch."

Appendix. 319

Not coming to any agreement, Mr. Eaton, on the part of the commissioners, and Major Denison on the part of the General Court, were instructed to prepare, each of them, a short draft to be presented to the court and elders. While Eaton was " clamorous for war," Denison did not advocate extreme measures, and it was undoubtedly greatly through his influence that the house of deputies communicated to the commissioners their resolve, " that according to their best apprehensions in the case they doe not understand wee are caled to make a present warr with the Dutch."

In the spring of this year, intelligence was brought that thousands of Indians had assembled at Piscataqua. Accordingly General Denison ordered out a scouting party of twenty-seven men, " to make a true discovery, and to quiet the minds of the inhabitants who were much distracted and taken of their employments." They were absent on service from Friday morning until Monday night, and were allowed as pay for each private, 1 sh., and two troopers 2 sh. 6d. per day. The alarm was without foundation.

He was appointed with three others to keep the county courts at Salisbury and Hampton.

In May, 1654, a committee of three was chosen, of which General Denison was one, " to examine, compare, reconcile, and place together, in good order, all former laws both printed and written." Whether the committee performed this labor or not, is uncertain. At any rate the following order was passed by the General Court four years afterward, May 26, 1658, " that Major General Daniel Denison diligently peruse, examine and weigh every law, and compare them with others of like nature; and such as are clear, plain and good, free from any just exception, to stand without any animadversion as approved. Such as are repealed or fit to be repealed, to be so marked, and the reason given; such as are obscure, contradictory, or seeming so, to be rectified, and the emendations prepared. When there is two or more laws about one and the same thing, to prepare a draught of one law, that may comprehend the same; to make a plain and easy table, and to prepare what else may present, in the perusing of them, to be necessary and useful, and make return at the next session of this court." The General entered upon this work with zeal, and in a few months produced the volume, which was at once printed. Two copies of the volume are still in existence. As compensation " for his great paines in transcribing the laws," the court granted him " a quarter part of Block Island," the remaining portions were granted to Endicott, Belingham, and Hathorne. These in turn sold the island to John Alcock, for the sum of £400 in 1660.

During the next month, by order of the court, he met Mr. Bradstreet and Mr. Symonds at Ipswich, " about a narrative in way of remonstrance of all matters respecting that which is charged on the General Court concerning the breach of the confederacy, for the vindication of this court's actions in such respects." This meeting was in reference to recent dissensions in the confederacy, in which Massachusetts had by her course of action, been accused by the other colonies of breaking the covenant. This narrative, together with answers to a letter received from the lord protector, were to be sent to Cromwell.

In 1655 he was on a committee appointed for the county of Essex, " for the procuring of suitable supplies," and " to consider of some such way as whereby both merchandizing may be encouraged, and the hands also of the husbandman may not wax weary in his employment."

Massachusetts, considering that she had a prior right to certain territory on the north east, claimed by representative of Gorges & Rigby, the court, at its session, October, 1657, appointed Gen. Denison, with Mr. Bradstreet and Mr. Hathorne, as commissioners to proceed to Kittery, and to confer with the inhabitants, who were dissatisfied with the existing state of affairs under which they lived. After long delay, and much consideration, Kittery submitted to the jurisdiction of Massachusetts. The commissioners next proceeded to Agamenticus (afterwards York,) and to other places, which were received on the same terms as Kittery.

As one of the confederate commissioners, to which office he was called in 1654, and in which he served faithfully until

Appendix. 321

1663, he addressing a letter to the Governor of Rhode Island, respecting the Quakers: "We therefore make it our request, that you as the rest of the colonies take such order herein that your neighbors may be freed from that danger; that you remove those Quakers that have been received, and for the future prohibit their coming among you. We further declare that we apprehend that it will be our duty seriously to consider what further provision God may call us to make to prevent the aforesaid mischief."

As commissioner with Mr. Bradstreet he dissented from the message and instructions given by their fellow commissioners of the other colonies, to his brother, Capt. George Denison, and two others, by which they were to go to Ninigret the Niantic sachem, and to the Narragansett chiefs, and warn them to abstain from hostilities against Uncas and against one another. An expedition, the command of which had been offered to Gen. Denison, and declined, had been sent a few years before, under Major Willard, against Ninigret. The result of this had been far from satisfactory. "There having been many messengers to this purpose," say the Massachusetts commissioners, "to the Indian sachems, but seldom observed by them, which now to renew again . . . can in reason have no other attendance in conclusion, than to render us low and contemptible in the eyes of the Indians, or engage us to vindicate our honor in a dangerous and unnecessary war upon Indian quarrels, the grounds whereof we can hardly ever satisfactorily understand."

In 1660, Gen. Denison joined the Ancient and Honorable Artillery Company, and the same year was elected commander, which was the first authentic instance of a person being admitted a member, and the same year admitted to its highest office.

"The monarchy having been now restored in the person of Charles II., the General Court of Massachusetts apprehending difficulties with the throne, proceeded to take certain precautions. At the close of the session of 1661, Gen. Denison with others was appointed a committee to consider and debate such matter or thing of public concernment, touching our patent laws, privileges and duty to his majesty, as they in their wisdom shall deem most expedient, and draw up the result of their apprehensions, and present the same to the next session for consideration and approbation, that so, (if the will of God be,) we may speak and act the same thing, becoming prudent, honest, conscientions and faithful men."

" The king having made demands of Massachusetts, through Secretary Morrice, among which was one ' express command and charge that four or five influential persons to be chosen by the Governor and Council should be sent to England forthwith, to attend upon his majesty,' the General Court at its session, Sept. 11th, 1666, appointed a committee to draw up a letter through Secretary Morrice, giving their reasons for not submitting to the mandates of the royal commissioners sent the year previous, and also replying at length to a proposal for an invasion of New France. In the debate, to which this letter gave rise, Gen. Denison and Mr. Bradstreet were much more compliant than the other magistrates, being confirmed in their views, perhaps, by the petitions which had come in from several towns, praying for submission to the king's demands."

" Major Gen. Denison declared his dissent from the letter to be sent to Secretary Morrice, as not being proportionate to the end desired, and he hopes intended, and desired it might be entered, viz., due satisfaction to his majesty and the preservation of the peace and liberty of this colony." " The king's commands pass anywhere," says Denison. " No doubt you may have a trial at law when you come in England if you desire it, and you may insist upon it and claim it. Prerogative is as necessary as law and is for the good of the whole, that there be always power in being to act, and where there is a right of power, it will be abused so long as 'tis in the hands of weak men, and the less pious the more apt to miscarry; but right may not be denied because it may be abused. If we shall refuse to answer here to commissioners, and in England also, what will the king say? Is it not plain that jurisdiction is denied to his majesty? Though no appeal lies to his majesty so to stop justice but it may require and answer thereto, so that our absolute power to determine must not abate the king's prerogative."

Appendix.

"The capture of New York by the Dutch in 1673, created an alarm among the English colonies, lest their dominion might also be invaded. Accordingly the Federal commissioners met at Hartford and recommended to the General Court of each of the colonies to provide means of defence The governor and Council of Massachusetts, at a meeting Aug. 4, 1673, ordered—"that for defence against the Dutch, in case of their appearance before the harbor, endeavors be used to set the three principal forts in order."

"1st. That the honored Governor and Major General shall be, and hereby is empowered, in case of any notice or appearance or assault of the enemy, to command such company of foot or horse as belong to the regiments of Suffolk, or Middlesex, to come in to the relief of the towns of Boston or Charlestown."

"6. That the Major of Essex regiment, Daniel Denison, Esq. shall and hereby is impowered and required to send relief into Salem and Marblehead."

"In the disastrous war with the Indians which broke upon the colonies in 1675, Gen. Denison, as might be supposed from his position, took an active part. There are several letters extant, relating to this latter portion of his life. These for the most part are well preserved, and the hand writing which is excellent, is as distinct as ever, although two centuries have fled since they were written. He was appointed commander-in-chief of the Massachusetts forces, June, 1675, as may be seen in the instructions given him by the Governor and Council; but as he was prevented by sickness from taking the field, Major Thomas Savage was substituted in his place.

"It would exceed the limits allotted to this sketch to give these official documents in detail. They serve to show that Gen. Denison was skillful with his pen, as well as with his sword, and that the authorities of the colony had the largest confidence in his abilities, and in his fidelity to public trusts.

"Oct. 12, 1676. The court appointed Gen'l Denison to proceed to Portsmouth, and to take chief command of the forces there destined for the war at the eastward. He was authorized 'to impress men, horses, ammunition and provisions, and as shall to him seem mete.'"

"In this connection, we extract the following from Hubbard's *Present State of New England:*

"The Governor and Council of the Massachusetts colony had at this time their hands full with the like attempts of Philip and his complices to the westward, yet were not unmindful of the deplorable condition of the eastern Plantations, having committed the care thereof to the respective regiments of the several counties on that side of the country, but more especially to the care and prudence of the honoured Major Daniel Deniron, the Major General of the whole colony, a gentleman who by his great insight in, and long experience of all martial affairs was every way accomplished for the managing that whole affair."

"Active operations against the enemy at the eastward were carried on until late in the autumn of 1676, under the direction of Gen. Denison. Magg, the Etechennie sachem, surrendered himself to the commander-in-chief at Portsmouth, and was sent to Boston, where a treaty was concluded, stipulating the cessation of hostilities, the restoration of prisoners, &c. This state of peace continued, however, only until the following spring, when hostilities were again commenced, and did not cease until the termination of the war in the spring of 1678. In the year 1677, Denison was not elected to the office of Major General, but during the remaining years of his life he filled that position. As one of the licensers of the press, with Bradstreet and Dudley, he authorizes the imprint and publication of Hubbard's Narrative, Mar. 29, 1677. In May of this year, he is one of three to grant permission to Indians to carry arms."

"The General Court granted to General Denison, Oct. 10, 1677, an island of 6 or 7 acres, opposite the middle of his farm for his distinguished services."

"Of the remaining years of Gen. Denison's life, we know but very little. As he was chosen Assistant the very year his death occurred, we may presume that the distressing disease of which he died did not prevent him from performing the public duties to which he was called, until very near the end. It is probable that he occupied the leisure moments of the latter portion of his active life in writing the treatise which he left at his decease, and which was published by his good pastor, Wm. Hubbard, two years after that event. The volume, which is entitled, "*Irenicon, or Salve for New England's Sore,*" is exceedingly rare, and is a good specimen of the quaint language of the day.

"In this he considers, 1. What our present maladies are intended in this discourse. 2. What might be the occasion thereof. 3. The danger. 4. The blameable causes. 5. The cure.

"Among the manifold symptoms of this disease, I apprehend none more threatening our dissolution, than the sad and unreasonable divisions about matters of religion. A receipt of these five simples without composition, accompanied with fasting and praying, till they are well digested, with God's blessing, may bring about the expected cure; for the Dose you need not trouble yourself, there is not danger of taking too much. And if this should fail, which I fear not, I have another receipt, but I fear it is somewhat corroding, which I hope I shall never have occasion to use, my lenitives working according to my expectation. So I take my leave, committing you to God and a good Nurse."

"During the last month of his life he was called upon to give his opinion in matters relating to the church at Andover."

"Gen. Denison died at Ipswich, Mass., Sept. 20, 1682. The death of so distinguished a public servant, must have called forth expressions of grief, not alone among his immediate family and townsmen, but throughout the colony.

That he was a man of distinguished abilities, and those of a most varied character, the services to which he was called continuously through a long life, abundantly testify. That he performed these services faithfully, and satisfactorily to his constituents, is shown by his constant re-election to offices of great public trust, even after it was acknowledged that he belonged to the moderate party, and when, by his speeches, he proved that he was ready to yield to the king's prerogative. Mr. Savage, in his life of Winthrop, speaks thus of Denison, "The moderate spirit by which he was actuated, had not a general spread, yet the continuance of his election to the same rank, when his sympathy was not, in relation to the controversy with the crown, in unison with that of the people, is evidence of the strong hold his virtue and public labors had acquired."

" Moreover, we have every reason to suppose that his character was strengthened and supported by religious influences, adding thereby to his eminence among men."

" It is much to be regretted that we have neither portrait nor description of the person of General Denison ; and of his private worth, we glean our knowledge chiefly from the funeral sermon preached by his pastor."

" The greater is our sorrow, who are now met together to solemnize the funeral of a person of so great worth, enriched with so many excellencies, which made him live neither undesired, nor die unlamented, nor go to his grave unobserved. . . ' Is there not a Prince and a great man fallen this day in Israel.' So in a sense it may be said here, a great man is fallen in our little Israel. Concerning the man whose funeral obsequies were lately celebrated amongst us, not to say more than is convenient, to prevent emulation in them that are surviving. His parts and abilities were well known amongst those with whom he lived, and might justly place him among the first three, having indeed many natural advantages above others for the more easy attaining of skill in every science."

" His military skill some years before his death advanced him to the conduct and command of the whole, which he was able to have managed with great exactness, yet was he not inferior in other sciences ; and as a good soldier of Christ Jesus he had attained to no small confidence in his last conflicts with the king of terrors, being not afraid to look death in the face, in cold blood, but with great composedness of mind received the last summons. For though he was followed with tormenting pain of the stone or strangury, that pursued him to the last, he neither expressed impatience under those grinding pains nor want of confidence, or comfort from his first seizure. . . . So having fought the good fight, run his race and finished his course, he quietly resigned up his spirit to God who gave it. His last thoughts and endeavors were for the good of the pub-

Appendix. 327

lic, as may be seen by the *Irenicon*, now lately found among his papers, which it is thought would be too much ingratitude to withhold from the view of all, any longer."

That his funeral services were conducted in a manner worthy of his distinguished rank and of the high estimation in which he was held, may be judged from the following copied from the Massachusetts archives:

"WHEREAS, it hath pleased the Lord, in his sovereign Providence, to take away our honored Daniel Denison, Esq., and in regard to his long continuance a Major General, it occasioned a very considerable charge at his funeral, and the annual income of his family being but small, the Magistrates judge meet that the Treasurer allow to his widow the full of this year's salary, until May next, and also twenty pounds in money to be paid the said widow, in pay of her said funeral charges.

The Magistrates have passed this, their brethren the Deputys hereto consenting.
EDWARD RAWSON, Sec'y.

Oct. 18, 1682. The Deputys consent not hereto.
WILLIAM TORREY, Clerk.

"Mrs. Denison survived her husband eight years. Of her life and character we know nothing with certainty. They had two children, John and Elizabeth. John married Martha, daughter of Deputy Governor Symonds, and had three children: one of whom, John, graduated at Harvard College, was chosen as colleague with Mr. Hubbard at Ipswich, and was much beloved by his people. His life was short. John, (senior,) died Jan. 9, 1671. Elizabeth married Rev. John Rogers, President of Harvard College."

ABSTRACT OF THE WILL OF DANIEL DENISON.

I, Daniel Denison of Ipswich in New England, being in good health and memory, doe thus ordaine my last will:

To my daughter, Mrs. Elizabeth Rogers, besides the portion of £120 and other kindness she hath already received, I give my farm of 500 acres lying upon Connecticut river above Northampton and Hatfield. Also, 500 acres granted me by the General Court in Oct., 1665, and £20 be payed her in lieu of so much given her by her grandfather Dudley. I give £5 to my grandchild Daniel Rogers, to be paid him at the age of 21 yeares, or sooner, if my executor see cause. To my wife Patience, I bequeath the rest of my estate in houses, lands, cattle, money, &c., for her support, and for the education and maintenance of my grandchild, John Denison, and for the relief of my grandchildren Daniel and Martha Denison, if they be in neede, for whose education and maintenance I have otherwise provided by a covenant made with Mr. Martyne, that married their mother. After the decease of my wife, I will that my grandchild, John Denison, have my farm at Chebacco, where he was borne, with all the implements of husbandry, also four and a half acres of land at Plum Island, lying against Grape Island, layd out at the right of the farm house. I will that my grandchild, Daniel Denison, have my farm at Merrimack of 600 acres, lying near Haveril bounds, which lands were promised their dear father upon his marriage. If either of my said grandchildren dye before they come to age, the survivor shall have two parts of what is bequeathed the other; and their sister Martha Denison, the other third part. If both dye, then Martha to have said farmes and land, except the four and a half acres of marsh, which I will to my grandchild, Elizabeth Rogers. In case my wife dye before said grandchildren come to age, their mother Mrs. Martha Martyne shall take upon her the care of their education, and for that end enjoy the benefit of their portions till they come of age, the boys at 21 years, the daughters 18 years; unless my wife see cause in her life time, or at her death, to dispose otherwise.

Remainder of estate, (after wife's decease,) leaving her liberty to gratify her children, or grandchildren as they shall best deserve, out of my stocke in her life, or at her death, to be divided into five equal parts (except my books, arms or artillery, which I will to my grandchildren, John and Daniel Denison, to be equally divided between them,) dau. Elizabeth Rogers and John and Daniel Denison, each one-fifth part, and grand hild Elizabeth Rogers one-fifth and one-half-fifth part, and grandchild Martha Denison, the other half-fifth part, to whom I have willed no larger a share, because I have provided otherwise that said Martha have £100 by Mr. Richard Martyne, her father-in-law. In case John or Daniel die before they receive their fifth part, the survivor, with their sister Martha, have that part equally divided between them, as also if Martha die in like manner, the brother have her portion; if both John and Daniel dye their fifth parts be to my daughter Elizabeth Rogers, and the two farms to their sister Martha, she paying Elizabeth Rogers £100 or the farm of 600 acres, at Merrimack within six months after demand made. In case said grandchildren all dye before the age of 21 years, leaving no issue, my daughter Elizabeth Rogers to have said two farms, she paying my grandchild Elizabeth Rogers at least £150, or the farm at Merrimack, as said grandchild shall choose. I make my wife Patience, executrix: my son, Mr. John Rogers and Capt. John Appleton, overseers.

18 July, 1673. Manu propria scripsi.

DANIEL DENISON.

In case my wife dye, and make no executors, I ordaine my two overseers, or either of them to be my executors.

July 17, 1679.   DANIEL DENISON.

Whereas, in the disposal of that part of my estate which I have willed to be divided into 5 equal parts, I have given my grandchild Martha Denison, but one half of a fifth part, and the other half to my grandchild, Elizabeth Rogers,

I have for good causes ordered that said Elizabeth have only one-fifth part, and that half of the fifth part given said grandchild be to my daughter Elizabeth Rogers, this I ordaine as a schedule to be affixed to my will.

Feb. 28, 1678. Manu propria scripsi.

DANIEL DENISON.

Having this day paid Mr. John Appleton who lately married my grandchild Elizabeth Rogers £50 in silver as a portion, and having given £8 in silver for her wedding clothes besides some other gifts, and whereas I have in the within will, given her but one-fifth part, and half a fifth part, of the remainder of my estate, and in the above written schedule retracted the bequest of the half-fifth part, and given the same to my daughter Elizabeth, I doe also declare my will and revoke said gift of one fifth part and give said part to my daughter Elizabeth Rogers over and above what else I have given her, leaving it to her to consider her daughter, now Elizabeth Appleton, as she shall see cause. This I ordaine as a seconde schedule to my will.

22 Dec., 1680. Manu propria scripsi.

DANIEL DENISON.

At a court held at Ipswich, 10 April, 1683, Mr. Major Samuel Appleton and Captaine Daniel Epps, appeared in court and made oath that sometime in the latter end of Sept, 1682, we were at the house of Major Daniel Denison, Esq., of Ipswich, he being sick of the disease whereof he died, yett of good understanding, did then declare unto us, that he had made several wills, but that which was the last dated, and had three latin words at the end of it, was the will he would have to stand. Capt. John Appleton appeared at the same court and (gave similar testimony,)

Accepted by the court. Attest: ROBERT LORD, Clerk.

INVENTORY OF ESTATE. 17 Oct., 1682. Amount £2105, 13s. Debts due the estate: money £28, 10s.; country pay £390, 8s., 2d; other debts which were thought on since said Inventory was taken: rates £1, 10s., country pay 3s.

Mrs. Patience Denison, executrix and relict of Major Denison, Esq., made oath before the worshipfull Samuel Appleton, Esq., and Maj. Robert Pike, Esq., that is a true inventory of her husband's estate, to the best of her knowledge.

14 April, 1683. Attest: ROBERT LORD, Clerk.

MAJOR GENERAL DANIEL DENISON'S DESCENDANTS.

1 DANIEL DENISON, (oldest son of William of Roxbury,) b. in 1612, was married about 1639, to Patience Dudley, dau. of Gov. Thomas Dudley, settled at Ipswich, Mass., in 1638. He d. Sept. 20, 1682. His wife d. Feb. 8, 1690. Their children :

 2 JOHN, b. 1640; *m.* Martha Symonds, 1664.
 3 ELIZABETH, b. 1641; *m.* John Rogers, President of Harvard College and a descendant of John Rogers the martyr.

Ex-Governor Dudley died in 1653, aged 77, and gave one-sixth of his estate to his daughter Patience Denison.

2 JOHN DENISON, (son of 1 Daniel,) b. 1640, *m.* Martha Symonds in 1664, and had :

 4 JOHN, b. 1665; *m.* Elizabeth Saltonstall, 1684.
 5 DANIEL, b. in 1667; no record.
 6 MARTHA, b. 1669; *m.* Matthew Whipple.

John Denison died in 1671, aged 31, and Martha, his widow, *m.* Richard Martyn.

3 ELIZABETH DENISON, (dau. of 1 Daniel,) b. 1641, *m.* Rev. John Rogers about 1660, lived at Cambridge, Mass. She d. in 1723, aged 82 ; he d. in 1684, aged 54 years. Their children :

 7 ELIZABETH, b. in 1661; *m.* John Appleton, 1680.
 8 MARGARET, b. 1664; *m.* 1st, Thomas Berry in 1682; 2d, John Leverett in 1697.
 9 JOHN, b. 1666; *m.* Martha Whittington.
 10 DANIEL, b. 1667; *m.* Sarah Appleton.
 11 NATHANIEL, b. 1669; *m.* Sarah Purkiss.
 12 PATIENCE, b. 1670; *m.* Benjamin Marston.

4 REV. JOHN DENISON, (son of 2 John,) b. 1665, *m.* Elizabeth Saltonstall, daughter of Nathaniel Saltonstall of Ipswich, about 1684, and had :

 13 RUTH, b. 1686; *m.* Joseph Kingsbury, 1706.
 14 JOHN, b. 1688; *m.* Mary Leverett, 1719.
 15 HANNAH, b. 1689; *m.* NathanielKingsbury, 1710.

Appendix. 331

Rev. John Denison died 1689, aged 24. He was assistant to Rev. William Hubbard of Ipswich, Mass., who died in 1704, age 83. Elizabeth, widow of Rev. John, *m.* Rev. Roland Cotton.

Charles Denison of Norwich, Conn., to whom we are indebted for most of the records of the descendants of Major General Daniel Denison, and many others of the descendants of Capt. George Denison, says of the above family record, " I have no certain authority for making Ruth and Hannah Denison, children of Rev. John and Elizabeth Denison, but as there is no record of any others of suitable age, and having record of the marriage at Haverhill of Ruth Denison and Joseph Kingsbury, Feb. 5th, 1706, and of Hannah Denison and Nathaniel Kingsbury, 1710, which Kingsburys were brothers, and settled in Norwich, Conn., I inferred their wives were sisters, and from their ages at death. I inferred they were daughters of Rev. John Denison. Nathaniel Kingsbury removed to Coventry, Conn. His wife Hannah, died 1772, aged 83. The birth of three of their children, viz.: John, b 1710, Nathaniel, b. 1710, Mary, b. 1713, are upon the Norwich records.

Deacon Joseph Kingsbury died Dec. 1757, age 75, at Norwich. His widow, Ruth Kingsbury, died May, 1779, age 93. Upon her grave stone in Franklin, (once a part of Norwich,) it reads, " She left 5 children, 61 grandchildren, 152 great grandchildren. The births of their children are upon the Norwich records."

The marriage of these sisters to brothers, at Haverhill, a neighboring town to Ipswich, the absence of any other family of Denisons in that region, and the correspondence of names, leave no reasonable doubt that the wives of the Kingsbury brothers were the daughters of 4 Rev. John Denison.

13 RUTH DENISON, (dau. of 4 Rev. John,) b. 1686, *m.* Joseph Kingsbury, Feb. 5, 1706, settled in Franklin, then a part of Norwich, Conn., about 1708. Joseph was a son of Joseph and Love Kingsbury, and was born Jan. 22, 1682. Their children were:

16 EPHRAIM, b. Jan. 4, 1707; *m.* Martha Smith, 1728; d. 1772.
17 HANNAH, b. March 1708; *m.* Jacob Hyde, 1727.
18 LOVE, b. 1710; *m.* Josiah Barker; d. 1778.

19 RUTH, b. 1712; *m.* Joshua Edgerton.
20 JOSEPH, b. 1714; *m.* Deliverance Squires, 1736.
22 EBENEZER, b. 1716; *m.* Priscilla Kingsbury.
23 ELEAZER, b. 1718; *m.*
24 EUNICE, b. 1722: *m.* John Barker.
25 DANIEL, b. 1724; *m.* Abigail Barlow.
26 TABITHA, b. 1726; *m.* ——— Waldo.
27 GRACE, twin, b. 1729; d. 1730.
28 JANE, twin, b. 1729; unmarried.
29 NATHANIEL, b. 1730; *m.* Sarah Hill.

14 JOHN DENISON, (son of 4 Rev. John,) b. 1688, *m.* Mary Leverett, 1719, and had :

30 JOHN, b. 1722; d. 1747, aged 25; unmarried.
31 MARY, b. 1724; *m.* John Wise.

John Denison graduated at Harvard College in 1710, was a representative of the General Court from Ipswich, 1716, '17 and '18, was Lieut. Colonel and High Sheriff of the County of Essex ; died 1724, age 35. His widow, Mary, *m.* Nathaniel Rogers, and died in 1756, aged 55.

30 REV. JOHN DENISON, (son of 14 John,) has a monument at Ipswich, Mass., with the following inscription :

" In memory of JOHN DENISON, A. M., only son of Col. John Denison, grandson of a minister of the same name, and a descendant of the renowned Major General Daniel Denison. An amiable young man and worthy of his ancestor. His genius, learning, and engaging manners spoke him the future joy of his native town. But heaven meant otherwise. He died in his 25th year, on the 25th of August, 1747."

His father, who was a lawyer, died before him, aged 35. In each generation of the descendants of Major General Daniel Denison, the male representative of the name was an only son. The line was as follows :

1. JOHN, only son of Major General Daniel.
2. REV. JOHN, only son of the above John.
3. JOHN, a lawyer, only son of Rev. John.
4. JOHN, only son of the lawyer. He was the young clergyman, who died unmarried at Ipswich, 1747, " last of his line."

7. ELIZABETH ROGERS, (dau of 3 Elizabeth,) b. 1661, *m.* Hon. John Appleton in 1680, and had :

Appendix. 333

32 ELIZABETH, b. 1682; *m.* Rev. Jabez Fitch, son of Rev. James of Norwich, Conn.
33 MARGARET, b. in 1691; *m.* C. Holyoke.
34 NATHANIEL, b. 1693; *m.* —— Gibbs.
35 DANIEL, b. 1695; *m.* Elizabeth Berry.
36 PRISCILLA, b. 1697; *m.* Robert Ward.
37 JOHN, b. in 1704.

Hon. John Appleton died in 1739, age 87 ; Elizabeth died in 1754, age 93.

8 MARGARET ROGERS, (dau. of 3 Elizabeth,) b. in 1664, *m.* Thomas Berry in 1682. Margaret Rogers Berry *m.* John Leverett in 1697, and had :

38 MARGARET, b. 1698; d. 1702.
39 MARY, b. 1699; d. 1699.
40 SARAH, b. 1700; *m.* —— Wigglesworth.
41 MARY, b. 1701; *m.* 14 John Denison.
42 JOHN, b. 1703; d. 1706.
43 PEYTON, b. 1704.
44 MARGARET, b. 1705; d. 1708.
45 JOHN, b. 1711.

John Leverett died 1724, age 62 ; Margaret, his wife, died 1720, age 55.

DESCENDANTS OF 50 DANIEL DENISON,
OF HAMPTON, CONN.

We suppose this Daniel Denison to be a son of 5 Daniel, who was brother of 4 Rev. John Denison, though a link is wanting in the documentary evidence, which we presume to be in existence, though we have not had opportunity to search for it. The evidences that support this theory are the following, and will pass for what they are worth.

1. It is settled that Daniel Denison of Hampton is not a descendant of Capt. George of Stonington. We started with this theory, and for a time thought we had traced his parentage to 177 John Denison of Saybrook, a grandson of Capt. George. But a thorough examination of the church and town records of Saybrook, Conn., showed, that 208 Daniel, son of

41

177 John, though born about the same time as Daniel of Hampton, married Mehitabel Foster and had six children who were accounted for at Saybrook. There is no evidence that 208 Daniel ever resided in any other place than Saybrook. The other Daniels, descendants of Capt. George, are accounted for in other places. This theory was abandoned.

2. There is nothing in the family records that we have found that forbids the theory that Daniel of Hampton was a son of 5 Daniel of Ipswich. He, No. 5. is mentioned in the will of his grandfather, Maj. Gen. Daniel: "I will that my grandchild, Daniel Denison, have my farme of Merrimack of 600 acres, lying near Haveril bounds, which lands were promised to their deare father upon his marriage." At the death of Gen. Denison in 1682, 5 Daniel was about 15 years of age. He would be of the usual marriageable age about 1690 to 95, and in the ordinary course would have taken possession of his 600 acre farm at Haverhill bounds about that time. Our records show that the Kingsbury brothers, found his neices 13 Ruth Denison, and 15 Hannah Denison in Haverhill, and in 1706 and 1710, married them and took them to live with them, the one in Franklin, and the other in Coventry, towns within eight or ten miles of Hampton. If 5 Daniel had a son Daniel it is quite probable that he went with his cousins Ruth and Hannah, a few years later perhaps, and that we find this son, in the person of Daniel Denison of Hampton. An examination of the Ipswich and Haverhill town and church records will probably determine the correctness of this theory.

3. We are informed by Rev. Andrew C. Denison of Middlefield, Conn., that tradition in the family traces their ancestry back to General Denison of Ipswich. Tradition handed down through only five generations, may be considered pretty good authority. Then the high respect in which the name Daniel has been held, is circumstantial evidence. There has been a Daniel in every generation at the Denison homestead in Hampton, from 1727 to the present day. This is what we should expect if Daniel of Hampton came from Ipswich stock. If this conjecture does not harmonize with "the last of the line" story upon the monument of Rev. John Denison of Ipswich, who died 1747, it

Appendix. 335

will not be the first time that gravestones have been found at fault. Providence may have been doing better things for the descendants of Gen. Denison in the wilderness of Hampton, than the stone-cutter knew of.

50 DANIEL DENISON, (son of 5 Daniel,) *m.* Hannah Crocker. Dec. 6, 1727. They lived at Hampton, Conn. He died at Windham of the bite of a rattlesnake, in 1732. His widow, Hannah, was appointed administratrix. Inventory £320. 6s.. 8d. By the division of the estate, Daniel Denison, Jr.'s share was £32, 4s., 8d. The share of Elizabeth and Hannah was £16, 2s, 4d. each. The widow had the balance, and married again, a Mr. Gibson. She probably died about 1752; as in that year it appears on the Windham records, that Elizabeth sold to her brother Daniel, her interest in her mother's thirds for £230, and upon Norwich records, Hannah sold her interest to Daniel for £270. The children were:

51 ELIZABETH, b. Sept. 5, 1728; *m.* Elisha Huntington of Lebanon, Mar. 1, 1749.
52 DANIEL, b. Dec. 5, 1730; *m.* Lydia Pearl of Windham, in 1753.
53 HANNAH, b. Feb. 22, 1731; *m.* Solomon Stoddard, 1757.

Upon the records of Windham there is a copy of a deed, dated 1725, of Daniel Denison of Norwich, for 100 acres of land in Windham, North or East Parish, now town of Hampton.

51 ELIZABETH DENISON, (dau. of 50 Daniel,) b. Sept. 5, 1728, *m.* Elisha Huntington, March 8, 1749, and had:

54 ELIZABETH, b. Jan. 23, 1750.
55 ELISHA, b. Sept. 15, 1751.

They lived probably in Norwich, as the above is from the Norwich records.

52 DANIEL DENISON, (son of 50 Daniel,) b. Dec. 5, 1730, *m.* Lydia Pearl, b. 1733, dau. of Timothy Pearl. They lived at Hampton, on the Denison homestead. She died in 1819, aged 76. He died Aug. 4, 1823, aged 93. They were married Nov. 27, 1753, and had:

56 DANIEL. b. Jan. 25, 1755; *m.* Lucy Clark.
57 HANNAH, b. Mar. 18, 1757; *m.* James Abbott.
58 DYER, b. Oct. 25, 1759; d. Jan. 13, 1772, aged 13.

Appendix.

53 HANNAH DENISON, (dau. of 50 Daniel,) b. Feb. 22, 1731, *m.* Solomon Stoddard, Jan. 5, 1757, and lived at Norwich.

56 DANIEL DENISON, (son of 52 Daniel,) b. Jan. 25, 1755, *m.* Lucy Clark, April 24, 1788, and had :

    59 LYDIA, b. July 20, 1789; *m.* Harry Fuller, 1828.
    60 DANIEL, b. Jun. 6, 1791; *m.* Susan Cunningham.
    61 LUCY, b. Jan. 16, 1798; *m.* Josiah Jackson.
    62 HANNAH, b. July, 1804; *m.* William Clark.

Daniel Denison died Nov. 10, 1822, aged 67. Lydia, his wife, died at Norwich, 1843, aged 76. He was a captain in the war of Independence.

57 HANNAH DENISON, (dau. of 52 Daniel,) b. March 18, 1757, *m.* James Abbott, Jan. 1st, 1778, and had :

    63 DANIEL.
    64 ELIJAH.

59 LYDIA DENISON, (dau. of 56 Daniel,) b. July 20, 1789, *m.* Harry Fuller in 1828, and had :

    65 JULIA, *m.* Daniel Hall, M. D.; d. early.
    66 MARY A., *m.* Leander W. Boynton of Hartford.

Lydia, wife of H. Fuller, died Feb. 5, 1838, aged 49.

60 DANIEL DENISON, (son of 56 Daniel,) b. June 6, 1791, *m.* Susan Cunningham of Pomfret, March 27, 1821. Children :

    67 ANDREW C., b. June 27, 1822; *m.* Catherine Coe.
    68 JAMES H., b. June 16, 1826; *m.* Caroline Sprague.
    69 MARY E., b. Aug. 5, 1828; a teacher, not married.
    70 JOHN C., b. Aug. 7, 1832; *m.* Elizabeth Goodenough.
    72 DANIEL, b. Sept. 4, 1838; *m.* Augusta Bryant.

Daniel died at Windham, Feb. 5, 1838. Peter Cunningham, the father of Susan, was a cousin of President John Adams, and captain of the U. S. ship Hazard in the Revolutionary war.

61 LUCY DENISON, (dau. of 56 Daniel,) b. Jan. 16, 1798, *m.* Josiah Jackson, April 9, 1827, and had :

    73 HORACE, b. Mar. 31, 1828; *m.* Jennette L. Fox, March 6, 1860; no children.
    74 EDWARD, b. Sept. 14, 1829; d. April 12, 1870; *m.* Adelaide Mandeville, July 4, 1860; 1 dau., d. young.
    75 HENRY, b. Aug. 9, 1834; *m.*; P. O., Willimantic, Conn.
    76 HELEN MARIA, b. Nov. 7, 1835; d. Oct. 17, 1836.
    77 DWIGHT, *m.*; lives in Hartford, Wis.

Appendix. 337

62 HANNAH DENISON, (dau. of 56 Daniel,) m. William Clark, May 29, 1832; lived at Windham; no children; both dead.

67 REV. ANDREW C. DENISON, (son of 60 Daniel,) b. June 27, 1822, m. Catherine Coe, dau. of Linus Coe of Middletown, Conn., May 25, 1853. He is pastor of the Congregational Church of Middlefield, Conn. He graduated at Yale College in 1847, and at Union Theological Seminary, N. Y., in 1849. He was ordained at Leicester, Mass., March 1, 1851, dismissed in 1856. He has since been Professor in the Theological Seminary in Charlotte, N. C., Pastor at Portland, Conn., and since 1868, has filled the pastorate at Middlefield. His first wife died Dec. 31, 1862, and he m. 2nd, Laura A. Nichols, May 20, 1867. His children :

    78 HENRY COE, b. Dec. 30, 1857; d. 1861.
    79 LINUS, b. Dec. 25, 1862.
    80 CHARLES N., b. May 10, 1868.

He m. 3d, Harriet L. Heart, in 1869, and had :

    81 CATHERINE MABEL, b. Dec. 8, 1870; d. Feb. 15, 1873.
    82 WILLIAM, b. Oct. 6, 1873.

68 JAMES H. DENISON, (son of 60 Daniel,) m. Catherine Wood, May 20, 1857; lives at Newark, N. J.

72 REV. DANIEL DENISON, (son of 60 Daniel,) b. Sept. 4, 1838, m. Augusta M. Bryant, Sept. 25, 1872. P. O., Cobalt, Conn. He was a graduate of Yale in 1860, of Andover Theological Seminary in 1864, and was ordained and installed as pastor of the 2nd church in Middle Haddam, Dec. 30, 1873, which office he still fills.

70 JOHN C. DENISON, (son of 60 Daniel,) b. Aug. 7, 1832, m. Elizabeth Goodenough, b. at Darien, N. Y., Aug. 10, 1840. They were married Aug. 10, 1859. P. O., Hartford, Wis. The children :

    83 ALICE, b. June 6, 1864; d. Oct. 6, 1867.
    84 CARRIE, b. April 8, 1870.

ROBERT DENISON OF MILFORD AND NEWARK.

1 ROBERT DENISON, who was settled in Milford, Conn., in 1645, was in no way connected with William of Roxbury. The Milford records do not say when he went there. He appears to have been a widower with two children, James and Mary. His son James settled in East Haven, Conn. Mary was married in Milford, and went with her husband to Newark, N. J. It seems that Robert Denison, m. a second wife, in Milford, whose name was Esther, and had five more children, four of them being recorded in Milford. In 1666, he went to Newark, N. J., with the first settlers of that place, and had assigned to him Lot No. 25, which adjoined that of Rev. Mr. Pierson, whose immediate neighbor on the other side was Robert Treat. Robert Denison died in Newark previous to 1676 ; for in that year, a survey was made for his widow Esther Denison. His children by the first wife :

    2 JAMES, m. Bethiah Boykom, Nov. 25, 1662.
    3 MARY, m. Robert Dalglish, about 1660.

By the second wife :

    4. JOHN, b. in 1654, in Milford. His will, made in Newark, in 1694, does not mention wife or child; but it names " sisters Esther, Hannah and Sarah," and " cousins John, Samuel and Esther, children of sister Mary."
    5 SAMUEL, b. in 1656, in Milford.
    6 ESTHER, b. in 1658, in Milford.
    7 HANNAH, b. in 1662, in Milford.
    8 SARAH, b. in Newark, probably.

3 MARY DENISON, (dau. of 1 Robert,) was married, about 1660 to Robert Dalglish or Douglas, and in 1666 went with him to Newark. She died in Newark previous to 1694. He died there after 1693. Their children :

    9 JOHN, b. about 1661; m. Sarah Ward, and had 5 children: Nathaniel, Samuel, Mary, Phebe, and Rachel.
    10 SAMUEL, m. Abigail Tompkins previous to 1688.
    11 ESTHER, b. in Newark, probably.

Appendix. 339

2 JAMES DENISON, (son of 1 Robert,) b. about 1638, probably, settled in East Haven, Conn., and was married to Bethiah Boykom, Nov. 25, 1662. His first appearance in the East Haven records shows, that in 1663, he bought " the shore of Wm. Andrews in Southend Neck." His children :

12 JAMES, b. August, 1664; d. young.
13 JOHN, b. November, 1665; d. young.
14 MARY, b. July 26, 1668.
15 SARAH, b. April 12, 1671; *m.* Joseph Sackett.
16 JAMES, b. Feb. 6, 1677; d. young.
17 JOHN, b. Feb. 6, 1677; *m.* Grace Brown.
18 ELIZABETH, b. Nov. 24, 1784; *m.* Samuel Harrison in 1707.
19 JAMES, b. Jan. 5, 1683.

17 JOHN DENISON, (son of 2 James,) b. Feb. 6, 1677, was married to Grace Brown, dau. of John and gr-dau. of Francis Brown. Their children :

20 ABIGAIL, b. Nov. 13, 1705; *m.* Daniel Granger.
21 SARAH, twin, b. May 10, 1708; *m.* Joseph Trowbridge.
22 JOHN, twin, b. May 10, 1708; d. young.
23 ELIZABETH, b. Aug. 28, 1710; *m.* Samuel Thompson.
24 MEHITABEL, b. Oct. 2, 1713; *m.* Samuel Hemenway.
25 MARY, b. March 29, 1716; *m.* John Woodward.

19 JAMES DENISON, Jr., (son of 2 James,) b. Jan. 5, 1683, was married in 1706 or 1707 ; but we have not learned either the exact date of the marriage or the name of his wife. He had these eight children :

26 JAMES, 3d, *m.* Sarah Smith.
27 DESIRE, *m.* Benjamin Smith.
28 SIBYL.
29 ABIGAIL.
30 JESSE, *m.* Abigail Hemenway, Aug. 25, 1740.
31 JOHN, *m.* Sarah Hough.
32 SARAH, *m.* Samuel Moultrop.
33 LYDIA, *m.* Jacob Goodell in 1755.

30 JESSE DENISON, (son of 19 James, Jr.,) was married, Aug. 25, 1740, to Abigail Hemenway of New Haven, Conn. One child :

34 ABIGAIL, b. in 1741; *m.* Simeon Bradley in 1759,

26 JAMES DENISON. 3d, (son of 19 James, Jr.) was married to Sarah Smith, and had these eight children :

35 SIBYL; d. young.
36 SARAH.

37 DESIRE, m. Ephraim Chedsey.
38 JESSE, m. Mabel Woodward; no child.
39 DOROTHY, d. young.
40 ABIGAIL.
41 LYDIA.
42 JAMES, d. young.

31 JOHN DENISON, (son of 19 James, Jr.,) manifestly had two wives; for he had fifteen children born in the years from 1748 to 1790. Of course, these were not all children of one marriage; but reports to us say only that he was married to Sarah Hough, who died Nov. 22, 1824. She appears to have been the second wife. Of the first wife we have learned nothing beyond the manifest fact that there was a first wife. He lived to be over 90 years old, and died in New Haven, Conn., March 1, 1814. His children:

43 JOHN, Jr., d. young.
44 OBEDIENCE.
45 ZINA, b. Jan. 7, 1751.
46 JAMES.
47 CHAUNCEY, m. Sarah Grannis in 1782.
48 SAMUEL.
49 LEVERETT, b. Aug. 26, 1767.
50 HANNAH, b. 1765.
51 LOIS, b. March 29, 1773.
52 SARAH.
53 JOHN, Jr., again.
54 DESIRE.
55 JESSE.
56 EPHRAIM.
57 EZEKIEL RICE, b. 1790.

The son Chauncey went to Litchfield, Conn., where his name appears in the town records.

45 ZINA DENISON, (son of 33 John,) b. Jan. 7, 1751, was married, May 2, 1774, to Martha Austin; lived in New Haven, Conn.; d. March 13, 1790. His children:

58 AUSTIN, b. Jan. 12, 1775; d. Aug. 11, 1812.
59 ABEL, b. Aug. 5, 1776; d. Feb. 15, 1813.
60 CHARLES, b. Feb. 23, 1778; d. June 25, 1825.
61 HENRY, b. Feb. 28, 1780; d. in 1847.
62 NANCY, b. Aug. 1, 1783; d. Feb. 4, 1822.
63 MARTHA, b. March 5, 1785; d. in 1868.
64 BETSEY, b. Jan. 26, 1787; d. in infancy.
65 BETSEY, b. Nov. 8, 1788; d. in 1856.

58 AUSTIN DENISON, (son of 45 Zina,) b. Jan. 12, 1775, was married to Martha Dwight, a niece of President Dwight of Yale College. They lived in New Haven, Conn. He died Aug. 12, 1812. They had three children:

66 MARY ELIZABETH, m. Oct. 24, 1825, Hon. Charles D. Shoemaker of Wilkesbarre, Pa. See his record, page 201.

Appendix. 341

67 MARTHA DWIGHT, *m* Gen. E. W. Sturtevant of Wilkesbarre, Pa.
68 ANOTHER CHILD, d. in infancy.

59 ABEL DENISON, (son of 45 Zina,) b. Aug. 5, 1776, was married to Mary Wetmore of Providence, R. I., and had these children:

69 MARY, *m.* Dr. J. B. Robertson; 3 ch.
70 CHARLES, *m.*; two daus., Rebecca and Maria.
71 ZINA, d. unmarried.

60 CHARLES DENISON, (son of 45 Zina,) b. Feb. 23, 1778, was twice married; first, to Hannah French; second to Mary Pynchon of Guilford, Conn. He was a lawyer in New Haven, Conn. He had three children, of whom we know nothing, except that one of them, Miss Sarah M. Denison, is still living in New Haven.

61 HENRY DENISON, (son of 45 Zina,) b. Feb. 28, 1780, was twice married: first, to Julia Ann Townsend, who d. Dec. 17, 1824; second, to Eliza Cunningham of Baltimore, who d. Feb. 22, 1866. He d. in 1847. He had eleven children:

72 JEREMIAH TOWNSEND.
73 ABEL, lives in Brooklyn, N. Y.
74 HENRY, *m.* Susan B. Giddings.
75 MARTHA, *m.* Rev. George W. Richards.
76 WILLIAM C., d. March, 1846, aged 22.
77 ELIZABETH A., d. unmarried.
78 ANNA G., (by second wife,) d. May 9, 1863.

There were four others, three of whom died in infancy.

63 MARTHA DENISON, (dau. of 45 Zina,) b. March 5, 1785, was married to Truman Woodward of Watertown, Conn., had five children:

79 TWINS. that died in infancy.
80 HANNAH.
81 GEORGE.
82 HENRY, d. when a young man.

72 JEREMIAH TOWNSEND DENISON, (son of 61 Henry,) was twice married: first, to Euretta Rosevelt, who had two children, Julia and John; second, to Esther Judson of Fairfield, Conn. The children:

83 JULIA, d. young.
84 JOHN, resides in California.

73 ABEL DENISON, (son of 61 Henry,) was married to Demetille Kroger, of Brooklyn, N. Y.; lives in Brooklyn; has had three children:

85 WILLIAM, b. at Brooklyn, N. Y.
86 NINA, d. young.
87 EVELYN, b. at Brooklyn, N. Y.

74 HENRY DENISON, JR., (son of 61 Henry) was married to Susan B. Giddings of Claremont, N. H. He lives at Elizabeth, N. J. Three children:

88 DOMIE, b. at Elizabeth, N. J.
89 EDWARD C., b. at Elizabeth, N. J.
90 ANOTHER, that d. in infancy.

49 LEVERETT DENISON, (son of 31 John,) b. Aug. 26, 1769, was married to Desire Page, in 1797. The children:

91 MALINDA, b. Jan. 30, 1799; d. in infancy.
92 MALINDA, twin, b. in 1800.
93 EURINDA, twin, b. in 1800.
94 URSENA, b. May 24, 1801.
95 POLLY, b. May 17, 1808.
96 FIDELIA, b. Oct. 2, 1812.

94 URSENA DENISON, (dau. of 49 Leverett,) b. May 24, 1801, was married to William S. Gilbert, March 1, 1825; lives at Hemlock Lake, N. Y. The children:

97 EMILY JANE, b. Feb. 17, 1826.
98 LUCIA SOPPIA, b. April 21, 1828.
99 MARY ELLEN, b Aug. 11, 1830.
100 WILLIAM HENRY, b. May 28, 1834.
101 CONGDON LEWIS, b. April 27, 1837.

51 LOIS DENISON, (dau. of 31 John.) b. March 29, 1773, was married, Aug. 27, 1799, to Edward D. Lake, who was born Jan. 12, 1775, in Stratford, Conn. They were married in Greenville, N. Y. In February, 1814, they settled on the farm in Ontario Co., N. Y., where they lived and died. Their children:

102 SALLY. b. Sept. 4, 1800; m. James McPherson.
103 JOHN, b. Aug. 2, 1802; d. Aug., 1802.
104 MINERVA, b. June 24, 1804; d. July 1, 1818.
105 MELINDA, b. Oct. 16, 1806; d. April 2, 1834.
106 ZOPHAR, b. Sept. 7, 1809; d. Jan. 1, 1825.
107 HARRIET, b. May 22, 1812; d. unmarried.
101 DENISON, b. Dec. 18, 1814; m. Harriet A. Arnold.

Lois (Denison) Lake, the first wife died Sept. 17, 1831; and Jan. 5, 1835, he m. second, Mrs. Mary H. Fessenden, b. Feb. 3, 1777. He d. March 27, 1864. She d. June 5, 1874. Of this family, only Sally and Denison were married.

Appendix. 343

102 SALLY LAKE, (dau. of 51 Lois and Edward D.,) b. Sept. 4, 1800, was married, April, 1820, to James McPherson. She had four children, and d. Dec. 15, 1830. The children :

> **109** MINERVA, b. about 1825, lives in Phelps, Ontario Co., N. Y.; unmarried.
> **110** JOHN E., lives in Hurley, Ulster Co., N. Y.
> **112** JAMES H., lives in Canandaigua, N. Y.
> **113** WILLIAM, the younge-t served in the war against rebellion, from the beginning, and died of wounds received in battle.

108 DENISON LAKE, (son of 51 Lois and Edward D.,) b. Dec. 18, 1814, was married, Feb. 10, 1841, to Harriet A. Arnold. He lives in Gorham, N. Y., on the farm that was owned and occupied by his father. His wife d. July 9, 1858, aged 38 years. Their children :

> **114** JOANNA A., b. Oct. 6, 1842; d. Dec. 22, 1862.
> **115** LOIS, b. May 13, 1844; d. July 18, 1855.
> **116** PHILAMELIA, b. Nov. 2, 1846; m. John C. Dwelle. They live at Cedar Keys Point, Chase Co., Kansas.

53 JOHN DENISON, JR., (son of 31 John,) was married Feb. 14, 1805, to Martha Coe, of Durham, N. Y., and had seven children :

> **117** LOUISA, b. Jan. 23, 1806; m. Orson Lyman.
> **118** EMELINE A., b. Aug. 18, 1807; m. Rev. L. H. Fellows of Vinton, Iowa, Sept. 19, 1833.
> **119** MARYETTE, b. Oct. 14, 1810; m. Silas E. Hollister.
> **120** CAROLINE, b. Aug. 25, 1813; d. unmarried, Dec. 16, 1832.
> **121** JOHN W., b. April 6, 1819; m. Mary A. Perkins.
> **122** DELIA M., b. Dec. 29, 1820; m. E. B. Warner of Cassopolis, Mich., March 24, 1862.
> **123** JULIUS C., b. Jan. 23, 1823; m. Cornelia Carter.

117 LOUISA DENISON, (dau. of 53 John, Jr.,) was married to Orson Lyman, of Warner, N. Y., Jan. 30, 1833. Four children :

> **124** SARAH LOUISE, b. Jan. 28, 1834; d. Dec. 25, 1851.
> **125** MARTHA HULDAH, b. Dec. 26, 1835.
> **126** MARY DELIA, b. Oct. 7, 1837; d. Oct. 3, 1840.
> **127** MARY DELIA, b. July 3, 1846.

119 MARYETTE DENISON, (dau. of 53 John, Jr.,) was married, June 5, 1834, to Silas E. Hollister, of Batavia, N. Y. Two children :

> **128** MARTHA MARYETTE, b. July 11, 1838.
> **129** SARAH DENISON, b. Jan. 25, 1847; d. Dec. 9, 1869.

121 JOHN W. DENISON, (son of 53 John, Jr.,) was married March, 1854, to Mary A. Perkins. He lives at Whitewater, Mich. The children:
    130 MARY LOUISA, b. July 9, 1857.
    131 HELEN ELIZABETH, b. March 7, 1859.
    132 JOHN JULIUS, b. Aug. 16, 1861.
    133 HATTIE, b. May 3, 1866.

123 JULIUS C. DENISON, (son of 53 John, Jr.,) was married Jan. 22, 1855, to Cornelia Carter; lived at Grand Rapids, Mich.; d. June, 1877. The children:
    134 LIBBIE, b. Sept. 8, 1857; d. Dec. 22, 1861.
    135 ARTHUR C., b. Nov. 10, 1861.
    136 HERBERT H., b. June 10, 1863; d. Sept. 26, 1865.
    137 EDWIN W., b. May 21, 1865; d. Oct., 1865.

57 EZEKIEL RICE DENISON, (son of 31 John,) b. April 14, 1790, was twice married: first, Sept. 27, 1812, to Abigail Adams who was b. July 14, 1792, and d. June 20, 1829; second, Jan. 23, 1834, to Catherine McArthur, who was b. June 24, 1796, and d. April 22, 1853. The children:
    138 JOHN H., b. Oct. 23, 1814.
    139 EZEKIEL L., b. Oct. 8, 1818.
    140 JULIETTE, b. July 27, 1820; d. June 20, 1827.
    141 HARRIETT A., b. Sept. 11, 1822; d. June 15, 1827.
    142 WILLIAM S., b. Dec. 24, 1824.
    143 JULIA F., b. Sept. 14, 1839.

142 WILLIAM S. DENISON, (son of 57 Ezekiel Rice,) was married, April 30, 1859, to Harriett Nicholson. The children:
    144 ELMER E., b. Oct. 22, 1860.
    145 JAMES A., b. Aug. 27, 1864.
    146 WILLIE F., b. Oct. 12, 1867.
    147 EVA F., b. Oct. 10, 1870.
    148 ABBIE C., b. Oct. 17, 1873.
    149 CHARLES O., b. Dec. 30, 1875.

55 JESSE DENISON, (son of 31 John,) was twice married: first, to a Miss Kelley; second, to Mary Coe. who was b. Feb. 20, 1785, and d. July 1, 1857. He lived in Florence, N. Y. Two children:
    150 SAMUEL, b. March 20, 1814; lives in Michigan.
    151 DANIEL L., b. Feb. 15, 1818.

151 DANIEL L. DENISON, (son of 55 Jesse,) was married, Dec. 14, 1856, to Widow Eliza J. Bennett, who d. March 9, 1872. He lives at Olivet, Michigan. Two children:
    152 DELLA MARY, b. Jan. 8, 1858.
    153 FREDERICK SAMUEL, b. Nov. 21, 1860.

GEORGE DENNISON OF ANNISQUAM.

1 GEORGE DENNISON, who was settled at Annisquam, Essex County, Mass., in 1725, came from Dublin, Ireland. He belonged to an English family that was settled at Dublin. The first mention made of him in the records here, is the statement that he was married at Gloucester, to Abigail Haradon, Jan. 14, 1725. In 1787, he built a house which is now standing, and inhabited by one of his descendants, in the 7th Ward of the City of Gloucester. He died March 14, 1748, aged 48 years. His wife died May 1, 1753. Their children:

2 GEORGE, b. Aug. 20, 1726; m. Thomasine Bradstreet.
3 ABNER, b. Oct. 2, 1730; m. Emma Lane.
4 ISAAC, b. Oct. 4, 1732; m. Mrs. Lucretia Day Edes.
5 DAVID, b. Aug. 6, 1734; m. Jenny Haradon.
6 JONATHAN, b. July 21, 1737; m. Jemima Haskell.
7 ABIGAIL, b. June 1, 1739.
8 SUSANNA, b. Jan. 21, 1741; d. Dec. 2, 1749.

One of the descendants of this George Dennison has sought to identify him with George Denison, son of George of Westerly. Of course no such identification is possible. That he came from Dublin, is suggested by this clause in his will: " and to my son George, I give my map of the City of Dublin." It must have been some special interest in Dublin which led him to procure and keep a map of that city. It is well understood among a portion of his descendants that he came from Dublin, and that he was or had been a shipmaster. In his will, he describes himself as " shoreman." He appears to have had considerable property when he came to Massachusetts. For most of the names and dates in this record of his descendants, we are indebted to a pamphlet of Mr. James W. Dennison of Annisquam, which does not include his Maine descendants.

2 GEORGE DENNISON, (son of 1 George,) b. Aug. 20, 1726, was married to Thomasine Bradstreet, and died when 32 years old. His children:

    9 SUSANNA, b. Dec. 25, 1749.
    10 BENJAMIN B., b. Jan. 4, 1752; *m.* Jenny Hale; had one child, Jane, b. Dec. 13, 1758.
    11 THOMASINE, b. March 15, 1758.

3 ABNER DENNISON, (son of 1 George,) b. Oct. 2, 1730, was married to Emma Lane, had four children, and then emigrated with his family to Maine. The children:

    12 ABIGAIL, b. June 17, 1752.
    13 ABNER, b. Sept. 2, 1759.
    14 GIDEON, b. 1761.
    15 EMMA, b. June 7, 1763.

5 DAVID DENNISON, (son of 1 George,) b. Aug. 6, 1734, was married to Jenny Haradon, about 1757, had four children, and emigrated to Maine. The children were:

    16 DAVID, b. Nov. 4, 1758; d. in 1759.
    17 DAVID, b. Aug. 15, 1760.
    18 GEORGE, b. May 19, 1762.
    19 JENNY, b. Jan. 10, 1764.

6 JONATHAN DENNISON, (son of 1 George,) b. July 21, 1737, was married to Jemima Haskell. He d. Dec. 27, 1774, aged 37 years. His children:

    20 ABIGAIL, b. May 2, 1769.
    21 ANNA, b. Nov. 29, 1770.
    22 ELIZABETH Goss, b. July 26, 1772.
    23 HANNAH, b. May 5, 1774.

4 ISAAC DENNISON, (son of 1 George,) b. Oct. 4, 1732, was married to Mrs. Lucretia Day Edes, and d. April 2, 1811. His children:

    24 ISAAC, b. Jan. 2, 1761; *m.* Sarah Rowe.
    25 ELIZABETH, b. July 31, 1762; *m.* William Rowe.
    26 WILLIAM, b. Feb. 21, 1764; d. April 20, 1782.
    27 JONATHAN, b. Nov. 5, 1765; *m.* Judith Stanwood.
    28 JAMES, b. May 31, 1770; *m.* Thomasine Griffin.

24 ISAAC DENNITON, JR., (son of 4 Isaac,) b. Jan 2, 1761, was married, in 1783, to Sarah Rowe, who was born June 16, 1763. He d. June 21, 1841. His children:

    29 ISAAC, 3d, b. Sept. 13, 1784; *m.* Mary C. Porter.
    30 SARAH, b. Sept. 26, 1785; *m.* Robert Hooper.
    31 WILLIAM, b. Sept. 25, 1788; d. Oct. 19, 1813.

32 James, b. Oct. 15, 1790; *m.* Mary Wheeler.
33 George, b. Nov. 20, 1792; *m.* Margaret Choate.
34 Jonathan, b. Nov. 30, 1794; *m.* Susan Fellows.
35 David, b. Jan. 28, 1797; *m.* Martha Story.
36 Elizabeth, b. Feb. 5, 1799; *m.* Joseph Fellows.
37 Rhoda, b. Feb. 3, 1802; *m.* Noah Griffin.
38 Mary, b. April 20, 1804; *m.* Thomas Chard.

28 James Dennison, (son of 4 Isaac,) b. May 31, 1770, was married to Thomasine Griffin, who was b. Jan. 28, 1777. He d. March 5, 1858 ; she d. June 11, 1839. Their children :

39 Tammy, b. Aug. 19, 1800; d. Sept. 25, 1815.
40 Lucretia, b. Feb. 8, 1802.
41 Judith, b. Oct. 7, 1803.
42 Abigail, b. May 11, 1805; *m.* Alanson Bingham.
43 Martha G., b. Dec. 25, 1807; *m.* William N. Parsons.
44 Tristram R., b. Dec. 1, 1810; *m.* Betsey Evans.
45 Elizabeth, b. March 27, 1813; *m.* Selden E. Willey.
46 Tammy, b. Nov. 12, 1815; *m.* George Woodward.
47 James W., b. May 11, 1818; *m.* Mrs. Mary A. Norwood Kerr; has one child, Carrie Louisa, b. July 21, 1866.

27 Jonathan Dennison, (son of 4 Isaac,) b. Nov. 5, 1765, was married to Judith Stanwood, about 1788. One child :

48 Jonathan, Jr., b. Sept. 15, 1789: *m.* twice.

48 Jonathan Dennison, Jr., (son of 27 Jonathan,) b. Sept. 15, 1789, was married, first, to Sally Parsons, who was b. Jan. 23, 1793. She had :

49 Sarah A., b. Aug. 17, 1816; *m.* George W. Banks.
50 Lucretia, b. Dec. 29, 1818; *m.* John Parsons.
51 Fidelia, b. Nov. 8, 1820; d. Oct. 19, 1821.
52 Serena, b. Aug. 1, 1822; *m.* Daniel Wheeler.
53 John P., b. Nov. 5, 1824; d. Feb. 5, 1826.

The wife, Sally Parsons, died Nov. 2, 1825 ; and he was married, second, to Mary J. Sweetser, who was b. Dec. 19, 1796. He d. March 10, 1874 ; she d. Sept. 23, 1876. Second wife's children :

54 Isaac Henry, b. July 27, 1827; d. Aug. 1, 1837.
55 Mary H., b. July 8, 1828; d. Oct. 17, 1828.
56 Mary, twin, b. Nov. 28, 1830.
57 Ellen, twin, b. Nov. 28, 1830.
58 Otis, b. April 7, 1832; d. Oct. 17, 1832.
59 Augusta I., b. Feb. 20, 1838.
60 Harriet, b. Oct. 15, 1840.

32 James Dennison, (son of 24 Isaac, Jr.,) b. Oct. 15, 1790, was married to Mary Wheeler, who was b. June 4, 1797.

He died July 25, 1855 ; she died Feb. 6, 1852. Their children :

- **61** JAMES, Jr., b. May 11, 1816; *m.* Susan Parsons.
- **62** ELIZABETH W., b. Jan. 10, 1818; *m.* Charles Wheeler.
- **63** MARY JANE, b. July 17, 1819; *m.* Nathaniel Paul.
- **64** WILLIAM, b. April 17, 1821; *m.* twice.
- **65** HOSEA BALLOU, b. Jan. 13, 1824; *m.* Justina Fernald.
- **66** WARREN, b. July 26, 1826; d. Jan. 6, 1832.
- **67** FRANKLIN. b. Jan. 11, 1829.
- **68** GEORGE W., b. Feb. 22, 1731; *m.* Ada Babson.
- **69** SUSAN BROWN, b. Aug. 7, 1833; d. Oct. 30, 1835.
- **70** OTIS, b. July 1, 1837; *m.* Mary Frances Slocomb.
- **71** ADELLA, b. Jan. 7, 1841; d. in 1841.

33 GEORGE DENNISON, (son of 24 Isaac, Jr.,) b. Nov. 20, 1792, was married to Margaret Choate about 1815, or 1816. He d. July 2, 1838. His children :

- **72** MARGARET A., b. June 18, 1817; *m.* Newell Burnham.
- **73** GEORGE G., b. Nov. 29, 1818; d. Dec. 18, 1830.
- **74** ELIZABETH, b. Sept. 18, 1829; d. in 1835.

34 JONATHAN DENNISON, (son of 24 Isaac, Jr.,) b. Nov. 30, 1794, was married about 1821, to Susan Fellows who was b. Sept. 16, 1794. He d. Nov. 30, 1859. She d. Oct. 28, 1861. Their children :

- **75** JONATHAN A., b. Dec. 16, 1822; *m.* Adaline Story.
- **76** JOHN W., b. Jan. 12, 1825; d. July 7, 1826.
- **77** JOHN W., b. May 10, 1828; *m.* Jane A. Lane.
- **78** SUSAN A. F., b. Aug. 31, 1832; *m.* John J. Knowlton.

35 DAVID DENNISON, (son of 24 Isaac, Jr.,) b. Jan. 28, 1797, was married to Martha Story about 1821. He d. Aug. 1, 1835. His children :

- **79** MARTHA, b. Dec. 11, 1823; *m.* John W. Legalloe.
- **80** DAVID, b. June 2. 1825; *m.* Mary O. Bragdon; one child, Charles E., b. Oct. 23, 1866.
- **81** ISAAC, b. Nov. 4, 1827; *m.* Ann A. Bragdon; one child, Edith, b. Aug. 3, 1548; d. Aug. 14, 1856.
- **82** ELIZA A., b. Sept. 17, 1829; *m.* Alfred J. Wiggin.
- **83** GEORGE G., b. Feb. 5, 1831; *m.* Charlotte A. Robinson.
- **84** CHARLES, b. July 15, 1833; *m.* Edith Lane.
- **85** EDWARD H., b. Dec. 2, 1835.

64 WILLIAM DENNISON, (son of 32 James,) b. April 17, 1821, was twice married : first, to M. Josephine Babson, who d. childless ; second, to Anna L. Downing, who has one child :

- **86** WILLIAM, b. Feb. 11, 1871.

Appendix. 349

44 TRISTRAM R. DENNISON, (son of 28 James,) b. Dec. 1, 1810, was married to Betsey Evans. Their children:

- **87** LOUISA, b. Nov. 4, 1838.
- **88** FRANCES, b. June 1, 1840; m. Frank L. Gilman.
- **89** TRISTRAM ROWE, b. July 8, 1842; d. July 3, 1845.
- **90** MARY E., b. Nov. 14, 1845; d. April 18, 1847.
- **91** BETSEY R., b. June 28, 1848; d. Sept. 29, 1871.
- **92** EDWARD C., b. April 11, 1852; d. Sept. 9, 1868.

61 JAMES DENNISON, JR., (son of 32 James,) b. May 11, 1816, was married to Susan Parsons. Their children:

- **93** JAMES EDWARD, b. Jan. 21, 1845; m. Maria E. Lincoln; one child, Edward B., b. Feb. 28, 1872.
- **94** ALBERT, b. April 1, 1846; m. Ellen Merrill.
- **95** EVELYN, b. Aug. 15, 1848; m. B. F. Ellery.
- **96** ANNIE, b. Nov. 14, 1850.
- **97** MINOR, b. May 16, 1853.
- **98** LEWIS FRED., b. Nov. 13, 1856; d. March 25, 1857.
- **99** FRANK WILLIAMS, b. March 24, 1859; d. Oct. 13, 1860.
- **100** IRVING CLIFFORD, b. Sept. 11, 1862; d. Oct. 25, 1862.

70 OTIS DENNISON, (son of 32 James,) b. July 1, 1837, was married to Mary Frances Slocumb. Their children:

- **101** FRANKLIN OTIS, b. Dec. 19, 1860; d. Aug., 1861.
- **102** EDITH MARION, b. Sept. 8, 1863; d. March, 1865.
- **103** FRANK, b. April 29, 1866.
- **104** HERBERT E., b. Nov. 23, 1868.
- **105** CHARLES H., b. March 13, 1873.

75 JONATHAN A. DENNISON, (son of 34 Jonathan,) b. Dec. 16, 1822, was married to Adaline Story. Their children:

- **106** WILLIAM A., b. May 18, 1845; m. Celia A. Woodward.
- **107** BERTHA E., b. Oct. 17, 1847; m. Fred. Davis.
- **108** ADALIZA, b. Sept. 1, 1849; d. Sept. 28, 1851.
- **109** ADALINE, b. Nov. 6, 1853; m. George W. Harvey.
- **110** SUSAN F., b. Nov. 23, 1855; m. Reuben Clark.

77 JOHN W. DENNISON, (son of 34 Jonathan,) b. May 10, 1828, was married to Jane A. Lane. He d. Nov. 2, 1868. Their children:

- **111** THOMAS S., b. July 16, 1856.
- **112** EMMA M.
- **113** FRANK L.
- **114** JOHN W.

83 GEORGE G. DENNISON, (son of 35 David,) b. Feb. 5, 1831, was married to Charlotte A. Robinson. Their children:

- **115** GEORGE, b. Feb. 23, 1853; m. Gertrude A. Harris.

116 CHARLOTTE E., b. Dec. 4, 1854.
117 GARDNER, b. Aug. 23, 1856.
118 AUGUSTUS, b. March 13, 1865.
119 ISAAC, b. Nov. 17, 1873.

84 CHARLES DENNISON, (son of 35 David,) b. July 15, 1833, was married to Edith Lane. Their children:

120 EDITH, b. June 1, 1872.
121 HELEN LANE, b. Sept. 8, 1874.
122 CHARLES H., b. Dec. 9, 1877.

106 WILLIAM A. DENNISON, (son of 75 Jonathan A.,) b. May 18, 1845, was married to Celia A. Woodward. The children:

123 WILLIAM S., b. July 4, 1869.
124 CARRIE A., b. May 2, 1871; d. March 31, 1873.
125 GRACE M., b. May 31, 1874.
126 ALICE M., b. Aug. 9, 1876.

Appendix. 351

ESTRAYS.

Under this head we print in the Appendix such family records as reached us too late to be printed in the body of the book ; also, some other records whose proper places we have not been able to determine with absolute certainty, although there is no doubt of their being records of descendants of Capt. George Denison. The numbering of the body of the of the book is continued in these " Estrays."

No. 1.
2732 DANIEL DENISON, 3rd.
(Daniel[4], Daniel[3], John[2], George[1].)
See Page 144.

Two months after the record of this Daniel Denison was printed on page 144, we received a communication which should have reached us long before it was printed. This communication, so far as it goes, enables us to correct and enlarge that record, as follows :

2732 DANIEL DENISON, 3rd, (oldest son of Daniel, Jr.,) b. Dec. 9, 1745, was married to Elizabeth Andross, in November, 1768. He lived in Vermont, went to Knox, N. Y., lived in Canada, went to Connecticut, went again to Vermont, and died there, Oct. 15, 1802, " in Bennington or in Pawlett." His widow lived with her son Asa, in Richmond, N. Y., and died there, June 11, 1826, aged 78 years. Their children :

    2983 ASA, b. May 16, 1770; *m.* Sylvia Horsford.
    2984 DANIEL, 4th, b. Jan. 1772; *m.* Lucy Avery.
    2985 STANTON, b. in 1774; d. unmarried.
    2986 ESTHER, b. in 1776; *m.* Minor Waldron, at Knox, N. Y.
    2987 ELIZABETH, b. about 1782; the date is uncertain.
    2987½W. WHEELER, b. Aug. 19, 1788; d. unmarried, aged 80.
    2987¾LAWTON, b. Dec. 19, 1791; drowned in the Ohio River.

Appendix.

2984 DANIEL DENISON, 4TH, (son of 2732 Daniel, 3d,) was married in 1794, in Connecticut, to Lucy Avery. After his marriage, with his brother Stanton who was never married, he emigrated to the New York wilderness. They settled at German Flats, Herkimer County; and there he died, Feb. 5, 1841. His children:

- **6163** JOHN, d. when 14 years old.
- **6164** PHEBE, m. J. B. Martin; d. in 1833.
- **6165** GEORGE, b. Jan. 26, 1799; d. in 1872.
- **6166** LUCY, m. Turner Peterson; d. in 1835.
- **6167** SALLY, m. Alvin Ford.
- **6168** EMELINE, m. Steven Joslyn; d. in 1832.

6165 GEORGE DENISON, (son of 2984 Daniel, 4th,) b. in Herkimer Co., N. Y., Jan. 26, 1799, was married June 21, 1818, to Lucy Ford. In 1845, he emigrated to McHenry Co., Ill., where he died Sept. 7, 1872. His wife Lucy, b. June 22, 1794, was still living in Feb., 1881. Their children:

- **6169** MARGARET, b. Feb. 1, 1821; m. Lorin Thomas, Sept. 1, 1844.
- **6170** JANE MARIA, b. Dec. 16, 1823; m. John P. Ransom, Dec. 28, 1842; d. March 21, 1849.
- **6171** DANIEL, b. Feb. 11, 1825; m. Julia A. Falkner.
- **6172** EMELINE, b. March 25, 1827; m. Dighton B. Chapman, Oct. 9, 1848; d. Oct. 30, 1867.
- **6173** LUCY ANN, b. Nov. 26, 1830; m. Mark Thompson, March 20, 1856.

6171 DANIEL DENISON, 5TH, (son of 6165 George,) b. Feb. 11, 1825, was married, July 23, 1856, to Julia A. Falkner, who was born Feb. 10, 1838. He lives in Richmond, McHenry Co., Ill., where he has a great farm, and is extensively engaged in the business of farming and stock raising. He has eight children:

- **6174** CLARENCE, b. July 16, 1858.
- **6175** JENNIE, b. Nov. 23, 1860.
- **6176** ELLA F., b. March 8, 1863.
- **6177** LINCOLN A., b. June 16, 1865.
- **6178** CORA B., b. April 10, 1867.
- **6179** IDA M., b. July 2, 1870.
- **6180** MARY E., b. Jan. 3, 1876.
- **6181** ZULA M., b. Sept. 4, 1878.

Appendix. 353

No. 2.
793 BENJAMIN GREEN DENISON.
See page 45.

The family record of Benjamin Green Denison, printed on page 45, is very incomplete, and, as far as it goes, greatly deficient. Since that was printed we have received his record in full, which we print here with new numbers:

793 BENJAMIN GREEN DENISON, (Jonathan^6, Daniel^5, Daniel^4, George^3, John^2, George^1,) b. Oct 30, 1793, was married to Abigail Babcock in 1815. She was born June 5th, 1794; is now living. He died June 17, 1870. Their children:

6182 SARAH, b. Oct. 28, 1816; *m.* William Whitbeck, Jan. 1, 1836. He was born April 10, 1816.
6183 BENJAMIN BARBER, *m.* Margaret Rysedorph; both deceased; had two children, Cathaline, and Helen Mar who d. young.
6184 SOPHRONIA, *m.* Daniel W. Streeter; three children; one living.
6185 CAROLINE, *m.* Thomas B. Simmons; six children, all now living.
6186 POLLY, deceased.
6187 GRISWOLD, b. Sept. 18, 1829; *m.* Susan M. Miles, Sept. 18, 1855. She was b. Aug. 8, 1835.
6188 SUSAN ESTHER, b. Feb. 15th, 1832; *m.* James H. Miller, Dec. 21, 1854. He was b. April 25, 1830.
6189 J. W. TYLER, b. Nov. 1, 1835, *m.* Ann Eliza Brewer, Jan 13, 1859. She was b. March 9, 1840.

6182 SARAH DENISON, (dau. of 793 Benj. Green,) b. Oct. 23, 1816, was married, Jan. 1, 1836, to William Whitbeck, who was born, April 10, 1816. Their children:

6190 RACHEL MARIA, b. Dec. 7, 1837; not living.
6191 MARY F., b. Aug. 26, 1839.
6192 JOHN BARBER, b. Feb. 27, 1843.
6193 SARAH C., b. Sept. 25, 1841.
6194 JANE ANN, b. March 26, 1846; not living.
6195 EUDORA F., b. May 26, 1848; not living.
6196 BENJAMIN DENISON, b. Feb. 27, 1851.
6197 WM. FRANKLIN, b. May 15, 1852; not living.
6198 GEORGE HENRY, b. Dec. 29, 1854; not living.
6199 ALBERTA, b. Nov. 24, 1856.
6200 WM. HENRY, b. Aug. 6, 1859.

6184 SOPHRONIA DENISON, (dau. of 793 Benj. Green,) *m.* Daniel W. Streeter; three children:

6201 WM. HENRY STREETER, d. April 5, 1871.
6202 HARVEY BENJ. STREETER.
6203 VICTOR D. STREETER, not living.

6185 CAROLINE DENISON, (dau. of 793 Benj. Green,) m. Thomas B. Simmons. Six children :

 6204 EDGAR.   **6207** ADDIE.
 6205 MARION.   **6208** JOHN THOMAS.
 6206 WM. HENRY. **6209** OSCAR D.

6187 GRISWOLD DENISON, (son of 793 Benj. Green,) b. Sept. 18, 1829, was married Sept. 18, 1859, to Susan M. Miles, who was b. Aug. 8, 1835 ; lives in Brooklyn, N. Y. Two children :

 6210 RACHEL ABIGAIL, b. Aug. 28, 1856; m. Charles A. Olcott, M. D., Dec. 15, 1880.
 6211 CHARLES HOWARD, b. Dec. 19, 1857.

6188 SUSAN ESTHER DENISON, (dau. of 793 Benj. Green,) b. Feb. 13, 1832, was married, Dec. 21, 1854, to James H. Miller, b. April 25, 1830. Their children :

 6212 TYLER D., b. Nov. 1, 1855; m. Mary B. Dikeman.
 6213 JOHN B., b. Jan. 20, 1858; m. Mary B. Connor.
 6214 MARY J., b. May 16, 1860.
 6215 GRACE M., b. April 5, 1868.

6189 J. W. TYLER DENISON, (son of 793 Benj. Green,) b. Nov. 1, 1835, was married, July 13, 1859, to Ann Eliza Brewer. Their children :

 6216 IDA BELL, b. Jan. 24, 1860; d. Jan. 14, 1865.
 6217 ALICE, b. July 4, 1861 ; d. Jan. 16, 1865.
 6218 BENJAMIN G., b. Jan. 6, 1863.
 6219 FRED. BREWER, b. July 16, 1865.
 6220 WILLIAM C., b. Nov. 6, 1867.
 6221 CAROLINE, b. April 27, 1869.
 6222 ADALINE S., b. April 10, 1870.
 6223 INFANT, b. Nov. 16, 1872; d. Nov. 18, 1872.
 6224 ANNIE MAY, b. Aug. 29, 1874.
 6225 EDNA, b. Jan. 23, 1878.

No. 3.
See page 119.

2449 JOSEPH NOYES, JR., (son of 2083 Prudence Denison and Joseph Noyes,) b. Sept. 30, 1768, was married Nov. 30, 1790, to Zurviah Wheeler ; lived in Stonington, Conn. The children :

 6226 WILLIAM AVERY, b. April 30, 1791.

Appendix. 355

6227 JOSEPH, b. Feb. 25, 1793; m. Grace B. Denison, dau. of Oliver.
6228 THOMAS, b. April 5, 1795; m. Eunice Denison, " "
6229 PAUL, b. March 5, 1797; m. Eunice Noyes.
6230 CYRUS, b. April 15, 1799.
6231 GEORGE W., b. Sept. 30, 1801; thrice married.
6232 NATHAN S., b. Jan. 7, 1804; m. Nancy Denison, dau. of Ethan.
6233 LUCY ANN, b. Nov. 21, 1805; m. Seth Williams.

Joseph Noyes, Jr., m. 2nd, Eunice Chesebro, dau. of William Chesebro', Jan. 29, 1811. Their children :

6234 ELISHA DENISON, b. Oct. 28, 1811; d. Oct. 24, 1834; m. Jane Russel; had 8 children.
6235 WILLIAM CHESEBRO', b. March 28, 1813.
6236 EPH. WILLIAMS, b. Nov. 11, 1814; d. Dec. 3, 1835.
6237 SILAS C., b. Oct. 18, 1816.
6238 REV. GURDON W., b. Aug. 13, 1818; m. Agnes McArthur. P. O., New Haven.
6239 EUNICE E., b. March 12, 1820.
6240 NANCY LORD, b. March 19, 1822; m. John S. Barber.
6241 T. EMILY, b. Nov. 3, 1823; m. C. G. Beebe, Sept. 28, 1843.
6242 CHARLOTTE A., b. April 3, 1826; m. Capt. David S. Babcock.

He died Aug. 24, 1831 ; his wife Eunice, died Nov. 4, 1844.

2450 AVERY NOYES, (son of 2083 Prudence Denison and Joseph Noyes,) b. Feb. 13, 1771, was married Feb. 13, 1799, to Polly Slack ; lived in Stonington, Conn. Their children :

6243 POLLY, b. Nov. 6, 1799; m. Abel Crandall.
6244 FANNY, b. April 20, 1801; m. John S. Moxley.
6245 PRUDENCE, b. June 5, 1803; not married.
6246 GRACE, b. March 13, 1805; d. Feb. 1, 1806.
6247 ANNA, b. Dec. 11, 1806; d. April 20, 1809.
6248 AVERY D., b. Oct. 1, 1808; m., and lives in Westerly, R. I.
6249 WILLIAM S., b. Jan. 2, 1811; m. Loisa Lamb.
6250 NANCY, b. July 18, 1813; m. Jonathan B. Stewart.
6251 CYRUS, b. Feb. 20, 1816; m. Bridget G. Denison.
6252 CAROLINE, b. Jan. 8, 1823; m. James Newcomb.
6253 SALLY, b. Nov. 10, 1818; m. Joseph Bishop.

6249 WILLIAM S. NOYES, (son of 2450 Avery,) m. Loisa Lamb, Nov. 6, 1836 ; lives at Mystic Bridge ; their children :

6254 WILLIAM AVERY, b. May 7, 1838; d. Jan. 25, 1840.
6255 MARIA LOUISA, b. Jan. 11, 1841; d. July 12, 1867; m. Wm. H. Davis.
6256 GEORGE WILLIAM, b. Nov. 14, 1844; m. Elizabeth Horn.
6257 MARY ELIZABETH, b. April 27, 1846.

356　　　　　　*Appendix.*

No. 4.

See page 27.

365½ MORRIS WILLIAMS DENISON, (Gideon H.[7], Jabez[6], Jabez[5], Jabez[4], John Jr.[3], Capt. John[2], George[1],) b. Oct. 31, 1825, was married to Mary A. Abell, Nov. 15, 1853. They live in Ada, Michigan, and have these children :

 6258 CHARLIE R., b. June 4, 1855; d. April 4, 1865.
 6259 HARLIE A., b. Oct. 14, 1866.
 6260 GETTIE B., b. October. 1867.

No. 5.

See page 55.

1067 CHARLES R. BEACH, (son of 1059 Nancy W. and Russell Beach,) b. 1849, was married to Ida M. Denison, at Saginaw, Mich. Their children :

 6261 GRACE MINERVA, b. March 21, 1876.
 6262 BESSIE WILLIAMS, b. April 19, 1880; d. Oct. 7, 1880.

No. 6.

See page 251.

5285 CHARLES R. GRIFFING, (son of 5266 Zelida Denison and Charles T. Griffing,) b. March 22, 1834, was married, Jan. 1, 1858, to Jennie R. White, in Chatfield, Minnesota. Their children :

 6263 CHARLES L., b. Sept. 27, 1858.
 6264 HORACE MANN, b. Nov. 27, 1859.
 6265 EFFIE E., b. Feb. 15, 1861.
 6266 HAROLD, b. July 4, 1869.
 And two daughters died in early infancy.

No. 7.

See page 44.

810 RHODA DENISON, (dau. of 792 Daniel,) b. at Berlin, N. Y., June 29, 1821, was married, Dec. 1, 1839, to Samuel Schuyler Streeter, b. at Berlin, April 13, 1818. They lived at Berlin. She d. there, Oct. 25, 1849. The children :

Appendix. 357

6267 ISABELLA JANE, b. Nov. 1, 1840.
6268 DANIEL DENISON, b. Aug. 19, 1843.
6269 MILFORD BARZALEEL, b. Sept. 1, 1847; unmarried.

6267 ISABELLA JANE STREETER, (dau. 810 Rhoda and S. S. Streeter,) b. Nov. 1, 1840, was married, Nov. 1, 1858, to Tracy D. Hull, had four children, and d. at Chicago, Ill., July 20, 1877. The children:

6270 KATE ISABELLA, b. Nov. 13, 1859.
6271 DANIEL DENISON, b. July 16, 1862.
6272 HARRY DOUGLASS, b. May 20, 1867.
6273 GERALDINE CHASE, b. Feb. 15, 1871.

6268 DANIEL DENISON STREETER, (son of 810 Rhoda and S. S. Streeter,) b. Aug. 19, 1843, was married, Dec. 13, 1866, at Kalamazoo, Mich., to Amelia T. Austin. Three children:

6274 FANNIE ISABELLA, b. April 18, 1867.
6275 WALTER WAKEFIELD, b. March 31, 1869; d. May 23, 1878.
6276 BLANCH WELLES, b. Oct. 10, 1873.

No. 8.

6276½ LUCRETIA DENISON, *m.* George Havens, Nov. 22, 1781. Their children:

6277 LUCRETIA, bapt. May 4, 1787.
6278 LOTTA, bapt. May 4, 1787.
6979 MIRIDE, bapt. May 4, 1787.
6280 LUCY, bapt. Dec. 20, 1789.

This was copied from the Westbrook church records, once a parish in Saybrook, Conn., where Samuel Denison, (George[2], George[1],) settled, and where some of his descendants still live. Lucretia Denison was without much doubt, a daughter of George Denison of Saybrook, who married Jemima Post. She was probably born about 1762, and her name was never recorded with the other children on the town books. George and Jemima were married in 1740, and were living in 1775, when they deeded land to their son Stephen.

No. 9.
See pages 226—7.

4782 BENADAM DENISON, JR., (son of 4776 Benadam,) b. in 1795, was married, first, to Lydia Boardman; and second, to Eliza Terrett. He lived in Halifax, Vt. We have sought the names and records of his children ; but promises have not been fulfilled. All we know is, that there was one child by the first marriage, as follows :

6281 GEORGE BOARDMAN DENISON, (son of 4782 Benadam, Jr.,) b. May 23, 1817, was married, Sept. 20, 1838, to Elizabeth Woodward, who was born in April, 1818. She d. June 21, 1848, and Dec. 21, 1848, he m. Jerua Warren, who was b. Aug. 27, 1824. He lives now in North Bernardston. His children :

 6282 CHARLES BOARDMAN, b. Jan. 17, 1840; m. Maria A. Barber.
 6283 HORACE WOODWARD, b. Jan. 15, 1842.
 6284 ARETUS LIVINGSTON, b. Jan. 12, 1844; m. Alma A. Clapp.
 6285 BENJAMIN FRANK., b. Dec. 15, 1845.
 6286 SILAS WARREN, b. July 5, 1850.

6282 CHARLES BOARDMAN DENISON, (son of 6281 George B.,) b. Jan. 17, 1840, m. Maria A. Barber, Dec. 31, 1864. Their children :

 6287 ARTHUR LIVINGSTON, b. Aug. 12, 1867.
 6288 FREDDIE BARBER, b. Dec. 8, 1868.

6284 ARETUS LIVINGSTON DENISON, (son of 6281 George B.,) b. Jan. 12, 1844, m. Alma A. Clapp, Dec. 7, 1873. Their children :

 6289 ELIZABETH LILIAN, b. Sept. 17, 1874.
 6290 ALTA JERUA, b. April 9, 1876.
 6291 MARION LOUISE, b. Dec. 23, 1877.
 6292 MELVIN ARETUS, b. June, 1879.

No. 10.

See page 259.

5446 DANIEL B. DENISON, (Daniel[6], George[5], Benadam[4], William[3], William[2], George[1],) b. Jan. 21, 1828, m. Lizzie H. Pierce of Chester, Vt., Jan. 1, 1869, and had :

 6293 A DAUGHTER, b. Jan, 10, 1870; d. March 1st, 1870.

Mrs. Lizzie Denison died Oct. 9, 1871.

5447 PAMELIA SUBMIT DENISON, (dau. of 5440 Daniel,) b. March 19, 1830, m. Nov. 24, 1851, Andrew O. Baker, b. March 9, 1827. They live in St. Johnsbury, Vt., and have had :

Appendix.

6294 WILLIAM, b. May 2, 1856; d. May 4, 1856.
6295 MINNIE FLORENCE, b. April 29, 1857.

The children were born at Holderness, N. H.

5452 HENRY CLAY DENISON, (Daniel[6], George[5], Benadam[4], William[3], William[2], George[1],) b. May 18, 1841, *m.* Emma F. Dewey of Queechy, Vt. They live at New Bedford, Mass, and have:

    6296 JENNIE FRANCES, b. June 6, 1865.
    6297 JOHN PORTER, b. Oct. 19, 1868.
    6298 MAY LOUISE, b. Nov. 25, 1872.
    6299 HELEN PAMELIA, b. March 7, 1875.

No. 11.
See page 198.

4173 ANN DENISON, (dau. of 3845 Nathan,) *m.* about 1762, Solomon Huntington, Jr, (son of Solomon and Mary Buckingham Huntington,) b. in Windham, Oct. 19, 1737, and had:

    6300 MINOR, b. April 22, 1763, went to Yarmouth, N. S., and *m.* Martha Walker in 1785. He is enrolled by Sabine in his history of the Loyalists. He d. in 1839, in Yarmouth, and his wife d. there some years later.
    6301 ALATHEA, b. Nov. 29, 1764; *m.* Medad Taylor, of Windham.
    6302 ELIZABETH, b. Jan. 15, 1767; *m.* Benj. Brewster, Oct. 25, 1809, and d. March 23, 1825; no children.
    6303 ANNA, b. April 7, 1770; *m.* Rev. Samuel Perkins, Feb. 24, 1793; lived in Windham, where she died April 17, 1829. Her husband d. Sept. 22, 1850, age 83. Their children were: 1st, Anna, who *m.* Sherman Converse of New Haven; 2nd, Samuel H., who graduated at Yale in 1818, and was a successful lawyer in Philadelphia; 3d, Horatio Nelson, d. in infancy; 4th, Harriet, the wife of Judge Clark of Windham.
    6304 SOLOMON, b. April 7, 1770; *m.* Anna Jones of New Haven, Oct. 25, 1801; lived in Mexico, N. Y.
    6305 JOSEPH DENISON, b. Oct. 28, 1778; *m.* Gratia Ann Weller of Westfield, who d. Dec. 19, 1853; lived in Lancaster and in Westfield, Mass.
    6306 MARY, b. Feb. 23, 1781; *m.* Hon. John Baldwin, Windham, a lawyer, judge of County Court, member of Congress, and who d. in Windham, March 27, 1850, age 78. She died April 20, 1814, having had two children: John, who lived in Windham, and Julia Ann, who d. June 14, 1806.

Anna Denison Huntington united with the Windham church in 1770, and died Sept. 9, 1807. Her husband died March 3, 1809.

Appendix.

No. 12.
DESCENDANTS OF JOSEPH DENISON OF WEST STAFFORD, CONN.

After extensive inquiries among his descendants, we are unable to fix the parentage of Joseph Denison of West Stafford, Conn. No one of them can tell who was his father or who was his mother. We have the age of himself and wife, as given in the records, that his wife was from New London, that they used to journey to New London and Stonington, to visit their kindred, on horseback, going through in a day; that he had a brother George, and another brother Stanton, which was probably a middle name.

His father belongs, properly, to the fourth generation from Capt. George, and is to be looked for among his great grandsons. We conjecture, and it is only a conjecture with slight data, that his father was 531 Wetherell Denison, whose record seems to be incomplete, and of whose children and descendants we have very incomplete accounts. Joseph, b. in 1744, would come in very properly after the birth of Wetherell's last child whose name is recorded, Sarah, b. May 31, 1743. He would have a brother George, and might have had a younger brother Stanton. It would account satisfactorily for his taking a wife in New London, Lydia Avery, whose parentage we have not yet discovered. Joseph died in 1828, and his wife in 1839, both in a good old age; and some of their grandchildren are still living, but no one of them can give the names of their great grandparents. The documents are probably in existence at the probate office in New London, and possibly in the records of the first church there, that will give light upon Joseph's parentage. There is no reasonable doubt that he is a descendant of Capt. George Denison.

6307 JOSEPH DENISON, b. in Stonington, 1744, *m.* Lydia Avery of New London, in 1775. She was born in 1755. They lived in West Stafford, Conn. He died July 27, 1828, aged 84; she died March 13, 1839, aged 84. Their children :

Appendix. 361

6308 LUCINDA, b. 1776; *m.* Leonard Smith.
6309 GEORGE, b. 1781.
6310 LYDIA, *m.* a Wardwell,
6311 SARAH, *m.* a McKenney.
6312 AMOS.
6313 CLARISSA, b. Nov. 13, 1789; *m.* John Bragg.
6314 JOSEPH, Jr , b. March 4, 1798.
6315 HANNAH M., b. 1797.
6316 RUBY E., b. Feb. 19, 1799; *m.* Benjamin Gold.
6317 ROBERT.

6308 LUCINDA DENISON, (dau. of 6307 Joseph,) b. in 1776, *m.* Leonard Smith, of West Springfield, Mass. She d. May 24, 1836, aged 80. Children :

6318 LEONARD, b. 1792.
6319 LUCINDA, b. 1795.
6320 ORIN, b. 1798.
6321 JONATHAN, b. 1800; P. O., Chicago, Ill.
6322 HENRY, d. young.
6323 CLARINDA, d. young.
6329 DENISON, b. 1703: d.
6330 JAMES M., b. 1806; P. O., Chicago. Ill.
6331 DELIA, twin, b. Sept. 4, 1817; *m.* Samuel Bascom, Belchertown, Mass.; no child.
6332 CELIA, twin, b. Sept. 4, 1817; *m.* Rufus Kingsbury; 2 children, Malisa and George.

6309 GEORGE DENISON, (son of 6307 Joseph,) b. 1781, *m.* Fannie Beaman. She died in 1858, aged 60 ; he died in 1858, aged 77. They lived at Warehouse Point, Conn., and had :

6333 HARRIET, b. Feb. 17, 1808; *m.* Samuel Converse of Somers.
6334 ELVIRA.
6335 ANGELINE.
6336 CHESTER.
6337 GILBERT, lives in California.
6338 GUILFORD.
6339 GAYLORD, b. 1823.
6340 MARIE S., b. June 17, 1825.
6341 LORENZO I., b. July 18, 1837.
6342 SANFORD.
6343 ALFRED, b. Oct. 30, 1832. P. O., Varville, Wis.

6313 CLARISSA DENISON, (dau of 6307 Joseph,) b. Nov. 13, 1789, *m.* John Bragg, Feb. 1, 1816. He d. Oct. 15, 1863, she d. June 7, 1875 ; they lived at Somers, Conn., and had :

6344 EMELINE, b. March 7, 1819.
6345 NOAH, b. June 11, 1824.

6344 EMELINE BRAGG, (dau. of 6313 Clarissa Denison,) b. March 7, 1819, *m.* Arnold Converse, Aug. 27, 1841. They live at Somers, Conn., and have :

 6346 JULIA M., b. Nov. 1, 1842; d. Feb. 15, 1848.
 6347 A SON, b. March 17, 1844; d. soon after birth.
 6348 A SON, b. Sept. 15, 1845; d. soon after birth.
 6350 A DAUGHTER, b. Aug. 1, 1846.
 6351 A DAUGHTER, b. July 17, 1847.
 6352 CARLOS A., b. Dec. 27, 1848; *m.* March 12, 1873.
 6353 EVERETT I., b. Sept. 11, 1850; d. Sept. 18, 1852.
 6354 GEORGE E., b. Nov. 9, 1853; d. Aug. 7, 1855.
 6355 LILLIAN C., b. Jan. 15, 1862; d. Sept. 17, 1862.
 6356 A DAUGHTER, b. March 9, 1857; d. Aug. 3, 1857.

6314 JOSEPH DENISON, JR., (son of 6307 Joseph,) b. Mar. 4, 1793; *m.* Adeline Adams, b. Dec. 16, 1812, Nov. 15, 1835; lived at Northfield, Vt., and had :

 6356½ ELVIRA, b. Oct. 31, 1836; d. April 12, 1850.
 6357 JOSEPH S., b. Sept. 11, 1838.
 6358 EMELINE, b. Dec. 17, 1840.
 6359 MARGARET, b. May 4, 1843.
 6360 ADORNO, b. Jan. 27, 1845; *m.* Addie V. Dalton, Dec. 5, 1872; lives at Middlesex, Vt.
 6361 ERSKINE, b, March 26, 1847.

6315 HANNAH M. DENISON, (dau. of 6307 Joseph,) b. 1797, *m.* Absalom Cady; lived at West Stafford, Conn. She d. March 19, 1835, aged 38 ; he d. in 1873, aged 83. Had :

 6362 HIRAM F., b. July 24, 1820.
 6363 CHARLANIA, b. Jan. 27, 1816; *m.* Holmes D. Sheldon, and had: Erwin, Ellen, Cady, and Denison.
 6364 ABNER L., b. Feb., 1825; d. Dec., 1866, age 40.
 6365 HANNAH A., b. May 22, 1827; *m.* Edwin Chaffee, West Stafford, Conn., and had Mahlon, Carlos, Abner, George, and Cora.

6316 RUBY E. DENISON, (dau. of 6307 Joseph,) b. Feb. 19, 1799, *m.* Benjamin Gold, March 12, 1815., lived at West Stafford, Conn. She d. Nov. 17, 1870. They had :

 6366 EMELINE S., b. Oct 19, 1816; *m.* Walter Ellis, Nov. 18, 1840. He d. Jan. 25, 1871.
 6367 BENJAMIN M., b. Aug. 4, 1822; *m.* Mary Brown, and had four children, viz , Alvin M., George, Milo, and Georgiana.
 6368 ALVIN B., b. Feb. 23, 1827.
 6369 CAROLINE C., twin, b. Sept. 30, 1832; d. Jan. 12, 1835.
 6370 ADELINE C., twin, b. Sept. 30, 1832; d. Jan. 26, 1835.

Appendix. 363

6317 ROBERT DENISON, (son of 6307 Joseph,) *m*. Mary Burpee, removed to the West, and had :

    6371 ARNOLD.   **6373** MARTHA.
    6372 MARY.   **6374** ALBERT.

6362 HIRAM F. CADY, (son of 6315 Hannah M. Denison,) b. July 24, 1820, *m*. Lucy Ingalls of Monson, Mass., June 30, 1852. She was b. July 21, 1834; lives at Kenosha, Wis., and has :

    6375 MARY, b. Nov. 27, 1853; *m*. Robert B. Yule, Sept. 14, 1871, and have Charles and Frank.
    6376 FLORENCE, b. Nov. 21, 1855; d. March 15, 1858.
    6377 CHARLES, b. Jan 29, 1869; d. Feb. 23, 1866.

6357 JOSEPH S. DENISON, (son of 6314 Joseph, Jr.,) b. Sept. 11, 1838; *m*. Nov. 25, 1862; lives at Northfield, Vt., and has :

    6378 CHARLES, b. Jan, 24, 1871.
    6379 FRANK, b. March 22, 1876.

6358 EMELINE DENISON, dau. of 6314 Joseph, Jr.,) b. Dec. 17, 1840, *m*. George W. Kingsbury, June 2, 1859. They live at Northfield, Vt., and have ,

    6380 DANIEL, b. Aug. 7, 1860.

6359 MARGARET DENISON, (dau. of 6314 Joseph, Jr.,) b. May 4, 1843, *m*. S. G. Winslow, March 19, 1860. They live in Pittsfield, N. H., and have :

    6381 CORA, b. April 24, 1863.
    6382 NELLIE, b. April 22, 1866.

6333 HARRIET A. DENISON, (dau. of 6309 George,) b. Feb. 17, 1808, *m*. Samuel Converse of Somers, Conn., Nov. 1, 1837. The children :

    6383 CLINTON C., b. April 29, 1839; d. June 9, 1871.
    6383½ CARLOS C., b May 21, 1841; d. Aug. 21, 1841.
    6384 CHARLES W., b. June 10, 1843.
    6385 LORENZO D., b. June 29, 1847.

6334 ELVIRA DENISON, (dau. of 6309 George,) *m*. Jacob Green, May 19, 1829. She d. June 30, 1834; he d. Aug. 1, 1870. The children :

    6386 GEORGE D., b. Dec. 21, 1831; m. Mary E. Smith, Oct. 18, 1870, and had Chester and Fannie; lives at Thompson, Conn.
    6387 CHESTER, b. June 13, 1834; d. Sept. 7, 1834.

6335 ANGELINE DENISON, (dau. of 6309 George,) *m.* Josiah Davis, and had:
  6388 ANGELINE.

6336 CHESTER DENISON, (son of 6309 George,) *m.* Mary Boyden. They live in Warren, Warren Co., Pa., and have:
  6389 CARRIE.   **6391** HENRY.
  6390 CHARLES.   **6392** MARY.

6337 GILBERT DENISON, (son of 6309 George,) *m.* Mary Ann Cadwell, and had:
  6393 JOHN.   **6395** ELLA.
  6394 LEON.

6338 GUILFORD DENISON, (son of 6309 George,) *m.* 1st, Julia Converse; 2d, Minerva Jones; lived at Somers, Conn., and had three children who died young.

6339 GAYLORD DENISON, (son of 6309 George,) b. 1823, *m.* Mrs. Sanford Denison, his brother's widow; lived at Somers, Conn., and had:
  6396 CHARLES DENISON, b. 1870.

6340 MARIE S. DENISON, (dau. of 6309 George,) b. June 17, 1825, *m.* Andrew A. Dwight, April 18, 1849. He d. March 10, 1865. They lived at Somers, Conn., and had:
  6397 GEORGE A., b. Sept. 5, 1850; d. Jan. 4, 1854.
  6398 JULIA S., b. Oct. 2, 1852.
  6399 MARIE S., b. May 27, 1856; d. July 27, 1857.

6341 LORENZO I. DENISON, (son of 6309 George,) b. July 18, 1837, *m.* Frances A. Turpin, April 14, 1859; they live at Warehouse Point, Conn., and have:
  6400 NELLIE F., b. Jan. 1, 1861.
  6401 WILLIAM H., b. July 25, 1864.
  6402 CHARLES B., Oct. 5, 1871.

6342 SANFORD DENISON, (son of 6309 George,) *m.* Emeline Shepherd in 1859. He d. in 1862. They lived in Somers, Conn., and had:
  6403 GEORGE, b. June, 1860.
  6404 ANGELINE, b. Oct., 1861.

Indexes.

I.
INDEX

To Names of Persons who were not Denisons, but were connected, by Marriage or Otherwise, with Denisons of this Genealogical Record.

[The figures refer to pages.]

A

Adams, Alice, 236.
Adams, Charlotte, 138.
Adams, Julius W.,179,180.
Adams, Victoria S., 133.
Ackart, Edward, 256, 257.
Allen, Alzina, 44, 45.
Allen, Mary L., 249.
Allen, Amos, 184.
Allen, Samuel B., 258.
Allen, Mr. A. W., 265.
Allen, Fanny, 235, 236.
Allen, Isaac, 43.
Allen, Emily L., 250, 252.
Allen, Mary, 23.
Allen, William, 43.
Andrews, Betsey E., 166, 168.
Andrews, Amos, 166.
Andrews, Mary Ann, 190.
Andross, Elizabeth, 131, 144.
Avery, Abigail, 121, 125.
Avery, Amy, 127.
Avery, Adeline L., 28, 29.
Avery, Benjamin, 231, 233.
Avery, Col. Ebenezer, 36.
Avery, Ebenezer, jr.,36,37.
Avery, Ebenezer, 59.
Avery, Katherine, 36, 38.
Avery, Erastus. 170.
Avery, Nathaniel, 282.

Avery, Eunice, 177.
Avery, Henry W., 169, 171.
Avery, Mary E., 169.
Avery, Nehemiah, 125.
Avery, David, (b. 1768,) 125.
Avery, David, (1817.) 239.
Avery, Jonathan, 84.
Avery, John, 10.
Avery, Lucy, (m.1807)283.
Avery, Jonas B., 59.
Avery, Lucy, (m.1773)234.
Avery, Mary, (1698) 84.
Avery, Mary, (b.1786)281, 293.
Avery, Mary, (1790) 38.
Avery, Park, 59.
Avery, Park W., 59.
Avery, Sarah, 120, 121.
Avery, Stephen, 125.
Avery, William, 121.
Ames, Eliza, 23.
Ashley, Vienna, 65.
Allison, Almira, 39, 41.
Allyn, Rev. Robert, 283, 284, 288.
Allyn, Charles, 284.
Allyn, Emeline Lucy, 284.
Almy, Eliza, 48, 51.
Aiken, John, 194.
Aiken, Sophia, 34.
Alden, Edmund B., 266.

Azeltine, Samuel, 153.
Azeltine, Sylvester H., 152, 153.

Abbott, Stephen, 199.
Arnold, Adela H., 25, 26.
Arnold, Mr. J. L., 151.
Arnold, Wilbur F., 216.
Aucutt, Gustavus, 168.
Austin, Henry R., 138.
Austin, Winnefred, 34.
Ausley, James G., 28.
Angus, Asa S., 65, 66, 68.
Angus, Dennis, 66.
Angus, John R., 68.
Angus, Mary J., 68.
Aumac, William, 268.
Asbury, John W., 253, 254.
Alderman, Rufus, 261.

B

Bacon, Orinda, 64.
Babcock, Abigail, 44, 45.
Babcock, Cynthia, 254, 249.
Babcock, Eveline F., 88.
Babcock, Harriet, 249.
Babcock, Mr. B. F., 92.
Babcock, Ruey, 281, 289.
Babcock, Giles, 96, 97.
Babcock, Mr. H., 86.
Babcock, Col. Henry, 177.
Babcock, Hannah, 87.
Babcock, Lucy, 281, 291.

368 Index.

Babcock, Raymond P.,201.
Babcock, May Denison,89.
Babcock, Maria, 255.
Babcock, Mary, (b. 1746) 86, 92.
Babcock, Mary, (b. 1761) 281, 283.
Babcock, Stephen, 193.
Babcock, William, 209.
Barnes, Emma, 267.
Bailey, Harriet P., 142.
Bailey, Francis B., 143.
Bailey, Isaac, (1702) 9.
Bailey, Isaac, (1820) 215, 216.
Bailey, Saxton, 8.
Bailey, Elizabeth, 60, 80.
Bailey, Rev. Rufus, 135, 142.
Bailey, Mary E., 142.
Bailey, Eleazer, 220, 221.
Bailey, Maria, 221.
Bayley, Clarrissa J., 39, 40.
Baylor, Charles G., 223.
Bailes, Mrs. C. W, 214.
Balcom, Susan E., 236.
Bayers, Edward, 70, 71.
Barrett, William, 258.
Baldwin, Wid. Ann, 35.
Baldwin Caroline. 25.
Baldwin, Edmund, 264.
Baldwin, Capt.David, 119.
Baldwin, Maj. John, 125, 127.
Baldwin, Priscilla, 234.
Baldwin, Daniel, 10, 127.
Baldwin, John Denison, 127, 128.
Baldwin, Daniel Avery, 127, 129.
Baldwin, Mary Ann, 127, 129.
Baldwin, John Stanton, 128.
Baldwin, Charles Clinton, 128, 129.
Baldwin, Capt.Theophilus, 132.
Baldwin, Eri G., 292.
Baldwin, Abigail, 35.

Ball, Albert P., 133.
Ballard, William W., 100.
Barnhart, Amarilla, 107.
Bartlett, Geo. C., 32.
Bradford, George H., 263.
Bradstreet, Rev.Simon, 17.
Brackett, Mary C., 287.
Barber, John, 38.
Barber, Ellen, 62.
Barker, Lucy A., 25, 26.
Bates, Mary C., 25.
Bates, Sally, 208.
Barnes, George, 194.
Barnes, Henry, 88.
Barnum, Mr. E. F., 187.
Blake, Alvin A., 31.
Barnes, Erastus, 162.
Bagley, Mary Ann, 133.
Barclay, Harriet, 165.
Blair, Maggie G., 111.
Blair, Adeline B., 260.
Blair, Sarah E., 271.
Blake, Bathsheba, 114,117.
Black, Samuel Gay, 72.
Brainard, John A., 23.
Bradley, Sarah, 62.
Bartholomew, Louise,260.
Baker, Betsey, 249.
Baker, Ereda, 289.
Batty, William, 268, 269.
Blauvelt, Charles, 268.
Bamman, AnnaMaria, 278.
Breed, Frances M., 158.
Breed, John, 11.
Bennett, Joseph, 96, 97.
Bennett, Barden, 266.
Bennett, Hon. Milo L.,135, 141.
Bennett, Hon. Edmund H. 141.
Bennet, Louis C., 238.
Bentley, Robert, 226.
Bentley, Mary C., 249.
Belden, Frank E., 163.
Belden, Mr. B. L., 257.
Belden, Nancy, 221.
Bemis, Alonzo, 109.
Bemis, Catherine, 100.
Bemis, Lauristine S., 109, 113.

Bemis, Frank T., 229.
Bement, Jeremy, 39, 42.
Beebe, Sarah, 54, 55.
Beach, Susan, 21.
Beach, Charles R, 55.
Beach, Russell, 55.
Beard, Ann M, 27.
Beckwith, Charlotte, 30.
Beckwith Lucretia, 30.
Benedict, Mary L, 38, 39.
Benton, Nelson, 240.
Bell, Mary, 18.
Bleeker, Sarah F., 96.
Breard, Lizzie, 267.
Brewster, Clara, 23.
Brewster, Daniel, 18.
Brewster, Dr. Wm.Barton, 94.
Bibbing, Lydia, 208.
Bills, Emeline, 208.
Bill, Gurdon, 170.
Bill, Frederick, 170.
Billings, Benjaman, 177, 183.
Billings, Elizabeth, 171.
Billings, Dell, 48, 50.
Billings, Sarah, 283, 286.
Billings, Ebenezer, jr., 17.
Billings, John, 9.
Billings, Joseph, 85, 86.
Billings, Martha, 196.
Billings, Mary, 234, 239.
Billings, Roger, 85.
Bicknell, Phebe, 152, 153.
Bickford, Delia, 118.
Bickford, Dr. Henry, 263.
Bishop, Jonathan, 32.
Briggs, Edward, 39, 42.
Briggs, Mary, 281, 282.
Briggs, Phebe, 291.
Briggs, Mary W., 48, 52.
Brigham, Jedediah, 59.
Bridges, Mr. J. D., 107.
Bingham, George, 208.
Bigelow, Ann Amelia, 136.
Bliss, Missouri, 145.
Bristol, Dea. Richard, 136.
Bristol, Charles N, 137.
Bristol, Ellen Ann, 137.
Bristol, Henry R., 137.

Index. 369

Bristol, Riley, 136, 137.
Bryan, Martha V., 189.
Bryant, David S., 122,123.
Bly, Mr. C., 44.
Bryson, Phebe, 68, 69.
Booker, Bowen, 271.
Borodell, Ann, 6, 7.
Borodell, John, 6.
Borden, Andrew, 72.
Borden, David, 72.
Borden, Perry, 67
Booth, Mary, 140, 141.
Booth, Laura, 260.
Boardman, Abigail, 127.
Boardman, Mary, 127.
Boardman, Lucy, 127.
Boardman, James, 127.
Boardman, Lydia, 227.
Bostwick, Sylvia, 178.
Boscawen, Dr. 181, 118.
Bolles, Nancy, 188.
Bolles, Enoch, 251.
Bothwell, Lucy, 194.
Bolton, John, 117, 118.
Bolton, George, 252.
Bonnell, Sarah H., 221,222.
Boyd, Chloe, 194
Boyce, Henry, 74.
Boynton, Luke, 107.
Blood, John, 186.
Blossom, David, 104.
Bloor, Jennie S., 256.
Blodgett, Joshua, 134.
Blodgett, Mary Esther,134.
Bowen, Alice E., 148.
Bower, Mr. S., 195.
Bower, Joseph, 195.
Bowman, Caroline, 199, 207.
Bowman, Derrick A., 203, 204.
Bowman, Ezekiel E., 205.
Brook, Eunice A., 286.
Brooks, John W., 79.
Browning, John, 147.
Brown, Charles, 63.
Brown, Catherine, 249, 250.
Brown, Fanny M., 123, 124.
Brown, Elias, (1770) 86.

Brown, Esther, 87.
Brown, James, jr. 14.
Brown, Enoch B., 278.
Brown, Joseph, 57.
Brown, Mercy, 13.
Brown, Morris E., 268,269.
Brown, Noyes, 12.
Brown, Louisa Keep, 287.
Brown, Noyes P., 275.
Brown, Bethany, 282.
Brown, Joanna, 134.
Brown, Eliza P., 275.
Brown, Elizabeth, 116,117.
Brown, Randall, 159.
Brown, Fanny Hazard,279.
Brown, Titus O., 109.
Brown, Sally, 114.
Brown, Rev. Oliver, 92.
Brown, Prudence, 101,119.
Brown, Stephen, 92.
Brown, Emily, 128.
Brown, John, 130, 131.
Brown, John (1831) 273.
Brown, Jerusha, 131.
Brown, Theody, 258.
Brown, Matthew, 130, 131.
Brown, Peleg, 178.
Brown, Ede, 179.
Brown, Esther, 179.
Brown, Prudence Dean, 188.
Brown, Fannie A., 104.
Brown, Eliza, 255.
Brown, Sarah, 255.
Brown, Elias, (1865) 257.
Buck, Sarah A., 268.
Buck, Cynthia, 268.
Buck, Catherine, 208.
Buckingham, Mr. R., 25.
Buckingham, Jemima, 31.
Burlingame, Mr., 59.
Burlingame, Nancy, 52.
Burnham, John A., 96, 97.
Burnell, Levi, 136.
Burnell, Joseph H., 136.
Burnell, Martha G., 136.
Burnell, Mary Elmira,136.
Burnell, Samuel Levi,136.
Burr, James, 2, 15, 220.
Burr, Eliza L., 221.

Burr, Lydia, 221.
Burr, Mrs J. H., 31.
Burrows, Caroline,268,269.
Burrows, Elam, 154, 159.
Burrows, Lura, 268, 269.
Burrows, Eunice E., 157.
Burrows, Benjamin, jr. 157.
Burrows, Mary E., 168.
Burrows, Enoch, 265, 277.
Burrows, Frances E., 162, 163.
Burrows, Eliza A., 162.
Burrows, Phebe, 159.
Burrows, Rev. Silas, 121, 122.
Burrows, Diana, 122.
Burrows Prudence M. 201.
Burrows, Hubbard, 234.
Burroughs, Ira, 242.
Buell, Mr. J. S., 22.
Buell, Mary Ann, 211.
Burdick, Caleb, 155.
Burdick, Jennie M., 111. 112.
Bushnell, Mary, 217.
Bushnell, Catherine, 225.
Bushnell, William, 224.
Bushnell, Eliza, 236, 238.
Bushnell, Sally, 29, 30.
Bundy, Ann, 262, 263.
Burwell, Julia A., 55, 56.
Burt, Edwin, 146.
Butt, Virginia E., 143.
Brush, Rosanna, 59.
Butterfield, Moses B., 172.
Butterfield, Mr. A. M., 260.
Butterfield, Mary S., 174.
Butterfield, Elizabeth S., 172.
Butler, Mary, 2-5.
Butler, Jerusha, 222, 223.
Butler, Elizabeth, 182.
Butler, Edward, 93.
Butler, Edward, jr., 94.
Butler, Caroline Hyde, 93.
Butler, Harriet D., 93.
Butler, Sarah C., 94.
Butler, Caroline Hyde, 2d, 95.
Butler, Frances L., 94.

Butler, Thomas, 92, 93.
Butler, TheodoreHunt,95.
Butler, Mary Hunt, 95.
Butler, Hunt Mills, 95.
Butler, Harriet D., 2d, 94.
Butler, Simeon, 93, 94.
Butler, Mrs. Mary(Hunt,) 94.
Butler, Theodore. 13, 192.
Butler, William, 257.
Burnett, Louisa, 241.
Burdon, Jane Pelton,279.
Budington, Jonathan,283, 288.
Budington, Mary Buckland, 288.
Budington, StephenBuckland, 289.

C

Caddock, Jesse, 261.
Caddock, Lydia, 261.
Campbell, Lucy B., 143.
Campbell, Prof. John L., 142.
Campbell, Mary E., 49.
Campbell, Ellen, 54.
Campbell, John C., 50.
Camp, Mary, 32.
Cameron, John S., 13.
Carew, Daniel, 13, 162.
Carew, SarahElizabeth,14.
Carew, Abbie C., 14.
Carey, Ann, 183, 198.
Carey, Caroline, 218.
Carleton, Charles Guy 93.
Carleton, Michael, 83.
Carpenter, James, 268.
Carpenter, Isabel, 268.
Carpenter, Hattie G., 111, 112.
Carroll, Emma, 242.
Carpenter, Samantha, 116.
Carpenter, Elizabeth, 198, 199.
Carpenter, Mary, 116.
Candee, Charles, 146.
Caton, William, 149, 151.
Casey, Phebe Jane, 149.
Catley, Ellen, 242.

Caldwell, James E., 94.
Caldwell, James A., 94.
Caldwell, Caroline E., 94.
Caldwell, Laura E., 94, 95.
Caulkins, Frances Manwaring, 7, 63.
Caulkins, Joshua, 62, 63.
Calkins, Catherine, 74.
Calkin, Benjamin H., 65.
Capps, Elizabeth W., 136, 137.
Caswell, Esther, 162.
Canad, Alvah, 208.
Carr, Seraphine S., 279.
Cahoon, Dr. C. S., 112.
Calverly, Philip, 114, 115.
Chandler, Rufus, 283.
Chandler, Rachel, 80.
Chandler, Bestey, 75.
Chalker, Elizabeth, 224.
Clark, Lucius P., 254, 255.
C'ark, Joseph, 221.
Clark, Chloe B., 224, 225.
Clark, George B., 160.
Clark, Irene, 210.
Clark, Albert C., 215.
Clark, Nettie E., 237.
Clark, Imogene Adell,279,
Clark, Dorcas, 213.
Clark, E. Parker, 171.
Clark, Jonathan, 21, 24.
Clark, Eliza R., 25, 28.
Clark, Henry H., 23.
Clark, Mr. J. H., 97.
Clark, Mary W., 97.
Clark, Henry, 276.
Champlin, Isaac, 179.
Champlin, John Denison, 179.
Champlin, John Denison, jr., 180.
Champlin, Christopher, jr. 175, 176.
Champlin, Susanna, 171.
Champlin, Mary, 74.
Chapin, Elizabeth M., 293.
Crandall, Rhoda, 52.
Crandall, Lucy, 45.
Crandall, Huldah, 283.
Crandall, Paul, 178.

Crary, Thomas, 132.
Crary, Nathan, 134.
Crary, Amos, (1811) 163, 164.
Crary, Benjamin, 86.
Crary, Peter, 92.
Crary, Capt. Henry, 256.
Crary, Polly, 38, 47.
Crary, Amos, (1756) 86.
Crary, Esther, 162.
Cram, Calvin, 113.
Cram, Henry, 213.
Chapman, Nathaniel, 209, 210.
Chapman, Juliana,210,212.
Chapman, Enoch, 7, 275.
Chapman, Caleb, 212.
Chapman, Frank, 252.
Chappell, William, 64.
Chappell, Mr. J. A., 154.
Chaple, Lemon, 28.
Chase, Henry S., 78.
Chase, Col. Champion S., 172.
Chase, Rachel, 243, 244.
Cranston, John H., 157.
Cranston, James H., 46.
Crane, Nancy, 66, 70.
Caswell, Mary E., 247.
Caswell, Rev. Henry, D.D. 247.
Chesebro', Nathaniel, 7, 8.
Chesebro', Nathaniel, jr., 7, 8, 10.
Chesebro', William, 8.
Chesebro', Margaret, 10.
Chesebro', Nathan, 10.
Chesebro', Samuel, 10.
Chesebro', Jabez, 11.
Chesebro', Mary, 1st, 12.
Chesebro', Mary, 2d, 14.
Chesebro', Ezra, 100.
Chesebro', James, 268.
Chesebro', Samuel R., 146.
Chesebro', Anna, 147, 131.
Chesebro', Amos, (1782) 147.
Chesebro', Daniel, 147.
Chesebro', Amos, (1851) 159.

Index.   371

Chesebro', Edmund, 160.
Chesebro', Hannah, 165.
Chesebro'. Denison. 273.
Chesebro', Arnold C., 122.
Chesebro', Mary, 3d, 130.
Chesebro', Sarah M., 130.
Chesebro'. Lydia, 132.
Chesebro', Elihu, 132.
Chesebro', Henry, 268.
Chesebro', Amira, 257,249.
Chesebro', Zebulon, 132.
Chesebro', Lucy, 226.
Chesebro', Sarah, 177.
Chesebro', Nathan, 177.
Cheney, Ellen, 55.
Cheney, David, 283, 284.
Clement. Alonzo, 40.
Cleveland, Widow, 74.
Cleveland, Mary, 92, 96.
Chittenden, Alfred, 211.
Chittenden, Rachel, 210, 211.
Chittenden, Julia, 215,219.
Chittenden, Lucius E.,139
Chittenden, Horace H.140.
Child, Gershom, 123.
Clickman, Peter. 130.
Clift, William, Sr., 125,126.
Clift, Rev. William, 126, 141, 89.
Clift, William, jr., 126.
Clift, George Denison,127.
Clift, Amos, 1st, 125.
Clift, Amos. 2d, 154, 160.
Clift, Amos, jr., 160.
Clift, Amos, 3d, 161.
Clift, Nathaniel, 154, 161.
Clift, Nathaniel, Jr., 162, 273, 274.
Clift, John G., 160.
Clift, John G., 2d, 161.
Clift, Waterman, 160.
Clift, Robert H., 161.
Clift, Charles Waterman, 161.
Clift, Frederic Denison, 161.
Clift, Mary Coit, 162.
Clift, Harriet W., 162.
Clift, William,(b.1805)162.

Clift, Eunice, 163.
Clift, Horace Hatch, 163.
Clift, Isaac Denison, 163.
Clift, Nancy D., 147.
Clift, Lydia, 89.
Clift, Esther W., 89.
Crickers, Sallie Ann, 260, 261.
Cook, Benjamin Ladd,191.
Cook, Olive P., 49, 50.
Cook, Wellington P., 55, 56.
Cook, Helen M., 33.
Cook, Francis. 67.
Cook, Bertha F., 95.
Cooper, Mercy S., 81, 83.
Cooper, Mr. A. B., 104.
Cole, Mr. H., 110.
Cole, Ira H, 219, 220.
Cole, Samuel, 289.
Cole, Louisa. 220.
Colver, Edwin, 62.
Copp, Joseph, 37.
Copp, David, 84.
Cobb, Oliver, 92.
Cobleigh, Freedom, 113.
Cobleigh, Diana. 113.
Cobleigh, Mary, 113.
Colton, Rev. Abisha, 114, 115.
Colton, Daniel, 114.
Collins, Widow, 73.
Collins, Adeline Eliza,137.
Collins, William, 122.
Collins, Maria, 273, 275.
Collins, Benj. F., 276, 277.
Cowles, Sally, 215.
Conable, Ezra, 283, 285.
Conable, Samuel Charles, 286.
Cooley, Lucy Burt, 283.
Cokelet, Sarah, 268.
Conkling, Abigail, 209.
Conklin, Betsey, 125.
Conklin, Mr. J. H., 126.
Coon, Alphonso, 252.
Cone, Susan C., 83.
Cone, Sylvester Wells, 81, 83.
Cone, Emeline A., 283.

Cone, Anna W., 83.
Connor, John, 269.
Coleman. Elmira, 58.
Colegrove, Amanda, 129.
Cogswell, Jane, 120.
Coggswell, Frederic, 190.
Coggswell, Samuel, 18.
Cogswell. Dorothy, 18.
Coger, Charles, 25, 27.
Coggill, Julia. 140.
Coats, Mary H., 134.
Coit, Benjamin, 86.
Coit, Mary, 10.
Coit, Rev. Joseph, 10.
Colt, Benjamin, 73, 74.
Colt, William, 73, 74.
Colvocoresses, Franka E., 180.
Cox, Thomas J., 272.
Cornell, Lydia A., 146.
Covill, Mr. H. W., 279.
Covell, Mary. 124.
Cottrell, Charles, 159.
Cottrell, Mary A., 276, 277.
Cottrell, Fanny E., 100.
Converse, Mr. M., 21.
Conway, Mary, 51.
Cowdry, Meribah, 53, 54.
Congdon, Cynthia, 268.
Cowee, James F., 47.
Coffell, Abigail, 67, 68.
Crocker, Sally, 142.
Crocker, Sarah M., 54.
Crocker, Ruth, 62.
Cross, Julia F , 65.
Cross, Nellie W., 83.
Crooks. Phebe, 145.
Culver, Edwin D., 46.
Culver, Sophia, 276.
Culver, Joshua, 18, 30.
Culver, Jonathan, 280.
Culver, Mr. J. E., 190.
Cushman, Wealthy, 75.
Cushman, Ralph. 287.
Cushman, Henry Clay,287.
Cushing, Kate, 113.
Curtis, Justine, 94.
Cutting, Joseph, 135, 139.
Cutler, Olive, 92.
Curran, Mr., 132.

Index

Crumb, Mary E., 54.

D

Dana, Mr. O. A., 77, 78.
Dana, Charles A., 82.
Dana, Junius, 82.
Dana, Anderson, 81, 82.
Davidson, Asa, 66. 68.
Davidson, Andrew, 66.
Davis, Amelia, 69.
Davis, Edwin G., 167.
Davis, Oscar B., 43.
Davis, James L., 271.
Davis, Mr. J. T., 44.
Davis, Mr. B. F. S., 156.
Davis, Thomas. 208.
Davis, Nancy, 148.
Davis, Joseph, 226, 228.
Davy, Isaiah, 39, 41.
Dabney, Rev. Wm. A.,143.
Dafoe, Cynthia M., 149,151.
Danforth, Sewall W., 109.
Danforth, Clara, 293.
Darling, Charles, 122.
Drake, Emilia, 76.
Draper, Mr. E. H., 277.
Dean, James, 9.
Dean, Rev. Paul, 75, 79.
Deane, Jesse, 99.
Deane, Dr. A. C., 109.
Bean, Mary F., 78.
Dean, Thankful, 266.
Dean, Christopher, 239.
Deeth, Henrietta, 203,205.
Denniston, Pauline, 87,89.
Dennis, Frances A., 284.
Denis, Francis B., 133.
Denny, Edward, 117.
Devine, Norman, 196.
Devine, Wilson D., 195.
Dexter, Mary M., 190,191.
Dexter, Elizabeth, 51.
Dewey, William, 249.
Dewey, Deborah, 243.
Dewey, William E., 255.
DeWitt, Adelia, 59.
DeWolf Robert, 70, 71.
Dibble, Mary, 48.
Dibble, Ichabod, 48. 51.
Dibble, Christina, 25, 26.

Dickson, David A., 72.
Dickerson, Mehetibel, 21.
Dickinson, Mary, 275.
Dickinson, Susan A., 155.
Dimon, Maria S., 163.
Dinehart, Mr. C. E., 197.
Dixon, William, 289.
Dixon. Nathan F., 280.
Dixon, Courtland P.,87,88.
Dixon, Nathan F., jr.,280, 281.
Dixon, Frances B., 281.
Dixon, Sally R., 281.
Dyer, Luther, 135, 140.
Dyer, Anne Abbott, 262, 263.
Doane, Anna, 224, 225.
Doane, Ann, 224.
Donley, John, 201.
Donley, Augusta, 201.
Donley, Elizabeth, 202.
Douglas, Daniel S., 22.
Douglas, Gertrude, 30.
Douglas, William. 35, 36.
Douglass, Archibald T.171.
Dodge, Hannah, 60, 84.
Dodge, Mr. E., 44.
Downing, Myra, 118.
Downer, Elizabeth A.,197, 198.
Dow, Caroline S., 235,237.
Dorrell, Celestina, 286,290.
DuBois, Carrie, 189.
Duboe, Rev. A. M., 52.
Dudley, Cecilia, 213.
Dudley, Gov. Thomas, 5.
Dudley, Patience, 5.
Dunbar, Mordecai,175,177.
Dunbar, Eunice, 244, 248.
Duncan, John T., 75, 76.
Dunham, Eliza, 51.
Dunham, Hetty, 51.
Dunning, Aurilla, 194.
Dupler, Dr., 271.
Du Vernett, Peter, 225.
Durrie, Miss H. K., 142.
Durkee, Keziah, 80.
Duyckinck, Whitehead Cornell, 95.
Drummond, Mr., 181.

E

Earl, Nathan, 48, 51.
Eastman. Rev. Cyrus L., 288.
Easton, Samuel, 53.
Eaton, Palmyra, 164.
Evans, Mary K., 113.
Evans, Ann C., 241.
Evans, Sarah A., 111, 112.
Evans, Mary, 241.
Evans, Dr. Samuel D., 164.
Evans, Edwin C., 242.
Eells, Benjamin, 92.
Eells, Edward, 101, 119.
Eells, Rev. Nathaniel, 92.
Eccleston, Wid.Mary Ann, 235.
Eccleston, Susan, 252.
Everett, Elizabeth, 75.
Everett, Sarah, 138.
Everett, Warren, 227.
Emerson, Abigail, 139.
Emerson, Lucy, 196.
Edgerton, Simeon, 35.
Elderkin, Susanna, 198, 208.
Elderkin, Joshua B., 198.
Edgecomb, Samuel, 121.
Estelle, J. B., 214.
Eldridge, Mrs.Abigail, 120.
Eldridge, Harriet, 185,188.
Eldridge, Lydia, 79.
Eldridge, Capt. Thomas, 124.
Eldredge, Abby, 255.
Eliot, Rev. John, 5.
Elliott, Smith D., 196.
Elliott, Mary, 254.
Eliot, Zebulon, 125.
Ellis, Anna, 211.
Ellis, Samuel, 187.
Ellison, Z. DeEtta, 256.
Ely, Aaron, 209.
Ely, Henry G., 263.
Ely, Phebe A., 185, 186.
Ely, Josiah G., 72, 80.
Eddy, Mary, 88.
Ensign, Jerusha, 57.
Edwards, Sarah, 135, 138.
Eggleston, Susan, 250.

Index.

F
Fairchild, Mary E., 55, 56.
Fairchild, Jane, 166, 168.
Farwell, Melinda, 288.
Farnesworth, Eleanor M., 197.
Falconer, Miss, 182.
Farley, Margaret, 43.
Fraser, Elizabeth, 39, 41.
Frasier, Betsey, 104.
Franklin, Esther, 267.
Faville, Mr. A. S., 165.
Farrer, Mr. E. M., 268.
Fay, Tim. P., 243.
Fay, Myra B., 247.
Ferguson, William E., 169.
Fellows, Laura, 206, 199.
Fellows, Priscilla, 265, 280.
Fellows, Isaac, 115.
Ferris, Alanson, 196, 197.
Ferrier, Thomas, 199.
Freeman, John Salter, 165.
Freeman, Huldah, 86.
Freeman, Mary Ellen, 165.
Fretz, Peter, 148.
Flett, William, 268, 270.
Fish, James Dean, 134.
Fish, Lavinia, 154, 156.
Fish, Hannah, 132, 169.
Fish, Julia, 159.
Fish, Bridget, 162.
Fish, Sanford, 28.
Fish, James, 275.
Fish, Lucy M., 38.
Fish, Edward, 227.
Fish, William, 42.
Fitch, Asahel, 194.
Fitch, William Reed, 194.
Fitch, Alvah, 194.
Fitch, Cynthia D., 194.
Fitch Charles D., 184.
Fitch, Polly, 195.
Fitch, James, jr., 171.
Fitch, James, 60.
Fitch, Elizabeth, 88, 89.
Fitzpatrick, Catherine, 62, 71.
Flint, Jennie, 39, 42.
Frink, Betsey M., 227.
Frink, Samuel, jr., 171.

Frink, Lizzie L., 264.
Frink, Elisha, 227.
Frink, Desire, 169.
Frink, Eunice, 127.
Frink, Stephen, 127.
Frink, Frederic, 127.
Frink, John, 69.
Fifield, Helen M., 117.
Fisher, Edwin, 109, 112.
Fisher, Mary O., 270, 272.
Fling, William, 134.
Flynn, Henry, 187.
Fyler, George, 114.
Fox, William H., 40.
Fox, William, 282.
Fox, Henry, 48, 50.
Fox, Sarah, 62, 66.
Fox, Dr. 145.
Forsyth, Jane, 161.
Forsyth, Cordelia, 245.
Forsyth, Thomas C., 160.
Forsyth, Lottie, 106.
Forsyth, Margaret Alice, 68.
Forsyth, Wid. C., 214.
Folger, William A., 73.
Foster, William, 42.
Foster, Mehitabel, 18, 19.
Fowler, Amos H., 227.
Fowler, Lucy A., 135.
Forbes, Frances S., 135, 143.
Force, Julia B., 134.
Ford, Cornelia D., 32.
Fopett, Miss C. M., 261.
Frost, Asenath, 145, 146.
Foot, Edward Y., 162.
Fuller, Hannah, 198.
Fuller, William, 71.
Fuller, Oliver, 71, 72.
Fuller, Mr. E. G., 67.
Funch, Frederic W., 275, 276.

G
Gallup, David L., 99.
Gallup, Elias, 100.
Gallup, Esther, 43.
Gallup, Euni e, 86.
Gallup, John, (1621) 9.

Gallup, John, (1870) 188.
Gallup, Joseph, 267, 268.
Gallup, Col. John, 131, 134.
Gallup, William, 243.
Gallup, Mary, 131, 163.
Gallup, John D., 153, 159.
Gallup, Mercy, 231.
Gallup, Lucy, 231, 234.
Gallup, Martha, (1820)255.
Gallup, Martha, (1742)183 193.
Gallup, Elisha, 265, 266.
Gallup, Daniel, 122.
Gallup, John D., 266.
Gallup, Prudence D., 129.
Gallup, Mary, (of Nova Scotia) 66, 68.
Gallaudet, Edward Minor, 244, 245.
Gallaudet, Alice C., 91.
Gardiner, Delia, 169.
Gardiner, Henry, 135.
Gardiner, Lydia, 233.
Gardner, Dr. Andrew J. 55.
Gardner, James R., 142.
Gardner, William, 131, 132.
Garfield, Ella L., 157.
Garfield, Isaac D., 244, 245.
Gaskill, Jabez, 22.
Gaskell, Stephen, 21, 22.
Gaskill, Olive E., 22.
Gano, Mary, 40.
Gage, Louisa, 79.
Gates, Gurdon, 159.
Gates, Zebediah, 154, 159.
Gay, Amos, 236.
Gaylord, Hannah, 53.
Graves, Libeus P., 40.
Graves, Parnell, 19, 20.
Graves Sereno W., 107, 108.
Graves, Ruth Ann. 260.
Graves, Nancy, 273.
Grange, Mary, 149.
Grange, William, 152.
Gray, Ann, 168.
Gray, Hon. H. H, 192.
Gray, Mary, 185.
Glaspie, William, 249, 250.

Index.

Galloway, Andrew, 177, 183.
Gladwin, Juliet, 31.
Grant, Joseph W., 247.
Grant, Oliver, 18.
Grant, David Denison, 247.
Grant, Thankful, 64.
Grant, Mr. D. W., 244, 247.
Grable, Mary, 272.
Geer, Charles, 258, 259.
Geer, Elisha, 86.
Geer, Martha, 86, 98.
Geer, John W., 87, 91.
Geer, Mary, 87.
Geer, Moses T., 99.
Gere, Nathan, 243.
Green, Franklin, 145.
Green, Allen, 254, 255.
Green, Cleora, 197.
Green, Mary E, 268.
Green, Mr. S. H., 190.
Green, John, 273.
Greene, Robert, 155, 156.
Green, Isaac, 143.
Green, Caleb, 282.
Green, Sarah, 38, 44.
Green, Sarah A., 273.
Green, Esther, 44.
Green, Ida A., 45.
Green, Mrs. S. A., 46.
Greenman, Mr. O. F., 42.
Greenlee, James A., 187.
Gillmar, George H., 72.
Gillmar, Lemuel L., 72.
Gillespie, Susan B., 262, 263.
Gillson, Lydia P., 160.
Gillson, Laura O., 122, 123.
Gibson, Mary Jane, 238.
Gilkey, Silas, 109.
Gile, Benjamin, 85.
Grinnell, Mary, 122.
Grinnell, Amos, 239.
Grinnell, Benjamin, 73, 74.
Gridley, Mercy B., 75.
Griswold, Fanny M., 32.
Griswold, Deborah, 60.
Griswold, Patience, 60, 72.
Griswold, Lucretia, 36.
Griswold, Joseph, 99, 100,

Griswold, Sylvanus, 74.
Griffing, Charles T., 250, 251.
Goodale, Francis H, 118.
Gooding, Emma, 165.
Gooding, Jasper A., 140.
Gooding, William, 139.
Goodman, Harriet M., 22, 23.
Goodrich, Norman, 250.
Goodrich, Esther K., 81, 83.
Godfrey, Hannah M., 47.
Gorham, Mercy, 6, 175.
Gorham, Capt. John, 175.
Goddard, Ebenezer, 177.
Goddard, Abigail, 125.
Godding, Diantha, 113.
Gonard Ella Frances, 137.
Goady, Jane, 221.
Gore, Aurelia, 124.
Gould, Rev. J. B., 188, 189.
Gowan, Addie H., 106.
Gronard, Ellen, 83.
Gordon, Eva, 150.
Gove, Sarah, 252.
Goodenow, Isaac T., 283.
Guernsey, Hoyt, 77.

H

Hallam, Edward, 34, 35.
Hallam, Harris, 55.
Hallum, Amos, 177.
Hallum, Elizabeth, 184.
Halsey, William, 10.
Halsey, Susan M., 73.
Halsey, Hannah, 80.
Haley, Elizabeth, 18.
Halliday, Edward, 188.
Halsted, Jefferson, 268.
Hamburger, Eliza, 41.
Hamilton, Rev. Henry H., 71.
Hamilton, Sloan, 260.
Hamilton, Nancy, 70.
Hamilton, Sophia, 70.
Hamilton, Oliver M., 293.
Hamlin, Edwin A., 212.
Hamley, Melissa J., 152.
Hammond, Mr., 59.
Handerson, Harriet M, 138,

Hancox, Frances, 273.
Hancock, Elvira, 289, 290.
Haltsman, Marinda, 207.
Hapgood, Elizabeth H. 289.
Hardy, Isaac, 144.
Hardy, Louisa, 145.
Harding, Jane, 174.
Harding, Wid. S., 31.
Hall, Harley M., 109.
Hartley, Ellen, 143.
Haughn, Jane, 207.
Hawley, Dr., 109.
Haverly, Eve, 135.
Haughton, Eunice, 281, 294.
Hazard, Esther K., 160.
Hazard, Mary Niles, 154.
Harris, Gibson, 34, 35.
Harris, Amasa, 66, 70.
Harris, Mrs. Mary, 34.
Harris, James F., 67.
Harris, John, 124, 216.
Harris, Eleanor C., 157, 158.
Harris, Lydia, 124.
Hart, Edmund B., 155.
Hart, Huldah, 20.
Harrington, Rev. R. B., 266.
Harvey, Lavinia, 91.
Haskell, Nahum, 77, 78.
Hacket, Alvin, 105, 106.
Hayden, John G., 24.
Haynes, Emily, 57.
Hayes, Adeline C., 26.
Haven, Philemon, 53.
Hawkins, Jason, 213.
Hattrick, Mary C., 182.
Hathaway, Lemira, 127, 128.
Haff, Ann M., 203, 204.
Hancock, William, 199, 200.
Hanover, Henry, 201, 202.
Hanover, Jane, 200, 202.
Hanks, Lucien Bonaparte, 279.
Hatch, Reuben, 132, 135.
Hatch, Fanny Newcomb, 136.
Hatch, Henry Denison, 136.

Index.

Hatch, Daniel D., 135.
Hatch, Frederick Wm. 137.
Hatch, Frederick, 137.
Hatch, Maria Allyn, 137.
Hatch, Ellen Ann, 137.
Hatch, Emily Stearns, 138.
Hatch, John, 138.
Hatch, John Chandler, 138.
Hatch, Dr. Horace, 138.
Hatch, Mary Yates, 139.
Hatch Elizabeth, 139.
Hatch, Fanny, 139.
Hatch, Aurora, 140.
Hatch, Harriet Hinckley, 140.
Hatch, Adeline, 141.
Hatch, Lucy C., 142.
Hatch, Albert G., 142.
Hatch, Joseph D., 143.
Hatch, Alfrederic, 143.
Hatch, Frank Everett, 138.
Hatch, Sarah E., 138.
Hatch, Thomas E., 138.
Hazen, Maria, 263.
Headley, Susan, 270.
Helm, Louisa, 194.
Hempstead, William S., 55.
Hempstead, Nathan, 62.
Henderson, Eliza Jane, 196, 197.
Henderson, Sarah M., 196.
Henderso., Sarah, 194, 195.
Hendee, Acsah, 266.
Henly, Commodore John D., 223.
Hershy, Angeline, 126.
Hester, George, 55, 56.
Hetrick, Dr. J. A. W., 164.
Heath, Sarah M., 99.
Heath, Margaret, 240.
Head, Pamelia L., 253, 259.
Henriques, George, 34.
Hewitt, Henry, 183, 184.
Hewitt, Elijah S., 247.
Hewitt, Henry Palmer, 155, 156.
Hewitt, Benjamin B., 131.
Hewitt, Maj. Israel, 11.

Hewitt, Phebe, 38.
Herrick, Edward, 85.
Herrick, Stephen, 85.
Heady, Morris, 272.
Hicks, Fanny C., 154, 155.
Hicks, Edwinia, 182.
Hickey, Margaret, 288.
Hicks, Edwin, 182.
Higbee, Rev. Edward Y., 223.
Hibbs, Samuel, 270.
Higgins, Mr. G. W., 110.
Higley, Iola, 74, 75.
Higby, Augustus, 105, 106.
High, Fanny, 93.
Hinckley, 226.
Hinckley, Samuel, 11.
Hilton, Delia, 214.
Hilton, Julia M., 214.
Hillard, William, 122, 125.
Hillyer, George R., 242.
Hinman, Charles, 41.
Hinman, Mr. W. G., 250.
Hitchcock, Frances Caroline, 289.
Hinsdale, Catherine, 62.
Hill, Eva, 51.
Hill, Olivia, 210, 211.
Hyde, Joshua Burrows, 278.
Hyde, Lucy Esther, 278.
Hyde, Harriet Elizabeth, 279.
Hyde, Rev. Edward Lawrence, 279.
Hyde, Rev. William P., 279.
Hyde, Ann, 61.
Hyde, John, 278.
Hyde, Daniel, 61.
Hyde, Theophilus R., 279.
Hyde, Walter, 61.
Hyde, Zelpha, 61.
Hyde, Dr. William, jr., 87, 88.
Hyde, Nancy, 239, 240.
Hypes, William, 284.
Holmes, Benjamin, 160.
Holmes, Daniel D., 133.
Holmes, Alonzo Lee, 133.

Holmes, Esther, 134.
Holmes, Wm. Henry, 133.
Holmes, Thomas, 127.
Holmes, Ellen, 188.
Holmes, Jeremiah, 159.
Holmes, Prudence, 231, 235.
Holmes, Benj. F., 167.
Holmes, Hiram C., 170.
Holmes, Hazard, 239, 243.
Holmes, Jeremiah, Sen., 132,
Holmes, Robert, 122, 124.
Holmes, Mr. J. W., 43.
Holmes, Polly C., 46.
Holmes, Mrs. Kendall, 67.
Holmes, Jabish, 88, 89.
Hovey, Silas P, 250.
Howe, Earl, 267, 268.
Howe, Henry C., 289, 290.
Hobart, Adaline C., 110.
Hoffman, Elias, 152, 153.
Holdredge, Capt. John, 162.
Holbrook, Desire, 25, 28.
Holbrook, Mary E., 13, 191.
Holden, Heman, 196.
Holden, Lavinia, 196.
Holman, Willard, 227.
Horsford, Sylvia, 144.
Hooper, Fanny, 139.
Hood, Phebe, 117, 118.
Howland, Abner, 112.
Hotchkiss, Hannah, 210.
Holt, Frances E., 28.
Hornaday, Mr. N., 286.
Hooker, William G, 251.
Hooker, Thomas, 52.
Hopkins, Pres. Mark, 79.
Hopson, Amelia A., 105.
Hopson, Rowena M., 106.
Hough, John, 35.
Hough, Jabez, 35, 36.
Hough, Elsie, 39.
Howell, Lucy E., 264.
Howell, Henry, 276.
Hoyt, Aaron, 115.
Hoyt, John F., 286.
Hoyt, Ruel, 64.
Howell, Sally M., 122, 123.
Howard, Emma A. 195, 107.

Index.

Howes, Moody, 116.
Hoxie, Benjamin F., 162.
Hoxie, Dr., 194.
Hull, Luther, 22
Hull, Daniel J., 47.
Hull, Dr. Emerson, 46.
Hull, Gideon, 216.
Hunt, Morton P., 163.
Hunt, Dorinda B., 206.
Hunt, Ella, 201.
Hunt, Elizabeth, 14.
Hunt, Betsey, 98.
Huntington, Hon. Roger, 248.
Huntington, Andrew, 62, 87.
Huntington, Emma L. 277.
Huntington, Solomon, 198.
Hunter, John H., 88, 90.
Hunton, Amelia Rosella, 108.
Hurd, Sarah, 76.
Hurd, Margaret A., 216.
Hurd, Mary, 219.
Hurlburt, Thomas, 114, 116.
Hurlburt, Elijah, 115.
Hurlburt, Thomas Stewart, 117.
Hurlburt, Samuel, 181, 182.
Hubbard, Rev. David B., 31.
Hughes, Augustus, 149, 150.
Hughes, Hannah, 149, 151.
Hughes, Mary Ellen, 188.
Hughes, William J., 149, 150.
Hulings, Ellen E., 199.
Humphrey, Harvey, 213.
Humphrey, Dovecine, 213.
Huested, Lyman, 213.

I

Ingalls, Walter, 123.
Ingraham, Caray, 249.
Ingraham, Anna, 181.
Ives, Dr. Levi, 200, 203.
Ives, Robert S., 203.
Isles, James, 242.

Irish, Elizabeth, 239, 240.
Irish, Phebe, 239, 242.
Irving, Sarah, 40.

J

Jackson, Thomas, 14.
Jackson, Rebecca, 95.
Jackson, Gen. W., 95.
James, Deborah, 194.
James, John, 87, 90.
James, Horatio T., 69, 70.
Jameson, John A., 244.
Jarvis, Mr. B. W., 147.
Jepson, Henry, 37.
Jerome, Waity, 53.
Jenks, Dr. John S., 258, 264.
Jenks, Dr. Nathaniel, 265.
Jenks, Isaac P., 116.
Jenks, Sally, 262.
Jennings, Morgan L., 196.
Jennings, Orville, 187.
Jennings, William, 296.
Johnson, Charles, 159.
Johnson, Elias P., 282.
Johnson, Frances, 199.
Johnson, Rachel M., 276.
Johnson, Geo. S., 152, 154.
Johnson, Marian, 64, 65.
Johnson, Mary E., 81.
Johnson, Samuel E., 94.
Johnson, Mr. E. B., 79.
Johnson, Simpson, 58.
Jones, Charlotte L., 167.
Jones, Darius, 135, 139.
Jones, Mrs. Elizabeth, 43.
Jones, Hannah, 38.
Jones, Mr. G. D., 46.
Jones, James, 38, 53.
Jones, James H., 53.
Jones, Roger, 38, 53.
Jones, Rebecca W., 200, 202.
Jones, Samuel, 210, 212.
Jones, Widow, 36.
Jones, Mary, 272.
Jones, Warren N., 256.

K

Knapp, Hannah, 221.

Kaulback, Hon. H. A. N., 70.
Keeler, Eliza, 74.
Kelley, Lucretia, 75, 78.
Kelley, William, 55.
Kelley, Elizabeth, 299, 213.
Kellogg, David, 235.
Kennedy, Capt., 62.
Keim, DeB. Randolph, 253.
Keyser, Jacob, 51.
Keyser, Hiram DeW., 188.
Kemp, Phebe J., 275.
Kemp, Ellen, 159.
Kendrick, Asa F., 273, 274.
Kendall, Elvira P., 110.
Kenyon, Louisa, 292.
Kenyon, Charles, 291.
Kenyon, Harriet, 123.
Kenyon, Aldridge, 238.
Kenney Thomas, 107.
Kinney, Rev. Pardon T., 188, 189.
Kinney, Ezra, 226, 228.
Kinney, Sarah, 228.
Kinney, Mary C., 127.
Kinney, George A., 124.
Kingsley, Joseph, 248.
Kinsley, James, 105, 106.
King, Thomas, 272.
King, Susan, 219.
Kilton, Mrs. Marcia, 240.
Kirkley, Ellen, 149, 150.
Kilbourne, Elizabeth, 263.
Kitchen, James, 272.
Kirtland, Hezekiah C., 217.
Kirtland, Ann M., 217.
Knight, William E., 147.
Kingsbury, George, 186, 187.
Kniskern, Louis H., 14.
Kyle, Martha, 81.
Koutz, Lizzie C., 191.
Knox, Martha, 197.
Krusan, Elizabeth, 270.

L

Lambdin, Hannah G., 241.
Lamphere, Gurdon M. 255.
Lamb, Clark, 111.
LaBarr, Eugene, 202.

Index. 377

Lambert, Amelia M., 248
Lambert, Joseph, 162.
LaGrange, Elizabeth E., 48, 49.
LaGrange, Abram, 48, 49.
La Roche, Pierre, 125, 141.
Lafoucade, Annie, 94.
Langworth, Carolina A., 254.
Lane, Daniel P., 220, 221.
Lance, Mr. O. M., 200.
Lane, Abigail, 29.
Lazelle, Otis J., 292.
Latham, Lucy, 36.
Latham, William, 122.
Latham, Jane, 159.
Latham, Hannah, 266, 267.
Latham, Benjamin, 159.
Latham, Daniel, 169, 171.
Latham, Alexander, 185.
Lathrop, Wealthy, 264.
Lathrop, John, 62, 63.
Lathrop, Elizabeth L., 96, 97.
Lathrop, Ann, 35.
Lathrop, Elisha, 35.
Latchley, John M., 70.
Laing, Hugh, 94.
Lankton, Nancy, 250, 252.
Lankton, Naomi, 250, 253.
Lay, Phebe, 6.
Lay, Robert, jr., 7.
Lay, Anna, 210.
Lay, Simeon, 222, 223.
Lawton, Joseph, 230.
Lawton, Rufus B., 123.
Latimer, Jonathan, 35, 36.
Latimer, Nancy, 265.
Latimer, Hannah, 61.
Laufman, Kate, 95.
Laud, Martha A., 230, 262.
Leach, George, 59.
Leard, John, 63.
Learned, Ebenezer, 182.
Lee, Malinda, 133, 132.
Lee, Lucy, 133.
Lee, Jedediah, 132.
Leeds, Frances A., 162.
Leeds, Hannah, 239.
Leet, Eleanor, 108.

Leavens, Frederick A., 220
Leavenworth, John, 194,
Leavenworth.
Leavenworth, Hiram, 196,
Leavenworth, Fanny, 196.
Leavenworth, Polly, 196.
Leavenworth, Clara, 197.
Leavenworth, Olivia, 197.
Leavenworth, Horace, 197.
Leavenworth, Mary I., 26.
Lemex, Harriet, 135, 142.
Ledyard, Nathaniel, 181, 182.
Ledyard, John, 182.
Ledyard, Betsey, 98.
Leland, Mary L., 284, 285.
Lewis, Eliza B., 51.
Lewis, Laura, 253.
Lewis, Lucy M., 159.
Lewis, Dr. Enos, 165, 167.
Lewis, Dea. Charles, 255, 249.
Lewis, Harriet L., 117.
Lewis, Sarah, 182.
Lewis, Jared, 221.
Lewis, Nathaniel, 256.
Lester, Elizabeth, 214.
Lester, Eliza, 54.
Leggett, William N., 67.
Leggett, Thomas, 271.
Letchworth, Susan, 293.
Lickens, Mr. J. W., 214.
Lincoln, Jonathan, 208.
Lindsey, Daniel, 143.
Lindsay, Lizzie, 244, 245.
Linton, Albert J., 55.
Lightbody, David, 39, 42.
Lillie, Hattie, 55.
Lines, Nabby, 104.
Lyman, Submit, 258.
Lyman, Rev. Horace, 75, 77.
Lynde, Thomas, 60.
Lock, William, 43.
Lord, Abner, 80.
Lohnds, Merinda, 28, 29.
Loomis, Mary, 33.
Loomis, Ann M., 207.
Loomis, Sally, 216.
Lonsdale, Helen Lea, 201.

Lott, George, 152.
Lovering, Mr. N. P., 142.
Lougee, James, 115, 116.
L'Homidieu, Enoch, 210.
Luce, Lieut. Stephen B., 223.
Lull, Mattie Jane, 137.
Ludlam, Isaac, 34.
Ludlow, Isaac, 34.

M

Mandeville, Margaret E., 273, 274.
Mallory, Charles H., 162, 163.
Mallory, Fanny, 88, 90.
Manton, Amy R., 157.
Mangum, Mattie, 242.
Manchester, William, 196.
Macomber, Widow L., 20.
Mather, Florilla, 57.
Marcutt, David, 109.
Martin, Benjamin C., 149.
Martin, Rufus, 28.
Martin, Julia A., 42.
Martin, Dr. John, 66.
Martin, Rachel, 67.
Martin, Sarah E., 292.
Manwaring, Christopher, 61, 62.
Manwaring, Christopher, 2nd, 62.
Manwaring, Robert, 62.
Manwaring, Frances, 63.
Manning, Henry C., 74.
Marsh, Robert G., 293.
Marsh, Benjamin, 19, 20.
Marsh, Joel, 134.
Masten, Mark P., 100.
Maples, William L., 250, 251.
Mason, Nehemiah (1722) 10.
Mason, Nehemiah, (1782) 185.
Mason, Lucy Ann, 215, 216.
Mason, Samuel, 11.
Mason, Wid. Elizabeth, 11.
Mason, Ann, 18.
Mason, Capt. John, 18.

Mason, Jere., 60.
Mattocks, Estelle, 113.
Matthews, Charles A., 191.
McLelland, Hon. Robert, 245.
McKim, Nancy, 148.
McComb, John N., 223.
McBride, Nancy, 148.
McDonald, John, 122.
McKim, John, 149.
McIntyre, Edmund, 114, 116.
McLelland Stitt, 71.
McGriffie, William A., 207.
McDaniel, Eunice, 82.
McQuin, Sarah M. R., 152.
McNeil, Charles, 98.
McEdwards, James, 196.
McKenzie, Daniel S., 250.
McAuliffe, John, 251.
McCabe, George, 261.
McGaffey, Martha, 262, 263.
McKunion, Robert, 263.
McClintock, Morris P., 266, 267.
McDonald, Rev. James, 278.
Mattison, Mr. D. O., 44.
Moxon, Abigail, 44, 46.
Moxon, Eveline, 45.
Maynard, Hannah Maria, 117.
Meach, Daniel, 86.
Meach, Hannah, 233.
Mead, Harriete, 145.
Meeker, Joseph, 54.
Meigs, Elizabeth, 43.
Meigs, General M. C., 223.
Mercer, William R., 201.
Messick, Mr. G. W., 253.
Meservey, Jefferson B., 157.
Merrill, Sherborn Sanborn, 165.
Merrill, Edwin R., 256, 257.
Messler, Maria, 213.
Merriam, Phebe, 272.
Merriam, George, 272.
Minor, Benjamin, 8, 9.

Minor, Simeon, 9.
Minor, Grace, 11.
Minor, James, 11.
Minor, Samuel, (1709) 17.
Minor, Samuel, (1739) 183, 184.
Minor, James O., 37.
Minor, Fanny, 74.
Minor, Mary, 203.
Minor, Mary, (1750) 79.
Minor, Mary, 235.
Minor, Francis W., 258.
Minor, Hattie Frances, 292.
Minor, Abigail, 87, 99.
Minor, Thomas, (1757) 101.
118.
Minor, Thomas, (1835) 258, 249.
Minor, Keturah, 100, 104.
Minor, Eliza A., 155.
Minor, Mary A , 257.
Minor, Isaac, 159.
Minor, Mr. J. D., 159.
Minor, Betsey, 211.
Minor, Mary, (1700) 175.
Minor, Prudence, 175, 183.
Minor, Frank, 249.
Minor, Sarah, 223.
Minor, Nathaniel, 178, 181.
Minor, Amos, 185.
Minor, Daniel, 234.
Minor, James, 234, 235.
Millard, Samuel N., 136.
Millard, Henry, 27.
Miller. Maj. Fred. E., 284, 285.
Miller, Frances, 74.
Miller, Netta Laura, 292.
Milden, Alonzo, 149.
Millet, Amos L., 110.
Mills, Charlotte, 215. 218.
Mills, Daniel M., 219.
Mills, Fanny Bell, 201.
Mills, Thomas Smith, 253.
Miles, Mr. E. B., 148.
Milton, Ann B., 218.
Middleton, Mary, 235.
Mitchell, John, 68.
Mooers, George, 266, 267.
Moore, Lydia, 35, 39.

Moore, Mary, 107.
Moore, William Flagg, 116.
Moore, Willard, 117.
Morehouse, Betsey, 194, 197.
Morehouse, Thomas, 60.
Morehouse, Miss A., 74.
Morse, Polly, 259.
Morse, Hannah, 161.
Morse, Louisa U., 194.
Mott, Jane N., 180.
Moss, Jesse L., 280, 281.
Moss, William C., 190, 191.
Monahan, William, 195.
Morey, Frank, 197.
Morgan, Mary, 233.
Morgan, John, 233.
Morgan, Willard, 291.
Morgan, Nancy E., 233.
Morgan, Charity, 160.
Morgan, William, (1698) 10.
Morgan, William, (1766) 37.
Moseman, Bessie G., 83.
Montague, Gertrude de la, 33.
Moriarty, John, 64.
Moon, Elizabeth, 71.
Mosely, Rachel, 192.
Mosher, Orin, 195.
Moulton, Julia G., 133.
Morrison, Adolphus F. 145.
Morrison, John, 145, 146.
Morrison, Laurena, 145.
Mumford, Rebecca, 100.
Munger, Charles S., 23, 24.
Munroe, Mary Jane, 107, 108.
Murdock, William, 210, 212.
Murphy, John F., 258.

N

Nash, Hannah, 268.
Newcomb, Fanny. 135.
Newcomb, Mr. J. H., 289, 290.
Newell, Electa, 104, 109.
Newell, Dr. Selim, 262, 263.

Index. 379

Newell, Roger, 57.
Nelson, Parmelia, 83.
Nevin, David, 206.
Newton, Lucius, 255.
Nichols, Charles, 169.
Niman, Mrs. J. P., 207.
Nichols, Mary E., 47.
Niles, Edmund, Jr., 40.
Niles Elisha, 234.
Niles, Anna T., 91.
Niles, Isabel, 44.
Niles, Nancy, 46.
Nightingale, Jerome, 107.
Nitchie, Elizabeth, 180.
Noble, Charles, 109.
Northrop, Henry S., 138.
Norton, Lydia, 49.
Noyes, Bridget, 10.
Noyes, Cyrus R., 157, 158.
Noyes, Elizabeth, 178, 181.
Noyes, Grace, 12.
Noges, Rev. James, 10, 12.
Noyes, Dr. James, 10 13, 177.
Noyes, Capt. Thomas, 178.
Noyes, James, 3d, 18.
Noyes, Nathan S., 99.
Noyes, Joseph, 101, 119.
Noyes, Joshua, 13, 192.
Noyes, James, (1752) 178.
Noyes, George W., 157, 158, 188.
Noyes, Rebecca, 178.
Noyes, Mary, 177.
Noyes, Jesse D., 275.
Noyes, Mary Stanton, 172.
Noyes. Sarah. 171.
Noyes, Nancy D., 273.
Noyes, Nathan, 159.
Noyes, Joseph, 273, 274.
Noyes, William D., 155, 156.
Noyes, Lydia S., 155.
Noyes, Thomas, 273, 275.
Noyes, James, (m. 1837) 240.

O
Oberlin, Louisa, 20.
Orcutt, Amanda, 49.

Orcutt, Ezra, 48.
Orcutt, Amy P., 50.
Orcutt, Emma C., 50.
Orcutt, Hannah E., 50.
Orcutt, Isaac D, 50.
Orcutt, James E., 49.
Orcutt, Josephine, 49.
Orcutt, Mary M., 50.
Osborn, Hiram, 152, 153.
Otis, Eunice, 132.
Overman, Emma, 225,
Owen, Galusha, 253, 250.
Owen, Jennie Amelia, 253.
Owen, Hattie G., 250, 251.

P
Page, Joseph, (1713) 9.
Page, Joseph, (1775) 235.
Page, Joseph, (1837), 146.
Paine, Anne, 81.
Paine, Stephen, 243.
Paine, Rosa, 197.
Packer, Elisha, 121.
Packer, Daniel, 234.
Packer, Helen, 268, 269.
Packer, Mary E., 161.
Palmer, Dea. Gershom, 11.
Palmer, Gershom, Jr. 12.
Palmer, Hannah, 12.
Palmer, Ichabod, 12.
Palmer, Luke, 13, 191.
Palmer, Luke, Jr., 13, 192.
Palmer, Hannah W., 13.
Palmer, Harriet N., 13.
Palmer, Sarah, 13.
Palmer, Grace Billings, 13.
Palmer, Nathaniel, 2nd, 12.
Palmer, Nathaniel, 3d, 13.
Palmer, Nehemiah, 9.
Palmer, Walter, 11.
Palmer, Saxton, 8.
Palmer, Dr. Nathan, 18.
Palmer, George, 87, 91.
Palmer, Denison, (1800)91.
Palmer Denison, (1869)237.
Palmer, Daniel, 84.
Palmer, Moses, 184.
Palmer, Dea. Noyes, 186.
Palmer, Warren, 273.
Palmer, Mary, 190.

Palmer, Clara, 273.
Palmer, Milcah, 66, 67.
Palmer, Theodocius, 66.
Palmer, Theo., 98.
Palmer, William L., 87, 88.
Palmer, Maria, 213.
Palmer, Huldah, 265, 276.
Palmer, Betsey, 215, 217.
Palmer, Abby, 265, 266.
Palmer, Deborah, 215, 218.
Palmer, Hannah, 275.
Palmer, Charles, 226, 228.
Palmer, Henry, 226, 228.
Palmer, Betsey, 280.
Palmer, Nathaniel, 181.
Palmer, Capt. Alexander S., 280.
Palmer, Betsey D., 192.
Palmatier. John, 48, 49.
Parrish, Mary R., 28.
Partlow, Adeline, 131.
Parke, Eliza, 257, 249.
Parke, Mary, 269.
Parke, Eunice, 235.
Parks, Jane, 136.
Passmore, John, 22.
Passmore, Mary, 270, 271.
Paul, Nancy, 195.
Parrison, Mary A., 149, 150.
Paterson, Thomas, 199, 293.
Paterson, Thomas, jr., 204.
Paterson, Elizabeth D., 204.
Paterson, William L., 204.
Paterson, Samuel, 204.
Paterson, Thomas N., 904.
Paterson, Nathan, 203.
Paterson, John D, 205.
Paterson, Sarah D., 205.
Paterson, Robert S., 205.
Paterson, Mary Ann, 205.
Paterson, Ezekiel M., 205.
Paterson, Christopher S., 81.
Plant, Ethiel, 210.
Platts, Elisha, 210, 211.
Platts, Temperance A., 215.
Platts, Eliza, 216.
Pratt, Lydia, 213.
Pratt, Dea. E., 18.
Pratt, Asa, 19, 24.

380 Index.

Pratt, Horatio N., 293,294.
Parker, Lewis, 250.
Peck, Mary, 80.
Peck, James, 13.
Peet, Rev. Stephen, 192.
Peet, Rev. Stephen D., 192.
Peet, Martha, 192.
Peet, Harriet, 192.
Peet, Emerson W., 192.
Peet, Joseph B., 192.
Perry, Jane, 151.
Perry, Hattie, 237.
Percival, Ruth, 132.
Peckham, Peleg, 253.
Peckham, Ella L. T., 128, 129.
Perrin, Lucy, 75, 77.
Pelton, Elizabeth, 24, 31.
Perkins, Dea. J., 74.
Perkins, Francis, 74.
Perkins, Dr., 57.
Perkins, Emma, 105, 106.
Phelps, Stiles, 181.
Phelps, William G., 203.
Phelps, Agnes E., 39, 40.
Phelps, Eleanor L., 39, 41.
Phelps, Dr. Charles, 86, 87.
Phelps, Hepzibah, 87.
Peters, Rev. Absalom, D.D., 135, 140.
Peters, Harriet Adaline, 140, 141.
Peters, Dr. George A., 140.
Peters, Mary Elizabeth, 141.
Peters, James Hugh, 141.
Peters, Bertha Borodell, 140.
Pearce, Christopher, 240.
Preston, Charles F., 166.
Preston, George, 227.
Pressure, Laura, 164.
Pendleton, Mr. W. W., 124.
Prentice, John, 155, 156.
Prentice, Mary Jane, 126.
Prentice, Jonas, 120, 121.
Prentice, Rufus, 228.
Prentice, George D., 228.
Prentice, Mary, (1700) 11.
Prentice, Mary, (1731) 85.

Prentice, Eleazer, 86.
Prentice, Samuel, 17, 18.
Peterson, Sarah J., 271.
Phillips, John, 266.
Price, Jane, 291.
Pierce, Mary Wilder, 133.
Pierce, Deborah, 163.
Pierce, Elizabeth, 113.
Pierce, Ethan, 100.
Pitcher, Viania, 130.
Pines, Susan, 68, 69.
Piper, Eugene, 260.
Pynchon, Cora N., 163.
Pyatte, John W., 167.
Ifonts, Dr. J. S., 200.
Potter, Martha, 82.
Potter, Edward, 224.
Potter, Robert, Esq., 177.
Pollack, Gertrude, 204.
Poole, George H., 98.
Polley, Lucretia, 105.
Popple, William, 98.
Post, Jemima, 209, 210.
Post, Joseph, 209.
Post, Temperance, 209.
Post, Abby, 22.
Post, Henry, 75, 76.
Post, Margaret, 29, 30.
Post, Mary, 24, 29, 31.
Post, Molly, 31.
Porter, Louisa A., 259.
Porter, Selden, 252.
Pomroy, Mary Lee, 133.
Pomroy, Selah J., 133.
Pomroy, Benjamin, 133.
Prosser, Caroline A., 261.
Purdy, John, 75, 79.
Purdy, Nelson P., 98.
Purdy, Henry D, 99.
Putney, Lydia, 113.
Pulman, Azuba E., 166.
Pulman, Maria L., 166.
Pulvers, William E., 169.
Purser, Martha, 182.
Plummer, William H., 96, 97.
Plumb, Albert, 283.
Plum, Ezra W., 292.

Q

Quimby, Elizabeth, 9.
Quigley, Sarah Jane, 221, 222.

R

Ralston, Jeannette B., 244, 245.
Ramsdell, Lydia W., 117, 118.
Randall, Rhoda, 226.
Randall, Charles, 67.
Randall, Abigail, 85.
Randall, Adelia M., 99.
Ranger, Catherine, 9.
Ransom, Judah, 74.
Ranney, John, 140.
Ramsey, Betsey Ann, 104.
Rathburn, Mary E., 72.
Raymond, Eleanor, 62.
Raymond, William, 62.
Reeves, James J., 95.
Reed, Eliza, 123.
Reed, Dimis, 243, 248.
Read, Thomas Buchanan, 94.
Read, John G., 79.
Reid, Alice Ida, 137.
Redfield, Lorenzo, 224.
Remington, Michael, 221, 222.
Remington, Samuel, 235.
Remington, Illustrious, 235.
Reilay, Gilbert, 199, 200.
Reilay, Margaret, 206.
Reynolds, Chauncey A., 199.
Reynolds, Julia, 28.
Reynolds, Albert, 43.
Reynolds, Enos, 242.
Rensehousen, Louisa H., 240.
Rice, Elias H., 215, 219.
Rice, Anna E., 76.
Richards, Samuel, 36.
Richardson, Samuel, 8.
Richardson, Rev. Geo. E., 287.
Richardson, Mr. W. G., 33.
Richardson, George, 282.

Index. 381

Richmond, Elizabeth, 149, 150.
Richmond, Mrs. Mary A., 286.
Richmond, Nelson, 149.
Richmond, Van Renseller, 98.
Ripley, Adeline, 74.
Rix, Elizabeth A., 248.
Rives, John F., 142.
Ryley, James, 158.
Root, Moses, 165, 168.
Robbins, Emma, 64, 65.
Robbins, Henry, 64, 65.
Robinson, Alvin T., 49, 50.
Robinson, David F., 57.
Robinson, Lucius F., 57.
Robinson, Henry C., 57.
Robinson, Mary C., 57.
Robin on, Sarah A., 57.
Robinson, Alfred S., 57.
Robinson, Mr. W. J., 181, 182.
Robinson, Sarah, 75.
Robinson, Ruth, 104, 107.
Robinson, Dr. Jefferson, 136.
Robinson, Wealthy, 115.
Roberts, Harrison, 196.
Rogers, John, 5.
Rogers, Prudence, 35.
Rogers, Samuel, 60, 61.
Rogers, Elizabeth, 62.
Rogers, Anna, 63, 64.
Rogers, Jeremiah, 73.
Rogers, Nathan, 73, 74.
Rogers, Ebenezer, 84.
Rogers, Isabella, 134.
Rogers, Dr. Samuel, 134.
Rogers, Robert, 115.
Rogers, Betsey, 129.
Rogers, Commodore John, 223.
Rogers, Rr. Admiral John, 223.
Rogers, Lieut. Henry, 223.
Roy, Hiram W., 40.
Roy, Rev. J. E., 136, 138.
Rollins, Russell, 57.
Rose, Beulah, 64.
Rose, William, 148.
Rose, Mary, 148.
Royall, Widow E. A., 247.
Ross, William H., 241.
Rhodes, Anthony, 104.
Rhodes, Paul, 93.
Rhodes, Charles D., 93.
Rhodes, Harriet A., 93.
Rhodes, Abby G., 93.
Russell, Catherine, 285.
Russell, Col. Giles, 177.
Russell, Rev. Ebenezer, 184.
Russell, Mrs. Content, 184.
Russell, Gertrude, 75.
Russell, Jane, 268.
Russell, Kate, 283.
Ruggles, Theodosia, 143.
Rutherford, John, 187.
Rumsey, John, 81.

S

Sabin, Charles, 236.
Sanders, Barton, 124.
Sanders, Albert, 124.
Saunders, Ella Maud, 111, 112.
Sanderson, Harriet, 262, 263.
Sandiforth, Rupert, 59.
Satterly, Rebecca, 18.
Sayre, Jane, 73.
Sargent, George I., 116.
Saterlee, Rebecca, 126.
Salisbury, Delia, 195.
Sappin, Amanda, 83.
Saxton, Capt. Joseph, 8.
Saxton, Mary, 8, 9.
Saxton, Jerusha, 9.
Saxton, Mercy, 9.
Sawyer, Mr. C. F., 289, 290.
Sawyer, Charlotte, 275.
Sawyer, Daniel, 208.
Sharpe Richard, 203, 206.
Sharpe, Alonzo T., 39.
Shaw, Mr. J., 44.
Shaw, Lizzie, 100.
Shay, Peter, 67.
Slater, Horatio N., 93.
Sharswood, George, 97.
Shannon, Mr. G. A., 40.
Stanley, Daniel, 145, 147.
Stanley, Almira, 145.
Stanton, Sarah, 6, 231.
Stanton, Sarah, 2nd, 8, 10.
Stanton, Thomas, jr., 6, 7, 10, 60.
Stanton, Thomas, 1st, 8.
Stanton, Samuel, 6.
Stanton, Anna, 7.
Stanton, Joseph, 8, 10.
Stanton, Hannah, 10, 127.
Stanton, Capt. Nathaniel, 10.
Stanton, Robert, 60.
Stanton, Joanna, 60.
Stanton, Mary, 120.
Stanton, Nathan, 172.
Stanton, Elizabeth, 172.
Stanton, Capt. Nathan, 228.
Stanton, Thomas, 4th, 175, 177.
Stanton, Anna, 177.
Stanton, Phineas, 177.
Stanton, Eunice, (*m*.1750) 178.
Stanton, Eunice, (*m*.1773) 243.
Stanton, Lois, 178.
Stanton, Frances, 180.
Stanton, Nathan, 4th, 185, 186.
Stanton, Eliza, 190.
Stanton, Paul B., 273.
Stanton, Charles T., 13.
Stanton, Joseph W., 13.
Stanton, John, 3d, 85, 86.
Stanton, Blandina, 97.
Stanton, Obedia'n, 239.
Standish, James, 236.
Standish, James L., 237.
Standish, Abbie S., 237.
Stannard, Timothy, 211.
Stannard, Edith L., 251.
Sparhawk, Phebe A., 138.
Sparhawk, Simeon, 171.
Spaulding, Amanda, 250.
Spaulding, Sarah, 81.
Starret, Sarah, 65.

382

Index.

Starr, Rachel, 35, 36.
Starr, Helen, 284.
Starr, Katherine, 36, 53.
Stark, Nancy, 130.
Swan, John, 3rd, 85.
Swan, Susanna, 85.
Swan, Susanna, 2d, 101, 114.
Swan, Thomas, 86, 90.
Swan, Thos, jr., 90.
Swan, Sarah Ann, 91.
Swan, Harriet, 280.
Swan, Joshua, 193.
Swan, Sarah A., 130.
Swan, Ann, 243.
Slack, Curtis O., 118.
Slack, Etherlinda, 270.
Slack, Polly, 119.
Slack, Anna, 265, 270.
Strader, George H., 105, 106.
Swagart, Clarissa, 58, 59.
Sprague, Benjamin, 183.
Slausen, John, 146.
Sellech, Maria E., 134.
Seagrave, Daniel, 117.
Seymour, Marshal, 148.
Seymour, Asa. 53, 56.
Seymour, Ann, 57.
Seabury, Isaac Crary, 51.
Sears, Mary, 73.
Selden, Susan, 64.
Sexton, Kellogg, 165.
Sheffield, George, 13, 192.
Sheffield, George W., 261.
Sheldon, James, 13, 14.
Sherburn, Henry, 147.
Sherman, Rev. Henry, 190, 192.
Sherman, Rebecca A., 192.
Sherman, Rebecca, 195.
Sherman, Levi, 194.
Sherman, Ruth, 48.
Sherman, Prudence, 61.
Spencer, Hannah, 12.
Spencer, Charlotte, 25.
Spencer, Lucy, 211.
Spencer, Rachel, 204.
Spencer, Horace, 236, 237.
Spence, Dr. Henry, 201.

Spence, Andrew, 222.
Schellinger, Isaac, 30.
Stewart, Highland H., 28.
Stewart, Thankful, 38, 52.
Stewart, Phineas, 276, 277.
Stewart, Alexander, 101, 119.
Stewart, Emma Sophia, 292.
Stewart, Dudley W., 157, 158.
Sweet, Holden, 44.
Sweet, James, 152, 153.
Streeter, Sarah M., 45.
Streeter, Aurora F., 46.
Stearns, Irving W., 202, 203.
Shearwood, Rebecca. 92.
Stevens, William, 105.
Stevens, Harriet, 78.
Stevens, Mary J., 78.
Stevens, William, 282.
Stevens, Mr. R. T., 260, 261, 262.
Stevens, Hamilton, 211.
Stevens, Mr. W. N., 191.
Stedman, Philamon, 289.
Stetson, Albert L., 137.
Shepardson, Maria, 270.
Shepardson, Jared, 271.
Shepardson, Joseph, 271.
Simpson, George, 293.
Simpson, Peter, 208.
Silliman, Lydia, 215, 217.
Sill, Elizabeth, (1740) 198.
Sill, Elizabeth, (1766) 80.
Sigorney, Angenette, 186.
Siple, Robert, 41.
Sisson, Ransom E., 49.
Sisson, Mary A., 49, 51.
Smith, David, 12, 99.
Smith, Catherine, 24.
Smith, Joseph A., 26.
Smith, Denton A., 41.
Smith, Philemon P., 50.
Smith, Lucius H., 48, 50.
Smith, Frederick, 50.
Smith, William, 58.
Smith, Lucy, 235, 236.
Smith, Dr. R. S., 289.

Smith, John, 108.
Smith, Amy, 78.
Smith, Mr. H. H., 78.
Smith, Joseph I., 283.
Smith, Joseph B., 83.
Smith, Nathan, (1767) 92.
Smith, Nathan, (1705) 120.
Smith, Sarah, 97.
Smith, Nathan, (1773) 92.
Smith, Nathan, (1724) 61, 121.
Smith, Arima, 104.
Smith, Mary Y., 135, 138.
Smith, Phebe, 154.
Smith, Betsey, 114, 115.
Smith, Harris T., 212.
Smith, Dea. Gilbert, 121, 132, 193.
Smith, Jane, 121.
Smith, Isaac, 120, 121.
Smith, Sarah, 121.
Smith, Patience, 215, 218.
Smith, Charles Dwight, 127, 129.
Smith, Hannah Amelia, 129.
Smith, Edna, 167.
Smith, Porter, 221.
Smith, Mr. J. B. H., 223.
Smith, Fred., 180.
Smith, Jabez, 177, 183.
Smith, Anna, 180.
Smith, Oliver, 121, 178, 180.
Smith, John B., 271.
Smith, Mary, 193.
Smith, Mr. C., 208.
Smith, Olive F., 194.
Smith, Eli, 194.
Smith, Elovsey, 194.
Smith, Oscar F., 197.
Smith, Thomas, 196.
Smith, Jane, 205.
Smith, Graty, 256.
Smith, Miss M. B., 256.
Smith, Harriel L., 257.
Smith, Elizabeth, 240, 250.
Smith, Keziah, 265, 281.
Shipman, Rev. N., 57, 58.
Skinner, Eliza, 244, 246.
Stillman, Mr. J.T., 254, 255.

Index. 383

Strickland, Esther, 266.
Strickland, Nathan, 237.
Strickland, Mary Ann, 171.
Sprigg. Mrs. Stella Mercer, 201.
Stille, Maria, 203.
Swifzer, Edward, 149.
Swisher, Rev. Isaac, 207.
Spicer, Prudence, 169, 170.
Snyder, Lany Ann, 166.
Snyder, Minnie, 250.
Snyder, Hugh L., 271.
Symonds, John, 5.
Stryker, Isabella, 264.
Scrymer, Estelle, 278.
Scott, Mary J., 148.
Scott, William, 213.
Scott, Hiram, 213.
Sorate, Lois, 98.
Short, Samuel D., 148, 151.
Short, Rebecca, 11.
Stocking, Dimis T., 39.
Stockwell, Abel, 215, 218.
Stockwell, Dr. Cyrus M., 218.
Shoemaker, Elijah, 198, 200.
Shoemaker, Charles D., 200.
Shoemaker, Robert C., 201.
Shoemaker, Frederick M., 201.
Shoemaker, Elizabeth, 201.
Shoemaker, Elijah, jr., 202.
Shoemaker, George, 202.
Shoemaker, Caroline (1816) 203.
Shoemaker, Caroline (1837) 202.
Shoemaker, Lazarus D., 202.
Shoemaker, Nathan, 202.
Shoemaker, Emma, 202.
Shoemaker, Austin D., 201.
Shoemaker, William M., 201.
Shoemaker, Frank L., 201.
Spooner, William L., 253.
Sloane, Thomas, 88.
Strong, Ella H., 244.

Strong, Mrs. Hannah, 124.
Strong, Freeman, 195.
Southworth, Mary Ann., 25.
Slosson, Edward, 91.
Shotwell, Charlotte, 206.
Stone, Chloe, 53, 58.
Stone, John, 73.
Storms, Cleanthe, 219.
Stoddard, Maria, 212.
Stoddard, Phebe A., 275, 276.
Stoddard, Sila, 109, 111.
Stoddard, Adaline, 113.
Storrs, Nathan, 190.
St. John, Ida May, 197.
Suffern, Martha, 188, 189.
Stuart, George H., 81.
Stuart, George H., jr., 82.
Stuart, Ellen, 81.
Stuart, Mary, 81, 82.
Schults, Charity, 48.
Struthers, James B., 251.

T

Taggart, Emma, 267.
Talt, George, 49.
Taugee, William R., 240.
Talbot, Wheaton, 289.
Taylor, Mr. F., 44.
Taylor, Mr. J. W., 75.
Taylor, Caroline W., 75.
Taylor, Rev. W. H., 136, 137.
Taylor, Anson H., 163,165.
Taylor, Anson H., jr., 165.
Taylor, Rev. Wm. A., 255.
Taylor, Mr. W. L., 251.
Thatcher, Stephen D., 96, 98.
Thaxter, Mary S., 110.
Teater, Sarah C., 222.
Terry, George W., 227.
Trescott, Minerva T., 203, 205.
Tenney, Sheldon, 116.
Tifft, Rhoda, 38, 46.
Tifft, Eleanor, 38, 47.
Tifft, Elizabeth I., 162, 163.
Tifft, Eliza, 188.

Tifft, Byron, 196.
Tifft, Oscar, 197.
Tripp, Molly, 25.
Tibbits, George, 79.
Tyler, Addie, 287.
Tyler, Jedidah, 21, 22.
Tyler, Samuel, 24.
Tyler, Abigail, 85, 120.
Tyler, Hannah, 86.
Tyler, Elizabeth, 134.
Tyler, Calvin, 266.
Tyler, Alice, 208.
Tyler, Pres. John, 208.
Tyler, William, 290.
Tyler, Moses, 209.
Tyson, Herbert S., 81, 82.
Tobias, Helen E., 27.
Tobey, Edward S., 82.
Tobey, Hannah B. S., 81,82.
Topping, Phebe, 73.
Topping, Maria, 74.
Town, Estelle, 45.
Town, Elizabeth, 88, 89.
Towner, Azubah, 211.
Towsley, Frank E., 111, 112.
Tod, George, 242.
Thompson, Bridget, 6.
Thompson, Anthony, 6.
Thomson, John, 6.
Thompson, William, 6.
Thompson, Mary, 61, 63.
Thompson, Hosea Q., 259.
Thompson, James, 37.
Thompson, Elizabeth, 147, 148.
Thompson, Alexander, 147, 148.
Thompson, David, 159.
Thompson, Dr. John D., 203, 205.
Thompson, Laura H., 115, 116.
Thompson, Harriet, 166.
Thompson, Joshua, 171.
Thompson, Col. Elias, 177.
Tompkins, Nelson C., 189.
Thorp, John, 207.
Thornton, William P., 196, 197.

384   Index.

Thornton, Frances E., 197. Viets, Louisa, 65. Wells, Cynthia, 113.
Thornton, Lucy, 265. Viets, Rev. Roger M., 65. Wells, William, 24.
Thomas, Lucy A., 287. Vincent, Dr. Ezra, 276, Wells, Lucy, 19.
Tuman, Mary, 63, 64.   277. Webster, Emma Abbott,
Tubbs, Benajah, 145, 146. Vose, Grace, 11.   259.
Turner, Daniel, 206, 199. Weidman, Jacob N., 48.
Turner, George D., 206. **W** Wetherell, Daniel, 34.
Turner, MargaretAnn,206. Wade, Esther, 63, 64. Westervelt, Emma M., 207.
Turner, Caroline, 166,167. Ward, Laura E., 79. Wetherhead, Joseph, 282.
Turner, Ezekiel, 183, 184. Ward, Albert S., 140, 141. Weaver, Ella, 261.
Turner, Mary, 235. Ward, Belle, 162. Wesler, Maria P., 214.
Thurber, John, 14. Wadhams, Esther W., 200, Welman, Libeus, 222.
Thurlow, Mary C.,   202. West, Miranda E., 242.
Tuttle, Mary, 212. Wadsworth, Capt. Alex- West, Lydia, 219.
Tuttle, Mr. J. L., 113.   ander, 223. West, Alfred, 256.
True, Hannah, 109, 113. Wakefield, Mary, 71. Wheeler, Anna, 10.
Tucker, Stephen, 127. Wallsworth, Eunice, 121. Wheeler, Mary, 24.
Tucker. Rev. Mark, 280. Wallace, Nellie, 167. Wheeler, Mr. F. M., 40.
Tucker, Mr. C. S., 110. Wallace, Elizabeth, 182. Wheeler, Richard A., 274.
Trumbull, J. Hammond, Wallace, Mary I., 204. Wheeler, Mr. A., 107.
   57, 91. Walworth, John, 72, 79. Wheeler, Mary Ann, 131.
Trumbull, Henry Clay, 91. Walcott, Gen. Roger, 61. Wheeler, Luke, 131.
Trumbull, Gurdon, 91. Warner, Albert B., 296. Wheeler, Martha, 85, 119.
Trumbull, Mary, 91. Warner, Ebenezer, 53, 58. Wheeler, Mrs. Bridget, 184.
Trumbull, Eliza N., 57. Warner, Rev. Pliny S.,276, Wheeler, John, 135, 132.
Trumbull, Eliza S., 57.   277. Wheeler, Capt. Thomas,
 Warner, Whipple, 111.   121.
U Waldron, Jonathan, 178, Wheeler, Esther, 120, 131.
Unger, Daniel, 149, 152.   179. Wheeler, Edward H., 268,
Underhill, Frank, 117. Wasson, Robert, 268.   269.
 Watrous, Maria, 216. Wheeler, Jonathan, 234,
V Watrous, Irwin S., 26.   235.
Vanblaricom, Rhoda H., Watkins, Edward, 19, 21. Whetmore, Daniel, 59.
   152. Watkins, Mary, 206. Whedon, Charles O., 284,
Van Zant, James, 272. Wattam, Martha, 148.   285.
Van Buren, Barout, 53,58. Ware, Clinton A., 290. Wilbur, Tony P., 39.
Van Derbogert, Nicholas, Walker, Eli I., 243, 254. Wilbur, Julia M., 157.
   147. Wasburn, Curtis D., 28. Wilcox, Charles B., 124.
Van Derbogert, William, Waterman, Ann, 35. Wilcox, James, 213.
   147, 148. Watson, Eusebia, 161. Wilcox, Harriet W., 273.
Van Derbogert, Susan,148. Watson, Susie W., 134. Willcox, Elisha, 236.
Van Derbogert, Ann, 148. Wattles, William, 60, 61. Willcox, Elias, 236.
Van Vulpin, Eva, 27. Weed, Hannah P., 13. Willcox, Elnathan,236,237.
Vandegrift, Olivia C., 187. Weed, William, 13. Willcox, Jesse H., 237.
Vanderpool, Henry, 239. Weeden, Sarah, 124. Wightman, Mary, 124.
Vanmeter, Nancy, 221. Welch, Prudence Ann, 160, Wightman, Mercy, 124.
Van Ryker, Mary, 162.   161. Wilgus, Nathaniel, 14.
Vaughn, Miss, 182. Welch, Lovisa, 48. Williams, Ellen, 88.
Vail, James W., 192. Welde, Elizabeth, 5. Williams, Amos D., 89.
Ventris, David B., 22, 23. Welde, Dorothy, 6. Williams, Ephraim, 87.

Index. 385

Williams, Ephraim, jr., 87.
Williams, Ephraim, 3d, 87, 88.
Williams Hepzibah, 87, 88.
Williams, Hannah E., 88.
Williams, EmelineP.,88,89.
Williams, Joseph P., 89.
Williams, Sarah P., 88.
Williams, Martha Jane, 90.
Williams, Charles P., 90, 163.
Williams, Henriette, 165.
Williams, Charlotte, 271.
Williams, Mr. B. F., 99.
Williams, Elisha, (m.1768) 265.
Williams, Elisha, (m.1807) 99, 100.
Williams, Elisha, (m.1741) 184.
Williams, Eliza, 99.
Williams, Eunice, (m.1817) 259, 260.
Williams, Eunice, (m.1800) 104, 107.
Williams, Isaac, 17, 18.
Williams, Rev. John K.,76.
Williams, Lydia, 19, 21.
Williams, Richard, 18.
Williams, Mrs. Polly, 47.
Williams, Mr. W. S., 22.
Williams, Widow, 38.
Williams, Thankful,85,101.
Williams, Eunice, (1773) 154.
Williams, Mrs. Jane, 154.
Williams, Amoretta, 152.
Williams, William S., 160.
Williams, Jesse, 270, 271.
Williams, Peleg, 122, 124.
Williams, Elizabeth, 281.
Williams, Sally, 125, 129.
Williams, Amelia E., 224.
Williams, Fanny, 132.
Williams, John, (1712)175,
Williams, John, (1770) 185.
Williams, Nehemiah, 177.
Williams, Seth, 275.
Williams, Hannah,185,190.
Williams, Mary, 271.
Williams, Martha, 234.272.
Williams, Martha,(m.1786) 265, 272.
Williams, Anna A., 236, 238.
Wing, Lydia, 22.
Winchester, Mrs. Jane A., 51.
Wilson, Sarah D., 100.
Wilson, Charles, 256.
Wilson, Chauncey, 134.
Wilson, Sally, 196.
Wilde, Sarah, 200.
Wise, Harriet, 123.
Wires, Rodney S., 143.
Willis, Millie, 260.
Willis, Herbert, 260.
Wills, J. Seward, 206.
Windover, Mary E., 149.
Willard, William, 222.
Withington, Mary, 98.
Whitman, Samuel, 79.
White, Samuel B., 33.
White, Solomon, 166, 168.
White, Jere., 166.
White, John H., 293, 294.
Whittlesey, Azariah, 225.
Whittaker, Emma, 191.
Wright, Washington, 211.
Wright, Caroline M., 212.
Wright, John, 145, 146.
Wright, Ezra, 25, 26.
Wright, William H., 40.
Wright, Mark, 71, 72.
Wright, Lucy L., 256, 257.
Whitney, Dr. E., 107.
Whitmore, Mary A., 34.
Wyness, Phebe, 215, 221.
Wyville,MargaretJ.,55,56.
Whitcomb, Miss C. C., 261.
Whitcraft, Miss, 271.
Whittle, Phineas R., 286.
Whittle, Mary Alice, 286.
Whitting, Emily, 292.
Wood, Samuel, 97.
Wood, Eugene, 43.
Wood, Zebediah, 35.
Wood, Sarah Frances, 147.
Wood, Mary, 147, 152.
Wood, Dr. John, 147.
Wood, Olive M., 227.
Wood, Charles G., 187.
Woony, James, 64.
Woodbury, Susan, 69, 70.
Woodbury, Rev. Webster, 114.
Woodmancy, Sylvester B. 250, 251.
Woodford, William S., 137.
Woodruff, Jane M., 73.
Woodruff, Sarah J., 284.
Woodruff, Polly, 145, 146.
Woodward, Aliph, 122.
Woodward, Samuel, 129.
Woodward, Benjamin, 227.
Woolworth, Hon. James M., 172.
Worthington, Fanny, 182.
Woodyard, Mary, 261.
Worden, Belinda, 291.

Y

Yaratau, Hattie, 118.
Yerrington, Jane B., 116.
Yocum, Mary J., 164.
York, Reuben W., 131.
Yorke, Allen, 235.
York, Thomas, 250, 253.
Young, Mr. D., 207.
Young, Ellen, 113.

II.

INDEX

OF FAMILY RECORDS OF PERSONS BEARING THE NAME OF

DENISON.

This Index is arranged Chronologically, and also according to Generations, following the order of the book,—the Descendants of Capt. John, George, and William, in parallel columns. There are generally but two references made in any individual case: first, when a child; second when head of a family.

[The figures refer to pages.]

FIRST GENERATION AND BEFORE.

DENISON, WILLIAM, 5.   DENISON, GEORGE, 6.
   DANIEL, 5.
   EDWARD, 5, 6.

SECOND GENERATION.

DENISON, ANN,   6, 11.   DENISON, JOHN,   6, 17.
   ANN BORODELL, 6, 7.   MARGARET, 6, 14.
   BORODELL, 6, 14, 171.   MERCY,   6.
   GEORGE,   6, 7, 225.   SARAH,   6, 7.
   HANNAH,   6. 7.   WILLIAM   6, 231.

THIRD GENERATION.

Descendants of John.	Descendants of George.	Descendants of William.
Denison, Ann, 17, 177.	Denison, Edward, 175, 177.	Denison, George, 231, 265.
Daniel, 17, 120.	Elizabeth, 175, 176.	Sarah, 231, 233.
George, 17, 34.	Desire, 175, 176.	William, jr., 231, 234.
John, 17, 18.	George, 175, 225.	
Phebe, 17, 17.	Joseph, 175, 183.	
Robert, 17, 60.	Mercy, 175, 177.	
Samuel, 17.	Samuel, 175, 208.	
Sarah, 17, 18.	Thankful, 175, 177.	
William, 17, 84.		

FOURTH GENERATION.

Descendants of John.
Denison, Abigail, 85, 85.
Abigail, 60, 61.
Abigail, 18.
Ann, 84.
Ann, 60, 60.
Ann, 35, 36.
Andrew, 60.
Avery, 85, 101.
Beebe, 120, 121.
Borodell, 35, 36.
Christopher, 85, 120.
Daniel, 35, 36.
Daniel, 120.
Daniel, 120, 131.
Daniel, 18, 19.
Desire, 85, 86.
Dorothy, 60.
Elizabeth, 60.
Esther, 120, 121.
George, 60.
Grace, 34, 35.
Hannah, 35, 35.
Jabez, 18, 24.
James, 18.
Joanna, 60.
John, 18. 18.
John, 60.
John, 85, 119.
John, 120, 125.
Lucy, 85, 85.
Lucy, 120, 121.
Lucy, 60, 61.
Mary, 60.
Mary, 84, 84, 85.
Mary, 120, 120.
Nathaniel, 60.
Phebe, 34, 35.
Phebe, 120.
Phebe, 84, 85.
Prudence, 120.
Robert, 60, 61.
Sarah, 35, 36.
Sarah, 60.
Sarah, 120.
Thankful, 85, 86.
Thomas, 60, 80.
Wetherell, 35, 59.
William, 85, 86.

Descendants of George.
Denison, Abby, 177, 183.
Ann, 184.
Amos, 183, 193.
Borodell, 183, 184.
Borodell, 226.
Christopher, 209, 213.
Desire, 177, 183.
Edward, 177.
Elizabeth, 209.
Elizabeth, 183, 184.
Elijah, 226.
Elisha, 177.
George, 226.
George, 209, 210.
Gideon, 209, 222,
Joanna, 183, 184.
Joanna, 209, 209.
Joseph, 226, 226.
John, 177, 177.
Joseph, 183, 184.
Mary, 177, 183.
Mary, 226.
Mary, 209.
Mercy, 209, 210.
Nathan, 183, 198.
Prudence, 226.
Prudence, 183.
Samuel, 209, 209.
Sarah, 226, 228.
Sarah, 209, 209.
Stephen, 209.
Thankful, 184.

Descendants of William.
Denison, Ann, 265.
Benadam, 234, 243.
David, 265, 281.
Esther, 234, 235.
Esther, 265.
George, 265, 265.
Jonathan, 234.
Lucy, 265.
Mary, 265.
Mercy, 265, 266.
Mercy, 234, 234.
Nathan, 234.
Samuel, 265.
Sarah, 234.
William, 265, 280.
William, 3d, 234, 234.

Index. 389

FIFTH GENERATION.

Descendants of John.
Denison, Abigail, 125.
    Abigail, 19, 24.
    Abigail, 80.
    Ann, 19.
    Anna, 125, 125.
    Ann B., 131, 134.
    Andrew, 61, 63.
    Andrew, 125, 129.
    Ashbel, 24, 33.
    Avery, 101, 119.
    Avery, 125.
    Beebe, 131, 165.
    Daniel, 131, 144.
    Daniel, 122, 122.
    Daniel, 36, 38.
    Daniel, 19, 19.
    Daniel, 61.
    David, 80, 81.
    David S., 62, 66.
    Deborah, 61, 62.
    Desire, 125.
    Desire, 101, 118.
    Dorothy, 24.
    Dorothy, 72.
    Ebenezer, 80.
    Ebenezer, 19, 21.
    Eleazer, 80.
    Elizabeth, 37, 38.
    Elizabeth, 61.
    Elisha, 101, 104.
    Esther, 131, 132.
    Esther, 59, 59.
    Eunice, 132, 135.
    Eunice, 62, 63.
    Frederick, 131, 169.
    George, 59, 59.
    Grace, 59.
    Gurdon, 62, 71.
    Hannah, 131, 134.
    Hannah, 37, 37.
    Henry, 131, 163.
    Hepzibah, 19.
    Isaac, 131, 154.
    Jabez, 24, 24.
    Jabez, 80.
    James, 24.
    James, 37.

Descendants of George.
Denison, Abigail, 209.
    Amos, 193.
    Amos, 185, 189.
    Amos, 198.
    Ann, 178, 181.
    Bridget, 185, 185.
    Christopher, 213, 213.
    Clarissa, 222.
    Content, 185, 185.
    Cynthia, 193.
    Desire, 222.
    Darius, 234, 239.
    Edmund, 210.
    Edward, 178.
    Eleazer, 198, 208.
    Elizabeth, 185.
    Elizabeth, 222.
    Elisha, 178, 181.
    Ephraim, 185.
    Ezra, 185.
    Ezra, 222.
    Eunice, 193, 193.
    Ezekiel, 210.
    George, 210.
    George, 226.
    George, 243, 258.
    Hannah, 210.
    Hetty, 222, 223.
    Gideon, 222, 223.
    James, 243, 243.
    Jedediah, 222, 224.
    Jemima, 210.
    Jeremiah, 223.
    Jesse, 178, 181.
    John, 178, 178.
    John, 213, 214.
    Joseph, 226.
    Joseph, 210, 210.
    Joseph, 198, 198.
    Joseph, 193, 193.
    Joseph, 185.

Descendants of William.
    Alice, 234, 249.
    Amy, 281.
    Andrew, 234.
    Benadam, 243, 248.
    Beebe, 234, 235.
    Darius, 234, 239.
    David, 281, 283.
    Desire, 281.
    Dorothy, 265.
    Dudley, 265.
    Edward, 281, 289.
    Elisha, 265.
    Emma, 281.
    Esther, 265, 277.
    Gilbert, 265, 276.
    George, 265, 266.
    George, 243, 258.
    George, 281, 291.
    Jabez, 281, 282.
    James, 243, 243.
    Jane, 265.
    John, 281, 293.

Index.

Fifth Generation Continued.

Descendants of John.
Denison, John, 24, 29.
John, 72, 73.
Julia, 125, 131.
Lucy, 19.
Lucy, 125.
Lucy, 59.
Lucy, 224.
Lydia, 59.
Mary, 122, 125.
Mary, 36, 37.
Mary, 61.
Mary, 125.
Mary, 131, 132.
Molly, 101, 118.
Mercy, 62.
Mercy, 101, 119.
Nathaniel, 80.
Nathan, 125.
Nathan, 101.
Patience, 72, 79.
Phebe, 19.
Phebe, 72, 80.
Phebe, 37, 37.
Phebe, 131, 132.
Prudence, 80.
Prudence, 101, 119.
Rachel, 37, 37.
Rebecca, 101.
Robert, 24.
Robert, 61.
Robert, 131, 147.
Samuel, 72, 74.
Samuel, 62.
Samuel, 37.
Sarah, 59.
Sarah, 62.
Sarah, 80.
Sarah, 125, 127.
Thomas, 36, 53.
Thankful, 101, 119.
William, 101, 114.
Zerviah, 101.

Descendants of George.
Denison, Lydia, 198.
Martha, 193, 193.
Mary, 178, 180.
Mary, 209.
Mary, 213.
Molly, 223.
Mercy, 178, 181.
Mercy, 210, 212.
Nathan. Col.198,198.
Nathaniel, 226, 226.
Peleg, 185, 185.
Prudence, 193, 193.
Rebecca, 178.
Saba, 210, 212.
Samuel, 209, 209.
Sarah, 209.
Sarah, 226, 228.
Stephen, 210, 211.
Thankful, 226.

Descendants of William.
Denison, Lucy, 243, 243.
Lucy, 265.
Mary, 280, 280.
Mercy, 234, 238.
Nathan, 265.
Oliver, 265, 272.
Priscilla, 280, 280.
Prudence, 234, 235.
Robert, 243, 245.
Samuel, 281, 294.
Wealthy, 281.
William, 265, 270.
William, 234.

SIXTH GENERATION.

Descendants of John.
Dennison, Abby, 99.
Abigail, 130.
Abigail, 114, 115.

Descendants of George.
Denison, Abigail, 224.
Abigail, 213.
Abigail, 209.

Descendants of William.
Denison, Abigail, 235.
Almira, 289.
Alice, 249, 255.

Index. 391

Sixth Generation Continued.

Descendants of John.	Descendants of George.	Descendants of William.
Denison, Abigail, 92, 96.	Denison, Amos, 190, 190.	Denison, Allen, 249, 257.
Abigail, 25.	Amos, 194, 195.	Amos B., 239.
Abigail, 66, 66.	Ann, 199, 206.	Amos, 258.
Alfred, 169.	Ann, 210, 211.	Amy, 291, 291.
Amelia, 71.	Asa, 209.	Andrew, 235.
Amy, 92, 93.	Bainai, 215, 217.	Anna, 243.
Amy, 98.	Bridget, 186, 186.	Ann, 248, 248.
Anna, 147.	Beckwith, 215, 219.	Ann B., 258.
Anna, 29.	Benadam, 226, 226.	Ann B., 293, 294.
Anna, 81.	Betsey P. 226, 228.	Arad Jos., 291, 291.
Ann B., 154, 159.	Charles, 194, 195.	Beebe, 235, 235.
Ann, 53, 53.	Charles W., 190, 190.	Belinda, 282.
Annie, 64.	Charles, 224, 224.	Benadam, 258, 259.
Asa S., 114, 115.	Christopher, 213, 213.	Benadam, 249, 249.
Asa, 144, 144.	Clorinda, 213.	Charles, 248.
Asenath, 38, 53.	Daniel, 209.	Charles H., 283, 286.
Asahel C., 114, 117.	Deborah, 212.	Clarissa, 283.
Ashbel, 33.	Debby, 212.	Content, 235.
Andrew, —.	Desire, 226.	Daniel, 258, 259.
Avery, 104, 107.		Darius, 239.
Beebe, 166, 166.		David, 283, 283.
Benjamin F. 130, 130.		David, 294.
Betsey, 92.		Deborah, 249, 255.
Betsey, 114. 116,		Desire, 283.
Betsey, 122.		Desire, 289.
Betsey, 169, 171.		Dimis, 243.
Catherine, 71.		
Charlotte, 75, 79.		
Charles, 33, 33.		
Charles H., 169.		
Charles, 59.		
Charles H., 130.		
Charles P., 92.		
Christopher, 63.		
Clarissa, 147.		
Dan, 29, 30.		
Daniel, 19.		
Daniel, 38, 38.		
Daniel, 53.		
Daniel, 98, 98.		
Daniel, 122.		
Daniel, 144, 144.		
Daniel, 154.		
Daniel, 163, 164.		
Daniel A., 169.		
David, 38, 47.		
David, 66, 67.		

392   *Index.*

Sixth Generation Continued.

Descendants of John.	Descendants of George.	Descendants of William.
Denison, David E., 81,83.	Denison, Edmund, 210, 211.	Denison, Edward, 289, 289.
Delia A., 169, 170.	Edward, 190.	Edward, 249.
Desire, 104, 104.	Edward, 178.	Elam W., 273, 273.
Desire, 130.	Edward, 224.	Elias, 249.
Dolly, 25.	Elisha, 181.	Elisha, 276.
Dorothy, 122, 124.	Eliza, 215, 216.	Eliza A., 249, 258.
Dorcas, 92, 92.	Elizabeth, 181, 182.	Elizabeth, 270, 272.
Ebenezer, 21, 21.	Elizabeth, 223, 223.	Elizabeth, 283, 287.
Ebenezer, 38, 43.	Elizabeth, 181.	Emeline, 249, 258.
Ebenezer, 154, 154.	Elizabeth, 213.	Emma, 289.
Edward, 99.	Elizabeth, 186.	Eunice, 235.
Elisha, 64.	Elizabeth, 198, 200.	Eunice, 289.
Elisha W., 154, 155.	Eunice, 178, 178.	Eunice, 243.
Elisha, 104, 107.	Eunice, 194.	Eunice W., 273, 275.
Eli, 25, 25.	Eunice P., 217.	Eunice, 293.
Elihu, 38, 52.	Esther, 226, 228.	Eunice, 294.
Elizabeth, 31.	Ezekiel, 210.	Fanny, 239, 243.
Elizabeth, 53, 56.	Ezra S., 190.	Gilbert, 293.
Elizabeth, 71, 72.	Ezra, 224.	Gilbert, 276, 276.
Elizabeth, 73, 74.	Gideon, 224.	Grace B., 273, 274.
Elizabeth, 74,	George, 199, 207.	Geo. W. Dr. 289, 298.
Elizabeth, 81.	George, 212.	Geo. W. Dr. 258, 260.
Elizabeth, 144.	George, 213.	George, 243.
Erastus, 169, 170.	George H., Rev. 224.	George, 291.
Esther, 163, 165.		George, 248.
Esther, 147.		George W., 249, 257.
Esther, 154, 159.		George, 266.
Esther, 59, 59.		George, 270.
Esther, 144, 148.		Gurdon, 270, 270.
Ethan A., 99, 99.		
Eunice, 104, 104.		
Eunice, 154, 161.		
Eunice, 66, 70.		
Ezra, 31, 32.		
Frances, 75, 79.		
Frances, 81, 83.		
Frederic, 154, 169.		
Frederic, 169.		
Fanny B., 99, 100.		
Fanny, 122, 124.		
George, 38.		
George W., 73.		
George, 81, 81.		
Gilbert P., 166, 168.		
Gideon, 163.		
Grace, 104.		
Grace, 53, 58.		

Index. 393

Sixth Generation Continued.

Descendants of John.	Descendants of George.	Descendants of William.
Denison, Griswold, 38, 46.	Denison, Hannah, 190.	Denison, Hannah S., 293,
Gurdon, 71, 71.	Hannah, 226.	Harriet, 248. [293.
Hannah, 92.	Hannah E., 190.	Henry, 235, 236.
Hannah, 98.	Henry, 223.	Henry, 266.
Hannah, 169.	Henry, 210, 211.	Henry, 276.
Hannah, 165, 168.	Isaac, 194.	Henry, 294.
Hannah, 104.	James, 213.	Huldah, 276, 277.
Hannah P., 99, 100.	Jemima, 210.	Jabez S., 291, 292.
Henry, 163, 163.	Jemima, 212.	Jabez, 282, 282.
Henry C., 74, 77.	Jedediah, 224, 224.	James, 243.
Hezekiah, 154.	Jeremiah, 224, 225.	James, 248.
Isaac, 63, 64.	Jesse, 215, 221.	James, 249, 254.
Isaac, 104, 109.	John, 199, 306.	Jane, 293.
Isaac, 154, 156.	John, 178, 179.	John A., 293.
Jabez, 25, 25.	John, 215, 215.	John, 294.
James P., 29, 29.	Joseph, 194, 197.	Jonathan, 249, 250.
Jane, 122.	Joseph, 185.	Jonathan, 258.
James, 64, 65.	Joseph, 210, 211.	Jos. Adam, 243, 244.
James, 59.	Julia, 212.	Joseph S., 249, 255.
Jeremiah, 166.	Lazarus, 198, 199.	Julia, 266.
John S., 73.	Lemuel, 194.	Joseph B., 283, 288.
John, 63, 64.	Leonard, 185, 186.	Justin W., 273, 275.
John, 75, 78.	Lois, 178, 179.	Lodowick, 239, 240.
John P., 81, 83.	Louisa, 223, 223.	Lucy, 270, 271.
John, 130, 130.	Lydia, 215.	Lucy, 243.
John, 166, 168.	Luther, 194, 197.	Lucy, 258, 264.
John, 19, 19.		Lucy, 248, 248.
John, 29, 29.		Lucy Ann. 249, 256.
Jonathan, 38, 44.		Luke P., 273.
Joseph, 92, 92.		
Katherine, 38, 53.		
Katherine, 53, 58.		
Keturah, 165, 167.		
Keturah, 19, 21.		
Lawton, 144.		
Latham, 38, 47.		
Lavinia, 16.		
Lois, 99, 100.		
Lois, 104.		
Lois, 163, 165.		
Lucy Ann, 130, 131.		
Lucy, 114, 116.		
Lucy, 25.		
Lydia, 21, 24.		
Lyman, 33, 34.		
Lyman, 114.		
Martha, 33.		

394　　　　　　　　　　*Index.*

Sixth Generation Continued.

Descendants of John.	Descendants of George.	Descendants of William.
Denison, Martha, 98.	Denison, Martha, 190, 192.	Denison, Marcia P., 273.
Martha, 147, 147.	Martha, 194, 194.	Martha, 249.
Mary, 29.	Mary, 178.	Martha, 273, 273.
Mary, 74.	Mary, 181.	Mason, Dr. 258, 264.
Mary, 64.	Mary, 226.	Matilda, 270, 271.
Mary, 92, 92.	Mary, 185, 186.	Matilda, 294.
Mary, 98.	Mary, 199, 203.	Mary, 282.
Mary, 163, 164.	Mehitabel, 181, 182.	Mary, 283, 285.
Mary, 114, 114.	Minerva, 223, 223.	Mary L., 293.
Marie, 71, 72.	Noyes, 185.	Mercy, 239, 239.
Mercy, 64.	Peleg, 185.	Mercy, 235.
Mercy, 154, 159.	Phebe, 181, 182.	Nancy, 270.
Mercy, 114.	Polly, 194, 195.	Nancy, 235.
Mehitabel, 29, 21.	Polly, 210.	Nancy, 283.
Mason, 29, 29.	Prudence, 194.	Nathan, 266.
Molly, 24.	Richard, 224.	Noyes P., 249, 257.
Moses T., 99.		Olive, 291, 291.
Nancy, 166, 168.		Oliver, 273, 273.
Nancy, 99, 100.		Phebe, 282.
Nancy, 122.		Polly, 235.
Nancy, 73, 74.		Polly, 239.
Nancy, 71, 71.		Prentice, 235.
Nathan, 104, 104.		Prudence, 235.
Nathan, 147, 148.		Prudence, 239, 239.
Nathan F., 169, 169.		Prudence, 266.
Nathaniel, 99.		Prudence, 282.
Olive, 66.		Robert, 249.
Oliver, 73.		Russel, 235.
Oliver, 122.		Ruey, 289.
Patience, 74.		
Phebe, 64.		
Phebe, 147, 147.		
Phebe, 73, 74.		
Polly, 147, 148.		
Prudence, 81.		
Prudence, 104, 114.		
Prudence, 71.		
Prudence, 66, 67.		
Rachel, 66.		
Rebecca, 114, 115.		
Rhoda, 25.		
Rensalaer, 147, 152.		
Robert, 25.		
Robert, 31, 31.		
Robert, 63, 64.		
Robert, 73.		
Robert, 147.		

Index.

Sixth Generation Continued.

Descendants of John.
Denison, Sally, 169.
  Sally, 130, 131.
  Sabra, 21.
  Samuel, 122, 122.
  Samuel, 38, 52.
  Samuel, 71.
  Samuel, 53.
  Samuel, 66, 67.
  Samuel, 73, 73.
  Samuel F., 92, 96.
  Sarah 66.
  Sarah, 74.
  Sarah, 92, 93.
  Sarah, 154, 159.
  Sarah, 163.
  Sherman, 66, 70.
  Simeon, 104.
  Sophia, 71.
  Sophia, 130.
  Starr, 53, 58.
  Stephen W., 130.
  Sylvester, 33.
  Thankful, 154, 160.
  Thankful, 104.
  Thankful, 114.
  Thomas, 38, 47.
  Thomas, 53, 54.
  Titus, 29, 30.
  Wells, 21, 22.
  W. Wheeler, 144.
  William A., 114.
  William, 71.
  William H., 74, 75.
  William H., 166.
  William, 98.
  William, 166.
  Zerviah, 104.

Descendants of George.
Denison, Samuel, 186.
  Samuel M. G., 185.
  Samuel, 209.
  Sarah P., 190, 191.
  Sarah, 199.
  Sarah, 215.
  William, 215, 216.
  William, 224.
  Zina, 213.
  Zina, 210, 212.

Descendants of William.
Denison, Samuel, 294.
  Sarah, 258, 259.
  Sophia, 276.
  Sophronia, 283, 288.
  Sophronia A. 293, 294
  Thankful, 266.
  Theody, 258.
  Thomas A., 293, 203.
  Thomas I., 273.
  Warren, 270, 271.
  William, 239, 242.
  William E. 249, 256.
  William G., 266, 266.
  William S., 270, 272.

SEVENTH GENERATION.

Descendants of John.
Denison, AbbyC., 155, 156.
  Abby Eliza, 99.
  Abigail, 64.
  Abigail, 68.
  Abraham, 22, 22.
  Achsa, 29.
  Adna C., 109, 113.

Descendants of George.
Denison, Achsa, 221.
  Albert E., Rev. 215,
  Alexander, 195. [216.
  Alford, 215.
  Almond, 195.
  Amanda, 207.
  Amanda, 213.

Descendants of William.
Denison, Abby Ann, 267,
  Abigail, 236.   [268.
  Adam B., 260.
  Adelaide L., 291, 292.
  Adeline, 268.
  Albert, 240, 240.
  Alice, 282, 282.

Index.

Seventh Generation Continued.

Descendants of John.
Denison, Ahirah, 145.
Alexander, 148, 150.
Alfred, 32.
Alice A., 167, 167.
Aliph, 122.
Alma, 43.
Almira A., 25.
Almira G., 85.
Almira, 109, 109.
Almond, 117, 117.
Alonzo, 47.
Alpha M., 117.
Alson, 46.
Alson, 52.
Alvin, 52.
Amanda, 115.
Amelia, 152, 153.
Amos, 148, 149.
Andrew, 130, 130.
Andrew, 64.
Andrew I., 167, 167.
Angeline, 148.
Angeline, 47.
Angeline, 149.
Ann B., 21, 21.
Ann B., 30.
Ann, 64.
Ann E., 96, 96.
Ann, 145, 145.
Ann E., 155.
Anna, 53.
Ansel, 29.
Ansel, 47.
Asa W., 25, 28.
Asa J., 145, 146.
Aseneth, 58.
Avery, Rev., 38, 39.
Avery, 43.
Avery, 53.
Beebe D., 166.
Benjamin G., 44, 45.
Betsey, 30, 30.
Betsey A., 98.
Bridget G., 157, 158.
Candace, 48, 56.
Caroline, 47.
Caroline, 73, 74.

Descendants of George.
Denison, Amelia S., 186.
Ann, 195.
Anna Caroline, 186.
Annis F., 227.
Ansel, 221, 222.
Amos E.W., 190, 191.
Asa C., 207.
Augusta E., 186.
Augusta M., 186, 187.
Benadam, 227.
Benjamin C. 199, 199.
Betsey, 227.
Binai, 215, 218.
Bridget, 188, 189.

Descendants of William.
Denison, Alice Dudley, 244, 247.
Alonzo C., 270, 270.
Allen Eugene, 256.
Amy S., 291, 292.
Andrew R., 291, 292.
Andrew J., 275.
Andrew J., 288.
Amos B., 286, 286.
Angeline M. 268, 269.
Ann B., 250, 253.
Ann E., 275.
Ann B., 282.
Ann Evelina, 272.
Ann Jenette, 254, 255.
Ann M., 260.
Ann M., 276, 277.
Avery I., 291, 292.
Benadam, 249.
Benadam, jr. 260, 260.
Benj. F., 262, 263.
Betsey P., 250, 253.
Betsey S., 266.

Index. 397

Seventh Generation Continued.

Descendants of John.
Denison, Caroline G., 96.
    Cassius A., 109.
    Catherine, —.
    Chas. Edward, 78, 78.
    Charles, 130.
    Charles, 130.
    Charles, 34.
    Charles, 54, 54.
    Charles E., 58.
    Charles P., 83.
    Charles, 33, 33.
    Charles C., 157.
    Charles M., 52.
    Charles B., 25, 28.
    Charlotte M., 25, 26.
    Charlotte R., 98, 98.
    Chloe, 58.
    Chloe, 145, 146.
    Clarissa, 22.
    Clarissa, 152, 153.
    Clarrissa, 32.
    Clarrissa, 39.
    Cornelia, 98.
    Cynthia, 145, 145.
    Cynthia, 31.
    Cyrus R., 107.
    Daniel, 38.
    Daniel, 48, 51.
    Daniel, 58, 59.
    Daniel, 39.
    Daniel, 53.
    Daniel, 54, 55.
    Daniel, 149, 15.
    Daniel, 44, 44.
    Daniel, 122.
    Daniel, 154.
    Daniel W., 22.
    Daniel A., 167.
    Daniel W., 157, 158.
    Datus, 152, 152.
    David, 32.
    David, 34.
    David, 44, 45.
    David, 81.
    David S., 67.
    Delina, 39.
    Derby, 32.

Descendants of George.
Denison, Caroline E., 197.
    Caroline E., 188, 189.
    Caroline, 190, 191.
    Charles, 211, 211.
    Charles, 199, 199.
    Charles, 227.
    Charles, 207.
    Charles C., 212.
    Charles Henry, 186.
    Charles S., 224, 224.
    Charles W. Rev. 190, 190.
    Clarissa, 225.
    Cynthia, 211.
    Daniel E., 188.
    Daniel S., 217.
    Dudley F., 227, 227.

Descendants of William.
Denison, Carrie J., 290.
    Celia B., 282, 282.
    Charles D., 272.
    Charles G., 260, 262.
    Charles G., 283.
    Charles H., 236.
    Charles H., 276.
    Charles H., 241, 242.
    Charles H., 286, 287.
    Charles O., 262, 263.
    Charles P., 276.
    Charles R., 270, 271.
    Charles K., 291.
    Charlotte A. 266, 267.
    Charlotte, 293.
    Charlotte A. 268, 269.
    Clara J., 293, 293.
    Clarissa, 273.
    Cyrus A., 257.
    Daniel B., 259.
    Daniel B., 262.
    Daniel M., 264, 264.
    Deborah, 249, 250.
    Deborah Ann, 256,
    David A., 283. [267.
    Darius C., 283.
    Darius, 241.
    Dewitt C., 262, 263.
    Dudley Chase, 244, 248.
    Dudley, 250, 250.

Index.

Seventh Generation Continued.

Descendants of John.
Denison, Duane, 164.
  Dudley, 122.
  Dudley C., 115, 116.
  Ebenezer, 154, 154.
  Ebenezer A., 43, 43.
  Edward C., 78.
  Edward R., 58.
  Edward, 71.
  Edward, 96, 97.
  Edward H., 75, 76.
  Edwin O., 167.
  Eli, 25.
  Eli, 130.
  Elias, 39.
  Elijah, 19, 19.
  Elijah B., 117, 118.
  Elihu, 53.
  Elisha, 64.
  Elisha A., 155, 155.
  Elisha M., 104, 104.
  Eliza, 92.
  Eliza H., 30.
  Eliza, 65, 66.
  Eliza, 68.
  Eliza 75, 76.
  Eliza, 115.
  Eliza, 149, 152.
  Eliza F., 157, 158.
  Elizabeth, 58.
  Elizabeth, 83.
  Elizabeth W., 78.
  Elizabeth, 152, 154.
  Emily, 54, 55.
  Emily F., 157, 158.
  Emily A., 170, 170.
  Emma A., 98.
  Emma, 169.
  Emma Wenham, 34.
  Erastus, 21.
  Erastus B., 167, 167.
  Erastus, 29.
  Erastus, 30.
  Eri, 44.
  Esther Ann, 83.
  Eunice M., 21.
  Eunice C., 155, 156.
  Eunice, 39, 42.
  Eunice M., 107.

Descendants of George.
Denison, Eber C., 215, 218.
  Edmund A., 211.
  Ede, 179.
  Edward, 179.
  Edwin, 197, 198.
  Elisha E., 186.
  Elisha, 190.
  Elisha I., 179.
  Eliza, 215, 216.
  Eliza, 190.
  Eliza A., 213.
  Elizabeth, 179, 180.
  Elizabeth, 225.
  Elizabeth C., 224, 224.
  Elizabeth C., 186, 187.
  Elizabeth, 199, 199.
  Elizabeth, 207.
  Elmina, 195.
  Elnathan, 221.
  Emily, 207.
  Emily M., 213.
  Emeline, 208.
  Esther 227.
  Erastus, 225.
  Erastus B., 217, 217.
  Eunice A., 179.
  Eunice, 227.
  Eunice P., 217.

Descendants of William.
Denison, Eber, 249, 249.
  Edgar, 273, 274.
  Elam, 273.
  Edward H., 289, 290.
  Elias, 242.
  Elias W., 275, 276.
  Elisha P., 275.
  Eliza, 236.
  Eliza, 240.
  Eliza A., 256, 257.
  Ellen D., 283.
  Ellen L., 289, 290.
  Elizabeth, 257.
  Elizabeth, 260, 261.
  Emeline, 260, 263.
  Emeline H., 283, 284.
  Emily, 236, 238.
  Emma J., 273, 274.
  Esther, 266, 267.
  Erastus, 268, 269.
  Etherlinda, 270.
  Eunice, 236, 237.
  Eunice, 244.
  Eunice, 260, 261.
  Eva J., 290, 290.

Index.

Seventh Generation Continued.

Descendants of John.

Denison, Euphemia, 67, 67.
  Evelina C., 96, 98.
  Frances D., 78, 78.
  Frances S., 78.
  Francis L., 75, 75.
  Frances Anna, 81.
  Frances M., 83.
  Frances J., 155, 156.
  Frances L., 157.
  Fanny, 75, 76.
  Fanny E., 73.
  Fanny Halsey, 34.
  Franklin B., 96.
  Frederick, 81.
  Frederick, Rev. 157,
  Furman, 47. [157.
  George, 38.
  George, 53.
  George, 47.
  George, 81.
  George Anson, 29.
  George Mason, 30, 30.
  George B., 52.
  George T., 46, 46.
  Gideon H., 25, 26.
  Gilbert W., 130.
  Gorham N. 44, 44.
  Gratia, 117.
  Gurnsey, 32 33.
  Harriet, 117, 118.
  Harriet, 83.
  Harriet M., 96, 97.
  Harriet H., 165.
  Hannah, 38.
  Hannah, 39.
  Hannah, 43.
  Hannah, 48.
  Hannah, 169, 169.
  Hannah F., 170, 170.
  Hannah M., 30.
  Harmon H., 164, 164.
  Henry C., 96.
  Henry C., 78.
  Henry W., 83.
  Henry, 164.
  Henry C., 77.
  Hiram C., 155, 155.

Descendants of George.

Denison, George, 212.
  George, 212.
  George B., 219, 219.
  George W., 186, 187.
  Hannah, 227.
  Hannah E., 188, 188.
  Harriet, 208.
  Harriet E., 188.
  Harriet E., 190.
  Harriet, 190, 191.
  Harvey H., 213.
  Harry C., 213, 214.
  Henrietta M. 186, 187.
  Henry, 207.
  Henry E., 212.
  Henry M., 208, 208.
  Henry S., 211.
  Hiram, 195, 195.
  Hiram, 199.
  Hiram, 215, 218.
  Howton, 207.
  Huldah A., 217.

Descendants of William.

Denison, Fidelia, 254, 255.
  Frances A., 266, 266.
  Frances E., 289, 290.
  Francis W., 257.
  Frank L., 241, 241.
  Frederic, 260.
  Fanny E., 257.
  Fannie S., 286, 286.
  George, 259, 259.
  George, 283, 284.
  George, 264.
  George, 267, 268.
  George, Rev. 244, 245.
  George, Rev. 293, 293.
  George P., 257.
  George H., 290.
  George M., 260, 262.
  George Jenks, 262.
  George S., 270, 270.
  George W., 291, 292.
  Georgiana S., 264.
  Gilbert P., 276.
  Guy, 241.
  H. Amira, 258.
  Hannah L., 236, 236.
  Henry S., 283.
  Hiram S., 283.
  Harriet A., 266.
  Harriet D., 236, 238.
  Harriet, 240.
  Harriet, 242.
  Harriet, 254.
  Helen J., 259, 259.
  Henry, 250, 252.
  Henry, 268, 269.
  Henry C., 276.
  Horace P., 256, 256.
  Huldah C., 283.

Seventh Generation Continued.

Descendants of John.
Denison, Hiram T., 166, 166.
    Holley, 47.
    Horace, 53.
    Horace A., 168.
    Isaac, 48, 49.
    Isaac A., 109, 113.
    Isaac W., 157, 157.
    Iola, 75, 76.
    Jabez, 25.
    Jabez W., 30.
    James A., 65, 65.
    James P., 164.
    James, 44, 44.
    James, 64, 64.
    James S., 52.
    James, 58.
    Jane Isabel, 96, 97.
    Jane M., 98, 98.
    Jedidah, 22, 23.
    Jerome B, 145.
    Jerusha H., 30.
    Jesse W., 48, 51.
    John, 19.
    John, 64.
    John, 29.
    John, 78.
    John C., 83.
    John W., 149, 152.
    John H., 64, 65.
    John J., 122, 123.
    John L., 157, 159.
    John M., 167.
    John Newton, 78, 78.
    John W., 107, 108.
    John H., 169.
    Jonathan, 44, 45.
    Joseph, 92.
    Joseph Allison, 70.
    Josephine, 108, 108.
    Julia Ann, 130.
    Julia Ann, 145.
    Julia Lavinia, 65.
    Katherine, 43.
    Katherine, 48, 51.
    Katherine, 52.
    Katherine, 53.
    Katherine, 54, 54.

Descendants of George.
Denison, Isaac, —
    James H., 219, 220.
    Jesse, 179.
    Jesse, 221.
    John, 179.
    John, 197, 197.
    John, 215, 217.
    John, 215, 215.
    John T. 217.
    Joseph, —.
    Julia M., 219.
    Juliaetta, 225.

Descendants of William.
Denison, James, 244, 247.
    James E., 250, 252.
    James Ray, 254.
    Jared 293.
    Jane, 236.
    Jane A., 264.
    Jane B., 276, 277.
    Jerome, 236, 238.
    Jesse, Rev., 250, 251.
    John, 293.
    John, 242.
    John H., 259.
    John W., 250, 253.
    John W., 260, 261.
    Jos. Adam, jr., 244, 244
    Joseph B., 291.
    Joseph, Rev. 233, 284.
    Joseph, 270.
    Joseph, 268, 269.
    Joseph W., 272.
    Julia, 236, 237.
    Julia Ann, 266, 267.
    Julia Ann, 267, 268
    Justin W., 275.

Seventh Generation Continued.

Descendants of John.
Denison, Katherine, 58.
  Latham, —.
  Laura E., 166, 166.
  Lavinia, 70.
  Lillie C., 167, 167.
  Linus S., 31, 31.
  Lizzie, 32.
  Lorena, 39.
  Lois W., 99, 100.
  Louisa A., 30.
  Louisa, 34.
  Louisa A., 54.
  Louisa A., 107, 107.
  Louis P , 67, 67.
  Lucius, 164.
  Lucius, 109, 109.
  Lucy, 19, 20.
  Lucy, 52.
  Lucy G., 170.
  Lucy P., 77, 78.
  Lucretia, 21.
  Lyman, 117, 117.
  Malvina C., 107,108.
  Margaret, 31, 31.
  Margaret, 67.
  Malverton H., 167.
  Martha, 21.
  Martha N., 64, 65.
  Martha K., 81, 81.
  Martha, 152, 153.
  Mary, 75, 76.
  Mary, 92.
  Mary, 21.
  Mary, 68.
  Mary, 48, 48.
  Mary C., 96, 97.
  Mary, 66.
  Mary, 70.
  Mary E., 96.
  Mary Jane, 130,130.
  Mary A., 13.
  Mary A., 107, 107.
  Mary Ann, 30.
  Mary B., 25, 27.
  Mary C., 96, 98.
  Mary Ann, 148, 151.
  Mary E., 170, 170.

Descendants of George.
Denison, Laura, 207.
  Laura A., 219.
  Leonard S., 186.
  Lewis, 221.
  Lester E., 215, 216.
  Lodemia, 221, 222.
  Lois, 179.
  Louisa, 211.
  Lucius, 208.
  Lydia, 215, 218.
  Lydia A., 217, 217.
  Lydia, 221.
  Maria Louisa, 225.
  Martha F., 195.
  Mary, 179, 179.
  Mary, 211.
  Mary, 215, 216.
  Mary, 188, 188.
  Mary, 195, 195.
  Mary, 195.
  Mary, 199, 199.
  Mary Augusta, 186.
  Mary Ann, 212, 212.
  Mary Ann, 213.
  Mary A., 225.
  Mary E., 217.
  Mary Lord, 186.
  Mary C., 190.
  Mary C., 219, 220.
  Mary W., 208.

Descendants of William.
Denison, Lafayette, 262,
  Lewis B., 260. [263.
  Lizzie E., 290.
  Louisa, 276.
  Louisa L., 283, 283.
  Lovilla, 293.
  Lucy A., 236, 236.
  Lydia L., 291, 292.
  Madison, 271.
  Maria R., 289, 290.
  Maria, 270, 270.
  Maria, 275, 275.
  Martha J., 266, 267.
  Marion H., 289.
  Martha Ann,273,274
  Marcia P., 273.
  Mary, 236, 236.
  Mary, 240.
  Mary, 258.
  Mary, 286.
  Mary, 276, 277.
  Mary Ann, 256, 256.
  Mary Ann, 259.
  Mary E., 241, 242.
  Mary B., 282.
  Mercy A., 275, 275.
  Minerva, 286.
  Miranda S., 250,253.

Seventh Generation Continued.

Descendants of John.
Denison, Mary E., 167.
    Mary E., 152, 153.
    Maria, 68.
    Maria, 109.
    Maria D., 164, 164.
    Maryette, 145, 147.
    Mason, 29.
    Mehitabel D., 21.
    Mercy W., 75.
    Minerva C., 109,112.
    Nancy, 39, 42.
    Nancy, 70.
    Nancy, 130.
    Nancy, 99, 99.
    Nancy C., 109, 109.
    Nathan,Rev.109,111.
    Nathaniel K., 29.
    Nellie S., 83.
    Ophelia, 81.
    Orpha, 43.
    Orrel, 47.
    Orvil W., 109.
    Oscar A., 109, 113.
    Patience, —.
    Paulina J., 169,169.
    Paul, 19.
    Pedy, 47.
    Phebe E., 155, 156.
    Phebe, 149, 151.
    Phebe T., 73.
    Phebe, 64.
    Phila, 75.
    Polly, 43, 44.
    Polly, 64.
    Polly, 44.
    Polly, 47.
    Prudence, 92.
    Pulaski, 96.
    Rachel, 67, 67.
    Rebecca, 70, 71.
    Rebecca, 46.
    Rebecca, 68.
    Rebecca N., 109,113.
    Reuben, 25, 26.
    Richard N., 64, 65.
    Rhoda, 39, 42.
    Rhoda, 47.

Descendants of George.
Denison, Nathan, 199.
    Nathan F., 195.
    Nathaniel, 179.
    Oliver C., 221, 222.
    Orville, 207.
    Peleg, 188, 189.
    Prudence C.,227, 227.
    Prudence S., 195.
    Rachel, 211.
    Rhoda, 227, 227.
    Roxena, 195.
    Rufus C., 225, 225.

Descendants of William.
Denison, Nancy, —.
    Nancy E., 283, 284.
    Nathan N., 273, 274.
    Noyes W., 256, 256.
    Noyes R., 257, 257.
    Oliver, 275, 275.
    Oliver, 260, 260.
    Oliver, 273, 273.
    Olivia, 254, 255.
    Orrin B., 254.
    Pamelia S., 259.
    Phebe, 242.
    Phebe M., 273.
    Polly, 260.
    Prudence, 242.
    Rachel Chase, 244.
    Robert S., 250, 252.
    Robert W., 258.
    Rowland S., 236,238.
    Russel A. 236.

Index.

Seventh Generation Continued.

Descendants of John.
Denison, Rhoda, 130.
    Robert Fordyce, 32.
    Robert W., 65.
    Robert S., 152, 152.
    Robert, 64.
    Robert, 149.
    Rosalie S., 109.
    Salmon S., 168, 168.
    Salah B., 154.
    Sally, 30.
    Sally, 52.
    Samuel D., Rev. 96,
    Samuel, 68, 69. [96.
    Samuel, 73.
    Samuel A., 117, 118.
    Samuel W., 122, 122.
    Sarah Ann, 31.
    Sarah H., 83.
    Sarah, 92.
    Sarah, 67, 67.
    Sarah A., 152.
    Sarah M., 155, 155.
    Sarah, 164.
    Sanford, 145.
    Smedley, 145, 146.
    Selden S., 22, 23.
    Silas, 122.
    Simeon M., 107, 107.
    Sherman, David, 70,
    Sophia, 70, 71. [70.
    Sophia, 115.
    Starr, 58, 58.
    Stephen A., 122, 124.
    Stratton, 115.
    Susanna, 33, 33.
    Sylvester, 34.
    Sylvia, 145, 146.
    Thomas, 25, 25.
    Thomas, 54, 54.
    Thomas C., 46, 48.
    Thomas, 58.
    Timothy T., 22, 23.
    Titus, 21.
    Titus K., 31.
    Thirza, 115, 116.
    Thankful, 53.
    Teresa, 47.

Descendants of George.
Denison, Sallyette, 197.
    Sally, 215, 219.
    Samantha, 207.
    Samuel, 179.
    Sarah, 199, 200.
    Sarah J., 195.
    Sarah S., 217.
    Sarah, 215.
    Sarah, 190.
    Socrates, 217, 217.
    Sophia, 195.
    Susan E., 211.
    Stanley, 207.
    Stephen B., 179.
    Sylvia, 211.
    Thomas, —

Descendants of William.
Denison, Sally, —.
    Sarah, 250, 251.
    Sarah A., 286.
    Sarah E., 273.
    Silas, 241.
    Stillman A., 241.
    Thomas J., 275.

404 *Index.*

Seventh Generation Continued.

Descendants of John.
Denison, Vine, 58.
  Wellington, 47.
  Wheeler, 25.
  Willard G., 164, 164.
  William, 25.
  William, 43.
  William, 64.
  William L., 30.
  William W., 122,123.
  William C., 96.
  William H., 98, 98.
  William Antil, 68 68.
  William C., Rev. 75.
  William Crane, 70.
  William S., 73, 73.
  William, 164.
  William H., 166,166.
  Wyllis N., 106.
  Zebediah, 145, 145.
  Ziba, 19, 20.

Descendants of George.
Denison, Una, 219.
  Wayman, 199.
  Wesley, 207, 207.
  William, —
  William, 221, 221.
  William, 208.
  William, Rev., 215, 216.
  William H., 211, 212.
  William W., 225.

Descendants of William.
Denison, Vashti L., 254.
  Warren, 271.
  Washington, 271.
  Willard A., 291,291.
  William, —
  William, jr., 242.
  William A., 256,256.
  William G., 262,263.
  William H., 236,237.
  William D., 264,264.
  William G., 266,267.
  William M., 293.
  William V., 241,241.
  Zelida, 250, 251.

EIGHTH GENERATION.

Descendants of John.
Denison, Abby J., 122, 123.
  Abby A., 22.
  Adah 118.
  Adaline M., 110.
  Adaline N., 111, 111.
  Addie, 158.
  Adelaide, 68.
  Adelaide, 124.
  Adelbert S., 113, 113.
  Adella M., 166.
  Admetus, 43.
  Albert H., 118.
  Adna T., 113.
  Alice M., 65.
  Alice, 23.
  Alice, 110, 110.
  Althea, 28.
  Alvina, 20.
  Albert, 155.
  Albert H., 155.
  Albert G., 44.
  Alexander, 152.
  Almond C., 117.

Descendants of George.
Denison, Adelia, 218.
  Alford M., 218.
  Alfred S., 220.
  Amelia P., 215.
  Amos, 191.
  Anna S., 189.
  Antoinette, 219.
  Augustus, 222.

Descendants of William.
Denison, Abbie A., 252.
  Abigail E., 251.
  Adeline 268.
  Adeline M., 256.
  Addie, 254.
  Addie E., 257.
  Albert, 292.
  Albert E., 240, 240.
  Alfred B., 260, 260.
  Alice, 244.
  Alice D., 247, 247.
  Alice C, 245.
  Alice T., 267.
  Andrew J., 288.
  Angeline, 269.
  Alonzo, 271.
  Ann B., 250.
  Ann B., 274.
  Ann E., 261.
  Ann M., 263.
  Anna, 269.
  Anna H., 288.
  Anna M., 262.

Index. 405

Eighth Generation Continued.

Descendants of John.
Denison, Alvira, 48.
  Alzina A., 46.
  Amelia T., 50.
  Annetta M., 153.
  Amie, 97.
  Amy, 157.
  Andrew, 123.
  Angeline M., 151.
  Angeline, 151.
  Ann B., 157.
  Anna, 97.
  Anna E., 152.
  Annie, 70.
  Anna C., 155.
  Ann E., 76, 76.
  Adolpha A., 152.
  Archibald, 66.
  Arthur, 118.
  Arthur L., 30.
  Arthur E., 110.
  Asa, 146.
  Asa Samuel A., 68.
  Asahel, 118.
  Aurelia, 79.
  Avery, 43.
  Avery E., 113, 113.
  Beebe, —.
  Benjamin T., 65.
  Benjamin F., 152.
  Betsey Ann, 105, 105.
  Betsey D., 168.
  Candace, 51.
  Caroline, 45.
  Caroline, 146.
  Caroline L., 97.
  Caroline N., 110, 110.
  Carrie, 117.
  Clara A., 79.
  Clara R., 114.
  Clarrissa, 23.
  Clarrissa P., 22.
  Charity, 48.
  Charles, 22.
  Charles, 66.
  Charles, 76.
  Charles, 78.
  Charles, 157.

Descendants of George.
Denison, Beckwith, 222.
  Caroline A., 189.
  Catherine, 222.
  Charles, 224.
  Charles, 198.
  Charles, 199.
  Char es H., 214.
  Charles B., 220.
  Charles W., 190.
  Charles M., 211.
  Charles W., 220.
  Clara P., 216.
  Cyrus H., 207.

Descendants of William.
Denison, Annie A., 238.
  Arthur A., 263.
  Belle E., 257.
  Belle, 260.
  Benjamin C., 241.
  Benjamin F., 263.
  Benjamin F., 264.
  Benadam, 261.
  Bertie R., 292.
  Burton, 242.
  Caroll, 292.
  Caroline E., 268.
  Carrie E., 262.
  Catherine A., 248.
  Catherine L., 253, 254
  Charles, Dr., 244.
  Charles, 251.
  Charles, 252.
  Charles F., 287, 287.
  Charles G., 241.
  Charles H., 256.
  Charles H., 240.
  Charles H., 262.
  Charles H., 271.
  Charles H., 251.
  Charles H., 292.
  Charles S., 237.
  Charles O., 263.
  Charles S., 245.
  Charles S., 284.
  Charles F., 252.
  Charles L., 262.
  Charles E., 261.
  Charles E., 264,
  Charlotte, 268.
  Clara, 261.
  Clara M., 252.
  Clara, 244, 245.
  Clara J., 274.
  Clark, 242.
  Cordelia E., 271.
  Cynthia L., 268.

406 Index.

Eighth Generation Continued.

Descendants of John.	Descendants of George.	Descendants of William.
Denison, Charles A., 22, 23.	Denison, Delia A., 195.	Denison, Daniel B., 269.
Charles D., 79.	Delaverge, 217.	Deville E., 256.
Charles F., 54, 54.	Daniel P., 217.	Dona E., 290.
Charles F., 34.	Dianthe, 217.	Dudley A., 250, 251.
Charles H., 39.	Eber, 218.	Dudley C., 252.
Charles H., 118.	Edgar, 189.	Dwight, 251.
Charles H., 155.	Edmund, 212.	Eber J., 250.
Charlie H., 167.	Edward L., 214.	Edward, 248.
Charles M., 68.	Eliza J., 222.	Edward, 269.
Charles M., 27, 27.	Elizabeth, 180.	Edward A., 261.
Charles M., 28, 29.	Elizabeth, 199.	Elam W., 274.
Charles W., 164.	Elizabeth, 208.	Eleanor P., 244.
Chloe A., 146.	Emily M., 214.	Elias S., 276.
Cynthia, 122.	Ellen E., 211.	Eliza, 244.
Daniel, 49, 49.	Elvira E., 219.	Eliza, 275.
Daniel, 55.	Enfield T., 211.	Elizabeth A., 241.
Daniel, 146.	Ephraim W., 191.	Elizabeth, 248.
Daniel, 144.	Erastus, 224.	Ella B., 264.
Daniel A., 39, 39.		Ella S., 264.
Daniel Eri, 44, 45.		Ellen F., 284, 285.
Daniel E., 149, 150.		Elmira I., 271.
Datus R., 152.		Eloise, 238.
David T., 39.		Emeline M., 261.
Deborah A., 164.		Emeline, 263.
Delilah E., 164.		Emma B., 252.
Diana, 124.		Emma J., 284, 285.
Ebenezer, —.		Erastus W., 250.
Edmund F., 97.		Estelle A., 276.
Edgar, 32.		Etherlinda, 271.
Edward R., 76.		Ettie M., 256.
Edward P., 157.		Eugene, 256.
Edward P., 26.		Eugene, 269.
Edward M., 130.		Eunice C., 271.
Edward, 48.		Eva E., 292.
Edwin, 69, 69.		
Edwin, 32.		
Edwin, 55, 56.		
Edwin, 117.		
Edwin N., 123, 123.		
Egbert, 34.		
Edwin C., 158.		
Ella E., 166.		
Eli, 25, 26.		
Elisha G., 105, 106.		
Elias B., 39, 41.		
Elias C., 155.		
Elias B., 110, 110.		

Index.

Eighth Generation Continued.

Descendants of John.	Descendants of George.	Descendants of William.
Denison, Ellen H., 23, 24.	Denison, Fannie R., 217.	Denison, Fanny, 244.
Ellen, 122.	Festus E., 218.	Fanny D., 288.
Ellen, 124.	Flora E., 197.	Frances R., 245.
Ellen, 146.	Florence, 198.	Frances F., 268, 270.
Ellen J., 23.	Francis M., 189.	Frank, 242,
Ellen J., 110, 110.	Frank E., 214.	Franklin, 244.
Eliza, 66.	Frank H., 220.	Franklin P., 276.
Eliza A., 111, 111.	Frederick H., 217.	Frank, 252.
Eliza J., 123.	Frederick W., 214.	Frank, 292.
Eliza M., 155.	Friend T., 214.	Frank A., 250.
Eliza, 157.		Frank A., 294.
Elizabeth L., 54.		Frank L., 261.
Elizabeth L., 98, 98.		Frank R., 238.
Elizabeth M., 54.		Frank E., 256.
Elizabeth A., 108.		Frank, 267.
Elizabeth, 149, 150.		Frank, 269.
Ella, 118.		Frederic, 238.
Elmer E., 164.		Frederick E., 240.
Emilie H., 118.		Frederick, 269.
Emily, 157.		
Emma, 65.		
Emma, 152.		
Emma A., 33.		
Emma J., 151.		
Emma J., 49.		
Emma J., 153.		
Emma N., 68.		
Emma M., 110.		
Emily C., 26, 26.		
Emily E., 68.		
Estelle, 124.		
Eudora, 124.		
Eudora E., 46.		
Eunice L., 108.		
Evalina T., 98.		
Ezra S., 22.		
Fannie E., 73.		
Fanny, 155.		
Frances, 75, 75.		
Frances L., 79.		
Frances E., 68.		
Frances M., 113.		
Frances, 146.		
Frances S., 23.		
Francis A., 105, 105.		
Francis C., 76.		
Francis W., 76, 76.		
Felix A., 26.		

Index.

Eighth Generation Continued.

Descendants of John.
Denison, Francelia, 117.
Frances R., —.
Frank, 66.
Frank, 51.
Franklin H., 155.
Frank H., 111, 112.
Frederic M., 30.
Frederic, 157.
Frederica, 157.
George, 66.
George, 164.
George, 149, 150.
George A., 68, 68.
George A., 124.
George G., 59.
George E., 22, 23.
George J., 39, 41.
George S.N., 111, 112.
George W., 64.
George W., 123, 124.
Gertrude, 34, 34.
Gorham N., 44, 44.
Guernsey H., 33.
Hannah B., 157, 157.
Hannah L., 152.
Harriet, 122.
Harriet P., 30.
Harriet B., 116.
Harriet S., 78.
Harriet B., 155, 155.
Harrietta, 145.
Harris A., 164.
Helen M., 108.
Helen M., 28, 28.
Henry, 97.
Henry H., 111, 112.
Henry C., 27, 27.
Henry M., 118.
Henry A., 39, 40.
Henry P., 150.
Henry E., 46, 47.
Henry S., 146, 146.
Herbert R., 110.
Herbert, 66.
Herbert, 69.
Herbert G., 76.
Hiram, 20, 20.

Descendants of George.
Denison, George, 199.
George, 220.
George S., 190.
George W., 225.
Gertrude, 220, 220.
Harriet G., 227.
Hattie M., 216.
Henrietta M., 227.
Henry, 216.
Henry G., 199.
Henry H., 207.
Hiram, 199.

Descendants of William.
Denison, George E., 237.
George L., 276.
George, 240.
George, 245.
George, 261.
George, 284.
George S., 244, 244.
George D., 245.
George B., 259.
George E., 261.
George M., 262.
George W., 269.
George W., 264.
Georgia, 264.
Georgiana K., 264.
Georgiana, 274.
Gertrude M., 248.
Gilbert H., 237, 237.
Gippie P., 241.
Harriet G., 256.
Harriet, D., 264.
Harriet E., 250.
Hatty O., 252.
Helen A., 259.
Helen, 261.
Henry, 252.
Henry, 268.
Henry, 269.
Henry H., 245, 246.
Henry W., 259.
Henry L., 284, 285.
Helen, 242,
Helen A., 238.
Helen C., 292.
Hinda, 242.
Horace, 240.

Index.

Eighth Generation Continued.

Descendants of John.
Denison, Howard, 51.
    Horace P., 26, 26.
    Huldah, 49, 49, 49.
    Huldah E., 113, 114.
    Ira W., 155.
    Isaac, —.
    Isaac M., 105, 106.
    Isaac W., 108.
    Isadora, 28.
    James, 65.
    James P., 55, 55.
    Jabez, —.
    Jabez D., 28, 29.
    Jacob H., 164.
    Jahn H., 105, 105.
    Jason, 105.
    James O., 39.
    James C., 51.
    Jane M., 28, 29.
    Jane, 48.
    Jane E., 154.
    James, 65.
    James R., 152.
    James R., 149, 149.
    James T. H., 158.
    Jarius N., 46.
    Jesse, 48.
    Jessie L., 52.
    Jedediah W., 55, 56.
    Jeptha S., 111.
    Jeptha C., 111, 112.
    John J., jr., 123, 124.
    John F., 23.
    John R., 118.
    John C., 117.
    John A., 149, 150.
    John H., 68, 69.
    John H., Rev., 79.
    John, 65.
    John B., 152.
    John B., 158.
    Jonathan G., 44.
    Joshua H., 154.
    Joseph, 69, 70.
    Joseph R., 108, 108.
    Julia, 66.
    Julia L., 114.

Descendants of George.
Denison, Imogene H., 227.
    James F., 220.
    Jane, 224.
    Jerome P., 214.
    Jesse, 222.
    John, 198.
    John, 191.
    John D., 191.
    John F., 207.
    John L., 216.
    John W., 180, 180.
    John D., 214.
    Joseph W., 211.
    Joseph K., 217.

Descendants of William.
Denison, Isaac G., 284.
    Imogene, 260.
    Ida, 260.
    Ida M., 256.
    James S., Dr., 253.
    James D., 252.
    James E., 250.
    James, 244, 245.
    Jane A., 263.
    Jesse L., 251.
    Jessie K., 252.
    Joseph A., 247.
    Joseph M., 260.
    Joseph D., 248, 248.
    Joseph B., 288.
    Joseph L., 269.
    Josephine, 241.
    Josie B., 276.
    John G., 274.
    John A., 286.
    John A., 293.
    John H., 248.
    John N., 253.
    Justin W., 274.

Index.

Eighth Generation Continued.

Descendants of John.
Denison, Julia P., 52, 52.
    Kate, 34.
    Kate S., 110, 110.
    Katie L., 114.
    Laura Glynn, 33.
    Lavinia F., 157.
    Learned B., 158.
    Leonard, 49.
    Leonard A., 49, 50.
    Lelia J., 33.
    Lewis, 20.
    Linus J., 31.
    Lois, 168.
    Louis P., 68.
    Louis A., 30.
    Louisa, 66.
    Louisa A., 55, 56.
    Louisa A., 105, 106.
    Lorenzo N., 39, 41.
    Loring G., 98.
    Lucilla C., 68.
    Lucius H., 110.
    Lucy, 20.
    Lucy, 66.
    Lydia, 98.
    Lydia A., 130.
    Lyman, 118.
    Lyman, 34, 34.
    Malvina C., 108, 108.
    Maria E., 124.
    Marshall, 28.
    Martha, 22, 22.
    Martha A., 46, 46.
    Martha J., 65.
    Martha A., 105, 106.
    Margaret, 44.
    Margaret, 44.
    Marietta, 55, 56.
    Mariana, 33.
    Maria L., 52.
    Marvin B., 158.
    Mary A., 26.
    Mary A., 68.
    Mary A., 108.
    Mary A., 123.
    Mary Ann G., 32, 32.
    Mary B., 124.

Descendants of George.
Denison, Laura V., 20.
    Leander C., 218.
    Leonard L., 207.
    Lewis, 222.
    Lewis B., 207.
    Lizzie, 198.
    Louisa, 212.
    Lucina, 218.
    Maria P., 199.
    Mary A., 225.
    Mary A., 222.
    Mary A., 222.
    Mary H., 199.
    Mary P., 190.
    Mary E., 216.
    Mary, 214.
    Mary, 220, 220.
    Minnie, 198.

Descendants of William.
Denison, Kate L., 262.
    Katie E., 252.
    Lafayette, 271.
    Laura A., 240.
    Lida, —.
    Lillian H., 238.
    Lizzie M., 238.
    Lizzie, 238.
    Loretta P., 292.
    Lottie L., 287.
    Luana, 242.
    Lucy, 244.
    Louise, 260.
    Lucy S., 238.
    Lucy D., 248.
    Lucy E., 250.
    Lucia M., 261.
    Lydia M., 274.
    Martha R., 252.
    Martha E., 262.
    Margaret, 288.
    Mary E., 251.
    Mary E., 240, 240.
    Mary E., 250.
    Mary J., 252.
    Mary L., 241.
    Mary L., 252.
    Mary L., 250, 251.
    Mary L., 257.
    Mary H., 245.
    Mary J., 252.
    Mary J., 287.
    Mary C., 247.
    Mary M., 288.
    M. Ella, 262.
    M. Jane, 269.
    Mary A., 250.
    Mary A., 252.
    Mary E., 263.
    Mary A., 268, 269.
    Mary, 261.
    Mary, 242.
    Mason, 264.
    Maud M., 290.
    Mille A., 264.

Index.

Eighth Generation Continued.

Descendants of John.
Denison, Mary M., 46.
    Mary M., 166.
    Mary L., 52, 52.
    Mary L., 27.
    Mary L., 51.
    Mary L., 154, 154.
    Mary O., 43.
    Mary E., 164.
    Mary E., 46, 46.
    Mary E., 130.
    Mary C., 59.
    Mary C., 96.
    Mary J., 68.
    Mary P., 154.
    Mary M., 111, 112.
    Mary, 146.
    Mary, 122, 122.
    Maryette, 44.
    Meribah D., 55.
    Minnie, 70.
    Minor, 48, 48.
    Morris W., 27.
    Myra, 118.
    Nancy, 69, 70.
    Nancy W., 55, 55.
    Nancy J., 149, 149.
    Nathan, 123.
    Nathan, 149, 149.
    Nathan H., 105, 106.
    Nathan L., 111.
    Nathan N., 110.
    Nathan W., 116.
    Nehemiah B., 23.
    Norah G., 33.
    Olive C., 28, 28.
    Oliver S., 23.
    Oscar J., 111, 111.
    Paul, 20, 20.
    Pardee N., 46, 46.
    Perry, 168.
    Phebe M., 154.
    Polly 44.
    Porter G., 46, 47.
    Rebecca, 44.
    Rhoda, 44.
    Richard W., 26.
    Rhoda E., 152.

Descendants of George.
Denison, Nancy, —.
    Nancy A., 189.
    Nancy P., 222.
    Olive M., 227.
    Phebe, 222.
    Phebe R., 222.
    Riley, 222.

Descendants of William.
Denison, Nancy, 274.
    Nellie A., 290.
    Newton, 245.
    Oliver, 274.
    Orpha L., 252, 252.
    Paul S., 274.
    Phebe E., 276.
    Phebe L., 241.
    Phebe M., 274.
    Philander C., 244.
    Riley, Capt., 271.
    Robert D., 252.
    Robert C., 259.
    Rosa M., 256.
    Rosa A., 264.

Index.

Eighth Generation Continued.

Descendants of John.
Denison, Rilan H., 105,107.
Robert, 149, 150.
Robert F., 32.
Robert S., 152.
Robert W., 153.
Rosalie H., 114.
Samantha L., 105, 106.
Sally M., 123, 123.
Samuel, 76.
Samuel, 96.
Samuel A., 69, 69.
Samuel, 122.
Samuel, 146.
Samuel C., 152.
Sarah, 48, 48.
Sarah, 45.
Sarah, 44.
Sarah, 146.
Sarah, 44.
Sarah A., 157.
Sarah J., 26.
Sarah M., 27, 27.
Sarah A., 68.
Sarah B., 97.
Sarah A., 149, 150.
Silas, 123.
Simeon, 105.
Sophronia J., 39, 41.
Stephen, 122.
Susan, 45.
Thomas, 55, 56.
Thalia A., 145.
Thomas L., 26.
Thomas N., 48.
Thomas D., 27, 27.
Thomas R., 39, 42.
Tyler, 45.
Walter, 34.
Walter, 66.
Walter, 117.
Wilhelmina, 68.
William, 66.
William, 149.
William, 75.
William, 130.
William A., 40, 51.
William A., 107,108.

Descendants of George.
Denison, Salome C., 217.
Samuel, 189.
Samuel H., 218.
Samuel G., 222.
Sarah, 222.
Sarah A., 216.
Sarah D., 191.
Simeon S., 219.
Sophia, 222.
Stephen B., 191.
Sylvester B., 220.
Walter, 222.
Walter P., 197.
William A., 216.
William H., 222.
William C., 207.
William, 218.
Winfield S., 222.

Descendants of William.
Denison, Sarah H., 261.
Sarah A., 263.
Sarah M., 252.
Sarah N., 253, 254.
Sidney J., 276,
Sina A., 271.
Susan, 244, 245.
Susan A., 241.
Susan C., 252.
Theodore M., 263.
Thomas J., 262.
Walter R , 252.
Wesley C., 263.
William, 241.
William, 250.
William B., 237.
William C., 287.
William H., 238.
William H., 263.
William H., 252.
William E., 256.
William N., 257.
William O., 260.
Willard, 291.
Winfield S., 271.
Virgie, 260, 260.

Index.

Eighth Generation Continued.

Descendants of John.
Denison, William A., 39,40.
    William B., 64.
    William B., 110,110.
    William W., 27.
    William C., 75.
    William C., 28, 28.
    William E., 73.
    William M., 30.
    William H., 123.
    William E., 32.
    William S., 131.
    William E., 33.
    William H., 68.
    William H., 123.
    William T., 54.
    William T., 76, 76.
    Willie H., 167.
    Willie S., 52.
    Willis S., 166.
    Vesta Ann, 59.
    Virginia, 33.

Descendants of George.

Descendants of William.

NINTH GENERATION.

Descendants of John.
Denison, Addie, 106.
    Addie C., 56.
    Adna A., 111.
    Adney N., 108.
    Alace, 55.
    Albert E., 150.
    Albert N., 111.
    Albert F., 66.
    Albert E., 45.
    Alexander F., 41.
    Alfred G., 45.
    Alpha J., 48.
    Alice M., 29.
    Alide E., 124.
    Allen, 106.
    Amos, 149.
    Anna T., 76.
    Annie C., 146.
    Anson 149.
    Archie S., 70.
    Arthur E., 108.
    Arthur P., 39.
    Augusta M, 146.

Descendants of George.
Denison, Alfred L., 219.
    Amos A., 191.

Descendants of William.

Index.

Ninth Generation Continued.

Descendants cf John.
Denison, Aurelia J., 150.
    Avery W., 39.
    Belle, 56.
    Bertie M., 28.
    Blanche A., 69.
    Burt M., 105.
    Burt N., 42.
    Byron R., 107.
    Byron F., 45.
    Calista E., 40.
    Carrie E., 20.
    Carrie A., 47.
    Carrie F., 32.
    Carrie L., 27.
    Celia L., 41.
    Charles, 29.
    Charles E., 69.
    Charles E., 5:.
    Charles E., 47.
    Clara, 40.
    Clara M., 124.
    Clara M., 23.
    Clarene, 144.
    Cora L., 108.
    Cora L., 105.
    Corilla E. A., 108.
    Cordelia S., 40.
    Cornelia A., 43.
    Delia A., 105.
    Delia L., 107.
    Daniel, 56.
    Daniel A., 54.
    Daniel F., 5:.
    David A., 41.
    Edgar F., 23.
    Edna A., 112.
    Edward E., 110.
    Effa A., 150.
    Eleanor F., 41.
    Elisha A., 106.
    Elisha A., 105.
    Elizabeth L., 54.
    Elizabeth A., 149.
    Elizabeth E., 40.
    Elizabeth M., 69.
    Ella, 112.
    Ella E., 105.
    Ellis F., 42.

Descendants of George.
Denison, Catherine N., 225.
    Charles A., 216.
    Eber W., 218.

Descendants of William.
Denison, Carrie, 238.
    Charles H., 287.
    Charles H., 240.
    Clara, 261.
    Dudley, 251.
    Dudley C., 246.
    Edgar R., 251.
    Edward T., 245.
    Elmer, 261.
    Emma, 261.
    Eunice D., 248.

Index.

Ninth Generation Continued.

Descendants of John.
Denison, Emeline R., 40.
    Elmetta J., 27.
    Elsie E., 39.
    Emma M., 150.
    Ernest, 41.
    Esther, 43.
    Eunice M., 39.
    Eva J., 149.
    Eva L., 27.
    Eva M., 113.
    Evalyn F., 40.
    Fannie D., 69.
    Fanny E., 124.
    Fanny G., 32.
    Flora B., 51.
    Francis M., 20.
    Frances A., 105.
    Frances E., 23.
    Frank D., —.
    Frank H., 41.
    Frank F., 39.
    Frank E., 69.
    Frank T., 51.
    Frederick P., 47.
    Freddie, 42.
    Frederick, 69.
    Frederick, 54.
    Frederick E., 54.
    Fred. C., 51.
    Frederick L., 41.
    Frederic R., 23.
    George H., 111.
    George H., 105.
    George H.. 47.
    George M., 146.
    George M., 105.
    George A., 69.
    Geo. B., 56.
    George P., 47.
    George W., 124.
    George W., 112.
    Grace E., 76.
    Grace, 56.
    Grace M., 110.
    Grace W., 23.
    Guy S., 105.
    Guy A., 105.

Descendants of George.

Descendants of William.
Denison, Frank, 285.
    George S., 245.
    George, 240.
    Gilbert H., 238.
    Grace M., 246.
    Harriet A., 251.

Index.

Ninth Generation Continued.

Descendants of John.
Denison, Haley N., 40.
    Hannah M., 150.
    Harry E., 56.
    Harry H., 112.
    Harry L., 69.
    Harriet A., 54.
    Henrie S., 69.
    Henry C., 40.
    Harvey S., —.
    Hattie L., 113.
    Hattie B., 56.
    Hattie G., 23.
    Herbert J., 112.
    Herbert, 40.
    Huldah M., 51.
    Ida M., 105.
    Ida M., 70.
    Ida M., 48.
    Ida B., 41.
    Inez M., 105.
    Imogene L., 106.
    James A., 29.
    James R., 40.
    James A., 69.
    James P., 47.
    Jennie V., 124.
    Jennie W., 56.
    Jennie R., 42.
    Jennie B., 40.
    Jessie C., 76.
    Jesse L., 56.
    John F., 65.
    John W., 69.
    Joseph G., 69.
    Joseph W., 70.
    Jennie R. 41.
    Julia B., 23.
    Julia E., 56.
    Kitty S., 41.
    Lavello, 28.
    Laura E., 51.
    Leo E., 112.
    Leland W., 111
    Leroy W., 56.
    Leslie E., 69.
    Lelia, 29.
    Lewis C., 55.
    Lillia M., —.

Descendants of George.
Denison, Irving, 219.
    John M., 180.
    Lewis L., 216.

Descendants of William.
Denison, Ireland, 285.
    Jessie H., 240.
    Janet J., 256.
    Jennie O., 251.
    Lindsey, 245.
    Lizzie L., 245.
    Lodema, 261.
    Lucy, 261.

Ninth Generation Continued.

Descendants of John.	Descendants of George.	Descendants of William.
Denison, Lillie J., 20.	Denison, Margaret L., 225.	Denison, Mary, 261.
Lillian E., 41.	Ruby E., 214.	Mary, 260.
Lillian A., 23.		Minnie, 261.
Lincoln, 144.		Nellie, 285.
Lincoln, 111.		Oliver, 261.
Lizzie M., 112.		Raymond C., 245.
Louisa G., 69.		Richard L., 245.
Louisa B., 32.		Rufus, 261.
Lulu E., 56.		
Lydia A., 106.		
Lydia J., 40.		
Maria M., 43.		
Mabel E., 112.		
Marguerite E., 112.		
Marshall H., 27.		
Martin E., 106.		
Martin, 55.		
Mary A., 149.		
Mary A., 56.		
Mary E., 150.		
Mary S., 112.		
Mary E., 43.		
Mary E., 32.		
Mary H., 113.		
Mary J., 108.		
Mary L., 106.		
Mary L., 42.		
Mary L., 28.		
Mary L., 27.		
Maud C., 69.		
Melvin J., 49.		
Minie G., 43.		
Minnie C., 27.		
Nancy L., 47.		
Nancy M., 150.		
Nathan F., 106.		
Nellie, 106.		
Nellie J., 70.		
Nellie A., 56.		
Nina F., 27.		
Olive A., 47.		
Perry M., 27.		
Phebe J., 149.		
Porter G., 47.		
Rena, 106.		
Rhoda E., 27.		
Riley E., 41.		

Index.

Ninth Generation Continued.

Descendants of John.
Denison, Robert F., 32.
  Robert L., 110.
  Robert F., 32.
  Roll F., 41.
  Roy, 42.
  Salinda, 41.
  Sarah A., 150.
  Sarah A., 41.
  Sarah C., 76.
  Sarah L., 43.
  Selina, 20.
  Silas E., 124.
  Simeon M., 108.
  Stewart M., 69.
  Susan L., 41.
  Theodore, 150.
  Victor V., 39.
  Waldo B., 42.
  Warren H., 51.
  Wellington J., 51.
  Will. F., 40.
  Willis, 20.
  William Z., 20.
  William H., 41.
  William H., 43.
  William, 49.
  William B., 111.
  William K., 110.
  William S., 108.
  William N., 69.
  Willie B., 69.
  Winifred T., 110.
  Zene M., 105.

Descendants of George.
Denison, William B., 225.

Descendants of William.
Denison, Warren, 261.
  William, 261.
  William, 261.
  William, 261.
  William, 260.
  William, 245.

TENTH GENERATION.

Descendants of John.
Denison, Ada L., 41.
  Benjamin H., 45.
  Carrie M., 41.
  Daniel S., 45.
  Edgar R., 45.

Descendants of John.
Denison, Ella M., 21.
  Hiram J., 21.
  Huldah J., 21.
  Lion K., 40.
  Luke, 40.

Descendants of John.
Denison, Mark, 40.
  Milford S., 45.
  Sarah A., 21.
  Silena, 21.

III.

INDEX
TO THE APPENDIX.

SKETCH OF CAPT. GEORGE DENISON,	297
His Courtship Letter to Bridget Thompson,	298
His Marriage to Ann Borodell,	299
His settlement at Stonington,	299
His home and farm,	300
His civil and military services,	304
His Will,	307
SKETCH OF CAPT. JOHN DENISON,	311
His Will,	314
SKETCH OF MAJOR GENERAL DANIEL DENISON,	315
His Will,	327
SKETCH OF DANIEL DENISON, of Hampton, Conn.,	333
SKETCH OF ROBERT DENISON, of Milford, Conn.,	338
SKETCH OF GEORGE DENNISON, of Annisquam, Mass.,	345
SKETCH OF JOSEPH DENISON, of West Stafford, Conn.,	360
ESTRAYS, received too late for the earlier pages,	351

DESCENDANTS OF MAJOR GENERAL DANIEL DENISON,
bearing the name of Denison.

Denison, Rev. Andrew C., 336, 337.
Alice, 337.
Carrie, 337.
Catherine M., 337.
Charles N., 337.
Daniel, Rev. 336, 337.
Daniel, 336, 336.
Daniel, 335, 336.
Daniel, 330, 333.
Daniel, 335, 335.
Denison, Dyer, 335.
Elizabeth, 330, 330.
Elizabeth, 335, 335.
Henry C., 337.
Hannah, 336, 337.
Hannah, 330.
Hannah, 335, 336.
Hannah, 335, 336.
John, 330, 330.
John, Rev., 330, 330.
John, Rev., 332, 332.
Denison, John, 330, 332.
John C., 336, 337.
James H., 336, 337.
Linus, 337.
Lucy, 336, 336.
Lydia, 336, 336.
Martha, 330.
Mary E., 336.
Ruth, 330, 331.
William, 337.

DESCENDANTS OF MAJOR GENERAL DANIEL DENISON,
bearing other Family Names.

Appleton, Elizabeth, 333.
   Margaret, 333.
   Nathaniel, 333.
   Daniel, 333.
   Priscilla, 333.
   John, 333.
Abbott, Daniel, 336.
   Elijah, 336.
Fuller, Julia, 336.
   Mary A., 336.
Huntington, Elizabeth, 335.
   Elisha, 335.
Jackson, Horace, 336.
   Edward, 336.
   Henry, 336.
   Helen M., 336.
   Dwight, 336.

Kingsbury, Ephraim, 331.
   Hannah, 331.
   Love, 331.
   Ruth, 332.
   Joseph, 332.
   Ebenezer, 332.
   Eleazer, 332.
   Eunice, 332.
   Daniel, 332.
   Tabitha, 332.
   Grace, 332.
   Jane, 332.
   Nathaniel, 332.
   John, 331.
   Nathaniel, 331.
   Mary, 331.

Leverett, Margaret, 333.
   Mary, 333.
   Sarah, 333.
   Mary, 333.
   John 333.
   Peyton, 333.
   Margaret, 333.
   John, 333.
Rogers, Elizabeth, 330.
   Margaret, 330.
   John, 330.
   Daniel, 330.
   Nathaniel, 330.
   Patience, 330.

DESCENDANTS OF ROBERT DENISON OF MILFORD,
bearing the Family Name.

Denison, Abel, 340, 341.
   Abel, 341, 341.
   Abigail, 339.
   Abigail, 339.
   Abigail, 339.
   Abigail, 340.
   Abbie C., 344.
   Anna G., 341.
   Arthur C., 344.
   Austin, 340.
   Betsey, 340.
   Caroline, 343.
   Charles O., 344.
   Charles, 340, 341.
   Charles, 341.
   Chauncy, 340.
   Daniel L., 344, 344.
   Della Mary, 344.
   Delia M., 343.
   Desire, 339.
   Desire, 340.
   Desire, 340.
   Dowie, 342.
   Dorothy, 340.
   Edward C., 342.
   Edwin W., 344.

Denison, Elizabeth, 339.
   Elizabeth, 339.
   Elizabeth A., 341.
   Emer E., 344.
   Emeline A., 343.
   Ephraim, 340.
   Esther, 338.
   Eurinda, 342.
   Evelyn, 342.
   Eva F., 344.
   Ezekiel R., 340, 344.
   Ezekiel L., 344.
   Fidelia, 342.
   Frederick S., 344.
   Hannah, 338.
   Hannah, 340.
   Harriet A., 344.
   Hattie, 344.
   Helen E., 344.
   Henry, 340, 341.
   Henry, 341, 342.
   Herbert H., 344.
   Jeremiah T., 341, 341.
   James, 338, 339.
   James, 339.
   James, 340.

Denison, James, 333.
   James, 340.
   James, 339, 339.
   James, 3d., 339.
   James A., 344.
   Jesse, 339.
   Jesse, 340.
   Jesse, 340, 344.
   John, 338, 339.
   John W., 343.
   John H., 344.
   John, 339, 343.
   John, 344.
   John J., 344.
   John, 339, 339.
   John, 339.
   John, jr., 340.
   John, 339.
   John, jr., 340.
   Julia, 341.
   Julia F., 344.
   Juliette, 334.
   Julius C., 343, 344.
   Leverett, 340, 342.
   Lois, 340.
   Libbie, 344.

Index. 421

Descendants of Robert Denison, of Milford, Continued.

Denison, Louisa, 343.	Denison, Mehitabel, 339.	Denison, Sarah, 339.
Lydia, 340.	Malinda, 342.	Sarah, 340.
Lydia, 339.	Nancy, 340.	Sibyl, 333.
Mercy, 338, 338.	Nina, 342.	Sibyl, 339.
Mary, 339.	Obedience, 340.	Ursena, 342, 342.
Mary, 339.	Polly, 342.	William C., 341.
Mary, 341.	Samuel, 338.	William, 342.
Mary E., 340.	Samuel, 340.	William S., 344, 344.
Mary L., 344.	Samuel, 344.	Willie F., 344.
Maryetta, 343.	Sarah, 338.	Zina, 340.
Martha, 341.	Sarah, 339.	Zina, 341.
Martha, 340, 341.	Sarah, 339.	
Martha D., 341.	Sarah, 339.	

DESCENDANTS OF ROBERT DENISON OF MILFORD,

bearing other names.

Dalglish, John, 338.	Lake, Harriet, 342.	Lake, William, 343.
Samuel, 338.	James H., 343.	Zophar, 342.
Esther, 338.	Joanna A., 343.	Lyman, Sarah L., 343.
Gilbert, Emily I., 342.	John E., 343.	Martha H., 343.
Lucia S., 342.	John, 342.	Mary D., 343.
Mary E., 342.	Lois, 343.	Woodward, Hannah, 341.
William H., 342.	Minerva, 342.	George, 341.
Congdon L., 342.	Minerva, 343.	Henry, 341.
Lake, Sally, 342.	Melinda, 342.	
Denison, 342.	Philamelia, 343.	

DESCENDANTS OF GEORGE DENNISON OF ANNISQUAM,

bearing the name of Dennison.

Dennison, Abigail, 347.	Dennison, Betsey R., 349.	Dennison, Elizabeth, 347.
Abigail 345.	Carrie A., 350.	Elizabeth W., 348.
Abigail, 346.	Charles H., 350.	Elizabeth G., 346.
Abigail, 346.	Charles H., 349.	Ellen, 347.
Abner, 345, 346.	Charles, 348, 350.	Emma, 346.
Abner, 346.	Charlotte E., 350.	Emma M., 349.
Adaline, 349.	David, 348.	Evelyn, 349.
Adaliza, 349.	David, 345, 246.	Edith M., 349.
Adella, 348.	David, 346.	Fidelia, 347.
Albert, 349.	David, 347.	Frances, 349.
Alice M., 350.	Edward H., 348.	Frank, 349.
Anna, 346.	Edward C., 349.	Frank L., 349.
Annie, 349.	Edith, 350.	Frank W., 349.
Augustus, 350.	Eliza A., 348.	Franklin, 348.
Augusta J., 347.	Elizabeth, 348.	Franklin O., 349.
Benjamin B., 346.	Elizabeth, 346.	George, 345, 346.
Bertha E., 349.	Elizabeth, 347.	George, 346.

52

Descendants of George Dennison, of Annisquam, Continued.

Dennison, Geo., 347, 348.
  George, 349.
  George G., 348.
  George G., 348.
  George W., 348.
  Gideon, 346.
  Grace M., 350.
  Gardner, 350.
  Helen L., 350.
  Hannah, 346.
  Harriet, 347.
  Herbert E., 349.
  Hosea B., 348.
  Isaac, 348.
  Isaac, 345, 346.
  Isaac, 346, 347.
  Isaac, 350.
  Isaac, 3d, 346.
  Isaac H., 347.
  Irving C., 349.
  James, 346, 347.
  James, 347.
  James, jr., 348, 349.
  James E., 349.

Dennison, Jas. W., 347.
  Jenny, 346.
  John P., 347.
  John W., 349.
  John W., 348.
  Jonathan, 345, 346.
  Jonathan, 346, 347.
  Jonathan, 347, 348.
  Jonathan jr., 347.347.
  Jonathan A., 348, 349
  Judith, 347.
  Lewis F., 349.
  Louisa, 349.
  Lucretia, 347.
  Lucretia, 347.
  Margaret A., 348.
  Mary, 347.
  Mary E., 349.
  Mary H., 347.
  Mary J., 348.
  Martha, 348.
  Martha S., 349.
  Minor, 349.
  Otis, 347.

Dennison, Otis, 348.
  Rhoda, 347.
  Sarah, 346.
  Sarah A., 347.
  Serena, 347.
  Susan F., 349.
  Susan A., 348.
  Susan B., 348.
  Susanna, 345.
  Susanna, 346.
  Tammy, 347.
  Tristam R., 347, 349.
  Tristam R., 349.
  Thomasine, 346.
  Thomas, 349.
  Warren, 348.
  William, 346, 348.
  William, 348.
  William, 346.
  William, 348.
  William A., 349, 350.
  William S., 350.

DESCENDANTS OF JOSEPH DENISON OF WEST STAFFORD,

Family Records.

Denison, Joseph, 5th, 360.
  George, 6th, 361.
  Joseph, jr., 6th, 362.
  Robert, 6th, 363.
  Joseph S., 7th, 363.
  Chester, 364.
  Gilbert, 364.
  Guilford, 364.

Denison, Gaylord, 364.
  Lorenzo J., 364.
  Sanford, 364.
  Bragg, Clarissa, 6th, 361.
  Converse, Emeline, 7th, 362
  Harriet A., 363.
  Cady, Hannah M., 362.
  Hiram F., 7th, 363.

Dwight, Marie S., 364.
Davis, Angeline, 364.
Gold, Ruby E., 6th, 362.
  Green, Elvira, 363.
Kingsbury, Emeline, 363.
Smith, Lucinda, 6th, 361.
Winslow, Margaret, 363.

ESTRAYS.

The following Family Records are found here:

Denison, Daniel, 3d, 351.
  Daniel 4th, 5th gen. 352.
  George, 6th g., 352.
  Daniel, 7th g., 352.
  Benj. Green, 7th, 353.
  Griswold, 8th, 354.
  J. W. T., 8th, 354.

Denison, Morris W., 8th, 356.
  Benadam, jr., 357.
  George B., 358.
  Charles B., 358.
  Aretus L., 358.
  Daniel B., 7th, 358.
  Henry C., 7th, 359.

Beach, Ida M., 8th, 356.
Baker, Pamelia S., 358.
Griffing, Chas. R., 8th, 356.
Havens, Lucretia D., 357.
Hull, Isabella J. S., 357.
Huntington, Ann D., 359.
Miller, Susan E., 8th, 354.
Noyes, Joseph, jr., 6th, 354.

Estrays, Continued.

Noyes, Avery, 6th, 355.
Noyes, William S., 7th, 355.
Streeter, Sophronia, 8th, 353.
Simmons, Caroline, 8th, 354.
Streeter, Rhoda D., 356. Daniel D., 357.
Whitbeck, Sarah D. 8th, 353.

GENERAL TABLE OF CONTENTS.

1. CAPT. GEORGE DENISON, His Father, His Brothers, and His Daughters, - - - - - pages 5 to 14
2. Capt. George's son CAPT. JOHN, - - - - - 15
3. Capt. John's son JOHN, JR., of Saybrook, - - - 18
4. "   "   GEORGE, of New London, - - - 34
5. "   "   ROBERT, of Mohegan, - - - - 60
6. "   "   WILLIAM, of North Stonington, - - 84
7. "   "   DEA. DANIEL, of Stonington, - - 120
8. Capt. George's son GEORGE, JR., - - - - - 173
9. George, Jr.'s son EDWARD, of Westerly, - - - - 177
10. "   "   JOSEPH, of Stonington, - - - - 183
11. "   "   SAMUEL, of Saybrook, - - - - 208
12. "   "   GEORGE, of Westerly, - - - - 225
13. Capt. George's son WILLIAM, - - - - - - 229
14. William's son WILLIAM, JR., of Stonington, - - - 234
15. "   "   GEORGE, of Stonington, - - - - 265
16. Appendix, - - - - - - - - - 296
16. Indexes, - - - - - - - from 365 to 423

ADDITIONAL ERRATA.

Page 46, No. 324, b. Dec. 13, should be b. Dec. 4.
" 73, third line from bottom, Franch should be French.
" 135, No. 2842, m. Frances not Francis Forbes.
" 158, No. 3393 Marvin should be Marion.
" 159, 12th line from bottom. John G. should be John D.
" 163, 4th line from bottom, John L. should be John Salter.
" 345, the date in line 6 should be 1727, not 1787.
" 410, in first column, Marvin B. should be Marion B.

www.ingramcontent.com/pod-product-compliance
Lightning Source LLC
Chambersburg PA
CBHW050326230426
43663CB00010B/1757